Bipolar Disorders: Clinical, Psychological and Biological Aspects

Bipolar Disorders: Clinical, Psychological and Biological Aspects

Edited by Francisco Watkins

hayle
medical

New York

Hayle Medical,
750 Third Avenue, 9th Floor,
New York, NY 10017, USA

Visit us on the World Wide Web at:
www.haylemedical.com

ISBN: 978-1-63241-586-8

Printed in China.

Cataloging-in-Publication Data

Bipolar disorders : clinical, psychological and biological aspects / edited by Francisco Watkins.
p. cm.
Includes bibliographical references and index.
ISBN 978-1-63241-586-8
1. Manic-depressive illness. 2. Depression, Mental. 3. Psychobiology. 4. Psychology, Pathological. 5. Physiology, Pathological. I. Watkins, Francisco.

RC516 .B57 2019
616.895--dc23

Table of Contents

Preface

This book has been a concerted effort by a group of academicians, researchers and scientists, who have contributed their research works for the realization of the book. This book has materialized in the wake of emerging advancements and innovations in this field. Therefore, the need of the hour was to compile all the required researches and disseminate the knowledge to a broad spectrum of people comprising of students, researchers and specialists of the field.

Bipolar disorder is a mental disorder, which causes periods of abnormally elevated mood and periods of depression. The elevated mood may be classified as mania or hypomania, depending on its severity and the presence or absence of signs of psychosis. An individual is likely to make quick decisions with little regard for consequences when in manic periods. During depression, negative outlook towards life, crying and poor eye contact with others are common. There is a high risk of suicide and self-harm in people with this disorder. Bipolar disorder may be caused due to genetic, environmental and neurological triggers. Abnormalities in the function or structure of certain brain circuits, and abnormal action and production of neurotransmitters may result in this disorder. Treatment usually follows a course of medications such as antipsychotics and mood stabilizers, and psychotherapy. This book covers in detail some existing theories and innovative concepts revolving around bipolar disorders. The objective of this book is to give a general view of the different clinical, psychological and behavioral aspects of bipolar disorders. It will help the readers in keeping pace with the rapid changes in this field.

At the end of the preface, I would like to thank the authors for their brilliant chapters and the publisher for guiding us all-through the making of the book till its final stage. Also, I would like to thank my family for providing the support and encouragement throughout my academic career and research projects.

Editor

Add-on treatment with *N*-acetylcysteine for bipolar depression: a 24-week randomized double-blind parallel group placebo-controlled multicentre trial (NACOS-study protocol)

Pernille Kempel Ellegaard[1,2,3*], Rasmus Wentzer Licht[4,5], Henrik Enghusen Poulsen[6,7], René Ernst Nielsen[4,5], Michael Berk[8,9,10], Olivia May Dean[8,9,10], Mohammadreza Mohebbi[11] and Connie Thuroee Nielsen[1,12]

Abstract

Background: Oxidative stress and inflammation may be involved in the development and progression of mood disorders, including bipolar disorder. Currently, there is a scarcity of useful treatment options for bipolar depressive episodes, especially compared with the efficacy of treatment for acute mania. *N*-Acetylcysteine (NAC) has been explored for psychiatric disorders for some time given its antioxidant and anti-inflammatory properties. The current trial aims at testing the clinical effects of adjunctive NAC treatment (compared to placebo) for bipolar depression. We will also explore the biological effects of NAC in this context. We hypothesize that adjunctive NAC treatment will reduce symptoms of depression, which will be reflected by changes in selected markers of oxidative stress.

Methods and analysis: In the study, we will include adults diagnosed with bipolar disorder, in a currently depressive episode. Participants will undertake a 20-week, adjunctive, randomized, double-blinded, parallel group placebo-controlled trial comparing 3 grams of adjunctive NAC daily with placebo. The primary outcome is the mean change over time from baseline to end of study on the Montgomery–Asberg Depression Rating Scale (MADRS). Among the secondary outcomes are mean changes from baseline to end of study on the Bech-Rafaelsen Melancholia Scale (MES), the Young Mania Rating Scale (YMRS), the WHO-Five Well-being Index (WHO-5), the Global Assessment of Functioning scale (GAF-F), the Global Assessment of Symptoms scale (GAF-S) and the Clinical Global Impression-Severity scale (CGI-S). The potential effects on oxidative stress by NAC treatment will be measured through urine and blood samples. DNA will be examined for potential polymorphisms related to oxidative defences.

Keywords: Bipolar disorder, Depression, Acetylcysteine, Oxidative stress, Inflammation, Urine, Blood, Treatment, Psychiatry, Genetics

Background

Bipolar disorder is generally characterized by recurrent episodes of mania (or hypomania) and major depression (Goodwin and Jamison 2007), with depressive phases being the dominant phase in terms of overall duration (Judd and Akiskal 2003).

In recent treatment guidelines for bipolar disorder, combinations of pharmacotherapy and psychotherapeutical treatments such as psychoeducation and individual or group-based psychotherapy are generally recommended (Fountoulakis et al. 2017). Regarding pharmacotherapy, combined use of various drugs is often beneficial in terms of both acute treatment response and for maintenance

*Correspondence: Pernille.ellegaard@rsyd.dk
[2] Research Unit, Mental Health Service Esbjerg, Gl. Vardevej 101, 6715 Esbjerg N, The Region of Southern Denmark, Denmark
Full list of author information is available at the end of the article

(Geddes et al. 2016). However, despite all efforts, treatment outcome is often inadequate, necessitating the development of new, more effective treatments. There a scarcity of effective treatments for the acute treatment of bipolar depression, in particular (Grunze et al. 2010).

Studies have indicated that oxidative stress and neuroinflammation seem to be linked to the pathophysiology of bipolar disorder (Andreazza et al. 2008; Berk et al. 2011). Recent studies have reported increased levels of oxidative stress markers in blood and urine samples from patients suffering from bipolar disorder (Andreazza et al. 2007, 2008; Munkholm et al. 2015; Jacoby et al. 2016). Furthermore, there is evidence that the level of oxidative stress may be a state marker in bipolar disorder (Munkholm et al. 2015; Fernandes et al. 2011; Polyakova et al. 2015).

The brain is thought to be especially vulnerable to oxidative stress due to its' high metabolic demands and its' limited capacity of defences such as glutathione (GSH), which is the central antioxidant in all tissues (Ballatori et al. 2009). Bipolar disorder is associated with decreased GSH levels, resulting in increased oxidative stress (Andreazza et al. 2008; Rosa et al. 2014; Brown et al. 2014; Soeiro-de-Souza et al. 2013). *N*-Acetylcysteine (NAC), the acetyl derivative of the amino acid cysteine, improves the L-cysteine supply, which increases GSH levels in the brain (Choy et al. 2010; Dean et al. 2009). Accordingly, NAC treatment appears to decrease oxidative stress and inflammation (Dean et al. 2011). Two previous clinical trials on NAC for bipolar disorder have shown significant effects on depressive symptoms (Berk et al. 2008, 2011).

Study rationale

Given the paucity of effective pharmacotherapy for bipolar depression, it seems warranted to test whether the previous positive findings of NAC for bipolar depression can be replicated in a Danish study sample. Furthermore, we wanted to go further than these studies by exploring the antioxidant effects of NAC in the context of the clinical trial. Finally, it would be useful for the development of new pharmacotherapies in general to test whether the potential antidepressant efficacy of NAC is linked to its antioxidant effects. In addition to the latter point, finding a relationship between the level of oxidative stress at baseline and the efficacy of NAC would be a step towards the goal of precision psychiatry (Fernandes et al. 2017).

Aims and objectives

The primary aim is to investigate the effects of adjunctive NAC treatment on depressive symptoms in participants diagnosed with bipolar depression. The secondary aims are to measure the biological effect of NAC treatment based on markers of oxidative stress in urine samples.

The study objectives are following:

Process aim 1

Assessing baseline adjusted between-group mean change between NAC and placebo group from baseline up till week 20 on The Montgomery–Asberg Depression Rating Scale score (MADRS) (Montgomery and Åsberg 1979).

Process aim 2

Assessing baseline adjusted between-group mean difference between NAC and placebo group from baseline up till week 20 on; the Bech-Rafaelsen Melancholia Scale (MES) (Bech 2002), the Young Mania Rating Scale (YMRS) (Young et al. 1978), the WHO-Five Well-being Index (WHO-5) (Staehr 1998), the Global Assessment of Functioning scale (GAF-F), The Global Assessment of Symptoms scale (GAF-S) (Jones et al. 1995) and the Clinical Global Impression-Severity scale (CGI-S) (Guy WNI-oMHPRBECDEP 1976).

Process aim 3

Assessing baseline adjusted between-group mean difference between NAC and placebo group from baseline up till week 20 in urine samples to explore biological correlation in DNA and RNA damage by oxidative stress.

Process aim 4

Assessing baseline adjusted between-group mean difference between NAC and placebo group from baseline up till week 24 on MADRS, MES, YMRS, WHO-5, GAF-F, GAF-S, CGI-S and urinary markers.

Process aim 5

Assessing baseline urinary markers to explore correlation in DNA and RNA damage by oxidative stress and the degree of depression severity.

Additionally, blood samples and DNA are collected for further explorations towards detecting potential genetic polymorphisms related to oxidative defences, but are currently stored.

Methods

Trial design

This is a 20-week randomized, double-blind, parallel group, placebo-controlled, multicentre trial, with a 4-weeks follow up after study treatment discontinuation. The protocol is developed in accordance with the Standard Protocol Items: Recommendations for Intervention Trials (SPIRIT) 2013 Guidelines (Chan et al. 2013). The study will follow the Consolidated Standards of Reporting Trials (CONSORT) guidelines to describe, report and publish the results (Schulz et al. 2010).

Visits and telephone calls

The study visits (outlined in Fig. 1) are planned to be at week 2, 10, 20 and 24 (± 7 days for each visit). Furthermore, participants will be contacted via telephone 6 and 15 weeks after inclusion (± 7 days). Telephone calls are conducted with participants to support adherence and provide an opportunity for participants to discuss any issues with the study (including adverse events).

Participant selection

The study participants will be recruited amongst in-and out patients from the Mental Health Services from three study centres covering three geographical areas (three cities in centre one and two, and one city in centre three). We plan to recruit participants over a study period of 2 years.

Participants assess for eligibility will be screened according to the inclusion and exclusion criteria.

Participant eligibility

Inclusion criteria

Participants will be included if they meet all of the following criteria:

- 18–64 years of age at baseline (inclusive).
- A diagnosis of bipolar disorder type I or II, current episode of depression according to Diagnostic and Statistical Manual of Mental Disorders 5 (DSM-V) (American Psychiatric Association 2000) (evaluated by using the M.I.N.I (International Neuropsychiatric Interview), version 5.0 in Danish (Sheehan et al. 1998).
- At least one documented affective episode within the last 6 months within the index period (depressive, manic or mixed), as judged by the principal investigator (according to the medical journal, and clinical interview based on the M.I.N.I
- Have had symptoms of depression for at least 4 weeks up till screening, and a Montgomery–Asberg Depression Rating Scale (MADRS) score of ≥ 18 (mild depression or more) at that time.
- Have given full oral and written informed consent.

Female participants should present a negative pregnant test at baseline and will be informed to use effective contraception throughout the study period.

Exclusion criteria

Participants will be excluded if they meet any of the following criteria:

- Have a daily intake of more than 500 mg NAC, 200 μM selenium, or 500 IU of vitamin E at screening.
- Have received electroconvulsive therapy (ECT) within the last 4 weeks prior to screening.
- Have epilepsy, chronic asthma or allergy towards NAC, as judged by investigator.
- Involuntary admitted, detainment or treated according to the statutes defined in the Mental Health Act.
- Cannot speak or understand the Danish language.
- Females planning pregnancy or breastfeeding during the timeframe of the study.

Discontinuation criteria

Participants will discontinue the study under the following circumstances:

- Withdrawal of consent.
- Discontinues study treatment for 7 or more consecutive days.

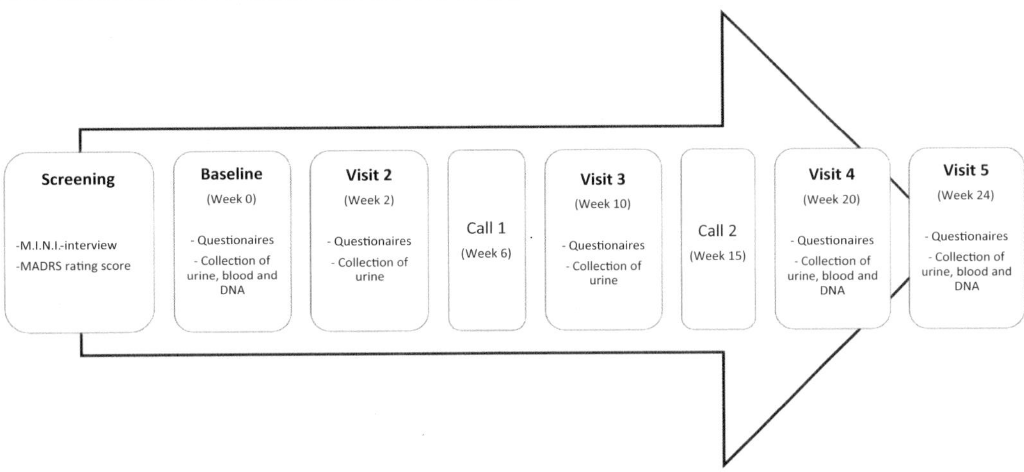

Fig. 1 Timeline with outcomes measures. *M.I.N.I-interview* Mini International Neuropsychiatric Interview, *MADRS* Montgomery–Asberg Depression Rating Scale

- Does not comply with the defined study visits (visits within 7 days prior or after the computer-generated date).
- Becomes pregnant, initiates breastfeeding, or wishes to become pregnant during the study period.
- Becomes hypersensitive to histamine, as judged by investigator.
- Develops serious adverse reaction/event (SAR/SAE) i.e. suspected to be associated with the study treatment, as judged by an investigator.
- Stops using effective contraception.
- Changes diagnosis during the study, and the primary diagnosis is no longer bipolar affective disorder.
- Involuntary admitted, detainment or treated according to the statutes defined in the Mental Health Act.
- Becomes increasingly suicidal during the study as judged by investigator.

Randomization

Participants will be randomized to NAC or placebo treatment by a computer-based random eight block number generator. The study participants will be randomised sequentially by the order they are enrolled into the trial. The randomization assignments will be hidden from the participants and the study investigators and raters. An independent pharmacy, Glostrup Pharmacy, will perform the randomization process, provide the randomization codes and the labelling of the tablet containers. The Coordinating Investigator (PKE) and Sponsor/Principal Investigator (CTN) will enrol and assign participants from two of the study centres, and the second Principal Investigator (REN) and a project nurse (HOE) will enrol and assign participants from the latter study centre.

Blinding procedure

The study medication is blinded to both study participants and the investigators. If un-blinding of one or more study participants is required, Glostrup Pharmacy hold the randomization list and can be contacted 24 h a day. Furthermore, the investigators have a sealed envelope with the randomization list, if there is a need for unblinding of any participants. To minimize the risk of participants comparing experiences, the study visits will be arranged staggered throughout the day and always separately. When all study participants have completed the trial, the study medication will be un-blinded.

Study treatment

Participants will be randomized to receive either NAC (National Center for Biotechnology Information 2017) or placebo in addition to their current pharmacotherapy and psychotherapy.

The study treatment powder (NAC and placebo) are imported and manufactured at Glostrup Pharmacy, which has manufacturing authorization, and all medication used is manufactured in accordance with good manufacturing practice (GMP) and good distribution practice (GDP).

The study medication is divided into nine, white containers containing 100 tablets each. The study medication is distributed twice during the 20 weeks, and receive 9 containers in total.

Participants will take three tablets containing 500 mg each, twice daily (3 g daily) for 20 weeks. NAC and placebo tablets have a similar appearance and have an added lemon odour, in order to camouflage the sulphur-containing odour of NAC.

ECT is not permitted 4 weeks prior to inclusion, but is allowed during the trial. Treating clinicians are allowed to change both psychopharmacy and psychotherapy during the trial at their discretion.

Treatment adherence

To enhance adherence, the participants will be offered a text message with two daily reminder messages on taking the study medication. The participants will be encouraged to return all remaining trial medication at the end of study participation. The returned tablet containers and the tables will all be counted and documented.

Outcome measures

The clinical and demographic data is obtained by the investigators through patient interviews and from hospital records. The biological data is obtained through laboratory analyses of blood and urine samples. An overview of the data collection process is displayed in Table 1.

Clinical outcome measures

The clinical measurements include scales of depressive symptoms (MADRS and MES), manic symptoms (YMRS), quality of life (WHO-5), symptoms- and social functioning level (GAF-S and GAF-F) and global clinical impression (CGI-S). All rating scales used in the study are assessed and validated in Danish.

Biological outcome measures

The biological data collected from the study participants will include urine and blood samples as well as DNA. The biological data will be applied to investigate markers of oxidative stress and inflammation. All biological materials (urine, blood and DNA) will be collected from not-fasting participants. The urine and blood samples are transferred to tubes, and all three biological materials are stored in hospital freezers until analysis.

Table 1 Overview of all measurements, instruments and time points

Variables	Sources	Study period					
		Enrolment	Intervention				Follow-up
		Screening	Baseline (week 0)	Visit 2 (week 2)	Visit 3 (week 10)	Visit 4 (week 20)	Visit 5 (week 24)
MADRS	Rater	X		X	X	X	X
MES, WHO-5, GAF-S, GAF-F, CGI-S YMRS	Rater/self-reported		X	X	X	X	X
M.I.N.I.-Interview	Rater	X					
Demographic (age, gender, height, inclusion site, etc.)	Self-reported		X				
Weight and BMI	Rater		X	X	X	X	X
Personal and demographic details (income source, education, relationship etc.)	Self-reported		X				
Family mental history	Self-reported		X				
Lifestyle information (smoking status, alcohol consumption and substance abuse)	Self-reported		X	X	X	X	X
Disorder information (no. of: episodes of depression, hypomania/mania, neutral mood, ECT, hospital admissions, suicidal thoughts, suicide attempts, etc.)	Self-reported/hospital record		X				
Medical conditions (Doctor diagnosed)	Self-reported		X				
Pharmacological treatment	Hospital record		X	X	X	X	X
Psychological treatment	Self-reported		X	X	X	X	X
Adverse events/reactions	Self-reported		X	X	X	X	X
Biography	Self-reported			X			
Urine samples	Laboratory		X	X	X	X	X
Blood samples	Laboratory		X			X	X
DNA	Laboratory		X			X	X

Screening pre-intervention, *Baseline* pre-intervention (week 0), *Visit 2* week 2, *Visit 3* week 10, *Visit 4* post-intervention (week 20), *Visit 5* follow-up (week 24), *Rater* coordinating investigator/project nurse, *MADRS* Montgomery-Åsberg Depression Rating Scale score, *MES* Bech-Rafaelsen Melancholia Scale, *WHO-5* World Health Organization well-being index, *GAF-S* The Global Assessment of Symptoms scale, *GAF-F* The Global Assessment of Functioning scale, *YMRS* Young Mania Rating Scale (YMRS), *CGI-S* The Clinical Global Impression-Severity scale (CGI-I), *M.I.N.I-interview* Mini International Neuropsychiatric Interview, *ECT* electroconvulsive therapy

Serious adverse reactions/events and adverse reactions/events

SARs, SAEs, Adverse Events (AE) and Adverse Reactions (AR) are defined according to good clinical practice (GCP), and assessed at each visit. Participants who discontinue study participation due to SAEs or SARs will be followed until the SAE/SAR has disappeared or the SAE/SAR is stable. Participants will be contacted with a few days after SAE/SAR and again after 4 weeks.

Data management

The trial is conducted in accordance with good clinical practice guidelines and Declaration of Helsinki, and will be monitoring by the GCP-unit at Odense University Hospital, Denmark. The study is approved before study initiation by the Regional Scientific Ethical Committees for Southern Denmark: 35664-20120177, the Danish Medicines Agency: 2012-004483-22, and Danish Data Protection Agency: 2008-58-0035. The trial is registered at ClinicalTrials.Gov: NCT02294591 and the European Clinical Trials Database, EudraCT: 2012-004483-22.

All data in the CRFs (Case Report Forms) are double entered in the database program *Research Electronic Data Capture* (REDCap) (Harris et al. 2009) by coordinating investigator (PKE).

Sample size and feasibility of recruitment

The sample size estimation was based on prior data from a similar clinical trial showing mean (SD) in MADRS score (from baseline to end of the study (week 24)) was decreased by around 10.0 ± 4.3 and increased by around 0.9 ± 2.6 (in respectively the NAC and the placebo group (Berk et al. 2008). Our sample size was calculated using a two-tailed independent sample t-test with 80% power to detect baseline-adjusted between-group mean difference at week 20, and a two-sided alpha-level of 0.05. To detect a between-group mean difference of change from baseline of at least 8 ± 10.0, 56 participants in total were required. Due to the expectation of a 40% drop-out rate we aim to recruit an overall of 78 study participants. To achieve an adequate number of participants, all in- and out-patients from the Mental Health Service included in the study having a bipolar disorder or suspect to have this disorder, are offered to participate.

Statistical analysis plan

A statistical significant difference in mean change on MADRS-score, between study groups, from baseline to end of study, is the primary outcome measure of the study. The remaining clinical and biological measures are secondary outcome measures and will be analysed using the same approach as the primary outcome. To investigate the difference in response and remission rates between study treatments at week 20 and 24, logistic regression models will be applied to estimate the odds ratios. The definition of a "responder" is a person which symptoms of depression has dropped 50% in MADRS-score from baseline to week 20 or 24, and "remitters" are defined as MADRS score < 10 (Hawley et al. 2002) at week 20 or 24. Data analysis will be conducted by the authors and a statistician. Between-group comparisons will be performed by applying Student t-tests, Mann–Whitney U tests, Chi square tests or Fishers exact test, whichever is most appropriate. The primary analysis for primary and secondary outcomes will be based on an Intention-To-Treat (ITT) analysis comprise all study participants completed the baseline measurements. A generalized estimating equation (GEE) (Feng et al. 2001) approach will be taken, and the likelihood-based linear mixed effects repeated measures (LMERM) analyses (Mallinckrodt et al. 2001; Laird and Ware 1982) is the primary analysis. The LMERM-analysis includes the fixed variable *study treatment, visits* as factor variable, and *treatment-by-visits* interaction (intervention impact). The LMERM includes all available data at each time point and is the preferred methods of analysing clinical trial data in psychiatry due to the fact that likelihood approach deals with missing data in follow-ups assuming missingness is at random. Planned comparisons will be done with the LMERM models to determine between-group differences in score change from baseline to week 2, week 10, week 20 and week 24. Additional per-protocol analysis includes participants who completed the study intervention. Sensitivity analysis will evaluate missing at random assumptions for missing follow-up data. Missing data will be imputed assuming Missing Not At Random (MNAR) in intervention, control and both arms respectively and robustness of finding under different MNAR assumptions will be examined.

Additionally, effect sizes will be reported using Cohen's guidelines (Cohen 1988). Dichotomous data will be presented as proportions, with 95% confidence interval, and reporting Chi square of Fishers's exact p-value where appropriate. Likelihood based generalized linear mixed repeated measures approach (GLMRM) with logit link will be used to compare dichotomous outcomes.

All tests of treatment effects will be conducted using a two-sided alpha level of 0.05. The statistical analysis will be conducted utilizing the statistical software program STATA IC, version 15 (StataCorp. Stata Statistical Software: Release 15 College Station, TX: StataCorp LP 2017). Statistical analysis plans can be obtained from the first author (PKE).

Discussion

In the current study, we will investigate the clinical effect of 3 g/day of adjunctive NAC treatment on symptoms of bipolar depression utilizing a randomized, double-blinded, parallel group, placebo-controlled design. People diagnosed with bipolar disorder predominantly experience depression, which is currently challenging to treat (Grande et al. 2016). It is evident that a large group of patients do not respond adequately to traditional pharmacotherapy and/or psychotherapy, which creates a need for novel treatment opportunities. If this trial indicates that NAC treatment significantly reduces symptoms of depression, NAC may become an important part of the pharmacotherapeutical options for bipolar disorder.

NAC is well-tolerated with few and often mild adverse events (Fernandes et al. 2016), and is available without prescription in many countries. The selected dosage in this trial has been well-tolerated in previous trials (Prado et al. 2015; Mardikian et al. 2007). NAC is hypothesized to decrease symptoms of depression at least in part due to its antioxidant properties. At present, few studies have investigated the effects of NAC in patients with bipolar depression, and the results have been mixed. Our study therefore will add to the limited clinical database (Berk et al. 2008, 2012).

The main strengths of the trial are the double-blinded design, with only two raters, and the possibility to do the study interviews in the patients' home, which should reduce drop-outs.

To increase adherence, the study medication is formulated as tablets instead of effervescent tablets, making is possible to take it along with existing medication. To reflect usual clinical practice, all kinds of non-study pharmaceutical treatment are allowed, including changes prior to and after inclusion. However, this may diminish the chances to detect a potential superiority of NAC over placebo.

The novelty of this study is the collection of several biological materials to explore the oxidative balance, inflammation and DNA damage related to the disorder and the treatment. Additionally, the study will shed light on the possible immune modulatory effects of NAC treatment. The markers may provide an insight to the potential mechanisms underlying the pathophysiology of BD.

Dissemination of results

The results from this study will be presented at national and international conferences and published in peer-reviewed journals.

Abbreviations

AE: adverse events; ANCOVA: ANalysis of COVAriance; AR: adverse reactions; CGI-S: Clinical Global Impression Scale-Severity scale; CONSORT: The Consolidated Standards of Reporting Trials; CRF: Case Report Form; CTN: Connie T. Nielsen; DSM-IV: Diagnostic and Statistical Manual of Mental Disorders 5; ECT: electroconvulsive therapy; GAF-F: Global Assessment of Functioning Scale; GAF-S: Global Assessment of Symptoms Scale; GCP: good clinical practice; GDP: good distribution practice; GEE: generalized estimating equation; GMP: good manufacturing practice; GSH: glutathione; HEP: Henrik E. Poulsen; HOS: Helle O. Soerensen; ITT: intention to treat; LMERM: linear mixed effects repeated measures; MADRS: Montgomery–Asberg Depression Rating Scale; M.B: Michael Berk; MES: Melancholia Scale; M.I.N.I-interview: Mini International Neuropsychiatric Interview; MNAR: missing nor at random; NAC: *N*-acetylcysteine; OMD: Olivia M. Dean; PKE: Pernille K. Ellegaard; REDCap: research electronics data capture; REN: René E. Nielsen; RWL: Rasmus W. Licht; SAE: serious adverse event; SAR: serious adverse reaction; SPIRIT: The Standard Protocol Items: Recommendations for Intervention Trials; WHO-5: WHO-5 Well-Being Index; YMRS: Young Mania Rating Scale.

Authors' contributions

The Vancouver Convention guidelines were applied (ICMJE 2017). PKE, CTN, RWL, HEP, MB and OMD conceptualized and designed the study. PKE and CTN raised funding and initiated the trial. PKE coordinated the trial, and conducted the trial together with CTN, REN and HOS. PKE drafted the manuscript; the remaining authors contributed to the manuscript and approved the final version. The Mental Health Service, The Region of Southern Denmark is the trial sponsor (psykiatrisygehuset@rsyd.dk). All authors read and approved the final manuscript.

Author details

[1] Institute of Regional Health Services Research, Faculty of Health Sciences, University of Southern Denmark, Odense, Denmark. [2] Research Unit, Mental Health Service Esbjerg, Gl. Vardevej 101, 6715 Esbjerg N, The Region of Southern Denmark, Denmark. [3] OPEN, Odense Patient Data Explorative Network, Odense University Hospital, Institute of Clinical Research, University of Southern Denmark, Odense, Denmark. [4] Unit for Psychiatric Research, Psychiatry, Aalborg University Hospital, Aalborg, Denmark. [5] Department of Clinical Medicine, Faculty of Medicine, Aalborg University, Aalborg, Denmark. [6] Clinical Pharmacology, Bispebjerg Frederiksberg Hospital, Copenhagen, Denmark. [7] Institute of Clinical Medicine, Faculty of Health and Medical Sciences, University of Copenhagen, Copenhagen, Denmark. [8] IMPACT Strategic Research Centre, School of Medicine, Barwon Health, Deakin University, Geelong, Australia. [9] Florey Institute for Neuroscience and Mental Health, University of Melbourne, Parkville, Australia. [10] Department of Psychiatry, University of Melbourne, Royal Melbourne Hospital, Parkville, Australia. [11] Biostatistics Unit, Faculty of Health, Deakin University, Geelong, Australia. [12] Mental Health Service Vejle, Odense, The Region of Southern Denmark, Denmark.

Acknowledgements

MB is supported by a NHMRC Senior Principal Research Fellowship (GNT1059660). OMD has received grant support from the Brain and Behavior Foundation, Simons Autism Foundation, Stanley Medical Research Institute, Deakin University, Lilly, NHMRC and Australasian Society for Bipolar and Depressive Disorders (ASBDD)/Servier. She has also received in kind support from BioMedica Nutracuticals, NutritionCare and Bioceuticals.

Competing interests

PK Ellegaard has received speaking fee from Lundbeck. RW Licht has received research grant from Glaxo Smith Kline, honoraria for lecturing from Pfizer, Glaxo Smith Kline, Eli Lilly, Astra-Zeneca, Bristol-Myers Squibb, Janssen Cilag, Lundbeck, Otsuka, Servier and honoraria from advisory board activity from Glaxo Smith Kline, Eli Lilly, Astra-Zeneca, Bristol-Myers Squibb, Janssen Cilag, and Sunovion. RE Nielsen has received research grants from H. Lundbeck and Otsuka Pharmaceuticals for clinical trials, received speaking fees from Bristol-Myers Squibb, Astra Zeneca, Janssen and Cilag, Lundbeck, Servier, Otsuka Pharmaceuticals, and Eli Lilly and has acted as advisor to Astra Zeneca, Eli Lilly, Lundbeck, Otsuka Pharmaceuticals, Takeda, and Medivir. Berk has received Grant/Research Support from the NIH, Cooperative Research Centre, Simons Autism Foundation, Cancer Council of Victoria, Stanley Medical Research Foundation, MBF, NHMRC, Beyond Blue, Rotary Health, Geelong Medical Research Foundation, Bristol Myers Squibb, Eli Lilly, Glaxo SmithKline, Meat and Livestock Board, Organon, Novartis, Mayne Pharma, Servier, Woolworths, Avant and the Harry Windsor Foundation, has been a speaker for Astra Zeneca, Bristol Myers Squibb, Eli Lilly, Glaxo SmithKline, Janssen Cilag, Lundbeck,

Merck, Pfizer, Sanofi Synthelabo, Servier, Solvay and Wyeth, and served as a consultant to Allergan, Astra Zeneca, Bioadvantex, Bionomics, Collaborative Medicinal Development, Eli Lilly, Grunbiotics, Glaxo SmithKline, Janssen Cilag, LivaNova, Lundbeck, Merck, Mylan, Otsuka, Pfizer and Servier. OM Dean has received grant support from the Brain and Behavior Foundation, Simons Autism Foundation, Stanley Medical Research Institute, Deakin University, Lilly, NHMRC and ASBDD/Servier. She has also received in kind support from Bio-Medica Nutracuticals, NutritionCare and Bioceuticals. HE Poulsen, M Mohebbi and CT Nielsen has no conflicts of interest to declare.

Funding

The trial has received grants from: The Psychiatry Research Foundation in Region of Southern Denmark, Ph.D. Scholarship from The University of Southern Denmark, Mental Health Service, Vejle and Beckett Foundation. All grants were unrestricted with respect to the development or execution of the trial, study design, analysis plan and dissemination of study results.

References

American Psychiatric Association. Diagnostic and statistical manual of mental disorders. In: Capter 6: Mood disorders, mixed episode. 4th text rev. ed2000.

Andreazza AC, Frey BN, Erdtmann B, Salvador M, Rombaldi F, Santin A, et al. DNA damage in bipolar disorder. Psychiatry Res. 2007;153(1):27–32.

Andreazza AC, Kauer-Sant'anna M, Frey BN, Bond DJ, Kapczinski F, Young LT, et al. Oxidative stress markers in bipolar disorder: a meta-analysis. J Affect Disord. 2008;111(2–3):135–44.

Ballatori N, Krance SM, Notenboom S, Shi S, Tieu K, Hammond CL. Glutathione dysregulation and the etiology and progression of human diseases. Biol Chem. 2009;390(3):191–214.

Bech P. The Bech-Rafaelsen Melancholia Scale (MES) in clinical trials of therapies in depressive disorders: a 20-year review of its use as outcome measure. Acta Psychiatr Scand. 2002;106:252–64.

Berk M, Copolov DL, Dean O, Lu K, Jeavons S, Schapkaitz I, et al. N-acetyl cysteine for depressive symptoms in bipolar disorder–a double-blind randomized placebo-controlled trial. Biol Psychiat. 2008;64(6):468–75.

Berk M, Dean O, Cotton SM, Gama CS, Kapczinski F, Fernandes BS, et al. The efficacy of *N*-acetylcysteine as an adjunctive treatment in bipolar depression: an open label trial. J Affect Disord. 2011b;135(1–3):389–94.

Berk M, Dean OM, Cotton SM, Gama CS, Kapczinski F, Fernandes B, et al. Maintenance *N*-acetyl cysteine treatment for bipolar disorder: a double-blind randomized placebo controlled trial. BMC Med. 2012;10:91.

Berk M, Kapczinski F, Andreazza AC, Dean OM, Giorlando F, Maes M, et al. Pathways underlying neuroprogression in bipolar disorder: focus on inflammation, oxidative stress and neurotrophic factors. Neurosci Biobehav Rev. 2011a;35(3):804–17.

Brown NC, Andreazza AC, Young LT. An updated meta-analysis of oxidative stress markers in bipolar disorder. Psychiatry Res. 2014;218(1–2):61–8.

Chan AW, Tetzlaff JM, Altman DG, Laupacis A, Gotzsche PC, Krleza-Jeric K, et al. SPIRIT 2013 statement: defining standard protocol items for clinical trials. Ann Intern Med. 2013;158(3):200–7.

Choy KH, Dean O, Berk M, Bush AI, van den Buuse M. Effects of *N*-acety-L-cysteine treatment on glutathione depletion and a short-term spatial memory deficit in 2-cyclohexene-1-one-treated rats. Eur J Pharmacol. 2010;649(1–3):224–8.

Cohen J. Statistical power analysis for the behavioral sciences. Hillsdale: Erlbaum Associates; 1988.

Dean O, Bush AI, Berk M, Copolov DL, van den Buuse M. Glutathione depletion in the brain disrupts short-term spatial memory in the Y-maze in rats and mice. Behav Brain Res. 2009;198(1):258–62.

Dean O, Giorlando F, Berk M. *N*-Acetylcysteine in psychiatry: current therapeutic evidence and potential mechanisms of action. J Psychiatry Neurosci. 2011;36(2):78–86.

Feng Z, Diehr P, Peterson A, McLerran D. Selected statistical issues in group randomized trials. Annu Rev Public Health. 2001;22:167–87.

Fernandes BS, Dean OM, Dodd S, Malhi GS, Berk M. *N*-Acetylcysteine in depressive symptoms and functionality: a systematic review and meta-analysis. J Clin Psychiatry. 2016;77(4):e457–66.

Fernandes BS, Gama CS, Cereser KM, Yatham LN, Fries GR, Colpo G, et al. Brain-derived neurotrophic factor as a state-marker of mood episodes in bipolar disorders: a systematic review and meta-regression analysis. J Psychiatr Res. 2011;45(8):995–1004.

Fernandes BS, Williams LM, Steiner J, Leboyer M, Carvalho AF, Berk M. The new field of 'precision psychiatry'. BMC Med. 2017;15(1):80.

Fountoulakis KN, Grunze H, Vieta E, Young A, Yatham L, Blier P, et al. The International College of Neuro-Psychopharmacology (CINP) Treatment Guidelines for Bipolar Disorder in Adults (CINP-BD-2017), part 3: the clinical guidelines. Int J Neuropsychopharmacol. 2017;20(2):180–95.

Geddes JR, Gardiner A, Rendell J, Voysey M, Tunbridge E, Hinds C, et al. Comparative evaluation of quetiapine plus lamotrigine combination versus quetiapine monotherapy (and folic acid versus placebo) in bipolar depression (CEQUEL): a 2 × 2 factorial randomised trial. Lancet Psychiatry. 2016;3(1):31–9.

Goodwin F, Jamison K. Manic-depressive illness: bipolar disorders and recurrent depression. Oxford: Oxford University Press; 2007.

Grande I, Berk M, Birmaher B, Vieta E. Bipolar disorder. Lancet. 2016;387(10027):1561–72.

Grunze H, Vieta E, Goodwin GM, Bowden C, Licht RW, Moller HJ, et al. The World Federation of Societies of Biological Psychiatry (WFSBP) guidelines for the biological treatment of bipolar disorders: update 2010 on the treatment of acute bipolar depression. World J Biol Psychiatry. 2010;11(2):81–109.

Guy WNIoMHPRBECDEP. ECDEU assessment manual for psychopharmacology. Rockville, Md.: US Dept. of Health, Education, and Welfare, Public Health Service, Alcohol, Drug Abuse, and Mental Health Administration, National Institute of Mental Health, Psychopharmacology Research Branch, Division of Extramural Research Programs; 1976.

Harris Paul A, Taylor Robert, Thielke Robert, Payne Jonathon, Gonzalez Nathaniel, Conde Jose G. Research electronic data capture (REDCap)—a metadata-driven methodology and workflow process for providing translational research informatics support. J Biomed Inform. 2009;42(2):377–81.

Hawley CJ, Gale TM, Sivakumaran T. Hertfordshire neuroscience research group. Defining remission by cut off score on the MADRS: selecting the optimal value. J Affect Disord. 2002;72(2):177–84.

ICMJE International Committee of Medical Journal Editors. Defining the Role of Authors and Contributors. 2017. http://www.icmje.org/recommendations/browse/roles-and-responsibilities/defining-the-role-of-authors-and-contributors.html.

Jacoby AS, Vinberg M, Poulsen HE, Kessing LV, Munkholm K. Increased DNA and RNA damage by oxidation in patients with bipolar I disorder. Transl Psychiatry. 2016;6(8):e867.

Jones SH, Thornicroft G, Coffey M, Dunn G. A brief mental health outcome scale-reliability and validity of the Global Assessment of Functioning (GAF). Br J Psychiatry. 1995;166(5):654–9.

Judd LL, Akiskal HS. Depressive episodes and symptoms dominate the longitudinal course of bipolar disorder. Curr Psychiatry Rep. 2003;5(6):417–8.

Laird NM, Ware JH. Random-effects models for longitudinal data. Biometrics. 1982;38(4):963–74.

Mallinckrodt CH, Clark WS, David SR. Accounting for dropout bias using mixed-effects models. J Biopharm Stat. 2001;11(1–2):9–21.

Mardikian PN, LaRowe SD, Hedden S, Kalivas PW, Malcolm RJ. An open-label trial of *N*-acetylcysteine for the treatment of cocaine dependence: a pilot study. Prog Neuropsychopharmacol Biol Psychiatry. 2007;31(2):389–94.

Montgomery SA, Åsberg M. A new depression scale designed to be sensitive to change. Br J Psychiatry. 1979;134:382–9.

Munkholm K, Poulsen HE, Kessing LV, Vinberg M. Elevated levels of urinary markers of oxidatively generated DNA and RNA damage in bipolar disorder. Bipolar Disord. 2015;17(3):257–68.

National Center for Biotechnology Information. PubChem Compound Database; CID=12035, *N*-acetyl-L-cysteine. 2017. https://pubchem.ncbi.nlm.nih.gov/compound/12035.

Polyakova M, Stuke K, Schuemberg K, Mueller K, Schoenknecht P, Schroeter ML. BDNF as a biomarker for successful treatment of mood disorders: a systematic and quantitative meta-analysis. J Affect Disord. 2015;174(174):432–40.

Prado E, Maes M, Piccoli LG, Baracat M, Barbosa DS, Franco O, et al. *N*-Acetylcysteine for therapy-resistant tobacco use disorder: a pilot study. Redox Rep. 2015;20(5):215–22.

Rosa AR, Singh N, Whitaker E, de Brito M, Lewis AM, Vieta E, et al. Altered plasma glutathione levels in bipolar disorder indicates higher oxidative stress; a possible risk factor for illness onset despite normal brain-derived neurotrophic factor (BDNF) levels. Psychol Med. 2014;44(11):2409–18.

Schulz KF, Altman DG, Moher D, Group C. CONSORT 2010 statement: updated guidelines for reporting parallel group randomised trials. BMJ. 2010;340:c332.

Sheehan DV, Lecrubier Y, Sheehan KH, Amorim P, Janavs J, Weiller E, et al. The Mini-International Neuropsychiatric Interview (M.I.N.I.): the development and validation of a structured diagnostic psychiatric interview for DSM-IV and ICD-10. J Clin Psychiatry. 1998;59(Suppl 20):22–33 **(quiz 4-57)**.

Soeiro-de-Souza MG, Andreazza AC, Carvalho AF, Machado-Vieira R, Young LT, Moreno RA. Number of manic episodes is associated with elevated DNA oxidation in bipolar I disorder. Int J Neuropsychopharmacol. 2013;16(7):1505–12.

Staehr JK. The use of well-being measures in primary health care—the DepCare project; in World Health Organization, Regional Office for Europe: Well-Being Mea-sures in Primary Health Care—the DepCare Project. Geneva: World Health Organization; 1998.

StataCorp. Stata Statistical Software: Release 15 College Station, TX: StataCorp LP; 2017. http://www.stata.com.

Young RC, Biggs JT, Ziegler VE, Meyer DA. A rating scale for mania: reliability, validity and sensitivity. Br J Psychiatry. 1978;133:429–35.

2

Actigraphy as an objective intra-individual marker of activity patterns in acute-phase bipolar disorder

Karoline Krane-Gartiser[1,2*], Andreas Asheim[3,4], Ole Bernt Fasmer[5,6], Gunnar Morken[1,2], Arne E. Vaaler[1,2] and Jan Scott[1,7]

Abstract

Background: Actigraphy could be an objective alternative to clinical ratings of motor activity in bipolar disorder (BD), which is of importance now that increased activity and energy are added as cardinal symptoms of (hypo)mania in the DSM-5 and commonly used rating scales give inadequate information about motor symptoms. To date, most actigraphy studies have been conducted in groups and/or used mean activity levels as the variable of interest. The novelty of this case series is therefore to indicate the potential of actigraphy and non-parametric analysis as an objective and personalized marker of intra-individual activity patterns in different phases of BD. To our knowledge, this is the first case series that provides an objective assessment of non-linear dynamics in within-person activity patterns during acute BD episodes.

Results: We report on three cases of bipolar I disorder with 24-h actigraphy recordings undertaken during the first few days of two or more separate admissions for an acute illness episode, including admissions for individuals in different phases of BD, or with different levels of severity in the same phase of illness. For each recording, we calculated mean activity levels over 24 h, but especially focused on key measures of variability and complexity in activity. Intra-individual activity patterns were found to be different according to phase of illness, but showed consistency within the same phase. With increasing psychotic symptoms, there was evidence of a lower overall level and greater irregularity in activity. As such, sample entropy (a measure of irregularity) may have particular utility in characterizing mania and psychotic symptoms, while assessment of the distribution of rest versus activity over 24 h may distinguish between phases of BD within an individual.

Conclusions: This case series indicates that objective, intra-individual, real-time recordings of patterns of activity may have clinical impact as a valuable adjunct to clinical observation and symptom ratings. We suggest that actigraphy combined with detailed mathematical analysis provides a biological variable that could become an important tool for developing a personalized approach to diagnostics and treatment monitoring in BD.

Keywords: Actigraphy, Bipolar disorder, Mania, Intra-individual, Variability, Non-linear dynamics, Biological variable, Objective markers, Personalized medicine

Background

Increased activity and energy are now included alongside mood changes as cardinal symptoms of (hypo)mania in the Diagnostic and Statistical Manual, 5th edition (DSM-5) (American Psychiatric Association 2013). A systematic review confirmed that empirical evidence supports this change in the 'criterion A' symptoms for (hypo) mania (Scott et al. 2016). However, it also highlighted that most instruments used to rate activity, energy and mood changes were not fit for this purpose in bipolar disorders (BD) (Scott et al. 2016). For example, an item response theory (IRT) analysis of the utility of the Young

*Correspondence: karoline.krane-gartiser@ntnu.no
[1] Department of Mental Health, NTNU, Norwegian University of Science and Technology, P.O. box 3250 Sluppen, 7006 Trondheim, Norway
Full list of author information is available at the end of the article

Mania Rating Scale and Montgomery–Asberg Depression Rating Scale indicated that both these widely used scales were poorly constructed and inefficient, (e.g., they contained several items that provided little or no psychometric information and only measured a narrow band of severity of symptoms) (Prisciandaro and Tolliver 2016). Given the renewed importance of accurately assessing activity patterns, it is pertinent to consider the role of intra-individual actigraphy as an adjunct to or an alternative rating of activity.

Actigraphy is a validated method for recording rest–activity patterns by non-invasive measurement of wrist movement (Ancoli-Israel et al. 2003) and has frequently been used for the objective measurement of sleep patterns, and to assess putative state or even trait markers of BD (Geoffroy et al. 2015; Ng et al. 2015). However, nearly all published studies have used between-group comparisons of rest–activity cycles recorded for about 1–14 days (usually BD cases versus controls), rather than examining repeated recordings of intra-individual activity over time (Scott et al. 2016; Gershon et al. 2015). There are a few exceptions, e.g., the earliest studies of actigraphy included repeated assessments of small samples of inpatients (Kupfer et al. 1974; Wehr et al. 1980; Wolff et al. 1985; Weiss et al. 1974), and a study of ten cases employed actigraphy to assess patient outcomes following lithium withdrawal (Klein et al. 1992). Nevertheless, the actiwatches available in the 1980s lacked sophistication and data analytic strategies may have been too simplistic. More recently, Salvatore et al. (2008) reported mean levels of activity and sleep in individuals in manic/mixed states and again after recovery. However, the study focused on group outcomes and crucially, mixed states and mania cases were grouped together, which recent research suggests may be inappropriate (Scott et al. 2017).

In summary, it is increasingly clear that simple measures, such as mean activity levels, do not capture the variability or complexity of activity patterns in BD sufficiently (Scott et al. 2016; Krane-Gartiser et al. 2014; De Crescenzo et al. 2016). To date, only one study has explored fluctuations in depressive symptoms by using within-person actigraphy alongside more sophisticated mathematical modeling, such as non-parametric analyses of activity patterns (Gershon et al. 2015). However, we could find no publications that specifically used non-linear dynamic analyses of within-person actigraphy recordings to determine the similarities or differences in intra-individual activity patterns during acute illness episodes. Given this omission from the literature, we report on three cases of BD-I that were hospitalized during an acute illness episode on two or more occasions. Intra-individual 24-h actigraphy provided objective recording of activity patterns for (a) different levels of symptom severity within the same illness episode, (b) relapses of the same phase of illness, or (c) relapses in different phases of BD.

Methods

The actigraphy research program at St. Olav's University Hospital in Trondheim, Norway, was approved by the Regional Ethical Committee of Central Norway (2011/137), and the study rationale, methodology and assessments used are detailed elsewhere (Scott et al. 2017; Krane-Gartiser et al. 2014, 2016).

Cases included in the current report were identified from individuals who gave written informed consent to participate in a series of case–control studies that involved 24-h actigraphy. Capacity to consent was evaluated by a clinical specialist in psychiatry or psychology, and patients who were judged unable to consent were not included. Individuals with a primary diagnosis of BD [according to a multi-disciplinary expert consensus that applied ICD-10 research diagnostic criteria (WHO 1993)] and actigraphy monitoring for at least two separate hospital admissions were selected. De-identified information regarding key aspects of the clinical history, psychiatric assessments and medical treatment during the recording periods were obtained from electronic medical case records, and sleep–wake cycle data were obtained from actigraphy recordings undertaken for 24 h via a wrist-worn actiwatch (Actiwatch Spectrum, Philips Respironics Inc., Murrysville PA, USA).

Activity measurements

Activity counts were recorded for 1-min intervals, and data were analyzed for the total recording time of 24 h. We calculated the following variables:

1. Mean activity level as counts per minute.
2. *Variability in activity* Reported as (a) the standard deviation in percent of mean activity (SD) as a measure of the intra-individual fluctuations from the mean, which is equivalent to the coefficient of variation; (b) the root mean squared successive difference (RMSSD) as a measure of the variability from minute to minute; (c) the RMSSD/SD ratio, which assesses the relationship between successive count variability and overall variability; and (d) a new estimate of activity level, namely the ratio between rest and activity which displays the temporal development of changes in activity levels over 24 h. Such a measure of activity is interesting to contrast with other measures that primarily track variability and regularity. The estimate is computed as the ratio of actigraphy samples being zero to non-zero within a time inter-

val. This ratio can vary between 0, no movement, and 1, continuous movement. By applying a shifting interval, with some smoothing (Ramsay and Silverman 2005), a continuous measure is obtained.

3. *Complexity* Sample entropy as a measure of pattern complexity or degree of regularity of the time series. This non-linear dynamical method examines even short time series for similar sequences at a certain temporal distance and calculates the probability that two sequences are self-similar. A high sample entropy value indicates less self-similarity or increased disorder (Richman and Moorman 2000), and such pattern irregularity has been found in several activated psychiatric conditions, e.g., activated depression, mania and schizophrenia (Krane-Gartiser et al. 2014, 2016; Hauge et al. 2011). Since extended periods of rest will yield low entropy, we plotted the rest/activity ratio alongside sample entropy curves to allow comparison of measures.

Results

Three cases had a diagnosis of BD-I and at least two actigraphy recordings and could be included. Details of clinical history and presentation are deliberately brief to maintain anonymity, but a summary of key clinical and actigraphy parameters are provided in Additional file 1: Tables S1–S3.

Case 1—repeated admissions during an episode of mania with psychosis (post-partum onset)

Case 1 was aged $\leq$ 30 years and had a history of hospitalization for mania 10 years prior to the current presentation. She had been well during her pregnancy (her first), but she was admitted within 1 week post-partum with mania and psychotic symptoms. The first actigraphy recording was on day 6 of the admission and the daily medication included olanzapine 5 mg and oxazepam 20 mg. The admission lasted for about 2 weeks.

Readmission occurred about 1 month later because of a severe relapse of the manic episode with more marked psychotic symptoms. After readmission, the daily medication changed to quetiapine 250 mg, clonazepam 2 mg, and zopiclone 7.5 mg at night as required. Actigraphy was undertaken on the 4th day of this admission, which lasted 6 weeks.

During the first admission (R1) the patient demonstrated a high mean level of activity over 24 h; the nocturnal sleep interval was short (about 5 h) and disrupted (Fig. 1, panel a). The recording from the second admission (R2) showed a lower 24-h mean activity level characterized by a longer sleep period at night (estimated 7.5 h), lower activity levels and shorter periods of increased activity (panel c). Figure 1 also shows more shifts between rest and activity during the daytime in R2 (panel d), as well as higher peaks of sample entropy compared to R1.

Case 2—mixed state

Case 2 was aged about 55 years and was hospitalized five times within 3 months due to a fluctuating mixed episode; three hospitalizations included actigraphy monitoring (R1, R2 and R3). The R2 monitoring was undertaken 3 weeks after R1, and R3 was undertaken 8 weeks after R2. R1 began on the third day of admission, and R2 and R3 on the second day of admission. The lifetime history indicated prior experience of psychotic symptoms (auditory hallucinations) and more than 10 hospitalizations in total (including an involuntary hospitalization for severe mania). No important history of alcohol or substance use and no major physical illnesses were reported. The daily medication regime at the actigraphy recordings were valproate 1500 mg, oxazepam 25 mg and quetiapine (R1: 600 mg, R2: 200 mg, R3: 500 mg).

The three actograms in Fig. 2 show consistent patterns across recordings with similar mean levels of activity and similar changes in the distribution of rest and activity periods. The variations in activity parameters may correspond to reported fluctuations in clinical symptoms over 24 h. The patient was experiencing visual hallucinations and paranoid delusions during R2 (Fig. 2, panels c and d), and there is evidence of a greater degree of inactivity during the daytime, with higher peaks of sample entropy (similar to the findings reported in Case 1).

Case 3—depression and mania

Case 3 was aged between 60 and 65 years. There was evidence of prior alcohol misuse, suicidal ideation and self-harm in the 40-year history of BD. Case 3 had a good response to lithium, but relapses had often followed relatively small modifications to prescribed dosages. The patient was initially admitted in a depressive episode; the daily medication regime at the time of the first actigraphy recording (day 2 of the admission) was quetiapine 275 mg and lithium 210 mg. The admission lasted about 6 weeks until remission. Due to renal complications of lithium, the medication regime was changed to quetiapine and lamotrigine during the admission.

Within 2 weeks, the patient became unwell and was readmitted with a manic episode with intermittent psychotic symptoms. Actigraphy was undertaken at day 2 of the admission; medication at the time of R2 included lamotrigine 200 mg, quetiapine 500 mg, and single doses of oxazepam and alimemazine. The patient improved gradually and was discharged after 10 weeks.

As shown in Fig. 3, the activity patterns in acute episodes of depression (R1) and mania (R2) are distinctly different [and, respectively, resemble previous findings

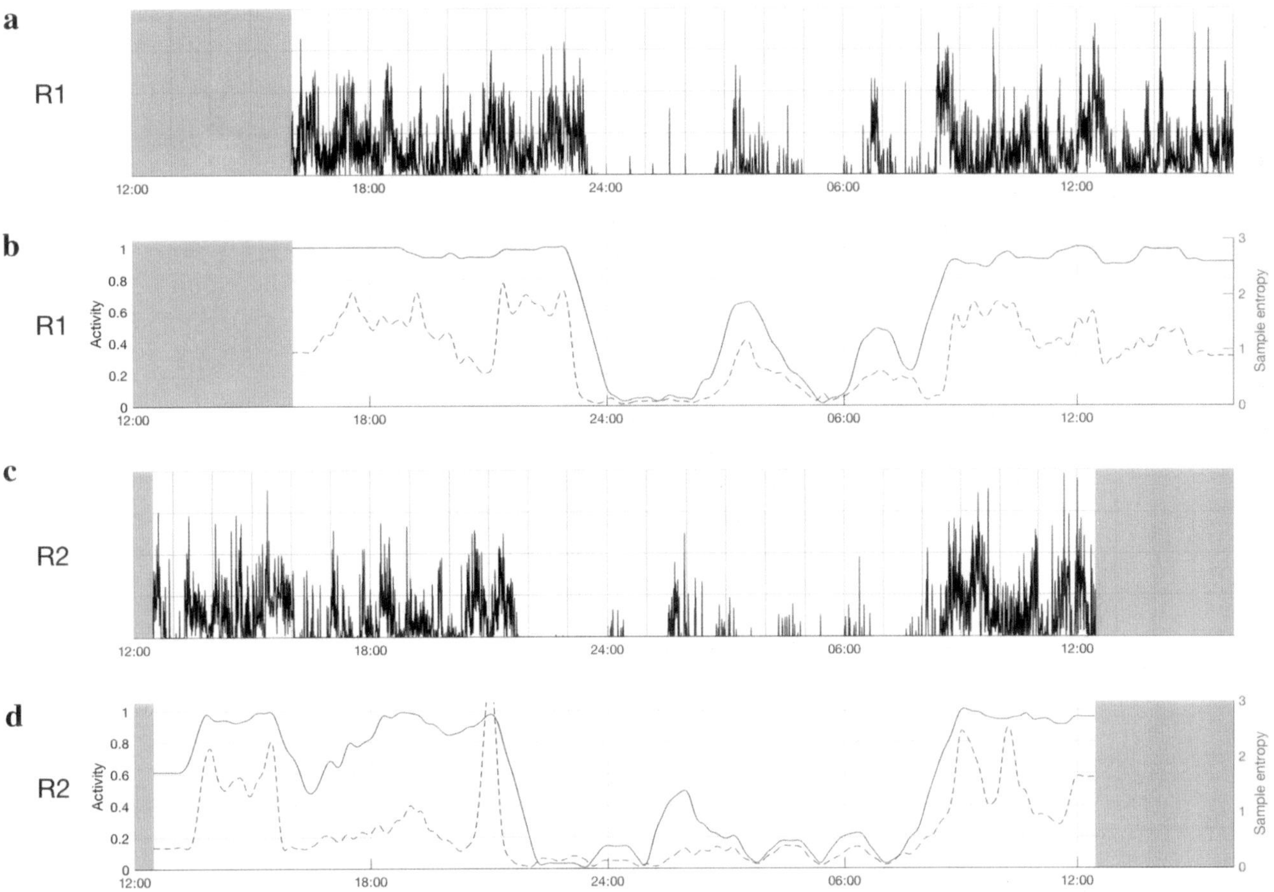

Fig. 1 Actigraphy data for two admissions for mania with psychotic symptoms (case 1). **a**, **b** Represent the first recording (R1) and **c**, **d** the second recording (R2). Time of day is shown at the bottom of each chart (24-h clock). Light grey parts at the beginning and end of each chart represent non-monitoring time; **a**, **c** are 24-h actograms: activity counts are shown as black, vertical lines on a scale from 0 to 500 counts. One square in the grid represents 1 h on a horizontal axis and 125 counts on a vertical axis. **b**, **d** The ratio between rest and activity as the fully drawn line (left axis) and sample entropy as the dotted line (right axis)

(Krane-Gartiser et al. 2014)]. As shown for R1, during depression, periods of motor activity are interspersed with frequent rest periods and the sample entropy is low. The peaks of sample entropy in the afternoon appear to correspond to clinically observed periods of increased anxiety and agitation. During the manic phase, R2 demonstrates an increased total mean level of activity, but also elevated sample entropy (indicating a more complex or irregular activity pattern).

Conclusions

This case series presents objective recordings of motor activity patterns in three individuals hospitalized with BD episodes and uses the data to indicate the potential of actigraphy combined with mathematical modeling as a within-person diagnostic marker of activity in different acute phases or presentations of BD.

The series of recordings demonstrate that intra-individual activity patterns differ between acute phases of BD, but show within-person consistency for the same phase of illness. For Cases 1 and 2, increasing psychotic symptoms within an episode translated into reduced mean activity levels (case 1), greater variation between rest and activity, and periods with distinctly increased irregularity in activity (sample entropy). Together, these results strengthen the hypothesis that individual movement patterns might be used as an adjunct to basic symptom ratings (e.g., self- or observer-reported mood) and provide a new biological variable for assessment of BD. Of course, to confirm whether this variable is a pure bipolar signal, larger cross-population studies in other psychiatric conditions such as unipolar depression and schizophrenia/schizoaffective disorder should be undertaken. Our data, along with the two recent studies of intra-individual

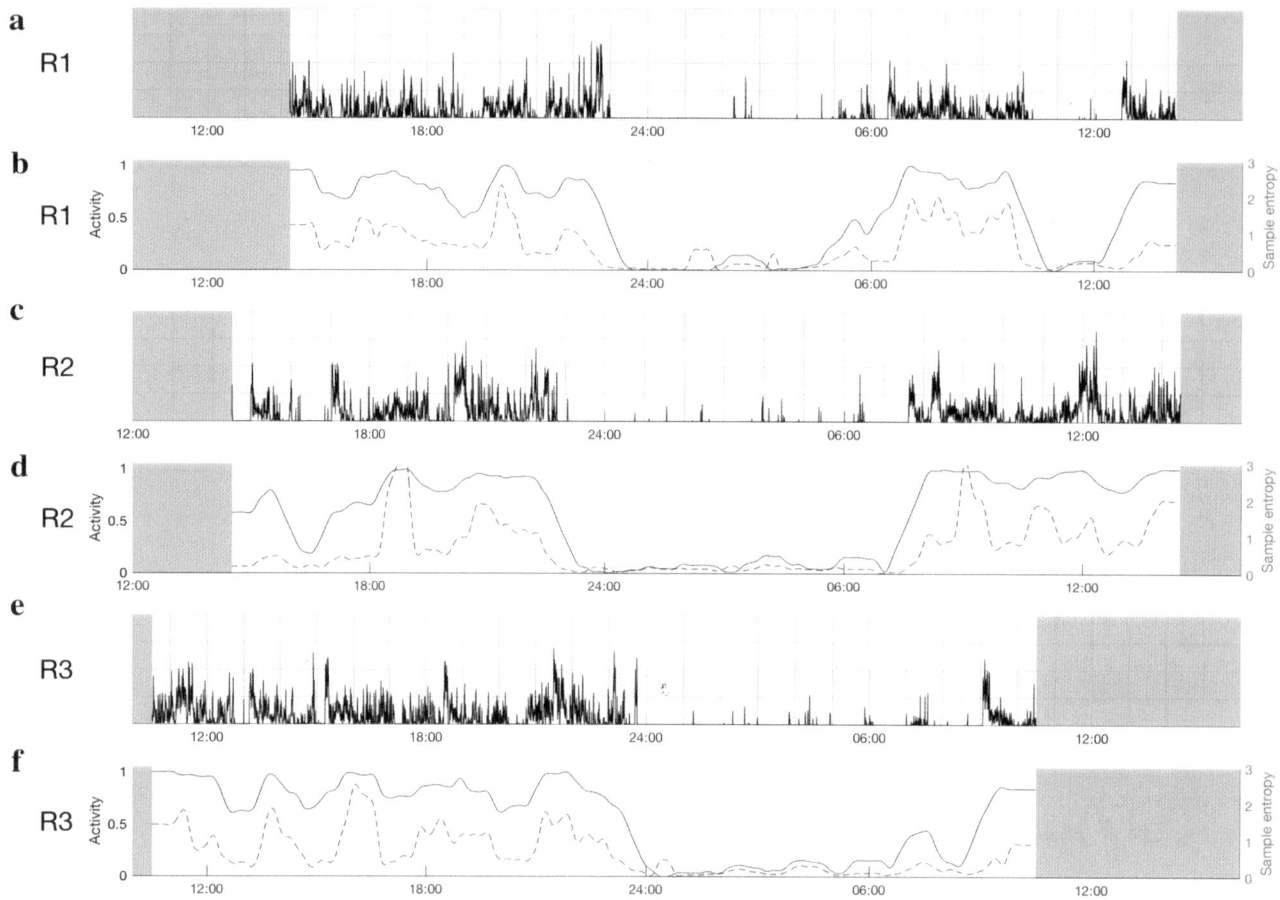

Fig. 2 Actigraphy data for three admissions for a mixed state (case 2). **a**, **b** Represent the first recording (R1); **c**, **d** the second recording (R2) and **e**, **f** the third recording (R3). Time of day is shown at the bottom of each chart (24-h clock). Light grey parts at the beginning and end of each chart represent non-monitoring time; **a**, **c**, **e** are 24-h actograms: activity counts are shown as black, vertical lines on a scale from 0 to 500 counts. One square in the grid represents 1 h on a horizontal axis and 125 counts on a vertical axis. **b**, **d**, **f** The ratio between rest and activity as the fully drawn line (left axis) and sample entropy as the dotted line (right axis)

actigraphy in BD (Gershon et al. 2015; Salvatore et al. 2008) indicate that findings from non-linear analysis of actigraphic data could be used to increase diagnostic validity, particularly if the analytical methods are elaborated further (Scott et al. 2016; Salvatore et al. 2008).

Sample entropy (as a measure of pattern irregularity) may be a particularly useful means of characterizing mania, which was also shown in our group study (Krane-Gartiser et al. 2014). With increasing symptom severity within a manic episode in the same individual, it was more complicated to identify robust differences in such a 24-h "snapshot" of activity, but peaks of increased sample entropy and lower energy are indicated as possibilities for further exploration of psychotic symptoms. While the sample entropy and rest/activity ratio appear to display a high degree of covariation in the plots and therefore should be contrasted, it may be that periods when these two measures deviate from each other are of particular interest. Peaks of sample entropy during a stable level of activity could potentially indicate more severe symptoms of psychosis and/or anxiety, as seems to be illustrated by the symptom changes in the three cases (panel d in Fig. 1, panel d in Fig. 2 and panels b and d in Fig. 3). Although the lower mean level of activity might be explained by medication changes (e.g., drugs that increased sedation), sample entropy is less likely to be influenced by pharmacological agents, but has previously been reported in non-manic psychotic patients (Krane-Gartiser et al. 2014; Hauge et al. 2011). Of course, the association between activity patterns and medication should be explored in future studies with larger samples to determine the true significance of irregular movements in psychosis.

This case series has several limitations, primarily related to its exploratory nature in a sample of three BD-I

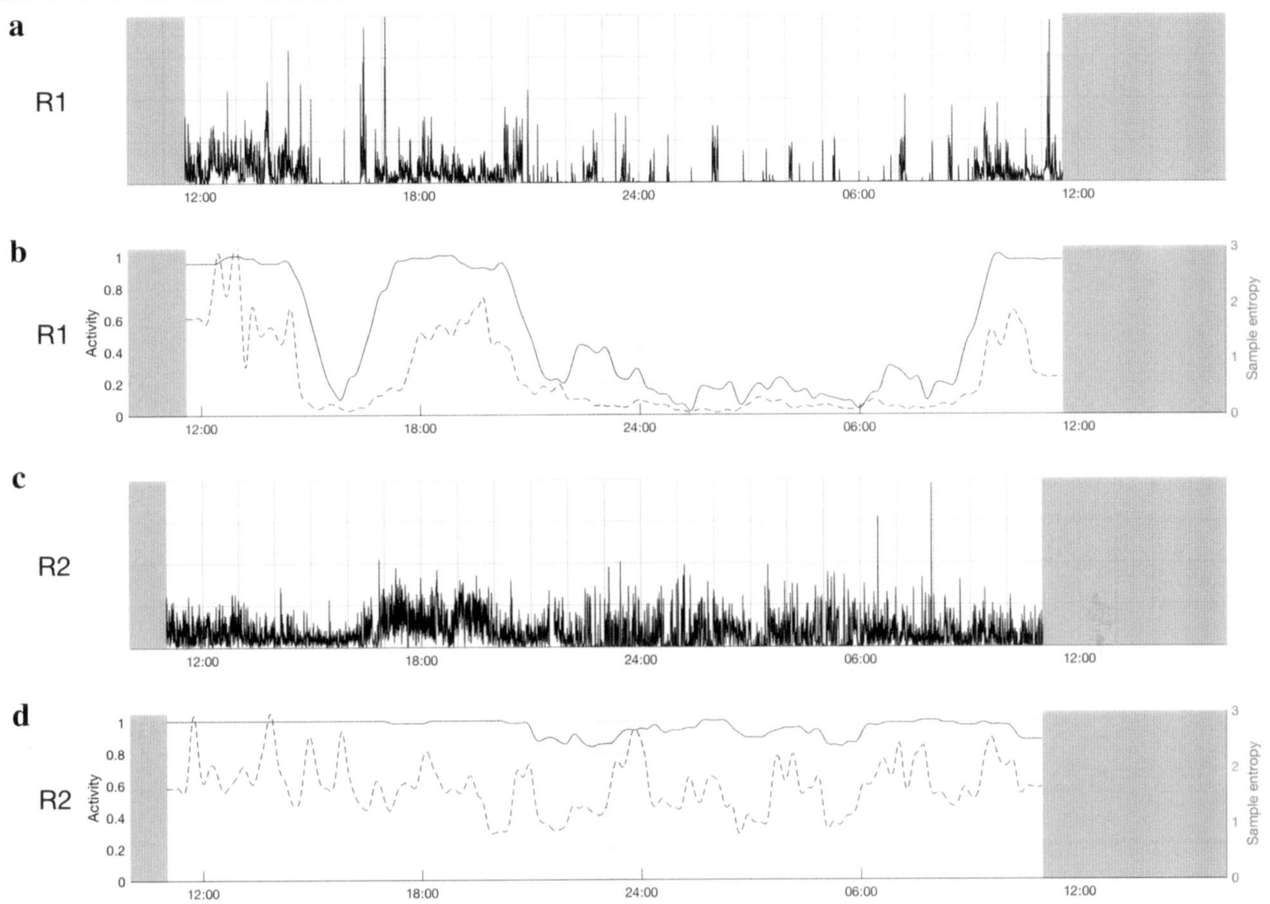

Fig. 3 Actigraphy data for two admissions due to depression and mania (case 3). **a**, **b** Represent the first recording (R1) and **c**, **d** the second recording (R2). Time of day is shown at the bottom of each chart (24-h clock). Light grey parts at the beginning and end of each chart represent non-monitoring time; **a**, **c** are 24-h actograms: activity counts are shown as black, vertical lines on a scale from 0 to 500 counts. One square in the grid represents 1 h on a horizontal axis and 125 counts on a vertical axis. **b**, **d** The ratio between rest and activity as the fully drawn line (left axis) and sample entropy as the dotted line (right axis)

cases. For example, we do not have repeated recordings of hypomania or euthymia, and we cannot take other confounders into account, e.g., some treatments prescribed during the admission may have masked true differences in activity patterns between recordings. Also, we do not have contemporaneous observer ratings or subjective reports of symptoms and thus cannot examine the associations (or direction of causality) between activity and mood changes. Furthermore, each recording was brief (24 h), and recordings over several days would provide more robust data. However, we could not find any published studies reporting non-linear dynamic analyses of repeated within-person recordings undertaken during separate admissions for acute phases of illness. As such, there are no intra-individual data in the literature that support or refute our findings. Long-term studies in larger samples are needed to determine whether real-time objective recordings of rest–activity cycles combined with non-linear analysis are a valuable addition to clinical observation. Actigraphy allows for ecological monitoring and therefore offers the possibility of clarifying the severity and subtype of episode objectively in an individual, which ultimately could be used to offer a biological variable for the assessment of the course and outcome of BD.

Abbreviations

BD: bipolar disorder; BD-I: bipolar disorder, type 1; DSM-5: Diagnostic and Statistical Manual of Mental Disorders, 5th edition; ICD-10: International Classification of Diseases, 10th revision; IRT: item response theory; R1: recording one; R2: recording two; R3: recording three; RMSSD: root mean squared successive difference; SD: standard deviation.

Authors' contributions

KKG, AV, OBF, and GM were involved in the design and planning of the original actigraphy studies with inpatients. KKG, JS and GM identified the hypotheses for the current study. AA, OBF, and KKG undertook the mathematical analyses. KKG and JS wrote the preliminary draft of the manuscript. All authors critically reviewed the drafts. All authors read and approved the final manuscript.

Author details

[1] Department of Mental Health, NTNU, Norwegian University of Science and Technology, P.O. box 3250 Sluppen, 7006 Trondheim, Norway. [2] Department of Psychiatry, St. Olav's University Hospital, Trondheim, Norway. [3] Department of Mathematical Sciences, NTNU, Norwegian University of Science and Technology, Trondheim, Norway. [4] Center for Health Care Improvement in Mid-Norway, St. Olav's University Hospital, Trondheim, Norway. [5] Section for Psychiatry, Department of Clinical Medicine, Faculty of Medicine and Dentistry, University of Bergen, Bergen, Norway. [6] Division of Psychiatry, Haukeland University Hospital, Bergen, Norway. [7] Academic Psychiatry, Institute of Neuroscience, Newcastle University, Newcastle upon Tyne, UK.

Acknowledgements

We are grateful to Kjetil Sørensen for managing the data collection and to Erlend Fasmer for making programs to extract actigraphy data.

Competing interests

JS is a visiting professor at NTNU. JS has received UK grant funding from the Medical Research Council (including for projects on actigraphy and bipolar disorders) and from the Research for Patient Benefit programme (PB-PG-0609-16166: Early identification and intervention in young people at risk of mood disorders).

Funding

St. Olavs University Hospital, NTNU—Norwegian University of Science and Technology and the Liaison Committee for education, research and innovation in Central Norway provided the funding of this work. They played no role in the design of the study, collection, analysis, interpretation of data or in writing the manuscript.

References

American Psychiatric Association. Diagnostic and statistical manual of mental disorders. 5th ed. Washington, DC: American Psychiatric Association; 2013.

Ancoli-Israel S, Cole R, Alessi C, Chambers M, Moorcroft W, Pollak CP. The role of actigraphy in the study of sleep and circadian rhythms. Sleep. 2003;26(3):342–92 **(PubMed PMID: 12749557, Epub 2003/05/17)**.

De Crescenzo F, Economou A, Sharpley AL, Gormez A, Quested DJ. Actigraphic features of bipolar disorder: a systematic review and meta-analysis. Sleep Med Rev. 2017;33:58–69 **(PubMed PMID: 28185811, Epub 2017/02/12)**.

Geoffroy PA, Scott J, Boudebesse C, Lajnef M, Henry C, Leboyer M, et al. Sleep in patients with remitted bipolar disorders: a meta-analysis of actigraphy studies. Acta Psychiatr Scand. 2015;131(2):89–99 **(PubMed PMID: 25430914, Epub 2014/11/29)**.

Gershon A, Ram N, Johnson SL, Harvey AG, Zeitzer JM. Daily actigraphy profiles distinguish depressive and interepisode states in bipolar disorder. Clin Psychol Sci. 2015;19:2015.

Hauge ER, Berle JO, Oedegaard KJ, Holsten F, Fasmer OB. Nonlinear analysis of motor activity shows differences between schizophrenia and depression: a study using Fourier analysis and sample entropy. PLoS ONE. 2011;6(1):e16291 **(PubMed PMID: 21297977, Pubmed Central PMCID: PMC3030566, Epub 2011/02/08)**.

Klein E, Lavie P, Meiraz R, Sadeh A, Lenox RH. Increased motor activity and recurrent manic episodes: predictors of rapid relapse in remitted bipolar disorder patients after lithium discontinuation. Biol Psychiatry. 1992;31(3):279–84 **(PubMed PMID: 1547301, Epub 1992/02/01)**.

Krane-Gartiser K, Henriksen TEG, Morken G, Vaaler A, Fasmer OB. Actigraphic assessment of motor activity in acutely admitted inpatients with bipolar disorder. PLoS ONE. 2014;9(2):e89574.

Krane-Gartiser K, Vaaler AE, Fasmer OB, Morken G. Distribution and characteristics of active and inactive periods distinguish unipolar depression with and without motor retardation. J Clin Psychiatry. 2016;77(6):841–2 **(PubMed PMID: 27337419, Epub 2016/06/24)**.

Kupfer DJ, Weiss BL, Foster G, Detre TP, McPartland R. Psychomotor activity in affective states. Arch Gen Psychiatry. 1974;30(6):765–8 **(PubMed PMID: 4832184, Epub 1974/06/01)**.

Ng TH, Chung KF, Ho FY, Yeung WF, Yung KP, Lam TH. Sleep-wake disturbance in interepisode bipolar disorder and high-risk individuals: a systematic review and meta-analysis. Sleep Med Rev. 2015;20:46–58 **(PubMed PMID: 25060968, Epub 2014/07/26)**.

Prisciandaro JJ, Tolliver BK. An item response theory evaluation of the young mania rating scale and the montgomery-asberg depression rating scale in the systematic treatment enhancement program for bipolar disorder (STEP-BD). J Affect Disord. 2016;205:73–80 **(PubMed PMID: 27420134, Pubmed Central PMCID: PMC5048523, Epub 2016/07/16)**.

Ramsay J, Silverman BW. Functional data analysis. 2nd ed. New York: Springer; 2005.

Richman JS, Moorman JR. Physiological time-series analysis using approximate entropy and sample entropy. Am J Physiol Heart Circ Physiol. 2000;278(6):H2039–49 **(PubMed PMID: 10843903, Epub 2000/06/14)**.

Salvatore P, Ghidini S, Zita G, De Panfilis C, Lambertino S, Maggini C, et al. Circadian activity rhythm abnormalities in ill and recovered bipolar I disorder patients. Bipolar Disord. 2008;10(2):256–65 **(PubMed PMID: 18271904, Epub 2008/02/15)**.

Scott J, Murray G, Henry C, Morken G, Scott E, Angst J, et al. Activation in bipolar disorders: a systematic review. JAMA Psychiatry. 2017;74(2):182–96 **(PubMed PMID: 28002572, Epub 2016/12/22)**.

Scott J, Vaaler AE, Fasmer OB, Morken G, Krane-Gartiser K. A pilot study to determine whether combinations of objectively measured activity parameters can be used to differentiate between mixed states, mania, and bipolar depression. Int J Bipolar Disord. 2017;5(1):5 **(PubMed PMID: 28155205, Epub 2017/02/06)**.

Wehr TA, Muscettola G, Goodwin FK. Urinary 3-methoxy-4-hydroxyphenylglycol circadian rhythm. Early timing (phase-advance) in manic-depressives compared with normal subjects. Arch Gen Psychiatry. 1980;37(3):257–63 **(PubMed PMID: 7362415, Epub 1980/03/01)**.

Weiss BL, Foster FG, Reynolds CF 3rd, Kupfer DJ. Psychomotor activity in mania. Arch Gen Psychiatry. 1974;31(3):379–83 **(PubMed PMID: 4606963, Epub 1974/09/01)**.

WHO. The ICD-10 classification of mental and behavioural disorders—diagnostic research criteria. Geneva: World Health Organization; 1993.

Wolff EA 3rd, Putnam FW, Post RM. Motor activity and affective illness. The relationship of amplitude and temporal distribution to changes in affective state. Arch Gen Psychiatry. 1985;42(3):288–94 **(PubMed PMID: 3977548, Epub 1985/03/01)**.

3

Animal models for bipolar disorder: from bedside to the cage

Dominik K. E. Beyer and Nadja Freund*

Abstract

Bipolar disorder is characterized by recurrent manic and depressive episodes. Patients suffering from this disorder experience dramatic mood swings with a wide variety of typical behavioral facets, affecting overall activity, energy, sexual behavior, sense of self, self-esteem, circadian rhythm, cognition, and increased risk for suicide. Effective treatment options are limited and diagnosis can be complicated. To overcome these obstacles, a better understanding of the neurobiology underlying bipolar disorder is needed. Animal models can be useful tools in understanding brain mechanisms associated with certain behavior. The following review discusses several pathological aspects of humans suffering from bipolar disorder and compares these findings with insights obtained from several animal models mimicking diverse facets of its symptomatology. Various sections of the review concentrate on specific topics that are relevant in human patients, namely circadian rhythms, neurotransmitters, focusing on the dopaminergic system, stressful environment, and the immune system. We then explain how these areas have been manipulated to create animal models for the disorder. Even though several approaches have been conducted, there is still a lack of adequate animal models for bipolar disorder. Specifically, most animal models mimic only mania or depression and only a few include the cyclical nature of the human condition. Future studies could therefore focus on modeling both episodes in the same animal model to also have the possibility to investigate the switch from mania-like behavior to depressive-like behavior and vice versa. The use of viral tools and a focus on circadian rhythms and the immune system might make the creation of such animal models possible.

Keywords: Translational, Human condition, Circadian rhythm, Dopamine, Immune system, Stress

Background

Bipolar disorder (BD) is characterized by recurrent episodes of manic and depressive states with intervening episodes of euthymia (normal mood) (Merikangas et al. 2007; Anderson et al. 2012; Phillips and Kupfer 2013). The symptomatology of BD is very heterogenic and heavily depends on the patient's state. Throughout manic episodes, people undergo euphoria, aggression, reduced need for sleep, high reward seeking, hypersexuality, and hyperactivity (Perry et al. 2010; Anderson et al. 2012; Cheniaux et al. 2014). In contrast, a state of depression includes anhedonia, increased sleep, reduced libido, feeling tired, and a greater risk of suicide among other symptoms (American Psychiatric Association 2013; Anderson et al. 2012). In addition, BD patients suffer from various cognitive deficits (Martínez-Arán et al. 2004; Savitz et al. 2005; Burdick et al. 2007; Goodwin et al. 2008). Established treatments for BD include mood stabilizers, such as lithium, anticonvulsants, like valproate, and antipsychotics. Current treatments, however, are not able to completely stabilize behavioral aberrations or to recover cognitive deficits (Grunze et al. 2013; van Enkhuizen et al. 2015a). Lithium, the first line medication for BD, is furthermore suspected to cause negative side effects, including cognitive impairment (Pachet and Wisniewski 2003; Holmes et al. 2008; Grunze et al. 2013). Besides the lack of novel developed therapeutics (Malkesman et al. 2009), current clinical criteria fail to diagnose milder symptoms of BD and therefore it can take years to finally diagnose this psychiatric disorder (Merikangas et al. 2011). Improvement of treatment and diagnosis options is crucial, particular given the high rate of

*Correspondence: Nadja.freund@rub.de
Experimental and Molecular Psychiatry, LWL University Hospital, Ruhr University Bochum, Universitätsstr. 150, 44801 Bochum, Germany

suicide attempts in patients with BD (Novick et al. 2010). A better understanding of cause and pathophysiology of the disease is needed to archive these improvements. Adequate animal models for BD will provide a useful tool to advance the knowledge on the underlying neurobiology of BD. Establishing animal models for psychiatric disorders, however, is a difficult task (Malkesman et al. 2009). Not only are the symptoms in patients with one disorder often quite broad and variable between patients, some symptoms used to diagnose psychiatric disorders in humans are not even possible to asses in animals, such as feelings of worthlessness or guilt (Malkoff-Schwartz et al. 1998; Nestler and Hyman 2010). Given its cyclical nature, BD is thereby especially hard to model (Gould and Einat 2007, 2014). So far BD is mainly investigated in separated animal models for either mania or depression (Einat 2014; van Enkhuizen et al. 2015a). The animal models mostly mimic some behavioral characteristics of BD, which are more or less easy to measure, such as overall locomotor activity, sexual behavior, aggression, risk taking, and decision making (Einat 2014; van Enkhuizen et al. 2015a; Harrison et al. 2016; Sharma et al. 2016). An animal model of BD in rodents, which models the whole complexity of symptoms, might never be possible. Nonetheless, it is still crucial to create and characterize new models for BD, which consistently tighten the gap between human pathophysiology and BD-like symptoms in animals. Animal models are an indispensable tool and a critical component in the preclinical research field. They allow developing new treatment and diagnosis options and therewith improving the lives of BD patients and can therefore not be replaced. Ideally, an adequate animal model of BD should include elements of the three axes of validity: face, predictive, and construct validity. Face validity indicates to which extent the model reflects characteristics of the human disease. Predictive validity refers to which degree the model will respond to an efficient treatment in humans. Construct validity reflects to which extent the model measures what it claims to be measuring (Einat 2014; Malkesman et al. 2009). The ideal animal model should therefore comply with the following requirements: (i) model BD-specific behavioral abnormalities with ideally all its facets; (ii) consider the cyclical nature of BD; (iii) be able to spontaneously switch between both episodes (all face validity); (iv) respond to current established treatment; and (v) due to the fact that not all BD patients respond to medications (Cipriani et al. 2011), reflect a distribution of responders and nonresponders (both predictive validity) (Einat 2014). This division would represent the result of clinical trials and therefore a group effect of treatment should still be observed. Additional prior determination of individual, untreated baseline measurements will be required to compare intra-individual differences before and after treatment of the animals to later successfully separate responders from nonresponders. It should furthermore (vi) be affected by pharmacological, environmental, or genetically manipulations in regard to the same mechanisms that are involved in human patients (face validity).

To date, no such animal model for BD exists. However, within the last couple of years several models were able to at least address some of the above-mentioned requirements and have therewith been able to improve our understanding of the neurobiology underlying BD. In this review, we will discuss various aspects that are affected in patients with BD, namely circadian rhythm, neurotransmitters focusing on the dopaminergic system, environment, and immune system. Disruptions and influences regarding these topics in patients will be compared to findings in animal models and we will illustrate how these findings have been used to develop animal models for the disorder.

Circadian rhythm

Aberrations of the sleep–wake cycle and circadian rhythms belong to primary symptoms of patients suffering from BD and are used as diagnostic criteria (Gonzalez 2014; Kripke et al. 2009; McCarthy and Welsh 2012; Wirz-Justice 2006). Patients display irregularities in daily biological rhythms including sleep, activity, body temperature, hormonal secretions, cell regeneration, and eating behavior (Bunney and Potkin 2008; Goetze and Tölle 1987; McClung 2007; Salvatore and Tohen 2007; Souetre et al. 1988; Takahashi et al. 2008). In addition, psychotherapeutic treatment (interpersonal and social rhythm therapy) with the aim of stabilizing and structuring daily routines and thereby enabling a normalized sleep–wake cycle is an effective therapeutic tool for mood stabilization and can reduce the number of manic and depressive episodes (Frank et al. 2000, 2007; Miklowitz et al. 2007). At the same time, mania can be induced by disruption of circadian rhythms (Bunney and Bunney 2000; McClung 2013). Circadian disruptions present in humans suffering from BD suggest an involvement of circadian clock genes in the pathogenesis of the disease (Cosgrove et al. 2016; Etain et al. 2011; Wirz-Justice 2006; McClung 2007; Frank et al. 2000). Indeed, BD symptoms are correlated with disruptions of the circadian rhythm and associated with a polymorphism of the *circadian locomotor output cycles kaput* (*Clock*) gene (Benedetti et al. 2003; Logan and McClung 2016; Serretti et al. 2003).

Targeting circadian rhythm genes to disrupt mechanisms regulating the circadian rhythm has been widely used to create animal models for BD (McClung et al. 2005; Mukherjee et al. 2010; Roybal et al. 2007). The master pacemaker of the circadian rhythm is localized in the suprachiasmatic nuclei and interconnects a complex network of transcriptional–translational activation and repression, resulting in an oscillating expression of clock genes over a period of 24 h (Takahashi et al. 2008). Several diverse preparations of *Clock* manipulation were used as animal models to study BD. The most common model is the *ClockΔ19* mutant mouse. These mice carry a deletion at exon 19 of the *Clock* gene, resulting in a dominant-negative protein, unable to activate transcription (King et al. 1997). Mutant mice exhibit mania-like behavior (Roybal et al. 2007) and altered sleep patterns (McClung 2013). The disruption of CLOCK resulted in lower immobility in the forced swim test, a greater preference for rewarding stimuli, such as sucrose solution and cocaine, a lower threshold within intra-cranial self-stimulation at lower drug doses, lowered anxiety levels, and less depressive-like behavior (McClung et al. 2005; Roybal et al. 2007). In addition, the *Clock* mutant mice exhibited deficits within the paired pulse inhibition paradigm (van Enkhuizen et al. 2013b). *ClockΔ19* mutant mice were also tested in the behavioral pattern monitor (BPM), a test to pattern and level of locomotor activity, exploratory behavior, and novelty seeking in humans and rodents (Perry et al. 2009; Young et al. 2007). While BD patients show increased exploration and goal-directed behavior, illustrated through linear and direct movements (Logan and McClung 2016; Minassian et al. 2011; Perry et al. 2009, 2010), the *ClockΔ19* mutant mice do not represent this specific exploration and goal-directed behavior. They exhibit more circumscribed, small-scale movements (Perry et al. 2009; van Enkhuizen et al. 2013b). In summary, the *ClockΔ19* mutant mice resemble various but not all behavioral aspects of BD mania in humans to its full extent. Another manipulation of *Clock*, which resulted in BD-relevant behavior, is the knock-down of CLOCK specifically in the ventral tegmental area (VTA) of mice (Mukherjee et al. 2010). The knock-down of *Clock* expression resulted in abnormal circadian rhythms, indicated by less robust activity in dark phases and enhanced activity in resting phases, less anxiety behavior, and increased locomotor activity in a novel environment. Despite the observed hyperactivity in a novel environment, the overall locomotor activity over a period of 24 h, however, was reduced (Mukherjee et al. 2010). In contrast to the previously observed less-depression-like behavior of the *ClockΔ19* mutant mice (Roybal et al. 2007), the CLOCK knock-down mice exhibited increased depression-like behavior in the forced swim and learned helplessness test and thereby express a mixed state of mania- and depression-like behavior (Mukherjee et al. 2010). Mukherjee and colleagues postulated, therefore, that CLOCK's functioning in the VTA is required for the regulation of mood-related behavior. This hypothesis is supported by the fact that over-expression of CLOCK in the VTA reduces hyperactivity and restores anxiety-related behavior almost to wild-type level in the *ClockΔ19* mutant mice (Roybal et al. 2007). Disrupted circadian rhythm in these animal models might create a vulnerable state with a greater sensitivity for addiction and mood disorders (Logan et al. 2014; Logan and McClung 2016). Commonly found in both *Clock* mice models is an enhanced dopamine (DA) release from neurons in the VTA, which is reflected, for example, in an increased dopaminergic cell firing rate (Coque et al. 2011; McClung et al. 2005; Mukherjee et al. 2010; Roybal et al. 2007). This functional linkage between the dopaminergic system (see "Dopaminergic pathways") and aberrant circadian rhythms connects two major pathways, which may be involved in the pathogenesis of BD and are often used as targets for the development of genetic or environmental animal models for BD. This involvement of the dopaminergic system supports the dopamine hypothesis (Berk et al. 2007) that hyper-dopaminergic transmission might be responsible for mania in humans and therefore also for mania-like behavior in animals.

Chronic lithium treatment was able to normalize various aspects of aberrant behavior in the *ClockΔ19* mutant mice (Coque et al. 2011; Roybal et al. 2007). Lithium's therapeutic efficacy might be due to its properties to lengthen the circadian period, which was observed across several species (Klemfuss 1992; Kripke et al. 1978). One well-studied potential target of lithium's action is the inhibition of glycogen synthase kinase-3 beta (GSK-3β) (Klein and Melton 1996; Serretti et al. 2009; but see also Agam and Azab 2016). GSK-3β is involved in various cell functions, like gene transcription, neurogenesis, and apoptosis (Doble and Woodgett 2003). GSK-3β is also able to regulate the circadian clock through phosphorylation of CLOCK and nuclear receptor subfamily1, group D, member1 (REV-ERBα) (Bellet and Sassone-Corsi 2010; Besing et al. 2015; Martinek et al. 2001; Yin et al. 2006) and thereby modulates the circadian rhythm (Besing et al. 2015). Synthetic inhibition of GSK-3β was able to mimic the effects of lithium and to prevent mania-like behavior, such as amphetamine-induced hyperactivity, in male C57BL/6J mice (Kozikowski et al. 2007). In addition, *gsk-3β* haploinsufficient mutant mice, lacking one copy of the gene coding for GSK-3β, show the same behavioral effects as lithium-treated mice (O'Brien et al. 2004). *gsk-3β* haploinsufficiency reduces exploratory behavior and immobility time in the forced swim test, comparable to treatment with lithium in wild-type mice, without affecting overall activity (O'Brien et al. 2004). Both manipulations of GSK-3β suggest that lithium's therapeutic effect as a mood stabilizer depends on inhibiting GSK-3β activity (O'Brien et al. 2011). Once again a manipulation of the circadian rhythm through transgenic mice over-expressing GSK-3β resulted in mania-like behavior (Prickaerts et al. 2006). The GSK-3β over-expressing mice exhibited hyperactivity, reduced immobility in the forced swim test, reduced habituation in the open field test, and increased acoustic startle response (Prickaerts et al. 2006). Patients in manic episodes opposingly exhibit reduced startle responses (Perry et al. 2001). Due to the nonspecific alterations of the dopaminergic system in the GSK-3β over-expressing mice, which are also recognizable in other psychiatric disorders, such as schizophrenia and attention-deficit hyperactivity disorder (ADHD), this animal model, however, lacks specificity for mania (Sharma et al. 2016).

An additional target of the circadian rhythm, which can be used to model BD-relevant behavior, is the extra-cellular-signal-regulated kinase (ERK) (Engel et al. 2008). The ERK pathway mediates proliferation, differentiation, and plasticity of neurons in the central nervous system (Thomas and Huganir 2004). ERKs are also involved in resetting the master pacemaker in the suprachiasmatic nucleus via photic input (Butcher et al. 2002; Coogan and Piggins 2004). Infusion of ERK inhibitor into the suprachiasmatic nucleus of mice prevents the activity rhythms shift, which is usually observed between light and dark phases (Butcher et al. 2002). A knock-out of the gene coding for ERK1 resulted in hyperactivity, enhanced goal-directed activity, increased risk taking or impulsivity, and increased reward-motivated behavior (Engel et al. 2008). In addition, the ERK1 pathway can be activated by lithium and valproate, but only valproate, not lithium, was able to reduce the behavioral abnormalities (Engel et al. 2008). The ERK pathway can in turn be activated by neurotrophins. One of these neurotrophins might play a role in the pathophysiology of BD, namely the brain-derived neurotrophic factor (BDNF) (Frey et al. 2013; Södersten et al. 2014). *BDNF* haploinsufficient mice indeed exhibit mania-like behavior, including hyperactivity, increased aggressive behavior, and appetite (Kernie et al. 2000; Lyons et al. 1999). Interestingly, even untreated *BDNF* haploinsufficient mice show reduced hippocampal volume and their CA3 dendritic arborizations resembled stressed wild-type mice, suggesting a role of BDNF in hippocampal dendritic remodeling (Magariños et al. 2011).

One downstream target of the ERK signaling pathway is B-cell lymphoma 2 (Bcl-2), which is involved in neuronal development, plasticity, and degeneration (Akhtar et al. 2004) through inhibition of apoptosis (Bold et al. 1999; Campani et al. 2001). Interestingly, lithium affects the Bcl-2 levels, with chronic lithium treatment increasing Bcl-2 levels in the brain of rats (Chen et al. 1999; Manji et al. 2000). Consistent with this effect of lithium is that transgenic over-expression of Bcl-2 in mice prevents neuronal death (Bonfanti et al. 1996) and acts protective against deleterious stress-induced neuronal endangerment (DeVries et al. 2001). Although BD is rather associated with neuroplasticity deficits than neurodegenerative events (Rajkowska 2002), cell death might play a role in the pathogenesis of BD (Lee et al. 2002). Bcl-2 manipulation might also be related to anxiety as mice with an additional *Bcl-2* transgene, and therefore elevated Bcl-2 levels, exhibited less anxiety behavior (Rondi-Reig et al. 1997; Rondi-Reig and Mariani 2002). On the other hand, mice with a heterozygous knock-out of the *Bcl-2* gene exhibit Bcl-2 deficiency and increased anxiety behavior (Einat et al. 2005). In addition, Bcl-2 heterozygous knock-out mice show some behaviors similar to mania, including increased reward seeking and amphetamine sensitization, and lithium pretreatment attenuated sensitization in these animals (Lien et al. 2008).

Another gene heavily involved in the regulation of circadian rhythms is *Dbp*. It encodes for the albumin D element-binding protein, a transcription factor that is regulated by the CLOCK protein (Ripperger et al. 2000; Wuarin et al. 1992). *Dbp* expression is affected in patients with BD and can furthermore be influenced by lithium treatment (Kittel-Schneider et al. 2015). A heterozygotous knock-out of DBP in mice induces a depressive-like phenotype indicated by reduced locomotor activity and diminished response to amphetamine. When exposed to environmental stress (see "Environment: stressors"), DBP knock-out mice show a switch in behavior and become hyperactive. This switch, which to some extend resembles the switch from depression to mania in BD patients, can be prevented by the administration of valproate (Le-Niculescu et al. 2008).

But even stressors alone (e.g., sleep deprivation) can disrupt the circadian clock resulting in changes of mood and even the induction of mania in BD patients (Colombo et al. 1999; Malkoff-Schwartz et al. 1998; Wright 1993). It is therefore possible that sleep deprivation paradigms can induce mania-like behavior in rodents. Indeed, wild-type rats after typically 72 h of sleep deprivation exhibited mania-like behavior, such as enhanced aggressive behavior and hypersexuality (Gessa et al. 1995; Hicks et al. 1979; Morden et al. 1968). But this behavioral phenotype lasted only for about 30 min. In addition, chronic lithium can reverse the mania-like behavior (Gessa et al. 1995). However, it should be noted that the disruption of regular sleep requires the usage of techniques that cause additional stress (i.e., immobilization, isolation, and the fear and experience of falling into water) (Logan and McClung 2016). Benedetti and colleagues used an improved protocol to minimize these additional stressors and still found mania-like behavior, such as increased locomotor activity and aggressive behavior (Benedetti et al. 2008). These results indicate that sleep deprivation alone is a sufficient stressor to induce BD-relevant behavior.

An additional possibility to affect the sleep–wake cycle is the high-frequency stimulation of the lateral hypothalamus, which resulted in mania-like behavior in rats (Abulseoud et al. 2014). The hypothalamic stimulated rats exhibited hyperactivity, such as increased grooming, and reduced resting phases, as well as hypersexuality, i.e., increased rearing and sexual self-stimulation. These behavioral characteristics could be attenuated through chronic lithium treatment.

Apart from the cycle of day and night, the changing of seasons and the associated photoperiod length can trigger changes in mood (Young and Dulcis 2015). Indeed, a seasonal pattern of the episodes of BD was identified in a proportion of patients (Schaffer et al. 2003), whereas depressive symptoms are more prevalent during winter months (Meesters and Gordijn 2016; Rosenthal et al. 1984). This seasonal effect might be due to shortening or lengthening of the day-lengths and the associated received illumination. Modified illumination in rats induced a switch in neurotransmitter expression. A long day period of 19 h of light resulted in a switch from DA to somatostatin expression in hypothalamic neurons after 1 week. The contrary effect was observed with a short day period of 5 h light (Dulcis et al. 2013). In addition, a matching pattern of receptor expression was observed: an increased expression of postsynaptic dopamine D2 receptors (D2R) was accompanied by the presynaptic increase in dopaminergic interneurons (Dulcis et al. 2013). Rats in the long day period exhibited more anxiety behavior in the elevated plus maze and more depressive-like behavior measured by increased immobile time in the forced swim test, whereas animals in the short day period displayed decreased anxiety-related behavior and less immobile time (Dulcis et al. 2013).

Disruption of the circadian rhythms has been widely used to induce BD-like behavior, mainly mania-like behavior (Table 1). Here it is to consider that the manipulations have been mainly conducted in nocturnal animals and results might not be comparable to mechanisms in diurnal humans (Challet 2007). Using diurnal rodent animal models could be beneficial in this field of research (Ashkenazy et al. 2009; Bilu et al. 2016; Einat et al. 2006; Leach et al. 2013). Nevertheless, effects are quite robust as various disruptions of one gene (i.e., *Clock*) as well as targeting related pathways or environmentally influence sleeping behavior result in similar effects (McClung et al. 2005; Mukherjee et al. 2010; Prickaerts et al. 2006; Roybal et al. 2007). Observations of depressive-like behavior after manipulations of circadian rhythms are rare. We see mixed behavior, some aspects of mania- and at the same time depressive-like behavior, in the *ClockΔ19* mutant mouse (Mukherjee et al. 2010). Similarly, manipulation of *Bcl-2*, a gene that has indirect connections with circadian rhythm pathways, can induce both behavioral states (Lien et al. 2008). Here it is important to note that elevated levels of Bcl-2 are associated with decreased anxiety (Rondi-Reig et al. 1997; Rondi-Reig and Mariani 2002), while Bcl-2 deficiency increases anxiety (Einat et al. 2005). The most promising model in terms of the cyclic characteristic of BD is the manipulation of length of day. Here we see depressive-like behavior when extending the day period and (at least) less depressive-like behavior when decreasing the day period (Dulcis et al. 2013).

Sensitization models and neurotransmitters in general

Nearly 100 years ago, Kraepelin made the observation that with an increasing number of episodes the course of the illness worsens, the so-called sensitization model of BD (Kraepelin 1909; Post 1992). Later on behavioral sensitization to psychostimulants in rodents was used to resemble the shortening of interepisodic intervals during the progression of BD in humans (Post 1990). Repeated administration of the same dose of cocaine induced hyperactivity and elevated stereotypy responses in rats (Kilbey and Ellinwood 1977; Post 1990). A drug-high state after the administration of psychostimulants was furthermore associated with increased aggression (Borison et al. 1978; Davies et al. 1974), a declined cognitive performance (Fries et al. 2015; Rygula et al. 2015) and deficits in prepulse inhibition (PPI) (Zheng et al. 2013). Several different psychostimulants were administrated to induce mania-like behavior. Apart from cocaine, the used substances were amphetamine (Frey et al. 2006), lisdexamfetamine dimesylate (Macêdo et al. 2013), and fenproporex in rats (Rezin et al. 2014), and alpha-lipoid acid (Macêdo et al. 2012) and GBR12909 in mice (Queiroz et al. 2015). All these substances resulted in mania-like behavior, which could be attenuated by mood stabilizers like valproate or lithium (Sharma et al. 2016).

Withdrawal from psychostimulants is accompanied by depressive-like behavior or at least an anhedonic state measured as reduced sexual behavior (Barr et al. 1999), elevated thresholds in self-stimulation (Markou and Koob 1991; Wise and Munn 1995), reduced activity (Paulson et al. 1991), decreased sucrose consumption (Barr and Phillips 1999), increased negative contrast (Barr and Phillips 2002), and increased anxiety (Mutschler and Miczek 1998). Immobility time in the forced swim test, however, depends on the administered does of amphetamine as well as the training procedure and was reported to be reduced during amphetamine withdrawal (Schindler et al. 1994) but also to be increased (Marszalek-Grabska et al. 2016). Withdrawal furthermore induces supersensitivity of serotoninergic neurons (Baumann and

Table 1 Summary of manipulable risk factors for BD and their influence on BD-relevant behavior

Manipulation	BD-relevant behavior	Neurobiology	References
Circadian rhythm			
ClockΔ19 mutant mice	Hyperactivity	Altered sleep pattern	(Coque et al. 2011; van Enkhuizen et al. 2013b; McClung 2013; McClung et al. 2005; Mukherjee et al. 2010; Roybal et al. 2007)
	Altered sleep pattern	Enhanced DA release	
	Greater preference for rewarding stimuli		
	Decreased anxiety behavior		
	Less depressive-like behavior		
	Impaired PPI		
CLOCK knock-down mice	Abnormal circadian rhythms		
	Less anxiety		
	Hyperactivity in novel environment but decreased overall hyperactivity		
	Increased depression-like behavior and helplessness		
GSK-3β haploinsufficient mutant mice	Reduced exploration	Affect gene transcription, neurogenesis, and apoptosis	(Besing et al. 2015; O'Brien et al. 2004, 2011; Prickaerts et al. 2006)
	Less helplessness		
	Normal overall activity		
GSK-3β over-expression mice	Hyperactivity	Alterations of dopaminergic system	
	Less helplessness		
	Reduced habituation		
	Increased acoustic startle response		
ERK1 knock-out mice	Hyperactivity	Shift of activity rhythm	(Engel et al. 2008)
	Enhanced goal-directed activity		
	Increased risk taking and impulsivity		
	Increased reward seeking		
BDNF haploinsufficient mutant mice	Hyperactivity	Decreased BDNF level following DA overactivity	(Kernie et al. 2000; Lyons et al. 1999; Magariños et al. 2011)
	Increased aggression		
	Elevated appetite	Decreased hippocampal volume	
		CA3 dendritic arborizations resemble stressed wild-type mice	
Bcl-2 heterozygous knock-out mice	Increased anxiety	Decreased *Bcl-2* level	(DeVries et al. 2001; Einat et al. 2005; Lien et al. 2008; Rondi-Reig et al. 1997; Rondi-Reig and Mariani 2002)
	Increased reward seeking	Acts protective against deleterious stress-induced neuronal endangerment	
	Increased amphetamine sensitization		
DBP heterozygotous knock-out mice	Hypoactivity		(Le-Niculescu et al. 2008)
	Diminished response to amphetamine		
	Environmental stress induce hyperactivity		

Table 1 continued

Manipulation	BD-relevant behavior	Neurobiology	References
Sleep deprivation	Hyperactivity Increased aggression Increased exploratory behavior Hypersexuality		(Benedetti et al. 2008; Gessa et al. 1995; Hicks et al. 1979; Malkoff-Schwartz et al. 1998; Morden et al. 1968)
High-frequency stimulation of the lateral hypothalamus	Hyperactivity Increased grooming Hypersexuality Reduced resting phases	Affects sleep–wake cycle	(Abulseoud et al. 2015; Abulseoud et al. 2014)
Photoperiod lengths	Anxiety behavior Helplessness	Neurotransmitter switching (DA ↔ somatostatin)	(Dulcis et al. 2013)
Sensitization models			
Administration of psychostimulants (amphetamine, cocaine)	Hyperactivity Increased aggression Stereotypies Increased hedonic behavior Disturbed sleep–wake cycle Declined cognitive performance Deficient PPI response	Increased synaptic DA and NE levels Disturbance of homeostatic mechanisms Alterations in BDNF level	(Borison et al. 1978; Davies et al. 1974; Frey et al. 2006; Fries et al. 2015; Gould et al. 2001; Kilbey and Ellinwood 1977; Macêdo et al. 2012, 2013; Post 1992; Post 1990; Queiroz et al. 2015; Rezin et al. 2014; Rygula et al. 2015; Seiden et al. 1993; Zheng et al. 2013)
Withdrawal following chronically psychostimulant administration	Hypoactivation Increased anxiety Anhedonia Increased negative contrast Decreased motivation	Supersensitivity of serotoninergic neurons a decrease in NE Reduced DA responsiveness	(Barr et al. 1999; Barr and Phillips 1999, 2002; Baumann and Rothman 1998; Markou and Koob 1991; Marszalek-Grabska et al. 2016; Mutschler and Miczek 1998; Paulson et al. 1991; Schindler et al. 1994; Schwartz et al. 1982; Wise and Munn 1995)
Dopaminergic pathways			
Increased D1R expression in the prefrontal cortex	Increased impulsivity Increased sexual behavior Hedonic behavior Addictive behavior	Decreased D2R in nucleus accumbens	(Freund et al. 2016; Sonntag et al. 2014)
Termination of previous D1R overexpression	Hypoactivity Anhedonic behavior Helplessness	Increased CREB in nucleus accumbens	(Freund et al. 2016)

Table 1 continued

Manipulation	BD-relevant behavior	Neurobiology	References
DAT knock-down mice	Hyperactivity in novel environments Increased risk behavior Hyperexploratory behavior Less anxiety Impaired decision making with a preference for high reward combined with high risk	Hyperdopaminergia	(Dulcis et al. 2013; van Enkhuizen et al. 2014b; van Enkhuizen et al. 2014a; Giros et al. 1996; Ralph et al. 2001; Ralph-Williams et al. 2003; Young et al. 2010, 2011; Zhuang et al. 2001)
DAT knock-out mice	Hyperactivity Sensorimotor deficits within PPI		
GluR6 knock-out mice	Hyperactivity Increased risk taking Elevated aggression Heightened responsivity to amphetamine Less anxiety		(Shaltiel et al. 2008)
Environmental stressors			
Prenatal stress	Hyperactivity in novel environment Hypersensitivity to amphetamine Anhedonia Increased helplessness Increased anxiety Impaired cognition including working memory deficits Decreased exploratory behavior Social withdrawal	Incomplete development of hippocampus and reduced weight of the prefrontal cortex and nucleus accumbens Alterations in HPA axis and neurotransmitter levels in early development Reduced BDNF levels Decreased Bcl-2 level Diminished neurogenesis Increased mGluR1 and mGluR2 Altered immune system Stimulating dopaminergic transmission	(Clarke and Schneider 1993; Coe et al. 2003; Diz-Chaves et al. 2012; Fatima et al. 2017; Frye and Wawrzycki 2003; Guan et al. 2013; Hao et al. 2010; Jia et al. 2015; Koehl et al. 1999; Lemaire et al. 2000; Lin et al. 2012; Lin and Wang 2014; Uno et al. 1990; Wakshlak and Weinstock 1990)
Postnatal stress	Hypoactivity Increased stereotypies Increased anxiety behavior Heightened response to acute stressor Elevated PPI response	Hippocampal development, memory, spatial and social learning, response to stress of the HPA axis Decreased BDNF level Neuronal atrophy Stimulating dopaminergic transmission	(Caldji et al. 2000b; Duman et al. 2016; Duman and Monteggia 2006; Huot et al. 2002; Huot et al. 2001; Kalinichev et al. 2002; Ladd et al. 2000, 2004; Lippmann et al. 2007; Magariños et al. 2011; McIntosh et al. 1999; Wigger and Neumann 1999)

Table 1 continued

Manipulation	BD-relevant behavior	Neurobiology	References
Chronic stress (through, e.g., repeated social defeat)	Depressive-like behavior Hypoactivity Reduced exploration Reduced aggression Hyposexuality Elevated anxiety Submissive behavior Social avoidance	Disrupted circadian rhythms and immune function	(Berton et al. 1998; Crawford et al. 2013; Hollis et al. 2010; Hollis and Kabbaj 2014; Leuner et al. 2014; Maier and Seligman 1976; Meerlo et al. 1996; Porsolt et al. 1977; Ruis et al. 1999; Steru et al. 1985; Tidey and Miczek 1997; Tornatzky and Miczek 1993; Wulsin et al. 2016)
Immune system			
Maternal immune activation	Increased locomotor response to amphetamine Increased repetitive and stereotypic behavior Increased anxiety Helplessness Disrupted sensorimotor gating Impaired working memory	Increased inflammation Increased striatal DA release	(Bakos et al. 2004; Cotter et al. 1995; Eßlinger et al. 2016; Fernández de Cossío et al. 2017; Kneeland and Fatemi 2013; Meyer et al. 2005; Remus and Dantzer 2016; Ronovsky et al. 2017; Rose et al. 2017; Shi et al. 2003; Wachholz et al. 2017; Zuckerman et al. 2003)

Rothman 1998), a transient decrease in norepinephrine (NE) in the hypothalamus, and a reduction in responsiveness to amphetamine in terms of DA concentrations in caudate-putamen and nucleus accumbens (Paulson et al. 1991). Even a switch in behavior has been shown in the same animal model. Anhedonic symptoms after withdrawal stabilize after a while (Paulson et al. 1991; Wise and Munn 1995). Morphine pretreated rats, furthermore, show a switch in β-endorphin-induced locomotor activity from being hyper-responsive to hypo-responsive when going through withdrawl (Schwartz et al. 1982).

The administration of psychostimulants affects several neurotransmitter systems which is in line with the fact that a number of neurotransmitters are affected in patients with BD (Barchas and Altemus 1999; Schildkraut 1965). Similarly, other pathways, e.g., the phosphoinositide cycle have been reported to be involved in BD and are targeted by treatment options for the disorder (Agam et al. 2002). A comprehensive overview of all these neurotransmitters and pathways would go beyond the scope of this review; therefore, we will give a brief overview on neurotransmitters and then focus on the dopaminergic system in "Dopaminergic pathways."

The cholinergic system seems to be predominantly involved in depressive-like symptoms in humans and animals. Manipulation of the cholinergic system through administration of arecoline, a direct agonist of cholinergic receptors, induced depression in both healthy controls and unmedicated euthymic BD patients (Nurnberger et al. 1983). Furthermore, affective disorder patients undergo exaggerated depressive responses to cholinergic agents compared to control groups. This hypersensitivity to cholinergic manipulations supports the hypothesis of a cholinergic imbalance during depressive episodes (van Enkhuizen et al. 2015b; Janowsky et al. 1994). Further evidence for the involvement of acetylcholine in BD comes from neuroimaging studies, where physostigmine, a cholinesterase inhibitor, resulted in elevated acetylcholine levels in the brain, counteracted mania, and induced depressive-like symptoms in both control and patients with affective disorders (Hannestad et al. 2013; Janowsky et al. 1972; Janowsky et al. 1974). Also reduced β_2 nicotinic acetylcholine receptor availability was observed in depressed BD patients compared to healthy and euthymic individuals (Hannestad et al. 2013). The brains of depressed patients contain elevated levels of choline, the precursor of acetylcholine (Steingard et al. 2000), supporting a hypercholinergic state during depressive episodes (van Enkhuizen et al. 2015b).

Animal models confirm the involvement of the cholinergic system in depression. The α7 nicotinic acetylcholine receptor agonist SSR180711 shows antidepressant-like effects in mice, indicated by reduced immobility time in the forced swim test (Andreasen et al. 2012). Interestingly, behaviorally effective doses of SSR180711 inhibited in part the serotonin reuptake (Andreasen et al. 2012). Another subtype-selective nicotinic acetylcholine receptor agonist acts antidepressive-like by reversing the escape deficits in the learned helplessness paradigm in rats (Ferguson et al. 2000). Furthermore, nicotine attenuates anhedonia-like behavior in rats (Andreasen et al. 2011) and depressive-like behavior in mice (Andreasen and Redrobe 2009). The withdrawal of chronic nicotine administration induces depressive-like behavior in mice, measured as increased immobility time in the force swim test (Roni and Rahman 2014). Another manipulation of the cholinergic system is the inhibition of acetylcholinesterase, which is degrading acetylcholine. This inhibition induces depressive- and anxiety-like behavior in mice (Mineur et al. 2013). Interestingly, both lithium and valproate increase the activity of acetylcholinesterase in the brain of rats (Varela et al. 2013).

The catecholaminergic system on the other hand is mainly involved in mania-like symptoms in humans as well as in animals. Elevated levels of both DA and NE could be observed in BD rapid cycling (Juckel et al. 2000) and normal cycling patients (Berk et al. 2007). Several antidepressants increase synaptic catecholamine (Salvi et al. 2008; Tanda et al. 1994) levels. Furthermore, as already mentioned above the psychostimulant amphetamine increases synaptic DA and NE levels through inhibition or reversing the corresponding reuptake mechanisms or elevated DA efflux (Berk et al. 2007; Raiteri et al. 1975; Schaeffer et al. 1976; Sulzer et al. 2005). Amphetamine not only induces mania-like behavior in animals but also causes manic symptoms in healthy humans and BD patients, such as decreased need for sleep, elevated mood, drive and energy and attention, sleep, sexual behavior, sensorimotor function, learning and memory are affected (Asghar et al. 2003; Berk et al. 2007; Corp et al. 2014; Cousins et al. 2009; Jacobs and Silverstone 1986; Nurnberger et al. 1982; Peet and Peters 1995; Seiden et al. 1993). These behavioral effects of amphetamine administration are not only a simple consequence of increased neurotransmitter levels but it is more likely that a disturbance of the homeostatic mechanisms, controlling the catecholamine levels, plays a key role for this dramatic mood shift (Anand et al. 1999; van Enkhuizen et al. 2015b; Young and Dulcis 2015). Comparable to the animal models psychotherapeutics, such as lithium and valproate, can also attenuate the amphetamine mania-relevant behavior in humans (Flemenbaum 1974; Silverstone et al. 1980; Van Kammen and Murphy 1975).

Several neurotransmitters are affected in BD and together with the high comorbidity of BD with substance abuse disorders (Kessler et al. 1997; Regier et al. 1990; Salloum et al. 2005) sensitization models have some face validity. They have for a long time also been the only BD animal models that show both phases, mania and depression, in the same animal model (Kato et al. 2007). On the other hand, the fact that psychostimulants act on numerous pathways hampers the investigation of the neurobiology underlying the observed behavioral changes. Therefore, more recent models for BD try to focus on one neurotransmitter system, primarily the dopaminergic system. Its involvement in BD and manipulations in animal models will be discussed in "Dopaminergic pathways."

Another limitation of the psychostimulant induced animal models for BD mania is that only a few simple aspects of human mania, like hyperactivity, are mimicked and even the amphetamine-induced hyperactivity is not specific for BD (Logan and McClung 2016; Rygula et al. 2015).

Dopaminergic pathways

Evidence from both human and animal studies suggests that BD is caused by an impaired neurotransmitter homeostasis (Berk et al. 2007). Clinical observations revealed that DA is altered in both episodes of BD. Thus, the dopamine hypothesis, claiming that dopaminergic transmission is disturbed depending on the mood phase, is one of the most promising hypotheses for the pathophysiology of BD (Berk et al. 2007). Manic episodes are associated with hyperdopaminergia. Increased dopaminergic transmission then induces homeostatic regulation mechanisms, which in a next step downregulate the post- and presynaptic sensitivity of receptors among other mechanisms. This downregulation results in an episode of decreased dopaminergic transmission, which is associated with the depressive episode of BD. This hypodopaminergic state activates then again the same homeostatic mechanisms, which now upregulate the key elements, resulting in another manic episode and thereby explaining the cyclic nature of the disease. A desynchronization of receptors and other key elements in different brain regions might be a possible explanation for euthymic episodes (Berk et al. 2007).

The dopaminergic system is involved in experiencing pleasure, mediating motivation (Bressan and Crippa 2005), impulsivity, risk behavior, and cognitive processes (Seamans and Yang 2004). Manipulation of the dopamine D1 receptor (D1R) in several species results in working memory deficits (Floresco and Phillips 2001; Goldman-Rakic 1999; Paspalas et al. 2013; Puig et al. 2014). Furthermore, increased D1R expression in the prefrontal cortex plays a role in impulsivity (Loos et al. 2010), cocaine addiction, sucrose preference, and high-risk behavior (Sonntag et al. 2014). All these behaviors are to a certain extent detectable in patients of BD, including increased risk for substance abuse (Messer et al. 2017), increased impulsivity in manic episodes (Logan and McClung 2016), or cognitive deficits (Cope et al. 2016). Indeed, elevations in D1R have been observed in BD patients via positron emission tomography and single-photon emission computed tomography (Gonul et al. 2009; Suhara et al. 1992; Yao et al. 2013). Also other dopamine receptors are altered in BD patients and might therefore play a role in the pathogenesis of the disease. The D2R density is elevated in the nucleus accumbens in bipolar patients with psychotic symptoms (Pearlson et al. 1995). Elevated DA levels in the urine were additionally observed in BD patients within manic episodes (Joyce et al. 1995). Alterations in the dopaminergic system through administration of psychostimulants result in a shift of neurotransmitter levels and manic behavior in humans (Cousins et al. 2009). DA levels can be affected through administration of L-DOPA, the precursor of DA, which is an established medication for Parkinson's disease (Berk et al. 2007). L-DOPA administration induced behavior similar to BD mania in these patients, such as increased sexual behavior, impulsivity, and risk taking (Berk et al. 2007; Claassen et al. 2011; van Praag and Korf 1975; Raja and Bentivoglio 2012). Not all, but some BD patients treated with different DA agonists, such as bromocriptine, also experienced manic episodes (Fisher et al. 1991; Gerner et al. 1976). BD depression can be treated with such agonists and resulted in an improvement of depressive symptoms (Goldberg et al. 2004; Zarate et al. 2004). On the other hand, manic symptoms of BD patients can be attenuated through administration of DA antagonists (Christie et al. 1989; Tohen et al. 2003; Vieta et al. 2005). Furthermore, antidepressants increase the dopaminergic transmission in the prefrontal cortex and nucleus accumbens as shown in rodents (Tanda et al. 1994). Alterations of functional DA transporter (DAT) levels, particularly reduced availability, were confirmed in BD patients via positron emission tomography (Anand et al. 2011), in postmortem tissue (Rao et al. 2012; Young and Dulcis 2015) and cell culture experiments (Horschitz et al. 2005).

A knock-down of DAT in mice with reduced DAT functioning to approximately 10% of wild-type level resulted in mania-like behavior, such as hyperactivity in novel environments (Zhuang et al. 2001), increased risk behavior in the Iowa Gambling Task (IGT) (Young et al. 2011), impaired decision making with a preference for high reward combined with high risk in the IGT (van Enkhuizen et al. 2014b), and a similar hyperexploratory behavior in the BPM as observed in humans but with less straight movements compared to BD patients (van Enkhuizen et al. 2014a; Perry et al. 2009; Young et al. 2010). But DAT knock-down mice fail to mimic the observed sensorimotor deficits in PPI observed in humans (Ralph-Williams et al. 2003). Alpha-methyl-*p*-tyrosine induced depletion of DA and was able to attenuate some of the behavioral abnormalities of the DAT knock-down mice (van Enkhuizen et al. 2014a), similar to the effect of chronic valproate treatment (van Enkhuizen et al. 2013a), whereas both treatments did not affect the exploration behavior. To sum up, this animal model is able to resemble various behavioral aspects of human BD mania (Cassidy et al. 1998; van Enkhuizen et al. 2015a). Interestingly, photoperiod length can influence the DAT level in the brain of rats (Dulcis et al. 2013), thereby again connecting the dopaminergic system and the circadian rhythm (see "Circadian rhythm") with the pathophysiology of BD. Possible critiques of the DAT knock-down mice are the clearly too low *DAT* expression compared with unmedicated BD patients, which is approximately 80% of healthy subjects (Anand et al. 2011; Young and Dulcis 2015) and that this animal model mimics only BD mania and not depression (van Enkhuizen et al. 2015a). Mania-like behavior, such as hyperactivity (Giros et al. 1996; Ralph et al. 2001) and sensorimotor deficits in PPI (Ralph et al. 2001), can also be induced through a complete knock-out of the *DAT* gene in mice. The pointed hyperactivity of these mice could be attenuated through the D1R antagonist SCH23390 (Ralph et al. 2001). PPI deficits could be diminished through clozapine and quetiapine, which are atypical antipsychotics used as an effective treatment for BD mania and schizophrenia (Powell et al. 2008), acting as antagonists of the D2R (Brust et al. 2015; Masri et al. 2008). However, the DAT knock-down and knock-out mice were also used as animal models for ADHD (Leo and Gainetdinov 2013) and schizophrenia (Gainetdinov et al. 2001). This is no surprise considering the fact that DA transmission is also involved in the pathogenesis of these disorders (Gainetdinov et al. 2001; Giros et al. 1996; Leo and Gainetdinov 2013; Sharma et al. 2016; Zhuang et al. 2001). Nevertheless, we want to point out that it is important to create specific animal models, which are able to model more facets of the complex behavior of each of these disorders and the cyclical nature of BD especially.

One different approach to recreate the cyclical nature of BD within one animal through manipulating the dopaminergic system was realized by Freund and colleagues, using an inducible lentiviral vector system. Over-expression of D1R in the medial prefrontal cortex of rats resulted in increased sexual behavior, increased sucrose preference, impulsivity, and increased drug-related behavior (Sonntag et al. 2014). The increased D1R expression in the medial prefrontal cortex was accompanied by decreased D2R expression in the nucleus accumbens. Even more interestingly, just the termination of this viral over-expression was sufficient enough to induce depressive-like behavior in the triadic paradigm of learned helplessness, reduced activity, and diminished sucrose preference (Freund et al. 2016). Termination of D1R over-expression furthermore increased levels of cAMP response element-binding protein (CREB) in nucleus accumbens (Freund et al. 2016). This animal model is therewith one of the few models, which is able to recreate the cyclical nature of BD. It furthermore supports the hypothesis that the homeostatic regulation of DA transmission plays a key role in the pathogenesis of BD (Berk et al. 2007).

Animal models that manipulate dopaminergic pathways mainly increased dopaminergic transmission and therewith induced mania-like behavior (Table 1). Inducible viral over-expression of D1R allowed investigating behavior after the termination of the over-expression (Freund et al. 2016). Results indicate that while increased dopaminergic transmission is associated with mania-like behavior the termination of increased dopaminergic transmission induces depressive-like behavior. Exact mechanisms leading to the observed behavioral changes are still unclear. Autoregulatory mechanism might have downregulated D1R expression during the viral over-expression causing reduced dopaminergic transmission after the termination of the over-expression. This explanation would be in line with Berk's dopamine hypothesis of BD (Berk et al. 2007). While this approach might be a promising new way to create an animal model for BD, further studies, e.g., on the models' susceptibility to treatment like lithium are necessary for better understanding of the underlying mechanisms.

Environment: stressors

Stressful life events in combination with genetic factors are a risk factor for the onset of psychiatric disorders (Afifi et al. 2009; Bebbington et al. 1984; Costello 1982; Kendler et al. 1999; Paykel 1978; Schmitt et al. 2014; Surtees et al. 1986). Environmental risk factors, causing these stressful experiences, are for example neglect during childhood, maternal loss, economic problems, family violence, abuse, sexual maltreatment, and many more (Bernstein et al. 2003; Brown et al. 2009; Kaufman and Charney 2001; Marangoni et al. 2016; Mullen et al. 1996). In fact almost two-third of BD patients sustained at least one negative or goal-attainment life event 6 months prior to the index or first occurred episode (Simhandl et al. 2015). Especially the first period of life plays an important role in the development of children (Vetulani 2013). Different types of maltreatment including physical, sexual, and emotional abuse or neglect in the early period of life (i.e., early live stress, ELS) are associated with mood disorders (Afifi et al. 2009; Green et al. 2010; Hovens et al. 2010; Leverich et al. 2002; McLaughlin et al. 2010). ELS in humans can lead to impaired cognitive functioning, exemplified in worse academic performance, impaired intellectual ability, language difficulties, and lower IQ (Cohen et al. 2008; De Bellis et al. 2009; van den Dries et al. 2010; Loman et al. 2009; Nelson et al. 2007). The risk to develop anxiety, depression, and psychoses in adulthood is particularly increased through ELS (Bebbington et al. 2004; Gilbert et al. 2009; Kaufman and Charney 2001; Mullen et al. 1996) and it is more likely that these illnesses are treatment resistant (Bryer et al. 1987; Nemeroff et al. 2003; Vetulani 2013). These long-lasting effects can occur through high or chronic levels of stress, because they might affect brain development and thereby mental health (Anda et al. 2006; De Bellis et al. 1999a; De Bellis et al. 1999b; Lupien et al. 2009; Maniglio 2009; McLaughlin et al. 2010; Pechtel and Pizzagalli 2011; Pirkola et al. 2005; Spataro et al. 2004; Teicher 2002). 32 percent of psychiatric disorders can be explained by childhood adverse experiences (Green et al. 2010; Pechtel and Pizzagalli 2011). These experiences influence also the overall lifespan, because humans, who experienced more than six traumatic events in their childhood, have an increased risk of dying approximately 20 years earlier (Anda et al. 2009; Brown et al. 2009).

The mother–infant interaction is very important not only for humans, but also for primates, rodents, or mammals in general for the development of the offspring and includes much more than just supply with nutrition (Gutman and Nemeroff 2002; Harlow and Zimmermann 1959; Heim and Nemeroff 2002; Kaffman and Meaney 2007; Mason and Berkson 1975; Meaney 2001; Tractenberg et al. 2016). Stressful events in the early period of life produce long-lasting effects on brain development in rodents (Caldji et al. 1998, 2000a; Francis and Meaney 1999; Romeo et al. 2003; Tractenberg et al. 2016), comparable to the effects observed in humans.

ELS in rodents can be induced as early as the prenatal period by stressing the pregnant damn, e.g., by restrain. Observed behavioral consequences of adult rats, which were prenatally stressed, can be identified as depressive-like, namely anhedonia, increased helplessness, indicated through increased immobility time in the forced swim test, increased anxiety behavior in the open field test, impaired cognition, decreased exploratory behavior, and social withdrawal (Fatima et al. 2017; Frye and Wawrzycki 2003; Hao et al. 2010; Jia et al. 2015; Lin et al. 2012; Lin and Wang 2014; Wakshlak and Weinstock 1990). Similar long-lasting effects on social behavior could be observed in prenatally stressed rhesus macaques (Clarke and Schneider 1993).

Prenatal stress is associated with alterations in the immune system (Diz-Chaves et al. 2012, see "Immune system") and HPA axis (Koehl et al. 1999), decreased neurogenesis in the hippocampus (Fatima et al. 2017; Lemaire et al. 2000; Lin and Wang 2014), and reduced BDNF levels (Jia et al. 2015; Lin and Wang 2014). In addition, the metabotropic glutamate receptor 1 (mGluR1) is increased in the hippocampus and prefrontal cortex and mGluR5 is increased in the striatum of prenatally stressed rats (Jia et al. 2015). Glutamate transporter expression is increased in adult prenatally stressed rats and therefore affects the whole glutamate neurotransmission long term, but only in the frontal cortex and hippocampus (Adrover et al. 2015). The glutamatergic system plays a critical role in the regulation of synaptic plasticity (D'Sa and Duman 2002; Manji et al. 2001). Chronic lithium and valproate treatment can down-regulate the synaptic expression of ionotropic glutamate receptors in hippocampal neurons of rats (Du et al. 2004; Gray et al. 2003) and the antidepressant imipramine has the opposite effect (Einat and Manji 2006; Gray et al. 2003). In addition, pharmacological inhibition of ionotropic glutamate receptors via several competitive and noncompetitive inhibitors attenuated amphetamine-induced hyperactivity in mice (Vanover 1998). Interestingly, a contrary effect occurs through manipulating the GluR6. Knock-out mice for the *GluR6* gene exhibited mania-like behavior, indicated through hyperactivity, heightened responsivity to amphetamine, increased risk-taking behavior, more aggressive, less immobility time in the forced swim test, and less anxiety behavior (Shaltiel et al. 2008). Lithium was able to attenuate these behavioral abnormalities (Shaltiel et al. 2008). Prenatal stress is in addition able to alter the circadian rhythm and corticosterone secretion through disturbance of the HPA axis in adult prenatally stressed rats (Koehl et al. 1999). One function of the HPA axis is the synthesis of cortisol, a glucocorticoid; especially, maternal glucocorticoid is crucial for fetal development, because it affects synaptic connections, density, and differentiation of postnatal development of the fetal hippocampus (Fatima et al. 2017; Trejo et al. 2000). An overall decrease in the number of neurons and overall size could be observed in fetal hippocampus of rhesus macaques, whose mothers were administrated excessive amounts of glucocorticoids during pregnancy (Uno et al. 1990). Similar effects of inhibited hippocampal neurogenesis, decreased hippocampal volume, and elevated cortisol levels were observed in juvenile rhesus macaques prenatally stressed via environmental alterations of the photoperiod (Coe et al. 2003). Hippocampal *Bcl-2* expression is also affected, namely decreased, in juvenile prenatally stressed offspring rats, exhibiting depressive-like behavior (Guan et al. 2013). Interestingly lithium, which attenuates mania-like behavior in animal models, increases the Bcl-2 level (Chen et al. 1999; Manji et al. 2000), indicating one way of lithium's therapeutic effects. In return, chronic stress during pregnancy affects not only the unborn pup, but also the mother. Stressed mother rats exhibit depressive-like behavior in the forced swim test, less maternal care, and a decrease in spine density in the medial prefrontal cortex (Leuner et al. 2014).

Not only prenatal but also postnatal stress, for example, induced through maternal separation of the pups from their mother for a defined amount of time (e.g., 2–4 h per day for up to 3 weeks) can result in long-lasting behavioral alterations. Early maternal separation (EMS) results in ELS and induces a conserved neural response, including a protest response and the feeling of despair in humans and animals (Hofer 2005). The mother's behavior has an influence on the brain development of the neonate. Hippocampal development, memory, spatial and social learning, and the response to stress of the HPA axis is affected by maternal licking and grooming of the offspring (Lévy et al. 2003; Lippmann et al. 2007; Liu et al. 1997, 2000; Vetulani 2013). This mother infant interaction has as well a physiological effect in rats and an interruption can result in alterations of the heart rate, hormone levels, and interestingly the circadian rhythm (Hofer 1970, 1975, 1976; Kuhn et al. 1990; Meaney et al. 1991; Stahl et al. 2002; Stanton and Levine 1990; Vetulani 2013). Rats exposed to chronic EMS exhibited hypoactivity, increased stereotypic behavior, abnormal anxiety behavior, abnormal HPA axis functioning, and heightened response to an acute stressor and an elevated acoustic startle response in adulthood (Caldji et al. 2000b; Huot et al. 2001; Kalinichev et al. 2002; Ladd et al. 2000, 2004; Lippmann et al. 2007; McIntosh et al. 1999; Wigger and Neumann 1999). Antidepressant treatment can attenuate these depressive-like behaviors induced by EMS (Cotella et al. 2013; Couto et al. 2012; El Khoury et al. 2006; Huot et al. 2001; MacQueen et al. 2003). The BDNF levels were decreased over a long period of time in the hippocampus of adult rats exposed to EMS (Lippmann et al. 2007), as well as in rats that were chronically stressed (Smith et al. 1995). Prolonged stress experiments indicate that inhibition of BDNF could cause neuronal atrophy or that BDNF is required for neuronal remodeling (Duman et al. 2016; Magariños et al. 2011). Indeed, long-lasting reduced BDNF levels in the hippocampus were associated with learning and memory deficits, as well as depressive-like behavior (Duman and Monteggia 2006; Huot et al. 2002; Lippmann et al. 2007). Furthermore, *BDNF* expression can be increased through chronic antidepressant treatment in rat hippocampus (Nibuya et al. 1995; Russo-Neustadt et al. 2000). In return, a single direct injection of BDNF into the hippocampus led to an antidepressant effect, indicated through comparable performances in the forced swim test and learned helplessness paradigm of rats chronically treated with antidepressants (Shirayama et al. 2002). This behavioral effect could not be recapitulated in mice with reduced *BDNF* expression (Saarelainen et al. 2003), suggesting that BDNF signaling is necessary for the antidepressant effect.

Interestingly, stress affects the dopaminergic system through stimulating dopaminergic transmission in the VTA of stressed rats (Di Chiara et al. 1999; Horger and Roth 1996; Nieoullon and Coquerel 2003; Yadid et al. 2001), which again links alterations in the dopaminergic system and stress to BD. In addition, humans and rodents are not only in these early stages of life highly vulnerable to stress, but also in adolescence. During this important time of brain development, neuroplasticity in stress regulatory circuits and HPA axis functioning are formed (Andersen 2003; Andersen and Teicher 2008; Eiland and Romeo 2013; Wulsin et al. 2016). Therefore, chronic stress exposure to rats in the late adolescence results in depressive-like behavior in adulthood (Wulsin et al. 2016). But the effects of environmental stressors can be so powerful to induce depressive-like phenotypes even in adult, normally raised rats. These stressors can be provided through several behavioral paradigms, such as the forced swim test (Porsolt et al. 1977), tail suspension test (Steru et al. 1985), and learned helplessness (Maier and Seligman 1976). Similar behavioral abnormalities, which can be described as depressive-like behavior, such as reduced locomotor and exploratory behavior, aggression, sexual behavior, elevated anxiety and submissive behavior, social avoidance, disrupted circadian rhythms, and immune function, can be induced through repeated exposure to social defeat in rats (Berton et al. 1998; Crawford et al. 2013; Hollis et al. 2010; Hollis and Kabbaj 2014; Meerlo et al. 1996; Ruis et al. 1999; Stefanski 2000; Tidey and Miczek 1997; Tornatzky and Miczek 1993). Another prominent stressor, sleep deprivation, was already discussed in "Circadian rhythm" and can result in mania-like behavior in rodents (Malkoff-Schwartz et al. 1998).

Environmental stress has been widely used to create animal models for depression. Paradigms like maternal separation (Tractenberg et al. 2016) or social defeat (Toyoda 2017) are well-established models that have revealed several neurobiological mechanisms that connect stress and the onset of depression. It is to mention, however, that we cannot distinguish between uni- and bipolar depressive-like behavior in these models. The administration of antidepressants in these models provides mixed results (Harrison and Baune 2014) but to our knowledge it did not result in the induction of mania-like behavior as sometimes seen in patients with BD. Lithium was able to prevent ELS-associated changes in the brain (Husum and Mathé 2002).

Environmental stressors can also induce mania-like behavior, e.g., by affecting circadian rhythms (Malkoff-Schwartz et al. 1998). A combination of circadian rhythm manipulation and environmental stressors (comparable to Le-Niculescu et al. 2008; see "Circadian rhythm") might therefore be useful to create a switch between both behavioral phases in animal models.

Immune system

During the past few years, it became more and more evident that the immune system plays an important role in psychiatric disorders including BD. First speculations started after epidemiological studies revealed that BD occurs more often in people born between December and March (Fuller Torrey et al. 1996), indicating that an infection of the mother during the winter months could contribute to the risk to develop BD. Indeed, several years later it was confirmed that an influenza infection during pregnancy increases the risk for the offspring to develop BD by fourfold (Parboosing et al. 2013). BD patients furthermore show an increased cerebrospinal fluid-to-serum ratio, which could be an indicator for a dysfunctional blood–brain barrier (Patel and Frey 2015; Zetterberg et al. 2014). However, not only the immune system predisposed to develop BD, but also changes in the immune system have been shown in patients diagnosed with BD. A persistent and low-grade pro-inflammatory state, which is more intense during mood episodes, especially manic episodes, and less intense in depressive episodes (Brietzke et al. 2009b; Modabbernia et al. 2013) has been revealed in these patients. Even euthymia has been associated with detectable peripheral pro-inflammatory activity (Brietzke et al. 2009a, 2009b). In support of these findings is the increased mortality rate of BD patients (Anda et al. 2009; Brown et al. 2009; Crump et al. 2013). Apart from suicide, this elevated mortality rate can be explained by additional natural causes of death associated with increased inflammation (Crump et al. 2013; Hoang et al. 2011; Kupfer 2005). Furthermore, the immunological response to stress is altered in patients with BD (Wieck et al. 2014). There are some findings showing that the number of past episodes could even be a key factor to understand the evolution of immunological changes in BD. In a study conducted by Maes and colleagues, they have found that the number of past depressive episodes positively correlates with pro-inflammatory cytokines (Maes et al. 2012). Indeed, elevated levels of pro-inflammatory cytokines were reported in BD patients (Goldstein et al. 2009; Haarman et al. 2014; Stertz et al. 2013). Interestingly, lithium is able to attenuate pro-inflammatory cytokines (Boufidou et al. 2004; Green and Nolan 2012; Himmerich et al. 2013; Patel and Frey 2015; Rowse et al. 2012; Wang et al. 2009; Zhang et al. 2009).

In animal models, maternal immune activation (MIA) and its consequences for the offspring has been intensively studied in the last two decades (Meyer 2014). Thereby, the immune system of the pregnant damn has mainly been stimulated with the human influenza virus (Cotter et al. 1995; Kneeland and Fatemi 2013), the immunostimulant Polyinosinic:polycytidylic acid (poly I:C) (Eßlinger et al. 2016; Rose et al. 2017; Shi et al. 2003), or bacterial lipopolysaccharide (Bakos et al. 2004; Fernández de Cossío et al. 2017) during different gestational stages. In adult animals that had been exposed to MIA sensorimotor gating, i.e., latent inhibition and the US-preexposure effect are disrupted, impairments in working memory are evident and the locomotor response to amphetamine is increased (Meyer et al. 2005). Furthermore, a reduction in social interactions in addition to increased repetitive and stereotypic behavior has been reported (Fernández de Cossío et al. 2017; Rose et al. 2017). Even depressive-like behavior including increased anxiety and helplessness (Meyer et al. 2005; Ronovsky et al. 2016) has been shown. Thereby, depressive-like behavior has also been reported in the second generation after MIA (Ronovsky et al. 2017). Taken together, MIA results in the development of several behavioral deficits that are associated with psychiatric disorders. Given the strong effect on sensorimotor gating and deficits in social behavior, MIA in animal models has mainly been associated with a schizophrenia-like phenotype (Meyer et al. 2005) or autism-related characteristics (Fernández de Cossío et al. 2017). An animal model for BD using MIA has never been proposed. At the same time, deficits in sensory gating have been implicated in patients with BD (Cheng et al. 2016), specifically during the acute mania phase (Kohl et al. 2013). Similarly, impairments in working memory (Dickinson et al. 2017) and social cognition (Hoertnagl et al. 2014) have been reported in patients with BD and animals after MIA (Fernández de Cossío et al. 2017; Meyer et al. 2005). Further findings on an increased striatal DA release following MIA (Zuckerman et al. 2003) are in line with the hypothesis that dopaminergic pathways are disrupted in BD (see "Dopaminergic pathways") and further support the fact that MIA might be useful to also create animal models for BD. Less research on disrupted behavior after an acute or chronic activation of the immune system in adult animals has been conducted. Nevertheless, there is evidence that even in adulthood activation of the immune system can induce depressive-like behavior and anxiety (Remus and Dantzer 2016; Wachholz et al. 2017). So far no reports on adult immune activation and mania-associated behaviors in animal models exist. An animal model of mania (induced by amphetamine; see "Sensitization models and neurotransmitters in general"), however, showed increased cytokine levels in plasma and brain, which could together with the mania-like behavior be reversed by lithium treatment (Valvassori et al. 2015). Even adult animals therefore show depressive-like behavior when manipulating the immune system and a mania-like phenotype in adult animals is associated with increased inflammation.

Taken together, there is growing evidence that the immune system plays an important role in BD. Animal models with an immune activation early in development (i.e., prenatally) show several behavioral changes that are associated with depression and mania. So far, however, no cycling between these two behavioral states has been shown after manipulation of the immune system and MIA has never been considered as a manipulation to create an animal model for BD.

Conclusions

BD was to some extent already described by ancient Greek scholars like Hippocrates and Aristoteles (Angst and Marneros 2001). Nevertheless, our current knowledge in the 21st century about the disorder is still limited. Given the fact that lithium, one of the top choice treatment options (Sani et al. 2017), was discovered by animal research (Cade 1949), animal models for the disorder can be a very useful tool to advance our knowledge. Indeed, several models have either confirmed findings from patients or even extended these findings by explaining the underlying neurobiological mechanisms. In this review, we could confirm that several affected areas and risk factors can be found in human patients as well as animal models for BD. Thereby, it can be noticed that all sections described here are connected with each other. Disruptions of circadian rhythms influence the dopaminergic system (Coque et al. 2011; McClung et al. 2005; Mukherjee et al. 2010; Roybal et al. 2007). DA in turn is well known as a key player in reward behavior and therewith drug use (Cooper et al. 2017). Substance abuse disorder is correlated with a stressful environment and stress increases the risk for relapse (Goldstein et al. 2008). Furthermore, stress and addiction induce similar epigenetic and neurobiological modifications (Cadet 2016; Moonat and Pandey 2012; Palmisano and Pandey 2017; Spanagel et al. 2014). Stress has an influence on the immune system (Stefanski 2000) and the immune system on the other hand is connected with pathways related to circadian rhythm (Dumbell et al. 2016). Manipulation in animal models therewith often results in an interplay of several affected factors. It therewith resembles the human condition and it strengthens the model. At the same time, when several mechanisms are affected, the exact mechanism underlying BD is hard to investigate. It is clear that BD is not caused by a single factor. Therefore animal models that cover a broad range of the disruptions observed in human patients might need manipulations in several areas. At the same time, single-factor manipulations would be the best way to confirm correlations between observed changes and the manipulation. Due to the complex etiology, biology and disease pattern of psychiatric diseases, animal models with targeted mutations involve some limitations. Therefore, it is unlikely that one genetic alteration within an animal model will be able to recapitulate all facets of human DSM-defined disorder symptomatology (Kaiser and Feng 2015). DSM-defined disorders often contain similar phenotypical features, which can be based on diverse biological factors. Nevertheless, most established animal models for BD use one manipulation to model just a partial list of symptoms (concentrating on either mania or depressive-like symptoms). This approach facilitates to connect behavioral outcomes to specific pathways and is an important tool to advance our knowledge of certain aspects. Nevertheless, the diverse character of behavior and even switch of behavior observed in patients is not considered in these models. Specifically for the investigation of this switch and its neurobiology, it is crucial to create animal models presenting mania- as well as depressive-like behavior (Nestler and Hyman 2010). So far, very few models were able to show a switch between mania- and depressive-like behaviors. Sensitization models show mania-like behavior following repeated administration of psychostimulants (see "Sensitization models and neurotransmitters in general") and depressive-like behavior during withdrawal (Antelman et al. 1998; Barr et al. 1999; Baumann and Rothman 1998; Marszalek-Grabska et al. 2016; Persico et al. 1995; Schwartz et al. 1982). However, psychostimulants target several neurotransmitter systems and therefore information on the neurobiology of BD we got from these models is limited. New techniques, namely the use of viral vector to induce genetic material into specific cells, might be promising for the development of new BD animal models reproducing the cyclic character of the disorder. D1R over-expression on glutamatergic cells in the medial prefrontal cortex induces mania-like behavior, while the single termination of this over-expression was sufficient enough to result in depressive-like behavior. It has to be noted, however, that this switch in behavior is not spontaneous as reported in BD patients. Apart from manipulating the dopaminergic system, circadian rhythms and the immune system seem to be promising targets for the development of animal models for BD. Investigating the neurobiology behind the induction of mania- or depressive-like behavior by extending or shortening the length of day might provide us with the switch between the two phases and will induce both phases one after the other in one animal. Similarly, inducing an increased state of inflammation followed by a decreased state of inflammation might reveal an animal model for BD showing the characteristic switch between mood phases.

As always, further research is needed. New technology, however, either in the field of animal research as well as for examining human patients is being established. Combining these techniques with new insights especially in the fields of immunology and circadian rhythms provides us with new tools to develop better models.

Abbreviations

ADHD: attention-deficit hyperactivity disorder; Bcl-2: B-cell lymphoma 2; BD: bipolar disorder; BDNF: brain-derived neurotrophic factor; BPM: behavioral pattern monitor; Clock: circadian locomotor output cycles kaput; CREB: cAMP response element-binding protein; D1R: dopamine D1 receptor; D2R: dopamine D2 receptor; DA: dopamine; DAT: dopamine transporter; ELS: early life stress; EMS: early maternal separation; ERK: extracellular-signal-regulated kinase; GSK-3β: glycogen synthase kinase-3 beta; HPA: hypothalamic–pituitary–adrenal; IGT: Iowa Gambling Task; mGluR: metabotropic glutamate receptor; MIA: maternal immune activation; NE: norepinephrine; poly I: C: polyinosinic:polycytidylic acid; PPI: prepulse inhibition; REV-ERBα: nuclear receptor subfamily1, group D, member1; VTA: ventral tegmental area.

Authors' contributions

NF and DKEB both contributed equally in writing this review. Both authors read and approved the final manuscript.

Competing interests

All authors declare that they have no competing interests.

References

Abulseoud OA, Camsari UM, Ruby CL, Mohamed K, Abdel Gawad NM, Kasasbeh A, et al. Lateral hypothalamic kindling induces manic-like behavior in rats: a novel animal model. Int J Bipolar Disord. 2014;2. http://www.ncbi.nlm.nih.gov/pmc/articles/PMC4452639/. Accessed 11 May 2017.

Abulseoud OA, Gawad NA, Mohamed K, Vadnie C, Camsari UM, Karpyak V, et al. Sex differences in mania phenotype and ethanol consumption in the lateral hypothalamic kindled rat model. Transl Psychiatry. 2015;5(3):e534.

Adrover E, Pallarés ME, Baier CJ, Monteleone MC, Giuliani FA, Waagepetersen HS, et al. Glutamate neurotransmission is affected in prenatally stressed offspring. Neurochem Int. 2015;88:73–87.

Afifi TO, Boman J, Fleisher W, Sareen J. The relationship between child abuse, parental divorce, and lifetime mental disorders and suicidality in a nationally representative adult sample. Child Abuse Negl. 2009;33(3):139–47.

Agam G, Azab AN. Whether lithium inhibits glycogen synthase kinase (GSK)-3β activity in vivo in humans is still an open question. Bipolar Disord. 2016;18(5):464–7.

Agam G, Shamir A, Shaltiel G, Greenberg ML. Myo-inositol-1-phosphate (MIP) synthase: a possible new target for antibipolar drugs. Bipolar Disord. 2002;4(Suppl 1):15–20.

Akhtar RS, Ness JM, Roth KA. Bcl-2 family regulation of neuronal development and neurodegeneration. Biochim Biophys Acta BBA-Mol Cell Res. 2004;1644(2–3):189–203.

American Psychiatric Association. Diagnostic and statistical manual of mental disorders. London: American Psychiatric Publishing; 2013.

Anand A, Darnell A, Miller HL, Berman RM, Cappiello A, Oren DA, et al. Effect of catecholamine depletion on lithium-induced long-term remission of bipolar disorder. Biol Psychiatry. 1999;45(8):972–8.

Anand A, Barkay G, Dzemidzic M, Albrecht D, Karne H, Zheng Q-H, et al. Striatal dopamine transporter availability in unmedicated bipolar disorder. Bipolar Disord. 2011;13(4):406–13.

Anda RF, Felitti VJ, Bremner JD, Walker JD, Whitfield C, Perry BD, et al. The enduring effects of abuse and related adverse experiences in childhood. Eur Arch Psychiatry Clin Neurosci. 2006;256(3):174–86.

Anda RF, Dong M, Brown DW, Felitti VJ, Giles WH, Perry GS, et al. The relationship of adverse childhood experiences to a history of premature death of family members. BMC Public Health. 2009;16(9):106.

Andersen SL. Trajectories of brain development: point of vulnerability or window of opportunity? Neurosci Biobehav Rev. 2003;27(1–2):3–18.

Andersen SL, Teicher MH. Stress, sensitive periods and maturational events in adolescent depression. Trends Neurosci. 2008;31(4):183–91.

Anderson IM, Haddad PM, Scott J. Bipolar disorder. BMJ. 2012;27(345):e8508.

Andreasen JT, Redrobe JP. Antidepressant-like effects of nicotine and mecamylamine in the mouse forced swim and tail suspension tests: role of strain, test and sex. Behav Pharmacol. 2009;20(3):286–95.

Andreasen JT, Henningsen K, Bate S, Christiansen S, Wiborg O. Nicotine reverses anhedonic-like response and cognitive impairment in the rat chronic mild stress model of depression: comparison with sertraline. J Psychopharmacol Oxf Engl. 2011;25(8):1134–41.

Andreasen JT, Redrobe JP, Nielsen EØ. Combined α7 nicotinic acetylcholine receptor agonism and partial serotonin transporter inhibition produce antidepressant-like effects in the mouse forced swim and tail suspension tests: a comparison of SSR180711 and PNU-282987. Pharmacol Biochem Behav. 2012;100(3):624–9.

Angst J, Marneros A. Bipolarity from ancient to modern times: conception, birth and rebirth. J Affect Disord. 2001;67(1–3):3–19.

Antelman SM, Caggiula AR, Kucinski BJ, Fowler H, Gershon S, Edwards DJ, et al. The effects of lithium on a potential cycling model of bipolar disorder. Prog Neuropsychopharmacol Biol Psychiatry. 1998;22(3):495–510.

Asghar SJ, Tanay VAMI, Baker GB, Greenshaw A, Silverstone PH. Relationship of plasma amphetamine levels to physiological, subjective, cognitive and biochemical measures in healthy volunteers. Hum Psychopharmacol. 2003;18(4):291–9.

Ashkenazy T, Einat H, Kronfeld-Schor N. Effects of bright light treatment on depression- and anxiety-like behaviors of diurnal rodents maintained on a short daylight schedule. Behav Brain Res. 2009;201(2):343–6.

Bakos J, Duncko R, Makatsori A, Pirnik Z, Kiss A, Jezova D. Prenatal immune challenge affects growth, behavior, and brain dopamine in offspring. Ann NY Acad Sci. 2004;1018(1):281–7.

Barchas JD, Altemus M. Monoamine hypotheses of mood disorders. 1999. https://www.ncbi.nlm.nih.gov/books/NBK28257/. Accessed 22 May 2017.

Barr AM, Phillips AG. Withdrawal following repeated exposure to d-amphetamine decreases responding for a sucrose solution as measured by a progressive ratio schedule of reinforcement. Psychopharmacology. 1999;141(1):99–106.

Barr AM, Phillips AG. Increased successive negative contrast in rats withdrawn from an escalating-dose schedule of D-amphetamine. Pharmacol Biochem Behav. 2002;71(1–2):293–9.

Barr AM, Fiorino DF, Phillips AG. Effects of withdrawal from an escalating dose schedule of d-amphetamine on sexual behavior in the male rat. Pharmacol Biochem Behav. 1999;64(3):597–604.

Baumann MH, Rothman RB. Alterations in serotonergic responsiveness during cocaine withdrawal in rats: similarities to major depression in humans. Biol Psychiatry. 1998;44(7):578–91.

Bebbington PE, Sturt E, Tennant C, Hurry J. Misfortune and resilience: a community study of women. Psychol Med. 1984;14(2):347–63.

Bebbington PE, Bhugra D, Brugha T, Singleton N, Farrell M, Jenkins R, et al. Psychosis, victimisation and childhood disadvantage: evidence from the second British national survey of psychiatric morbidity. Br J Psychiatry J Ment Sci. 2004;185:220–6.

Bellet MM, Sassone-Corsi P. Mammalian circadian clock and metabolism—the epigenetic link. J Cell Sci. 2010;123(Pt 22):3837–48.

Benedetti F, Serretti A, Colombo C, Barbini B, Lorenzi C, Campori E, et al. Influence of CLOCK gene polymorphism on circadian mood fluctuation and illness recurrence in bipolar depression. Am J Med Genet Part B Neuropsychiatr Genet. 2003;123B(1):23–6.

Benedetti F, Fresi F, Maccioni P, Smeraldi E. Behavioural sensitization to repeated sleep deprivation in a mice model of mania. Behav Brain Res. 2008;187(2):221–7.

Berk M, Dodd S, Kauer-Sant'Anna M, Malhi GS, Bourin M, Kapczinski F, et al. Dopamine dysregulation syndrome: implications for a dopamine hypothesis of bipolar disorder. Acta Psychiatr Scand. 2007;116:41–9.

Bernstein DP, Stein JA, Newcomb MD, Walker E, Pogge D, Ahluvalia T, et al. Development and validation of a brief screening version of the childhood trauma questionnaire. Child Abuse Negl. 2003;27(2):169–90.

Berton O, Aguerre S, Sarrieau A, Mormede P, Chaouloff F. Differential effects of social stress on central serotonergic activity and emotional reactivity in Lewis and spontaneously hypertensive rats. Neuroscience. 1998;82(1):147–59.

Besing RC, Paul JR, Hablitz LM, Rogers CO, Johnson RL, Young ME, et al. Circadian rhythmicity of active GSK3 isoforms modulates molecular clock gene rhythms in the suprachiasmatic nucleus. J Biol Rhythm. 2015;30(2):155–60.

Bilu C, Einat H, Kronfeld-Schor N. Utilization of diurnal rodents in the research of depression. Drug Dev Res. 2016;77(7):336–45.

Bold RJ, Hess KR, Scott Pearson A, Grau AM, Sinicrope FA, Jennings M, et al. Prognostic factors in resectable pancreatic cancer: p53 and Bcl-2. J Gastrointest Surg. 1999;3(3):263–77.

Bonfanti L, Strettoi E, Chierzi S, Cenni MC, Liu X-H, Martinou J-C, et al. Protection of retinal ganglion cells from natural and axotomy-induced cell death in neonatal transgenic mice overexpressing bcl-2. J Neurosci. 1996;16(13):4186–94.

Borison RL, Sabelli HC, Maple PJ, Havdala HS, Diamond BI. Lithium prevention of amphetamine-induced "manic" excitement and of reserpine-induced "depression" in mice: possible role of 2-phenylethylamine. Psychopharmacology. 1978;59(3):259–62.

Boufidou F, Nikolaou C, Alevizos B, Liappas IA, Christodoulou GN. Cytokine production in bipolar affective disorder patients under lithium treatment. J Affect Disord. 2004;82(2):309–13.

Bressan RA, Crippa JA. The role of dopamine in reward and pleasure behaviour–review of data from preclinical research. Acta Psychiatr Scand Suppl. 2005;427:14–21.

Brietzke E, Kauer-Sant'anna M, Teixeira AL, Kapczinski F. Abnormalities in serum chemokine levels in euthymic patients with bipolar disorder. Brain Behav Immun. 2009a;23(8):1079–82.

Brietzke E, Stertz L, Fernandes BS, Kauer-Sant'Anna M, Mascarenhas M, Vargas AE, et al. Comparison of cytokine levels in depressed, manic and euthymic patients with bipolar disorder. J Affect Disord. 2009b;116(3):214–7.

Brown DW, Anda RF, Tiemeier H, Felitti VJ, Edwards VJ, Croft JB, et al. Adverse childhood experiences and the risk of premature mortality. Am J Prev Med. 2009;37(5):389–96.

Brust TF, Hayes MP, Roman DL, Watts VJ. New functional activity of aripiprazole revealed: robust antagonism of D2 dopamine receptor-stimulated Gβγ signaling. Biochem Pharmacol. 2015;93(1):85–91.

Bryer JB, Nelson BA, Miller JB, Krol PA. Childhood sexual and physical abuse as factors in adult psychiatric illness. Am J Psychiatry. 1987;144(11):1426–30.

Bunney WE, Bunney BG. Molecular clock genes in man and lower animals: possible implications for circadian abnormalities in depression. Neuropsychopharmacology. 2000;22(4):335–45.

Bunney JN, Potkin SG. Circadian abnormalities, molecular clock genes and chronobiological treatments in depression. Br Med Bull. 2008;86:23–32.

Burdick KE, Braga RJ, Goldberg JF, Malhotra AK. Cognitive dysfunction in bipolar disorder: future place of pharmacotherapy. CNS Drugs. 2007;21(12):971–81.

Butcher GQ, Doner J, Dziema H, Collamore M, Burgoon PW, Obrietan K. The p42/44 mitogen-activated protein kinase pathway couples photic input to circadian clock entrainment. J Biol Chem. 2002;277(33):29519–25.

Cade JFJ. Lithium salts in the treatment of psychotic excitement. Med J Aust. 1949;2(10):349–52.

Cadet JL. Epigenetics of stress, addiction, and resilience: therapeutic implications. Mol Neurobiol. 2016;53(1):545–60.

Caldji C, Tannenbaum B, Sharma S, Francis D, Plotsky PM, Meaney MJ. Maternal care during infancy regulates the development of neural systems mediating the expression of fearfulness in the rat. Proc Natl Acad Sci. 1998;95(9):5335–40.

Caldji C, Diorio J, Meaney MJ. Variations in maternal care in infancy regulate the development of stress reactivity. Biol Psychiatry. 2000a;48(12):1164–74.

Caldji C, Francis D, Sharma S, Plotsky PM, Meaney MJ. The effects of early rearing environment on the development of GABAA and central benzodiazepine receptor levels and novelty-induced fearfulness in the rat. Neuropsychopharmacol. 2000b;22(3):219–29.

Campani D, Esposito I, Boggi U, Cecchetti D, Menicagli M, De Negri F, et al. Bcl-2 expression in pancreas development and pancreatic cancer progression. J Pathol. 2001;194(4):444–50.

Cassidy F, Murry E, Forest K, Carroll BJ. Signs and symptoms of mania in pure and mixed episodes. J Affect Disord. 1998;50(2–3):187–201.

Challet E. Minireview: entrainment of the suprachiasmatic clockwork in diurnal and nocturnal mammals. Endocrinology. 2007;148(12):5648–55.

Chen G, Zeng WZ, Yuan PX, Huang LD, Jiang YM, Zhao ZH, et al. The mood-stabilizing agents lithium and valproate robustly increase the levels of the neuroprotective protein bcl-2 in the CNS. J Neurochem. 1999;72(2):879–82.

Cheng C-H, Chan PY, Liu CY, Hsu SC. Auditory sensory gating in patients with bipolar disorders: a meta-analysis. J Affect Disord. 2016;203:199–203.

Cheniaux E, Filgueiras A, da Silva RD, Silveira LAS, Nunes ALS, Landeira-Fernandez J. Increased energy/activity, not mood changes, is the core feature of mania. J Affect Disord. 2014;152–154:256–61.

Christie JE, Whalley LJ, Hunter R, Bennie J, Fink G. Sulpiride treatment of acute mania with a comparison of the effects on plasma hormone concentrations of lithium and sulpiride treatment. J Affect Disord. 1989;16(2–3):115–20.

Cipriani A, Barbui C, Salanti G, Rendell J, Brown R, Stockton S, et al. Comparative efficacy and acceptability of antimanic drugs in acute mania: a multiple-treatments meta-analysis. Lancet Lond Engl. 2011;378(9799):1306–15.

Claassen DO, van den Wildenberg WPM, Ridderinkhof KR, Jessup CK, Harrison MB, Wooten GF, et al. The risky business of dopamine agonists in Parkinson disease and impulse control disorders. Behav Neurosci. 2011;125(4):492–500.

Clarke AS, Schneider ML. Prenatal stress has long-term effects on behavioral responses to stress in juvenile rhesus monkeys. Dev Psychobiol. 1993;26(5):293–304.

Coe CL, Kramer M, Czéh B, Gould E, Reeves AJ, Kirschbaum C, et al. Prenatal stress diminishes neurogenesis in the dentate gyrus of juvenile rhesus monkeys. Biol Psychiatry. 2003;54(10):1025–34.

Cohen NJ, Lojkasek M, Zadeh ZY, Pugliese M, Kiefer H. Children adopted from China: a prospective study of their growth and development. J Child Psychol Psychiatry. 2008;49(4):458–68.

Colombo C, Benedetti F, Barbini B, Campori E, Smeraldi E. Rate of switch from depression into mania after therapeutic sleep deprivation in bipolar depression. Psychiatry Res. 1999;86(3):267–70.

Coogan AN, Piggins HD. MAP kinases in the mammalian circadian system–key regulators of clock function. J Neurochem. 2004;90(4):769–75.

Cooper S, Robison AJ, Mazei-Robison MS. Reward circuitry in addiction. Neurother: Neurother J Am Soc Exp; 2017.

Cope ZA, Powell SB, Young JW. Modeling neurodevelopmental cognitive deficits in tasks with cross-species translational validity. Genes Brain Behav. 2016;15(1):27–44.

Coque L, Mukherjee S, Cao J-L, Spencer S, Marvin M, Falcon E, et al. Specific role of VTA dopamine neuronal firing rates and morphology in the reversal of anxiety-related, but not depression-related behavior in the clockΔ19 mouse model of mania. Neuropsychopharmacology. 2011;36(7):1478–88.

Corp SA, Gitlin MJ, Altshuler LL. A review of the use of stimulants and stimulant alternatives in treating bipolar depression and major depressive disorder. J Clin Psychiatry. 2014;75(9):1010–8.
Cosgrove VE, Kelsoe JR, Suppes T. Toward a valid animal model of bipolar disorder: how the research domain criteria help bridge the clinical-basic science divide. Biol Psychiatry. 2016;79(1):62–70.
Costello CG. Social factors associated with depression: a retrospective community study. Psychol Med. 1982;12(2):329–39.
Cotella EM, Mestres Lascano I, Franchioni L, Levin GM, Suárez MM. Long-term effects of maternal separation on chronic stress response suppressed by amitriptyline treatment. Stress Amst Neth. 2013;16(4):477–81.
Cotter D, Takei N, Farrell M, Sham P, Quinn P, Larkin C, et al. Does prenatal exposure to influenza in mice induce pyramidal cell disarray in the dorsal hippocampus? Schizophr Res. 1995;16(3):233–41.
Cousins DA, Butts K, Young AH. The role of dopamine in bipolar disorder. Bipolar Disord. 2009;11(8):787–806.
Crawford LK, Rahman SF, Beck SG. Social stress alters inhibitory synaptic input to distinct subpopulations of raphe serotonin neurons. ACS Chem Neurosci. 2013;4(1):200–9.
Crump C, Sundquist K, Winkleby MA, Sundquist J. Comorbidities and mortality in bipolar disorder: a Swedish national cohort study. JAMA Psychiatry. 2013;70(9):931–9.
D'Sa C, Duman RS. Antidepressants and neuroplasticity. Bipolar Disord. 2002;4(3):183–94.
Davies C, Sanger DJ, Steinberg H, Tomkiewicz M, U'Prichard DC. Lithium and alpha-methyl-p-tyrosine prevent "manic" activity in rodents. Psychopharmacologia. 1974;36(3):263–74.
De Bellis MD, Baum AS, Birmaher B, Keshavan MS, Eccard CH, Boring AM, et al. Developmental traumatology part I: biological stress systems. Biol Psychiatry. 1999a;45(10):1259–70.
De Bellis MD, Keshavan MS, Clark DB, Casey BJ, Giedd JN, Boring AM, et al. A.E. bennett research award. Developmental traumatology. Part II: brain development. Biol Psychiatry. 1999b;45(10):1271–84.
De Bellis MD, Hooper SR, Spratt EG, Woolley DP. Neuropsychological findings in childhood neglect and their relationships to pediatric PTSD. J Int Neuropsychol Soc. 2009;15(6):868–78.
de Fernández Cossío L, Guzmán A, van der Veldt S, Luheshi GN. Prenatal infection leads to ASD-like behavior and altered synaptic pruning in the mouse offspring. Brain Behav Immun. 2017;63:88–98.
DeVries AC, Joh HD, Bernard O, Hattori K, Hurn PD, Traystman RJ, et al. Social stress exacerbates stroke outcome by suppressing Bcl-2 expression. Proc Natl Acad Sci USA. 2001;98(20):11824–8.
Di Chiara G, Loddo P, Tanda G. Reciprocal changes in prefrontal and limbic dopamine responsiveness to aversive and rewarding stimuli after chronic mild stress: implications for the psychobiology of depression. Biol Psychiatry. 1999;46(12):1624–33.
Dickinson T, Becerra R, Coombes J. Executive functioning deficits among adults with bipolar disorder (types I and II): a systematic review and meta-analysis. J Affect Disord. 2017;15(218):407–27.
Diz-Chaves Y, Pernía O, Carrero P, Garcia-Segura LM. Prenatal stress causes alterations in the morphology of microglia and the inflammatory response of the hippocampus of adult female mice. J Neuroinflamm. 2012;20(9):71.
do Couto FS, Batalha VL, Valadas JS, Data-Franca J, Ribeiro JA, Lopes LV. Escitalopram improves memory deficits induced by maternal separation in the rat. Eur J Pharmacol. 2012;695(1–3):71–5.
Doble BW, Woodgett JR. GSK-3: tricks of the trade for a multi-tasking kinase. J Cell Sci. 2003;116(7):1175–86.
Du J, Gray NA, Falke CA, Chen W, Yuan P, Szabo ST, et al. Modulation of synaptic plasticity by antimanic agents: the role of AMPA glutamate receptor subunit 1 synaptic expression. J Neurosci Off J Soc Neurosci. 2004;24(29):6578–89.
Dulcis D, Jamshidi P, Leutgeb S, Spitzer NC. Neurotransmitter switching in the adult brain regulates behavior. Science. 2013;340(6131):449–53.
Duman RS, Monteggia LM. A neurotrophic model for stress-related mood disorders. Biol Psychiatry. 2006;59(12):1116–27.
Duman RS, Aghajanian GK, Sanacora G, Krystal JH. Synaptic plasticity and depression: new insights from stress and rapid-acting antidepressants. Nat Med. 2016;22(3):238–49.
Dumbell R, Matveeva O, Oster H. Circadian clocks, stress, and immunity. Front Endocrinol. 2016;7:37.
Eiland L, Romeo RD. Stress and the developing adolescent brain. Neuroscience. 2013;26(249):162–71.
Einat H. New ways of modeling bipolar disorder. Harv Rev Psychiatry. 2014;22(6):348–52.
Einat H, Manji HK. Cellular plasticity cascades: genes-to-behavior pathways in animal models of bipolar disorder. Biol Psychiatry. 2006;59(12):1160–71.
Einat H, Yuan P, Manji HK. Increased anxiety-like behaviors and mitochondrial dysfunction in mice with targeted mutation of the Bcl-2 gene: further support for the involvement of mitochondrial function in anxiety disorders. Behav Brain Res. 2005;165(2):172–80.
Einat H, Kronfeld-Schor N, Eilam D. Sand rats see the light: short photoperiod induces a depression-like response in a diurnal rodent. Behav Brain Res. 2006;173(1):153–7.
El Khoury A, Gruber SHM, Mørk A, Mathé AA. Adult life behavioral consequences of early maternal separation are alleviated by escitalopram treatment in a rat model of depression. Prog Neuropsychopharmacol Biol Psychiatry. 2006;30(3):535–40.
Engel SR, Creson TK, Hao Y, Shen Y, Maeng S, Nekrasova T, et al. The extracellular signal-regulated kinase pathway contributes to the control of behavioral excitement. Mol Psychiatry. 2008;14(4):448–61.
Eßlinger M, Wachholz S, Manitz M-P, Plümper J, Sommer R, Juckel G, et al. Schizophrenia associated sensory gating deficits develop after adolescent microglia activation. Brain Behav Immun. 2016;58:99–106.
Etain B, Milhiet V, Bellivier F, Leboyer M. Genetics of circadian rhythms and mood spectrum disorders. Eur Neuropsychopharmacol. 2011;21(Supplement 4):S676–82.
Fatima M, Srivastav S, Mondal AC. Prenatal stress and depression associated neuronal development in neonates. Int J Dev Neurosci. 2017;4(60):1–7.
Ferguson SM, Brodkin JD, Lloyd GK, Menzaghi F. Antidepressant-like effects of the subtype-selective nicotinic acetylcholine receptor agonist, SIB-1508Y, in the learned helplessness rat model of depression. Psychopharmacology. 2000;152(3):295–303.
Fisher G, Pelonero AL, Ferguson C. Mania precipitated by prednisone and bromocriptine. Gen Hosp Psychiatry. 1991;13(5):345–6.
Flemenbaum A. Does lithium block the effects of amphetamine? A report of three cases. Am J Psychiatry. 1974;131(7):820–1.
Floresco SB, Phillips AG. Delay-dependent modulation of memory retrieval by infusion of a dopamine D1 agonist into the rat medial prefrontal cortex. Behav Neurosci. 2001;115(4):934–9.
Francis DD, Meaney MJ. Maternal care and the development of stress responses. Curr Opin Neurobiol. 1999;9(1):128–34.
Frank E, Swartz HA, Kupfer DJ. Interpersonal and social rhythm therapy: managing the chaos of bipolar disorder. Biol Psychiatry. 2000;48(6):593–604.
Frank E, Swartz HA, Boland E. Interpersonal and social rhythm therapy: an intervention addressing rhythm dysregulation in bipolar disorder. Dialogues Clin Neurosci. 2007;9(3):325–32.
Freund N, Thompson BS, Sonntag K, Meda S, Andersen SL. When the party is over: depressive-like states in rats following termination of cortical D1 receptor overexpression. Psychopharmacology. 2016;233(7):1191–201.
Frey BN, Valvassori SS, Réus GZ, Martins MR, Petronilho FC, Bardini K, et al. Effects of lithium and valproate on amphetamine-induced oxidative stress generation in an animal model of mania. J Psychiatry Neurosci JPN. 2006;31(5):326–32.
Frey BN, Andreazza AC, Houenou J, Jamain S, Goldstein BI, Frye MA, et al. Biomarkers in bipolar disorder: a positional paper from the international society for bipolar disorders biomarkers task force. Aust NZ J Psychiatry. 2013. doi:10.1177/0004867413478217.
Fries GR, Valvassori SS, Bock H, Stertz L, da Silva Magalhães PV, Mariot E, et al. Memory and brain-derived neurotrophic factor after subchronic or chronic amphetamine treatment in an animal model of mania. J Psychiatr Res. 2015;68:329–36.
Frye CA, Wawrzycki J. Effect of prenatal stress and gonadal hormone condition on depressive behaviors of female and male rats. Horm Behav. 2003;44(4):319–26.
Fuller Torrey E, Rawlings RR, Ennis JM, Merrill DD, Flores DS. Birth seasonality in bipolar disorder, schizophrenia, schizoaffective disorder and stillbirths. Schizophr Res. 1996;21(3):141–9.
Gainetdinov RR, Mohn AR, Caron MG. Genetic animal models: focus on schizophrenia. Trends Neurosci. 2001;24(9):527–33.

Gerner RH, Post RM, Bunney WE. A dopaminergic mechanism in mania. Am J Psychiatry. 1976;133(10):1177–80.

Gessa GL, Pani L, Fadda P, Fratta W. Sleep deprivation in the rat: an animal model of mania. Eur Neuropsychopharmacol. 1995;5(Supplement 1):89–93.

Gilbert R, Widom CS, Browne K, Fergusson D, Webb E, Janson S. Burden and consequences of child maltreatment in high-income countries. Lancet. 2009;373(9657):68–81.

Giros B, Jaber M, Jones SR, Wightman RM, Caron MG. Hyperlocomotion and indifference to cocaine and amphetamine in mice lacking the dopamine transporter. Nature. 1996;379(6566):606–12.

Goetze U, Tölle R. Circadian rhythm of free urinary cortisol, temperature and heart rate in endogenous depressives and under antidepressant therapy. Neuropsychobiology. 1987;18(4):175–84.

Goldberg JF, Burdick KE, Endick CJ. Preliminary randomized, double-blind, placebo-controlled trial of pramipexole added to mood stabilizers for treatment-resistant bipolar depression. Am J Psychiatry. 2004;161(3):564–6.

Goldman-Rakic PS. The "psychic" neuron of the cerebral cortex. Ann NY Acad Sci. 1999;868(1):13–26.

Goldstein BI, Strober MA, Birmaher B, Axelson DA, Esposito-Smythers C, Goldstein TR, et al. Substance use disorders among adolescents with bipolar spectrum disorders. Bipolar Disord. 2008;10(4):469–78.

Goldstein BI, Kemp DE, Soczynska JK, McIntyre RS. Inflammation and the phenomenology, pathophysiology, comorbidity, and treatment of bipolar disorder: a systematic review of the literature. J Clin Psychiatry. 2009;70(8):1078–90.

Gonul AS, Coburn K, Kula M. Cerebral blood flow, metabolic, receptor, and transporter changes in bipolar disorder: the role of PET and SPECT studies. Int Rev Psychiatry Abingdon Engl. 2009;21(4):323–35.

Gonzalez R. The relationship between bipolar disorder and biological rhythms. J Clin Psychiatry. 2014;75(4):323–31.

Goodwin GM, Martinez-Aran A, Glahn DC, Vieta E. Cognitive impairment in bipolar disorder: neurodevelopment or neurodegeneration? An ECNP expert meeting report. Eur Neuropsychopharmacol. 2008;18(11):787–93.

Gould TD, Einat H. Animal models of bipolar disorder and mood stabilizer efficacy: a critical need for improvement. Neurosci Biobehav Rev. 2007;31(6):825–31.

Gould TJ, Keith RA, Bhat RV. Differential sensitivity to lithium's reversal of amphetamine-induced open-field activity in two inbred strains of mice. Behav Brain Res. 2001;118(1):95–105.

Gray NA, Du J, Falke CS, Yuan P, Manji HK. Lithium regulates total and synaptic expression of the AMPA glutamate receptor GluR2 in vitro and in vivo. Ann NY Acad Sci. 2003;1003:402–4.

Green HF, Nolan YM. GSK-3 mediates the release of IL-1β, TNF-α and IL-10 from cortical glia. Neurochem Int. 2012;61(5):666–71.

Green JG, McLaughlin KA, Berglund PA, Gruber MJ, Sampson NA, Zaslavsky AM, et al. Childhood adversities and adult psychopathology in the national comorbidity survey replication (NCS-R) I: associations with first onset of DSM-IV disorders. Arch Gen Psychiatry. 2010;67(2):113.

Grunze H, Vieta E, Goodwin GM, Bowden C, Licht RW, Möller H-J, et al. The world federation of societies of biological psychiatry (WFSBP) guidelines for the biological treatment of bipolar disorders: update 2012 on the long-term treatment of bipolar disorder. World J Biol Psychiatry. 2013;14(3):154–219.

Guan L, Jia N, Zhao X, Zhang X, Tang G, Yang L, et al. The involvement of ERK/CREB/Bcl-2 in depression-like behavior in prenatally stressed offspring rats. Brain Res Bull. 2013;99:1–8.

Gutman DA, Nemeroff CB. Neurobiology of early life stress: rodent studies. Semin Clin Neuropsychiatry. 2002;7(2):89–95.

Haarman BC, der Lek Riemersma-Van RF, de Groot JC, Ruhé HG, Klein HC, Zandstra TE, et al. Neuroinflammation in bipolar disorder—A [(11)C]-(R)-PK11195 positron emission tomography study. Brain Behav Immun. 2014;40:219–25.

Hannestad JO, Cosgrove KP, DellaGioia NF, Perkins E, Bois F, Bhagwagar Z, et al. Changes in the cholinergic system between bipolar depression and euthymia as measured with [123I]5IA single photon emission computed tomography. Biol Psychiatry. 2013;74(10):768–76.

Hao LY, Hao XQ, Li SH, Li XH. Prenatal exposure to lipopolysaccharide results in cognitive deficits in age-increasing offspring rats. Neuroscience. 2010;166(3):763–70.

Harlow HF, Zimmermann RR. Affectional responses in the infant monkey: orphaned baby monkeys develop a strong and persistent attachment to inanimate surrogate mothers. Science. 1959;130(3373):421–32.

Harrison EL, Baune BT. Modulation of early stress-induced neurobiological changes: a review of behavioural and pharmacological interventions in animal models. Transl Psychiatry. 2014;4(5):e390.

Harrison PJ, Cipriani A, Harmer CJ, Nobre AC, Saunders K, Goodwin GM, et al. Innovative approaches to bipolar disorder and its treatment. Ann NY Acad Sci. 2016;1366(1):76–89.

Heim C, Nemeroff CB. Neurobiology of early life stress: clinical studies. Semin Clin Neuropsychiatry. 2002;7(2):147–59.

Hicks RA, Moore JD, Hayes C, Phillips N, Hawkins J. REM sleep deprivation increases aggressiveness in male rats. Physiol Behav. 1979;22(6):1097–100.

Himmerich H, Bartsch S, Hamer H, Mergl R, Schönherr J, Petersein C, et al. Impact of mood stabilizers and antiepileptic drugs on cytokine production in-vitro. J Psychiatr Res. 2013;47(11):1751–9.

Hoang U, Stewart R, Goldacre MJ. Mortality after hospital discharge for people with schizophrenia or bipolar disorder: retrospective study of linked English hospital episode statistics, 1999–2006. BMJ. 2011;13(343):d5422.

Hoertnagl CM, Oberheinricher S, Hofer A. Soziale Kognition bei PatientInnen mit affektiven Störungen: Teil II: Bipolar affektive Störung. Neuropsychiatrie. 2014;28(2):84–91.

Hofer MA. Physiological responses of infant rats to separation from their mothers. Science. 1970;168(3933):871–3.

Hofer MA. Studies on how early maternal separation produces behavioral change in young rats. Psychosom Med. 1975;37(3):245–64.

Hofer MA. The organization of sleep and wakefulness after maternal separation in young rats. Dev Psychobiol. 1976;9(2):189–205.

Hofer MA. The psychobiology of early attachment. Clin Neurosci Res. 2005;4(5–6):291–300.

Hollis F, Kabbaj M. Social defeat as an animal model for depression. ILAR J. 2014;55(2):221–32.

Hollis F, Wang H, Dietz D, Gunjan A, Kabbaj M. The effects of repeated social defeat on long-term depressive-like behavior and short-term histone modifications in the hippocampus in male Sprague-Dawley rats. Psychopharmacology. 2010;211(1):69–77.

Holmes MK, Erickson K, Luckenbaugh DA, Drevets WC, Bain EE, Cannon DM, et al. A comparison of cognitive functioning in medicated and unmedicated subjects with bipolar depression. Bipolar Disord. 2008;10(7):806–15.

Horger BA, Roth RH. The role of mesoprefrontal dopamine neurons in stress. Crit Rev Neurobiol. 1996;10(3–4):395–418.

Horschitz S, Hummerich R, Lau T, Rietschel M, Schloss P. A dopamine transporter mutation associated with bipolar affective disorder causes inhibition of transporter cell surface expression. Mol Psychiatry. 2005;10(12):1104–9.

Hovens JGFM, Wiersma JE, Giltay EJ, van Oppen P, Spinhoven P, Penninx BWJH, et al. Childhood life events and childhood trauma in adult patients with depressive, anxiety and comorbid disorders vs. controls. Acta Psychiatr Scand. 2010;122(1):66–74.

Huot RL, Thrivikraman KV, Meaney MJ, Plotsky PM. Development of adult ethanol preference and anxiety as a consequence of neonatal maternal separation in long evans rats and reversal with antidepressant treatment. Psychopharmacology. 2001;158(4):366–73.

Huot RL, Plotsky PM, Lenox RH, McNamara RK. Neonatal maternal separation reduces hippocampal mossy fiber density in adult Long Evans rats. Brain Res. 2002;950(1–2):52–63.

Husum H, Mathé AA. Early life stress changes concentrations of neuropeptide Y and corticotropin-releasing hormone in adult rat brain. Lithium treatment modifies these changes. Neuropsychopharmacology. 2002;27(5):756–64.

Jacobs D, Silverstone T. Dextroamphetamine-induced arousal in human subjects as a model for mania. Psychol Med. 1986;16(2):323–9.

Janowsky D, Davis J, El-Yousef MK, Sekerke HJ. A cholinergic–adrenergic hypothesis of mania and depression. Lancet. 1972;300(7778):632–5.

Janowsky DS, El-Yousef MK, Davis JM. Acetylcholine and depression. Psychosom Med. 1974;36(3):248–57.

Janowsky DS, Overstreet DH, Nurnberger JI. Is cholinergic sensitivity a genetic marker for the affective disorders? Am J Med Genet. 1994;54(4):335–44.

Jia N, Li Q, Sun H, Song Q, Tang G, Sun Q, et al. Alterations of group I mGluRs and BDNF associated with behavioral abnormity in prenatally stressed offspring rats. Neurochem Res. 2015;40(5):1074–82.

Joyce PR, Fergusson DM, Woollard G, Abbott RM, Horwood LJ, Upton J. Urinary catecholamines and plasma hormones predict mood state in rapid cycling bipolar affective disorder. J Affect Disord. 1995;33(4):233–43.

Juckel G, Hegerl U, Mavrogiorgou P, Gallinat J, Mager T, Tigges P, et al. Clinical and biological findings in a case with 48-hour bipolar ultrarapid cycling before and during valproate treatment. J Clin Psychiatry. 2000;61(8):585–93.

Kaffman A, Meaney MJ. Neurodevelopmental sequelae of postnatal maternal care in rodents: clinical and research implications of molecular insights. J Child Psychol Psychiatry. 2007;48(3–4):224–44.

Kaiser T, Feng G. Modeling psychiatric disorders for developing effective treatments. Nat Med. 2015;21(9):979–88.

Kalinichev M, Easterling KW, Plotsky PM, Holtzman SG. Long-lasting changes in stress-induced corticosterone response and anxiety-like behaviors as a consequence of neonatal maternal separation in Long-Evans rats. Pharmacol Biochem Behav. 2002;73(1):131–40.

Kato T, Kubota M, Kasahara T. Animal models of bipolar disorder. Neurosci Biobehav Rev. 2007;31(6):832–42.

Kaufman J, Charney D. Effects of early stress on brain structure and function: implications for understanding the relationship between child maltreatment and depression. Dev Psychopathol. 2001;13(3):451–71.

Kendler KS, Karkowski LM, Prescott CA. Causal relationship between stressful life events and the onset of major depression. Am J Psychiatry. 1999;156(6):837–41.

Kernie SG, Liebl DJ, Parada LF. BDNF regulates eating behavior and locomotor activity in mice. EMBO J. 2000;19(6):1290–300.

Kessler RC, Crum RM, Warner LA, Nelson CB, Schulenberg J, Anthony JC. Lifetime co-occurrence of DSM-III-R alcohol abuse and dependence with other psychiatric disorders in the national comorbidity survey. Arch Gen Psychiatry. 1997;54(4):313–21.

Kilbey MM, Ellinwood EH. Reverse tolerance to stimulant-induced abnormal behavior. Life Sci. 1977;20(6):1063–75.

King DP, Zhao Y, Sangoram AM, Wilsbacher LD, Tanaka M, Antoch MP, et al. Positional cloning of the mouse circadian clock gene. Cell. 1997;89(4):641–53.

Kittel-Schneider S, Schreck S, Ziegler C, Weißflog L, Hilscher M, Schwarz R, et al. Lithium-induced clock gene expression in lymphoblastoid cells of bipolar affective patients. Pharmacopsychiatry. 2015;48(4–5):145–9.

Klein PS, Melton DA. A molecular mechanism for the effect of lithium on development. Proc Natl Acad Sci. 1996;93(16):8455–9.

Klemfuss H. Rhythms and the pharmacology of lithium. Pharmacol Ther. 1992;56(1):53–78.

Kneeland RE, Fatemi SH. Viral infection, inflammation and schizophrenia. Prog Neuropsychopharmacol Biol Psychiatry. 2013;5(42):35–48.

Koehl M, Darnaudéry M, Dulluc J, Van R, Moal ML, Maccari S. Prenatal stress alters circadian activity of hypothalamo-pituitary- adrenal axis and hippocampal corticosteroid receptors in adult rats of both gender. J Neurobiol. 1999;40(3):302–15.

Kohl S, Heekeren K, Klosterkötter J, Kuhn J. Prepulse inhibition in psychiatric disorders—apart from schizophrenia. J Psychiatr Res. 2013;47(4):445–52.

Kozikowski AP, Gaisina IN, Yuan H, Petukhov PA, Blond SY, Fedolak A, et al. Structure-based design leads to the identification of lithium mimetics that block mania-like effects in rodents. possible new GSK-3beta therapies for bipolar disorders. J Am Chem Soc. 2007;129(26):8328–32.

Kraepelin E. Psychiatrie. ein Lehrbuch für Studierende und Ärzte/von Emil Kraepelin. Leipzig Barth; 1909. http://widgets.ebscohost.com/prod/customerspecific/s9118275/vpn.php?url=http://search.ebscohost.com/login.aspx?direct=true&db=cat04752a&AN=rub.1372991&lang=de&site=eds-live.

Kripke DF, Mullaney DJ, Atkinson M, Wolf S. Circadian rhythm disorders in manic-depressives. Biol Psychiatry. 1978;13(3):335–51.

Kripke DF, Nievergelt CM, Joo E, Shekhtman T, Kelsoe JR. Circadian polymorphisms associated with affective disorders. J Circadian Rhythm. 2009;23(7):2.

Kuhn CM, Pauk J, Schanberg SM. Endocrine responses to mother-infant separation in developing rats. Dev Psychobiol. 1990;23(5):395–410.

Kupfer DJ. The increasing medical burden in bipolar disorder. JAMA. 2005;293(20):2528–30.

Ladd CO, Huot RL, Thrivikraman KV, Nemeroff CB, Meaney MJ, Plotsky PM. Long-term behavioral and neuroendocrine adaptations to adverse early experience. Prog Brain Res. 2000;122:81–103.

Ladd CO, Huot RL, Thrivikraman KV, Nemeroff CB, Plotsky PM. Long-term adaptations in glucocorticoid receptor and mineralocorticoid receptor mRNA and negative feedback on the hypothalamo-pituitary-adrenal axis following neonatal maternal separation. Biol Psychiatry. 2004;55(4):367–75.

Leach G, Adidharma W, Yan L. Depression-like responses induced by daytime light deficiency in the diurnal grass rat (*Arvicanthis niloticus*). PLoS ONE. 2013;8(2):e57115.

Lee AL, Ogle WO, Sapolsky RM. Stress and depression: possible links to neuron death in the hippocampus. Bipolar Disord. 2002;4(2):117–28.

Lemaire V, Koehl M, Moal ML, Abrous DN. Prenatal stress produces learning deficits associated with an inhibition of neurogenesis in the hippocampus. Proc Natl Acad Sci. 2000;97(20):11032–7.

Le-Niculescu H, McFarland MJ, Ogden CA, Balaraman Y, Patel S, Tan J, et al. Phenomic, convergent functional genomic, and biomarker studies in a stress-reactive genetic animal model of bipolar disorder and co-morbid alcoholism. Am J Med Genet Part B Neuropsychiatr Genet. 2008;147B(2):134–66.

Leo D, Gainetdinov RR. Transgenic mouse models for ADHD. Cell Tissue Res. 2013;354(1):259–71.

Leuner B, Fredericks PJ, Nealer C, Albin-Brooks C. Chronic gestational stress leads to depressive-like behavior and compromises medial prefrontal cortex structure and function during the postpartum period. PLoS ONE. 2014;9(3):e89912.

Leverich GS, McElroy SL, Suppes T, Keck PE, Denicoff KD, Nolen WA, et al. Early physical and sexual abuse associated with an adverse course of bipolar illness. Biol Psychiatry. 2002;51(4):288–97.

Lévy F, Melo AI, Galef BG, Madden M, Fleming AS. Complete maternal deprivation affects social, but not spatial, learning in adult rats. Dev Psychobiol. 2003;43(3):177–91.

Lien R, Flaisher-Grinberg S, Cleary C, Hejny M, Einat H. Behavioral effects of Bcl-2 deficiency: implications for affective disorders. Pharmacol Rep. 2008;60(4):490–8.

Lin Y-L, Wang S. Prenatal lipopolysaccharide exposure increases depression-like behaviors and reduces hippocampal neurogenesis in adult rats. Behav Brain Res. 2014;1(259):24–34.

Lin Y-L, Lin S-Y, Wang S. Prenatal lipopolysaccharide exposure increases anxiety-like behaviors and enhances stress-induced corticosterone responses in adult rats. Brain Behav Immun. 2012;26(3):459–68.

Lippmann M, Bress A, Nemeroff CB, Plotsky PM, Monteggia LM. Long-term behavioural and molecular alterations associated with maternal separation in rats. Eur J Neurosci. 2007;25(10):3091–8.

Liu D, Diorio J, Tannenbaum B, Caldji C, Francis D, Freedman A, et al. Maternal care, hippocampal glucocorticoid receptors, and hypothalamic-pituitary-adrenal responses to stress. Science. 1997;277(5332):1659–62.

Liu D, Diorio J, Day JC, Francis DD, Meaney MJ. Maternal care, hippocampal synaptogenesis and cognitive development in rats. Nat Neurosci. 2000;3(8):799–806.

Logan RW, McClung CA. Animal models of bipolar mania: the past, present and future. Neuroscience. 2016;3(321):163–88.

Logan RW, Williams WP, McClung CA. Circadian rhythms and addiction: mechanistic insights and future directions. Behav Neurosci. 2014;128(3):387–412.

Loman MM, Wiik KL, Frenn KA, Pollak SD, Gunnar MR. Postinstitutionalized children's development: growth, cognitive, and language outcomes. J Dev Behav Pediatr. 2009;30(5):426–34.

Loos M, Pattij T, Janssen MCW, Counotte DS, Schoffelmeer ANM, Smit AB, et al. Dopamine receptor D1/D5 gene expression in the medial prefrontal cortex predicts impulsive choice in rats. Cereb Cortex. 2010;20(5):1064–70.

Lupien SJ, McEwen BS, Gunnar MR, Heim C. Effects of stress throughout the lifespan on the brain, behaviour and cognition. Nat Rev Neurosci. 2009;10(6):434–45.

Lyons WE, Mamounas LA, Ricaurte GA, Coppola V, Reid SW, Bora SH, et al. Brain-derived neurotrophic factor-deficient mice develop aggressiveness and hyperphagia in conjunction with brain serotonergic abnormalities. Proc Natl Acad Sci. 1999;96(26):15239–44.
Macêdo DS, Medeiros CD, Cordeiro RC, Sousa FC, Santos JV, Morais TA, et al. Effects of alpha-lipoic acid in an animal model of mania induced by d-amphetamine. Bipolar Disord. 2012;14(7):707–18.
Macêdo DS, de Lucena DF, Queiroz AIG, Cordeiro RC, Araújo MM, Sousa FC, et al. Effects of lithium on oxidative stress and behavioral alterations induced by lisdexamfetamine dimesylate: relevance as an animal model of mania. Prog Neuropsychopharmacol Biol Psychiatry. 2013;3(43):230–7.
MacQueen GM, Ramakrishnan K, Ratnasingan R, Chen B, Young LT. Desipramine treatment reduces the long-term behavioural and neurochemical sequelae of early-life maternal separation. Int J Neuropsychopharmacol. 2003;6(4):391–6.
Maes M, Mihaylova I, Kubera M, Ringel K. Activation of cell-mediated immunity in depression: association with inflammation, melancholia, clinical staging and the fatigue and somatic symptom cluster of depression. Prog Neuropsychopharmacol Biol Psychiatry. 2012;36(1):169–75.
Magariños AM, Li CJ, Gal Toth J, Bath KG, Jing D, Lee FS, et al. Effect of brain-derived neurotrophic factor haploinsufficiency on stress-induced remodeling of hippocampal neurons. Hippocampus. 2011;21(3):253–64.
Maier SF, Seligman ME. Learned helplessness: theory and evidence. J Exp Psychol Gen. 1976;105(1):3–46.
Malkesman O, Austin DR, Chen G, Manji HK. Reverse translational strategies for developing animal models of bipolar disorder. Dis Model Mech. 2009;2(5–6):238–45.
Malkoff-Schwartz S, Frank E, Anderson B, Sherrill JT, Siegel L, Patterson D, et al. Stressful life events and social rhythm disruption in the onset of manic and depressive bipolar episodes: a preliminary investigation. Arch Gen Psychiatry. 1998;55(8):702–7.
Maniglio R. The impact of child sexual abuse on health: a systematic review of reviews. Clin Psychol Rev. 2009;29(7):647–57.
Manji HK, Moore GJ, Chen G. Lithium up-regulates the cytoprotective protein Bcl-2 in the CNS in vivo: a role for neurotrophic and neuroprotective effects in manic depressive illness. J Clin Psychiatry. 2000;61(Suppl 9):82–96.
Manji HK, Drevets WC, Charney DS. The cellular neurobiology of depression. Nat Med. 2001;7(5):541–7.
Marangoni C, Hernandez M, Faedda GL. The role of environmental exposures as risk factors for bipolar disorder: a systematic review of longitudinal studies. J Affect Disord. 2016;15(193):165–74.
Markou A, Koob GF. Postcocaine anhedonia. An animal model of cocaine withdrawal. Neuropsychopharmacology. 1991;4(1):17–26.
Marszalek-Grabska M, Gibula-Bruzda E, Jenda M, Gawel K, Kotlinska JH. Memantine improves memory impairment and depressive-like behavior induced by amphetamine withdrawal in rats. Brain Res. 2016;1(1642):389–96.
Martinek S, Inonog S, Manoukian AS, Young MW. A role for the segment polarity gene shaggy/GSK-3 in the drosophila circadian clock. Cell. 2001;105(6):769–79.
Martínez-Arán A, Vieta E, Reinares M, Colom F, Torrent C, Sánchez-Moreno J, et al. Cognitive function across manic or hypomanic, depressed, and euthymic states in bipolar disorder. Am J Psychiatry. 2004;161(2):262–70.
Mason WA, Berkson G. Effects of maternal mobility on the development of rocking and other behaviors in rhesus monkeys: a study with artificial mothers. Dev Psychobiol. 1975;8(3):197–211.
Masri B, Salahpour A, Didriksen M, Ghisi V, Beaulieu J-M, Gainetdinov RR, et al. Antagonism of dopamine D2 receptor/β-arrestin 2 interaction is a common property of clinically effective antipsychotics. Proc Natl Acad Sci. 2008;105(36):13656–61.
McCarthy MJ, Welsh DK. Cellular circadian clocks in mood disorders. J Biol Rhythms. 2012;27(5):339–52.
McClung CA. Circadian genes, rhythms and the biology of mood disorders. Pharmacol Ther. 2007;114(2):222–32.
McClung CA. How might circadian rhythms control mood? Let me count the ways. Biol Psychiatry. 2013;74(4):242–9.
McClung CA, Sidiropoulou K, Vitaterna M, Takahashi JS, White FJ, Cooper DC, et al. Regulation of dopaminergic transmission and cocaine reward by the Clock gene. Proc Natl Acad Sci USA. 2005;102(26):9377–81.
McIntosh J, Anisman H, Merali Z. Short- and long-periods of neonatal maternal separation differentially affect anxiety and feeding in adult rats: gender-dependent effects. Dev Brain Res. 1999;113(1–2):97–106.
McLaughlin KA, Green JG, Gruber MJ, Sampson NA, Zaslavsky AM, Kessler RC. Childhood adversities and adult psychiatric disorders in the national comorbidity survey replication II: associations with persistence of DSM-IV disorders. Arch Gen Psychiatry. 2010;67(2):124–32.
Meaney MJ. Maternal care, gene expression, and the transmission of individual differences in stress reactivity across generations. Annu Rev Neurosci. 2001;24:1161–92.
Meaney MJ, Viau V, Bhatnagar S, Betito K, Iny LJ, O'Donnell D, et al. Cellular mechanisms underlying the development and expression of individual differences in the hypothalamic-pituitary-adrenal stress response. J Steroid Biochem Mol Biol. 1991;39(2):265–74.
Meerlo P, Overkamp GJF, Daan S, Van Den Hoofdakker RH, Koolhaas JM. Changes in behaviour and body weight following a single or double social defeat in rats. Stress Amst Neth. 1996;1(1):21–32.
Meesters Y, Gordijn MC. Seasonal affective disorder, winter type: current insights and treatment options. Psychol Res Behav Manag. 2016;30(9):317–27.
Merikangas KR, Akiskal HS, Angst J, Greenberg PE, Hirschfeld RMA, Petukhova M, et al. Lifetime and 12-month prevalence of bipolar spectrum disorder in the national comorbidity survey replication. Arch Gen Psychiatry. 2007;64(5):543–52.
Merikangas KR, Jin R, He J-P, Kessler RC, Lee S, Sampson NA, et al. Prevalence and correlates of bipolar spectrum disorder in the world mental health survey initiative. Arch Gen Psychiatry. 2011;68(3):241–51.
Messer T, Lammers G, Müller-Siecheneder F, Schmidt R-F, Latifi S. Substance abuse in patients with bipolar disorder: a systematic review and meta-analysis. Psychiatry Res. 2017;8(253):338–50.
Meyer U. Prenatal Poly(I:C) exposure and other developmental immune activation models in rodent systems. Biol Psychiatry. 2014;75(4):307–15.
Meyer U, Feldon J, Schedlowski M, Yee BK. Towards an immuno-precipitated neurodevelopmental animal model of schizophrenia. Neurosci Biobehav Rev. 2005;29(6):913–47.
Miklowitz DJ, Otto MW, Frank E, Reilly-Harrington NA, Wisniewski SR, Kogan JN, et al. Psychosocial treatments for bipolar depression: a 1-year randomized trial from the systematic treatment enhancement program. Arch Gen Psychiatry. 2007;64(4):419–26.
Minassian A, Henry BL, Young JW, Masten V, Geyer MA, Perry W. Repeated assessment of exploration and novelty seeking in the human behavioral pattern monitor in bipolar disorder patients and healthy individuals. PLoS ONE. 2011;6(8):e24185.
Mineur YS, Obayemi A, Wigestrand MB, Fote GM, Calarco CA, Li AM, et al. Cholinergic signaling in the hippocampus regulates social stress resilience and anxiety- and depression-like behavior. Proc Natl Acad Sci USA. 2013;110(9):3573–8.
Modabbernia A, Taslimi S, Brietzke E, Ashrafi M. Cytokine alterations in bipolar disorder: a meta-analysis of 30 studies. Biol Psychiatry. 2013;74(1):15–25.
Moonat S, Pandey SC. Stress, epigenetics, and alcoholism. Alcohol Res Curr Rev. 2012;34(4):495–505.
Morden B, Mullins R, Levine S, Cohen H, Dement W. Effect of REM deprivation on the mating behavior of male rats. Psychophysiology. 1968;5:241–2.
Mukherjee S, Coque L, Cao J-L, Kumar J, Chakravarty S, Asaithamby A, et al. Knockdown of Clock in the ventral tegmental area through RNA interference results in a mixed state of mania and depression-like behavior. Biol Psychiatry. 2010;68(6):503–11.
Mullen PE, Martin JL, Anderson JC, Romans SE, Herbison GP. The long-term impact of the physical, emotional, and sexual abuse of children: a community study. Child Abuse Negl. 1996;20(1):7–21.
Mutschler NH, Miczek KA. Withdrawal from a self-administered or non-contingent cocaine binge: differences in ultrasonic distress vocalizations in rats. Psychopharmacology. 1998;136(4):402–8.
Nelson CA, Zeanah CH, Fox NA, Marshall PJ, Smyke AT, Guthrie D. Cognitive recovery in socially deprived young children: the Bucharest early intervention project. Science. 2007;318(5858):1937–40.
Nemeroff CB, Heim CM, Thase ME, Klein DN, Rush AJ, Schatzberg AF, et al. Differential responses to psychotherapy versus pharmacotherapy in

patients with chronic forms of major depression and childhood trauma. Proc Natl Acad Sci USA. 2003;100(24):14293–6.
Nestler EJ, Hyman SE. Animal models of neuropsychiatric disorders. Nat Neurosci. 2010;13(10):1161–9.
Nibuya M, Morinobu S, Duman RS. Regulation of BDNF and trkB mRNA in rat brain by chronic electroconvulsive seizure and antidepressant drug treatments. J Neurosci. 1995;15(11):7539–47.
Nieoullon A, Coquerel A. Dopamine: a key regulator to adapt action, emotion, motivation and cognition. Curr Opin Neurol. 2003;16(Suppl 2):S3–9.
Novick DM, Swartz HA, Frank E. Suicide attempts in bipolar I and bipolar II disorder: a review and meta-analysis of the evidence. Bipolar Disord. 2010;12(1):1–9.
Nurnberger JI, Gershon ES, Simmons S, Ebert M, Kessler LR, Dibble ED, et al. Behavioral, biochemical and neuroendocrine responses to amphetamine in normal twins and "well-state" bipolar patients. Psychoneuroendocrinology. 1982;7(2–3):163–76.
Nurnberger JI, Jimerson DC, Simmons-Alling S, Tamminga C, Nadi NS, Lawrence D, et al. Behavioral, physiological, and neuroendocrine responses to arecoline in normal twins and "well state" bipolar patients. Psychiatry Res. 1983;9(3):191–200.
O'Brien WT, Harper AD, Jové F, Woodgett JR, Maretto S, Piccolo S, et al. Glycogen synthase kinase-3beta haploinsufficiency mimics the behavioral and molecular effects of lithium. J Neurosci. 2004;24(30):6791–8.
O'Brien WT, Huang J, Buccafusca R, Garskof J, Valvezan AJ, Berry GT, et al. Glycogen synthase kinase-3 is essential for β-arrestin-2 complex formation and lithium-sensitive behaviors in mice. J Clin Invest. 2011;121(9):3756–62.
Pachet AK, Wisniewski AM. The effects of lithium on cognition: an updated review. Psychopharmacology. 2003;170(3):225–34.
Palmisano M, Pandey SC. Epigenetic mechanisms of alcoholism and stress-related disorders. Alcohol Fayettev N. 2017;60:7–18.
Parboosing R, Bao Y, Shen L, Schaefer CA, Brown AS. Gestational influenza and bipolar disorder in adult offspring. JAMA Psychiatry. 2013;70(7):677–85.
Paspalas CD, Wang M, Arnsten AFT. Constellation of HCN channels and cAMP regulating proteins in dendritic spines of the primate prefrontal cortex: potential substrate for working memory deficits in schizophrenia. Cereb Cortex. 2013;23(7):1643–54.
Patel JP, Frey BN. Disruption in the blood-brain barrier: the missing link between brain and body inflammation in bipolar disorder? Neural Plast. 2015;2015:708306.
Paulson PE, Camp DM, Robinson TE. Time course of transient behavioral depression and persistent behavioral sensitization in relation to regional brain monoamine concentrations during amphetamine withdrawal in rats. Psychopharmacology. 1991;103(4):480–92.
Paykel ES. Contribution of life events to causation of psychiatric illness. Psychol Med. 1978;8(2):245–53.
Pearlson GD, Wong DF, Tune LE, Ross CA, Chase GA, Links JM, et al. In vivo D2 dopamine receptor density in psychotic and nonpsychotic patients with bipolar disorder. Arch Gen Psychiatry. 1995;52(6):471–7.
Pechtel P, Pizzagalli DA. Effects of early life stress on cognitive and affective function: an integrated review of human literature. Psychopharmacology. 2011;214(1):55–70.
Peet M, Peters S. Drug-induced mania. Drug Saf. 1995;12(2):146–53.
Perry W, Minassian A, Feifel D, Braff DL. Sensorimotor gating deficits in bipolar disorder patients with acute psychotic mania. Biol Psychiatry. 2001;50(6):418–24.
Perry W, Minassian A, Paulus MP, Young JW, Kincaid MJ, Ferguson EJ, et al. A reverse-translational study of dysfunctional exploration in psychiatric disorders: from mice to men. Arch Gen Psychiatry. 2009;66(10):1072–80.
Perry W, Minassian A, Henry B, Kincaid M, Young JW, Geyer MA. Quantifying over-activity in bipolar and schizophrenia patients in a human open field paradigm. Psychiatry Res. 2010;178(1):84–91.
Persico AM, Schindler CW, Zaczek R, Brannock MT, Uhl GR. Brain transcription factor gene expression, neurotransmitter levels, and novelty response behaviors: alterations during rat amphetamine withdrawal and following chronic injection stress. Synapse. 1995;19(3):212–27.
Phillips ML, Kupfer DJ. Bipolar disorder diagnosis: challenges and future directions. Lancet. 2013;381(9878):1663–71.
Pirkola S, Isometsä E, Aro H, Kestilä L, Hämäläinen J, Veijola J, et al. Childhood adversities as risk factors for adult mental disorders: results from the health 2000 study. Soc Psychiatry Psychiatr Epidemiol. 2005;40(10):769–77.
Porsolt RD, Le Pichon M, Jalfre M. Depression: a new animal model sensitive to antidepressant treatments. Nature. 1977;266(5604):730–2.
Post RM. Sensitization and kindling perspectives for the course of affective illness: toward a new treatment with the anticonvulsant carbamazepine. Pharmacopsychiatry. 1990;23(01):3–17.
Post RM. Transduction of psychosocial stress into the neurobiology of recurrent affective disorder. Am J Psychiatry. 1992;149(8):999–1010.
Powell SB, Young JW, Ong JC, Caron MG, Geyer MA. Atypical antipsychotics clozapine and quetiapine attenuate prepulse inhibition deficits in dopamine transporter knockout mice. Behav Pharmacol. 2008;19(5–6):562–5.
Prickaerts J, Moechars D, Cryns K, Lenaerts I, van Craenendonck H, Goris I, et al. Transgenic mice overexpressing glycogen synthase kinase 3β: a putative model of hyperactivity and mania. J Neurosci. 2006;26(35):9022–9.
Puig MV, Rose J, Schmidt R, Freund N. Dopamine modulation of learning and memory in the prefrontal cortex: insights from studies in primates, rodents, and birds. Front Neural Circuits. 2014;8(93). http://www.frontiersin.org/neural_circuits/10.3389/fncir.2014.00093/abstract.
Queiroz AIG, de Araújo MM, da Silva Araújo T, de Souza GC, Cavalcante LM, Machado MD, et al. GBR 12909 administration as an animal model of bipolar mania: time course of behavioral, brain oxidative alterations and effect of mood stabilizing drugs. Metab Brain Dis. 2015;30(5):1207–15.
Raiteri M, Bertollini A, Angelini F, Levi G. d-Amphetamine as a releaser or reuptake inhibitor of biogenic amines in synaptosomes. Eur J Pharmacol. 1975;34(1):189–95.
Raja M, Bentivoglio AR. Impulsive and compulsive behaviors during dopamine replacement treatment in Parkinson's disease and other disorders. Curr Drug Saf. 2012;7(1):63–75.
Rajkowska G. Cell pathology in bipolar disorder. Bipolar Disord. 2002;4(2):105–16.
Ralph RJ, Paulus MP, Fumagalli F, Caron MG, Geyer MA. Prepulse inhibition deficits and perseverative motor patterns in dopamine transporter knock-out mice: differential effects of D1 and D2 receptor antagonists. J Neurosci. 2001;21(1):305–13.
Ralph-Williams RJ, Paulus MP, Zhuang X, Hen R, Geyer MA. Valproate attenuates hyperactive and perseverative behaviors in mutant mice with a dysregulated dopamine system. Biol Psychiatry. 2003;53(4):352–9.
Rao JS, Kellom M, Reese EA, Rapoport SI, Kim H-W. Dysregulated glutamate and dopamine transporters in postmortem frontal cortex from bipolar and schizophrenic patients. J Affect Disord. 2012;136(1–2):63–71.
Regier DA, Farmer ME, Rae DS, Locke BZ, Keith SJ, Judd LL, et al. Comorbidity of mental disorders with alcohol and other drug abuse. Results from the epidemiologic catchment area (ECA) study. JAMA. 1990;264(19):2511–8.
Remus JL, Dantzer R. Inflammation models of depression in rodents: relevance to psychotropic drug discovery. Int J Neuropsychopharmacol. 2016;19(9). https://academic.oup.com/ijnp/article/19/9/pyw028/2488254/Inflammation-Models-of-Depression-in-Rodents. Accessed 23 May 2017.
Rezin GT, Furlanetto CB, Scaini G, Valvassori SS, Gonçalves CL, Ferreira GK, et al. Fenproporex increases locomotor activity and alters energy metabolism, and mood stabilizers reverse these changes: a proposal for a new animal model of mania. Mol Neurobiol. 2014;49(2):877–92.
Ripperger JA, Shearman LP, Reppert SM, Schibler U. CLOCK, an essential pacemaker component, controls expression of the circadian transcription factor DBP. Genes Dev. 2000;14(6):679–89.
Romeo RD, Mueller A, Sisti HM, Ogawa S, McEwen BS, Brake WG. Anxiety and fear behaviors in adult male and female C57BL/6 mice are modulated by maternal separation. Horm Behav. 2003;43(5):561–7.
Rondi-Reig L, Mariani J. To die or not to die, does it change the function? Behavior of transgenic mice reveals a role for developmental cell death. Brain Res Bull. 2002;57(1):85–91.
Rondi-Reig L, Lemaigre Dubreuil Y, Martinou JC, Delhaye-Bouchaud N, Caston J, Mariani J. Fear decrease in transgenic mice overexpressing bcl-2 in neurons. Neuroreport. 1997;8(11):2429–32.
Roni MA, Rahman S. The effects of lobeline on nicotine withdrawal-induced depression-like behavior in mice. Psychopharmacology. 2014;231(15):2989–98.

Ronovsky M, Berger S, Molz B, Berger A, Pollak DD. Animal models of maternal immune activation in depression research. Curr Neuropharmacol. 2016;14(7):688–704.
Ronovsky M, Berger S, Zambon A, Reisinger SN, Horvath O, Pollak A, et al. Maternal immune activation transgenerationally modulates maternal care and offspring depression-like behavior. Brain Behav Immun. 2017;63:127–36.
Rose DR, Careaga M, Van de Water J, McAllister K, Bauman MD, Ashwood P. Long-term altered immune responses following fetal priming in a non-human primate model of maternal immune activation. Brain Behav Immun. 2017;63:60–70.
Rosenthal NE, Sack DA, Gillin JC, Lewy AJ, Goodwin FK, Davenport Y, et al. Seasonal affective disorder. A description of the syndrome and preliminary findings with light therapy. Arch Gen Psychiatry. 1984;41(1):72–80.
Rowse AL, Naves R, Cashman KS, McGuire DJ, Mbana T, Raman C, et al. Lithium controls central nervous system autoimmunity through modulation of IFN-γ signaling. PLoS ONE. 2012;7(12):e52658.
Roybal K, Theobold D, Graham A, DiNieri JA, Russo SJ, Krishnan V, et al. Mania-like behavior induced by disruption of CLOCK. Proc Natl Acad Sci USA. 2007;104(15):6406–11.
Ruis MA, te Brake JH, Buwalda B, De Boer SF, Meerlo P, Korte SM, et al. Housing familiar male wildtype rats together reduces the long-term adverse behavioural and physiological effects of social defeat. Psychoneuroendocrinology. 1999;24(3):285–300.
Russo-Neustadt AA, Beard RC, Huang YM, Cotman CW. Physical activity and antidepressant treatment potentiate the expression of specific brain-derived neurotrophic factor transcripts in the rat hippocampus. Neuroscience. 2000;101(2):305–12.
Rygula R, Szczech E, Kregiel J, Golebiowska J, Kubik J, Popik P. Cognitive judgment bias in the psychostimulant-induced model of mania in rats. Psychopharmacology. 2015;232:651–60.
Saarelainen T, Hendolin P, Lucas G, Koponen E, Sairanen M, MacDonald E, et al. Activation of the TrkB neurotrophin receptor is induced by antidepressant drugs and is required for antidepressant-induced behavioral effects. J Neurosci. 2003;23(1):349–57.
Salloum IM, Cornelius JR, Daley DC, Kirisci L, Himmelhoch JM, Thase ME. Efficacy of valproate maintenance in patients with bipolar disorder and alcoholism: a double-blind placebo-controlled study. Arch Gen Psychiatry. 2005;62(1):37–45.
Salvatore P, Tohen M. Khalsa H-MK, Baethge C, Tondo L, Baldessarini RJ. Longitudinal research on bipolar disorders. Epidemiol Psichiatr Soc. 2007;16(2):109–17.
Salvi V, Fagiolini A, Swartz HA, Maina G, Frank E. The use of antidepressants in bipolar disorder. J Clin Psychiatry. 2008;69(8):1307–18.
Sani G, Perugi G, Tondo L. Treatment of bipolar disorder in a lifetime perspective: is lithium still the best choice? Clin Drug Investig. 2017. doi:10.1007/s40261-017-0531-2.
Savitz J, Solms M, Ramesar R. Neuropsychological dysfunction in bipolar affective disorder: a critical opinion. Bipolar Disord. 2005;7(3):216–35.
Schaeffer JC, Cho AK, Fischer JF. Inhibition of synaptosomal accumulation of l-norepinephrine II: N-aryloxyalkylphentermines, quaternary d-amphetamines, and 3-aryloxypropylamines. J Pharm Sci. 1976;65(1):122–6.
Schaffer A, Levitt AJ, Boyle M. Influence of season and latitude in a community sample of subjects with bipolar disorder. Can J Psychiatry. 2003;48(4):277–80.
Schildkraut JJ. The catecholamine hypothesis of affective disorders: a review of supporting evidence. Am J Psychiatry. 1965;122(5):509–22.
Schindler CW, Persico AM, Uhl GR, Goldberg SR. Behavioral assessment of high-dose amphetamine withdrawal: importance of training and testing conditions. Pharmacol Biochem Behav. 1994;49(1):41–6.
Schmitt AR, Brewer JD, Bordeaux JS, Baum CL. Staging for cutaneous squamous cell carcinoma as a predictor of sentinel lymph node biopsy results: meta-analysis of american joint committee on cancer criteria and a proposed alternative system. JAMA Dermatol. 2014;150(1):19–24.
Schwartz JM, Ksir C, Koob GF, Bloom FE. Changes in locomotor response to beta-endorphin microinfusion during and after opiate abstinence syndrome—a proposal for a model of the onset of mania. Psychiatry Res. 1982;7(2):153–61.
Seamans JK, Yang CR. The principal features and mechanisms of dopamine modulation in the prefrontal cortex. Prog Neurobiol. 2004;74(1):1–58.
Seiden LS, Sabol KE, Ricaurte GA. Amphetamine: effects on catecholamine systems and behavior. Annu Rev Pharmacol Toxicol. 1993;33:639–77.
Serretti A, Benedetti F, Mandelli L, Lorenzi C, Pirovano A, Colombo C, et al. Genetic dissection of psychopathological symptoms: insomnia in mood disorders and CLOCK gene polymorphism. Am J Med Genet B Neuropsychiatr Genet. 2003;121B(1):35–8.
Serretti A, Drago A, De Ronchi D. Lithium pharmacodynamics and pharmacogenetics: focus on inositol mono phosphatase (IMPase), inositol poliphosphatase (IPPase) and glycogen sinthase kinase 3 beta (GSK-3 beta). Curr Med Chem. 2009;16(15):1917–48.
Shaltiel G, Maeng S, Malkesman O, Pearson B, Schloesser RJ, Tragon T, et al. Evidence for the involvement of the kainate receptor subunit GluR6 (GRIK2) in mediating behavioral displays related to behavioral symptoms of mania. Mol Psychiatry. 2008;13(9):858–72.
Sharma AN, Fries GR, Galvez JF, Valvassori SS, Soares JC, Carvalho AF, et al. Modeling mania in preclinical settings: a comprehensive review. Prog Neuropsychopharmacol Biol Psychiatry. 2016;3(66):22–34.
Shi L, Fatemi SH, Sidwell RW, Patterson PH. Maternal influenza infection causes marked behavioral and pharmacological changes in the offspring. J Neurosci. 2003;23(1):297–302.
Shirayama Y, Chen AC-H, Nakagawa S, Russell DS, Duman RS. Brain-derived neurotrophic factor produces antidepressant effects in behavioral models of depression. J Neurosci. 2002;22(8):3251–61.
Silverstone T, Fincham J, Wells B, Kyriakides M. The effect of the dopamine receptor blocking drug pimozide on the stimulant and anorectic actions of dextroamphetamine in man. Neuropharmacology. 1980;19(12):1235–7.
Simhandl C, Radua J, König B, Amann BL. The prevalence and effect of life events in 222 bipolar I and II patients: a prospective, naturalistic 4 year follow-up study. J Affect Disord. 2015;1(170):166–71.
Smith MA, Makino S, Kvetnansky R, Post RM. Stress and glucocorticoids affect the expression of brain-derived neurotrophic factor and neurotrophin-3 mRNAs in the hippocampus. J Neurosci. 1995;15(3 Pt 1):1768–77.
Södersten K, Pålsson E, Ishima T, Funa K, Landén M, Hashimoto K, et al. Abnormality in serum levels of mature brain-derived neurotrophic factor (BDNF) and its precursor proBDNF in mood-stabilized patients with bipolar disorder: a study of two independent cohorts. J Affect Disord. 2014;160:1–9.
Sonntag KC, Brenhouse HC, Freund N, Thompson BS, Puhl M, Andersen SL. Viral over-expression of D1 dopamine receptors in the prefrontal cortex increase high-risk behaviors in adults: comparison with adolescents. Psychopharmacology. 2014;231(8):1615–26.
Souetre E, Salvati E, Wehr TA, Sack DA, Krebs B, Darcourt G. Twenty-four-hour profiles of body temperature and plasma TSH in bipolar patients during depression and during remission and in normal control subjects. Am J Psychiatry. 1988;145(9):1133–7.
Spanagel R, Noori HR, Heilig M. Stress and alcohol interactions: animal studies and clinical significance. Trends Neurosci. 2014;37(4):219–27.
Spataro J, Mullen PE, Burgess PM, Wells DL, Moss SA. Impact of child sexual abuse on mental health. Br J Psychiatry. 2004;184(5):416–21.
Stahl CE, Redei E, Wang Y, Borlongan CV. Behavioral, hormonal and histological stress markers of anxiety-separation in postnatal rats are reduced by prepro-thyrotropin-releasing hormone 178-199. Neurosci Lett. 2002;321(1–2):85–9.
Stanton ME, Levine S. Inhibition of infant glucocorticoid stress response: specific role of maternal cues. Dev Psychobiol. 1990;23(5):411–26.
Stefanski V. Social stress in laboratory rats: hormonal responses and immune cell distribution. Psychoneuroendocrinology. 2000;25(4):389–406.
Steingard RJ, Yurgelun-Todd DA, Hennen J, Moore JC, Moore CM, Vakili K, et al. Increased orbitofrontal cortex levels of choline in depressed adolescents as detected by in vivo proton magnetic resonance spectroscopy. Biol Psychiatry. 2000;48(11):1053–61.
Stertz L, Magalhães PVS, Kapczinski F. Is bipolar disorder an inflammatory condition? The relevance of microglial activation. Curr Opin Psychiatry. 2013;26(1):19–26.
Steru L, Chermat R, Thierry B, Simon P. The tail suspension test: a new method for screening antidepressants in mice. Psychopharmacology. 1985;85(3):367–70.
Suhara T, Nakayama K, Inoue O, Fukuda H, Shimizu M, Mori A, et al. D1 dopamine receptor binding in mood disorders measured by positron emission tomography. Psychopharmacology. 1992;106(1):14–8.

Sulzer D, Sonders MS, Poulsen NW, Galli A. Mechanisms of neurotransmitter release by amphetamines: a review. Prog Neurobiol. 2005;75(6):406–33.

Surtees PG, Miller PM, Ingham JG, Kreitman NB, Rennie D, Sashidharan SP. Life events and the onset of affective disorder: a longitudinal general population study. J Affect Disord. 1986;10(1):37–50.

Takahashi JS, Hong H-K, Ko CH, McDearmon EL. The genetics of mammalian circadian order and disorder: implications for physiology and disease. Nat Rev Genet. 2008;9(10):764–75.

Tanda G, Carboni E, Frau R, Di Chiara G. Increase of extracellular dopamine in the prefrontal cortex: a trait of drugs with antidepressant potential? Psychopharmacology. 1994;115(1–2):285–8.

Teicher MH. Scars that won't heal: the neurobiology of child abuse. Sci Am. 2002;286(3):68–75.

Thomas GM, Huganir RL. MAPK cascade signalling and synaptic plasticity. Nat Rev Neurosci. 2004;5(3):173–83.

Tidey JW, Miczek KA. Acquisition of cocaine self-administration after social stress: role of accumbens dopamine. Psychopharmacology. 1997;130(3):203–12.

Tohen M, Goldberg JF, Gonzalez-Pinto Arrillaga AM, Azorin JM, Vieta E, Hardy-Bayle M-C, et al. A 12-week, double-blind comparison of olanzapine vs haloperidol in the treatment of acute mania. Arch Gen Psychiatry. 2003;60(12):1218–26.

Tornatzky W, Miczek KA. Long-term impairment of autonomic circadian rhythms after brief intermittent social stress. Physiol Behav. 1993;53(5):983–93.

Toyoda A. Social defeat models in animal science: what we have learned from rodent models. Anim Sci. 2017;88(7):944–52.

Tractenberg SG, Levandowski ML, de Azeredo LA, Orso R, Roithmann LG, Hoffmann ES, et al. An overview of maternal separation effects on behavioural outcomes in mice: evidence from a four-stage methodological systematic review. Neurosci Biobehav Rev. 2016;68:489–503.

Trejo JL, Cuchillo I, Machín C, Rúa C. Maternal adrenalectomy at the early onset of gestation impairs the postnatal development of the rat hippocampal formation: effects on cell numbers and differentiation, connectivity and calbindin-D28k immunoreactivity. J Neurosci Res. 2000;62(5):644–67.

Uno H, Lohmiller L, Thieme C, Kemnitz JW, Engle MJ, Roecker EB, et al. Brain damage induced by prenatal exposure to dexamethasone in fetal rhesus macaques. I. Hippocampus. Dev Brain Res. 1990;53(2):157–67.

Valvassori SS, Tonin PT, Varela RB, Carvalho AF, Mariot E, Amboni RT, et al. Lithium modulates the production of peripheral and cerebral cytokines in an animal model of mania induced by dextroamphetamine. Bipolar Disord. 2015;17(5):507–17.

van den Dries L, Juffer F, van Ijzendoorn MH, Bakermans-Kranenburg MJ. Infants' physical and cognitive development after international adoption from foster care or institutions in China. J Dev Behav Pediatr. 2010;31(2):144–50.

van Enkhuizen J, Geyer MA, Kooistra K, Young JW. Chronic valproate attenuates some, but not all, facets of mania-like behaviour in mice. Int J Neuropsychopharmacol. 2013a;16(5):1021–31.

van Enkhuizen J, Minassian A, Young JW. Further evidence for ClockΔ19 mice as a model for bipolar disorder mania using cross-species tests of exploration and sensorimotor gating. Behav Brain Res. 2013b;15(249):44–54.

van Enkhuizen J, Geyer MA, Halberstadt AL, Zhuang X, Young JW. Dopamine depletion attenuates some behavioral abnormalities in a hyperdopaminergic mouse model of bipolar disorder. J Affect Disord. 2014a;155:247–54.

van Enkhuizen J, Henry BL, Minassian A, Perry W, Milienne-Petiot M, Higa KK, et al. Reduced dopamine transporter functioning induces high-reward risk-preference consistent with bipolar disorder. Neuropsychopharmacology. 2014b;39(13):3112–22.

van Enkhuizen J, Geyer MA, Minassian A, Perry W, Henry BL, Young JW. Investigating the underlying mechanisms of aberrant behaviors in bipolar disorder from patients to models: rodent and human studies. Neurosci Biobehav Rev. 2015a;58:4–18.

van Enkhuizen J, Janowsky DS, Olivier B, Minassian A, Perry W, Young JW, et al. The catecholaminergic-cholinergic balance hypothesis of bipolar disorder revisited. Eur J Pharmacol. 2015b;15(753):114–26.

Van Kammen DP, Murphy DL. Attenuation of the euphoriant and activating effects of d- and l-amphetamine by lithium carbonate treatment. Psychopharmacologia. 1975;44(3):215–24.

van Praag HM, Korf J. Central monoamine deficiency in depressions: causative of secondary phenomenon? Pharmakopsychiatr Neuropsychopharmakol. 1975;8(5):322–6.

Vanover KE. Effects of AMPA receptor antagonists on dopamine-mediated behaviors in mice. Psychopharmacology. 1998;136(2):123–31.

Varela RB, Valvassori SS, Lopes-Borges J, Fraga DB, Resende WR, Arent CO, et al. Evaluation of acetylcholinesterase in an animal model of mania induced by D-amphetamine. Psychiatry Res. 2013;209(2):229–34.

Vetulani J. Early maternal separation: a rodent model of depression and a prevailing human condition. Pharmacol Rep. 2013;65(6):1451–61.

Vieta E, Ros S, Goikolea JM, Benabarre A, Popova E, Comes M, et al. An open-label study of amisulpride in the treatment of mania. J Clin Psychiatry. 2005;66(5):575–8.

Wachholz S, Knorr A, Mengert L, Plümper J, Sommer R, Juckel G, et al. Interleukin-4 is a participant in the regulation of depressive-like behavior. Behav Brain Res. 2017;30(326):165–72.

Wakshlak A, Weinstock M. Neonatal handling reverses behavioral abnormalities induced in rats by prenatal stress. Physiol Behav. 1990;48(2):289–92.

Wang Y, Huang W, Wang C, Tsai C, Chen C, Chang Y, et al. Inhibiting glycogen synthase kinase-3 reduces endotoxaemic acute renal failure by down-regulating inflammation and renal cell apoptosis. Br J Pharmacol. 2009;157(6):1004–13.

Wieck A, Grassi-Oliveira R, do Prado CH, Rizzo LB, de Oliveira AS, Kommers-Molina J, et al. Pro-inflammatory cytokines and soluble receptors in response to acute psychosocial stress: differential reactivity in bipolar disorder. Neurosci Lett. 2014;580:17–21.

Wigger A, Neumann ID. Periodic maternal deprivation induces gender-dependent alterations in behavioral and neuroendocrine responses to emotional stress in adult rats. Physiol Behav. 1999;66(2):293–302.

Wirz-Justice A. Biological rhythm disturbances in mood disorders. Int Clin Psychopharmacol. 2006;21(Suppl 1):S11–5.

Wise RA, Munn E. Withdrawal from chronic amphetamine elevates baseline intracranial self-stimulation thresholds. Psychopharmacology. 1995;117(2):130–6.

Wright JB. Mania following sleep deprivation. Br J Psychiatry J Ment Sci. 1993;163:679–80.

Wuarin J, Falvey E, Lavery D, Talbot D, Schmidt E, Ossipow V, et al. The role of the transcriptional activator protein DBP in circadian liver gene expression. J Cell Sci Suppl. 1992;16:123–7.

Wulsin AC, Wick-Carlson D, Packard BA, Morano R, Herman JP. Adolescent chronic stress causes hypothalamo-pituitary-adrenocortical hyporesponsiveness and depression-like behavior in adult female rats. Psychoneuroendocrinology. 2016;65:109–17.

Yadid G, Overstreet DH, Zangen A. Limbic dopaminergic adaptation to a stressful stimulus in a rat model of depression. Brain Res. 2001;896(1–2):43–7.

Yao J, Pan Y, Ding M, Pang H, Wang B. Meta-analysis shows dopamine receptor D1 gene polymorphism is associated with bipolar disorder but not with schizophrenia. Psychiatry Res. 2013;210(3):1324–5.

Yin L, Wang J, Klein PS, Lazar MA. Nuclear receptor Rev-erbalpha is a critical lithium-sensitive component of the circadian clock. Science. 2006;311(5763):1002–5.

Young JW, Dulcis D. Investigating the mechanism(s) underlying switching between states in bipolar disorder. Eur J Pharmacol. 2015;15(759):151–62.

Young JW, Minassian A, Paulus MP, Geyer MA, Perry W. A reverse-translational approach to bipolar disorder: rodent and human studies in the behavioral pattern monitor. Neurosci Biobehav Rev. 2007;31(6):882–96.

Young JW, Goey AKL, Minassian A, Perry W, Paulus MP, Geyer MA. The mania-like exploratory profile in genetic dopamine transporter mouse models is diminished in a familiar environment and reinstated by subthreshold psychostimulant administration. Pharmacol Biochem Behav. 2010;96(1):7–15.

Young JW, van Enkhuizen J, Winstanley CA, Geyer MA. Increased risk-taking behavior in dopamine transporter knockdown mice: further support for a mouse model of mania. J Psychopharmacol Oxf Engl. 2011;25(7):934–43.

Zarate CA, Payne JL, Singh J, Quiroz JA, Luckenbaugh DA, Denicoff KD, et al. Pramipexole for bipolar II depression: a placebo-controlled proof of concept study. Biol Psychiatry. 2004;56(1):54–60.

Zetterberg H, Jakobsson J, Redsäter M, Andreasson U, Pålsson E, Ekman CJ, et al. Blood-cerebrospinal fluid barrier dysfunction in patients with bipolar disorder in relation to antipsychotic treatment. Psychiatry Res. 2014;217(3):143–6.

Zhang P, Katz J, Michalek SM. Glycogen synthase kinase-3β (GSK3β) inhibition suppresses the inflammatory response to Francisella infection and protects against tularemia in mice. Mol Immunol. 2009;46(4):677–87.

Zheng W, Zeng Z, Bhardwaj SK, Jamali S, Srivastava LK. Lithium normalizes amphetamine-induced changes in striatal FoxO1 phosphorylation and behaviors in rats. Neuroreport. 2013;24(10):560–5.

Zhuang X, Oosting RS, Jones SR, Gainetdinov RR, Miller GW, Caron MG, et al. Hyperactivity and impaired response habituation in hyperdopaminergic mice. Proc Natl Acad Sci USA. 2001;98(4):1982–7.

Zuckerman L, Rehavi M, Nachman R, Weiner I. Immune activation during pregnancy in rats leads to a postpubertal emergence of disrupted latent inhibition, dopaminergic hyperfunction, and altered limbic morphology in the offspring: a novel neurodevelopmental model of schizophrenia. Neuropsychopharmacolog. 2003;28(10):1778–89.

4

Cognitive functioning following stabilisation from first episode mania

Rothanthi Daglas[1,2], Kelly Allott[1,2], Murat Yücel[3], Lisa P. Henry[1], Craig A. Macneil[4], Melissa K. Hasty[4], Michael Berk[1,2,5,6,7] and Sue M. Cotton[1,2*]

Abstract

Background: The purpose of this study was to examine cognitive functioning in people following first-episode mania relative to a demographically similar healthy control group.

Methods: Forty-one patients, who had recently stabilised from a first manic episode, and twenty-one healthy controls, were compared in an extensive cognitive assessment.

Results: First-episode mania participants had significantly lower Full-Scale IQ (FSIQ) relative to healthy controls; however, this finding could be driven by premorbid differences in intellectual functioning. There were no significant differences between groups in Verbal IQ (VIQ) and Performance IQ (PIQ). First-episode mania participants performed significantly poorer than healthy controls in processing speed, verbal learning and memory, working memory, and cognitive flexibility with medium-to-large effects. There were no group differences in other measures of cognition.

Conclusions: Participants following first-episode mania have poorer global intelligence than healthy controls, and have cognitive difficulties in some, but not all areas of cognitive functioning. This highlights the importance of early intervention and cognitive assessment in the early course of the disorder.

Keywords: Bipolar disorder, Cognition, Depression, Manic, Remission

Background

Cognitive impairments during euthymia in people in all stages of bipolar disorder have been reported by several meta-analyses, with findings of medium to large effect in processing speed, verbal learning and memory, non-verbal memory, working memory, verbal fluency, sustained attention and executive functions (Arts et al. 2008; Bora et al. 2009; Bourne et al. 2013; Mann-Wrobel et al. 2011). There has been limited research conducted on cognitive functioning during the early stages of the illness, thus the timing and onset of cognitive change remains unclear.

Recently, two meta-analyses on adults with first episode bipolar disorder (including any polarity of illness) have identified impairments in most cognitive domains relative to healthy control (HC) participants (Bora and Pantelis 2015; Lee et al. 2014). However, a recent systematic review on first episode mania (FEM) that included adolescents as well as adult samples, revealed discrepancies between study findings across most cognitive domains, apart from a consistently reported deficit in working memory during remission, and that verbal fluency and non-verbal memory remained intact (Daglas et al. 2015). The literature regarding intelligence in FEM has revealed that patients perform worse than HCs in global IQ (Elshahawi et al. 2011; López-Jaramillo et al. 2010), and on measures of non-verbal intelligence (Hellvin et al. 2012; Torres et al. 2010); however, the studies in FEM (included in the systematic review) had not controlled for the differences observed between FEM and HC groups in IQ, which may have contributed to the inconsistencies between study findings (Daglas et al. 2015). This is in contrast to a meta-analysis that reported preserved current IQ in people with established bipolar disorder (Bora et al. 2009). Moreover, there appears to be a bi-modal pattern regarding school performance in asymptomatic adolescents (aged 15–16 years) who later

*Correspondence: smcotton@unimelb.edu.au
[2] Centre for Youth Mental Health, University of Melbourne, 35 Poplar Road, Parkville, VIC 3052, Australia
Full list of author information is available at the end of the article

develop bipolar disorder. Those with the highest school grades displayed a nearly fourfold increased risk of developing the disorder by age 31, whilst those with the lowest school performance were found to have close to a twofold increased risk (MacCabe et al. 2010). Predictors of lower intellectual functioning in individuals with bipolar disorder include an earlier age of onset, greater number of prior episodes and hospitalisations (Denicoff et al. 1999).

Although cognitive deficits have been identified during remission in bipolar disorder, the effects of intelligence, residual symptoms, medication use, number of hospitalisations and number of past episodes may impact upon the findings (Bourne et al. 2013; Donaldson et al. 2003; Nehra et al. 2006; Thompson et al. 2005; Torres et al. 2010). The first diagnostic episode for bipolar I disorder enables the assessment of cognitive functioning prior to the effects of covariates such as prolonged medication use and recurrent manic episodes. Most of the studies conducted to date have included adult samples with FEM (Daglas et al. 2015) and have not considered that the incidence of FEM is greatest between 16 and 30 years (Kennedy et al. 2005), and that there may be developmental differences in cognition between younger and older populations.

Thus, the aim of the current study was to examine cognitive functioning of young people (15–25 years) following FEM relative to a demographically similar HC group. The cognitive domains considered were processing speed, attention, sustained attention, verbal learning and memory, non-verbal learning and memory, working memory, verbal fluency and executive functions. Due to diagnostic instability in the early phases of the illness, and that an accurate diagnosis is on average delayed for 7.5 years in people with bipolar disorder, any presentation of FEM will be considered in this study (Ghaemi et al. 1999; Schimmelmann et al. 2005). It was hypothesised that FEM participants would perform significantly worse than HCs in processing speed, attention, sustained attention, verbal learning and memory, working memory and executive functions; and that the groups would not significantly differ in verbal fluency and non-verbal memory. Furthermore, FEM participants were expected to perform more poorly than HCs in full-scale IQ (FSIQ) and performance IQ (PIQ), but that the groups would have similar verbal IQ (VIQ).

Methods

Design

This study involved secondary analysis of baseline data from a single-blinded Randomised Control Trial (RCT) conducted at Orygen, The National Centre of Excellence in Youth Mental Health, Melbourne, Australia. The focus of the trial was on the effectiveness of quetiapine fumarate compared to lithium carbonate monotherapy for the maintenance treatment of FEM over a 12-month period. This trial was registered with the Australian and New Zealand Clinical Trials Registry ACTRN12607000639426. Neuropsychological data were also collected on a separate HC group that was not part of the RCT, using the same time-points and measures.

Sample and setting

The FEM patients were recruited between 2006 and 2013 from outpatient clinics of OYH and Monash Health, located within the Western, North Western and South Eastern suburbs of Melbourne, respectively. To satisfy inclusion criteria for the RCT, the FEM patients were required to have: (1) clinically stabilised from a first treated manic episode on a combination of quetiapine and lithium for a least 1 month prior to randomisation (stabilisation of mental state was based on clinical judgment by the treating clinicians on the basis of a global clinical assessment); (2) met Diagnostic and Statistical Manual of Mental Disorders-Fourth Edition-Text Revision (DSM-IV-TR; APA, 2000) criteria for bipolar I disorder, schizoaffective disorder-bipolar type, or a substance-induced mood disorder; (3) scored a minimum of 20 on the Young Mania Rating Scale (YMRS) during the first manic episode; and (4) been aged 15–25 years at the time of recruitment.

FEM patients were excluded if they had a clinically relevant systemic medical disorder, biochemical or haematological abnormalities or unstable diabetes mellitus, were pregnant or lactating, had a sensitivity or allergy to components of lithium or quetiapine, were non-fluent in English, had a history of epilepsy, were at immediate risk of harm to self or others, or had an organic mental disease including intellectual disability (FSIQ < 70). The use of potent cytochrome P450 inhibitors and inducers was also prohibited during the study.

HCs were matched as closely as possible to the FEM group in age, sex and premorbid intelligence, and were recruited from similar regions of Melbourne through advertisements in a freely distributed newspaper at inner-city metro stations of Melbourne, the Orygen website, and by word of mouth. Due to recruitment feasibility, FEM and HC participants were recruited at a ratio of 2:1. Individuals interested in participating contacted the researchers and were given a detailed description of the study. Prior to providing informed consent, the HCs were assessed for current or past mental health disorders with the screening tool of the Structured Clinical Interview (Patient Edition) for DSM-IV-TR. HCs were excluded if they had a history of, or current mental health disorder, substance abuse or dependence, an FSIQ < 70, or were not 15–25 years of age.

Measures

Neuropsychological measures

One assessor (RD) was trained in standardised neuropsychological testing and clinical assessment of this clinical population and conducted all assessment components of the study. The neuropsychological battery was administered in the same order for all participants and consisted of psychometrically robust, valid and standardised tests. Cognitive functions that were assessed included intelligence, processing speed, attention span, sustained attention, verbal learning and memory, non-verbal learning and memory, working memory, verbal fluency and executive functions.

Intelligence

To measure estimated premorbid intelligence, the Wechsler Test of Adult Reading (WTAR) was used (The Psychological Corporation 2001). As a measure of current intelligence, the Wechsler Abbreviated Scale of Intelligence (WASI) was utilised (The Psychological Corporation 1999). From the WASI, FSIQ, VIQ and PIQ scores were derived.

Processing speed

Four tests of processing speed were administered, including Trail Making Test—part A (TMT-A) (Reitan 1955), WAIS-III Digit Symbol Coding (Wechsler 1997), the computerised Go/No-Go test to assess the reaction time for go responses (see Takagi et al. 2011), and the Cogstate$_{TM}$ Detection task (see Hammers et al. 2011, 2012).

Attention

Attention span was assessed with WAIS-III Digit Span-forward (Wechsler 1997). The computerised Stroop task for congruent responses, Go/No-Go test for missed go responses (see Takagi et al. 2011), and Cogstate$_{TM}$ Identification task were used as measures of focused attention (see Hammers et al. 2011, 2012).

Sustained attention

A shorter version of the original Attention Network Test (ANT) was used to measure sustained attention (Fan et al. 2005).

Verbal learning and memory

The Rey auditory verbal learning test (RAVLT) was administered to test verbal learning and memory (Lezak 1983; Rey 1958). The correct recall of words in trial 1 was used as a test of immediate memory, and the total correct recall of the same list of words in five consecutive trials was used to measure verbal learning. Delayed verbal recall was measured by the recall of the same list of words after a 20-min interval.

Non-verbal learning and memory

The computerised Cogstate$_{TM}$ One-card leaning task (OCL) (see Hammers et al. 2011, 2012) and the Cogstate$_{TM}$ Groton Maze Learning Test (GMLT)—delayed recall were used as measures of non-verbal learning and memory (see Snyder et al. 2005).

Working memory

The WAIS-III Digit Span-backward was used to measure working memory capacity (Wechsler 1997).

Verbal fluency

The Controlled Oral Word Association Test was used to measure semantic (animal category) and phonemic (FAS) verbal fluency (see Mitrushina et al. 2005).

Executive functioning

The Trail Making Test—part B (TMT-B) was utilised to measure cognitive flexibility (Reitan 1955). To assess inhibitory control, computerised versions of the Stroop and Go/No-Go tasks were used (see Takagi et al. 2011). The Cogstate$_{TM}$ GMLT was used as a test of spatial problem solving (see Snyder et al. 2005).

Clinical measures

The clinical scales used to assess psychiatric symptomatology included: the YMRS (Young et al. 1978); the Montgomery–Åsberg Depression Rating Scale (MADRS) (Montgomery and Asberg 1979); the Brief Psychiatric Rating Scale (BPRS), total scores and positive psychotic scores (including the 4 subscales: unusual thought content, hallucinations, suspiciousness and conceptual disorganisation) (Overall and Gorham 1962); and the Clinical Global Impression scale—modified for bipolar disorder (CGI-BP) (Spearing et al. 1997).

Procedure

The trial adhered to Good Clinical Practice guidelines, and was approved by the Human Research Ethics Committees of Melbourne Health (HREC 2006.644) and Monash Health (06138B). All participants or legal guardians (on behalf of participants under 18 years of age) provided voluntary informed consent. Patients who were treated with a combination of quetiapine and lithium for their first acute episode of mania were referred to the study by the treating psychiatrist or case manager. Once patients had clinically stabilised and were transferred to outpatient care, they were provided with a full description of the study. Cognitive and clinical assessments occurred once the patients had stabilised and had commenced monotherapy. The clinical assessment was conducted on the same day as the cognitive assessment for most FEM participants (41%). Thirty-one percent of the

FEM participants had the clinical assessment within the first week, 15% within the 2-weeks and 13% over 2-weeks of cognitive testing. The time-point for the structured clinical interview for DSM-IV-TR was within 2–4 weeks of the cognitive testing.

Data analysis

All statistical analyses were conducted using IBM® SPSS® Statistics Version 22.0. Descriptive statistics were calculated for demographic variables, and illness characteristics. Independent samples *t* test and Chi-square (χ^2) analyses were performed to assess for between-group differences on demographic variables. Several outliers were identified by box plots, and skewness and kurtosis values revealed that the cognitive data were differentially distributed within the two groups. Therefore, non-parametric Mann–Whitney *U* tests were utilised to compare groups for each cognitive measure. To control for the effects of multiple comparisons, family-wise error adjustments were made per cognitive domain ($\alpha = .05$/number of cognitive measures per domain). To determine absolute values for effect size (*r*), *z* scores were divided by the square root of *N* ($r = Z/\sqrt{N}$), as used for non-parametric tests (Fritz et al. 2012). According to Cohen's (1998) guidelines for *r*, a small effect size is 0.1, medium effect size is 0.3 and a large effect size is 0.5 (Coolican 2009). The relationship between clinical symptom rating (YMRS, MADRS, BPRS and BPRS—positive psychotic scores) and cognitive functioning was assessed using Pearson's correlation on any measure that showed a significant difference between FEM participants and HCs following family-wise adjustment.

Results

The cohort included sixty-one patients who had recently stabilised from their first treated manic episode. Of the 61 FEM patients, 7 were excluded due to not adhering to the randomised medication allocation, 2 were deemed too unwell to participate by their treating psychiatrist, 5 relapsed prior to the first assessment, and 6 withdrew consent or disengaged from the service. In total, 41 FEM participants and 21 HCs were included in the study.

Sample characteristics

Demographic and illness characteristics are presented in Table 1. The FEM and HC groups did not differ significantly in age, sex and premorbid intelligence. However, the difference observed between groups in premorbid

Table 1 Participant demographics and illness characteristics

Demographics variables	FEM ($n = 41$)	HC ($n = 21$)	Statistics	*p* value
Age, M (SD)	21.32 (2.26)	21.14 (2.54)	*t* test	0.784
Sex, male, n (%)	32 (78)	11 (52.38)	$\chi^{2\,c}$	0.074
Premorbid intelligence[a]				
Based on WTAR UK norms, M (SD)	94.9 (13.81)	101.70 (9.65)	*t* test	0.054
Education level				
Less than 12 years, n (%)	16 (39)	2 (7)	χ^2	0.032
12 years, n (%)	7 (17)	3 (14)		
More than 12 years, n (%)	18 (44)	16 (76)		
Diagnosis				
Bipolar I disorder[b], n (%)	35 (85)			
Substance-induced mood disorder, n (%)	4 (10)			
Schizoaffective disorder- bipolar type, n (%)	2 (5)			
Symptom rating				
YMRS, total, M (SD)	2.51 (3.57)			
MADRS, total, M (SD)	7.39 (8.95)			
BPRS, total, M (SD)	33.24 (9.32)			
BPRS, positive psychotic subscale, M (SD)	4.63 (1.64)			
CGI-BP, mania severity, M (SD)	1.15 (.573)			
CGI-BP, depression severity, M (SD)	2.05 (1.563)			
CGI-BP, overall severity, M (SD)	2.02 (1.491)			

FEM first episode mania, *HC* healthy controls, *WTAR* Wechsler Test of Adult Reading, *YMRS* Young Mania Rating Scale, *MADRS* Montgomery–Åsberg Depression Rating Scale, *BPRS* Brief Psychiatric Rating Scale, *CGI-BP* Clinical Global Impression scale for bipolar illness, *t test* independent samples *t* test, χ^2 Chi-square test

[a] Missing data (FEM, $n = 1$; HC, $n = 1$)

[b] Diagnosis of bipolar I disorder confirmed by treating clinician ($n = 1$)

[c] Continuity correction

intelligence was of moderate effect ($d = 0.57$). On average the HC group had spent more years in education than the FEM group. The largest percentage of FEM patients had a diagnosis of bipolar I disorder (85%), 10% had a substance-induced mood episode and 5% were diagnosed with schizoaffective disorder-bipolar type. All FEM participants had experienced a manic or mixed episode with psychotic features.

On average the FEM participants were in remission from acute mania (YMRS, $M = 2.51$, SD = 3.57), did not have positive psychotic symptomatology in the BPRS ($M = 4.63$, SD = 1.64), and were rated normal/not ill in mania severity on the CGI-BP ($M = 1.15$, SD = 0.573). However, the FEM participants were on average mildly depressed (MADRS, $M = 7.39$, SD = 8.95), as also identified in the BPRS total psychopathology rating ($M = 33.24$, SD = 9.32). FEM participants were considered minimally ill in depression severity ($M = 2.05$, SD = 1.56), and in overall bipolar disorder severity on the CGI-BP ($M = 2.02$, SD = 1.49).

Cognitive functioning

The median and minimum/maximum scores for each group per cognitive measure and the associated test statistics and effect sizes are presented in Table 2.

Intelligence

FEM participants had significantly lower FSIQ ($p = .014$) and PIQ ($p = .046$) than HCs, with medium ($r = .31$) and small to medium effect ($r = .26$), respectively. However, PIQ did not remain significant after family-wise adjustment (i.e. $\alpha/3$). There was no significant difference between groups in VIQ ($p = .084$).

Processing speed

A highly significant group difference was observed between groups on the TMT-A ($p < .001$) and digit symbol coding ($p = .002$), even after family-wise adjustment (i.e. $\alpha/4$). FEM patients performed substantially slower than HCs with a large ($r = .57$) and medium ($r = .40$) effect size, respectively.

There were no significant differences between groups in 'go' reaction time ($p = .480$) or Cogstate^{TM} Detection time ($p = .668$).

Attention

The groups did not differ significantly on Digit Span-forward ($p = .532$), missed go responses ($p = .753$), Stroop congruent total errors ($p = .928$) or in Cogstate$_{TM}$ Identification time ($p = .487$).

Sustained attention

FEM and HC groups performed similarly in ANT alerting ($p = .785$), orienting ($p = .677$) and executive control ($p = .081$). There was no significant difference between groups in total errors for the no cue ($p = .593$), spatial cue ($p = .351$), double cue ($p = .850$), congruent ($p = .248$) and incongruent ($p = .432$) conditions.

Verbal learning and memory

FEM patients recalled significantly fewer words in trial 1 of the RAVLT relative to HCs ($p = .002$), of medium effect ($r = .39$). FEM patients recalled significantly fewer words than HCs in trials 1–5 ($p < .001$) and in delayed verbal recall ($p < .001$), which were both of a medium to large effect size ($r = .47$). These differences remained significant after family-wise adjustment (i.e. $\alpha/3$).

Non-verbal learning and memory

There were no significant group differences in the OCL task ($p = .609$) or in the GMLT-delayed recall ($p = .187$).

Working memory

FEM patients had poorer working memory capacity than HCs, with a highly significant difference between groups in Digit Span-backward ($p = .001$) with medium to large effect ($r = .44$).

Verbal fluency

There was no significant difference between groups in phonemic fluency ($p = .122$). FEM participants produced significantly fewer words than HCs in semantic fluency ($p = .045$), though, this difference did not remain significant after family-wise adjustment (i.e. $\alpha/2$).

Executive functions

A large difference was observed in cognitive flexibility with FEM patients performing worse than HCs in TMT-B ($p = .004$), even after family-wise adjustment (i.e. $\alpha/5$), with a medium effect size ($r = .37$).

Groups did not differ significantly with respect to response inhibition in Go/No-Go false alarm responses ($p = .063$), in Stroop incongruent total errors ($p = .974$), or in Stroop effect ($p = .794$). Additionally, no significant group differences were observed in spatial problem solving as assessed by GMLT ($p = .502$).

Relationship between clinical symptomatology and cognition

A significant negative correlation was found between rating scores on the YMRS and the RAVLT trial 1 ($p = .033$) with a moderate effect size ($r = -.333$). There also was a significant negative relationship between symptom rating on the YMRS and scores on the RAVLT

Table 2 Cognitive functioning in participants following FEM relative to healthy controls

	FEM Median (min–max)	HC Median (min–max)	Test statistic	Value	*df*	*p* value	Effect size
Intelligence (WASI)[a]							
Verbal IQ	102 (63–128)	109 (96–130)	M–W	297.5	61	.084	0.22
Performance IQ	104 (75–128)	115 (90–129)	M–W	280	61	.046	0.26
Full-scale IQ	107 (70–128)	113 (98–126)	M–W	250.5	61	.014	0.31
Processing speed							
Trail Making Test-A[a]	31 (19–72)	22 (13–41)	M–W	120.5	61	< .001	0.57
Digit symbol coding[a]	73 (30–106)	80 (60–125)	M–W	207	61	.002	0.4
Go/No-Go[b], go reaction time	294.96 (238.13–424.11)	304.91 (258.77–387.96)	M–W	355	60	.480	0.09
Cogstate[c], detection reaction time	2.44 (2.32–2.69)	2.43 (2.36–2.59)	M–W	362	58	.668	0.06
Attention							
Digit Span forward[a]	8 (4–12)	10 (5–12)	M–W	370	61	.532	0.08
Go/No-Go[b], go misses	0 (0–8)	0 (0–6)	M–W	382	60	.753	0.04
Stroop[d], congruent errors	2.5 (0–15)	2 (0–13)	M–W	374.5	58	.928	0.01
Cogstate[c], identification reaction time	2.66 (2.55–2.91)	2.66 (2.54–2.80)	M–W	345.5	58	.487	0.09
Sustained attention[e]							
ANT, alerting reaction time	44.61 (− 99.46 to 162.3)	38.56 (− 21.45 to 97.28)	M–W	373	59	.785	0.04
ANT, orienting reaction time	164.15 (13.67–316.42)	159.54 (15.70–232.76)	M–W	364	59	.677	0.05
ANT, executive control reaction time	226.74 (6.37–794.91)	189.81 (84.25–273.07)	M–W	281	59	.081	0.23
ANT, no cue errors	1 (0–5)	1 (0–3)	M–W	358	59	.593	0.07
ANT, spatial cue errors	1 (0–5)	1 (0–2)	M–W	335.5	59	.351	0.12
ANT, double cue errors	1 (0–5)	1 (0–10)	M–W	378.5	59	.850	0.02
ANT, congruent errors	0 (0–2)	0 (0–3)	M–W	329.5	59	.248	0.15
ANT, incongruent errors	3 (0–9)	2.5 (0–13)	M–W	341.5	59	.432	0.1
Verbal learning and memory[a]							
Rey auditory verbal learning test[e]—trial 1	6 (3–12)	7.5 (4–12)	M–W	215	61	.002	0.39
Rey auditory verbal learning test[e]—trials 1-5	52 (26–66)	59.50 (42–71)	M–W	170.5	61	< .001	0.47
Rey auditory verbal learning test[e]—delayed recall	11 (3–15)	14 (10–15)	M–W	174	61	< .001	0.47
Non-verbal learning and memory							
Cogstate, one-card learning[f]	1.01 (0.26–1.22)	1.03 (0.82–1.12)	M–W	339.5	57	.609	0.07
Cogstate, Groton Maze Learning Test, delayed, errors[g]	6 (0–24)	4 (0–11)	M–W	291.5	57	.187	0.17
Working memory							
Digit Span backward[a]	4 (1–10)	7 (3–12)	M–W	186.5	61	.001	0.44
Verbal fluency[a]							
FAS	37 (17–59)	43 (17–58)	M–W	309.5	61	.122	0.2
Animal category	21 (11–32)	23 (16–27)	M–W	280	61	.045	0.26
Executive functions							
Trail Making Test-B[h]	75 (31–215)	51 (30–116)	M–W	207	60	.004	0.37
Go/No-Go[b], no-go false alarms	9.5 (2–21)	6.5 (1–16)	M–W	282	60	.063	0.24

Table 2 continued

	FEM Median (min–max)	HC Median (min–max)	Test statistic	Value	*df*	*p* value	Effect size
Stroop effect[d], reaction time	360.02 (97.20–603.79)	380.58 (115.75–618.27)	M–W	364	58	.794	0.03
Stroop[d], incongruent errors	7 (1–26)	6 (3–24)	M–W	378	58	.974	< 0.01
Cogstate[c], Groton Maze Learning Test, errors	54 (23.00–142.00)	51.00 (32.00–115.00)	M–W	347	58	.502	0.09

FEM first episode mania, *HC* healthy controls, *ANT* attention network test, *M–W* Mann–Whitney *U* test

ANT, alerting reaction time = no cue reaction time – double cue reaction time

ANT, orienting reaction time = double cue reaction time – spatial cue reaction time

ANT, executive control reaction time = incongruent trials reaction time – congruent trials reaction time

ANT, no cue errors = total errors for the no cue conditions

ANT, spatial cue errors = total errors for the spatial cue conditions

ANT, double cue errors = total errors for the double cue conditions

ANT, congruent errors = total errors for the congruent trials

ANT, incongruent errors = total errors for the incongruent trials

Stroop effect = incongruent condition reaction time – congruent condition reaction time

Stroop, congruent errors = total errors for the congruent trials

Stroop, incongruent errors = total errors for the incongruent trials

Go/No-Go, go reaction time = reaction time for go responses

Go/No-Go, no-go false alarms = sum of false responses to no-go stimulus

Go/No-Go, go misses = sum of missed responses to go stimulus

[a] Missing data (HC, $n = 1$)

[b] Missing data (FEM, $n = 1$; HC, $n = 1$)

[c] Missing data (FEM, $n = 5$)

[d] Missing data (FEM, $n = 3$; HC, $n = 1$)

[e] Missing data (FEM, $n = 2$; HC, $n = 1$)

[f] Missing data (FEM, $n = 4$; HC, $n = 1$)

[g] Missing data (FEM, $n = 5$; HC, $n = 1$)

[h] Missing data (HC, $n = 2$)

trials 1–5 ($p = .029$), which was of a moderate effect size ($r = -.342$). Furthermore, a significant negative correlation was found between general psychopathology rating (BPRS total) and the RAVLT trials 1–5 ($p = .008$), which was of a moderate to large effect size ($r = -.408$). There were no other significant correlations found between clinical symptom rating scales and cognition.

Discussion

The purpose of this study was to investigate cognitive functioning in youth following FEM. FEM patients were found to have lower FSIQ than HCs. While the groups were statistically matched in estimated premorbid intelligence, the difference in premorbid IQ was of medium effect and so the difference in current FSIQ may be driven by true pre-existing group differences or the inherent difficulties encountered matching FEM and HC on premorbid intelligence. Furthermore, FEM patients were still within the average intelligence range when compared to norms of people from a similar age group. Furthermore, the groups did not significantly differ in verbal and performance IQ after controlling for multiple comparisons. Previous research has been mixed showing that patients following FEM had poorer global intellectual functioning compared to HCs (Elshahawi et al. 2011; López-Jaramillo et al. 2010) and that FEM patients and HCs did not differ in verbal IQ, though FEM patients performed more poorly than HCs in subtests of performance IQ, including Block Design (Hellvin et al. 2012) and spatial reasoning (Hellvin et al. 2012; Torres et al. 2010).

Our findings indicate that FEM patients displayed cognitive impairments in some, but not all areas of cognitive functioning. First, as expected FEM patients performed worse than HCs in tests of processing speed, verbal learning and memory, working memory and cognitive flexibility. Second, phonemic verbal fluency and non-verbal learning and memory were not impaired relative to HCs; and differences observed in sematic verbal fluency were no longer apparent after family-wise adjustment. Contrary to our hypothesis, there were no group differences found in attention span, sustained attention or in the computerised tests of psychomotor speed and response inhibition. Although findings in the literature examining cognitive functioning in the early stages of bipolar disorder is somewhat mixed (Daglas et al. 2015), the results from the current study are generally comparable to the majority of research findings in FEM.

Regarding processing speed, Elshahawi et al. (2011) also revealed impairments in FEM patients relative to HCs as assessed by TMT-A and Digit Symbol Coding. Additionally, Hellvin et al. (2012) found that FEM patients performed worse than HCs in Digit Symbol Coding, whilst reporting no difference between groups in Stroop performance. On the other hand, Torres et al. (2010) found that FEM patients and HCs performed alike in both Stroop and in TMT-A. Another study by López-Jaramillo et al. (2010) reported a similar performance between FEM patients and HCs in TMT-A and in Digit Symbol Coding; however, this study had recruited relatives of the FEM patients as HCs, which may have influenced their findings. It has been reported that first-degree relatives of people with bipolar I disorder have a slower ability to process information than those without a family history of psychiatric illnesses (Antila et al. 2007).

Deficits in working memory have been reported by most first episode studies across the bipolar disorder spectrum relative to HCs (Barrett et al. 2009; Elshahawi et al. 2011; Hellvin et al. 2012; Hill et al. 2009; López-Jaramillo et al. 2010). However, two studies that assessed working memory using the letter–number sequencing (LNS) task failed to find a significant difference between groups (Torres et al. 2010; Zanelli et al. 2010). An explanation for this may be that FEM patients may have a weaker activation of the phonological loop required for verbal memory encoding (as in the Digit Span task), but may have maintained the ability to process more complex information, such as the interaction required between visuospatial functions, processing speed, and working memory when switching between letters and numbers in LNS (Crowe 2000; Haut et al. 2000).

Our study revealed that FEM patients had deficits in verbal learning and memory, but spared non-verbal learning and memory. Notably, when either mania or general psychopathology symptoms increased, verbal learning and memory performance decreased. Similar to our findings, Torres et al. (2010) reported that patients who had recently experienced a first episode of mania recalled significantly fewer words than HCs. Whilst, another study failed to find a significant difference between groups in total words recalled (trials 1–5), there were a significantly higher percentage of FEM patients (24%) who had clinically impaired verbal learning on the task (1.5 standard deviations below the mean of the HC group) than HCs (5%) (Hellvin et al. 2012). Impairments in delayed verbal recall have also been reported by previous studies in people with bipolar disorder experiencing their first episode of mania or psychosis (Hellvin et al. 2012; Zanelli et al. 2010).

Most research on first episode patients across the bipolar spectrum has revealed that non-verbal learning and memory remains intact (Hellvin et al. 2012; López-Jaramillo et al. 2010; Torres et al. 2010; Zanelli et al. 2010). Only one study of patients with bipolar disorder in remission from their first episode of psychosis identified a deficit in non-verbal memory (Barrett et al. 2009). Furthermore, a study on individuals at ultra-high risk for psychosis identified impaired visual reproduction relative to HCs, in patients who later developed a first episode of psychosis (Brewer et al. 2005). A deficit in non-verbal memory has also been identified in patients with recurrent bipolar disorder (Arts et al. 2008). Thus, dysfunction in non-verbal memory may reflect a deficit primarily related to psychosis or more chronic forms of bipolar disorder that appears to remain unaffected following FEM.

Our finding that attention was not impaired is consistent with the majority of first episode studies in bipolar disorder (Hellvin et al. 2012; Hill et al. 2009; López-Jaramillo et al. 2010; Torres et al. 2010). Although one study identified impairment in attention span in FEM patients relative to HCs, this study was limited by their recruitment of hospital employees from the same hospital as the FEM patients for the HC group, and therefore may not have been truly representative of the general population (Elshahawi et al. 2011).

Furthermore, our finding of no deficit in sustained attention is contrary to a previous study by Torres et al. (2010), who found that FEM patients performed significantly worse in this domain than HCs. The inconsistency between these study findings may be largely attributed to the different tests that were administered. The sustained attention task used in the current study required the unique activation of alerting, orienting and executive control pathways, which is a variation from more commonly used tests of sustained attention such as the rapid visual information processing task. However, as there has only been one previous study that has assessed sustained attention in FEM, further studies are required in respect to this domain.

In accordance with the recent systematic review on FEM (Daglas et al. 2015), both phonemic and semantic verbal fluency remained intact in the current study of FEM patients. Whilst a recent meta-analysis in the first episode bipolar disorder identified deficits in verbal fluency, these were of small effect and were observed in only two studies (Lee et al. 2014). However, these studies had compared adult FEM patients to a poorly matched HC group in age, sex and/or education level (Nehra et al. 2006; Zanelli et al. 2010).

Furthermore, we identified that there were no impairments in most domains of executive function, except for cognitive flexibility. Cognitive inflexibility has been reported in the acute state of FEM (Fleck et al. 2008). Most studies on patients following FEM have reported that cognitive flexibility remained intact relative to HCs (Hellvin et al. 2012; López-Jaramillo et al. 2010; Torres et al. 2010), with the exception of Elshahawi et al. (2011) who identified deficits in cognitive flexibility during remission in patients who had FEM with psychotic features relative to HCs. Most studies in FEM during the acute state (Lebowitz et al. 2001) and in remission (López-Jaramillo et al. 2010; Torres et al. 2010) are in support of our finding that response inhibition is not impaired following FEM. The deficits in response inhibition identified by one study of FEM patients who were predominantly depressed at the time of testing may have been reflective of the ongoing mood symptoms (Hellvin et al. 2012). A study by Malhi et al. (2007) identified that depressed patients with bipolar disorder had significantly poorer response inhibition than HCs, a finding that was not observed for either the euthymic or hypomanic groups.

The decline in cognitive functioning with illness progression has been elucidated by studies comparing FEM patients to those with multiple episodes (Elshahawi et al. 2011; Hellvin et al. 2012; López-Jaramillo et al. 2010; Torres et al. 2010). Relative to findings of widespread cognitive impairments in people with chronic forms of bipolar disorder, our findings suggest that specific deficits in processing speed, verbal learning and memory, working memory and cognitive flexibility might occur from the early stages of the illness. It may be postulated that the impairments reported in attention, sustained attention, non-verbal memory, verbal fluency and other executive functions may result from recurrent episodes (Bora et al. 2009; Bourne et al. 2013; Mann-Wrobel et al. 2011; Torres et al. 2007), as reported deficits in these domains are largely inconsistent in studies in FEM (Daglas et al. 2015). Neuroimaging studies have provided evidence in support of neuroprogression in bipolar disorder, with findings of prefrontal, cerebellum volume and ventricular abnormalities seen in patients with recurrent episodes relative to first episode patients or HCs (DelBello et al. 1999; Mills et al. 2005; Strakowski et al. 2002). Some structural brain abnormalities pertaining to the subgenual prefrontal cortex, have also been identified early in the course of the illness, which may reflect the cognitive deficits in the specific domains observed by studies in FEM (Strakowski et al. 2005).

Amongst the strengths of this study is the relatively large sample size of a specified group of psychiatric patients recruited from a naturalistic treatment environment. Given the sample size, post hoc power analyses indicated that we had sufficient power at .80 to detect moderate to large effects when α was set at .05. Additionally, in this study we administered an extensive cognitive battery, which covered several cognitive domains and included computerised cognitive testing to increase sensitivity in identifying deficits. Importantly, the FEM participants were matched as closely as possible to the HC group in age and sex. We also attempted to match the groups as closely as possible on premorbid intelligence; however, the FEM group had an average premorbid intelligence score 6.8 lower than the HC. Although the between-group difference in premorbid intelligence was not statistically significant, it was of moderate effect and might have explained the differences between groups in specific cognitive domains. It was not possible to control for premorbid intelligence and other factors (e.g. education) in non-parametric analyses. However, it is argued, that clinically such a difference is not necessarily meaningful and both groups had mean premorbid intelligence scores that would be considered in the average or normal range. Also highlighted are the difficulties matching patient and healthy control groups on such variables.

Other limitations included that stabilisation from acute mania was based on clinical judgment without use of an objective mania cut-off score, and on average the FEM participants were mildly depressed. Medication effects may have influenced cognitive functioning; it would be methodologically ideal but ethically questionable to include a medication-naive group. Although this study utilised a catchment area service, the generalisability of our results is limited to individuals who had stabilised from a FEM with psychotic features, representing the more severe end of the bipolar spectrum. The findings of this study are also not generalisable to people following stabilisation from first episode mania on other medications. Additionally, this study did not exclude FEM participants with comorbidities such as substance abuse disorders, which may have impacted the findings. Also, due to the cross-sectional nature of this study, it is not possible to assess whether cognitive deficits existed prior to FEM.

Conclusions

Our findings revealed lower global intelligence in people following FEM may be evident prior to the onset of FEM, as well as specific cognitive deficits in processing speed, verbal learning and memory, working memory, and cognitive flexibility. These findings highlight the necessity of cognitive testing early in the course of the disorder. Amid the clinically relevant findings of this study, the differences observed in verbal learning and memory compared to non-verbal learning and memory may inform tailored interventions to address potential difficulties in functioning in people with FEM. Future research on the trajectory of cognitive functioning following FEM and the associated effects of treatment medications over time is warranted.

Authors' contributions

MB, MY, MKH, CAM, SMC and LPH were involved in the original study design and conduct of the project. RD, was a PhD candidate who collected the data, analysed the data and prepared the first draft of the paper; SMC was her principal supervisor and MB, KA,\ and MY were co-supervisors. All authors read and approved the final manuscript.

Author details

[1] Orygen, The National Centre of Excellence in Youth Mental Health, 35 Poplar Road, Parkville, VIC 3052, Australia. [2] Centre for Youth Mental Health, University of Melbourne, 35 Poplar Road, Parkville, VIC 3052, Australia. [3] Brain and Mental Health Laboratory, School of Psychological Sciences & Monash Biomedical Imaging Facility, Monash University, Clayton, Australia. [4] Orygen Youth Health-Clinical Program, 35 Poplar Road, Parkville 3052, Australia. [5] IMPACT Strategic Research Centre, School of Medicine, Deakin University, PO Box 281, Geelong 3220, Australia. [6] Barwon Health and the Geelong Clinic, Swanston Centre, PO Box 281, Geelong, VIC 3220, Australia. [7] Florey Institute for Neuroscience and Mental Health, Kenneth Myer Building, Royal Parade, Parkville, Australia.

Acknowledgements

None.

Competing interests

Sue Cotton is supported by a NHMRC Career Development Fellowship 1061998. Kelly Allott is supported by a Ronald Philip Griffiths Fellowship, The University of Melbourne. Murat Yücel is supported by a NHMRC Senior Research Fellowship 1021973. Michael Berk is supported by a NHMRC Senior Principal Research Fellowship 1059660, and has received Grant/Research Support from the NIH, Cooperative Research Centre, Simons Autism Foundation, Cancer Council of Victoria, Stanley Medical Research Foundation, MBF, NHMRC, Beyond Blue, Rotary Health, Geelong Medical Research Foundation, Bristol Myers Squibb, Eli Lilly, Glaxo SmithKline, Meat and Livestock Board, Organon, Novartis, Mayne Pharma, Servier and Woolworths, has been a speaker for Astra Zeneca, Bristol Myers Squibb, Eli Lilly, Glaxo SmithKline, Janssen Cilag, Lundbeck, Merck, Pfizer, Sanofi Synthelabo, Servier, Solvay and Wyeth, and served as a consultant to Astra Zeneca, Bioadvantex, Bristol Myers Squibb, Eli Lilly, Glaxo SmithKline, Janssen Cilag, Lundbeck Merck and Servier. For the remaining authors, none were declared. This article is the authors' original work, has not received prior publication, and is not under consideration for publication elsewhere.

Funding

This study involved baseline analyses from an RCT that received an investigator-initiated grant by AstraZeneca. This funding source had no influence on the study design and was not involved in data collection, data analysis and interpretation of the results.

References

Antila M, Tuulio-Henriksson A, Kieseppä T, Soronen P, Palo OM, Paunio T, Haukka J, Partonen T, Lönnqvist J. Heritability of cognitive functions in families with bipolar disorder. Am J Med Genet Part B Neuropsychiatr Genet. 2007;144B(6):802–8. doi:10.1002/ajmg.b.30538.

Arts B, Jabben N, Krabbendam L, van Os J. Meta-analyses of cognitive functioning in euthymic bipolar patients and their first-degree relatives. Psychol Med. 2008;38(6):771–85. doi:10.1017/S0033291707001675.

Barrett SL, Mulholland CC, Cooper SJ, Rushe TM. Patterns of neurocognitive impairment in first-episode bipolar disorder and schizophrenia. Br J Psychiatry. 2009;195(1):67–72. doi:10.1192/bjp.bp.108.054874.

Bora E, Pantelis C. Meta-analysis of cognitive impairment in first-episode bipolar disorder: comparison with first-episode schizophrenia and healthy controls. Schizophr Bull. 2015. doi:10.1093/schbul/sbu198.

Bora E, Yucel M, Pantelis C. Cognitive endophenotypes of bipolar disorder: a meta-analysis of neuropsychological deficits in euthymic patients and their first-degree relatives. J Affect Disord. 2009;113(1–2):1–20. doi:10.1016/j.jad.2008.06.009.

Bourne C, Aydemir Ö, Balanzá-Martínez V, Bora E, Brissos S, Cavanagh JT, Clark L, Cubukcuoglu Z, Dias VV, Dittmann S, Ferrier IN. Neuropsychological testing of cognitive impairment in euthymic bipolar disorder: an individual patient data meta-analysis. Acta Psychiatr Scand. 2013;128(3):149–62. doi:10.1111/acps.12133.

Brewer WJ, Francey SM, Wood SJ, Jackson HJ, Pantelis C, Phillips LJ, Yung AR, Anderson VA, McGorry PD. Memory impairments identified in people at ultra-high risk for psychosis who later develop first-episode psychosis. Am J Psychiatry. 2005;162(1):71–8. doi:10.1176/appi.ajp.162.1.71.

Coolican H. Research methods and statistics in psychology. London: Hodder; 2009.

Crowe SF. Does the letter number sequencing task measure anything more than digit span? Assessment. 2000;7(2):113–7.

Daglas R, Yucel M, Cotton S, Allott K, Hetrick S, Berk M. Cognitive impairment in first episode mania: a systematic review of the evidence. Int J Bipolar Disord. 2015;3:9. doi:10.1186/s40345-015-0024-2.

DelBello MP, Strakowski SM, Zimmerman ME, Hawkins JM, Sax KW. MRI analysis of the cerebellum in bipolar disorder: a pilot study. Neuropsychopharmacology. 1999;21(1):63–8. doi:10.1016/S0893-133X(99)00026-3.

Denicoff KD, Ali SO, Mirsky AF, Smith-Jackson EE, Leverich GS, Duncan CC, Connell EG, Post RM. Relationship between prior course of illness and neuropsychological functioning in patients with bipolar disorder. J Affect Disord. 1999;56(1):67–73.

Donaldson S, Goldstein LH, Landau S, Raymont V, Frangou S. The Maudsley Bipolar Disorder Project: the effect of medication, family history, and duration of illness on IQ and memory in bipolar I disorder. J Clin Psychiatry. 2003;64(1):86–93.

Elshahawi HH, Essawi H, Rabie MA, Mansour M, Beshry ZA, Mansour AN. Cognitive functions among euthymic bipolar I patients after a single manic episode versus recurrent episodes. J Affect Disord. 2011;130(1–2):180–91. doi:10.1016/j.jad.2010.10.027.

Fan J, McCandliss BD, Fossella J, Flombaum JI, Posner MI. The activation of attentional networks. Neuroimage. 2005;26(2):471–9. doi:10.1016/j.neuroimage.2005.02.004.

Fleck DE, Shear PK, Madore M, Strakowski SM. Wisconsin Card Sorting Test performance in bipolar disorder: effects of mood state and early course. Bipolar Disord. 2008;10(4):539–45. doi:10.1111/j.1399-5618.2008.00582.x.

Fritz CO, Morris PE, Richler JJ. Effect size estimates: current use, calculations, and interpretation. J Exp Psychol Gen. 2012;141(1):2–18. doi:10.1037/a0024338.

Ghaemi SN, Sachs GS, Chiou AM, Pandurangi AK, Goodwin K. Is bipolar disorder still underdiagnosed? Are antidepressants overutilized? J Affect Disord. 1999;52(1–3):135–44.

Hammers D, Spurgeon E, Ryan K, Persad C, Barbas N, Heidebrink J, Darby D, Giordani B. Validity of a brief computerized cognitive screening test in dementia. J Geriatr Psychiatry Neurol. 2012;25(2):89–99. doi:10.1177/0891988712447894.

Hammers D, Spurgeon E, Ryan K, Persad C, Heidebrink J, Barbas N, Albin R, Frey K, Darby D, Giordani B. Reliability of repeated cognitive assessment of dementia using a brief computerized battery. Am J Alzheimers Dis Other Dement. 2011;26(4):326–33. doi:10.1177/1533317511411907.

Haut MW, Kuwabara H, Leach S, Arias RG. Neural activation during performance of number–letter sequencing. Appl Neuropsychol. 2000;7(4):237–42. doi:10.1207/S15324826AN0704_5.

Hellvin T, Sundet K, Simonsen C, Aminoff SR, Lagerberg TV, Andreassen OA, Melle I. Neurocognitive functioning in patients recently diagnosed with bipolar disorder. Bipolar Disord. 2012;14(3):227–38. doi:10.1111/j.1399-5618.2012.01004.x.

Hill SK, Reilly JL, Harris MS, Rosen C, Marvin RW, Deleon O, Sweeney JA. A comparison of neuropsychological dysfunction in first-episode psychosis patients with unipolar depression, bipolar disorder, and schizophrenia. Schizophr Res. 2009;113(2–3):167–75. doi:10.1016/j.schres.2009.04.020.

Kennedy N, Everitt B, Boydell J, van Os J, Jones PB, Murray RM. Incidence and distribution of first-episode mania by age: results from a 35 year study. Psychol Med. 2005;35:855–63. doi:10.1017/S0033291704003307.

Lebowitz BK, Shear PK, Steed MA, Strakowski SM. Verbal fluency in mania: relationship to number of manic episodes. Neuropsychiatry Neuropsychol Behav Neurol. 2001;14(3):177–82.

Lee RS, Hermens DF, Scott J, Redoblado-Hodge MA, Naismith SL, Lagopoulos J, Griffiths KR, Porter MA, Hickie IB. A meta-analysis of neuropsychological functioning in first-episode bipolar disorders. J Psychiatr Res. 2014;57C:1–11. doi:10.1016/j.jpsychires.2014.06.019.

Lezak MD. Neuropsychological assessment. 2nd ed. New York: Oxford University Press; 1983.

López-Jaramillo C, Lopera-Vásquez J, Gallo A, Ospina-Duque J, Bell V, Torrent C, Martínez-Arán A, Vieta E. Effects of recurrence on the cognitive performance of patients with bipolar I disorder: implications for relapse prevention and treatment adherence. Bipolar Disord. 2010;12(5):557–67. doi:10.1111/j.1399-5618.2010.00835.x.

MacCabe JH, Lambe MP, Cnattingius S, Sham PC, David AS, Reichenberg A, Murray RM, Hultman CM. Excellent school performance at age 16 and risk of adult bipolar disorder: national cohort study. Br J Psychiatry. 2010;196(2):109–15. doi:10.1192/bjp.bp.108.060368.

Malhi GS, Ivanovski B, Hadzi-Pavlovic D, Mitchell PB, Vieta E, Sachdev P. Neuropsychological deficits and functional impairment in bipolar depression, hypomania and euthymia. Bipolar Disord. 2007;9(1–2):114–25. doi:10.1111/j.1399-5618.2007.00324.x.

Mann-Wrobel MC, Carreno JT, Dickinson D. Meta-analysis of neuropsychological functioning in euthymic bipolar disorder: an update and investigation of moderator variables. Bipolar Disord. 2011;13(4):334–42. doi:10.1111/j.1399-5618.2011.00935.x.

Mills NP, Delbello MP, Adler CM, Strakowski SM. MRI analysis of cerebellar vermal abnormalities in bipolar disorder. Am J Psychiatry. 2005;162(8):1530–2. doi:10.1176/appi.ajp.162.8.1530.

Mitrushina M, Boone KB, Razani J, D'Elia LF. Handbook of normative data for neuropsychological assessment. 2nd ed. New York: Oxford University Press; 2005.

Montgomery SA, Asberg M. A new depression scale designed to be sensitive to change. Br J Psychiatry. 1979;134:382–9.

Nehra R, Chakrabarti S, Pradhan BK, Khehra N. Comparison of cognitive functions between first- and multi-episode bipolar affective disorders. J Affect Disord. 2006;93(1–3):185–92. doi:10.1016/j.jad.2006.03.013.

Overall JE, Gorham DR. The brief psychiatric rating scale. Psychol Rep. 1962;10(3):799–812.

Reitan RM. The relation of the trail making test to organic brain damage. J Consult Psychol. 1955;19(5):393–4.

Rey A. L'examen clinique en psychologie. Paris: Presse Universitaire de France; 1958.

Schimmelmann BG, Conus P, Edwards J, McGorry PD, Lambert M. Diagnostic stability 18 months after treatment initiation for first-episode psychosis. J Clin Psychiatry. 2005;66(10):1239–46.

Snyder PJ, Werth J, Giordani B, Caveney AF, Feltner D, Maruff P. A method for determining the magnitude of change across different cognitive functions in clinical trials: the effects of acute administration of two different doses alprazolam. Hum Psychopharmacol. 2005;20(4):263–73. doi:10.1002/hup.692.

Spearing MK, Post RM, Leverich GS, Brandt D, Nolen W. Modification of the clinical global impressions (CGI) scale for use in bipolar illness (BP): the CGI-BP. Psychiatry Res. 1997;73(3):159–71.

Strakowski SM, Delbello MP, Adler CM. The functional neuroanatomy of bipolar disorder: a review of neuroimaging findings. Mol Psychiatry. 2005;10(1):105–16. doi:10.1038/sj.mp.4001585.

Strakowski SM, DelBello MP, Zimmerman ME, Getz GE, Mills NP, Ret J, Shear P, Adler CM. Ventricular and periventricular structural volumes in first- versus multiple-episode bipolar disorder. Am J Psychiatry. 2002;159(11):1841–7.

Takagi M, Lubman DI, Cotton S, Fornito A, Baliz Y, Tucker A, Yucel M. Executive control among adolescent inhalant and cannabis users. Drug Alcohol Rev. 2011;30(6):629–37. doi:10.1111/j.1465-3362.2010.00256.x.

The Psychological Corporation. Wechsler abbreviated scale of intelligence. San Antonio: Author; 1999.

The Psychological Corporation. Wechsler test of adult reading. San Antonio: Author; 2001.

Thompson JM, Gallagher P, Hughes JH, Watson S, Gray JM, Ferrier IN, Young AH. Neurocognitive impairment in euthymic patients with bipolar affective disorder. Br J Psychiatry. 2005;186:32–40. doi:10.1192/bjp.186.1.32.

Torres IJ, Boudreau VG, Yatham LN. Neuropsychological functioning in euthymic bipolar disorder: a meta-analysis. Acta Psychiatr Scand Suppl. 2007;434:17–26. doi:10.1111/j.1600-0447.2007.01055.x.

Torres IJ, DeFreitas VG, DeFreitas CM, Kauer-Sant'Anna M, Bond DJ, Honer WG, Lam RW, Yatham LN. Neurocognitive functioning in patients with bipolar I disorder recently recovered from a first manic episode. J Clin Psychiatry. 2010;71(9):1234–42. doi:10.4088/JCP.08m04997yel.

Wechsler D. Wechsler adult intelligence scale. 3rd ed. San Antonio: The Psychological Corporation; 1997.

Young RC, Biggs JT, Ziegler VE, Meyer DA. A rating scale for mania: reliability, validity and sensitivity. Br J Psychiatry. 1978;133:429–35.

Zanelli J, Reichenberg A, Morgan K, Fearon P, Kravariti E, Dazzan P, Morgan C, Zanelli C, Demjaha A, Jones PB, Doody GA, Kapur S, Murray RM. Specific and generalized neuropsychological deficits: a comparison of patients with various first-episode psychosis presentations. Am J Psychiatry. 2010;167(1):78–85. doi:10.1176/appi.ajp.2009.09010118.

5

The association between mood state and chronobiological characteristics in bipolar I disorder: a naturalistic, variable cluster analysis-based study

Robert Gonzalez[1*], Trisha Suppes[2], Jamie Zeitzer[2], Colleen McClung[3], Carol Tamminga[4], Mauricio Tohen[5], Angelica Forero[1], Alok Dwivedi[6] and Andres Alvarado[6]

Abstract

Background: Multiple types of chronobiological disturbances have been reported in bipolar disorder, including characteristics associated with general activity levels, sleep, and rhythmicity. Previous studies have focused on examining the individual relationships between affective state and chronobiological characteristics. The aim of this study was to conduct a variable cluster analysis in order to ascertain how mood states are associated with chronobiological traits in bipolar I disorder (BDI). We hypothesized that manic symptomatology would be associated with disturbances of rhythm.

Results: Variable cluster analysis identified five chronobiological clusters in 105 BDI subjects. Cluster 1, comprising subjective sleep quality was associated with both mania and depression. Cluster 2, which comprised variables describing the degree of rhythmicity, was associated with mania. Significant associations between mood state and cluster analysis-identified chronobiological variables were noted. Disturbances of mood were associated with subjectively assessed sleep disturbances as opposed to objectively determined, actigraphy-based sleep variables. No associations with general activity variables were noted. Relationships between gender and medication classes in use and cluster analysis-identified chronobiological characteristics were noted. Exploratory analyses noted that medication class had a larger impact on these relationships than the number of psychiatric medications in use.

Conclusions: In a BDI sample, variable cluster analysis was able to group related chronobiological variables. The results support our primary hypothesis that mood state, particularly mania, is associated with chronobiological disturbances. Further research is required in order to define these relationships and to determine the directionality of the associations between mood state and chronobiological characteristics.

Keywords: Bipolar disorder, Actigraphy, Rhythm, Sleep, Activity, Cluster analysis, Mood state

Background

Chronobiological disturbances are key features of bipolar disorder (Association AP 2013). Empirical data continue to mount implicating these disruptions as components of the pathophysiology of the illness (Gonzalez 2014). A significant body of research suggests a relationship between chronobiological disturbances and mood state in bipolar disorder. For example, disruptions of social rhythms have been associated with the emergence of affective episodes (Malkoff-Schwartz et al. 1998), particularly mania (Malkoff-Schwartz et al. 1998, 2000). A link between psychomotor activity and mood state has also been suggested (Wehr et al. 1980; Teicher 1995). Sleep disturbances have been shown to correlate with affective states (Eidelman et al. 2010) and increased symptom

*Correspondence: Robert99.Gonzalez@ttuhsc.edu; r2gonz@rocketmail.com
[1] Department of Psychiatry, Texas Tech University Health Sciences Center El Paso, El Paso, TX, USA
Full list of author information is available at the end of the article

severity (Eidelman et al. 2010; Gruber et al. 2009) and may increase the susceptibility toward developing mania (Bunney et al. 1972; Sitaram et al. 1978). Chronobiological disruptions of physiological functioning have also been noted in relation to affective states in bipolar disorder (Pflug et al. 1981).

Multiple models have been proposed to explain the chronobiological disruptions associated with bipolar disorder (Gonzalez 2014). Some of the most compelling evidence indicates an inherent instability in the biological rhythms of those suffering from the illness. In support of this premise is the wide degree of variability in biological rhythms that has been reported in bipolar disorder (Pflug et al. 1981; Krane-Gartiser et al. 2014; Jones et al. 2005). This variability has been observed in the psychomotor activity patterns related to the illness. For example, patients suffering from bipolar disorder demonstrate greater variability (Krane-Gartiser et al. 2014; Jones et al. 2005), less stable rhythmicity (Krane-Gartiser et al. 2014; Jones et al. 2005), greater fragmentation (Jones et al. 2005), and lower relative activity amplitude (Rock et al. 2014) in locomotor activity when compared to controls. Disturbances in the rhythmic expression of locomotor activity have also been reported in affective states in bipolar disorder (Salvatore et al. 2008; Gonzalez et al. 2014). Prior research has demonstrated that a greater severity of manic symptoms is related to less robust locomotor activity rhythms (Gonzalez et al. 2014). These findings have led some to hypothesize that less robust rhythms are a predisposing factor toward developing mood state symptomatology in patients suffering from affective disorders (Reinberg et al. 2007).

Various chronobiological disturbances have been reported in bipolar disorder, including characteristics associated with general activity levels, sleep, and rhythmicity. There is a paucity of research examining how these variables are interrelated and how they are collectively associated with clinical characteristics of the illness. Variable cluster analysis is a method for grouping variables based on the similarity of their characteristics and identifies the most representative variables in clusters. This statistical approach is a dimension reduction technique, similar in approach to principal component analysis. Variable cluster analysis not only identifies the interrelationships between variables, but also overcomes the problem of interpretation related to principal component analysis. The identification of subgroups via general cluster analysis is relatively common. For example, cluster analysis has been used to identify patient subgroups in affective disorders based on chronobiological characteristics in order to determine relationships with physiological markers of rhythmicity (Carpenter et al. 2017). However, no previous studies have used a variable cluster analysis approach to determine the most salient chronobiological characteristics among a large dimension of variables in association with mood state. While previous studies have focused on the individual relationships between affective state and chronobiological characteristics, to the best of our knowledge, no study has yet to assess how these different types of chronobiological disturbances may be interrelated in their association with mood state. The aim of this study was, therefore, to conduct a variable cluster analysis in order to ascertain how chronobiological traits collectively are associated with affect. Our goal in conducting a variable cluster analysis was also to reduce the number of related variables associated with mood state and to determine the chronobiological markers most representative of these relationships. Based on our previous study that demonstrated a relationship between a lower degree of robustness in the rhythmicity of psychomotor activity and the severity of mania (Gonzalez et al. 2014), we hypothesized that a greater degree of manic symptomatology is associated disturbances of rhythm.

Methods

Study description

The protocol is a 1-week naturalistic study designed to assess chronobiological characteristics using actigraphy and clinical measures in bipolar I disorder (BDI) subjects under ambulatory conditions.

Subjects

DSM-IV-TR Axis I diagnosis of BDI was confirmed by the Structured Clinical Interview for DSM-IV Axis I Disorders (SCID-I/P) (Ventura et al. 1998) or Mini International Neuropsychiatric Interview (MINI) (Sheehan et al. 1998). Subjects with a history of neurological impairment or uncontrolled medical conditions with the potential to disrupt biological rhythms, current use of hypnotic agents for sleep, and a history of substance abuse or dependence 1 month prior to study participation were excluded from the study. Subjects with current lifestyle demands (i.e., work, school) requiring shift work or diurnal changes in work schedule and those undergoing travel involving three or more time zones occurring 4 weeks prior to or during the course of the study were also excluded from the participation. Patients were recruited from county and community hospitals, university medical centers, and community mental health clinics between the dates of March 2009 to January 2016. The study was approved by the University of Texas Southwestern Medical Center, University of Texas Health Sciences Center San Antonio, and Texas Tech University Health Sciences Center El Paso institutional review boards and was consistent with standard for the ethical conduct of human research. Written informed consent was obtained for all subjects. In addition to the previous reported sample (Gonzalez et al. 2014), an additional 63 BDI subjects were included for analysis. Given the increased number of variables assessed and in order to ensure consistency, analyses defining chronobiological characteristics were conducted de novo in all subjects.

Demographic and clinical characteristics

For purposes of cofactor analysis, information regarding age, gender, and current medication status, including the classes of medications currently in use, was collected. The severity of manic and depressive symptoms was defined by using the Young Mania Rating Scale (Young et al. 1978) and 30-Item Inventory of Depressive Symptomatology (Rush et al. 1996), respectively.

Clinical assessments of sleep and rhythm

Clinical assessments were also used to assess sleep and rhythm characteristics. These included the 5-Item Social Rhythm Metric (SRM-5) (Monk et al. 2002), designed to capture the degree of lifestyle regularity, and the Pittsburgh Sleep Quality Index (PSQI) (Buysse et al. 1989) that characterizes general sleep health (PSQI scores > 5 are associated with disrupted sleep). Sleep diaries were collected to help confirm estimated sleep periods (Gonzalez et al. 2013).

Actigraphy

Basic Motionlogger actigraph units (Ambulatory Monitoring, Inc., Ardsley, NY) were used to collect data regarding locomotor activity. Subjects wore actigraph units on the non-dominant wrist. Data were recorded in proportional integral mode (PIM) and sampled in 60-s epochs. Summary statistics characterizing psychomotor activity, sleep parameters, and rhythmicity were calculated from the raw motor activity data using Action 4 circadian rhythm analysis software and Action W-2 software (Ambulatory Monitoring, Inc., Ardsley, NY).

Summary statistics assessing the intensity and rate of change of physical activity included *activity mean* (average daily minutes of physical activity), *activity median* (median daily minutes of physical activity), *acceleration index* (change in activity rate during interval; an estimate of physical activity intensity), and *activity index* (percentage of time in minutes where activity levels were recorded at greater than zero). Sleep-based statistics included *sleep percent* (average of the percentage of minutes scored as sleep), and *sleep efficiency* (proportion of the total sleep time to time in bed), and *average daily sleep time* (sleep time; average daily minutes scored as sleep). Rhythm-based variables included *amplitude* (difference between the peak and the mean activity values as determined via cosinor analysis), *mesor* (circadian rhythm-adjusted mean activity value based on cosinor analysis), *circadian quotient* (CQ; cosinor analysis-based amplitude to mesor ratio; an estimation of how well circumscribed periods of activity are during the course of the day and used as a proxy for the robustness of rhythms), *goodness-of-fit* (GOF; measure of how well the activity data fits the cosine function which can be taken as an indicator of strength of rhythm), and *24-h correlation* (autocorrelation of a time series with its own past and future values that may be taken as an indicator of the degree of rhythmicity), *interdaily stability* (IS; the stability of activity rhythm between days), *intradaily variability* (IV; fragmentation of activity within a 24-h period), and *relative amplitude* (RA; average for the ratio of the most active 10-h period and least active 5-h period).

Statistical analysis

Descriptive statistics were generated for demographic and sample characteristics, actigraphic assessments, and clinical scales. Quantitative variables were described using mean and standard deviation (SD). Categorical variables were summarized using frequencies and percentages.

In order to reduce the dimension and determine clustering of chronobiological variables, a variable cluster analysis (proc varclus) was conducted. Cluster scores were generated using the standardized scores for the chronobiological variables and the coefficients obtained from the principal component method. The representative variable for each cluster (smallest $1-R^2$ within each cluster) was also identified. Ordinary linear regression analyses adjusting for age, gender, and medication classes in use (lithium, anticonvulsants, antidepressants, antipsychotics, and benzodiazepines) were conducted to determine the associations between mood state, as defined by YMRS and IDS-30-C scores, and identified clusters. To assess the relationships between mood state and variable cluster analysis-identified chronobiological characteristics, both Pearson's correlations and adjusted linear regression analyses were conducted. In order to determine the effects of multiple testing, these analyses were also conducted with all 17 chronobiological variables considered individually. Benjamini–Hochberg procedure was used to adjust for false-positive probability in the adjusted linear regression modeling. All the statistical analyses were carried out using SAS 9.4. *p* values less than or equal to 5% were considered as significant variables.

Results

Sample characteristics

A total of 105 BDI subjects were included for analysis. Sample characteristics are summarized in Table 1. The

Table 1 Sample characteristics

	Mean ± standard deviation or *N* (%)
Demographic characteristics	
Age (in years)	41.20 ± 11.34
Gender	
Female	66 (62.86%)
Male	39 (37.14%)
Race	
Caucasian	57 (54.29%)
Hispanic	35 (33.33%)
African-American	13 (12.38%)
Clinical characteristics	
Mood state	
YMRS	14.62 ± 9.27
IDS-30-C	24.52 ± 12.18
Psychiatric medication status	
Medicated	90 (86.54%)
Unmedicated	14 (13.64%)
Lithium	19 (18.10%)
Anticonvulsants	56 (53.33%)
Antidepressants	45 (42.86%)
Antipsychotics	55 (52.38%)
Benzodiazepines	26 (24.76%)
Actigraphic assessments	
Interdaily stability (IS)	0.52 ± 0.15
Intradaily variability (IV)	0.67 ± 0.20
Relative amplitude (RA)	0.80 ± 0.14
Goodness-of-fit (GOF)	0.46 ± 0.13
Sleep efficiency	66.02 ± 13.55
Sleep percent	31.42 ± 7.08
Average daily sleep time (in hours)	7.49 ± 2.19
24-h correlation	0.25 ± 0.13
Mesor	2925.24 ± 1604.64
Amplitude	2159.33 ± 1235.05
Circadian quotient (CQ)	0.74 ± 0.17
Activity mean	2843.84 ± 1565.51
Activity median	1852.60 ± 1614.06
Acceleration index	38.26 ± 115.35
Activity index	65.48 ± 29.87
Clinical chronobiological assessments	
5-Item Social Rhythm Metric (SRM-5)	3.79 ± 1.30
Pittsburgh Sleep Quality Index (PSQI)	10.30 ± 4.04

Summarizes the sample characteristics. This includes demographic information, clinical characteristics, and actigraphic measurements

YMRS Young Mania Rating Scale, *IDS-30-C* 30-Item Inventory of Depressive Symptomatology

cohort was mostly middle-aged, Caucasian, and female, with most participants being on psychiatric medications during the study. The average YMRS and IDS-30-C scores were 17.44 ± 9.16 and 23.80 ± 11.61, respectively. This reflects mania in the mild-to-moderate range and depression of moderate severity. The mean PSQI and SRM-5 scores were 10.30 ± 4.04 and 3.79 ± 1.30, respectively. The majority of the sample (91.35%) had a PSQI score > 5 which is indicative of disrupted sleep. The mean observational period was 7.5 days. Subjects were taking a mean of 1.95 ± 1.13 psychiatric medications (median = 2, minimum = 0, maximum = 4).

Clustering of chronobiological markers

Variable cluster analysis identified five cluster groups (Table 2). Cluster groups were characterized by subjective sleep disruption (Cluster 1), the rhythmicity and regularity of daily activity patterns (Cluster 2), rate of change and magnitude of movement (Cluster 3), objective measurements of sleep (Cluster 4), and the fitted daily activity amplitude, activity levels and fragmentation of activity within a 24-h period (Cluster 5). The most representative variables for Clusters 1 through 5 were PSQI, IS, acceleration index, sleep time, and mesor, respectively. The variation and proportion explained by the five clusters was 12.77 and 75.0%, respectively.

Relationships between mood state and identified clusters

After adjusting for age, gender, and medication class, Cluster 1, comprising solely PSQI, was positively associated with both YMRS (RC = 0.027, $p = 0.012$) and IDS-30-C (RC = 0.024, $p = 0.005$) scores. Cluster 2 was negatively associated with YMRS scores (RC = − 0.033, $p = 0.0001$). In addition, female gender was associated with increased Cluster 2 score (RC = 0.461, $p = 0.016$).

Associations between mood state and individual chronobiological characteristics

The results from analyses assessing the relationship between mood state and cluster analysis-identified chronobiological variables are represented in Table 3. On unadjusted Pearson's correlations, YMRS was negatively correlated with all variable cluster analysis-identified variables and IDS-30-C was associated with PSQI. After adjusting for age, gender, and medication class, YMRS was negatively associated with IS, RA, GOF, CQ, and PSQI with a trend toward association with SRM-5. IDS-30-C was positively associated with PSQI. After correcting for possible false discovery rate, YMRS remained significantly associated with IS, RA, CQ with a trend toward significance with PSQI. IDS-30-C remained associated with PSQI. In this modeling, associations between variable cluster analysis-identified chronobiological characteristics and both gender and medication class were noted (Table 4). A positive association was noted with female gender. Lithium was positively associated with several markers of rhythm. Antidepressants

Table 2 Cluster analysis results

Cluster	Variable	Standardized scoring coefficients	*R*-squared with		$1-R^2$	Variation explained by clusters	Proportion explained by clusters
			Own Cluster	Next Closest	Ratio		
Cluster 1	PSQI	1.00	1.00	0.08	*0.00**	6.12	0.36
Cluster 2	IS	0.23	0.84	0.25	*0.22**	8.6	0.51
	RA	0.21	0.69	0.16	0.37		
	GOF	0.24	0.86	0.48	0.28		
	24-h correlation	0.22	0.74	0.40	0.43		
	CQ	0.20	0.61	0.21	0.49		
	SRM-5	0.11	0.18	0.05	0.87		
Cluster 3	Acceleration index	0.53	0.90	0.01	*0.10**	10.36	0.61
	Activity index	– 0.53	0.90	0.04	0.11		
Cluster 4	Sleep efficiency	0.31	0.38	0.07	0.66	11.87	0.70
	Sleep percent	0.45	0.82	0.21	0.23		
	Sleep time	0.45	0.80	0.05	*0.21**		
Cluster 5	IV	0.24	0.44	0.28	0.77	12.77	0.75
	Mesor	0.23	0.95	0.15	*0.05**		
	Amplitude	0.23	0.88	0.39	0.20		
	Activity mean	0.23	0.91	0.13	0.11		
	Activity median	– 0.16	0.88	0.16	0.14		

The results of the principal components-based cluster analysis (proc varclus) of chronobiological variables. Five cluster groups were identified. Summarized are the variables that comprise the clusters, the standardized scoring coefficients, and the representative chronobiological variables for each cluster (smallest $1-R^2$ within each cluster). * and italic font denotes most representative variable in the cluster. Presented are the values for the variation and proportion of the variation explained in the sample based on the number of chronobiological clusters considered. Demonstrated are the variation and proportion of variation explained in the sample when considering successive clusters. The total variation and total proportion of the sample explained when including all five clusters were 12.77 and 75.00%, respectively

IS interdaily stability, *IV* intradaily variability, *RA* relative amplitude, *CQ* circadian quotient, *GOF* goodness-of-fit, *SRM-5* 5-Item Social Rhythm Metric, *PSQI* Pittsburgh Sleep Quality Index

Table 3 Relationships between mood and cluster analysis-identified chronobiological characteristics

Variables	YMRS			IDS-30-C		
	Unadjusted correlations *r* (*p* value)	Adjusted linear regression RC (*p* value)	BHC *p* value	Unadjusted correlations *r* (*p* value)	Adjusted linear regression RC (*p* value)	BHC *p* value
IS	*– 0.331 (0.0007)**	*– 0.004 (0.005)**	*0.030**	0.0005 (0.995)	0.001 (0.25)	0.956
RA	*– 0.391 (< 0.0001)**	*– 0.005 (0.0003)**	*0.0021**	– 0.064 (0.523)	0.001 (0.268)	0.956
GOF	*– 0.333 (0.0006)**	*– 0.003 (0.017)**	0.051[a]	– 0.099 (0.32)	– 0.00 (0.956)	0.956
CQ	*– 0.217 (0.027)**	*– 0.005 (0.006)**	*0.030**	0.057 (0.565)	0.002 (0.181)	0.956
24-h correlation	*– 0.317 (0.001)**	– 0.003 (0.623)	0.623	– 0.152 (0.124)	– 0.00 (0.623)	0.956
SRM-5	*– 0.218 (0.0325)**	– 0.026 (0.09)[a]	0.180	– 0.038 (0.696)	0.004 (0.741)	0.956
PSQI	*0.351 (0.0003)**	*0.111 (0.012)**	*0.048**	*0.396 (< 0.0001)**	*0.099 (0.005)**	*0.035**

The relationships between mood rating scale scores and variables characterizing biorhythms. Unadjusted correlations as well as linear regression results adjusted for age, gender, and medication class use (lithium, anticonvulsants, antidepressants, antipsychotics, benzodiazepines) are shown. *r* denotes correlation coefficient and RC denotes regression coefficient

IS interdaily stability, *IV* intradaily variability, *RA* relative amplitude, *CQ* circadian quotient, *GOF* goodness-of-fit, *SRM-5* 5-Item Social Rhythm Metric, *PSQI* Pittsburgh Sleep Quality Index, *YMRS* Young Mania Rating Scale, *IDS-30-C* 30-Item Inventory of Depressive Symptomatology. *BHC* Benjamini–Hochberg Correction for multiple testing

* and italic font denotes statistical significance

[a] Denotes a trend toward significance

demonstrated negative associations with rhythm markers and positive associations with PSQI scores. Both variable cluster analysis and individual variable analyses identified the same associations between mood state and chronobiological characteristics (Additional file 1: Table S1). Given the reduction in the number of variables, the variable cluster analysis approach proved to be more powerful when correcting for false discovery rate. Since subjects were on a variable number of medications, exploratory analyses were conducted to assess the impact that the number of medications had on the expression of chronobiological variables. These analyses demonstrated that the class of psychiatric medication used had a greater effect on the associations between mood state and chronobiological characteristics than did the number of medications currently in use (Additional file 2: Table S2).

Discussion

To the best of our knowledge, this is the first study to examine the application of variable cluster analysis in determining the relationships between mood state and chronobiological characteristics in BDI. Variable cluster analysis was able to successfully identify and cluster chronobiological variables with related characteristics. A strength of this approach was highlighted by the ability of the variable cluster analysis to group variables characterizing similar phenomena even with variables being calculated via different mathematical models and algorithms (Ancoli-Israel et al. 2003). By implementing a variable cluster analysis, the number of targeted variables was able to be significantly reduced. This reduction in the number of variables increased the power to detect significant associations between mood state and chronobiological variables secondary to the more favorable multiple testing adjustment profile. Furthermore, this technique was able to identify the most representative variables associated with their respective clusters.

The findings of this study support our overarching hypothesis that mania is associated with disturbances of rhythm. Cluster 2, which comprised variables describing the robustness and degree of rhythmicity, was associated with mania. While all six variables in Cluster 2 demonstrated associations with mania, two of these variables may be of particular importance. IS was significantly associated with YMRS scores in all analyses and was identified by cluster analysis as the most representative variable in its cluster. Lower IS has been associated with bipolar disorder subjects as compared to controls (Jones et al. 2005) with evidence suggesting that this actigraphy variable may have predictive value for determining the risk of relapse (Novak et al. 2014). A recent study also identified IS as a potential phenotype in bipolar disorder pedigrees with an associated locus on chromosome 12 (Pagani et al. 2016). RA was also significantly associated with YMRS scores on all analyses. This variable demonstrated the highest degree of significance in association with mania. A lower RA has been reported in bipolar disorder subjects as compared to controls (Rock et al. 2014; Ng et al. 2015) and in individuals at risk for developing the illness (Ankers and Jones 2009).

Study findings also showed associations between mood state and subjective assessments of sleep. Cluster 1, comprising subjective sleep quality as measured via PSQI,

Table 4 Associations between cofactors and chronobiological variables

	IS RC (*p* value)	RA RC (*p* value)	GOF RC (*p* value)	CQ RC (*p* value)	24-h correlation RC (*p* value)	SRM-5 RC (*p* value)	PSQI RC (*p* value)
Medications							
Li	0.07 (0.054)[a]	0.06 (0.082)[a]	*0.07 (0.037)**	0.04 (0.377)	*0.07 (0.023)**	0.11 (0.725)	1.57 (0.127)
AC	− 0.03 (0.20)	− 0.03 (0.255)	− 0.02 (0.335)	0.008 (0.806)	− 0.03 (0.228)	− 0.06 (0.813)	− 0.18 (0.821)
AD	− 0.05 (0.078)[a]	*− 0.07 (0.004)**	*− 0.05 (0.031)**	− 0.04 (0.178)	*− 0.05 (0.03)**	− 0.39 (0.128)	1.46 (0.07)[a]
AP	0.00 (0.974)	0.02 (0.322)	− 0.02 (0.355)	− 0.03 (0.322)	− 0.03 (0.168)	0.05 (0.859)	− 0.37 (0.646)
BZD	− 0.03 (0.378)	− 0.03 (0.295)	− 0.01 (0.691)	− 0.01 (0.766)	− 0.01 (0.751)	− 0.42 (0.15)	1.24 (0.176)
Other covariates							
Age	0.0004 (0.75)	− 0.001 (0.198)	− 0.0003 (0.769)	− 0.0002 (0.86)	− 0.001 (0.272)	0.014 (0.19)	0.042 (0.235)
Gender (female)	*0.074 (0.015)**	0.052 (0.062)[a]	*0.072 (0.004)**	*0.09 (0.007)**	*0.054 (0.034)**	0.172 (0.517)	0.23 (0.779)

The table highlights the associations between cofactors and chronobiological variables identified via cluster analysis. Results are presented as regression coefficients (RC) and associated *p* values

Li lithium, *AC* anticonvulsants, *AD* antidepressants, *AP* antipsychotics, *BZD* benzodiazepines. *IS* interdaily stability, *IV* intradaily variability, *RA* relative amplitude, *CQ* circadian quotient, *GOF* goodness-of-fit, *SRM-5* 5-Item Social Rhythm Metric, *PSQI* Pittsburgh Sleep Quality Index

* and italic font denotes statistical significance

[a] Denotes a trend toward significance

was associated with both mania and depression. While subjectively assessed sleep disturbances were associated with the severity of affective symptoms, no associations between objectively determined, actigraphy-based sleep variables and affective states were noted. Although contrary to some previous reports (Eidelman et al. 2010a, b; Gruber et al. 2009; Hudson et al. 1992), our findings are in line with research demonstrating a discrepancy between objective and subjective assessments of sleep in patients suffering from bipolar disorder (Gonzalez et al. 2013; Harvey et al. 2005; Armitage et al. 1997; Rotenberg et al. 2000; Tsuchiyama et al. 2003) and suggest that rhythm disturbances may be a more robust characteristic of the disorder than sleep disturbances (Jones et al. 2005).

In our sample, we found no relationships between mood state and variables characterizing intensity or rate of change of activity. While not in accord with some previous studies (Wehr et al. 1980; Teicher 1995; Klein et al. 1992), the findings suggest, as other investigators have reported, that it is a less robust rhythm of psychomotor activity that is a key characteristic of the illness (Krane-Gartiser et al. 2014; Jones et al. 2005; Rock et al. 2014) and one which is associated with mania (Gonzalez et al. 2014).

The results also point to additional factors that may impact the expression of biological rhythms in bipolar disorder. For example, relationships between gender and chronobiological characteristics were demonstrated. Given other studies which suggest that gender and chronobiological characteristics can mediate the expression of mood disorders (White et al. 2016), further research is required to determine these relationships. Psychiatric medications can significantly alter chronobiology in this clinical population (Dallaspezia and Benedetti 2015). Our findings indicate that medication class, more than the number of medications in use, accounted for these effects. Results from statistical modeling testing the relationships between mood state and cluster analysis-identified chronobiological variables noted that lithium may have a stabilizing effect on rhythms while antidepressants may have the opposite effect (Dallaspezia and Benedetti 2015). Lithium has been found to lengthen the circadian periods (Johnsson et al. 1983). These relationships may have clinical and therapeutic implications. For example, in patients suffering from bipolar depression, lithium has been associated with phase delays (Campbell et al. 1989). In addition, bipolar patients with a shorter circadian period may respond positively to lithium (Kripke et al. 1978). Lithium may also exert its therapeutic effects by decreasing the sensitivity of melatonin secretion to nocturnal light exposure (Hallam et al. 2005). Some antidepressants have been shown to cause phase advancements (Sprouse et al. 2006) and shorten circadian periods (Nomura et al. 2008). Antidepressants, however, can have a variable impact on chronobiology (Duncan 1996). Interestingly, antidepressants that cause phase delays have been associated with improvements in sleep continuity (Duncan 1996).

Limitations and future directions

While promising, these results must be viewed in the context of the studies limitations and with an eye on future areas of research. A primary study limitation is the cross-sectional design that does not allow us to infer causal relationships between rhythm disturbances and mood state. Longitudinal studies are, therefore, required to determine the directionality and the temporal relationship between mood and chronobiological characteristics in bipolar disorder. Some limitations are associated with the naturalistic design of the study. Subsequent studies should more carefully account for clinical and demographic characteristics, such as social schedules (i.e., school and or employment, family responsibilities, weekend or holiday schedules) and clinical factors (i.e., body mass index), which may impact chronobiology in the illness. The use of psychiatric medications is also a limitation of the study. While we were able to account for the medication class and number of psychiatric medications used, we were not able to examine dosages or the complexity of medication regimens. Since various psychiatric medications can alter chronobiological functioning (Duncan 1996), future research should aim to address this limitation. Also, it should be noted that rhythmicity of locomotor activity is only considered a proxy for circadian rhythmicity. More definitive studies (Hida et al. 2012) are, therefore, required to fully characterize physiological markers of circadian rhythms.

Conclusions

Variable cluster analysis proved to be a statistical methodology able to group chronobiological variables based on related characteristics in BDI. These clusters and the individual markers comprising them were able to demonstrate relationships with affective symptomatology. The findings of the present study are in line with a growing body of literature identifying a relationship between chronobiological disturbances and bipolar disorder. The results support our primary hypothesis that mania is associated with rhythm disturbances. Both depression and mania were also associated with subjective assessments of sleep. The findings also suggest that other demographic and clinical characteristics, such as gender and psychiatric medication use, may affect the relationship between chronobiology and mood state. Further research is required in order to define these relationships and to determine the directionality of the associations between mood state and chronobiological disruptions in bipolar disorder.

Abbreviations

BDI: bipolar I disorder; IS: interdaily stability; IV: intradaily variability; RA: relative amplitude; CQ: circadian quotient; GOF: goodness-of-fit; SRM-5: 5-Item Social Rhythm Metric; PSQI: Pittsburgh Sleep Quality Index; YMRS: Young Mania Rating Scale; IDS-30-C: 30-Item Inventory of Depressive Symptomatology; *r*: correlation coefficient; RC: regression coefficient.

Authors' contributions

RG is the principal investigator of this research protocol. He was involved in the project design, statistical analysis, sample recruitment and assessment. He is the corresponding and primary author of this manuscript. TS and CM contributed to the study design and contributed to the preparation of the manuscript. JZ contributed to the analysis of the data interpretation to the preparation of the manuscript. CT and MT assisted in the protocol implementation and sample recruitment. AF conducted subject assessments and data collection and assisted with analysis of actigraphy data. AD and AA conducted the statistical analysis and participated in manuscript preparation. All authors read and approved the final manuscript.

Author details

[1] Department of Psychiatry, Texas Tech University Health Sciences Center El Paso, El Paso, TX, USA. [2] VA Palo Alto Health Care System, Department of Psychiatry and Behavioral Sciences, Stanford University School of Medicine, Palo Alto, CA, USA. [3] Department of Psychiatry, University of Pittsburgh Medical Center, Pittsburgh, PA, USA. [4] Department of Psychiatry, University of Texas, Southwestern Medical School, Dallas, TX, USA. [5] Department of Psychiatry, University of New Mexico Medical School, Albuquerque, NM, USA. [6] Department of Biomedical Sciences, Texas Tech University Health Sciences Center El Paso, El Paso, TX, USA.

Competing interests

The authors declare that they have no competing interests.

Funding

The study was funded by the Brain and Behavior Foundation (NARSAD Young Investigator Award), two National Institutes of Mental Health Grants (T32-MH067543-05 and RO1-MH0698567), and institutional funds (allocated to Dr. Gonzalez) made available through Texas Tech University Health Sciences Center El Paso. The funding sources played no role in conceptualizing or designing the research project, analyzing or interpreting the data, or in drafting the manuscript.

References

Ancoli-Israel S, Cole R, Alessi C, Chambers M, Moorcroft W, Pollak CP. The role of actigraphy in the study of sleep and circadian rhythms. Sleep. 2003;26(3):342–92.

Ankers D, Jones SH. Objective assessment of circadian activity and sleep patterns in individuals at behavioural risk of hypomania. J Clin Psychol. 2009;65(10):1071–86.

Armitage R, Trivedi M, Hoffmann R, Rush AJ. Relationship between objective and subjective sleep measures in depressed patients and healthy controls. Depress Anxiety. 1997;5(2):97–102.

Association AP. Diagnostic and statistical manual of mental disorders. 5th ed. Arlington: American Psychiatric Publishing; 2013.

Bunney WE Jr, Goodwin FK, Murphy DL, House KM, Gordon EK. The "switch process" in manic-depressive illness. II. Relationship to catecholamines, REM sleep, and drugs. Arch Gen Psychiatry. 1972;27(3):304–9.

Buysse DJ, Reynolds CF 3rd, Monk TH, Berman SR, Kupfer DJ. The Pittsburgh Sleep Quality Index: a new instrument for psychiatric practice and research. Psychiatry Res. 1989;28(2):193–213.

Campbell SS, Gillin JC, Kripke DF, Janowsky DS, Risch SC. Lithium delays circadian phase of temperature and REM sleep in a bipolar depressive: a case report. Psychiatry Res. 1989;27(1):23–9.

Carpenter JS, Robillard R, Hermens DF, Naismith SL, Gordon C, Scott EM, et al. Sleep-wake profiles and circadian rhythms of core temperature and melatonin in young people with affective disorders. J Psychiatr Res. 2017;94:131–8.

Dallaspezia S, Benedetti F. Chronobiology of bipolar disorder: therapeutic implication. Curr Psychiatry Rep. 2015;17(8):606.

Duncan WC Jr. Circadian rhythms and the pharmacology of affective illness. Pharmacol Ther. 1996;71(3):253–312.

Eidelman P, Talbot LS, Gruber J, Harvey AG. Sleep, illness course, and concurrent symptoms in inter-episode bipolar disorder. J Behav Ther Exp Psychiatry. 2010a;41(2):145–9.

Eidelman P, Talbot LS, Gruber J, Hairston I, Harvey AG. Sleep architecture as correlate and predictor of symptoms and impairment in inter-episode bipolar disorder: taking on the challenge of medication effects. J Sleep Res. 2010b;19(4):516–24.

Gonzalez R. The relationship between bipolar disorder and biological rhythms. J Clin Psychiatry. 2014;75(4):e323–31.

Gonzalez R, Tamminga C, Tohen M, Suppes T. Comparison of objective and subjective assessments of sleep time in subjects with bipolar disorder. J Affect Disord. 2013;149:363–6.

Gonzalez R, Tamminga CA, Tohen M, Suppes T. The relationship between affective state and the rhythmicity of activity in bipolar disorder. J Clin Psychiatry. 2014;75(4):e317–22.

Gruber J, Harvey AG, Wang PW, Brooks JO 3rd, Thase ME, Sachs GS, et al. Sleep functioning in relation to mood, function, and quality of life at entry to the Systematic Treatment Enhancement Program for Bipolar Disorder (STEP-BD). J Affect Disord. 2009;114(1–3):41–9.

Hallam KT, Olver JS, Horgan JE, McGrath C, Norman TR. Low doses of lithium carbonate reduce melatonin light sensitivity in healthy volunteers. Int J Neuropsychopharmacol. 2005;8(2):255–9.

Harvey AG, Schmidt DA, Scarna A, Semler CN, Goodwin GM. Sleep-related functioning in euthymic patients with bipolar disorder, patients with insomnia, and subjects without sleep problems. Am J Psychiatry. 2005;162(1):50–7.

Hida A, Kitamura S, Mishima K. Pathophysiology and pathogenesis of circadian rhythm sleep disorders. J Physiol Anthropol. 2012;31:7.

Hudson JI, Lipinski JF, Keck PE Jr, Aizley HG, Lukas SE, Rothschild AJ, et al. Polysomnographic characteristics of young manic patients. Comparison with unipolar depressed patients and normal control subjects. Arch Gen Psychiatry. 1992;49(5):378–83.

Johnsson A, Engelmann W, Pflug B, Klemke W. Period lengthening of human circadian rhythms by lithium carbonate, a prophylactic for depressive disorders. Int J Chronobiol. 1983;8(3):129–47.

Jones SH, Hare DJ, Evershed K. Actigraphic assessment of circadian activity and sleep patterns in bipolar disorder. Bipolar Disord. 2005;7(2):176–86.

Klein E, Lavie P, Meiraz R, Sadeh A, Lenox RH. Increased motor activity and recurrent manic episodes: predictors of rapid relapse in remitted bipolar disorder patients after lithium discontinuation. Biol Psychiatry. 1992;31(3):279–84.

Krane-Gartiser K, Henriksen TE, Morken G, Vaaler A, Fasmer OB. Actigraphic assessment of motor activity in acutely admitted inpatients with bipolar disorder. PLoS ONE. 2014;9(2):e89574.

Kripke DF, Mullaney DJ, Atkinson M, Wolf S. Circadian rhythm disorders in manic-depressives. Biol Psychiatry. 1978;13(3):335–51.

Malkoff-Schwartz S, Frank E, Anderson B, Sherrill JT, Siegel L, Patterson D, et al. Stressful life events and social rhythm disruption in the onset of manic and depressive bipolar episodes: a preliminary investigation. Arch Gen Psychiatry. 1998;55(8):702–7.

Malkoff-Schwartz S, Frank E, Anderson BP, Hlastala SA, Luther JF, Sherrill JT, et al. Social rhythm disruption and stressful life events in the onset of bipolar and unipolar episodes. Psychol Med. 2000;30(5):1005–16.

Monk TH, Frank E, Potts JM, Kupfer DJ. A simple way to measure daily lifestyle regularity. J Sleep Res. 2002;11(3):183–90.

Ng TH, Chung KF, Ho FY, Yeung WF, Yung KP, Lam TH. Sleep-wake disturbance in interepisode bipolar disorder and high-risk individuals: a systematic review and meta-analysis. Sleep Med Rev. 2015;20:46–58.

Nomura K, Castanon-Cervantes O, Davidson A, Fukuhara C. Selective serotonin reuptake inhibitors and raft inhibitors shorten the period of Period1-driven circadian bioluminescence rhythms in rat-1 fibroblasts. Life Sci. 2008;82(23–24):1169–74.

Novak D, Albert F, Spaniel F. Analysis of actigraph parameters for relapse prediction in bipolar disorder: a feasibility study. Conf Proc IEEE Eng Med Biol Soc. 2014;2014:4972–5.

Pagani L, Clair PAS, Teshiba TM, Service SK, Fears SC, Araya C. Genetic contributions to circadian activity rhythm and sleep pattern phenotypes in pedigrees segregating for severe bipolar disorder. Proc Natl Acad Sci USA. 2016;113(6):E754–61.

Pflug B, Johnsson A, Ekse AT. Manic-depressive states and daily temperature. Some circadian studies. Acta Psychiatr Scand. 1981;63(3):277–89.

Reinberg AE, Ashkenazi I, Smolensky MH. Euchronism, allochronism, and dyschronism: is internal desynchronization of human circadian rhythms a sign of illness? Chronobiol Int. 2007;24(4):553–88.

Rock P, Goodwin G, Harmer C, Wulff K. Daily rest-activity patterns in the bipolar phenotype: a controlled actigraphy study. Chronobiol Int. 2014;31(2):290–6.

Rotenberg VS, Indursky P, Kayumov L, Sirota P, Melamed Y. The relationship between subjective sleep estimation and objective sleep variables in depressed patients. Int J Psychophysiol. 2000;37(3):291–7.

Rush AJ, Gullion CM, Basco MR, Jarrett RB, Trivedi MH. The inventory of depressive symptomatology (IDS): psychometric properties. Psychol Med. 1996;26(3):477–86.

Salvatore P, Ghidini S, Zita G, De Panfilis C, Lambertino S, Maggini C, et al. Circadian activity rhythm abnormalities in ill and recovered bipolar I disorder patients. Bipolar Disord. 2008;10(2):256–65.

Sheehan DV, Lecrubier Y, Sheehan KH, Amorim P, Janavs J, Weiller E, et al. The mini-international neuropsychiatric interview (MINI): the development and validation of a structured diagnostic psychiatric interview for DSM-IV and ICD-10. J Clin Psychiatry. 1998;59(Suppl 20):22–33 **(quiz 4–57)**.

Sitaram N, Gillin JC, Bunney WE Jr. The switch process in manic-depressive illness. Circadian variation in time of switch and sleep and manic ratings before and after switch. Acta Psychiatr Scand. 1978;58(3):267–78.

Sprouse J, Braselton J; Reynolds L. Fluoxetine modulates the circadian biological clock via phase advances of suprachiasmatic nucleus neuronal firing. Biol Psychiatry. 2006;60(8):896–9.

Teicher MH. Actigraphy and motion analysis: new tools for psychiatry. Harv Rev Psychiatry. 1995;3(1):18–35.

Tsuchiyama K, Nagayama H, Kudo K, Kojima K, Yamada K. Discrepancy between subjective and objective sleep in patients with depression. Psychiatry Clin Neurosci. 2003;57(3):259–64.

Ventura J, Liberman RP, Green MF, Shaner A, Mintz J. Training and quality assurance with the structured clinical interview for DSM-IV (SCID-I/P). Psychiatry Res. 1998;79(2):163–73.

Wehr TA, Muscettola G, Goodwin FK. Urinary 3-methoxy-4-hydroxyphenylglycol circadian rhythm. Early timing (phase-advance) in manic-depressives compared with normal subjects. Arch Gen Psychiatry. 1980;37(3):257–63.

White KH, Rumble ME, Benca RM. Sex differences in the relationship between depressive symptoms and actigraphic assessments of sleep and rest-activity rhythms in a population-based sample. Psychosom Med. 2016;79(4):479–84.

Young RC, Biggs JT, Ziegler VE, Meyer DA. A rating scale for mania: reliability, validity and sensitivity. Br J Psychiatry. 1978;133:429–35.

6

Childhood maltreatment and the medical morbidity in bipolar disorder: a case–control study

Georgina M. Hosang[1*], Helen L. Fisher[2], Rudolf Uher[3], Sarah Cohen-Woods[4], Barbara Maughan[2], Peter McGuffin[2] and Anne E. Farmer[2]

Abstract

Background: Childhood maltreatment (abuse and neglect) can have long-term deleterious consequences, including increased risk for medical and psychiatric illnesses, such as bipolar disorder in adulthood. Emerging evidence suggests that a history of childhood maltreatment is linked to the comorbidity between medical illnesses and mood disorders. However, existing studies on bipolar disorder have not yet explored the specific influence of child neglect and have not included comparisons with individuals without mood disorders (controls). This study aimed to extend the existing literature by examining the differential influence of child abuse and child neglect on medical morbidity in a sample of bipolar cases and controls.

Methods: The study included 72 participants with bipolar disorder and 354 psychiatrically healthy controls (average age of both groups was 48 years), who completed the Childhood Trauma Questionnaire, and were interviewed regarding various medical disorders.

Results: A history of any type of childhood maltreatment was significantly associated with a diagnosis of any medical illness (adjusted OR = 6.28, 95% confidence intervals 1.70–23.12, $p = 0.006$) and an increased number of medical illnesses (adjusted OR = 3.77, 95% confidence intervals 1.34–10.57, $p = 0.012$) among adults with bipolar disorder. Exposure to child abuse was more strongly associated with medical disorders than child neglect. No association between childhood maltreatment and medical morbidity was detected among controls.

Conclusions: To summarise, individuals with bipolar disorder who reported experiencing maltreatment during childhood, especially abuse, were at increased risk of suffering from medical illnesses and warrant greater clinical attention.

Keywords: Bipolar disorder, Childhood maltreatment, Medical illness, Physical health, Child abuse, Child neglect, Childhood adversity

Background

Bipolar disorder is associated with substantial morbidity and mortality (Kupfer 2005); for instance people with bipolar disorder die up to 14 years younger than the general population (Chang et al. 2011). Premature mortality among individuals with this illness cannot be explained by suicide alone (Hoang et al. 2011) but has been attributed to the high rates of medical illnesses in this group (Crump et al. 2013). The rates of a myriad of medical disorders (e.g. diabetes, stroke, thyroid disease and cardiovascular disease) have been reported to be significantly elevated among people with bipolar disorder compared to the general population (Forty et al. 2014; Perron et al. 2009).

Little is known about the factors that are associated with the high medical burden in bipolar disorder, although the implications are huge for the individual, their families and society as a whole. The available evidence suggests that multiple factors are likely to

*Correspondence: g.hosang@qmul.ac.uk
[1] Psychology Department, Goldsmiths, University of London, Lewisham Way, London SE14 6NW, UK
Full list of author information is available at the end of the article

contribute to the medical morbidity in bipolar disorder (and other serious mental illnesses), the factors which have received the most attention include side effects of psychotropic medications, unhealthy life style choices and issues with health care provision for this group. Various side effects are associated with psychotropic medication, such as mood stabilisers and antipsychotics which are commonly used to treat bipolar disorder, the most pertinent to this context include weight gain and insulin resistance (Newcomer 2007). Such side effects are risk factors for diabetes and cardiovascular disease (Correll et al. 2015) and thus may explain the high rates of these illnesses in people with bipolar disorder. Smoking, unhealthy diet and physical inactivity are lifestyle choices and habits which are prevalent in people with bipolar disorder (Scott and Happell 2011) but are also known risk factors for physical illnesses, such as diabetes and coronary heart disease, thus these lifestyle choices may explain the comorbidity between these illnesses and bipolar disorder (De Hert et al. 2011). A small but growing body of research suggests that people with serious mental illnesses are less likely to receive standard levels of care (De Hert et al. 2011). For instance, low rates of surgical interventions for coronary heart disease (e.g. stenting) and screening for metabolic abnormalities associated with diabetes are recorded for people with mental illnesses including bipolar disorder (De Hert et al. 2011). This is despite the fact that such illnesses are highly prevalent in this population. A factor which has received less attention in this context is the influence of childhood adversity. Preliminary research suggests that the experience of childhood maltreatment may contribute to the medical morbidity observed in bipolar disorder (Post et al. 2013), but these findings await replication and extension.

Childhood maltreatment encompasses both abuse (e.g. sexual, emotional and physical abuse) and neglect (lack of provision for the individual's needs by their caregiver, including food, shelter and support) (Norman et al. 2012). Childhood maltreatment can be considered a plausible risk factor for the comorbidity between medical illnesses and bipolar disorder based on two lines of evidence. First, childhood maltreatment is associated with lasting changes or abnormalities in a number of biological systems or processes detected in adulthood (Gonzalez 2013; Danese and Lewis 2016). For instance, increased inflammatory cytokines are exhibited by maltreated individuals both as children (Slopen et al. 2013) and adults (Baumeister et al. 2016). Elevated inflammation has also been implicated in bipolar disorder (Leboyer et al. 2012) and a series of medical illnesses, such as diabetes, arthritis and certain cancers (Couzin-Frankel 2010) and thus could explain the comorbidity between the two disorder groups. Moreover, there is evidence that people with mood disorders and a history of childhood maltreatment exhibit particularly pronounced elevation in inflammation levels (Danese et al. 2008, 2011). For example, maltreated individuals with depression have significantly increased inflammation levels compared to those with depression only, a history of childhood maltreatment only and those without either (controls) (Danese et al. 2011).

Secondly, childhood maltreatment is associated with an increased risk of medical illnesses (Hosang et al. 2013; Scott et al. 2011) and bipolar disorder (Fisher and Hosang 2010; Palmier-Claus et al. 2016) in adulthood. The results from several studies have gone further and shown that childhood maltreatment is linked to the co-occurence of medical illnesses and mood disorders (including bipolar disorder) (Lu et al. 2008; McIntyre et al. 2012). To date only one study has examined this relationship in bipolar disorder specifically and found that childhood adversity is significantly related to the diagnosis of medical illnesses in adulthood, including diabetes, cardiovascular disease and asthma (Post et al. 2013).

The limited available research in this area has not explored the specific role of child neglect but has focused on broadly defined childhood maltreatment (McIntyre et al. 2012), or childhood adversity which includes child abuse, parental psychopathology and violence in the home (Lu et al. 2008; Post et al. 2013). Exposure to child neglect has been related to a number of medical illnesses, such as cardiovascular disease, diabetes and osteoarthritis in adulthood (Norman et al. 2012; Scott et al. 2011) and therefore is a crucial construct to consider in this context. Furthermore, previous studies examining the medical morbidity in bipolar disorder have not included comparisons with control groups (Post et al. 2013), thus it remains unclear whether the relationship between child adversity (including childhood maltreatment) and medical illnesses is specific to or greater among people with bipolar disorder relative to the general population.

To address the methodological gaps in the literature, the current study aimed to investigate the association between a history of child maltreatment and the diagnosis of medical illnesses in adulthood among people with bipolar disorder compared to unaffected controls (those without a personal or family history of a psychiatric illness). The differential influence of child abuse and child neglect on the diagnosis of medical illnesses was also examined in this context. It is hypothesised that both child abuse and neglect will be more significantly associated with medical illnesses in the bipolar disorder group compared to controls.

Methods

Participants

A total of 426 participants were included in this study, 354 (58% females, $N = 205$) of which were psychiatrically healthy controls and 72 (78% females, $N = 56$) were diagnosed with bipolar disorder (see Table 1). The participants with bipolar disorder were aged between 29 and 72 years, with a mean of 48.4 years (SD = 9.43). Participants with bipolar disorder were enrolled in the BADGE (gene-environment interplay in bipolar affective disorder) study (see Hosang et al. 2012) and were recruited by re-contacting bipolar cases from the Bipolar affective disorder case–control study (BaCCs) (see Gaysina et al. 2009; Hosang et al. 2017). Participant recruitment for BACCs was mainly via psychiatric outpatient clinics with the rest enlisted through media advertisement and self-help groups in the UK. All participants with bipolar disorder met DSM-IV criteria for bipolar I or bipolar II disorder ascertained via the schedules for clinical assessment in neuropsychiatry interview (see "Measures" section), and were Caucasian to control for population stratification since they were originally recruited from a genetic association study (see Gaysina et al. 2009). Participants were excluded if their bipolar episodes only occurred in relation to substance misuse or a physical disorder or if they had a personal or family history of schizophrenia. Participants with bipolar disorder were not experiencing a mood

Table 1 Comparison of reports of each medical condition and history of childhood maltreatment between bipolar disorder cases and unaffected controls

	Bipolar cases, *N* (%) [*N* = 72]	Controls, *N* (%) [*N* = 354]	Statistic	*p* value
Female	56 (78)	205 (58)	$\chi^2(1) = 9.34$	*0.002*
Age at assessment [mean (SD)]	48.36 (9.42)	47.73 (9.15)	$t(395) = 0.52$	0.60
At least one medical illness	42 (58)	96 (27)	$\chi^2(1) = 26.61$	*<0.001*
Number of medical illnesses				
None	30 (42)	259 (73)		
1	21 (29)	78 (22)		
2 or more	21 (29)	17 (4)	$\chi^2(2) = 49.88$	*<0.001*
Different types of medical illnesses				
Heart problems (i.e. stroke, angina and heart attack)	1 (1)	2 (1)	Two-tailed fisher's exact	0.427
Asthma	15 (21)	31 (9)	$\chi^2(2) = 9.06$	*0.003*
Diabetes (types I and II)	5 (7)	7 (2)	Two-tailed fisher's exact	*0.036*
Arthritis	17 (24)	23 (7)	$\chi^2(2) = 20.60$	*<0.001*
Hypertension	16 (22)	32 (9)	$\chi^2(2) = 10.40$	*0.001*
Epilepsy or convulsions	3 (4)	0 (0)	Two-tailed fisher's exact	*0.005*
Osteoporosis	3 (4)	3 (0.9)	Two-tailed fisher's exact	0.063
Multiple sclerosis	0 (0)	0 (0)	–	
Emphysema or chronic bronchitis	5 (7)	14 (4)	$\chi^2(2) = 1.26$	0.263
Postherpetic neuralgia	0 (0)	2 (0.6)	Two-tailed fisher's exact	1.00
Childhood maltreatment				
Any type of childhood maltreatment (abuse and/or neglect)[a, b]	37 (51)	64 (18)	$\chi^2(1) = 36.70$	*<0.001*
Any type of child abuse[a, c]	31 (43)	41 (12)	$\chi^2(1) = 42.20$	*<0.001*
Physical abuse	8 (11)	13 (4)	$\chi^2(1) = 6.99$	*0.008*
Emotional abuse	20 (28)	23 (7)	$\chi^2(1) = 35.13$	*<0.001*
Sexual abuse	20 (28)	20 (6)	$\chi^2(1) = 34.16$	*<0.001*
Any type of child neglect[a, d]	20 (28)	36 (10)	$\chi^2(1) = 16.25$	*<0.001*
Physical neglect	10 (14)	64 (6)	$\chi^2(1) = 5.04$	*0.025*
Emotional neglect	19 (26)	28 (8)	$\chi^2(1) = 20.71$	*<0.001*

Significant *p* values are italicised

N number of participants, *SD* standard deviations, % percentage, *P* probability due to chance

[a] These figures are not the sum of the derived variables as some participants report experiencing more than one type of maltreatment

[b] Childhood maltreatment was considered present if any type of child abuse or neglect were rated as moderate or severe

[c] Child abuse was considered present if any form of child abuse was rated as moderate or severe

[d] Child neglect was considered present if physical or emotional neglect was rated as moderate or severe

episode at either of their assessments for the BaCCs and BADGE studies.

The controls were a sub-sample of a case–control genetic association study on unipolar depression that provided information on their experience of maltreatment during childhood (see Fisher et al. 2013). The controls were aged between 24 and 68 years with a mean of 47.7 years (SD = 9.15). They were recruited through UK general medical practices and excluded if they had a personal or family history (among first degree relatives) of any psychiatric disorder. Given that participants were drawn from genetic association studies they were Caucasian to control for population stratification. All participants were aged 18 years or over and provided written informed consent after the nature of the study and procedures were fully explained. All studies received ethical approval from either King's College Hospital or the Joint from South London and Maudsley and Institute of Psychiatry Research Ethics Committees. All procedures contributing to this work were conducted in accordance with the Declaration of Helsinki in 1975 (revised in 2008), and the ethical standards of the national and institutional committees on human experimentation.

Measures

Bipolar disorder diagnosis

The Schedules for Clinical Assessment in Neuropsychiatry (SCAN), Version 2.1 interview (Wing et al. 1990) was used to ascertain a lifetime DSM-IV diagnosis of bipolar disorder. The presence and severity of the psychopathology items were rated for the worst depressive and manic episodes, separately.

History of childhood maltreatment

All participants completed the 28-item Childhood Trauma Questionnaire (CTQ) (Bernstein et al. 2003), which was used to record the experience of five types of childhood maltreatment (i.e. physical abuse, sexual abuse, emotional abuse, physical neglect and emotional neglect). A total of 5 items were used to measure each type of maltreatment, which were rated on a 5-point Likert scale ranging from 1 (never true) to 5 (very often true). The cut-offs for moderate to severe levels of each type of maltreatment were employed in this study in accordance with the manual (Bernstein et al. 2003). The five types of childhood maltreatment rated as moderate or severe were categorised into abuse (i.e. sexual, emotional and/or physical abuse) and neglect (emotional and/or physical neglect). Good psychometric properties have been reported for this instrument, for instance there is high concordance between CTQ scores and therapists' ratings of childhood maltreatment (Bernstein et al. 2003). Moreover, good test–retest reliability has been found using this instrument in a sample of people with bipolar disorder (Shannon et al. 2016).

Medical history

All participants completed a self-report questionnaire to determine the lifetime presence of various medical illnesses (Farmer et al. 2008; Forty et al. 2014). Participants were asked whether they had been formally diagnosed with any of the following illnesses: heart problems (i.e. stroke, angina and heart attack), asthma, diabetes (I and II), arthritis (i.e. osteoarthritis, rheumatoid arthritis and other types of arthritis), hypertension, epilepsy or convulsions, osteoporosis, multiple sclerosis, emphysema or chronic bronchitis, or post herpetic neuralgia. Trained research assistants administered the questionnaire to all participants, which involved confirming that a formal diagnosis of the illness was provided by a medical professional (e.g. General Practitioner or medical consultant). Good concordance between the self-report of medical illnesses using this interview and practitioner ratings have been found (Farmer et al. 2008).

Analyses

Group differences were tested using Chi-square (χ^2) tests, one-way ANOVAs and independent sample t tests. The Fisher's exact test was conducted if a χ^2 test could not be used (e.g. expected values were less than 5). Case–control differences concerned with the association between childhood maltreatment and medical illnesses were examined using two approaches. First, using logistic regression models when at least one medical disorder was examined and second, ordinal logistic regression models when the number of medical illnesses was the focus (none, 1 and 2 or more illnesses). Gender and age were entered as covariates, along with child maltreatment, bipolar disorder status, as well as the interaction between childhood maltreatment and bipolar disorder status. Three parallel models (for each approach) were undertaken to investigate the effect of any type of childhood maltreatment, child abuse and child neglect. Given the relatively small bipolar disorder sample size and uneven distribution of some variables, we estimated the variance in the regression models with non-parametric bootstrap with replacement (1000 replications) to obtain empirical standard error estimates without making distributional assumptions. All statistical tests were performed in STATA version 14.0; the conventional level of significance, $p < 0.05$, was used in this study.

Results

There was no significant age difference between the controls and participants with bipolar disorder ($t(393) = 0.60$, p = NS), but there was a significantly higher proportion of females in the bipolar group relative to the controls ($\chi^2(1) = 9.34$, $p = 0.002$). The percentage of participants reporting each medical illness and different types of childhood maltreatment are presented in Table 1. The most commonly reported medical illnesses in the sample were arthritis, asthma and hypertension. The relatively low number of participants that recorded being diagnosed with each medical illness prevented the examination of associations between specific disorders and childhood maltreatment. Thus the remaining analyses focused on either the diagnosis of *at least one* or *the number of* (none, 1 and 2 or more) medical illnesses.

There were no gender differences in the diagnosis of at least one ($\chi^2(1) = 0.08$, $p =$ NS) or the number of medical disorders ($\chi^2(1) = 0.29$, $p =$ NS). Those individuals that reported receiving a diagnosis of at least one medical disorder were significantly older than those without a diagnosis ($t(393) = 4.05$, $p < 0.001$). A similar pattern was observed when the number of medical illnesses were examined ($F(2, 392) = 9.92$, $p < 0.001$): participants that reported 1 (mean age = 49.73 years, SD = 8.14) or at least 2 (mean age = 52.54 years, SD = 9.54) medical disorders were significantly older than the individuals that recorded none (mean age = 46.53 years, SD = 9.19) according to a Tukey post hoc test ($p = 0.009$, $p < 0.001$, respectively).

Significantly more participants with bipolar disorder reported being diagnosed with at least one medical illness compared to controls ($\chi^2(1) = 26.61$, $p < 0.001$) and they also reported to have significantly more medical illnesses relative to controls ($\chi^2(2) = 49.88$, $p < 0.001$). The rates of all types of childhood maltreatment were significantly greater among the bipolar group compared to the controls (see Table 1). A moderate correlation between child abuse and neglect was detected in the entire sample (Pearson's $r(426) = 0.33$, $p < 0.001$).

Logistic regression models were conducted to explore the interaction between bipolar disorder status and the history of childhood maltreatment on the diagnosis of at least one medical illness, and ordinal logistic regression models were undertaken to examine the number of medical disorders (gender and age were included as covariates in the analyses), the results of which are presented in Table 2. Bipolar disorder status significantly interacted with both the exposure to any type of childhood maltreatment and child abuse on the diagnosis of at least one and the increased number of medical illnesses (see Table 2). The results remained significant for child abuse even when the effects of child neglect were controlled for (at least one medical illness: adjusted OR = 5.90, 95% confidence intervals (CI) 1.31–26.62, $p = 0.021$; number of medical disorders: adjusted OR = 4.85, 95% CI 1.30–18.06, $p = 0.019$). Although exposure to child neglect was associated with higher odds of having a medical illness with bipolar disorder, the results failed to reach conventional levels of significance (at least one medical illness: adjusted OR = 4.32, 95% CI 0.96–19.47, $p = 0.057$; number of medical disorders: adjusted OR = 3.30, 95% CI 0.89–12.22, $p = 0.075$).

Further examination of the interactions showed that exposure to any type of childhood maltreatment, child abuse and child neglect were significantly associated with higher odds of having at least one and a greater number of medical illnesses in the bipolar group but not for the controls (see Table 3). The percentage of bipolar cases

Table 2 Main and interaction effects of bipolar disorder diagnosis and childhood maltreatment on the diagnoses of medical illnesses

	Adjusted OR[a]	95% confidence intervals		*p* value
		Lower	Upper	
At least one medical illness				
Main effects				
Bipolar disorder diagnosis	3.80	2.13	6.77	*<0.001*
Childhood maltreatment[b]	2.05	1.24	3.40	*0.006*
Child abuse[c]	2.14	1.23	3.70	*0.007*
Child neglect[d]	2.24	1.18	4.24	*0.013*
Interaction effects				
Bipolar disorder × childhood maltreatment	6.43	1.70	24.31	*0.006*
Bipolar disorder × abuse	6.31	1.46	27.24	*0.014*
Bipolar disorder × neglect	4.32	0.96	19.47	0.057
Number of medical illnesses				
Main effects				
Bipolar disorder diagnosis	4.81	2.71	8.53	*<0.001*
Childhood maltreatment	1.59	1.05	2.40	*0.028*
Child abuse	1.78	1.11	2.85	*0.016*
Child neglect	1.89	1.14	3.13	*0.014*
Interaction effects				
Bipolar disorder × childhood maltreatment	4.97	1.39	17.76	*0.014*
Bipolar disorder × abuse	5.23	1.32	20.75	*0.019*
Bipolar disorder × neglect	3.30	0.89	12.22	0.075

Significant *p* values are italicised

OR odds ratio derived from binary logistic regression for 'at least one medical illness' and from ordinal logistic regression for 'number of medical illnesses', *P* probability due to chance

[a] Adjusted for the effects of gender and age

[b] Childhood maltreatment was considered present if any type of child abuse or neglect were rated as moderate or severe

[c] Child abuse was considered present if any form of child abuse was rated as moderate or severe

[d] Child neglect was considered present if physical or emotional neglect was rated as moderate or severe

Table 3 Relationship between childhood maltreatment and medical illnesses, presented separately for participants with bipolar disorder and controls

	Participants with bipolar disorder			Controls		
	Adjusted OR[a]	95% confidence interval	*p* value	Adjusted OR[a]	95% confidence interval	*p* value
At least one medical illness						
Any type of childhood maltreatment[b]	6.28	1.70–23.12	*0.006*	0.92	0.47–1.81	0.809
Child abuse[c]	4.99	1.32–18.75	*0.017*	0.81	0.36–1.84	0.616
Child neglect[d]	4.78	1.09–20.86	*0.038*	1.12	0.49–2.56	0.794
Number of medical illnesses						
Any type of childhood maltreatment	3.77	1.34–10.57	*0.012*	0.89	0.47–1.69	0.714
Child abuse	3.75	1.29–10.86	*0.015*	0.83	0.36–1.90	0.651
Child neglect	2.91	1.11–7.62	*0.029*	1.05	0.48–2.30	0.899

Significant *p* values are italicised

OR odds ratio derived from binary logistic regression for 'at least one medical illness' and from ordinal logistic regression for 'number of medical illnesses', *P* probability due to chance

[a] Adjusted for the effects of gender and age

[b] Childhood maltreatment was considered present if any type of child abuse or neglect were rated as moderate or severe

[c] Child abuse was considered present if any form of child abuse was rated as moderate or severe

[d] Child neglect was considered present if physical or emotional neglect was rated as moderate or severe

and controls with medical illnesses by each type of childhood maltreatment is visually presented in Fig. 1. Given that there were a restricted number of participants that reported experiencing each type of child abuse (i.e. sexual, physical and emotional) and neglect (i.e. emotional and physical), analyses examining their individual and interactional effects were not possible.

Discussion

This study found a significant relationship between childhood maltreatment and medical illnesses in adulthood among individuals with bipolar disorder but not in unaffected controls. When the analyses were stratified by the type of childhood maltreatment the results were strongest for child abuse rather than child neglect. This is the first study to explore child neglect in this context using both controls and participants with bipolar disorder. Our findings are consistent with previous studies that have focused on mood disorders (Lu et al. 2008; McIntyre et al. 2012) and bipolar disorder specifically (Post et al. 2013). For instance, broadly defined childhood adversity, which includes child abuse (verbal, physical and sexual) and parental psychiatric diagnosis, but not child neglect, was found to be significantly associated with the overall number of medical illnesses in a sample of over 900 people with bipolar disorder (Post et al. 2013). Childhood adversity was also found to be significantly associated with specific medical illnesses in this group including arthritis, asthma, hyper- and hypo-tension (Post et al. 2013). However the results from the present investigation add to this literature by showing that the relationship between childhood maltreatment and medical illnesses is especially pertinent to bipolar disorder compared to controls.

Although the relationship between childhood maltreatment and medical illnesses in adulthood has been established in the general population (Scott et al. 2011), this relationship maybe particularly relevant to bipolar disorder for two reasons. First, high rates of childhood maltreatment have been found among people with bipolar disorder (Fisher and Hosang 2010; Palmier-Claus et al. 2016). Childhood maltreatment has also been associated with a worse clinical course among people with bipolar disorder, such as, earlier age of onset and more mood episodes (Agnew-Blais and Danese 2016). Such clinical course characteristics have also been linked to the medical morbidity in bipolar disorder (Magalhães et al. 2012). Bringing together these lines of research it is possible that childhood maltreatment may lead to an unfavourable clinical course in bipolar disorder that in turn contributes to the high medical burden observed in this illness. Although the exact mechanism that underpins this relationship is unclear, it has been postulated that it may reflect shared biological vulnerabilities, such as disruption in inflammation and oxidative systems (Magalhães et al. 2012). Alternatively, the more severe clinical course associated with childhood maltreatment (Agnew-Blais and Danese 2016) is likely to increase the need for medication treatment. The side effects of mood stabilisers and antipsychotics, include weight gain and insulin resistance (Newcomer 2007) are linked to various medical conditions, such as diabetes (Newcomer 2007), potentially explaining the link between childhood maltreatment and physical illnesses in bipolar disorder but may

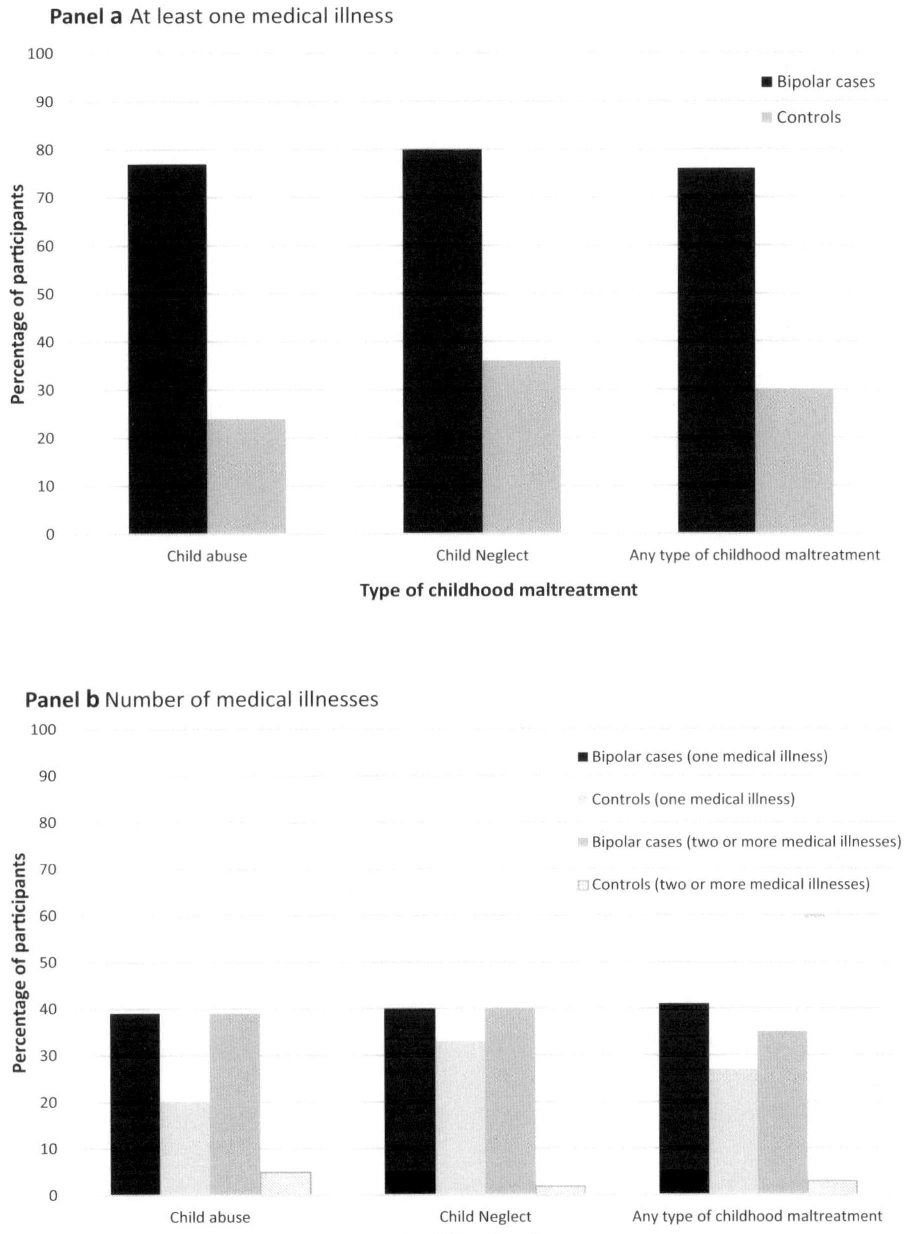

Fig. 1 Percentage of participants with medical illnesses by type of childhood maltreatment experienced. The *y*-axis presents the percentage of participants with medical illnesses by the different types of childhood maltreatment groups (child abuse, child neglect and any type of childhood maltreatment) for bipolar cases and controls. **a** The diagnosis of at least one medical illness and **b** the number of medical illnesses (one and two or more)

have also attenuated the results here. Although in the current study all of the participants with bipolar disorder were on long-term medication regimens for their psychiatric illness; therefore this confounding effect is unlikely here, but more research is needed to clarify this issue.

Second, the biological sequelae of childhood maltreatment, such as increased inflammation levels (Baumeister et al. 2016) are also evident in bipolar disorder (Leboyer et al. 2012) and various medical illnesses, particularly autoimmune diseases, such as arthritis and type I diabetes (Couzin-Frankel 2010). Research indicates that elevated inflammation is particularly pronounced among maltreated individuals with mood disorders even when compared to those who have a history of child abuse and neglect (Danese et al. 2008, 2011), thus potentially increasing the risk of such medical illnesses. For example, the results from one study found that inflammation levels were significantly higher among those with a history of childhood maltreatment and depression relative to those with depression only, childhood maltreatment only and controls (without either) (Danese et al. 2011). The biological consequences of childhood maltreatment in bipolar disorder warrants further research attention to better understand the possible mechanisms that underlie its high medical burden.

The results from the current investigation provide a novel contribution to the field by helping to show differential relationships between child abuse, child neglect and medical illnesses in bipolar disorder. Previous studies examined these adversities under one overarching construct of childhood maltreatment or did not explore the impact of child neglect separately (Lu et al. 2008; McIntyre et al. 2012; Post et al. 2013). The results of the present study suggest that the effect of child abuse on medical illnesses is not only significant but may also be stronger than that of child neglect in bipolar disorder. This is consistent with the results of previous studies which have shown that child abuse is associated with a list of medical disorders whereas neglect is linked to only a limited number of illnesses (Scott et al. 2011; Norman et al. 2012). It is possible that unhealthy lifestyles may explain the stronger association between the experience of child abuse and medical disorders compared to child neglect. For example, smoking is a major risk factor for a series of medical disorders (Ezzati et al. 2002), and has been significantly associated with child abuse but not child neglect (Norman et al. 2012). The exact mechanisms behind the link between child abuse and the medical burden in bipolar disorder is unclear and warrants further investigation. The limited sample size of the bipolar group may have impacted on the study's power and is likely to have contributed to the non-significant interaction effect of child neglect and bipolar disorder status on the diagnosis of medical illnesses. Future research focusing on the biological, psychological and behavioural correlates of child abuse using larger samples would be especially informative.

With replication, the findings of this study are clinically valuable since they can be used to identify a subgroup of people with bipolar disorder (those with a history of childhood maltreatment) who are at risk of poor health (Post et al. 2013) and worse clinical course (Agnew-Blais and Danese 2016). These results underscore the need for routine assessment of childhood maltreatment history in clinical practice, which would assist with the early recognition of an 'at risk' group who would benefit most from targeted prevention and intervention efforts. Family therapy or psychoeducation focused on improving the social support provided to people with bipolar disorder maybe particularly beneficial. This suggestion is based on research that shows that social support influences the risk of relapse in bipolar disorder and mediates the effect of childhood maltreatment on physical health in adulthood (Herrenkohl et al. 2016).

There are a number of strengths of this study including the use of a well-characterised bipolar disorder sample and screened controls that completed validated instruments. But several limitations of the current study should be considered when interpreting the findings. First, the limited sample size of the bipolar group may reduce the power to detect significant effects and the ability to generalise our results. Participants with bipolar disorder in this study were recruited from across the UK through psychiatric outpatient clinics and self-help groups, so are not entirely biased or unrepresentative. Future studies should use a larger case–control sample to confirm the associations observed in this investigation. Second, childhood maltreatment and medical illnesses were assessed using self-report which has been associated with various problems (e.g. reporting accuracy) (Reuben et al. 2016). Retrospective self-report questionnaires used to assess childhood maltreatment are commonly used in both epidemiological and psychiatric studies (Norman et al. 2012; Agnew-Blais and Danese 2016). Moreover, childhood maltreatment data yielded from self-report show high concordance with case notes (Fisher et al. 2011) and therapists' ratings (Bernstein et al. 2003). Substantial agreement between the self-report medical interview used here and the health practitioner reports of the diagnoses of medical disorders has been reported (Farmer et al. 2008). Nonetheless, it would be useful for future studies to replicate the findings of the present study using practitioner reports of medical illnesses, and prospective objective assessment of childhood maltreatment.

Finally, the incidence of several medical illnesses, particularly heart problems was relatively low especially compared to other studies, this precluded the examination of the specific association between childhood maltreatment and particular medical illnesses. This may have been the result of the age of the sample (median age 49 years, range 24–72 years), with the majority of participants outside of the median age of onset (58–64 years) for various heart problems, including coronary heart disease and stroke (Terry et al. 2004). But the prevalence of arthritis, hypertension and asthma in the current study is comparable to those reported in previous investigations (McIntyre et al. 2006; Perron et al. 2009). Future studies should explore the influence of childhood maltreatment on the medical morbidity in bipolar disorder using an older sample.

To summarise, this is one of a limited number of studies that has examined the relationship between childhood maltreatment and the medical morbidity in bipolar disorder. This study extends previous work by exploring the differential relationship between child abuse and neglect and in this context using a sample of controls and individuals with bipolar disorder. The results of this study showed that childhood maltreatment is significantly associated with medical ill health among people with bipolar disorder but not controls. On further examination of the data, child abuse showed the strongest association with medical illnesses compared to child neglect. With more research these findings can be used to identify individuals who would benefit most from prevention and intervention efforts.

Abbreviations

SCAN: schedules for clinical assessment in neuropsychiatry interview; CTQ: Childhood Trauma Questionnaire; BADGE: gene-environment interplay in bipolar affective disorder; BaCCs: bipolar affective disorder case–control study.

Authors' contributions

GMH conducted the analyses for the manuscript, interpreted the results and drafted the manuscript. BM, PM and AF worked on the conception and design of the study and critically revising the manuscript in preparation for submission. HF, SC-W and UR were involved in the data analysis, interpretation of the findings and drafting the manuscript. All authors read and approved the final manuscript.

Author details

[1] Psychology Department, Goldsmiths, University of London, Lewisham Way, London SE14 6NW, UK. [2] MRC Social, Genetic and Developmental Psychiatry Centre, Institute of Psychiatry, Psychology & Neuroscience, King's College London, De Crespigny Park, London SE5 8AF, UK. [3] Department of Psychiatry, Dalhousie University, 5909 Veterans' Memorial Lane, Halifax, NS B3H 2E2, Canada. [4] School of Psychology, Flinders University, GPO Box 2100, Adelaide, SA 5001, Australia.

Acknowledgements

We would like to thank the members of the Radiant Team who were involved with the data collection and management of the studies and all of the individuals who participated in the research.

Competing interests

The authors declare that they have no competing interests.

Funding

The bipolar case–control genetic association study was funded by an unrestricted grant from GlaxoSmithKline Research and Development. Funding for the depression case–control study was provided by the UK Medical Research Council (MRC; G0701420). The BADGE study was supported by an Interdisciplinary Ph.D. studentship from the UK Economic Social Research Council (ESRC) and MRC to Dr. Hosang. Prof. Uher is supported by the Canada Research Chairs program (http://www.chairs-chaires.gc.ca/him) and Dr. Fisher is supported by an MQ Fellows Award (MQ14F40). The sources of funding had no involvement in the study design, data collection or decision to submit for publication.

References

Agnew-Blais J, Danese A. Childhood maltreatment and unfavourable clinical outcomes in bipolar disorder: a systematic review and meta-analysis. Lancet Psychiatry. 2016;3(4):342–9.

Baumeister D, Akhtar R, Ciufolini S, Pariante CM, Mondelli V. Childhood trauma and adult inflammation: a meta-analysis of peripheral C-reactive protein, interleukin-6 and tumour neurosis factor-α. Mol Psychiatry. 2016;21:642–9.

Bernstein DP, Stein JA, Newcomb MD, Walker E, Pogge D, Ahluvalia T, et al. Development and validation of a brief screening version of the Childhood Trauma Questionnaire. Child Abuse Negl. 2003;27(2):169–90.

Chang CK, Hayes RD, Perera G, Broadbent MTM, Fernandes AC, Lee WE, et al. Life expectancy at birth for people with serious mental illness and other major disorders from a secondary mental health care case register in London. PLoS ONE. 2011;6(5):e19590.

Correll CU, Detraux J, De Lepeleire J, De Hert M. Effects of antipsychotics, antidepressants and mood stabilizers on risk for physical diseases in people with schizophrenia, depression and bipolar disorder. World Psychiatry. 2015;14(2):119–36.

Couzin-Frankel J. Inflammation bares a dark side. Science. 2010;330:1621.

Crump C, Sundquist K, Winkleby MA, Sundquist J. Comorbidities and mortality in bipolar disorder: a Swedish national cohort study. JAMA Psychiatry. 2013;70(9):931–9.

Danese A, Caspi A, Williams B, Ambler A, Sugden K, Mika J, et al. Biological embedding of stress through inflammation processes in childhood. Mol Psychiatry. 2011;16:244–6.

Danese A, Lewis S. Psychoneuroimmunology of early-life stress: the hidden wounds of childhood trauma. Neuropsychopharmacology. 2017;42:99–114.

Danese A, Moffitt TE, Pariante CM, Ambler A, Poulton R, Caspi A. Elevated inflammation levels in depressed adults with a history of childhood maltreatment. Arch Gen Psychiatry. 2008;65(4):409–15.

Ezzati M, Lopez AD, Rodgers A, Vander Hoorn S, Murray CJ. Selected major risk factors and global and regional burden of disease. Lancet. 2002;360(9343):1347–60.

Farmer A, Korszun A, Owen MJ, Craddock N, Jones L, Jones I, et al. Medical disorders in people with recurrent depression. Br J Psychiatry. 2008;192(5):351–5.

Fisher H, Hosang G. Childhood maltreatment and bipolar disorder: a critical review of the evidence. Mind Brain J Psychiatry. 2010;1(1):1–11.

Fisher HL, Cohen-Woods S, Hosang GM, Korszun A, Owen M, Craddock N, et al. Interaction between specific forms of childhood maltreatment and the serotonin transporter gene (5-HTT) in recurrent depressive disorder. J Affect Disord. 2013;145(1):136–41.

Fisher HL, Craig TK, Fearon P, Morgan K, Dazzan P, Lappin J, et al. Reliability and comparability of psychosis patients' retrospective reports of childhood abuse. Schizophr Bull. 2011;37(3):546–53.

Forty L, Ulanova A, Jones L, Jones I, Gordon-Smith K, Fraser C, et al. Comorbid medical illness in bipolar disorder. Br J Psychiatry. 2014;205(6):465–72.

Gaysina D, Cohen-Woods S, Chow PC, Martucci L, Schosser A, Ball HA, et al. Association of the dystrobrevin binding protein 1 gene (DTNBP1) in a bipolar case–control study (BACCS). Am J Med Genet B Neuropsychiatr Genet. 2009;150B(6):836–44.

Gonzalez A. The impact of childhood maltreatment on biological systems: implications for clinical interventions. Paediatr Child Health. 2013;18(8):415–8.

Herrenkohl TI, Jung H, Klika JB, Mason WA, Brown EC, Leeb RT, et al. Mediating and moderating effects of social support in the study of child abuse and adult physical and mental health. Am J Orthopsychiatry. 2016;86(5):573–83.

De Hert M, Correll CU, Bobes J, Cetkovich-Bakmas M, Cohen D, Asai I, et al. Physical illness in patients with severe mental disorders. I. Prevalence, impact of medications and disparities in health care. World Psychiatry. 2011;10(1):52–77.

Hoang U, Stewart R, Goldacre MJ. Mortality after hospital discharge for people with schizophrenia or bipolar disorder: retrospective study of linked English hospital episode statistics, 1999–2006. BMJ. 2011;343:d5422.

Hosang GM, Fisher HL, Cohen-Woods S, McGuffin P, Farmer AE. Stressful life events and catechol-*O*-methyl-transferase (COMT) gene in bipolar disorder. Depress Anxiety. 2017;34:419–26.

Hosang GM, Johnson SL, Kiecolt-Glaser J, Di Gregorio MP, Lambert DR, Bechtel MA, et al. Gender specific association of child abuse and adult cardiovascular disease in a sample of patients with basal cell carcinoma. Child Abuse Negl. 2013;37(6):374–9.

Hosang GM, Uher R, Maughan B, McGuffin P, Farmer AE. The role of loss and danger events in symptom exacerbation in bipolar disorder. J Psychiatr Res. 2012;46(12):1584–9.

Kupfer DJ. The increasing medical burden in bipolar disorder. JAMA. 2005;293(20):2528–30.

Leboyer M, Soreca I, Scott J, Frye M, Henry C, Tamouza R, et al. Can bipolar disorder be viewed as a multi-system inflammatory disease? J Affect Disord. 2012;141:1–10.

Lu W, Mueser KT, Rosenberg SD, Jankowski MK. Correlates of adverse childhood experiences among adults with severe mood disorders. Psychiatr Serv. 2008;59(9):1018–26.

Magalhães PV, Kapczinski F, Nierenberg AA, Deckersbach T, Weisinger D, Dodd S, et al. Illness burden and medical comorbidity in the systematic treatment enhancement program for bipolar disorder. Acta Psychiatr Scand. 2012;125(4):303–8.

McIntyre RS, Konarski JZ, Soczynska JK, Wilkins K, Panjwani G, Bouffard B, et al. Medical comorbidity in bipolar disorder: implications for functional outcomes and health service utilization. Psychiatr Serv. 2006;57(8):1140–4.

McIntyre RS, Soczynska JK, Liauw SS, Woldeyohannes HO, Brietzke E, Nathanson J, et al. The association between childhood adversity and components of metabolic syndrome in adults with mood disorders: results from the international mood disorders collaborative project. Int J Psychiatry Med. 2012;43(2):165–77.

Newcomer JW. Antipsychotic medications: metabolic and cardiovascular risk. J Clin Psychiatry. 2007;68(Suppl 4):8–13.

Norman RE, Byambaa M, De R, Butchart A, Scott J, Vos T. The long-term health consequences of child physical abuse, emotional abuse, and neglect: a systematic review and meta-analysis. PLoS Med. 2012;9(11):e1001349.

Palmier-Claus JE, Berry K, Bucci S, Mansell W, Varese F. Relationship between childhood adversity and bipolar affective disorder: systematic review and meta-analysis. Br J Psychiatry. 2016;209(6):454–9.

Perron BE, Howard MO, Nienhuis JK, Bauer MS, Woodward AT, Kilbourne AM. Prevalence and burden of general medical conditions among adults with bipolar I disorder: results from the national epidemiologic survey on alcohol and related conditions. J Clin Psychiatry. 2009;70(10):1407–15.

Post RM, Altshuler LL, Leverich GS, Frye MA, Suppes T, McElroy SL, et al. Role of childhood adversity in the development of medical co-morbidities associated with bipolar disorder. J Affect Disord. 2013;147(1–3):288–94.

Reuben A, Moffitt TE, Caspi A, Belsky DW, Harrington H, Schroeder F, et al. Lest we forget: comparing retrospective and prospective assessments of adverse childhood experiences in the prediction of adult health. J Child Psychol Psychiatry Allied Discipl. 2016;57(10):1103–12.

Scott D, Happell B. The high prevalence of poor physical health and unhealthy lifestyle behaviours in individuals with severe mental illness. Issues Ment Health Nurs. 2011;32(9):589–97.

Scott KM, Von Korff M, Angermeyer MC, Benjet C, Bruffaerts R, de Girolamo G, et al. Association of childhood adversities and early-onset mental disorders with adult-onset chronic physical conditions. Arch Gen Psychiatry. 2011;68(8):838–44.

Shannon C, Hanna D, Tumelty L, Waldron D, Maguire C, Mowlds W, et al. Reliability of reports of childhood trauma in bipolar disorder: a test–retest study over 18 months. J. Trauma Dissociation. 2016;17(4):511–9.

Slopen N, Kubzansky LD, McLaughlin KA, Koenen KC. Childhood adversity and inflammatory processes in youth: a prospective study. Psychoneuroendocrinology. 2013;38(2):188–200.

Terry DF, Wilcox MA, McCormick MA, Perls TT. Cardiovascular disease delay in centenarian offspring. J Gerontol Ser A. 2004;59(4):385–9.

Wing JK, Babor T, Brugha T, Burke J, Cooper JE, Giel R, et al. Schedules for clinical assessment in neuropsychiatry. Arch Gen Psychiatry. 1990;47(6):589–93.

7

Control charts for monitoring mood stability as a predictor of severe episodes in patients with bipolar disorder

Maria D. L. A. Vazquez-Montes[1*], Richard Stevens[1], Rafael Perera[1], Kate Saunders[2] and John R. Geddes[2]

Abstract

Background: Recurrent mood episodes and subsyndromal mood instability cause substantial disability in patients with bipolar disorder. Early identification of mood episodes enabling timely mood stabilization is an important clinical goal. This study investigates the ability of control chart methodology to predict manic and/or depressive episodes by applying Shewhart's control rules to weekly self-reported scores from mania and depression questionnaires.

Methods: Shewhart's control rules were applied to weekly self-reported scores from the Altman Self-Rating Mania Scale (ASRM) and the Quick Inventory of Depressive Symptomatology—Self-Report (QIDS) collected from 2001 to 2012 as part of the OXTEXT programme. Manic and depressive episodes were defined as an ASRM score $\geq$ 10 or a QIDS score $\geq$ 15, respectively. An episode-free run-in period of eight consecutive weeks without an episode of either type was used to calibrate control charts. Shewhart's rules were then applied to follow-up data. Their sensitivity and positive predictive value for predicting manic or depressive episodes within the next 4 weeks were calculated focusing on the first episode. Secondary analyses varying control chart type, length of episode-free run-in period, time frames to evaluate diagnostic accuracy, thresholds defining either manic or depressive episodes, and missing data methods were performed.

Results: Data from 146 participants (37% men) were included. The mean age was 43.4 (SD = 13.3) years. The median follow-up was 10 (IQR 5–40) weeks for mania and 10 (IQR 5–23) weeks for depression. A total of 53 (36%) participants had a manic episode and 67 (46%) had a depressive episode. For manic episodes, the sensitivity and positive predictive value of Shewhart's control rules were 30% (95% CI 19–45%) and 7% (95% CI 5–9%), and for depressive episodes, 33% (95% CI 22–46%) and 9% (95% CI 6–12%), respectively. Results from secondary analyses were similar to these.

Conclusions: Tele-monitoring with control rules has the potential to predict about one-third of manic or depressive episodes before they occur, at the cost of a high false positive rate. Given the severe consequences of manic and depressive episodes, this trade-off may be desirable.

Keywords: Bipolar disorder, Episode prediction, Mood variability, Control charts, Shewhart's control rules, Sensitivity, Positive predictive value

Background

Bipolar disorder is a mental illness characterized by recurrent manic and depressive symptoms occurring as both acute episodes and subsyndromal mood instability. It has a prevalence of approximately 1–2% in the general population (Mayora et al. 2013) and is the mental disorder with the highest suicide rate (Hawton et al. 2005). Recurrent episodes and mood instability cause substantial disability and so prevention of severe episodes and mood stabilization are important therapeutic targets.

Conventional treatments for bipolar disorder include a combination of drugs [lithium being the most commonly used (Geddes et al. 2004)] and psychotherapy (Geddes

*Correspondence: maria.vazquezmontes@phc.ox.ac.uk
[1] Nuffield Department of Primary Care Health Sciences, University of Oxford, Radcliffe Observatory Quarter, Woodstock Road, Oxford OX2 6GG, UK
Full list of author information is available at the end of the article

et al. 2013). As a means to prevent relapse, current treatment research is focusing on understanding mood variability (Bonsall et al. 2012). Efforts have been directed towards development of technology for continuous monitoring of more objective parameters to aid treatment (e.g. voice frequency readers, wrist-worn activity monitors, mobile electro-dermal activity sensors) (Mayora et al. 2013). The use of text messaging and email has been implemented for weekly self-report of mood scores, for instance by the OXTEXT programme (https://oxfordhealth.truecolours.nhs.uk/www/en/; Bopp et al. 2010). Such approaches are beneficial as retrospective accounts are inherently unreliable, unable to measure temporal variation or to identify mood instability that is mild but nevertheless functionally significant. Remote monitoring methodologies are a mechanism to reduce this recall bias and give us greater insight into the dynamic nature of mood instability in daily life.

Prediction models for episodes have so far considered covariates correlated with symptom severity, treatment complexity, or remission to predict long-term outcomes (Busch et al. 2012). However, variability between severe episodes has not been considered as a potential predictor. Control charts are a tool focused on the variability of a process which can potentially be used to identify when an episode is about to occur.

Control charts are widely used in industry. They are a visual display of a process over time combined with algorithms called 'control rules' designed to distinguish systematic change in the underlying process from random noise. A run-in period of data collected under stability informs the user of the inherent variability of the process. This variability is used to calculate control limits usually as 1, 2, and 3 deviations from the mean. Control charts are subsequently applied to prospectively monitor the process stability and control. Their application in medicine has expanded in recent years (Thor et al. 2007; Mohammed et al. 2008) in topics as varied as maintaining quality of electronic medical records (Siregar et al. 2013), evaluating performance in cardiac surgery (Smith et al. 2013), or managing patients with asthma (Alemi and Neuhauser 2004). They have been shown to be effective tools in the management of other medical conditions. In particular, they are useful for immediate detection of unusual change allowing for early intervention and prevention (Smith et al. 2013).

This study investigates the ability of the control chart methodology to predict manic or depressive episodes in patients with bipolar disorder by applying Shewhart's control rules to weekly self-reported scores from mania and depression self-measurement questionnaires. The main analysis considers control charts based on mean and standard deviation across all patients' episode-free run-in periods. The sensitivity and positive predictive value (PPV) of Shewhart's control rules for predicting manic or depressive episodes within the next 4 weeks are reported. Secondary analyses using a longer episode-free run-in period, different control chart types, different time frames to evaluate diagnostic accuracy parameters, lower thresholds defining episodes of either type, and missing data methods were also performed.

Methods

Data

The OXTEXT programme, funded by the UK National Institute of Health Research, investigates the benefit of self-monitoring in people with bipolar disorder using the True Colours self-management system (https://oxfordhealth.truecolours.nhs.uk/www/en/). Participants in the programme were prompted weekly by text messages or email to complete and return self-measurement questionnaires.

Mania was assessed using the Altman Self-Rating Mania Scale (ASRM) (Altman et al. 1997). This scale is formed of five items evaluating mood, self-confidence, sleep disturbance, speech, and activity level over the past week. Each item can take a value between 0 and 4. The total score for this scale ranges from 0 to 20. Higher scores indicate higher manic mood severity. A manic episode was defined as any instance where the ASRM score was greater or equal to 10, which is a pragmatic cut point to reflect clinically significant mania observed in the wider OXTEXT cohort (judged by OXTEXT programme experts).

Depression is assessed using the Quick Inventory of Depressive Symptomatology—Self Report (QIDS) (Rush et al. 2000). This scale is formed of 16 items evaluating nine symptom domains for depression according to DSM-IV (Association AP 1994) in the past week: sad mood, concentration, self-criticism, suicidal ideation, interest, energy/fatigue, sleep disturbance (initial, middle, and late insomnia or hypersomnia), decrease or increase in appetite or weight, and psychomotor agitation or retardation. Each domain can take a value between 0 and 3. The total score for this scale ranges from 0 to 27. Higher scores indicate higher severity of depression. A depressive episode was defined as any instance where the QIDS score was greater or equal to 15, which is the cut point defined as that for severe depression (Rush et al. 2003; University of Pittsburgh Epidemiology Data Centre 2017).

Data inclusion criteria were based on ASRM and QIDS scores submitted on the same date. Initial non-responses, assumed to be a participant's training period, were excluded. When a participant submitted several responses for a particular scale at a given time point, the average of these observations was included in the analysis. When repeated measurements occurred for a period of time, the most complete data were selected for that period. For participants who had a gap of 28 days or more since the last observation, data from the first record after the gap were selected. After this initial data selection, only participants with 12 or more records were considered, including only those who had a period of eight consecutive weeks without either a severe mania or depression episode (see below the definition of mania and depression episodes) after which period data were limited up to the first severe episode. Figure 1 gives a schematic representation of this inclusion/exclusion process. We will refer to the retained sample as the "short run-in period cohort".

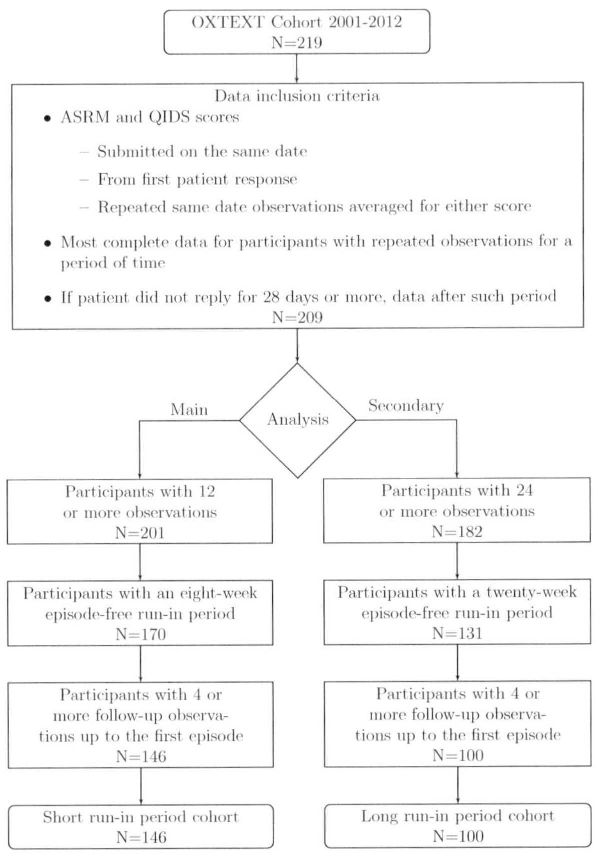

Fig. 1 Flow diagram of data inclusion. Data were selected from the starting OXTEXT cohort 2001–2012 according to inclusion criteria designed to reduce missing data. Cohorts for the main and secondary analyses were then selected based on the number of available individual observations such that every participant included had a period of eight consecutive weeks without either a manic or depressive episode (episode-free run-in period) and at least four follow-up observations up to the first episode

Control charts

For each of ASRM and QIDS, we developed four types of control charts, based on the same dataset: X-bar charts, personalized X-bar charts, individual-moving range charts, and run sum charts. An episode-free run-in period was defined as the first eight consecutive weeks without an episode of either type. A minimum of 50% observed values during the 8 weeks was required to establish the episode-free run-in period for each scale.

X-bar charts (Shewhart 1931) assume an underlying normal distribution of the data to define control limits as follows. The mean and standard deviation (SD) of the scores over the episode-free run-in period was calculated for all participants. The average, across all participants, of these means and SDs were subsequently used as global mean and SD to calculate universal upper control limits as the global mean plus one, two, or three global SDs. Lower control limits were not considered given that the medical interest in the context of bipolar disorder lies in detecting unusually high values, referred to as out-of-control values in the quality control literature (Montgomery 2013). To construct personalized X-bar charts, the control limits were calculated for each participant based on his/her mean score and SD over his/her episode-free run-in period. Figure 2 shows an example of an X-bar control chart for randomly generated ARSM data (mean = 5, SD = 3.3 points).

Individual-moving range charts are recommended in industry when single measurements are collected at a given time (Levinson 2010) as it happens with the monitoring of bipolar disorder patients. They are a pair of charts in which the first one displays the individual observations, with control limits based on their average and standard deviation estimated using the average moving range of pairs of consecutive measurements. The second chart displays the moving ranges, with control limits calculated using the average moving range and its estimated standard deviation. The function *qcc()* in R can be used to automatically calculate the limits and control charts themselves.

Run sum charts (Reynolds 1971; Aguirre-Torres and Reyes-López 1999) are also a pair of personalized charts, named X-bar and R charts, used to assess changes in the mean and dispersion of the process due to special causes. These charts do not use Shewhart's control rules separately. Instead, they incorporate a simple automatic procedure in which weights previously assigned to each control chart zone are added up depending on where the data, sampled beforehand, fall. Starting at zero, weights are added for all observations on the same side of the central line of the chart. Once an observation falls on the opposite side of the central line, the sum is reset to the weight associated with the control zone where the

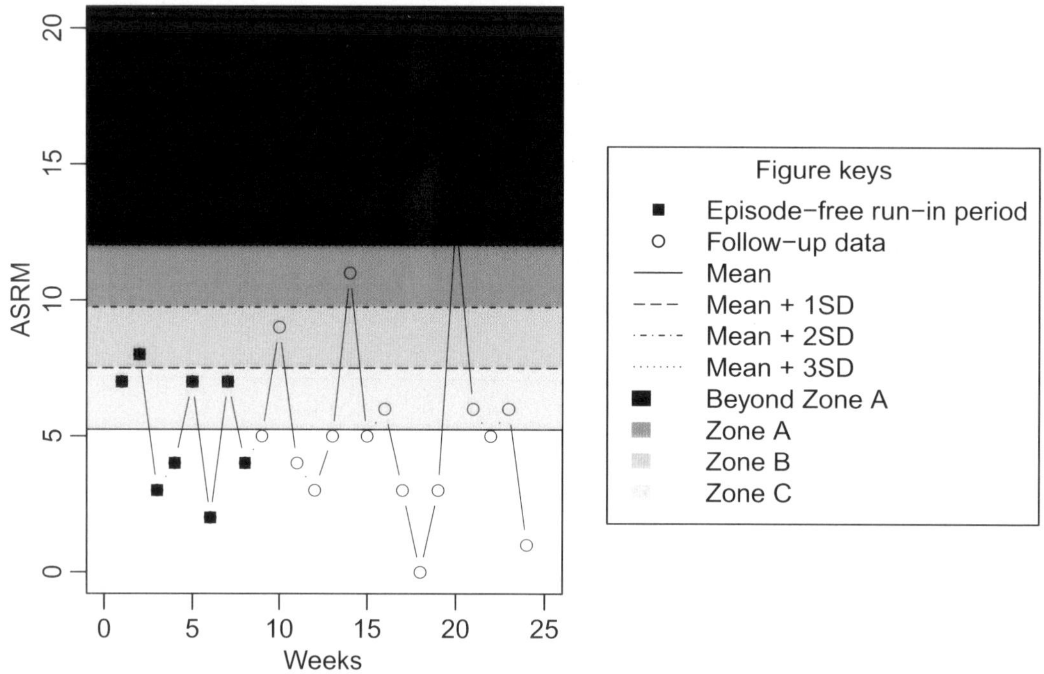

Fig. 2 Control chart and control chart zones. A control chart is a graphical representation of a process over time, for instance weekly ASRM scores, where control limits defined by the number of standard deviations from the mean are highlighted. The areas between the control limits define control zones used to subsequently apply control rules that will allow the user to identify observations potentially showing a special cause variability and not simply random variability. This study considered only control zones above the mean, because in the context of bipolar disorder unusually high mood scores are of greater interest than low ones. This figure shows an X-bar chart for randomly generated ARSM scores (mean = 5, SD = 3.3)

observation fell. The latter is also done when the total sum of weights exceeds a pre-specified threshold. In such case, a special variation cause is identified at the point where the threshold was overcome. In this work, Reynolds' (1971) weights and threshold were considered. These are: 0 for observations in Zone C, 1 for observations in Zone B, 2 for observations in Zone A, and 3 for observations beyond Zone A (control zones are represented in Fig. 2 and explained in more detail in the next section); threshold 5. Aguirre-Torres and Reyes-López (1999) demonstrated that this score system is less sensitive to small changes in dispersion and is likely to reduce the amount of false alarms. They also introduced a procedure to construct the R chart that allows using the same score system in both run sum charts. We followed the procedure to construct the charts described in detail in Aguirre-Torres and Reyes-López (1999). Both run sum charts are based on the average and range of rational subgroups which are groups of successive observations from the same patient. We selected the minimum possible rational subgroup size that these charts allow: two observations. Because the run sum procedure can only be applied when data are observed, we assessed these charts on the following scenarios: (1) only available data are used, ignoring episode-free run-in periods; (2) all data used, with missing data imputed through last value carried forward procedure and ignoring episode-free run-in periods; (3) episode-free run-in periods used to define the control zones, using mean imputation if data missing, and the run sum procedure was carried out over follow-up data (a) available, and (b) imputed using last value carried forward. The charts were considered independently and jointly.

Control limits and rules

All control charts were divided into zones covering the area above the mean (see Fig. 2), except for run sum charts that consider the area below the mean too. A measurement was defined to be: 'beyond zone A' if it lay more than 3 SD values above the mean (or 3SD values below the mean); 'in zone A' if it lay between 2 and 3 SD values above the mean (or between 2 and 3 SD values below the mean); 'in zone B' if it lay between 1 and 2 SD values above the mean (or between 1 and 2 SD values below the mean); 'in zone C' if it lay up to 1 SD above the mean (or up to 1 SD below the mean).

This study looked individually at the five control rules listed in Fig. 3 and also at the case when any of the five rules was activated. For its generality, the results presented in this manuscript are based on the 'any rule'

Control rules investigated in this study

Rule	Definition
1	1 observation beyond zone A
2a	2 of 3 successive observations in zone A
2b	4 of 5 successive observations in zone B or beyond
2c	8 successive observations above the mean
3	6 successive strictly increasing (moving average) observations

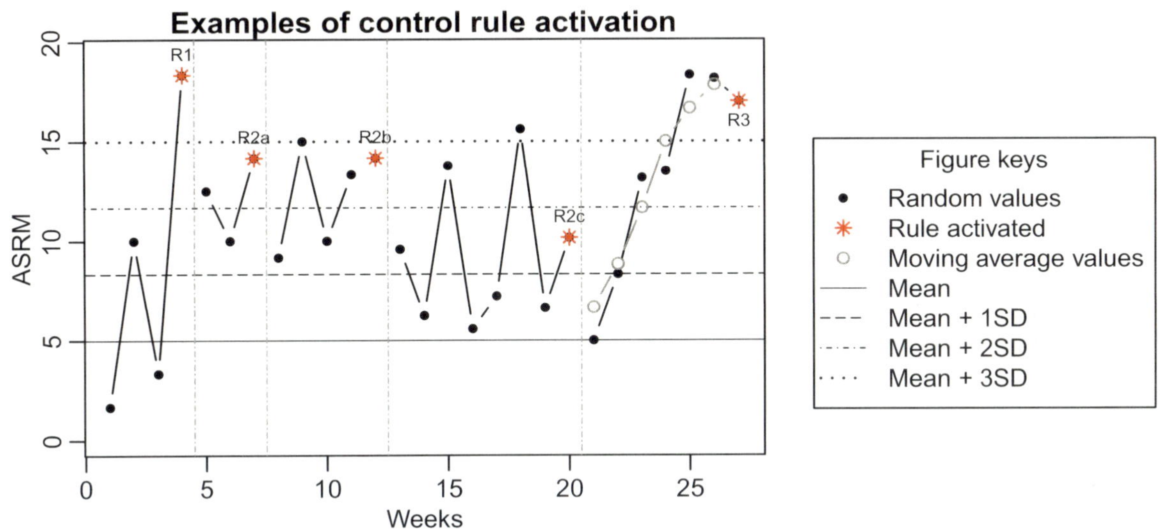

Fig. 3 Control rules investigated in this study and examples of control rule activation. ASRM scores were randomly generated with mean = 5 and SD = 3.3. Independent sections where each of the five control rules investigated in this study was activated are shown. A control rule was said to be activated on the observation by which all its conditions were satisfied

context. Results for the individual rules are shown in Additional files 1 and 2 for universal and personalized X-bar charts; and Additional files 3 and 4 for individual-moving range charts. Rules 1, 2a, 2b, and 2c are the usual first four Shewhart's rules (Kane 1989). Shewhart's rule 3 (6 successive increasing observations above the mean or 6 successive decreasing observations below the mean) was modified to be six successive strictly increasing observations above the mean, where the observations were transformed to the moving average of each observation and the observations on either side. A control rule was said to be activated on the observation by which all its conditions were satisfied. Figure 3 also shows examples of rule activation for randomly generated ASRM scores with mean = 5 and SD = 3.3 points.

For each of ASRM and QIDS, we calculated the sensitivity and positive predictive value of Shewhart's control rules for predicting manic or depressive episodes as follows. The sensitivity of control rule methodology for predicting clinical episodes was defined as the percentage of episodes that were preceded by activation of a rule in the previous 4 weeks across all participants. The positive predictive value (PPV) of control rule methodology was defined as the percentage of control rule activations that were succeeded by an episode within the next 4 weeks across all participants. To avoid introducing bias, activated rules that coincided with an episode were excluded from the analysis of PPV. Figure 4 shows an example in which the sensitivity and PPV of Shewhart's control rules to predict depressive episodes in the next 4 weeks based on 'any rule' and using universal X-bar charts (with mean = 6.2 and SD = 2.5) are calculated. For this example, a random sample of four anonymized patients was extracted from the QIDS data imputed using last value carried forward (see "Secondary analyses" for details regarding this dataset). All depressive episodes and points where a rule was activated are highlighted differentiating between rules pre-episode and rules coinciding with an episode. Focusing on the first episode ever, the window of 4 weeks pre-episode to assess sensitivity is also indicated. In this example, there were a total of four depressive episodes, two of which were preceded by the activation of a rule in the previous 4 weeks. This gives a sensitivity of 50%. As for PPV, a total of 13 pre-episode

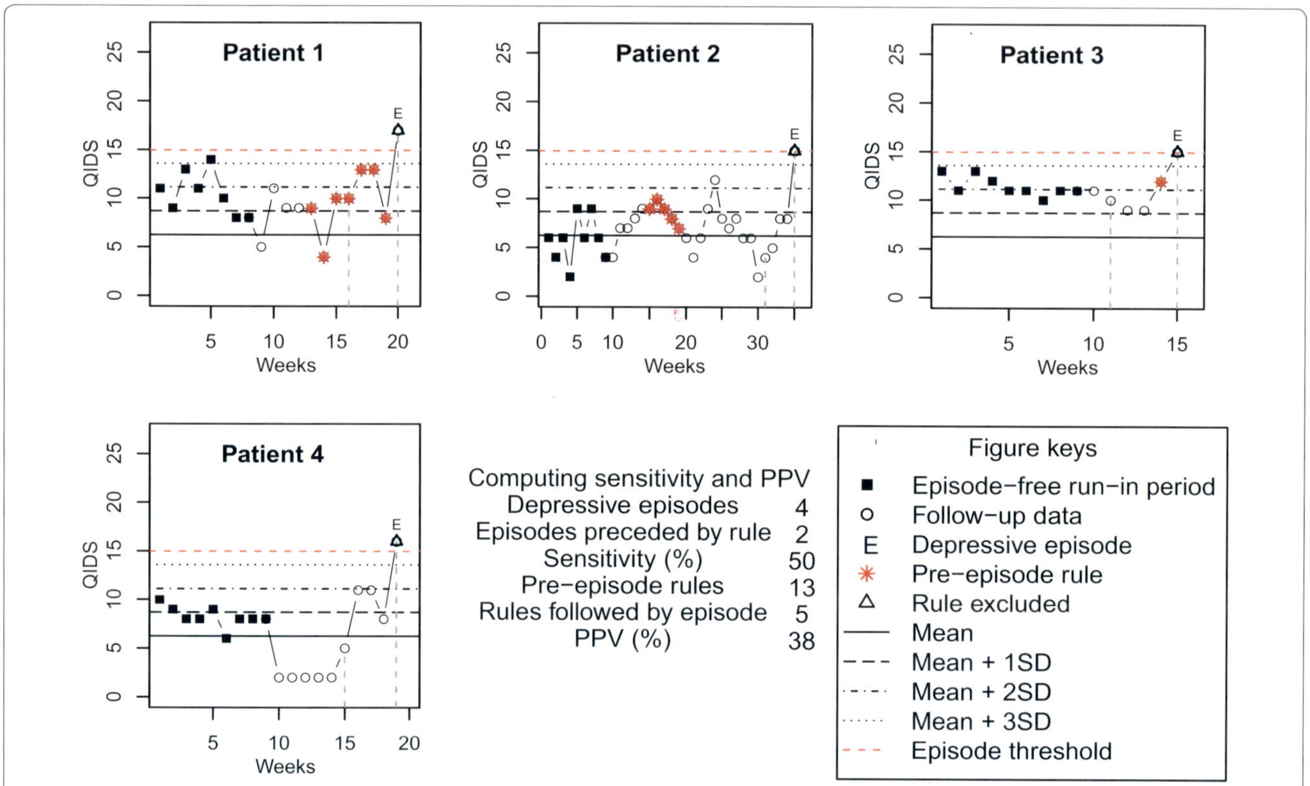

Fig. 4 Example of sensitivity and positive predictive value calculation. Calculation of the sensitivity and positive predictive value of Shewhart's control rules to predict a depressive episode in the next 4 weeks using universal X-bar charts (with mean = 6.2 and SD = 2.5) across a sample of four anonymized patients. QIDS data used in this plot have been imputed using last value carried forward

rules were activated, 5 of which were succeeded by an episode in the next 4 weeks, giving a PPV of 38%.

For comparison, Fig. 5 shows the corresponding calculation procedure when personalized X-bar charts are used. Given that the episode-free run-in period of each patient is used to define his/her own control chart, the control zones are different for all patients. In this particular example, both sensitivity and PPV values are smaller than the values obtained when universal control charts are used (see Fig. 4).

The sensitivity and PPV associated with run sum charts were calculated in a similar manner to the one described above, assuming that a rule was activated at the point where a special variation cause was identified.

Main analysis

The main analysis considered X-bar charts with universal limits (i.e. based on the global mean and SD of either ASRM or QIDS scores) applied to non-imputed data from the short run-in period cohort. Missing responses were coded as − 1 and Shewhart's control rules applied to the corresponding recoded dataset. We focused on the sensitivity and PPV of 'any rule' activated. That is, to calculate the sensitivity value, all rules activated within the previous 4 weeks of an episode were counted independently of the type of rule. Similarly, to calculate the PPV, for all rules activated the total number of times an episode occurred within the following 4 weeks was summed. For both metrics, the counting process was performed across all patients.

Secondary analyses

We performed a secondary analysis evaluating the effect of the initial episode-free run-in period's length increasing this length to 20 weeks. A different subsample was used extracted from the OXTEXT cohort, following similar criteria as for the main analysis except that only participants with 24 or more records were considered, selecting those with 20 consecutive weeks without either a severe mania or depression episode, prior to start of follow-up. Participants' data were limited to the first severe episode as before. We will refer to this sample as the "long run-in period cohort". There was an overlap between the short and long run-in period cohorts, as described in Fig. 1.

The impact of missing data was investigated using the last value carried forward (LVCF) imputation method, assuming that a participant's scores remained constant

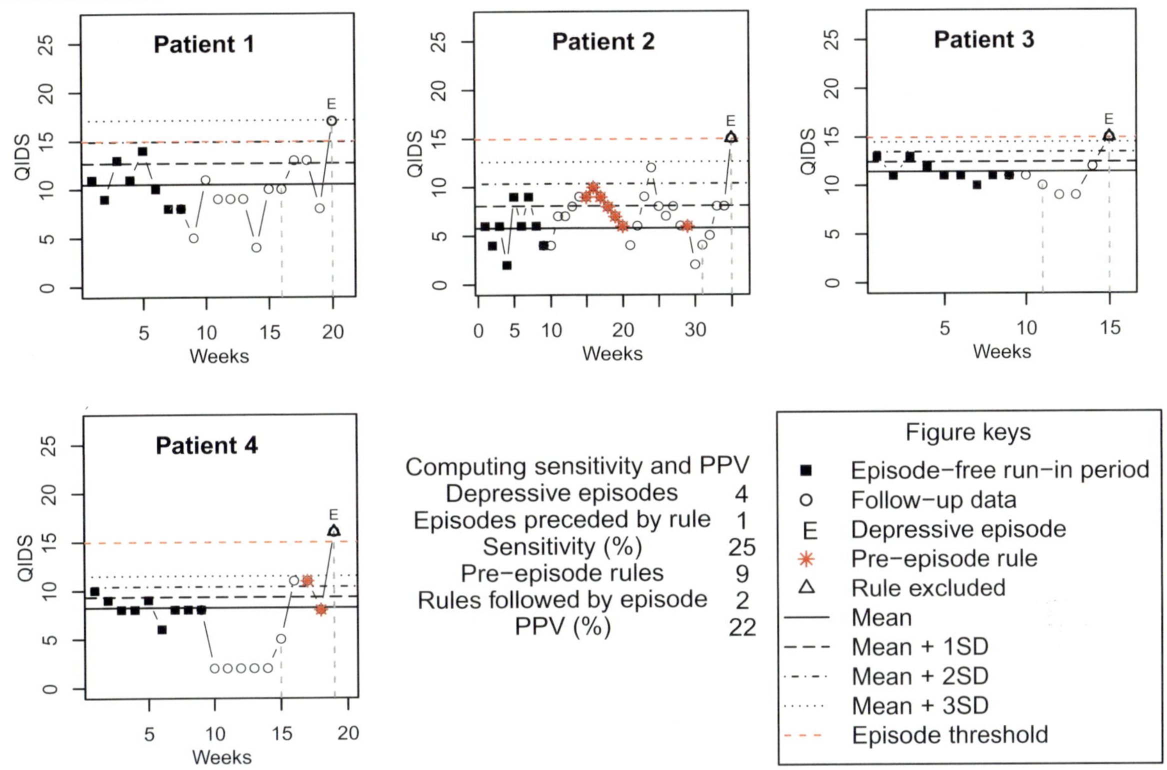

Fig. 5 Example of sensitivity and positive predictive value calculation using personalized control charts. Calculation of the sensitivity and positive predictive value of Shewhart's control rules to predict a depressive episode in the next 4 weeks using personalized X-bar charts for the same data used in Fig. 4

until the next response was observed. All analyses were repeated using personalized X-bar charts, individual-moving range charts, and run sum charts. To explore the effect of the threshold used to define an episode on the performance of Shewhart's control rules, the cohort extractions and, subsequently, application of universal control charts were repeated using a cutoff of 11 for QIDS [this covers moderate and severe depressive episodes (University of Pittsburgh Epidemiology Data Centre 2017)] and a cutoff of 6 for ASRM [only one point above that recommended by Altman et al. (1997)].

Manic episodes appeared to be occurring less frequently than depressive episodes; thus, we performed a post hoc analysis evaluating the sensitivity and PPV of Shewhart's control rules to detect a manic episode within the next 8 weeks for all scenarios considered in this study.

Data extraction was carried out in Stata/SE 12.0 (StataCorp 2011). All other analyses were performed in R 3.0.1 (R Core Team 2013). Calculation of 95% confidence intervals for proportions was done using the prop. Test R function. We used the Wilcoxon rank sum test to compare the number of weeks to first episode and to first rule activation in the short- and long run-in period cohorts.

Results

Main analysis

An OXTEXT cohort of 219 participants with data recorded from 2001 to 2012, with median (IQR) follow-up of 60 (24–127) weeks, was available for this study. A sample of 146 participants was extracted for the main analysis following the inclusion criteria described in Fig. 1 (short run-in period cohort). Table 1 shows the baseline and episode-free run-in period characteristics for this sample. In particular, the overall episode-free run-in period mean (SD) was 2.0 (1.7) points for ASRM and 6.2 (2.5) points for QIDS.

The median (IQR) waiting time from the first week after the episode-free run-in period to the first episode was 10.3 (5.3–39.6) weeks for ASRM and 10.5 (5.1–22.7) weeks for QIDS. A total of 53 (36%) participants had at least one manic episode and 67 (46%) participants had at least one depressive episode. As for the median (IQR) warning time from rule activation to episode, this was 1 (0–15) week for ASRM and 0 (0–4.5) weeks for QIDS. The average percentage of missing values was 21% (95% CI 17.8–24.2%) for ASRM and 28% (95% CI 23.9–32.1%) for QIDS, respectively.

Table 1 Participant and episode-free run-in period characteristics

Baseline participant characteristics	Short run-in period cohort[a] $N = 146$	Long run-in period cohort[b] $N = 100$
Males, *n* (%)	53 (37)	40 (41)[c]
Age, years, mean (SD)	43.4 (13.3)	44.5 (13.5)
White, *n* (%)	139 (97)	94 (96)[c]
Education, *n* (%)		
O-level/GCSE or fewer years	18 (13)	12 (12)
A-level/AS levels/Scottish Highers/HND/BTEC	24 (17)	17 (18)
Degree (includes NVQ level 5)	56 (40)	35 (36)[c]
Post-graduate degree	43 (30)	33 (34)[c]
Occupation, *n* (%)		
Disabled	1 (1)	1 (1)[c]
Housewife/homemaker	9 (6)	7 (7)[c]
Full-time student	16 (11)	9 (9)[c]
Unemployed	27 (19)	16 (17)[c]
Retired	11 (8)	9 (9)[c]
Employed	76 (54)	54 (56)[c]
Diagnosis, *n* (%)		
Bipolar disorder type I	80 (58)	60 (65)[c]
Bipolar disorder type II	53 (38)	30 (32)[c]
Bipolar disorder not otherwise specified	5 (4)	3 (3)[c]
Depression history		
Episodes, median (IQR)	10 (6–20)	10 (6–17.5)
Age of impairment, years, mean (SD)	21.7 (9.0)	23.1 (9.8)
Duration of illness, years, median (IQR)	19 (10–30)	18 (10–31)
Hospital admissions, yes, *n* (%)	63 (43)	41 (41)
Mania history		
Episodes, median (IQR)	10 (4–20)	9 (4–15)
Age of impairment, years, mean (SD)	27.2 (11.4)	28.7 (11.7)
Duration of illness, years, median (IQR)	13 (6–25)	12 (6–26)
Hospital admissions, yes, *n* (%)	46 (32)	33 (33)
Alcohol use, yes, *n* (%)	109 (86)	71 (85)[c]
Smoker, yes, *n* (%)	80 (56)	54 (55)[c]
Episode-free run-in period characteristics		
Number of prompts, mean (SD)	9 (1.1)	22.2 (2)
Percentage of missing values, mean (SD)	10 (14)	13 (14)
ASRM score across participants		
Mean score, mean (SD)	2.0 (1.6)	1.8 (1.4)
Standard deviation of score, mean (SD)	1.7 (1.0)	1.6 (0.9)
QIDS score across participants		
Mean score, mean (SD)	6.2 (2.7)	5.1 (2.4)
Standard deviation of score, mean (SD)	2.5 (1.2)	2.5 (1.0)

n number of observed values, *SD* standard deviation, *IQR* interquartile range

[a] Short run-in period cohort is the cohort for the main analysis defined by an episode-free run-in period 8 weeks long

[b] Long run-in period cohort is the cohort for secondary analysis defined by an episode-free run-in period 20 weeks long

[c] Percentages calculated over the total observed values

Tables 2 and 3 show the sensitivity and PPV of Shewhart's control rules for ASRM and QIDS, respectively, for all analyses (except for run sum charts) focusing on 'any rule'. Results for individual and moving range charts are presented independently. Results obtained by simultaneously using both charts were similar to when only the moving range chart was used and thus omitted for simplicity. Additional files 5 and 6 contain the

Table 2 Shewhart's control rules sensitivity and PPV for predicting manic episodes within the next 4 weeks

	Manic episodes	Episodes preceded by any rule activation		Rules activated	Rules followed by an episode	
	n	*n*	Sensitivity% (95% CI)	*n*	*n*	PPV% (95% CI)
Universal X-bar charts						
Short run-in period cohort						
Original data[a]	53[a]	16[a]	30 (19, 45)[a]	439[a]	29[a]	7 (5, 9)[a]
LVCF imputed data	53	18	34 (22, 48)	755	47	6 (5, 8)
Long run-in period cohort						
Original data	25	14	56 (35, 75)	548	22	4 (3, 6)
LVCF imputed data	25	15	60 (39, 78)	958	35	4 (3, 5)
Personalized X-bar charts						
Short run-in period cohort						
Original data	53	15	28 (17, 43)	666	29	4 (3, 6)
LVCF imputed data	53	18	34 (22, 48)	1052	42	4 (3, 5)
Long run-in period cohort						
Original data	25	10	40 (22, 61)	421	15	4 (2, 6)
LVCF imputed data	25	12	48 (28, 68)	711	25	4 (2, 5)
Individual-moving range charts						
Short run-in period cohort						
Original data						
Individual chart	53	17	32 (20, 46)	944	35	4 (3, 5)
Moving range chart	53	22	42 (28, 56)	1333	49	4 (3, 5)
LVCF imputed data						
Individual chart	53	20	38 (25, 52)	1415	49	3 (3, 5)
Moving range chart	53	27	51 (37, 65)	2027	76	4 (3, 5)
Long run-in period cohort						
Original data						
Individual chart	25	10	40 (22, 61)	635	23	4 (2, 5)
Moving range chart	25	13	52 (32, 72)	1078	27	3 (2, 4)
LVCF imputed data						
Individual chart	25	11	44 (25, 65)	1012	34	3 (2, 5)
Moving range chart	25	15	60 (39, 78)	1697	44	3 (2, 3)

PPV positive predictive value, *CI* confidence interval, *LVCF* last value carried forward

[a] Results from main analysis

results for run sum charts. In the main analysis, applying universal X-bar charts on non-imputed data from the short run-in period cohort, the sensitivity of Shewhart's control rules to detect a manic episode within the next 4 weeks was 30% (95% CI 19–45%). The PPV was 7% (95% CI 5–9%). The sensitivity of Shewhart's control rules to detect a depressive episode within the next 4 weeks was 33% (95% CI 22–46%), whereas the corresponding PPV was 9% (95% CI 6–12%).

Secondary analyses

The long run-in period cohort was formed of 100 participants. The baseline characteristics for this sample were similar to those for the short run-in period cohort (see Table 1). Twenty-five (25%) participants experienced a manic episode and 32 (32%) a depressive episode. The average percentage of missing data at follow-up was smaller than in the short run-in period cohort for both scales [3% (95% CI − 7 to 14%) less for ASRM; 4% (95% CI − 8 to 16%) less for QIDS]. Both the median time to first episode and warning time after first rule activation were higher for the ASRM scale in the long run-in period cohort than in the short run-in period cohort (34 vs 10.3 weeks, Wilcoxon rank sum test p value = 0.043; 13 vs 1 week, Wilcoxon rank sum test p value = 0.060, respectively). The correspondent values for QIDS were similar to those in the short run-in period cohort. In other words, in the study at hand, manic episodes occurred less frequently than depressive episodes.

Table 3 Shewhart's control rules sensitivity and PPV for predicting depressive episodes within the next 4 weeks

	Depressive episodes	Episodes preceded by any rule activation		Rules activated	Rules followed by an episode	
	n	*n*	Sensitivity % (95% CI)	*n*	*n*	PPV % (95% CI)
Universal X-bar charts						
Short run-in period cohort						
Original data[a]	67[a]	22[a]	33 (22, 46)[a]	395[a]	34[a]	9 (6, 12)[a]
LVCF imputed data	67	27	40 (29, 53)	777	51	7 (5, 9)
Long run-in period cohort						
Original data	32	11	34 (19, 53)	456	19	4 (3, 7)
LVCF imputed data	32	11	34 (19, 53)	924	20	2 (1, 3)
Personalized X-bar charts						
Short run-in period cohort						
Original data	67	12	18 (10, 30)	520	21	4 (3, 6)
LVCF imputed data	67	15	22 (13, 53)	848	33	4 (3, 5)
Long run-in period cohort						
Original data	32	11	34 (19, 53)	430	26	6 (4, 9)
LVCF imputed data	32	10	31 (17, 50)	749	27	4 (2, 5)
Individual-moving range charts						
Short run-in period cohort						
Original data						
Individual chart	67	13	19 (11, 31)	785	26	3 (2, 5)
Moving range chart	67	38	57 (44, 69)	3790	119	3 (3, 4)
LVCF imputed data						
Individual chart	67	17	25 (16, 38)	1222	42	3 (3, 5)
Moving range chart	67	44	66 (53, 77)	5170	160	3 (3, 4)
Long run-in period cohort						
Original data						
Individual chart	32	12	38 (22, 56)	749	30	4 (3, 6)
Moving range chart	32	22	69 (50, 83)	3246	61	2 (1, 2)
LVCF imputed data						
Individual chart	32	12	38 (22, 56)	1170	33	3 (2, 4)
Moving range chart	32	23	72 (53, 86)	4451	75	2 (1, 2)

PPV positive predictive value, *CI* confidence interval, *LVCF* last value carried forward

[a] Results from the main analysis

Table 4 presents the differences between the results from the main analysis, using universal X-bar charts on non-imputed data from the short run-in period cohort, and each of the secondary analyses over non-imputed data, except for run sum charts results which use a different procedure to determine rule activations. For all secondary analyses using X-bar charts, the corresponding 95% confidence intervals indicated that the sensitivity of Shewhart's control rules to detect manic or depressive episodes within the next 4 weeks was similar to the sensitivity obtained in the main analysis [median absolute difference = 4.7% (IQR 1.5–15.5%)]. However, the sensitivity values over the long run-in period cohort were consistently larger than in the main analysis, with the largest difference being + 26% (95% CI − 0.2 to 51.8%) when universal X-bar charts were used over ASRM data. The smallest difference was − 15% (95% CI − 30.9 to 1.1%) when personalized X-bar charts were used over short run-in period QIDS data. Individual charts performed similar to personalized X-bar charts. Moving range charts returned consistently larger sensitivity values than individual charts and universal and personalized X-bar charts. As for run sum charts, the sensitivity values were also consistently larger than for universal and personalized X-bar charts, with combination of run sum X-bar and R charts showing greater values than for each of these charts separately.

Regarding PPVs, smaller values were observed in all secondary analyses, with a median absolute difference of 4.1% (IQR 2.9–5.4%). In particular, for ASRM data, PPVs

Table 4 Difference (95% confidence interval) between main and secondary analysis results over non-imputed data

	Non-imputed ASRM		Non-imputed QIDS	
	Sensitivity	PPV	Sensitivity	PPV
Universal X-bar charts				
Short run-in period (main analysis)	0 (0, 0)	0 (0, 0)	0 (0, 0)	0 (0, 0)
Long run-in period	25.8 (– 0.2, 51.8)	– 2.6 (– 5.6, 0.5)	1.5 (– 20.0, 23.0)	– 4.4 (– 8.0, – 0.9)
Personalized X-bar charts				
Short run-in period	– 1.9 (– 21.1, 17.3)	– 2.3 (– 5.2, 0.7)	– 14.9 (– 30.9, 1.1)	– 4.6 (– 8.0, – 1.1)
Long run-in period	9.8 (– 16.0, 35.6)	– 3.0 (– 6.2, 0.1)	1.5 (– 20.0, 23.0)	– 2.6 (– 6.4, 1.3)
Individual-moving range charts				
Short run-in period cohort				
Individual chart	1.9 (– 17.6, 21.4)	– 2.9 (– 5.7, – 0.1)	– 13.4 (– 29.6, 2.8)	– 5.3 (– 8.5, – 2.1)
Moving range chart	11.3 (– 8.7, 31.3)	– 2.9 (– 5.6, – 0.2)	53.7 (39.7, 67.8)	– 5.5 (– 8.4, – 2.5)
Long run-in period cohort				
Individual chart	9.8 (– 16.0, 35.6)	– 3.0 (– 5.9, – 0.1)	4.7 (– 17.8, 27.2)	– 4.6 (– 7.9, – 1.3)
Moving range chart	21.8 (– 4.3, 47.9)	– 4.1 (– 6.8, – 1.4)	35.9 (14.0, 57.8)	– 6.7 (– 9.7, – 3.8)

Numbers in this table can be interpreted as difference of proportions (proportion in the secondary analysis minus proportion in the main analysis) and its corresponding 95% confidence interval. A negative value indicates that the result observed in the secondary analysis was smaller than in the main analysis

ASRM Altman Self-Rating Mania Scale, *QIDS* Quick Inventory of Depressive Symptomatology—Self-Report, *PPV* positive predictive value

over the long run-in period cohort were smaller than in the short run-in period cohort, with a minimum difference of – 2.3% (95% CI – 5.2 to 0.7%) showed by personalized X-bar charts, and a maximum difference of – 4.1% (95% CI – 6.8 to – 1.4%) showed by moving range charts. There was not a clear pattern over QIDS, where the minimum difference was – 2.6% (95% CI – 6.4 to – 1.3%) showed by personalized X-bar charts, and the maximum difference was – 6.7% (95% CI – 9.7 to – 3.8%) showed by moving range charts. PPVs for sum rum charts were also smaller than those from the main analysis.

Increasing the time to evaluate the diagnostic accuracy of Shewhart's control rules to predict manic episodes from 4 to 8 weeks (see Additional file 7), varying the type of chart or the length of episode-free period returned similar results to those from the main analysis. Imputing the last observed value improved the sensitivity of Shewhart's rules, but not their PPV. The differences were non-significant, as indicated by the corresponding 95% CI is in Table 4. Reducing the cutoff to define episodes of either type had an impact on the sample size, and total number of episodes, for both cohorts. After applying the data extraction procedure described in Fig. 1, the number of patients in the short episode-free run-in period cohort changed from 146 (53 episodes) to 99 (48 episodes) in the ASRM dataset, and from 146 (67 episodes) to 96 (57 episodes) in the QIDS dataset. In the long episode-free run-in period cohort, the number of patients changed from 100 (25 episodes) to 65 (28 episodes) in the ASRM dataset, and from 100 (32 episodes) to 68 (37 episodes) in the QIDS dataset. The sensitivity of any rule when using universal control charts was slightly improved under this scenario, but not their PPV. This was true for both scales (see Additional file 8).

Discussion

We have used control chart methodology to identify changes in mood scores in people with bipolar disorder that could indicate the emergence of a clinically important manic or depressive episode. We estimate that Shewhart's control rules have sensitivity of 30 and 33% for manic and depressive episodes, so that approximately one-third of episodes are detected in advance. We also estimate that the positive predictive values are less than 10%, so that many 'false positive' alerts would occur in addition to those genuinely detecting an emerging clinical episode. Given the very significant impact major mood episodes can have on patient's lives, being able to prevent episodes is a desirable feature of this statistical tool even though the proportion of false alarms is high. There is potential to improve the sensitivity at the expense of further false alarms, for example by using alternative control rules or different methods to calibrate the chart, as shown in Tables 2, 3 and 4.

Although approximately two-thirds of episodes would not be detected in advance by the control rules, telemonitoring itself could detect all episodes, as defined here, at least at the moment of occurrence. Mood episodes usually last longer than a week (Solomon et al. 2010); thus, control chart methodology becomes a useful tool to provide treatment as soon as the symptoms arise. As the analysis was performed considering the scales separately, mixed episodes were not explored, nor episode length.

To the best of our knowledge, no previous attempt has been made to use control charts to aid the management of patients with bipolar disorder. We report the analysis of four types of control charts based on a normality assumption. We also explored the potential use of attribute charts for which the strong, and possibly unrealistic, assumption of the ASRM and QIDS scores following a binomial distribution is required. The binomial parameter n was taken as the maximum possible score (i.e. $n = 20$ for ASRM; $n = 27$ for QIDS), and the proportion parameter was estimated as the sum of scores over the episode-free run-in period divided by n times the episode-free run-in period length. Upper control limits were then calculated as the 68th, 95th, and 99th‰ of the corresponding binomial distribution, with the mean being equal to n times the estimated proportion. This type of charts was evaluated in a personalized setting only. The results were similar to those obtained for personalized X-bar charts and are mentioned here for completion (data available on request). In summary, our analysis shows that personalized and universal X-bar control limits charts have no effect on the sensitivity and PPV of Shewhart's control rules. The sensitivity of Shewhart's control rules is greater when using more ad hoc charts like the individual-moving range charts, but at the cost of even lower PPV than what was observed for universal and personalized X-bar charts. Moreover, these types of charts require consecutive observations, a characteristic which represents a potential practical disadvantage when monitoring bipolar patients due to the likelihood of missing data. The latter is also true for run sum charts which incorporate a much simpler procedure to identify out-of-control observations and present very high sensitivity values, although much lower PPVs than those from our main analysis. Universal X-bar charts have the advantage of providing an a priori tool for the monitoring of bipolar disorder patients that can be used straightforwardly.

The length of the episode-free run-in period used to construct the control charts also did not affect the results for either score. Missing data in the context of bipolar disorder is an important factor to consider given their potential informative nature. Due to the characteristics of bipolar disorder, patients with severe symptoms are less likely to respond when an action is required as loss of insight is a common symptom. For instance, a correlation between missing values and the standard deviation of sleep ratings has been observed (Moore et al. 2014). For these reasons, a secondary analysis evaluating the effect of missing data was performed using the LVCF method. LVCF is considered conservative and the advantages of methods like mixed models (Stevens et al. 2010) have previously been shown (Hamer and Simpson 2009). However, this method was implemented here due to its simplicity and potentially small bias (Glasziou et al. 2008). The use of mean imputation methods would have required a careful evaluation of linearity and possibly data transformation due to the nonlinear pattern observed in ASRM and QIDS scores (Moore et al. 2012a, b). The results after LVCF imputation were similar to those from the main analysis. Looking at individual rules, we observed that Rule 1 contributed the most towards the overall sensitivity and PPV reported here, whereas Rule 3 contributed the least. However, looking at the activation of any rule increases the possibility of predicting an episode by considering a greater variety of data patterns than a single rule would. For this reason, results in this paper are based on 'any rule' activation. An exploratory analysis of the impact of the threshold employed to define an episode of either type was performed. However, consensus on the threshold to be used to define either depressive or manic episodes should be achieved previous to constructing the control charts as suggested in this work, because the episode-free run-in period, from which the control chart defining parameters are obtained, is highly dependent on such thresholds.

The impact of medication type in the prediction performance of control chart methodology was not explored in this study. However, it is expected that as patients' responses to different medication types vary, also the signals detected by the control charts would differ between medication types. Further investigating whether this methodology could perform better when used jointly with a specific medication type could be part of an improved treatment delivery.

The study was performed using available observational data. It is possible that selection bias is present in the results shown. External validation or simulation confirming the findings would complement this analysis. The effect of participants' clinical and demographic characteristics on the predictive ability of Shewhart's control rules was also not explored in this work. It is likely that taking them into account when applying control chart methodology could have resulted in a larger PPV. Busch et al. (2012) investigated the prediction accuracy for remission of random effect regression models fitted to mood scores obtained through the Montgomery-Asberg Depression Rating Scale and Young Mania Rating Scale at quarterly time points over a year. They found that prediction models that include more complete medical information have a good prediction accuracy, which is higher than those models including limited information with non-significantly different accuracy in the longer term.

Ratheesh et al. (2015) identified six instruments that predict the onset of bipolar disorder. The sensitivity and PPV of such instruments varied from 33 to 100 and from 16.7 to 72.7%, respectively. These instruments were evaluated on younger participants than those included in this study. These samples were either university students, offspring of patients with a diagnosis of bipolar disorder, or people presenting bipolar disorder symptoms at baseline. Thus, the reported sensitivity and PPVs and the corresponding values obtained in this study are not directly comparable.

Bonsall et al. (2012) focused on QIDS scores fitting different nonlinear time series to two clinically identified groups of patients (those with relatively stable or unstable mood scores) using a small sample size. The present analysis shows that control charts can equally be applied to both ASRM and QIDS scores with similar results. The nonlinear nature of the data was considered by exploring universal and personalized control limits and also by assuming a binomial distribution of the data with results also similar to the main analysis presented here.

Moore et al. (2012a, b) also used time series methodology to model QIDS scores looking at the correlation between the scale domains. They found that sleep and appetite/weight is the pair of less correlated factors and sleep variability is inversely correlated with irregularity of data. The current analysis is based on total scores which is what clinicians look at in the first instance in practice. Moreover, total scores summarize the effect of the individual domains.

Although the control charts constructed in this study are based on a sufficiently inclusive cohort, it is desirable to calculate the universal control limits based on a more representative sample. A meta-analysis to obtain more representative summary statistics for ASRM and QIDS scores could be a next step to achieve this. A randomized study of the utility of control charts in the clinical practice would provide evidence of the potential advantages of basing an intervention system on the data provided by control charts.

A further question is the possibility of defining a single control chart that combines the manic and depressive scores. We have analysed the performance of Shewhart's control rules applied independently to depressive and manic scores. However, given the nature of bipolar disorder, there is an apparent negative interaction between these and in mixed affective states patients can experience both manic and depressive symptoms concurrently.

Finally, having a small PPV and thus a large amount of false alarms could be due to process autocorrelation. This methodological issue could be approached by exploring the use of time series and residual control charts, as suggested by Moran and Solomon (2013).

Conclusions

Control charts are a visual display of data that can aid patients and clinicians to systematically identify when a patient should seek and receive clinical advice to prevent manic and depressive episodes. Shewhart's control rules are designed to separate random variability from special cause changes in processes. Thus, mood scores activating any of these rules will usually tend to be beyond the control limits indicating that the patient is getting worse. In most cases, this signal alarm can occur before the mood scores reach the threshold value defining an episode as the PPV found in this work indicates. The universal control charts constructed in this study can easily be implemented in the form of a programme that prospectively monitors regular mood scores sent electronically. This potentially provides clinicians with a practical tool to manage patients with bipolar disorder.

Additional files

Additional file 1. Sensitivity and PPV of individual Shewhart's control rules for predicting manic episodes within the next four weeks using universal and personalized X-bar charts.

Additional file 2. Sensitivity and PPV of individual Shewhart's control rules for predicting depressive episodes within the next four weeks using universal and personalized X-bar charts.

Additional file 3. Sensitivity and PPV of individual Shewhart's control rules for predicting manic episodes within the next four weeks using individual-moving range charts.

Additional file 4. Sensitivity and PPV of individual Shewhart's control rules for predicting depressive episodes within the next four weeks using individual-moving range charts.

Additional file 5. Sensitivity and PPV of run sum procedure for predicting manic episodes within the next four weeks.

Additional file 6. Sensitivity and PPV of run sum procedure for predicting depressive episodes within the next four weeks.

Additional file 7. Shewhart's control rules sensitivity and PPV for predicting manic episodes within the next eight weeks.

Additional file 8. Sensitivity and PPV of any Shewhart's control rule for predicting manic and depressive episodes within the next four weeks, when a depressive episode is defined as a QIDS score ≥ 11 and a manic episode is defined as an ASRM score ≥ 6.

Abbreviations

ASRM: Altman Self-Rating Mania Scale; CI: confidence interval; DSM-IV: Diagnostic and Statistical Manual of Mental Disorders, 4th edition; IQR: interquartile range; LVCF: last value carried forward; OXTEXT: study about the benefit of self-monitoring in people with bipolar disorder using the True Colours self-management system (https://oxfordhealth.truecolours.nhs.uk/www/en/); PPV: positive predictive value; QIDS: quick inventory of depressive symptomatology self-report; SD: standard deviation.

Authors' contributions

RS, RP, and JRG made contributions to conception and design of the study. JRG contributed with data acquisition. MAVM performed the statistical analysis and drafted the manuscript. RS and RP provided statistical input and JRG and KEAS provided clinical input for data interpretation. All authors contributed to the final manuscript. All authors read and approved the final manuscript.

Author details

[1] Nuffield Department of Primary Care Health Sciences, University of Oxford, Radcliffe Observatory Quarter, Woodstock Road, Oxford OX2 6GG, UK.
[2] Department of Psychiatry, Warneford Hospital, University of Oxford, Warneford Lane, Oxford OX3 7JX, UK.

Acknowledgements

The authors thank Clare Bankhead for her helpful comments and proofreading the manuscript; Joshua Wallace for facilitating the access to and understanding of the OXTEXT database; Paul Moore and Hugo Maruri-Aguilar for helpful discussions during initial data analysis; Amy Bilderbeck for helpful comments on early manuscript versions. The authors also wish to thank the reviewers for their helpful suggestions to improve the manuscript.

Competing interests

The authors declare that they have no competing interests.

Funding

This research was part funded by the National Institute of Health Research (NIHR) National School of Primary Care: Department of Health, UK, by the NIHR Health Technology Assessment Programme, and by the NIHR Biomedical Research Centre, Oxford. This paper also presents independent research funded by the NIHR under its Programme Grants for Applied Research Programme (Reference Number RP-PG-0108-10087). KEAS and JRG are supported by a Wellcome Trust Strategic Award (CONBRIO: Collaborative Network for Bipolar Research to Improve Outcomes). The views expressed are those of the authors and not necessarily those of the NHS, the NIHR, or the Department of Health. Neither agency had any role in the design of the study, data collection, analysis, or interpretation, nor in the writing or decision to submit the manuscript for publication.

References

Aguirre-Torres V, Reyes-López D. Run sum charts for both X and R. Qual Eng. 1999;12(1):7–12.

Alemi F, Neuhauser D. Time-between control charts for monitoring asthma attacks. Jt Comm J Qual Saf. 2004;30(2):95–102.

Altman EG, Hedeker D, Peterson JL, Davis JM. The Altman Self-Rating Mania Scale. Biol Psychiatry. 1997;42(10):948–55.

Association AP. Diagnostic and statistical manual of mental disorders (DSM-IV). 4th ed. Washington, DC: American Psychiatric Association; 1994.

Bonsall MB, Wallace-Hadrill SM, Geddes JR, Goodwin GM, Holmes EA, editors. Nonlinear time-series approaches in characterizing mood stability and mood instability in bipolar disorder. In: Proc R Soc B. The Royal Society; 2012.

Bopp JM, Miklowitz DJ, Goodwin GM, Stevens W, Rendell JM, Geddes JR. The longitudinal course of bipolar disorder as revealed through weekly text messaging: a feasibility study. Bipolar Disord. 2010;12(3):327–34.

Busch AB, Neelon B, Zelevinsky K, He Y, Normand S-LT. Accurately predicting bipolar disorder mood outcomes—implications for the use of electronic databases. Med Care. 2012;50(4):311.

Geddes JR, Miklowitz DJ. Treatment of bipolar disorder. Lancet (London, England). 2013;381(9878):1672–82.

Geddes JR, Burgess S, Hawton K, Jamison K, Goodwin GM. Long-term lithium therapy for bipolar disorder: systematic review and meta-analysis of randomized controlled trials. Am J Psychiatry. 2004;161(2):217–22.

Glasziou PP, Irwig L, Heritier S, Simes RJ, Tonkin A. Monitoring cholesterol levels: measurement error or true change? Ann Intern Med. 2008;148(9):656–61.

Hamer RM, Simpson PM. Last observation carried forward versus mixed models in the analysis of psychiatric clinical trials. Am J Psychiatry. 2009;166(6):639–41.

Hawton K, Sutton L, Haw C, Sinclair J, Harriss L. Suicide and attempted suicide in bipolar disorder: a systematic review of risk factors. J Clin Psychiatry. 2005;66(6):693–704.

Kane VE. Defect prevention: use of simple statistical tools: solutions manual. New York: CRC Press; 1989.

Levinson WA. Statistical process control for real-world applications. USA: CRC Press; 2010.

Mayora O, Arnrich B, Bardram J, Dräger C, Finke A, Frost M, et al. Personal health systems for bipolar disorder anecdotes, challenges and lessons learnt from monarca project. In: Pervasive computing technologies for healthcare (PervasiveHealth), 2013 7th international conference on. IEEE; 2013.

Mohammed M, Worthington P, Woodall W. Plotting basic control charts: tutorial notes for healthcare practitioners. Qual Saf Health Care. 2008;17(2):137–45.

Montgomery DC. Introduction to statistical quality control. 7th ed. London: Wiley; 2013.

Moore PJ, Little MA, McSharry PE, Geddes JR, Goodwin GM. Forecasting depression in bipolar disorder. IEEE Trans Biomed Eng. 2012a;59(10):2801–7.

Moore PJ, Little MA, McSharry PE, Geddes JR, Goodwin GM. Corrections to "forecasting depression in bipolar disorder" [Oct 12, 2801–2807]. IEEE Trans Biomed Eng. 2012b;59(12):3550.

Moore PJ, Little MA, McSharry PE, Goodwin GM, Geddes JR. Correlates of depression in bipolar disorder. Proc R Soc Lond B Biol Sci. 2014;281(1776):20132320.

Moran JL, Solomon PJ. Statistical process control of mortality series in the Australian and New Zealand Intensive Care Society (ANZICS) adult patient database: implications of the data generating process. BMC Med Res Methodol. 2013;13(1):1.

R Core Team. R: a language and environment for statistical computing. Vienna: R Foundation for Statistical Computing; 2013.

Ratheesh A, Berk M, Davey CG, McGorry PD, Cotton SM. Instruments that prospectively predict bipolar disorder—a systematic review. J Affect Disord. 2015;179:65–73.

Reynolds JH. The run sum control chart procedure. J Qual Technol. 1971;3(1):23–7.

Rush AJ, Carmody T, Reimitz PE. The inventory of depressive symptomatology (IDS): clinician (IDS-C) and self-report (IDS-SR) ratings of depressive symptoms. Int J Methods Psychiatr Res. 2000;9(2):45–59.

Rush AJ, Trivedi MH, Ibrahim HM, Carmody TJ, Arnow B, Klein DN, et al. The 16-Item quick inventory of depressive symptomatology (QIDS), clinician rating (QIDS-C), and self-report (QIDS-SR): a psychometric evaluation in patients with chronic major depression. Biol Psychiatry. 2003;54(5):573–83.

Shewhart WA. Economic control of quality of manufactured product. Milwaukee: ASQ Quality Press; 1931.

Siregar S, Roes KC, van Straten AH, Bots ML, van der Graaf Y, van Herwerden LA, et al. Statistical methods to monitor risk factors in a clinical database. Circ Cardiovasc Qual Outcomes. 2013;6(1):110–8.

Smith IR, Gardner MA, Garlick B, Brighouse RD, Cameron J, Lavercombe PS, et al. Performance monitoring in cardiac surgery: application of statistical process control to a single-site database. Heart Lung Circ. 2013;22(8):634–41.

Solomon DA, Leon AC, Coryell WH, Endicott J, Li C, Fiedorowicz JG, et al. Longitudinal course of bipolar I disorder: duration of mood episodes. Arch Gen Psychiatry. 2010;67(4):339–47.

StataCorp. Stata statistical software: release 12. College Station: StataCorp LP; 2011.

Stevens RJ, Oke J, Perera R. Statistical models for the control phase of clinical monitoring. Statistical methods in medical research. 2010.

Thor J, Lundberg J, Ask J, Olsson J, Carli C, Härenstam KP, et al. Application of statistical process control in healthcare improvement: systematic review. Qual Saf Health Care. 2007;16(5):387–99.

University of Pittsburgh Epidemiology Data Centre. IDS/QIDS Instruments in English and Multiple Translations. 2017. http://www.ids-qids.org/index.html.

Resilience concepts in psychiatry demonstrated with bipolar disorder

David G. Angeler[1*], Craig R. Allen[2] and Maj-Liz Persson[3]

Abstract

Background: The term resilience describes stress–response patterns of subjects across scientific disciplines. In ecology, advances have been made to clearly distinguish resilience definitions based on underlying mechanistic assumptions. Engineering resilience (rebound) is used for describing the ability of subjects to recover from adverse conditions (disturbances), and is the rate of recovery. In contrast, the ecological resilience definition considers a systemic change: when complex systems (including humans) respond to disturbances by reorganizing into a new regime (stable state) where structural and functional aspects have fundamentally changed relative to the prior regime. In this context, resilience is an emergent property of complex systems. We argue that both resilience definitions and uses are appropriate in psychology and psychiatry, but although the differences are subtle, the implications and uses are profoundly different.

Methods: We borrow from the field of ecology to discuss resilience concepts in the mental health sciences.

Results: In psychology and psychiatry, the prevailing view of resilience is adaptation to, coping with, and recovery (engineering resilience) from adverse social and environmental conditions. Ecological resilience may be useful for describing vulnerability, onset, and the irreversibility patterns of mental disorders. We discuss this in the context of bipolar disorder.

Conclusion: Rebound, adaptation, and coping are processes that are subsumed within the broader systemic organization of humans, from which ecological resilience emanates. Discerning resilience concepts in psychology and psychiatry has potential for a mechanistically appropriate contextualization of mental disorders at large. This might contribute to a refinement of theory and contextualize clinical practice within the broader systemic functioning of mental illnesses.

Keywords: Ecological resilience, Engineering resilience, Stress-recovery, Bipolar disorder, Mental disorders, Ecological theory, Interdisciplinary research

Background

The concept of resilience has increased in use across scientific disciplines (e.g., ecology, social sciences, health sciences, etc). However, with the increased use of the concept, different definitions have been forwarded (Angeler and Allen 2016). These definitions often have different meanings but are frequently used interchangeably within and across scientific disciplines. This results, in many cases, in the loss of clarity of resilience concepts (Brand and Jax 2007), and may lead to an improper characterization of pattern–process (stress–response) relationships.

In psychology and psychiatry, resilience is very broadly defined as an individual's positive *adaptation* (for definition of terms in italics see Table 1) to life tasks under stressful and adverse social situations (Goldberg and Williams 1988; Luthar 2003; Haddadi and Besharat 2010; Pęciłło 2016). Resilience is positive growth or adaptation that mediates rates of *recovery* following periods of homeostatic disruption (Richardson 2002). The concept describes a dynamic process of a person's *coping capacity* related to risk factors. Risk factors are stressful life events

*Correspondence: david.angeler@slu.se
[1] Department of Aquatic Sciences and Assessment, Swedish University of Agricultural Sciences, PO Box 7050, 750 07 Uppsala, Sweden
Full list of author information is available at the end of the article

Table 1 Overview and definitions of terms used in this paper adapted from Angeler and Allen (2016)

Term	Definition
Adaptation (Psychology)	Psychological adaptation is the dynamic process, grounded in a person's intellect and emotions, which maintains a balance in their mental and emotional states, and in their interactions with their social and cultural environments
Recovery (Engineering resilience)	Engineering resilience is synonymous to recovery and focuses on the return of structural and functional attributes of systems to pre-disturbance conditions following a disturbance. The unit of measurement is time of recovery. This definition assumes that systems are characterized by a single equilibrium and therefore fails to account for the potential for alternative regimes of the same system. In bipolar disorder, recovery from a depression or (hypo) manic episode can be regarded as engineering resilience
Coping capacity	The ability of patients to use available resources (clinical practices), skills (learning) and awareness (self-knowledge) to face and manage adverse situations. The strengthening of coping capacities is a means to build resilience to the effects of mental health symptoms and stressful social and other external situations
Response ability	Response ability is a combination of awareness and capability, which is influenced by people's personalities. Capabilities can be any form of intellect or a physical aspect, and awareness any form of knowledge and experience. Increasing awareness and capability result in increased response ability and determine the speed and magnitude of recovery from, and adaptation to, stressful situations
Ball-in-cup heuristic	This model is commonly applied in ecology to demonstrate resilience concepts. The possibility of complex systems to exist in alternative regimes is shown by different cups. The shape of the cups symbolizes the basin of attraction (stability characteristics of these alternative regimes): deeper and wider cups symbolize a higher resilience of an alternative regime relative to cups that are smaller and shallower. The cup shape can be considered analogous to people's personalities that influence their adaptation and coping abilities with, for instance, bipolar disorder (see text). The ball symbolizes dynamic stress–response patterns: (1) engineering resilience after disturbances (i.e., when the ball stays within the cup, and (2) ecological resilience when a disturbance threshold is passed (i.e., when the ball rolls to another cup))
Alternative regime	A potential alternative configuration in terms of structural and functional patterns and processes of a system. Alternative regimes are explicit in ecological resilience. In bipolar disorder, the healthy and diseased states can be considered alternative regimes
Ecological resilience	Ecological resilience is a measure of the amount of stress needed to change a complex system from one set of processes and structures to a different set of processes and structures. In bipolar disorder, it is the amount of stress needed to change a patient's health status from a healthy regime to a permanently diseased regime
Regime shift	A shift in regime is a persistent change in the structure, function, and mutually reinforced processes or feedbacks of a complex system. The change of regimes, or the shift, usually occurs when a change in an internal process (feedback) or a disturbance (external shock) triggers a completely different system behavior. In bipolar disorder, a regime shift occurs when the disorder is triggered in a person
Coerced resilience	Management interventions in an undesired regime to approach conditions of a desired regime. In bipolar disorder, clinical treatment ameliorates symptomatology and aims at approximating conditions of healthy individuals. Coerced resilience means that (1) permanent treatment is needed, (2) that treatment does not restore a healthy regime, and (3) that cessation of treatment restores the full-blown symptomatology of bipolar disorder
Stable equilibrium	Relatively stable system dynamics, which are controlled by a specific set of structural and functional patterns, processes, and feedbacks. In bipolar disorder, mood swings comprise stable equilibrium dynamics within the diseased regime
Emergent properties	A complex systemic feature that cannot be explained by the sum of individual system components. In bipolar disorder, the diseased regime emerges from the complex interplay between genetic, physiological, brain-structural, behavioral, and personality traits of patients, and their interactions with social and environmental factors. This complex interplay determines the symptomatology and their recurrence dynamics
Feedbacks	In ecological systems feedbacks arise from the set of interactions between patterns and processes. Feedbacks control an effect by influencing and being influenced by the process which gave rise to it. A positive feedback enhances or amplifies these processes, while negative feedbacks have the opposite effects. Positive and negative feedbacks generally do not imply any judgment of value regarding the desirability of the effects or outcomes (e.g., healthy vs. diseased regime in bipolar disorder). Positive feedbacks are of most interest in resilience theory; these help maintain structure, function, and processes in specific alternative regimes

(e.g., health problems, financial hardship, or problems at work or with family relationships; Rutter 2008) and an increased possibility of a person to develop a mental health condition (e.g., inherited vulnerability from a parent; Duffy et al. 2016).

Resilience is often conceptualized as existing along a continuum of vulnerability. Individuals with low vulnerability have a high resistance to psychopathology, although they are not entirely invulnerable to the development of a psychiatric disorder (Goldberg 1972). Such resistant individuals are often referred to as being resilient (e.g., Tiet et al. 1998). This resilience can be related to the concept of *response ability*, which has been defined as a combination of awareness and capability (Campbell 2011). Increasing awareness and capability result in increased response ability. It is determined by people's personalities, which influence their capability (i.e., any form of intellect or a physical aspect) and awareness, which depends on their knowledge, learning and experience (Campbell 2011). In addition to individual´s personality traits (neuroticism, hyperthymia, extravertedness, humor) other factors (social support, harsh childhood) influence resilience. The complex combination of factors determines whether or not, or how fast people recover from stressful life events (Bonanno 2004; Bonanno and Mancini 2008). That is, although some people resist stressful events, others need time to recover competent functioning, while others may permanently suffer from such events (for instance, when incurable bipolar disorder is triggered).

A concept related to adaptation, coping, and response ability in the mental health sciences is "*engineering resilience*" in ecology. Engineering resilience is synonymous with recovery, bounce back and resiliency (Angeler and Allen 2016), and is frequently shown as a *ball-in-cup heuristic* (Fig. 1a). In this heuristic, recovery is symbolized with the ball moving away from and then returning to its original position after disturbances (Fig. 1a). Recovery, or engineering resilience, is a dynamic process of both persons and ecosystems in response to disturbances, and

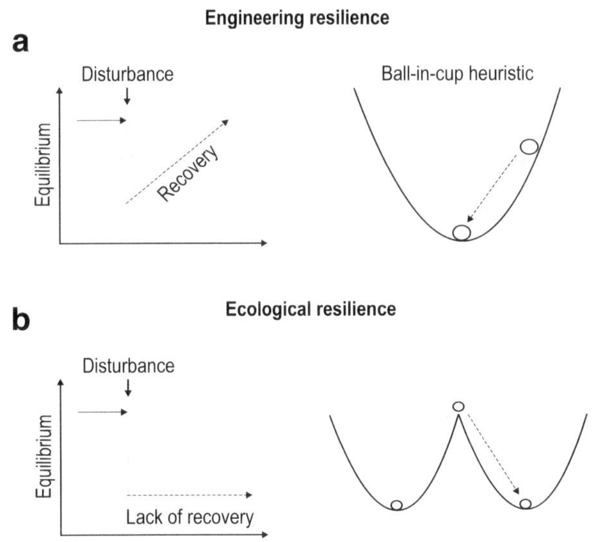

Fig. 1 Schematic distinguishing between (**a**) recovery (engineering resilience) and (**b**) ecological resilience. Panels on the left show subject (humans, ecosystems) trajectories before (full black arrow), during (gray arrow), and after disturbances (black broken arrow). Panels on the right express these dynamics with ball-in-cup heuristics commonly used in ecology. In the case of recovery/engineering resilience, the ball rolls back to its equilibrium position after a disturbance. In the case of ecological resilience, the ball rolls over the cup's brink and falls into a new cup. This cup represents an alternative stable system regime from which recovery to the previous regime is impossible. This is symbolized with the ball not rolling back to the previous cup

the speed and the magnitude of recovery from stressful events depend on traits in both cases (response ability in people [Campbell 2011]; biodiversity in ecosystems [Nash et al. 2016]).

It follows that inherent in the psychological and psychiatric view of resilience is one's ability to adapt to, cope with and bounce back from a negative experience by restoring well-being and social and self-functioning of individuals. That is, in psychology and psychiatry, coping, adaptation, and recovery are linked resilience aspects used to describe patients' abilities to deal with adverse conditions. However, sometimes subjects suffer chronically from traumatic events. In such cases, implications of resilience concepts and treatment alternatives are quite different. When a full recovery of subjects is not tenable, treatment is reactive and focuses on alleviating symptoms of mental illness through medication and therapy (developing adaptation and coping skills). This suggests that the engineering resilience, adaptation, and coping aspects of resilience are useful for describing the ability of patients to deal with symptoms of mental disorders. However, these concepts frequently fail to characterize the broader systemic aspects of stress–response patterns related to psychological and psychiatric phenomena, an observation true in ecology as well.

Ecologists have become increasingly aware that ecological (e.g., lakes) and other complex systems of people and nature frequently do not bounce back after disturbances (Allen et al. 2014). Instead, when their adaptive capacity to stress is exhausted, they reorganize in an *alternative system regime* once a disturbance threshold has been passed (Fig. 1b). An alternative system regime means that basic structural (e.g., species assemblages) and functional patterns and processes (e.g., production of food and fiber) are distinctly different compared to the system regime that existed prior to passing the disturbance threshold. Ecologist use the term "*ecological resilience*," when a system reorganizes in an alternative regime rather than bounces back after disturbances (Holling 1973).

There are striking similarities between ecological systems and humans in terms of the complexity of responses to adverse conditions (disturbances). In this paper, we point out the utility of the ecological resilience definition for describing some psychological and psychiatric phenomena; for instance, bipolar disorder. We contend that similar to ecological systems, resilience in bipolar disorder and other mental illnesses is an emergent phenomenon, which allows for the existence of alternative healthy and diseased regimes in patients that develop disorders. That is, both the systemic complexity of bipolar disorder (vulnerability, onset, irreversibility) and clinical interventions to ameliorate symptoms of the disorder well align with the ecological resilience definition. We argue that engineering resilience, adaptation, and coping are processes that are subsumed within the broader systemic organization of bipolar disorder that ecological resilience characterizes, and that these different definitions of resilience are therefore not mutually exclusive. We contend that discerning ecological and engineering resilience, and related concepts (adaptation, coping) in psychology and psychiatry, has potential for a mechanistically appropriate contextualization of mental disorders and psychological phenomena at large. This might contribute to a refinement of theory in the mental health sciences and contextualize and unify clinical practice (preventative *vs* reactive treatment) within the broader systemic functioning of mental illnesses.

Bipolar disorder and resilience

Bipolar or manic–depressive disorder is an affective disorder characterized by pronounced mood swings with recurrent cycles of (hypo)mania (increased energy levels, decreased need for sleep, racing thoughts, pressure of speech, frequent agitation, confusion and distraction, heightened libido, and in extreme forms, hallucinations and delusions), and severe depression episodes (chaos, emotional emptiness, despair, self-stigma, doom, anhedonia, guilt, monochromatic world view, suicidal ideology) (Goodwin and Jamison 2007). The disorder comprises a spectrum wherein (hypo)manic and depression symptoms manifest with high variability and magnitude among patients, and these symptoms often co-occur (mixed states) (Phelps 2006). The illness affects between 3 and 8% of the human population (Goodwin and Jamison 2007), although these numbers may be higher because current diagnostic problems complicate differentiating between unipolar and bipolar depression (Bauer and Pfennig 2005).

Bipolar disorder, like many other mental disorders, has an underlying genetic component that increases the vulnerability to, and triggers, the disorder, frequently in adolescence or early adulthood, and often in response to stressful life experiences (Goodwin and Jamison 2007). This vulnerability can be visualized with a shallower bottom in the ball-in-cup heuristic (Fig. 2a-c), relative to a person without this vulnerability (deeper bottom of cup in Fig. 2d). That is, the heuristic exemplifies that people without bipolar vulnerability are more likely to rebound from stressful life events (engineering resilience) compared to people vulnerable to bipolarity. Note that, for simplicity, Fig. 2 is meant for demonstration only and therefore does not represent bipolar disorder as a spectrum illness with different degrees of people's vulnerability to develop the disorder (Phelps 2006).

Given the susceptibility of people with disposition to bipolar disorder, the illness becomes eventually expressed after a threshold of stressful live events has been passed. This can be symbolized with the ball rolling into another cup (Fig. 2a). This indicates that the patient has undergone a *"regime shift,"* whereby his or her functioning becomes critically conditioned by the symptomatology of the disorder after this shift. Because bipolar disorder has no cure, the ball-in-cup heuristic is useful for highlighting that the patient has moved to a permanent (diseased) regime from which recovery to the symptom free health status prior to the outbreak of the disorder is highly unlikely (Fig. 2b).

Medication and different forms of therapy (psychotherapy, cognitive behavioral therapy, exercise) are common approaches to treat the symptoms of bipolar disorder (Phelps 2006). Although effective in terms of improving patients personal and interpersonal functioning, they do not cure the illness. That is, there is no full "functional restoration" of patients that would indicate recovery from the disorder, despite clinical interventions (i.e., return from the deep to the shallow cup in Fig. 2b). Psychiatrists are well aware that clinical treatment ameliorates the symptoms of bipolar disorder, rather than fully restores cognitive, behavioral, and functional characteristics prior to those before the onset of the disorder. From an ecological resilience point of view, clinical interventions can be considered a "coercion" of the diseased regime [*coerced resilience* (Rist et al. 2014)], by targeting the approximation of desired functionality of patients comparable to healthy individuals. This coercion is symbolized by the full arrow in Fig. 2b pushing the ball close to the regime before the outbreak of the disorder. That treatment is only a coerced condition of the disease regime is evident by the well-known fact that, for instance, breakthrough depression events can occur despite clinical treatment (Miklowitz and Gitlin 2015). These breakthrough depressions are indicative of the stability of the diseased regime. The notion of clinical treatment of bipolar disorder being a coerced condition of the diseased regime also helps explain why individuals that cease medication revert to express the full-blown symptomatology of (hypo)manic and depressive episodes of the disorder. This is symbolized with the dotted arrow in Fig. 2b. This further indicates the stability of the diseased regime.

Such coerced regimes are also observed in ecological systems. In boreal lakes, acidified rain has altered the pH, a measure of acid content, of lakes necessitating expensive and difficult additions of lime to restore pH levels toward neutrality (Angeler and Goedkoop 2010). However, like bipolar human subjects, the rehabilitation is temporary and requires constant management input

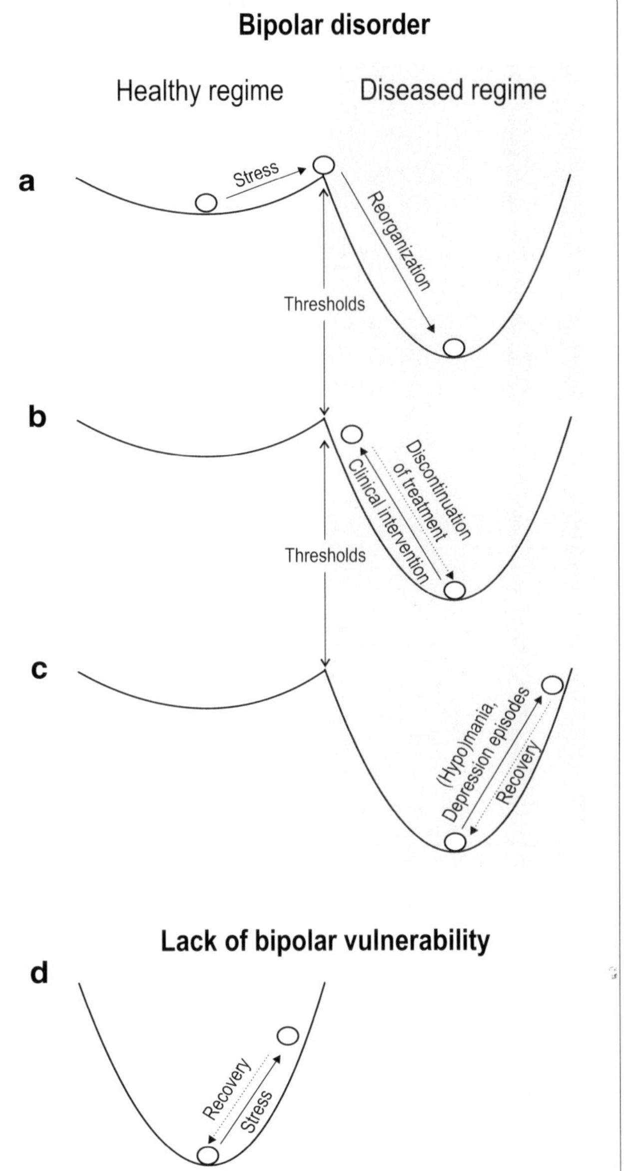

Fig. 2 Ball-in-cup heuristic in the context of bipolar disorder. **a** Individual with bipolar vulnerability (symbolized with the shallow cup). Stressful life events trigger the chronic, incurable disorder (symbolized with the ball rolling from the healthy into a new (diseased) regime once a stress threshold has been passed). **b** Bipolar individual receiving healthcare (medication, therapy). Clinical intervention does not restore the regime prior to the outbreak of the disorder (no recovery). Instead, it ameliorates symptoms and increases personal and interpersonal functioning of the patient within the diseased regime (full arrow). Discontinuing clinical treatment (dotted arrow) eventually restores the full symptomatology. **c** Engineering resilience subsumed within ecological resilience: shown are stress-recovery patterns related to episodes of (hypo)mania and depression in the diseased regime. **d** Individual without bipolar vulnerability (i.e., in a healthy regime) recovering from adverse situations (stress). The lack of vulnerability is also symbolized by the absence of a diseased regime (gray dotted cup). Note that similar to persons without disposition to bipolar disorder, stress–response dynamics also occur in the healthy regime of patients with bipolar disorder (not shown in the figure)

(lime treatment). Cessation of liming often leads to the reestablishment of the acidified lake conditions (Clair and Hindar 2005).

Following the ecological resilience definition, the acidified regimes of boreal lakes and the diseased regime of bipolar disorder are systemic features wherein patterns and processes operate in a *stable equilibrium*. In bipolar disorder, these pattern–process relationships are manifested in the expression of symptoms (patterns) and their recurrence (dynamic process). The deviations from relative symptom free periods to episodes of depression or (hypo)mania that are inherent in the mood swings, whether or not the patient receives clinical treatment, are a central part in this dynamic process. These deviations, which impair the patients functioning, are followed by periods of recovery whereby the patient's health improves. This recovery is indicative of engineering resilience, and because recovery patterns differ between patients as a function of their coping and adaptation potential, recovery time (i.e., recovery as a process rate) can vary substantially. Taken together, this suggests that engineering resilience is subsumed within ecological resilience, meaning that deviations and recovery from equilibrium conditions can occur within both the healthy and diseased alternative regimes (Fig. 2c, d). However, engineering resilience fails to describe the return from the diseased regime to the healthy regime (Fig. 2a).

Understanding engineering resilience as a rate of recovery is mechanistically relatively simple and easy to measure. In contrast, ecological resilience as an *emergent systemic property* is a highly complex phenomenon, which complicates the prediction when a shift to an alternative regime can occur. This complexity results from the interaction of many factors that create positive *feedbacks* that are critical in maintaining ecological resilience (Angeler and Allen 2016). The cessation of treatment leading to a return of symptoms in the bipolar disorder or the increase in acidity in the boreal lake examples suggests that in both cases, we are able to manage engineering resilience (with clinical interventions or liming, respectively), but that we still lack the ability and knowledge to fully restore the feedbacks that would lead to a self-maintaining healthy regime in bipolar patients or a non-acidified, circumneutral regime of lakes. However, in bipolar disorder, different forms of psychotherapy, including psychoeducation, cognitive behavioral therapy and mindfulness-based cognitive therapy, have positive effects in terms of increased time to mood episode relapse or recurrence and improved depressive and anxiety symptoms (Salcedo et al. 2016). Similarly, adjunctive psychotherapy can be effective in treating manic symptoms (Miklowitz 2008), which confers significant advantages in preventing hospitalization for a mood episode (Solomon et al. 2008). Studies also highlighted the relevance of age, reporting faster functional recovery of older patients from a manic episode after first hospitalization relative to younger individuals (Tohen et al. 2000, 2003). Other factors such as shorter duration of the illness, higher social class, and treatment compliance may also influence recovery (Keck et al. 1998). Taken together, these observations suggest that clinical approaches (therapy, medication, exercise, mindfulness) together with environmental and personal factors may potentially gradually change some of the emergent properties of bipolar disorder (e.g., self-awareness of the precursor of the disorder, skills to prevent relapses). In turn, this might modulate the feedbacks of the diseased regime and influence resilience to bipolar episodes. This change of feedbacks and emergent properties (adaptation, coping ability) can be symbolized with a changing cup shape in the ball-in-cup heuristic (Fig. 3). The decreasing depth of the cups over time symbolizes that coping capacities and adaptation are strengthened and engineering resilience increased. This is shown with shorter arrows to maintain the coerced state of relative well-being in the diseased regime of bipolar disorder (Fig. 3).

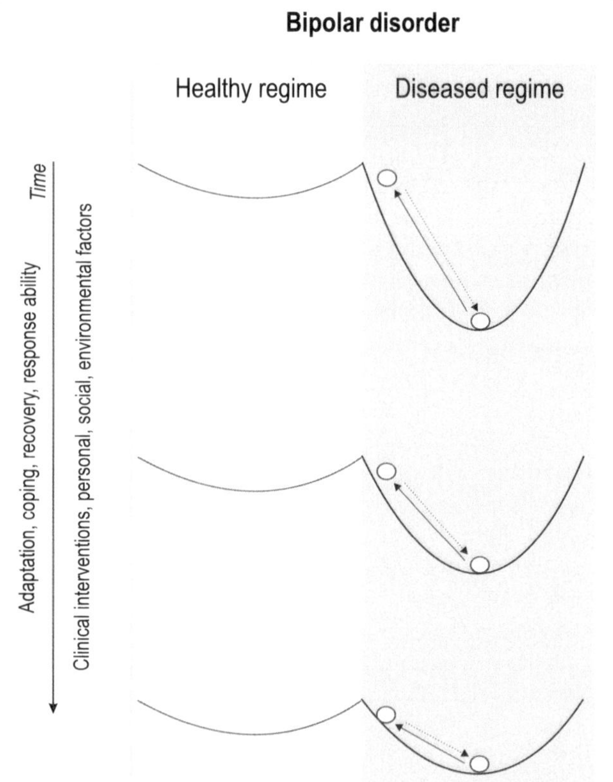

Fig. 3 Ball-in-cup heuristic showing how clinical practices among other factors can contribute to improve patients' capacities to cope with, adapt to, and recover from mood episodes in the coerced state in the diseased regime of bipolar disorder by modulating the shape of the cup (basin of attraction)

Conclusion

This paper argues that engineering and ecological resilience definitions used in ecology are appropriate in psychology and psychiatry, and although the differences are subtle, their implications and uses are profoundly different. Resilience concepts used in the mental health sciences that focus on dynamic processes (engineering resilience or rebound, adaptation to, and coping with stressful events) are subsumed within ecological resilience, an emergent phenomenon that emphasizes the existence of alternative regimes in bipolar disorder. In this context, deviations from and recovery to equilibrium conditions (engineering resilience) can be observed within the healthy and diseased regimes of patients. However, engineering resilience, adaptation, and coping capacity fail to capture the nonlinear dynamics that occur when a patient enters an alternative mental health regime, and the permanence or semipermanence of alternative regimes. This misrepresents the dynamics of complex systems, such as ecosystems and human brains.

Bipolar disorder can be considered the emergent phenomenon of the existence and interactions of a healthy and diseased regime. From a normative perspective, the healthy regime is desired, and the diseased regime undesired. In this context, the ecological resilience concept provides advantages over other resilience definitions to contextualize theory and management of the disorder, which differs between the healthy and the diseased regimes. Management of the healthy regime mainly requires proactive, preventative approaches to recognize bipolar vulnerability, reduce the risk of the disorder to become triggered, and foster the resilience of the healthy regime. Brain-structural and functional assessments are available to assess such risks (Frangou 2012; Frangou et al. 2017; Singh et al. 2014). For instance, Frangou (2012) showed that increased brain insular volume, decreased activation within the posterior and inferior parietal regions, and reduced fronto-insular and fronto-cingulate connectivity were risk factors in relatives of bipolar patients. Similarly, atypical patterns of prefrontal and subcortical intrinsic connectivity have been found in the healthy offspring of parents with bipolar disorder (Singh et al. 2014). There is also accruing evidence of a number of measurable and potentially modifiable markers of vulnerability and developing illness in youth at familial risk for bipolar disorder. These markers include in some high-risk children of bipolar-affected parents (Duffy et al. 2016): (1) sleep and anxiety disorders that precede mood disorders by several years and reflect an increased vulnerability, (2) early exposure to adverse situations like exposure to illness or neglect from a parent, (3) an increased risk of psychopathology manifested at behavioral and biological levels resulting from increased stress reactivity, (4) interrelated risk factors stemming from psychological processes (reward sensitivity, unstable self-esteem, rumination, and positive self-appraisal are risk factors for mood disorders), and (5) risk related to disturbances in circadian rhythm and immune dysfunction. Identifying such markers can be used for the development of specific early interventions that might reduce the risk of bipolar disorder to become triggered in people, particularly in youths with a high vulnerability (Duffy et al. 2016). Early warnings of bipolar vulnerability are especially required for youth because early onset of bipolar disorder might herald a more severe disease course in terms of chronicity and comorbidity (Perlis et al. 2004). In contrast, the diseased regime requires reactive approaches to ameliorate symptoms of the disorder and improve personal and interpersonal functioning of patients through different forms of therapy, medication, and exercise. These approaches have proven very useful to improve patients' coping capacities and adaptation abilities, and facilitate faster recovery from episodes.

In summary, ecological resilience characterizes the broader systemic complexity and functioning of bipolar disorder and allows contextualizing resilience definitions. The ecological resilience definition emphasizes that both adaptation within single regimes and transformation between regimes, rather than adaptation alone, are critical elements in the functioning of complex systems. Discerning resilience concepts in psychology and psychiatry might contribute to a mechanistically appropriate characterization of the complexity inherent in bipolar disorder and mental illnesses at large. Such distinctions can also help to contextualize and unify clinical practice (preventative vs. reactive treatment) within the broader systemic functioning of mental illnesses.

Authors' contributions

DGA conceived the study and wrote the paper. CRA and MLP have contributed to idea development and the writing. All authors read and approved the final manuscript.

Author details

[1] Department of Aquatic Sciences and Assessment, Swedish University of Agricultural Sciences, PO Box 7050, 750 07 Uppsala, Sweden. [2] U.S. Geological Survey, Nebraska Cooperative Fish and Wildlife Research Unit, School of Natural Resources, University of Nebraska–Lincoln, Lincoln, NE, USA. [3] PRIMA Adult Psychiatric Ward, Katrinebergsvägen 6, 117 43 Stockholm, Sweden.

Acknowledgements

The constructive criticism by two anonymous reviewers helped improve the paper. The Nebraska Cooperative Fish and Wildlife Research Unit is jointly supported by a cooperative agreement between the United States Geological Survey, the Nebraska Game and Parks Commission, the University of Nebraska–Lincoln, the United States Fish and Wildlife Service, and the Wildlife Management Institute.

Competing interests

The authors declare that they have no competing interests.

Funding

August T. Larsson Foundation, NJ Faculty, Swedish University of Agricultural Sciences.

References

Allen CR, Angeler DG, Garmestani AS, Gunderson LH, Holling CS. Panarchy: theory and applications. Ecosystems. 2014;17:578–89.

Angeler DG, Allen CR. Quantifying resilience. J Appl Ecol. 2016;53:617–24.

Angeler DG, Goedkoop W. Biological responses to liming in boreal lakes: an assessment using plankton, macroinvertebrate and fish communities. J Appl Ecol. 2010;47:478–86.

Bauer M, Pfennig A. Epidemiology of bipolar disorders. Epilepsia. 2005;46:8–13.

Bonanno GA. Loss, trauma, and human resilience: have we underestimated the human capacity to thrive after extremely aversive events? Am Psychol. 2004;59:20–8.

Bonanno GA, Mancini AD. The human capacity to thrive in the face of potential trauma. Pediatrics. 2008;121:369–75.

Brand FS, Jax L. Focusing the meaning(s) of resilience: resilience as a descriptive concept and a boundary object. Ecol Soc. 2007;12:23.

Campbell JE. Teachers and mental health: the art of accurate speech and other ways to help students (children) not become psychiatric patients. Bloomington: AuthorHouse; 2011.

Clair TA, Hindar A. Liming for the mitigation of acid rain effects in freshwaters: a review of recent results. Environ Rev. 2005;13:91–128.

Duffy A, Jones S, Goodday S, Bentall R. Candidate risks indicators for bipolar disorder: early intervention opportunities in high-risk youth. Int J Neuropsychopharmacol. 2016;19:1.

Frangou S. Brain structural and functional correlates of resilience to bipolar disorder. Front Human Neurosci. 2012;5:184.

Frangou S, Dima D, Jogia J. Towards person-centered neuroimaging markers for resilience and vulnerability in bipolar disorder. Neuroimage. 2017;145:230–7.

Goldberg D. The detection of psychiatric illness by questionnaire: a technique for the identification and assessment of non-psychotic psychiatric illness. London: Oxford University Press; 1972.

Goldberg D, Williams P. A user's guide to the General Health Questionnaire. Windsor: NFER-Nelson; 1988.

Goodwin FK, Jamison KR. Manic-depressive illness: bipolar disorders and recurrent depression. New York: Oxford University Press; 2007.

Haddadi P, Besharat MA. Resilience, vulnerability and mental health. Procedia Soc Behav Sci. 2010;5:639–42.

Holling CS. Resilience and stability of ecological systems. Ann Rev Ecol Syst. 1973;4:1–23.

Keck PE, McElroy SL, Strakowski SM, West SA, Sax KW, Hawkins JM, Bourne ML, Haggard P. 12-month outcome of patients with bipolar disorder following hospitalization for a manic or mixed episode. Am J Psychiatry. 1998;155:646–52.

Luthar SS. Resilience and vulnerability: Adaptation in the context of childhood adversities. Cambridge: Cambridge University Press; 2003.

Miklowitz, DJ. Adjunctive psychotherapy for bipolar disorder: state of the evidence. Am J Psychiatry. 2008;165:1408–19.

Miklowitz DJ, Gitlin MJ. Clinician's guide to bipolar disorder. New York: Guilford Press; 2015.

Nash KL, Graham NAJ, Jennings S, Wilson SK, Bellwood DR. Herbivore cross-scale redundancy supports response diversity and promotes coral reef resilience. J Appl Ecol. 2016;53:646–55.

Pęciłło M. The concept of resilience in OSH management: a review of approaches. Int J Occup Saf Ergon. 2016;22:291–300.

Perlis RH, et al. Long-term implications of early onset in bipolar disorder: data from the first 1000 participants in the systematic treatment enhancement program for bipolar disorder (STEP-BD). Biol Psychiatry. 2004;55:875–81.

Phelps J. Why am I still depressed? Recognizing and managing the ups and downs of Bipolar II and soft bipolar disorder. New York: McGraw-Hill; 2006.

Richardson GE. The metatheory of resilience and resiliency. J Clin Psychol. 2002;58:307–21.

Rist L, Felton A, Nyström M, Troell M, Sponseller RA, Bengtsson J, Österblom H, Lindborg R, Tidåker P, Angeler DG, Milestad R, Moen J. Applying resilience thinking to production systems. Ecosphere. 2014;5:1.

Rutter M. Developing concepts in developmental psychopathology. In: Hudziak JJ, editor. Developmental psychopathology and wellness: Genetic and environmental influences. Washington, DC: American Psychiatric Publishing; 2008. p. 3–22.

Salcedo S, Gold AK, Sheikh S, Marcus PH, Nierenberg AA, Deckersbach T, Sylvia LG. Empirically supported psychosocial interventions for bipolar disorder: current state of the research. J Affect Disord. 2016;201:203–14.

Singh MK, Chang KD, Kelley RG, Saggar M, Reiss AL, Gotlib IH. Early signs of anomalous neural functional connectivity in healthy offspring of parents with bipolar disorder. Bipolar Disord. 2014;16:678–89.

Solomon DA, Keitner GI, Ryan CE, Kelley J, Miller IW. Preventing recurrence of bipolar I mood episodes and hospitalizations: family psychotherapy plus pharmacotherapy versus pharmacotherapy alone. Bipolar Disord. 2008;10:798–805.

Tiet QQ, Bird HR, Davies M, Hoven C, Cohen P, Jensen PS, Goodman S. Adverse life events and resilience. J Am Acad Child Adolesc Psychiatry. 1998;37:1191–200.

Tohen M, et al. Two-year syndromal and functional recovery in 219 cases of first-episode major affective disorder with psychotic features. Am J Psychiatry. 2000;157:220–8.

Tohen M, et al. The McLean-Harvard first-episode mania study: prediction of recovery and first recurrence. Am J Psychiatry. 2003;12:2099–107.

Regularity of self-reported daily dosage of mood stabilizers and antipsychotics in patients with bipolar disorder

Maximilian Pilhatsch[1*], Tasha Glenn[2], Natalie Rasgon[3], Martin Alda[4], Kemal Sagduyu[5], Paul Grof[6], Rodrigo Munoz[7], Wendy Marsh[8], Scott Monteith[9], Emanuel Severus[1], Rita Bauer[1], Philipp Ritter[1], Peter C. Whybrow[10] and Michael Bauer[1]

Abstract

Background: Polypharmacy is often prescribed for bipolar disorder, yet medication non-adherence remains a serious problem. This study investigated the regularity in the daily dosage taken of mood stabilizers and second generation antipsychotics.

Methods: Daily self-reported data on medications taken and mood were available from 241 patients with a diagnosis of bipolar disorder who received treatment as usual. Patients who took the same mood stabilizer or second generation antipsychotic for $\geq$ 100 days were included. Approximate entropy was used to determine serial regularity in daily dosage taken. Generalized estimating equations were used to estimate if demographic or clinical variables were associated with regularity.

Results: There were 422 analysis periods available from the 241 patients. Patients took drugs on 84.4% of days. Considerable irregularity was found, mostly due to single-day omissions and dosage changes. Drug holidays (missing 3 or more consecutive days) were found in 35.8% of the analysis periods. Irregularity was associated with an increasing total number of psychotropic drugs taken ($p = 0.009$), the pill burden ($p = 0.026$), and the percent of days depressed ($p = 0.049$).

Conclusion: Despite low missing percent of days, daily drug dosage may be irregular primarily due to single day omissions and dosage changes. Drug holidays are common. Physicians should expect to see partial adherence in clinical practice, especially with complex drug regimens. Daily dosage irregularity may impact the continuity of drug action, contribute to individual variation in treatment response, and needs further study.

Keywords: Bipolar disorder, Mood stabilizers, Second generation antipsychotics, Polypharmacy, Adherence

Background

Drug regimens for the treatment of bipolar disorder are increasing in complexity. Polypharmacy, defined as two or more psychotropic medications, is prescribed to the majority of inpatients and outpatients, including the elderly (Weinstock et al. 2014; Bjørklund et al. 2016; Bauer et al. 2013a; Peselow et al. 2016; Kleimann et al. 2016; Golden et al. 2017; Rej et al. 2017; Kessing et al. 2016). A minority of patients, ranging from 18 to 36% in recent studies, are prescribed four or more psychotropic medications (Bauer et al. 2013a; Weinstock et al. 2014; Golden et al. 2017; Goldberg et al. 2009). The use of evidence-based combination therapies may improve treatment response, and many drug combinations are included as first and second-line recommendations in international guidelines for the treatment of bipolar disorder (Parker et al. 2017; Fountoulakis et al. 2017). The challenges of polypharmacy include unproven

*Correspondence: maximilian.pilhatsch@uniklinikum-dresden.de
[1] Department of Psychiatry and Psychotherapy, Medical Faculty, University Hospital Carl Gustav Carus, Technische Universität Dresden, Fetscherstr. 74, 01307 Dresden, Germany
Full list of author information is available at the end of the article

combination therapies, limited available evidence, increased risks of serious adverse reactions and drug interactions, and patient costs (Kukreja et al. 2013; Sachs et al. 2014).

Less than half of patients with bipolar disorder are estimated to be adherent with prescribed treatments, with most having intermittent or partial adherence that fluctuates over time (García et al. 2016; Pompili et al. 2009; Scott and Pope 2002; Kessing et al. 2007). Medication non-adherence in bipolar disorder is associated with an increased risk of relapse, hospitalization, and suicide (Hassan and Lage 2009; Hong et al. 2011; Gonzalez-Pinto et al. 2006; Schuepbach et al. 2008). Medication adherence is difficult to measure, and all methods have strengths and weaknesses (Hawkshead and Krousel-Wood 2007; Pearson et al. 2007; Levin et al. 2015; Sajatovic et al. 2010). Clinical studies of adherence generally involve subjective scales completed by patients or physicians, which quantify missing days, doses or attitudes (Pompili et al. 2009; Baldessarini et al. 2008; Jónsdóttir et al. 2010). We previously measured the regularity in the daily dosage taken of mood stabilizers (lithium and anticonvulsants) using self-reported data (Bauer et al. 2013b). Dosage regularity measures daily changes and enhances understanding beyond the basic percent of missing days. Considerable irregularity in the daily dosage of mood stabilizers was found in patients missing less than 14% of days (Bauer et al. 2013b). Both the total number of psychotropic medications and the pill burden were associated with increased irregularity. The purpose of this study is to repeat the regularity analysis including second-generation antipsychotics as well as traditional mood stabilizers.

Methods

All data were obtained from outpatients, aged 18 years or older, who agreed to record mood, sleep, and medications taken daily using ChronoRecord software (Bauer et al. 2004, 2008). All the participants were volunteers, primarily recruited by the prescribing psychiatrist, who were informed about the study prior to providing written informed consent. The study was approved by local institutional review boards. The diagnosis was made by the prescribing psychiatrist at a clinical interview, and the patient received pharmacological treatment as usual throughout the study. Data were obtained from 666 patients, of which 480 had a diagnosis of any bipolar disorder based on DSM IV or DSM 5 criteria, and returned $\geq$ 30 days of data.

Patient data entry

Patents received about a half hour of training on the use of ChronoRecord software, in person or by telephone, before entering data. During the training session, a medication list was created for each patient. The medication list includes all drugs prescribed for bipolar disorder and any other prescribed or over-the-counter (OTC) drugs that the patient felt impacted their mood. The prescribed psychotropic drugs were selected from a list in the software, displayed by both brand and generic names. The patient could add a drug not included in the software list, and could modify the list of drugs taken at any time. For each selected drug, the pill strength was chosen from a list of available strengths. Every day, for each drug, the patient entered the total number of pills taken. Patients could enter partial pills (1/4, 1/2, or 3/4) for tablets but not capsules. If a drug was not taken, the patient entered 0 pills for that drug for that day. A missing day of data was also treated as if no pills were taken. Data not entered on 1 day could be entered at a later date. The software includes error checking to prevent entry for a future date, and to verify entry of a large number of pills for a drug.

In addition to medications, the patients entered mood, sleep, and significant life events daily, and weight weekly into the ChronoRecord software. ChronoRecord uses a 100-unit visual analog scale between the extremes of mania and depression to rate mood. Based upon the prior validation studies (Bauer et al. 2004, 2008), a mood entry less than 40 was considered depression, 40–60 euthymia, and greater than 60 hypomania/mania. The depression ratings varied from mild (entry of 20–39) to moderate–severe (entry of 0–19), and the mania ratings varied from hypomania (entry of 61–80) to moderate-severe (entry of 81–100).

Drugs analyzed

The drugs analyzed were traditional mood stabilizers as in the prior analysis: lithium, valproate, lamotrigine, carbamazepine, oxcarbazepine (Bauer et al. 2013b), and second generation antipsychotics: aripiprazole, olanzapine, risperidone, quetiapine, ziprasidone, paliperidone, asenapine, lurasidone, and clozapine. The analysis of the total psychotropic drugs taken and the daily pill burden also included antidepressants, benzodiazepines, typical antipsychotics, insomnia medications, other anticonvulsants (topirimate, gabapentin, pregabalin, tiagabine, levetiracetam, zonisamide), thyroid hormones and estrogens.

Regularity analysis using ApEn

Regularity in the daily medication dosage was calculated using Approximate Entropy (ApEn) as in the prior studies (Bauer et al. 2013b, c). ApEn is a family of statistics that measure serial regularity in a time series, are model independent, and can be used with datasets that are small and noisy (Pincus 1991; Pincus et al. 1991). Regularity can be thought of as the tendency that values within a time series remain the same on incremental comparisons (Pincus 1991; Pincus et al. 1991). ApEn computes a single positive value, with 0 indicating a completely regular sequence, and with increasingly larger numbers signifying greater serial irregularity. The estimated value of the ApEn (m, r, N) depends on: m the pattern length used for prediction of the subsequent value, r the level of noise filtering, and N the number of data values in the run to be compared. The ApEn noise filtering compares the difference between the data in each sequence of m days of data (Pincus et al. 1991). Conceptually, when the absolute value of the difference is greater than the noise filter level, the ApEn statistic is incremented. Otherwise, the difference is treated as noise and ignored. The level of noise filtering was calculated as a percent of the individual subjects' standard deviation (Pincus et al. 1993). For this analysis, the parameters included were $m = 1$ day, $r = 0.2 \times$ SD in daily drug dosage, and $N = 100$ days.

The calculated value of ApEn is dependent upon the order of the data in the time series. Changing the order of the data will likely change the calculated value of ApEn. In contrast, the calculated value of the familiar mean and standard deviation will be identical for a set of data in a time series regardless of the order of the data. ApEn is a valuable measure of the daily dosage fluctuations found with partial adherence (Bauer et al. 2013b, c). For example, the ApEn would be 0 if the patient made no changes to the daily dosage or discontinued a medication, and would be largely unaffected by a prescription change if the patient keeps taking the new dosage (Bauer et al. 2013b).

Per patient regularity analysis

For every drug included in the ApEn analysis, the time span for taking the drug was determined for each patient. If the time span was $\geq$ 100 days, the ApEn was calculated for the first 100 days of data. Patients who took more than one drug for $\geq$ 100 days could have more than one ApEn analysis. Of the 480 patients with bipolar disorder, 241 patients took at least one drug for sufficient length of time for analysis. For the 241 patients, 422 ApEn sequences were calculated.

Statistics

Descriptive statistics for the demographic and clinical characteristics of the 241 patients were calculated. For each patient, for each 100-day ApEn period, the percent of days with depressed, euthymic and manic/hypomanic mood were determined. Drug holidays, defined as missing 3 or more consecutive days (Urquhart 1998), were determined for each patient during the 100-day period. The daily pill burden was defined as total number of pills for all psychotropic medications. For each patient, for each 100-day ApEn period, the mode of the daily number of psychotropic medications, daily pill burden, and daily dosage were calculated. The mode is the most frequent value in a series of numbers, and was chosen as a proxy for the prescribed daily number of medications, pill burden and daily dosage. The mean values for the entire sample were calculated using the modal values for each patient.

Since one patient could have more than one ApEn analysis, generalized estimating equations (GEE) were used to adjust model coefficients and standard errors for within-patient correlation. To estimate if demographic or clinical variables were associated with ApEn, GEE models were used with ApEn as the dependent variable and an independent working correlation structure (Pan and Connett 2002). GEE models were also used to estimate if demographic or clinical variables were associated with the percent of missing doses or with drug holidays. SPSS Version 24 was used for all analyses.

Results

422 ApEn sequences were calculated from the 241 patients. Of the 241 patients, 158 (66%) were recruited from a university mood clinic and 83 (34%) from a private practice. The demographic characteristics of the 241 patients are shown in Table 1. During the 100-day periods, the patients were euthymic 71.6% of days, depressed 20.9% of days, and hypomanic/manic 7.5% of days. The 241 patients returned a mean of 389 (SD 567) days of data.

Medications

The medications taken by the 241 patients are summarized in Table 2. The patients took a mean of 3.9 psychotropic medications, with a mean pill burden of 7.2 for these drugs. Many of the 241 patients were taking more than one mood stabilizer or antipsychotic, or changed medication, such that 121 (50%) of the patients had 1 ApEn analysis, 72 (30%) had 2 ApEn analysis, 40 (17%) had 3 ApEn analyses, and 8 (3%) had > 3 ApEn analyses.

Missing days and drug holidays

Overall, the patients took medication on a mean of 84.4% of days. Missing drug data occurred frequently within the 100-day analysis periods. There was at least one single day omission in 64.7% of the 422 analyses periods. The percent of days of missing drug data was associated with the percent of days depressed ($p = 0.046$), and inversely associated with the percent of days euthymic ($p = 0.047$).

One or more drug holidays were found in 151 (35.8%) of the 422 analysis periods. Of the 151 analysis periods containing a drug holiday, more than one drug holiday

Table 1 Patient demographics (N = 241)

Demographic	N	%
Gender (N = 242)		
Male	70	29
Female	171	71
Diagnosis (N = 240)		
BP I	145	60
BP II	86	36
BP NOS	9	4
Marital status (N = 223)		
Married	111	50
Divorced	29	13
Single	83	37
Employment status (N = 207)		
Working full-time	94	45
Disabled	52	25
Other	61	30
Education (N = 225)		
High school	29	13
Some college	72	32
College graduate	124	55
	Mean	*SD*
Age (N = 241)	41.2	10.9
Age of onset (N = 225)	22.6	10.5
Hospitalizations (N = 218)	2.8	4.7
Years of illness (N = 225)	18.9	12.1

was present in 57 (37.8%). Taking a drug holiday was associated with working full time ($p = 0.005$), and the total number of psychotropic drugs ($p = 0.043$).

Regularity analysis

For the 422 100-day analyses periods, the ApEn values ranged between 0 and 0.94, with a mean of 0.21 (SD 0.18). For the 422 analyses, the ApEn was between 0 and 0.2 for 240 (56.9%), between 0.2 and 0.4 for 128 (30.3%), and > 0.4 for 54 (12.8%). The ApEn was 0 (no change to daily dosage) in 56 (13.3%) of the analyses.

ApEn is directly related to the percent of days of missing doses ($p < 0.001$). However, even patients with a low percent of days missing doses may have irregular daily dosages. Figure 1 includes examples graphs of patients with irregular daily dosage, despite low missing days of data, and one example of how a patient may have both a larger number of missing days, and variable dosage.

The factors other than missing days of data that were associated with increasing irregularity are shown in Table 3. The total number of psychotropic drugs ($p = 0.009$), the pill burden ($p = 0.026$), and the percent of days depressed ($p = 0.049$) were all associated with irregularity. The percent of days euthymic was inversely related to irregularity ($p = 0.028$). No other clinical or demographic variables were associated with irregularity.

Table 2 Psychotropic medications taken during the 100-day analyses periods (N = 241)

Medication	N	%		
Taking antidepressants	122	51		
Taking benzodiazepines	55	23		
Taking insomnia medications	22	9		
All medications[a]	**Mean**	**SD**		
Total number of medications	3.9	2.0		
Total pill burden	7.2	4.8		
Antipsychotic/mood stabilizer[b]	**N in analysis**	**Mean dosage (mg)**	**Dosage SD**	**Pct days missing**
Aripiprazole	28	15.5	11.3	15.4
Risperidone	17	1.6	1.4	19.5
Quetiapine	48	268.4	202.0	22.3
Ziprasidone	12	141.6	59.4	12.9
Olanzapine	17	8.4	5.4	13.5
Lithium	99	914.6	320.6	15.1
Valproate	45	1107.2	599.0	12.8
Carbamazepine	15	798.1	386.1	5.1
Oxcarbazepine	14	938.1	605.6	26.1
Lamotrigine	119	231.9	129.4	13.5

[a] Only psychotropic drugs

[b] Only including drugs with $\geq$ 10 analysis periods

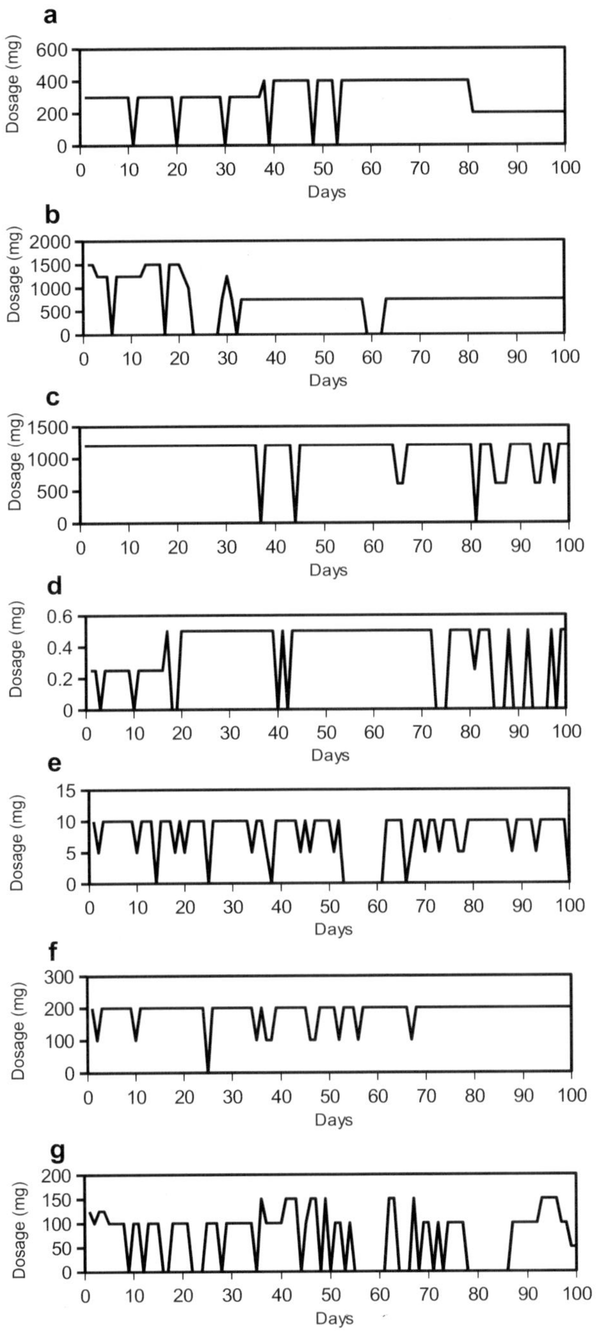

Fig. 1 Example ApEn, adherence and drug holiday values for 100 days of data. In **a–f**, patients have few missing days but irregular daily dosage (high ApEn). In **g**, the patient has both a large number of missing days and irregular daily dosage. **a** Lamotrigine. ApEn 0.3432 with 94% adherence and 0 drug holidays. **b** Valproate. ApEn 0.4836 with 87% adherence and 2 drug holidays. **c** Lithium. ApEn 0.3511 with 97% adherence and 0 drug holidays. **d** Risperidone. ApEn 0.6007 with 80% adherence and 4 drug holidays. **e** Asenapine. ApEn 0.7117 with 86% adherence and 1 drug holiday. **f** Lamotrigine. ApEn 0.3756 with 99% adherence and 0 drug holidays. **g** Lamotrigine. ApEn 0.9428 with 65% adherence and 4 drug holidays

Discussion

Patients with bipolar disorder in this study were motivated to actively participate in their care, and took medication on about 84% of days. Yet, even among this group, despite the low percent of missing days, there was considerable irregularity in the daily dosage taken. Days of missing doses, primarily single day omissions, and changes to the daily dosage were the primary cause of the irregularity. Additionally, there was at least one drug holiday in 35.8% of the analysis periods. These results are consistent with our prior studies, and there are many implications of these findings (Bauer et al. 2013b, c).

It is challenging for the physician to reliably assess patient adherence and the link between non-adherence and inadequate response. Irregularity in the daily dosage may be a contributing factor. Most psychiatrists prefer to assess adherence of patients with bipolar disorder by asking the patient (Vieta et al. 2012), but physician perceptions are often incorrect and optimistic (Velligan et al. 2009; Baldessarini et al. 2008). For example, physicians overestimated adherence with second-generation antipsychotics, primarily by patients with bipolar disorder, as compared to claims data (Stephenson et al. 2012). For 97 patients who went to an emergency room for an exacerbation of psychosis, including 26 with bipolar disorder, staff assessments of adherence and non-adherence were correct 41.5 and 75% of the time respectively, when compared to plasma antipsychotic levels (Lopez et al. 2017).

In this study, single day omissions occurred frequently. Some drugs and formulations are more forgiving about dosage omissions than others, varying with the pharmacokinetic and pharmacodynamic properties (Osterberg et al. 2010; Urquhart 1998). With a forgiving drug, the duration of action is much longer than the dosage interval, so an occasional missed dose is unlikely to interrupt therapeutic activity (Osterberg et al. 2010). Recently, the number of drug formulations that require less frequent dosing has increased, including formulations for psychotropic drugs. While a less frequent dosing regimen generally increases adherence (Saini et al. 2009; Claxton et al. 2001), it may not improve outcomes (Comté et al. 2007; Richter et al. 2003; Vrijens et al. 2014; Vrijens and Heidbuchel 2015; Harden 2017; Bialer 2007). For example, the consequences of missing one dose of a once-daily drug may be more deleterious to the continuity of therapeutic action than missing one dose of a twice-daily drug (Osterberg et al. 2010; Hughes 2006; Urquhart and Vrijens 2006). However, extended release formulations that reduce fluctuations in plasma concentration may improve the forgiveness of once-daily drugs (Pellock and Brittain 2016; Chen et al. 2013; Brittain and Wheless 2015).

Table 3 Estimated coefficients of parameters associated with daily dosage irregularity for mood stabilizers and second generation antipsychotics[a]

Parameter	Coefficient estimate	Standard error	95% Wald confidence interval		Coefficient significance	
			Lower	Upper	Wald chi square	p
Total pill burden[b]	0.005	0.002	0.001	0.010	4.944	0.026
Total number of medications[b]	0.015	0.006	0.004	0.027	6.771	0.009
Percent days depressed	0.001	0.001	4.137E−6	0.003	3.867	0.049
Percent days euthymic	− 0.001	0.001	− 0.002	0.000	4.845	0.028
Percent days manic	0.001	0.001	− 0.001	0.003	1.870	0.171

[a] (422 100-day analyses periods). GEE model estimated ApEn (1, 0.2 * SD, 100) using the listed parameter with an independent working correlation structure for each model

[b] Psychotropic medications only

The relatively large number of drug holidays reported in this study, with a dosing interruption of 3 or more days, are of considerable concern. The rapid discontinuation of a psychotropic drug may trigger immediate withdrawal symptoms or delayed rebound phenomena, related to complex factors including pharmacokinetic and pharmacodynamic properties of a drug formulation, and individual metabolism (Baldessarini et al. 1999; Cerovecki et al. 2013; Franks et al. 2008; Fava et al. 2015; Correll 2010; Osterberg et al. 2010). After a drug holiday, patients often resume taking the full-strength dosage, including of drugs that are slowly titrated upward. Re-starting a drug after a long lapse may trigger first-dose effects (Urquhart 1998). Given the frequent use of polypharmacy, drug holidays may impact the potential for drug interactions (Spina et al. 2016). There is a need for increased understanding of the clinical impacts of repeated starting and stopping of mood stabilizers and antipsychotic drugs, in various product formulations (Osterberg et al. 2010; Hughes 2008; Samtani et al. 2012). In this study, taking a drug holiday was associated with working full time, suggesting that some patients may doubt they need ongoing treatment (Clatworthy et al. 2009), or lack insight into the value of medications (Copeland et al. 2008). In prior research, employment was not associated with psychotropic medication adherence (Bulloch and Patten 2010; Razzano et al. 2005, Sajatovic et al. 2006).

In addition to dosage omissions, changes to the daily dosage contributed to the irregularity. The patients in this study took polypharmacy with a mean of 3.9 psychotropic medications for bipolar disorder, and a mean pill burden of 7.2. Both the number of psychotropic medications and the pill burden were associated with irregularity in daily dosage. Research in a wide range of chronic medical illnesses has found that medication regimen complexity decreases adherence (Ingersoll and Cohen 2008). Some patients with bipolar disorder may have trouble integrating a complex drug regimen into their daily routine (Sajatovic et al. 2009; Wagner and Ryan 2004), especially those with a disorganized lifestyle (Frank et al. 2006). Even patients intent on adhering often forget about doses, especially on days with unexpected schedule interruptions (Dunbar-Jacob and Mortimer-Stephens 2001; Bulloch and Patten 2010), which usually results in underdosing but sometimes overdosing.

Other factors contribute to irregular daily dosages. Patients may have an "as needed" approach to dosing, taking doses to treat symptoms or lessen side effects (Dunbar-Jacob and Mortimer-Stephens 2001; Marder 2003; Pound et al. 2005). Recent societal emphasis on self-management may be encouraging self-experimentation (Swan 2013). Some patients want to take as little medication as possible (Pound et al. 2005). Consistent with our prior studies, depressive symptoms were associated with increased irregularity (Bauer et al. 2013b, c). In other research, depressive symptoms were associated with non-adherence in bipolar disorder (Belzeaux et al. 2013; Johnson et al. 2007), as well chronic medical conditions (Grenard et al. 2011).

Several issues may impact the generalizability of this study. No data were available on the rate and characteristics of patients who were asked but declined to participate in the study. A large percentage of patients were recruited from university clinics, which may not reflect other settings. In the current study, more females than males were included, and patients varied in the phase of illness and disease severity. However, the demographic characteristics of the patients who use ChronoRecord are similar to those reported for other studies of bipolar disorder (Bauer et al. 2012). Since taking a mood stabilizer or antipsychotic for 100 days was required for analysis, the least adherent patients were excluded. However, even higher irregularity in daily dosage would be expected from patients who are less adherent.

There are other limitations to this study. All data were self-reported. However, review articles about the measurement of medication adherence have found moderate-to-high concordance between self-reported patient questionnaires and diaries, and electronic monitoring (Garber et al. 2004; Shi et al. 2010; Monnette et al. 2018). In a study of patients with bipolar disorder, good agreement was found between patient questionnaires and serum levels of psychotropic medications (Jónsdóttir et al. 2010). This study underestimated regimen complexity since medications taken for general medical reasons and OTC drugs were not included. Other aspects of drug regimen complexity such as administration instructions, and dosage timing were not available. Some of the dosage changes may have been prescribed by the physician. Only oral medications were included in this study. Different formulations of the same medication, such as pill size and ease of swallowing, are known to impact adherence but were not considered (Bhosle et al. 2009; Fields et al. 2015). The specific drug regimens were not investigated but are highly variable in clinical practice, including different combinations of medication classes and drugs (Bauer et al. 2013a).

It is important to put the findings of this study into context. In this sample of patients with bipolar disorder who were motivated to participate in their care, there was considerable irregularity in daily dosage. However, partial adherence is also routinely found in patients with chronic medical conditions who do not have mental illness (Osterberg and Blaschke 2005; Brown et al. 2016). Even in a monitored environment, less than 70% of over 16,000 patients with various medical conditions enrolled in 95 clinical studies were fully adherent (Vrijens and Urquhart 2014; Blaschke et al. 2012). The clinician treating patients with bipolar disorder should expect a level of nonadherence including dosage omissions, changes, and drug holidays, even among patients determined to recover. If the patient's condition is such that exceptional adherence is required, such as approaching no missing dosages, intensive educational measures, and customization of the individual's regimen are required. These findings also confirm the need for careful evaluation of newly appearing or worsening symptoms.

Conclusion

In conclusion, considerable irregularity in daily dosage of mood stabilizers and antipsychotic medications was found despite a low percent of missing days. The total number of psychotropic drugs, pill burden and depression were associated with increased irregularity. The irregularity in daily dosage was primarily due to single day omissions and dosage changes. Drug holidays were also present. These findings may contribute to understanding the individual variation in treatment response seen in clinical practice. Physicians should expect to see partial adherence with treatments for bipolar disorder. More understanding of the impacts of daily irregularity on specific drugs and formulations is needed.

Authors' contributions

MP, MB, TG and PW worked on the conception and design of the study, interpreted the results and drafted the manuscript. TG performed the analyses. NR, MA, KS, PG, RM; WM, SM, ES, RB, and PR performed data collection, and interpretation of the findings. All authors read and approved the final manuscript.

Author details

[1] Department of Psychiatry and Psychotherapy, Medical Faculty, University Hospital Carl Gustav Carus, Technische Universität Dresden, Fetscherstr. 74, 01307 Dresden, Germany. [2] ChronoRecord Association Inc., Fullerton, CA, USA. [3] Department of Psychiatry and Behavioral Sciences, Stanford School of Medicine, Palo Alto, CA, USA. [4] Department of Psychiatry, Dalhousie University, Halifax, NS, Canada. [5] Department of Psychiatry, University of Missouri Kansas City School of Medicine, Kansas City, MO, USA. [6] Mood Disorders Center of Ottawa, University of Toronto, Toronto, Canada. [7] Department of Psychiatry, University of California San Diego, San Diego, CA, USA. [8] Department of Psychiatry, University of Massachusetts, Worcester, MA, USA. [9] Michigan State University College of Human Medicine, Traverse City Campus, Traverse City, MI, USA. [10] Department of Psychiatry and Biobehavioral Sciences, Semel Institute for Neuroscience and Human Behavior, University of California Los Angeles (UCLA), Los Angeles, CA, USA.

Acknowledgements

We acknowledge support by the Open Access Publication Funds of the TU Dresden.

Competing interests

The authors declare that they have no competing interests.

Funding

Open Access publication was funded by Publication Funds of the TU Dresden.

References

Baldessarini RJ, Tondo L, Viguera AC. Discontinuing lithium maintenance treatment in bipolar disorders: risks and implications. Bipolar Disord. 1999;1:17–24.

Baldessarini RJ, Perry R, Pike J. Factors associated with treatment nonadherence among US bipolar disorder patients. Hum Psychopharmacol. 2008;23:95–105.

Bauer M, Grof P, Gyulai L, Rasgon N, Glenn T, Whybrow PC. Using technology to improve longitudinal studies: self-reporting with ChronoRecord in bipolar disorder. Bipolar Disord. 2004;2004(6):67–74.

Bauer M, Wilson T, Neuhaus K, Sasse J, Pfennig A, Lewitzka U, et al. Self-reporting software for bipolar disorder: validation of ChronoRecord by patients with mania. Psychiatry Res. 2008;159:359–66.

Bauer M, Glenn T, Keil M, Bauer R, Marsh W, Grof P, et al. Brief depressive symptoms in patients with bipolar disorder: analysis of long-term self-reported data. Aust N Z J Psychiatry. 2012;46:1068–78.

Bauer M, Glenn T, Alda M, Sagduyu K, Marsh W, Grof P, et al. Drug treatment patterns in bipolar disorder: analysis of long-term self-reported data. Int J Bipolar Disord. 2013a;1:5.

Bauer M, Glenn T, Alda M, Sagduyu K, Marsh W, Grof P, et al. Regularity in daily mood stabilizer dosage taken by patients with bipolar disorder. Pharmacopsychiatry. 2013b;46:163–8.

Bauer R, Glenn T, Alda M, Sagduyu K, Marsh W, Grof P, et al. Antidepressant dosage taken by patients with bipolar disorder: factors associated with irregularity. Int J Bipolar Disord. 2013c;1:26.

Belzeaux R, Correard N, Boyer L, Etain B, Loftus J, Bellivier F, et al. Depressive residual symptoms are associated with lower adherence to medication in bipolar patients without substance use disorder: results from the FACE-BD cohort. J Affect Disord. 2013;151:1009–15.

Bhosle M, Benner JS, Dekoven M, Shelton J. Difficult to swallow: patient preferences for alternative valproate pharmaceutical formulations. Patient Prefer Adherence. 2009;3:161–71.

Bialer M. Extended-release formulations for the treatment of epilepsy. CNS Drugs. 2007;21:765–74.

Bjørklund L, Horsdal HT, Mors O, Østergaard SD, Gasse C. Trends in the psychopharmacological treatment of bipolar disorder: a nationwide register-based study. Acta Neuropsychiatr. 2016;28:75–84.

Blaschke TF, Osterberg L, Vrijens B, Urquhart J. Adherence to medications: insights arising from studies on the unreliable link between prescribed and actual drug dosing histories. Annu Rev Pharmacol Toxicol. 2012;52:275–301.

Brittain ST, Wheless JW. Pharmacokinetic simulations of topiramate plasma concentrations following dosing irregularities with extended-release vs. immediate-release formulations. Epilepsy Behav. 2015;52:31–6.

Brown MT, Bussell J, Dutta S, Davis K, Strong S, Mathew S. Medication adherence: truth and consequences. Am J Med Sci. 2016;351:387–99.

Bulloch AG, Patten SB. Non-adherence with psychotropic medications in the general population. Soc Psychiatry Psychiatr Epidemiol. 2010;45:47–56.

Cerovecki A, Musil R, Klimke A, Seemüller F, Haen E, Schennach R, et al. Withdrawal symptoms and rebound syndromes associated with switching and discontinuing atypical antipsychotics: theoretical background and practical recommendations. CNS Drugs. 2013;27:545–72.

Chen C, Wright J, Gidal B, Messenheimer J. Assessing impact of real-world dosing irregularities with lamotrigine extended-release and immediate-release formulations by pharmacokinetic simulation. Ther Drug Monit. 2013;35:188–93.

Clatworthy J, Bowskill R, Parham R, Rank T, Scott J, Horne R. Understanding medication non-adherence in bipolar disorders using a necessity-concerns framework. J Affect Disord. 2009;116:51–5.

Claxton AJ, Cramer J, Pierce C. A systematic review of the associations between dose regimens and medication compliance. Clin Ther. 2001;23:1296–310.

Comté L, Vrijens B, Tousset E, Gérard P, Urquhart J. Estimation of the comparative therapeutic superiority of QD and BID dosing regimens, based on integrated analysis of dosing history data and pharmacokinetics. J Pharmacokinet Pharmacodyn. 2007;34:549–58.

Copeland LA, Zeber JE, Salloum IM, Pincus HA, Fine MJ, Kilbourne AM. Treatment adherence and illness insight in veterans with bipolar disorder. J Nerv Ment Dis. 2008;196:16–21.

Correll CU. From receptor pharmacology to improved outcomes: individualising the selection, dosing, and switching of antipsychotics. Eur Psychiatry. 2010;25(Suppl 2):S12–21.

Dunbar-Jacob J, Mortimer-Stephens MK. Treatment adherence in chronic disease. J Clin Epidemiol. 2001;54(Suppl 1):S57–60.

Fava GA, Gatti A, Belaise C, Guidi J, Offidani E. Withdrawal symptoms after selective serotonin reuptake inhibitor discontinuation: a systematic review. Psychother Psychosom. 2015;84:72–81.

Fields J, Go JT, Schulze KS. Pill properties that cause dysphagia and treatment failure. Curr Ther Res Clin Exp. 2015;77:79–82.

Fountoulakis KN, Grunze H, Vieta E, Young A, Yatham L, Blier P, Kasper S, Moeller HJ. The International College of Neuro-Psychopharmacology (CINP) treatment guidelines for bipolar disorder in adults (CINP-BD-2017), part 3: the clinical guidelines. Int J Neuropsychopharmacol. 2017;20:180–95.

Frank E, Gonzalez JM, Fagiolini A. The importance of routine for preventing recurrence in bipolar disorder. Am J Psychiatry. 2006;163:981–5.

Franks M, Macritchie KA, Mahmood T, Young AH. Bouncing back: is the bipolar rebound phenomenon peculiar to lithium? A retrospective naturalistic study. J Psychopharmacol. 2008;22:452–6.

Garber MC, Nau DP, Erickson SR, Aikens JE, Lawrence JB. The concordance of self-report with other measures of medication adherence: a summary of the literature. Med Care. 2004;42:649–52.

García S, Martínez-Cengotitabengoa M, López-Zurbano S, Zorrilla I, López P, Vieta E, et al. Adherence to antipsychotic medication in bipolar disorder and schizophrenic patients: a systematic review. J Clin Psychopharmacol. 2016;36:355–71.

Goldberg JF, Brooks JO 3rd, Kurita K, Hoblyn JC, Ghaemi SN, Perlis RH, et al. Depressive illness burden associated with complex polypharmacy in patients with bipolar disorder: findings from the STEP-BD. J Clin Psychiatry. 2009;70:155–62.

Golden JC, Goethe JW, Woolley SB. Complex psychotropic polypharmacy in bipolar disorder across varying mood polarities: a prospective cohort study of 2712 inpatients. J Affect Disord. 2017;221:6–10.

Gonzalez-Pinto A, Mosquera F, Alonso M, López P, Ramírez F, Vieta E, et al. Suicidal risk in bipolar I disorder patients and adherence to long-term lithium treatment. Bipolar Disord. 2006;8:618–24.

Grenard JL, Munjas BA, Adams JL, Suttorp M, Maglione M, McGlynn EA, et al. Depression and medication adherence in the treatment of chronic diseases in the United States: a meta-analysis. J Gen Intern Med. 2011;26:1175–82.

Harden CL. Generic modified-release antiepileptic drugs: no difference within formulations, but important differences across formulations. Epilepsy Curr. 2017;17:29–31.

Hassan M, Lage MJ. Risk of rehospitalization among bipolar disorder patients who are nonadherent to antipsychotic therapy after hospital discharge. Am J Health Syst Pharm. 2009;66:358–65.

Hawkshead J, Krousel-Wood MA. Techniques for measuring medication adherence in hypertensive patients in outpatient settings. Disease Manag Health Outcomes. 2007;15:109–18.

Hong J, Reed C, Novick D, Haro JM, Aguado J. Clinical and economic consequences of medication non-adherence in the treatment of patients with a manic/mixed episode of bipolar disorder: results from the European Mania in Bipolar Longitudinal Evaluation of Medication (EMBLEM) study. Psychiatry Res. 2011;190:110–4.

Hughes D. Less is more: medicines that require less frequent administration improve adherence, but are they better? Pharmacoeconomics. 2006;24:211–3.

Hughes DA. Estimation of the impact of noncompliance on pharmacokinetics: an analysis of the influence of dosing regimens. Br J Clin Pharmacol. 2008;65:871–8.

Ingersoll KS, Cohen J. The impact of medication regimen factors on adherence to chronic treatment: a review of literature. J Behav Med. 2008;31:213–24.

Johnson FR, Ozdemir S, Manjunath R, Hauber AB, Burch SP, Thompson TR. Factors that affect adherence to bipolar disorder treatments: a stated-preference approach. Med Care. 2007;45:545–52.

Jónsdóttir H, Opjordsmoen S, Birkenaes AB, Engh JA, Ringen PA, Vaskinn A, et al. Medication adherence in outpatients with severe mental disorders: relation between self-reports and serum level. J Clin Psychopharmacol. 2010;30:169–75.

Kessing LV, Sondergard L, Kvist K, Andersen PK. Adherence to lithium in naturalistic settings: results from a nationwide pharmacoepidemiological study. Bipolar Disord. 2007;9:730–6.

Kessing LV, Vradi E, Andersen PK. Nationwide and population-based prescription patterns in bipolar disorder. Bipolar Disord. 2016;18:174–82.

Kleimann A, Schrader V, Stübner S, Greil W, Kahl KG, Bleich S, et al. Psychopharmacological treatment of 1650 in-patients with acute mania-data from the AMSP study. J Affect Disord. 2016;191:164–71.

Kukreja S, Kalra G, Shah N, Shrivastava A. Polypharmacy in psychiatry: a review. Mens Sana Monogr. 2013;11:82–99.

Levin JB, Sams J, Tatsuoka C, Cassidy KA, Sajatovic M. Use of automated medication adherence monitoring in bipolar disorder research: pitfalls, pragmatics, and possibilities. Ther Adv Psychopharmacol. 2015;5:76–87.

Lopez LV, Shaikh A, Merson J, Greenberg J, Suckow RF, Kane JM. Accuracy of clinician assessments of medication status in the emergency setting: a comparison of clinician assessment of antipsychotic usage and plasma level determination. J Clin Psychopharmacol. 2017;37:310–4.

Marder SR. Overview of partial compliance. J Clin Psychiatry. 2003;64(Suppl 16):3–9.

Monnette A, Zhang Y, Shao H, Shi L. Concordance of adherence measurement using self-reported adherence questionnaires and medication monitoring devices: an updated review. Pharmacoeconomics. 2018;36:17–27.

Osterberg L, Blaschke T. Adherence to medication. N Engl J Med. 2005;353:487–97.

Osterberg LG, Urquhart J, Blaschke TF. Understanding forgiveness: minding and mining the gaps between pharmacokinetics and therapeutics. Clin Pharmacol Ther. 2010;88:457–9.

Pan W, Connett JE. Selecting the working correlation structure in generalized estimating equations with application to the lung health study. Statistica Sinica. 2002;12:475–90.

Parker GB, Graham RK, Tavella G. Is there consensus across international evidence-based guidelines for the management of bipolar disorder? Acta Psychiatr Scand. 2017;135:515–26.

Pearson CR, Simoni JM, Hoff P, Kurth AE, Martin DP. Assessing antiretroviral adherence via electronic drug monitoring and self-report: an examination of key methodological issues. AIDS Behav. 2007;11:161–73.

Pellock JM, Brittain ST. Use of computer simulations to test the concept of dose forgiveness in the era of extended-release (XR) drugs. Epilepsy Behav. 2016;55:21–3.

Peselow ED, Naghdechi L, Pizano D, IsHak WW. Polypharmacy in maintenance of bipolar disorder. Clin Neuropharmacol. 2016;39:132–4.

Pincus SM. Approximate entropy as a measure of system complexity. Proc Natl Acad Sci USA. 1991;88:2297–301.

Pincus SM, Gladstone IM, Ehrenkranz RA. A regularity statistic for medical data analysis. J Clin Monit. 1991;7:335–45.

Pincus SM, Cummins TR, Haddad GG. Heart rate control in normal and aborted-SIDS infants. Am J Physiol. 1993;264:R638–46.

Pompili M, Serafini G, Del Casale A, Rigucci S, Innamorati M, Girardi P, et al. Improving adherence in mood disorders: the struggle against relapse, recurrence and suicide risk. Expert Rev Neurother. 2009;9:985–1004.

Pound P, Britten N, Morgan M, Yardley L, Pope C, Daker-White G, et al. Resisting medicines: a synthesis of qualitative studies of medicine taking. Soc Sci Med. 2005;61:133–55.

Razzano LA, Cook JA, Burke-Miller JK, Mueser KT, Pickett-Schenk SA, Grey DD, et al. Clinical factors associated with employment among people with severe mental illness: findings from the employment intervention demonstration program. J Nerv Ment Dis. 2005;193:705–13.

Rej S, Herrmann N, Shulman K, Fischer HD, Fung K, Gruneir A. Current psychotropic medication prescribing patterns in late-life bipolar disorder. Int J Geriatr Psychiatry. 2017;32:1459–65.

Richter A, Anton SF, Koch P, Dennett SL. The impact of reducing dose frequency on health outcomes. Clin Ther. 2003;25:2307–35.

Sachs GS, Peters AT, Sylvia L, Grunze H. Polypharmacy and bipolar disorder: what's personality got to do with it? Int J Neuropsychopharmacol. 2014;17:1053–61.

Saini SD, Schoenfeld P, Kaulback K, Dubinsky MC. Effect of medication dosing frequency on adherence in chronic diseases. Am J Manag Care. 2009;15:e22–33.

Sajatovic M, Bauer MS, Kilbourne AM, Vertrees JE, Williford W. Self-reported medication treatment adherence among veterans with bipolar disorder. Psychiatr Serv. 2006;57:56–62.

Sajatovic M, Ignacio RV, West JA, Cassidy KA, Safavi R, Kilbourne AM, et al. Predictors of nonadherence among individuals with bipolar disorder receiving treatment in a community mental health clinic. Compr Psychiatry. 2009;50:100–7.

Sajatovic M, Velligan DI, Weiden PJ, Valenstein MA, Ogedegbe G. Measurement of psychiatric treatment adherence. J Psychosom Res. 2010;69:591–9.

Samtani MN, Sheehan JJ, Fu DJ, Remmerie B, Sliwa JK, Alphs L. Management of antipsychotic treatment discontinuation and interruptions using model-based simulations. Clin Pharmacol. 2012;4:25–40.

Schuepbach D, Novick D, Haro JM, Reed C, Boeker H, Noda S, et al. Determinants of voluntary vs. involuntary admission in bipolar disorder and the impact of adherence. Pharmacopsychiatry. 2008;41:29–36.

Scott J, Pope M. Nonadherence with mood stabilizers: prevalence and predictors. J Clin Psychiatry. 2002;63:384–90.

Shi L, Liu J, Koleva Y, Fonseca V, Kalsekar A, Pawaskar M. Concordance of adherence measurement using self-reported adherence questionnaires and medication monitoring devices. Pharmacoeconomics. 2010;28:1097–107.

Spina E, Pisani F, de Leon J. Clinically significant pharmacokinetic drug interactions of antiepileptic drugs with new antidepressants and new antipsychotics. Pharmacol Res. 2016;106:72–86.

Stephenson JJ, Tunceli O, Gu T, Eisenberg D, Panish J, Crivera C, et al. Adherence to oral second-generation antipsychotic medications in patients with schizophrenia and bipolar disorder: physicians' perceptions of adherence vs. pharmacy claims. Int J Clin Pract. 2012;66:565–73.

Swan M. The quantified self: fundamental disruption in big data science and biological discovery. Big Data. 2013;1:85–99.

Urquhart J. Pharmacodynamics of variable patient compliance: implications for pharmaceutical value. Adv Drug Deliv Rev. 1998;33:207–19.

Urquhart J, Vrijens B. 'Hedged' prescribing for partially compliant patients. Clin Pharmacokinet. 2006;45:105–8.

Velligan DI, Weiden PJ, Sajatovic M, Scott J, Carpenter D, Ross R, et al. The expert consensus guideline series: adherence problems in patients with serious and persistent mental illness. J Clin Psychiatry. 2009;70(Suppl 4):1–46.

Vieta E, Azorin JM, Bauer M, Frangou S, Perugi G, Martinez G, et al. Psychiatrists' perceptions of potential reasons for non- and partial adherence to medication: results of a survey in bipolar disorder from eight European countries. J Affect Disord. 2012;143:125–30.

Vrijens B, Heidbuchel H. Non-vitamin K antagonist oral anticoagulants: considerations on once- vs. twice-daily regimens and their potential impact on medication adherence. Europace. 2015;17:514–23.

Vrijens B, Urquhart J. Methods for measuring, enhancing, and accounting for medication adherence in clinical trials. Clin Pharmacol Ther. 2014;95:617–26.

Vrijens B, Claeys MJ, Legrand V, Vandendriessche E, Van de Werf F. Projected inhibition of platelet aggregation with ticagrelor twice daily vs. clopidogrel once daily based on patient adherence data (the TWICE project). Br J Clin Pharmacol. 2014;77:746–55.

Wagner GJ, Ryan GW. Relationship between routinization of daily behaviors and medication adherence in HIV-positive drug users. AIDS Patient Care STDS. 2004;18:385–93.

Weinstock LM, Gaudiano BA, Epstein-Lubow G, Tezanos K, Celis-Dehoyos CE, Miller IW. Medication burden in bipolar disorder: a chart review of patients at psychiatric hospital admission. Psychiatry Res. 2014;216:24–30.

10

The clinical trajectory of emerging bipolar disorder among the high-risk offspring of bipolar parents: current understanding and future considerations

A. Duffy[1*], C. Vandeleur[2], N. Heffer[3] and M. Preisig[2]

Abstract

Background: Relatively little is known about the onset of bipolar disorder, yet the early illness course is already associated with significant morbidity and mortality. Therefore, characterizing the bipolar illness trajectory is key to risk prediction and early intervention advancement.

Main body: In this narrative review, we discuss key findings from prospective longitudinal studies of the high-risk offspring of bipolar parents and related meta-analyses that inform us about the clinical trajectory of emerging bipolar disorder. Challenges such as phenotypic and etiologic heterogeneity and the non-specificity of early symptoms and syndromes are highlighted. Implications of the findings for both research and clinical practice are discussed.

Conclusion: Bipolar disorder in young people at familial risk does not typically onset with a hypomanic or manic episode. Rather the first activated episode is often preceded by years of impairing psychopathological states that vary over development and across emerging bipolar subtype. Taking heterogeneity into account and adopting a more comprehensive approach to diagnosis seems necessary to advance earlier identification and our understanding of the onset of bipolar disorder.

Keywords: Bipolar disorder, Early course, Antecedents, Stages, Illness trajectory, High-risk, Offspring

Background

Bipolar disorder is a heterogeneous and genetically complex illness (McGuffin et al. 2010). Currently, the diagnosis is based on the manifestation of at least one manic (bipolar I) or hypomanic and depressive episode (bipolar-II). However, prospective studies provide substantial evidence that the first activated (manic or hypomanic) episode is often preceded by one or several depressive episodes typically in adolescence, and not uncommonly by much earlier childhood clinical antecedents (Duffy et al. 2014; Egeland et al. 2012; Mesman et al. 2013). Further, it is estimated to take over a decade from the onset of the first activated episode to recognition of the bipolar diagnosis, and much longer still from the onset of impairing symptoms (Egeland et al. 2000; Judd and Akiskal 2003). This diagnostic delay is associated with devastating consequences including inappropriate treatment, increased hospitalization, medical comorbidity, treatment refractoriness, addiction, school drop-out, underemployment, and suicide (Judd et al. 2005; Keck et al. 2008).

Therefore, earlier identification of emergent bipolar disorder and advances in understanding the nature of illness onset are key research priorities. An important strategic aim to attain these goals is mapping risk processes and markers of illness activity over the trajectory of illness development—from well but at risk, to full-blown illness. An informative approach to accomplish this aim is to prospectively study the high-risk offspring of bipolar parents from childhood over the peak risk period for

*Correspondence: anne.duffy@queensu.ca
[1] Student Wellness Centre, Department of Psychiatry, Queen's University, 146 Stuart Street, Kingston, ON K7L3N6, Canada
Full list of author information is available at the end of the article

illness onset. (i.e., adolescence and early adulthood). This design allows for parallel, real-time assessment of risk factors and potential confounds—allowing for the separation of trait from state, critical to the task of identifying risk markers and endophenotypes. Ultimately, this advance will inform the development and timing of specific early interventions; thereby reducing the proportion of individuals reaching end-stage illness and developing a progressive illness course.

Methods

We completed a selective narrative review of published studies that inform us about the emerging clinical trajectory of bipolar disorder. Included studies (listed in Table 1) had to be prospective and longitudinal in design, include the offspring of at least one parent with bipolar disorder, and report on clinical outcomes at the syndrome level. The purpose of this narrative review is, therefore, to summarize the available evidence informing the clinical picture of emerging bipolar disorder and highlight the importance of heterogeneity in this work. We also discuss how risk factors such as family history can be used to differentiate the early bipolar illness trajectory from otherwise non-specific clinical presentations. Finally, we discuss the clinical and research implications of these findings, highlighting knowledge gaps and future challenges.

Results and discussion

Emerging bipolar disorder

Bipolar disorder runs in families and a confirmed history in a first-degree relative is the single most robust predictor of illness risk. Based on data from published family studies and a meta-analysis, a first degree relative of a bipolar patient has an estimated eight- to tenfold lifetime risk of developing bipolar disorder and a two to threefold lifetime risk of developing a depressive disorder compared to the general population (Duffy et al. 2000; Wilde et al. 2014). However, recent evidence from two large family studies found an increase of major depressive disorder only among adult family members of bipolar-II but not bipolar-I probands, suggesting the independence of familial aggregation of bipolar-I and major depressive disorder (Vandeleur et al. 2014; Merikangas et al. 2014). The discrepant results of these recent compared to earlier family studies is most likely explained by differential methodological approaches—that is a mixture of probands with both bipolar-I and bipolar-II disorders, as well as the use of RDC criteria and different diagnostic measures. Depressive disorders that share a bipolar diathesis (i.e., in relatives of bipolar probands) or represent the emerging course (i.e., in subjects that later develop bipolar disorder) have been described as having an early adolescent onset, a highly recurrent course, and not uncommonly include psychotic features, activated symptoms and evidence of paradoxical worsening on antidepressants (Strober and Carlson 1982; O'Donovan et al. 2008).

There are a number of risk modifiers that can be used to individualize the estimated risk of developing bipolar disorder for individuals from specific families. For example, high penetrance across multiple generations, an earlier age of onset in the proband bipolar patient, and assortative mating all increase the risk estimate (Duffy et al. 2000). Additionally, early adversity in the form of abuse, neglect, increased exposure to active parental illness, and attachment difficulties have been associated with an increased risk and an earlier age of onset of bipolar disorder, possibly through epigenetic mechanisms (Goodday et al. 2015; Duffy et al. 2016; Doucette et al. 2016; Petronis 2010; Post et al. 2016; Bagot and Meaney 2010).

Given the high estimated heritability of bipolar disorder (Smoller and Finn 2003), children of bipolar parents are an important and informative high-risk population. Prospective study of the emerging clinical course in children of parents with well-characterized bipolar disorder, alongside assessment of other important risk factors, is the best way to disentangle primary illness development from burden of illness effects. There are now a number of published international prospective longitudinal offspring studies (Table 1) (Duffy et al. 2014; Egeland et al. 2012; Mesman et al. 2013; Birmaher et al. 2009; Preisig et al. 2016; Nurnberger et al. 2011). Each study varies in terms of recruitment and assessment methods, yielding differences in risk modifiers such as the age of onset and comorbidity in the proband parents, degree of assortative mating, proportion of intact families, and level of education and income of the family. The nature of the comparator (control) group also differs across high-risk studies.

Nonetheless, there are several key findings regarding the children at confirmed familial risk that can be summarized as follows: (i) anxiety and sleep disorders in childhood increase the risk of subsequent major mood disorders 2.5- to 3-fold compared to high-risk offspring without these antecedents (Nurnberger et al. 2011; Duffy et al. 2013); (ii) ADHD and behavioural disorders are not consistently elevated in high-risk offspring after adjustment for family factors (socioeconomic status, cultural context, ADHD and other comorbid psychiatric disorders in bipolar and other parents) and bipolar subtype (psychotic spectrum illness) (Egeland et al. 2012; Birmaher et al. 2009; Nurnberger et al. 2011; Duffy 2012; Axelson et al. 2015); (iii) increased exposure in childhood to active parental illness (Goodday et al. 2015) and earlier age of onset of parental bipolar disorder (Preisig et al.

Table 1 An overview of prospective bipolar offspring studies: study characteristics and psychopathology outcomes

Published work	Cohort characteristics					Parental characteristics				Offspring characteristics				
	Country of origin	Type of cohort	Years of follow-up	Follow-up interval (# interviews)	Drop-out rate (%)	*n*	BD index parent	BD mother (%)	Recruitment	*n*	Mean age at last assessment (range)	Diagnostic interview	Most recent offspring diagnoses % (controls)	Early course of BD
Duffy et al. (1998, 2014)	Canada	Dynamic[a]	Up to 16 (mean 6.3)	Annually	9	113	45% BDI 43% BDII 12% RMDD[d]	52	Outpatient specialty clinics; lithium responders and non-responders	229	22.6 (7–25)	K-SADS-PL; SADS-L	22% BDI, II, NOS, SCZBD (0%) 32% MDD (3%) 20% adjustment (41%) 9% minor mood (2%) 23% anxiety (12%) 30% SUD (16%) 11% neuro dev (6%) 2% DBD (0%)	84% index episode depressive Mean onset 16 ± 4 years Latency 4 years to hypo/mania Mean onset hypo/mania 20 years 0 pre-pubertal hypo/mania Antecedent anxiety predicted 2.5-fold-risk major mood disorder
Wals et al. (2001); Mesman et al. (2013)	The Netherlands	Fixed[b]	12	Baseline, 1–5, 12-years (4)	23	93	75% BDI 25% BDII	60	72% patient association 28% outpatient clinic	108	28.0 (22–33)	K-SADS-PL; SCID	12% BDI, II, SCZBD 17% MDD 4% adjustment 29% minor mood 25% anxiety 23% SUD 5% ADHD, 7% DBD	88% index episode depressive Mean onset 15 ± 5 years Latency 5 years to hypo/mania Median onset hypomania 17 years Median onset mania 20 years 0 pre-pubertal hypo/mania

Table 1 continued

Published work	Cohort characteristics					Parental characteristics				Offspring characteristics				
	Country of origin	Type of cohort	Years of follow-up	Follow-up interval (# interviews)	Drop-out rate (%)	*n*	BD index parent	BD mother (%)	Recruitment	*n*	Mean age at last assessment (range)	Diagnostic interview	Most recent offspring diagnoses % (controls)	Early course of BD
Egeland et al. (2003, 2012)	USA	Fixed	16	Annually (16)	0	15	100% BDI	43	Genetic linkage research; Amish community	115	59% within 'window of risk' period (13–29)	CARE - interview	7% BDI (1%), 39% Risk rating (16%)	Median onset hypo/mania 18 years 0 pre-pubertal hypo/mania All preceded by anxiety/dep 0 evidence of SMD in childhood 0 DBD, ADHD, irritability Episodic childhood internalizing-symptoms Shift in adolescence to externalizing-symptoms
Birmaher et al. (2009); Axelson et al. (2015)	USA	Fixed	Mean 6.8	Mean 2.5 years (mean# interviews 2.7)	9	236	72% BDI 28% BDII	81	53% advertisement 31% adult BD studies 16% outpatient clinics	356	18.1 (± 4.8)	K-SADS-PL; SCID	8% BD (1%), 11% BDNOS (1%) 19% MDD (14%), 10% Dep NOS (7%) 40% anxiety (22%) 20% SUD (10%) 31% ADHD (18%), 27% DBD (15%) 35% ODD/CD (19%)	Mean onset hypo/mania 13 years Mean onset MDD 14 years 33% index hypo/mania < 10 years 53% onset hypo/mania < 12 years

Table 1 continued

Published work	Cohort characteristics					Parental characteristics				Offspring characteristics				
	Country of origin	Type of cohort	Years of follow-up	Follow-up interval (# interviews)	Drop-out rate (%)	*n*	BD index parent	BD mother (%)	Recruitment	*n*	Mean age at last assessment (range)	Diagnostic interview	Most recent offspring diagnoses % (controls)	Early course of BD
Nurnberger et al. (2011)	USA	Fixed	2–3	Baseline, 1–2-years (3)	No info	88 proband[c]	88.5% BDI 7% BDII 4.5% SCZBD	No info	Outpatient clinic; research studies	141	17 (12–21 baseline)	K-SADS-BP; 65% by telephone	9% BDI, II, NOS (0%) 16% MDD (4%) 18% SUD (9%) 8% ADHD (6%), 11% DBD (8%)	Median onset hypomania 16 years Median onset mania 13 years 5% of BD had onset ≤ 12 years Antecedent anxiety predicted a 2.5-fold-risk major mood disorder Antecedent externalising disorders predicted 3.5-fold-risk major mood disorder
Vandeleur et al. (2014); Preisig et al. (2016)	Switzerland	Dynamic	Mean 10.6	Every 3 years (mean # interviews 3.3)	33	81	65.5% BDI 12.5% BDII 22% SCZBD	58	Inpatient and outpatient clinics	145	21.1 (16–28)	K-SADS-E	12% BDI, II (4%) 17% BPS (5%) 37% MDD (38%) 44% anxiety (38%) 28% SUD (19%) 17% ADHD (13%) 15% ODD (13%)	Mean onset hypo/mania 16 years (median = 15 years) Mean onset MDD 13 years (median = 13 years) 61% index episode depressive 19.4% onset hypo/mania < 12 years

ADHD attention deficit (hyperactivity) disorder, *BD* bipolar disorder, *BD-NOS* bipolar disorder not otherwise specified, *BD I* bipolar I disorder, *BD II* bipolar-II disorder, *BPS* bipolar spectrum disorder, *CD* conduct disorder, *DBD* disruptive behavioral disorder, *Dep-NOS* depression not otherwise specified, *MDD* major depressive disorder, *Neuro-dev* neurodevelopmental disorder, *ODD* oppositional defiant disorder, *SCZBD* schizoaffective disorder bipolar type, *SUD* substance use disorder

[a] *Dynamic* continuous enrolment and follow-up from entry

[b] *Fixed* enrolment at time 1 and then follow-up

[c] *Proband* for 81% of offspring the proband was the parent

[d] *RMDD* recurrent major depressive disorder in 1st degree relatives of BD probands

2016) appear to increase the risk of psychopathology in high-risk offspring.

Several offspring studies, but not all (Axelson et al. 2015), confirm the prominence of depressive mood disorders early in the course of emergent bipolar disorder, typically manifesting at the syndrome level in early to mid-adolescence (Duffy et al. 2009, 2014; Mesman et al. 2013; Nurnberger et al. 2011). To wit, the Dutch, multisite US, and Canadian offspring studies reported that in the vast majority of cases, the initial major mood episode in those offspring who developed bipolar disorder was depressive in polarity (Duffy et al. 2014; Mesman et al. 2013; Nurnberger et al. 2011). Interestingly, despite repeated prospective direct assessment of children at confirmed familial risk, these studies have almost uniformly found no support for the proposed pre-pubertal or very early onset bipolar disorder subtype (Duffy et al. 2014; Egeland et al. 2012; Mesman et al. 2013). For example, the mean age of onset of the first diagnosable activated episode across studies at last report ranged from 13 to 20 years (Duffy et al. 2014; Mesman et al. 2013; Nurnberger et al. 2011). The BIOS study stands apart somewhat from these other published studies reporting that, in those offspring who developed BD, 50% had mania prior to age 12 (compared to 0% in other studies) and 50% debuted with a depressive episode (compared to over 80% in other studies) (Axelson et al. 2015). It is possible that these differences reflect differences in study populations (Birmaher et al. 2009)—BIOS families had significantly lower SES, higher rates of comorbidity in the BD parent, and more assortative mating as indicated by high rates of psychiatric illness in the other (non-bipolar) parent compared to the Canadian, Dutch and Amish studies (Duffy et al. 2014; Egeland et al. 2012; Mesman et al. 2013). The Swiss study found the mean age of onset of the first diagnosable activated episode was age 16 (SD 5.1 years), of which 61% debuted with a depressive episode. Six cases (19.4%) of mania/hypomania were found prior to age 12, but 5 out of these 6 children had experienced early trauma just before the reported onset of mania/hypomania. The mean age of onset of the first activated manic/hypomanic episode in the remaining offspring was 17.5 (SD 4.3) years. With longer follow-up, the mean age of onset of first activated episode will likely increase further as new onsets continue to occur and as evidenced in the updated reports from the Dutch and Canadian studies (Duffy et al. 2014; Mesman et al. 2013).

A preliminary analysis of the trajectory of emerging bipolar disorder based on the Canadian Flourish high-risk offspring cohort was consistent with a progressive sequence of psychopathology over development (see Fig. 1 reproduced with permission (Duffy 2014)). Further evidence supported that bipolar disorder varies in presentation within families and in course and treatment response between families, highlighting important aspects of phenotypic and etiologic heterogeneity. The best-fit model supported a shift from non-specific childhood antecedent syndromes (i.e., sleep problems, anxiety, and in the lithium non-responsive bipolar subtype, neurodevelopmental disorders) to internalizing symptoms under stress (i.e., sensitivity), to depressive disorders and finally on to the manifestation of the first activated episode.

This conceptual model of the trajectory of emerging bipolar disorder is consistent with several of the main observations among the high-risk studies, namely that: (i) bipolar disorder does not typically begin with a manic episode and is often presaged by childhood antecedent conditions and years of depressive episodes with more proximal subsyndromal hypomanic symptoms; (ii) childhood sleep and internalizing disorders likely have different significance in children with a confirmed familial risk of bipolar disorder compared to children without this risk; (iii) depressive episodes in adolescents at confirmed familial risk of bipolar disorder may represent emerging bipolar disorder or at least an increased likelihood of a bipolar predisposition; (iv) manic-like presentations in very young children without a confirmed family history of bipolar disorder may index a set of disorders or problems unrelated to bipolar disorder.

Findings from a recent meta-analysis indicate that there is substantive heterogeneity in prodromal symptom profiles and duration preceding an index manic episode (Van Meter et al. 2016). All but one of the studies included in this meta-analysis relied on retrospective data, often based on structured self-report symptom rating scales. Further, recall was over variable periods of time and often in patients whose most recent episode was manic. All of these methodological aspects are potential sources of bias. These limitations notwithstanding, common prodromal or proximal symptoms (> 50%) included excessive energy and goal directedness, talkativeness and pressured speech, elated mood, insomnia, depressed mood, diminished ability to think, and academic and work difficulties (Van Meter et al. 2016).

The Amish high-risk offspring study was the first to report that sensitivity by nature (i.e., stress reactivity) and episodic internalizing anxiety and depressive symptoms shifted into episodic activated symptom clusters over development and more proximal to the onset of bipolar disorder (Egeland et al. 2003, 2012). The episodic recurrent nature of these symptoms, combined with the confirmed familial risk of bipolar disorder in multiple generations, increases the likelihood that these otherwise non-specific manifestations reflect the bipolar diathesis.

Recently, the BIOS study showed that parent-reported internalizing symptoms and child-reported affective lability predicted onset of the first manic episode; the latter in part through an association with more proximal manic symptoms (Hafeman et al. 2016). The Flourish Canadian study observed that while the median age of onset of clinically assessed hypomanic symptoms in that offspring cohort was 16.4 years, the range was large (between 6 and 30 years). On average, these clinically significant hypomanic symptom onset prior but proximal to the index depressive episode (median onset age 16.8 years), and several years before the onset of the first diagnosable hypo/manic episode (median age of onset 18.4, bipolar I, and 21, bipolar-II) (Goodday et al. 2015). A recent report also found that high-risk offspring of bipolar parents had more severe depressive episodes and were more likely to experience mixed (activated) symptoms compared to low-risk depressed controls (Diler et al. 2017).

Cognitive function has been a focus of studies aimed at predicting risk and describing the early course of psychotic spectrum disorders, including bipolar disorder. Evidence from prospective studies, reviews, and a meta-analysis support distinctly different trajectories of cognitive function in schizophrenia and bipolar disorder over the emerging course of illness onset (Lewandowski et al. 2011; Trotta et al. 2015). Specifically, lower general intelligence and poorer school performance is evident pre-morbidly in children who later develop schizophrenia (MacCabe and Murray 2004; MacCabe et al. 2010). Further, at an early age, children who develop psychosis have evidence of pre-morbid cognitive deficits in verbal learning, working memory, attention, processing speed and executive function, along with "soft" neurological deficits, including problems with coordination and fine motor control (Owens and Johnstone 2006; Cannon et al. 2002). School performance, social functioning and cognitive deficits worsen through the school years leading up to the first psychotic break (Lewandowski et al. 2011). The trajectory of premorbid abnormal and deteriorating cognition and function across a number of domains, taken together with childhood neurological abnormalities, are consistent with a neurodevelopmental hypothesis of schizophrenia (Owens and Johnstone 2006; Clarke et al. 2012).

In contrast, based on prospective studies, the academic performance, cognitive function, and neurodevelopmental history of children who go on to develop bipolar disorder is comparable to that of the general population (Lewandowski et al. 2011; Trotta et al. 2015). Children who develop bipolar disorder do not manifest the same degree of lower and declining intellectual functioning or school performance as seen in children who develop schizophrenia (MacCabe et al. 2010; Cannon et al. 2002; Murray et al. 2004). Rather than reflecting the illness predisposition, cognitive deficits in bipolar disorder appear to largely manifest after illness onset (Lewandowski et al. 2011) and relate to aspects of the nature of the illness course, such as the number and polarity of mood episodes, polypharmacy, psychosis, antipsychotic treatment, and medical comorbidity (Berk et al. 2011; Hajek et al. 2013a, b; Calkin et al. 2015). However, it should be noted that studies have typically not considered heterogeneity of bipolar illness. Specifically, there is evidence to suggest that the psychotic spectrum bipolar subtype, as indexed by non-response to lithium prophylaxis, is characterized by learning disabilities, academic problems and ADHD in childhood—a point of overlap with the psychotic illness trajectory and differentiation from the early developmental history of those who develop classic lithium-responsive manic-depressive illness (Duffy 2012, 2015).

Alongside the evolution of clinical symptoms and syndromes, there is accruing evidence of the importance of psychological risk processes in the onset of bipolar disorder. These psychological risk processes in part overlap with those predicting unipolar depression in that children at genetic risk for bipolar disorder have unstable self-esteem and abnormal styles of self-regulation including excessive rumination (Jones et al. 2006a; Pavlickova et al. 2014). Additional psychological targets are suggested by studies showing that young people with hypomanic personality traits show abnormal reward responsivity, (Meyer et al. 1999) impulsiveness, (Mason et al. 2012) and abnormal interpretation of activated internal states, (Jones et al. 2006b) and that young people with abnormal sensitivity to reward and goal-striving are at elevated risk of developing BD symptoms (Alloy et al. 2012). It is possible that different psychological risk processes are important at different stages in the emerging clinical trajectory of specific subtypes of bipolar disorder and could be important intervention targets (Duffy et al. 2016).

Conclusions

There is evidence from a number of longitudinal high-risk offspring studies that the index manic or hypomanic episode typically manifests in mid-late adolescence and early adulthood. Despite the fact that DSM considers the activated episode to be the cardinal indicator of bipolar illness, prospective high-risk studies show that activated episodes are often preceded by years of clinically significant psychopathology at both the syndrome and symptom levels. Internalizing symptoms, emotional sensitivity and sleep and anxiety disorders in childhood, followed by depressive disorders and more proximal prodromal hypomanic symptoms manifest prior to the

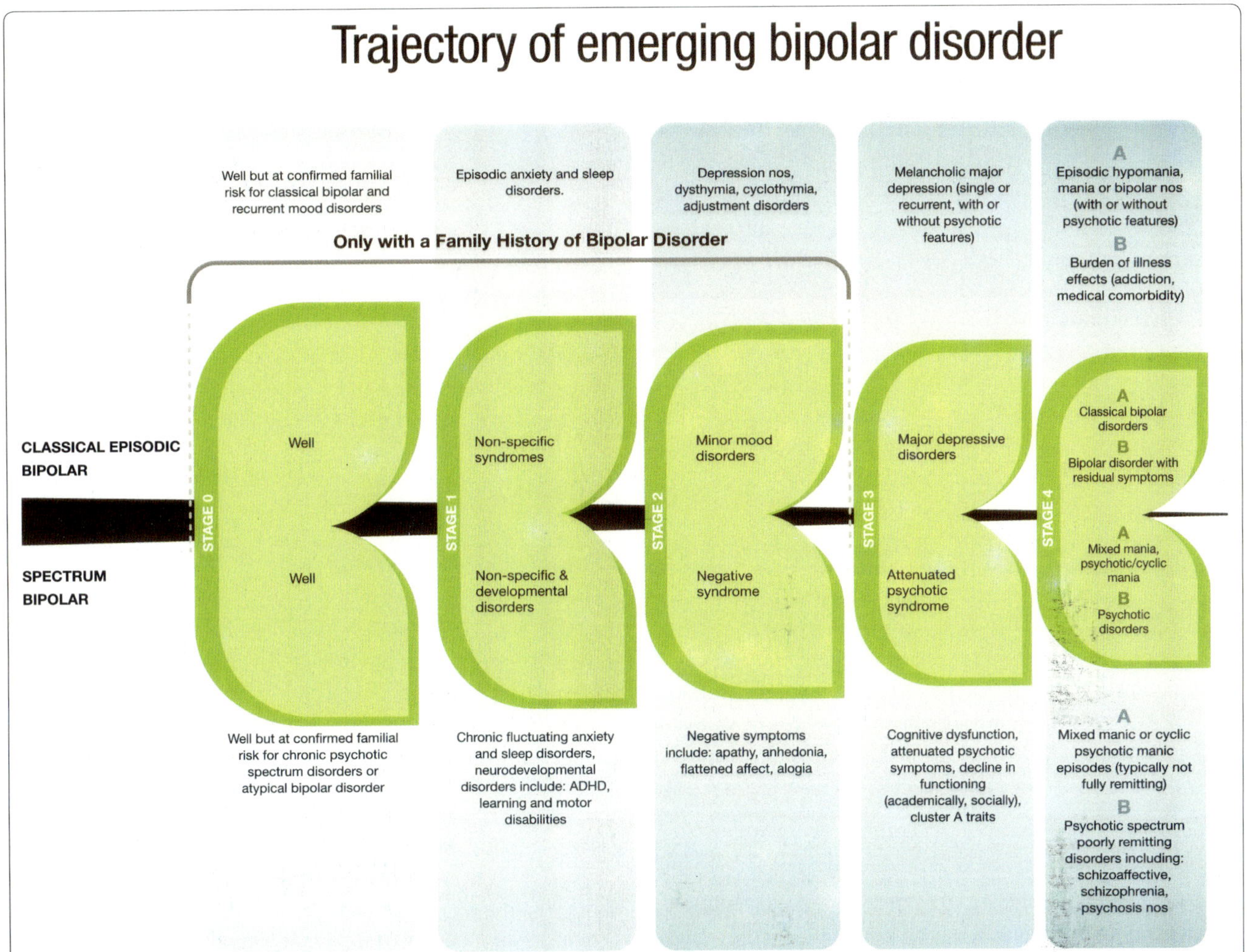

Fig. 1 The trajectory of emerging bipolar disorder in two subtypes of high-risk offspring

full-threshold hypo/manic episode. Antecedent symptoms and syndromes may have a different predictive meaning in children at confirmed familial risk of bipolar disorder compared to children without this risk. Further, there is accumulating evidence for the importance of rumination, self-appraisal processes, impulsivity, and reward sensitivity in the development of bipolar disorder and these psychological risk processes may have different importance at different stages of the bipolar illness trajectory. In contrast to psychotic illnesses, cognitive deficits in bipolar disorder emerge after full-blown illness onset and are likely more related to mixed burden of illness effects, emphasizing the importance of accurate early identification and effective early intervention.

Clinical implications

The observations from prospective high-risk studies can inform prevention and early intervention strategies at both the program and individual patient levels. While there are some practical and conceptual reasons for separating adult and youth psychiatric services, it is clear that this separation is detrimental when it comes to youth from families with a high risk of developing major psychiatric disorders. Therefore, closer collaboration between child and adult psychiatric services and other medical programs seems crucial—both to identify children at risk given a confirmed family history and to work to improve the mental health of affected parents with children (this may be especially important for bipolar mothers with children). In addition, further development of programs designed specifically targeting symptomatic transitional aged youth (15–25 years) is a necessity. These programs should offer engaging and accessible psychoeducation and support programs to mitigate risk factors and bolster resilience including healthy coping with stress, mood regulation, and avoidance of substance use. These community-based programs should have direct access to subspecialty early intervention programs that provide timely expert assessment and evidence-based care to those with emergent illness, especially those with a confirmed familial risk of major psychiatric illness and/or suicide.

At an individual level, to more accurately predict risk, prognosis, and treatment response in young people, who often have limited and seemingly non-specific clinical presentations, the current approach to diagnosis should be supplemented with other predictive information including: penetrance and nature of psychiatric illnesses in relatives, age on onset of illness in first-degree relatives, developmental history, psychosocial risk exposures, and the clinical course of emerging psychopathology. The outcome of this more comprehensive approach will earlier illness identification, more effective and better-tolerated interventions, and improved long-term outcomes for patients.

Research gaps and next directions

Longitudinal studies of children of well-characterized bipolar parents and their adult relatives will advance understanding of pathophysiological mechanisms, translating predisposition to illness onset and identifying more homogeneous bipolar subtypes. Prospective offspring studies make possible the mapping of changes in multilevel indicators of illness risk from pre-morbid states to prodromes and finally to illness onset. Early risk exposures (trauma, abuse, exposure to parental active illness), psychological risk processes, and biological markers can be mapped to the emerging clinical course through parallel studies. Understanding the nature of the illnesses segregating in family members and the family environment is also an important contributor to risk and outcomes in the children. These studies can also advance understanding of complex pathways leading to complications and comorbidities of bipolar disorder such as substance use, suicide and cardiovascular illness.

To advance, future research will need to consider the effect of heterogeneity on outcomes. As currently defined, bipolar disorder is a broad diagnostic category comprised of different illness subtypes with varying pathophysiology as evidenced by differences in clinical course, family history, treatment response, genetic, and neurobiological findings (etiologic heterogeneity) (Manchia et al. 2013; Angst et al. 2004). One type of bipolar disorder appears related to psychotic illness with early adolescent onset of psychotic manic or mixed episodes, male preponderance, neurodevelopmental comorbidity, poor quality of remission, family history of psychotic or chronic mood disorders and failure to fully respond to lithium prophylaxis (Grof et al. 2009; Alda 2004). By contrast, another type of bipolar disorder is consistent with the Kraepelin description of classical manic-depressive illness characterized by a highly recurrent course, predominance of depressive episodes, good quality of spontaneous remission, equal sex ratio, family history of episodic mood disorders, and an excellent response to lithium prophylaxis (Grof et al. 2009; Alda 2004).

There is also evidence of phenotypic heterogeneity in that the bipolar trait presents differently in affected relatives within the same families, who presumably share the same illness subtype or trait. Furthermore, the spectrum of illness (phenotypic spectrum) differs between subtypes. For example, relatives of patients with a classical lithium-responsive manic-depressive illness manifest high rates of episodic major depression and bipolar I and II disorders, while relatives of patients with psychotic spectrum bipolar disorder have elevated rates of chronic illnesses including neurodevelopmental disorders (autism, learning disabilities, ADHD), schizoaffective illness, chronic depression, and psychosis (Duffy and Grof 2001; Rice et al. 1987).

More recently, early intervention research concerning psychotic disorders has focused on studying heterogeneous populations of youth at clinical high-risk of developing psychosis. While this approach has been very helpful in identifying individuals manifesting high-risk mental states warranting intensive surveillance and clinical intervention, the approach is not likely robust enough to inform the identification and validation of biomarkers or to understand the translation of genetic predisposition into illness onset. To advance our understanding of bipolar disorder onset, it will be necessary to start from parents with well-characterized bipolar illness that can be organized into more homogeneous subtypes. Refined illness phenotypes have a higher likelihood of mapping to changes in underlying genetic and neurobiological markers and thereby identifying specific intervention targets. Whilst findings may not be directly generalizable to heterogeneous at risk and clinical populations, it is a necessary approach to advance our understanding of the pathophysiology driving emerging illness. Similar approaches have been very productive in differentiating illness subtypes and identifying susceptibility genes and biological markers associated with illness progression in other areas such as autism (Loth et al. 2017), dementia (Meeter et al. 2017), and cancer research (Zabor and Begg 2017).

Authors' contributions

All authors have participated in contributing their outcomes and writing of this manuscript. All authors have provided consent for this submission. All authors read and approved the final manuscript.

Author details

[1] Student Wellness Centre, Department of Psychiatry, Queen's University, 146 Stuart Street, Kingston, ON K7L3N6, Canada. [2] Department of Psychiatry Lausanne, University Hospital of Lausanne, Lausanne, Switzerland. [3] Medical Sciences Division, University of Oxford, Oxford, UK.

Acknowledgements
We thank the families who were involved in this research.

Competing interests
The authors declare that they have no competing interests.

Funding
The Flourish Offspring study is funded by a grant from the Canadian Institutes for Health Research (CIHR) PJT# 152976. The Lausanne–Geneva high-risk study was and is supported by five grants from the Swiss National Foundation (SNF: #3200-040677, #32003B-105969, and #32003B-118326 to F. Ferrero; #3200-049746 and #3200-061974 to M. Preisig), two grants for a national research project *"The Synaptic Bases of Mental Diseases"* (#125759 and #158776 to P. Magistretti) financed by the Swiss National Foundation, and a grant from GlaxoSmithKline Clinical Genetics.

References

Alda M. The phenotypic spectra of bipolar disorder. Neuropsychopharmacology. 2004;14:94–9.

Alloy LB, Bender RE, Whitehouse WG, et al. High behavioral approach system (BAS) sensitivity, reward responsiveness, and goal-striving predict first onset of bipolar spectrum disorders: a prospective behavioral high-risk design. J Abnorm Psychol. 2012;121:339–51.

Angst J, Gerber-Werder R, Zuberbuhler HU, et al. Is bipolar I disorder heterogeneous? Eur Arch Psychiatry Clin Neurosci. 2004;254:82–91.

Axelson D, Goldstein B, Goldstein T, et al. Diagnostic precursors to bipolar disorder in offspring of parents with bipolar disorder: a longitudinal study. Am J Psychiatry. 2015;172:638–46.

Bagot RC, Meaney MJ. Epigenetics and the biological basis of gene x environment interactions. J Am Acad Child Adolesc Psychiatry. 2010;49:752–71.

Berk M, Kapczinski F, Andreazza AC, et al. Pathways underlying neuroprogression in bipolar disorder: focus on inflammation, oxidative stress and neurotrophic factors. Neurosci Biobehav Rev. 2011;35:804–17.

Birmaher B, Axelson D, Monk K, et al. Lifetime psychiatric disorders in school-aged offspring of parents with bipolar disorder: the Pittsburgh bipolar offspring study. Arch Gen Psychiatry. 2009;66:287–96.

Calkin CV, Ruzickova M, Uher R, et al. Insulin resistance and outcome in bipolar disorder. Br J Psychiatry. 2015;206:52–7.

Cannon M, Caspi A, Moffitt TE, et al. Evidence for early-childhood, pan-developmental impairment specific to schizophreniform disorder: results from a longitudinal birth cohort. Arch Gen Psychiatry. 2002;59:449–56.

Clarke MC, Kelleher I, Clancy M, Cannon M. Predicting risk and the emergence of schizophrenia. Psychiatr Clin North Am. 2012;35:585–612.

Diler RS, Goldstein TR, Hafeman D, et al. Characteristics of depression among offspring at high and low familial risk of bipolar disorder. Bipolar Disord. 2017;19(5):344–52.

Doucette S, Levy A, Flowerdew G, et al. Early parent-child relationships and risk of mood disorder in a Canadian sample of offspring of a parent with bipolar disorder: findings from a 16-year prospective cohort study. Early Interv Psychiatry. 2016;10:381–9.

Duffy A. The nature of the association between childhood ADHD and the development of bipolar disorder: a review of prospective high-risk studies. Am J Psychiatry. 2012;169:1247–55.

Duffy A. Toward a comprehensive clinical staging model for bipolar disorder: integrating the evidence. Can J Psychiatry Revue Canadienne de Psychiatrie. 2014;59:659–66.

Duffy A. Early identification of recurrent mood disorders in youth: the importance of a developmental approach. Evid-Based Ment Health. 2015;18:7–9.

Duffy A, Alda M, Hajek T, Grof P. Early course of bipolar disorder in high-risk offspring: prospective study. Br J Psychiatry. 2009;195:457–8.

Duffy A, Alda M, Kutcher S, Fusee C and Grof P. Psychiatric symptoms and syndromes among adolescent children of parents with lithium-responsive or lithium-nonresponsive bipolar disorder. Am J Psychiatry. 1998;155:431–3.

Duffy A, Grof P. Psychiatric diagnoses in the context of genetic studies of bipolar disorder. Bipolar Disord. 2001;3:270–5.

Duffy A, Grof P, Robertson C, Alda M. The implications of genetics studies of major mood disorders for clinical practice. J Clin Psychiatry. 2000;61:630–7.

Duffy A, Horrocks J, Doucette S, Keown-Stoneman C, McCloskey S, Grof P. Childhood anxiety: an early predictor of mood disorders in offspring of bipolar parents. J Affect Disord. 2013;150:363–9.

Duffy A, Horrocks J, Doucette S, Keown-Stoneman C, McCloskey S, Grof P. The developmental trajectory of bipolar disorder. Br J Psychiatry. 2014;204:122–8.

Duffy A, Jones S, Goodday S, Bentall R. Candidate risks indicators for bipolar disorder: early intervention opportunities in high-risk youth. Int J Neuropsychopharmacol. 2016. doi:10.1093/ijnp/pyv071.

Egeland JA, Endicott J, Hostetter AM, Allen CR, Pauls DL, Shaw JA. A 16-year prospective study of prodromal features prior to BPI onset in well Amish children. J Affect Disord. 2012;142:186–92.

Egeland JA, Hostetter AM, Pauls DL, Sussex JN. Prodromal symptoms before onset of manic-depressive disorder suggested by first hospital admission histories. J Am Acad Child Adolesc Psychiatry. 2000;39:1245–52.

Egeland JA, Shaw JA, Endicott J, et al. Prospective study of prodromal features for bipolarity in well Amish children. J Am Acad Child Adolesc Psychiatry. 2003;42:786–96.

Goodday S, Levy A, Flowerdew G, et al. Early exposure to parental bipolar disorder and risk of mood disorder: the Flourish Canadian prospective offspring cohort study. Early Interv Psychiatry. 2015. doi:10.1111/eip.12291.

Grof P, Duffy A, Alda M, Hajek T. Lithium response across generations. Acta Psychiatr Scand. 2009;120:378–85.

Hafeman DM, Merranko J, Axelson D, et al. Toward the definition of a bipolar prodrome: dimensional predictors of bipolar spectrum disorders in at-risk youths. Am J Psychiatry. 2016;173:695–704.

Hajek T, Calkin C, Blagdon R, Slaney C, Alda M. Type 2 diabetes mellitus: a potentially modifiable risk factor for neurochemical brain changes in bipolar disorders. Biol Psychiatry. 2013a;77(33):295–303.

Hajek T, Cullis J, Novak T, et al. Brain structural signature of familial predisposition for bipolar disorder: replicable evidence for involvement of the right inferior frontal gyrus. Biol Psychiatry. 2013b;73:144–52.

Jones SH, Tai S, Evershed K, Knowles R, Bentall R. Early detection of bipolar disorder: a pilot familial high-risk study of parents with bipolar disorder and their children. Bipolar Disord. 2006a;8:362–72.

Jones S, Mansell W, Waller L. Appraisal of hypomania-relevant experiences: development of a questionnaire to assess positive self-dispositional appraisals in bipolar and behavioural high risk samples. J Affect Disord. 2006b;93:19–28.

Judd LL, Akiskal HS. The prevalence and disability of bipolar spectrum disorders in the US population: re-analysis of the ECA database taking into account subthreshold cases. J Affect Disord. 2003;73:123–31.

Judd LL, Akiskal HS, Schettler PJ, et al. Psychosocial disability in the course of bipolar I and II disorders: a prospective, comparative, longitudinal study. Arch Gen Psychiatry. 2005;62:1322–30.

Keck PE Jr, Kessler RC, Ross R. Clinical and economic effects of unrecognized or inadequately treated bipolar disorder. J Psychiatr Pract. 2008;14(Suppl 2):31–8.

Lewandowski KE, Cohen BM, Ongur D. Evolution of neuropsychological dysfunction during the course of schizophrenia and bipolar disorder. Psychol Med. 2011;41:225–41.

Loth E, Charman T, Mason L, et al. The EU-AIMS longitudinal European autism project (LEAP): design and methodologies to identify and validate stratification biomarkers for autism spectrum disorders. Mol Autism. 2017;8:24.

MacCabe JH, Lambe MP, Cnattingius S, et al. Excellent school performance at age 16 and risk of adult bipolar disorder: national cohort study. Br J Psychiatry. 2010;196:109–15.

MacCabe JH, Murray RM. Intellectual functioning in schizophrenia: a marker of neurodevelopmental damage? J Intell Disabil Res. 2004;48:519–23.

Manchia M, Cullis J, Turecki G, Rouleau GA, Uher R, Alda M. The impact of phenotypic and genetic heterogeneity on results of genome wide association studies of complex diseases. PLoS ONE. 2013;8:e76295.

Mason L, O'Sullivan N, Blackburn M, Bentall R, El-Deredy W. I want it now! Neural correlates of hypersensitivity to immediate reward in hypomania. Biol Psychiatry. 2012;71:530–7.

McGuffin P, Perroud N, Uher R, et al. The genetics of affective disorder and suicide. Eur Psychiatry. 2010;25:275–7.

Meeter LH, Kaat LD, Rohrer JD, van Swieten JC. Imaging and fluid biomarkers in frontotemporal dementia. Nat Rev Neurol. 2017;13:406–19.

Merikangas KR, Cui L, Heaton L, et al. Independence of familial transmission of mania and depression: results of the NIMH family study of affective spectrum disorders. Mol Psychiatry. 2014;19:214–9.

Mesman E, Birmaher BB, Goldstein BI, et al. Categorical and dimensional psychopathology in Dutch and US offspring of parents with bipolar disorder: a preliminary cross-national comparison. J Affect Disord. 2016;205:95–102.

Mesman E, Nolen WA, Reichart CG, Wals M, Hillegers MH. The Dutch bipolar offspring study: 12-year follow-up. Am J Psychiatry. 2013;170:542–9.

Meyer B, Johnson S, Carver C. Exploring behavioural activation and inhibition sensitivities among college students at-risk for mood disorders. J Psychopathol Behav Assess. 1999;21:275–92.

Murray RM, Sham P, Van Os J, Zanelli J, Cannon M, McDonald C. A developmental model for similarities and dissimilarities between schizophrenia and bipolar disorder. Schizophr Res. 2004;71:405–16.

Nurnberger JIJ, McInnis M, Reich W, Kastelic E, Wilcox HC, Glowinski A, et al. A high-risk study of bipolar disorder. Childhood clinical phenotypes as precursors of major mood disorders. Arch Gen Psychiatry. 2011;68:1012–20.

Owens DG, Johnstone EC. Precursors and prodromata of schizophrenia: findings from the Edinburgh high risk study and their literature context. Psychol Med. 2006;36:1501–14.

O'Donovan C, Garnham JS, Hajek T, Alda M. Antidepressant monotherapy in pre-bipolar depression; predictive value and inherent risk. J Affect Disord. 2008;107:293–8.

Pavlickova H, Turnbull O, Myin-Germeys I, Bentall RP. The inter-relationship between mood, self-esteem and response styles in adolescent offspring of bipolar parents: an experience sampling study. Psychiatry Res. 2015;225(3):563–70. doi:10.1016/j.psychres.2014.11.046.

Petronis A. Epigenetics as a unifying principle in the aetiology of complex traits and diseases. Nature. 2010;465:721–7.

Post RM, Altshuler LL, Kupka R, et al. Age of onset of bipolar disorder: combined effect of childhood adversity and familial loading of psychiatric disorders. J Psychiatr Res. 2016;81:63–70.

Preisig M, Strippoli MP, Castelao E, et al. The specificity of the familial aggregation of early-onset bipolar disorder: a controlled 10-year follow-up study of offspring of parents with mood disorders. J Affect Disord. 2016;190:26–33.

Rice J, Reich T, Andreasen NC, et al. The familial transmission of bipolar illness. Arch Gen Psychiatry. 1987;44:441–7.

Smoller JW, Finn CT. Family, twin, and adoption studies of bipolar disorder. Am J Med Genet Part C, Semin Med Genet. 2003;123C:48–58.

Strober M, Carlson G. Predictors of bipolar illness in adolescents with major depression: a follow-up investigation. Adolesc Psychiatry. 1982;10:299–319.

Trotta A, Murray RM, MacCabe JH. Do premorbid and post-onset cognitive functioning differ between schizophrenia and bipolar disorder? A systematic review and meta-analysis. Psychol Med. 2015;45:381–94.

Van Meter AR, Burke C, Youngstrom EA, Faedda GL, Correll CU. The bipolar prodrome: meta-analysis of symptom prevalence prior to initial or recurrent mood episodes. J Am Acad Child Adolesc Psychiatry. 2016;55:543–55.

Vandeleur CL, Merikangas KR, Strippoli MP, Castelao E, Preisig M. Specificity of psychosis, mania and major depression in a contemporary family study. Mol Psychiatry. 2014;19:209–13.

Wals M, Hillegers MH, Reichart CG, Ormel J, Nolen WA, Verhulst FC. Prevalence of psychopathology inchildren of a bipolar parent. J Am Acad Child Adolesc Psychiatry. 2001;40:1094–102.

Wilde A, Chan HN, Rahman B, et al. A meta-analysis of the risk of major affective disorder in relatives of individuals affected by major depressive disorder or bipolar disorder. J Affect Disord. 2014;158:37–47.

Zabor EC, Begg CB. A comparison of statistical methods for the study of etiologic heterogeneity. Stat Med. 2017. doi:10.1002/sim.7405.

11

Clinical correlates of age at onset distribution in bipolar disorder: a comparison between diagnostic subgroups

Mirko Manchia[1,2*], Giuseppe Maina[3], Bernardo Carpiniello[1], Federica Pinna[1], Luca Steardo[4], Virginia D'Ambrosio[3], Virginio Salvi[3], Martin Alda[5], Alfonso Tortorella[4] and Umberto Albert[6]

Abstract

Background: Admixture analysis of age at onset (AAO) has helped delineating the clinical profile of early onset (EO) bipolar disorder (BD). However, there is scarce evidence comparing the distributional properties of AAO as well as the clinical features of EO BD type 1 (BD1) with EO BD type 2 (BD2). To this end, we studied 515 BD patients (224 BD1, 279 BD2, and 12 BD not otherwise specified [NOS]) diagnosed according to DSM-IV-TR criteria.

Methods: AAO was defined as the first reliably diagnosed hypo/manic or depressive episode according to diagnostic criteria. We used normal distribution mixture analysis to identify subgroups of patients according to AAO. Models were chosen according to the Schwarz's Bayesian information criteria (BIC). Clinical correlates of EO were analysed using univariate tests and multivariate logistic regression models.

Results: A two normal components model best fitted the observed distribution of AAO in BD1 (BIC = −1599.3), BD2 (BIC = −2158.4), and in the whole sample (BIC = −3854.9). A higher number of EO BD2 patients had a depression-(hypo)mania-free interval (DMI) course, while a higher rate of (hypo)mania-depression-free interval (MDI) course was found in EO BD1. EO BD2 had also a higher rate of comorbidity with alcohol dependence compared to EO BD1. The latter finding was confirmed by multivariate logistic regression analysis.

Conclusions: In conclusion, both BD1 and BD2 had bimodal AAO distributions, but EO subgroups had a diagnostic-specific clinical delineation.

Keywords: Mood disorders, Diagnostic subtypes, Early onset, Retrospective study, Admixture analysis

Background

Bipolar disorder (BD) is a heritable psychiatric illness characterised by cyclic mood episodes of opposite polarity alternating with intervals of well-being (Goodwin and Jamison 2007). As in other psychiatric complex genetic diseases, the relatively high clinical heterogeneity of BD might have hindered the identification of molecular and clinical determinants of risk as well as of predictors of treatment outcome (Alda 2004). The magnitude of clinical heterogeneity might be reduced by studying subgroups of BD patients sharing specific clinical characteristics such as patterns of treatment response (Alda et al. 2005), mood incongruent psychosis (Goes et al. 2007), or early illness onset (Jamain et al. 2014). Indeed, the extensive analysis of age at onset (AAO) BD subgroups through admixture analysis has shown clinical (Bellivier et al. 2001; Lin et al. 2005; Manchia et al. 2008; Tozzi et al. 2011; Ortiz et al. 2011) and genetic (Etain et al. 2006; Severino et al. 2009; Etain et al. 2010; Belmonte et al. 2011) characteristics specific, particularly, to early onset (EO) BD.

As the vast majority of studies investigated BD type 1 (BD1) samples, it remains to be established, however, whether this clinical delineation of EO is present also in BD type 2 (BD2) patients. Furthermore, the distributional

*Correspondence: mirkomanchia@unica.it; Mirko.Manchia@dal.ca
[1] Section of Psychiatry, Department of Medical Science and Public Health, University of Cagliari, Via Liguria, 13, 09127 Cagliari, Italy
Full list of author information is available at the end of the article

properties of AAO have never been investigated in samples exclusively composed of BD2 patients.

Methods

Aims

The primary aim of the present study was to test whether BD1 and BD2 differed in terms of AAO distributions. The secondary objective was to test whether EO had clinical characteristics specific for each diagnostic subgroup. To this end, we (i) studied the AAO distribution of each diagnostic subgroup with mixture modelling; (ii) compared the AAO distributions identified in BD1 and BD2; (iii) analyzed the pattern of associations of a set of demographic and clinical variables with EO in each diagnostic subgroup; and (iv) compared the clinical association patterns between EO BD1 and EO BD2.

Patient population and assessment instruments

Our sample consisted of 515 unrelated patients with BD. Two hundred and twenty-four were diagnosed with BD1, while 279 had a diagnosis of BD2, and 12 had a diagnosis BD not otherwise specified (NOS). All subjects were of Italian ancestry. Patients were recruited at the Anxiety and Mood Disorders Unit, University of Turin, Italy and at the Department of Psychiatry, University of Naples SUN, Napoli, Italy. Certified psychiatrists with at least 4 years of postgraduate clinical experience performed the clinical assessment of patients. All potential interviewers met prior to study beginning and underwent a common extensive training prior to conducting the assessments. They were trained in the use of a common semi-structured interview that was used to collect (a) socio-demographic data (age, gender, marital status, years of education, and occupational status); (b) diagnosis (current and lifetime), which were performed according to the Diagnostic and Statistical Manual of Mental Disorders (DSM)-IV-Text Revision (TR) criteria (American Psychiatric Association 2000) using the structured clinical interview for DSM-IV-TR Axis I disorders (SCID-I/P) (First et al. 2002); (c) clinical data including AAO. In addition, a systematic review of patients' medical records helped clinicians to establish AAO and corroborate data concerning clinical characteristics of the disorder emerging from direct interview. Age at onset was defined as the first reliably diagnosed hypo/manic or depressive episode meeting the diagnostic criteria. External corroboration for AAO was obtained, whenever possible, by directly interviewing, with patient's consent, a first-degree family member or other significant individuals. For the purposes of the present study, we included only subjects for whom it was possible to establish AAO with complete agreement between the information provided by patients and their relatives. Age at interview was defined as the age at which subjects were first assessed by a clinician at each research centre.

In the early phase of the study, inter-rater reliability of the diagnosis of Axis I disorders with the SCID-I was ascertained. The inter-rater reliability was found to be good: Cohen kappa coefficient was 0.89 for the presence of any current or lifetime Axis I disorder.

Data analysis

We used Gaussian distribution mixture analysis to test whether we could identify subgroups of patients according to the AAO. We investigated a range of number of AAO groups (1–9). The choice of the mixture model that best fit the distribution of AAO was made according to the Schwarz's Bayesian information criteria (BIC). Specifically, the analysis performed with the "Mclust" (Fraley and Raftery 1999; Fraley et al. 2014) package implemented in R (R Development Core Team 2008) indicates the best model as the one with the highest BIC among the fitted models (Fraley and Raftery 2007). This package estimates parameters of the model using an expectation–maximization (EM) algorithm. Cut-off points were derived using the Gaussian cumulative distribution function of estimated AAO mixture function and calculating each data point's probability of belonging to each class. Specifically, once the mixture model parameters were estimated, we calculated the posterior probability of any data point. The resulting probabilities were then compared in order to establish which class the data point belonged to. Gaussian mixture analysis (both number of components and parameters estimates) was also replicated and confirmed with the "Mixtools" R package (Benaglia et al. 2009). We used Kolmogorov–Smirnov (K–S) test to determine whether the Gaussian cumulative distribution function of estimated AAO mixture identified in BD1 patients was significantly different from the one identified in BD2 patients. Further, we used K–S to test for differences in the AAO Gaussian cumulative distribution function of estimated AAO mixture between participating research centres. We tested the association of continuous and categorical clinical variables with AAO subgroups using univariate analysis (t test or χ^2 test as appropriate). The independent variables tested included sex, age at interview, diagnosis, illness duration, presence of family history of any DSM-IV-TR psychiatric disorder, presence of family history of BD and any DSM-IV-TR mood disorders, number of manic/hypomanic, depressive and mixed episodes, type of clinical course cycle [i.e. (hypo)mania-depression-free interval (MDI), depression-(hypo)mania-free interval (DMI), irregular cycling, continuous cycling, rapid cycling], presence of lifetime suicidal behaviour, lifetime comorbidity with substance (other than alcohol) dependence, and lifetime comorbidity with drug and/or alcohol dependence. Statistical significance was set at $\alpha = 0.05$. Only clinical variables presenting a statistical significant association with an AAO subgroup ($p < 0.05$) of each diagnostic sample (BD1 and BD2) were entered into a backward stepwise multivariate binary logistic model to account for possible intercorrelations. All statistical analyses, except for mixture modelling, were performed with STATA/SE 12.0.

Results

Age at onset distribution: Gaussian mixture analysis

The BD1 sample (99 males and 125 females) had a mean age at interview (±SD) of 47.2 years (±13.0) and a mean AAO of 26.7 years (±9.2). A two normal components model best fitted the observed distribution of AAO (BIC = −1599.3) (Fig. 1). Models with three and four components did not improve the fit (Table 1).

The EO component had a mean AAO of 22.6 years (±4.8), while the late onset (LO) component had a mean AAO of 35.1 years (±10.1) comprising 67% and 33% of the population proportion, respectively. The cut-off point, derived by the Gaussian cumulative distribution function of the latter estimated AAO function, was at 32 years for BD1 (EO group <32 years; LO group ≥32 years) with 169 patients in the EO group and 55 in the LO group.

The BD2 sample (114 males and 165 females) had a mean age at interview of 50.6 years (±14.8) and a mean AAO of 30.6 years (±12.7). The observed distribution of AAO was also best fitted by a two normal components model (BIC = −2158.4) (Fig. 2).

No improvement of the fit was observed with three and four components models (Table 1). The BD2 sample had an EO component with mean AAO of 20.9 years (±4.1) and a LO component with mean AAO of 38.2 years (±11.8) with population proportions of 44% and 56%, respectively. The cut-off point, derived by the Gaussian cumulative distribution function of this estimated AAO function, was at 28 years (EO group <28 years; LO group ≥28 years). The EO group comprised 142 patients, while the LO group included 137 patients.

Kolmogorov–Smirnov test showed that the Gaussian cumulative distribution functions of estimated AAO mixture of BD1 and BD2 differed significantly ($D = 0.18$, $p < 0.00001$) (Fig. 3). Conversely, there was no significant difference between the Gaussian cumulative distributions

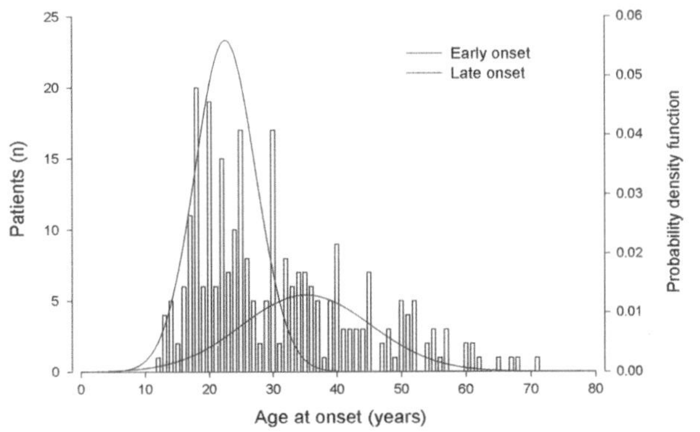

Fig. 1 Age at onset distribution in bipolar disorder type 1 patients ($N = 224$). Gaussian probability density function was derived by the estimated age at onset mixture function in bipolar disorder type 1 patients

Table 1 Age at onset distributions identified by Gaussian mixture analysis in bipolar disorder type 1 and type 2 and in the whole sample

Mixture model	BIC	Model components	Mean	SD	Proportion (%)
Bipolar disorder type 1 sample ($n = 224$)					
M1	−1637.7	1st component	26.7	9.1	100.0
M2	*−1599.4*	*1st component*	*22.6*	*4.8*	*66.9*
		2nd component	*35.1*	*10.1*	*33.1*
M3	−1611.0	1st component	18.7	3.0	27.1
		2nd component	25.6	4.4	45.7
		3rd component	36.6	10.1	27.2
M4	−1624.0	1st component	17.9	2.6	23.1
		2nd component	23.8	3.1	28.2
		3rd component	28.8	5.9	33.4
		4th component	40.9	9.9	15.3
Bipolar disorder type 2 sample ($n = 279$)					
M1	−2218.4	1st component	30.6	12.6	100.0
M2	*−2158.4*	*1st component*	*20.9*	*4.1*	*44.0*
		2nd component	*38.2*	*11.8*	*56.0*
M3	−2163.2	1st component	19.3	3.3	33.1
		2nd component	28.4	6.1	33.7
		3rd component	44.0	11.0	33.2
M4	−2177.7	1st component	17.6	2.5	22.8
		2nd component	23.0	2.8	24.7
		3rd component	32.2	4.4	22.7
		4th component	45.6	10.3	29.8
Total bipolar disorder sample ($n = 515$)					
M1	−3986.7	1st component	29.0	11.5	100.0
M2	*−3854.9*	*1st component*	*21.9*	*4.6*	*55.0*
		2nd component	*37.6*	*11.5*	*45.0*
M3	−3856.0	1st component	19.2	3.2	28.9
		2nd component	26.5	5.6	40.6
		3rd component	41.5	11.2	30.6
M4	−3868.3	1st component	17.8	2.6	22.8
		2nd component	23.3	3.1	28.0
		3rd component	31.1	5.1	24.0
		4th component	43.4	10.9	25.2

Best fitting mixture models are typed in italics

M model, *BIC* Bayesian information criteria, *SD* standard deviation

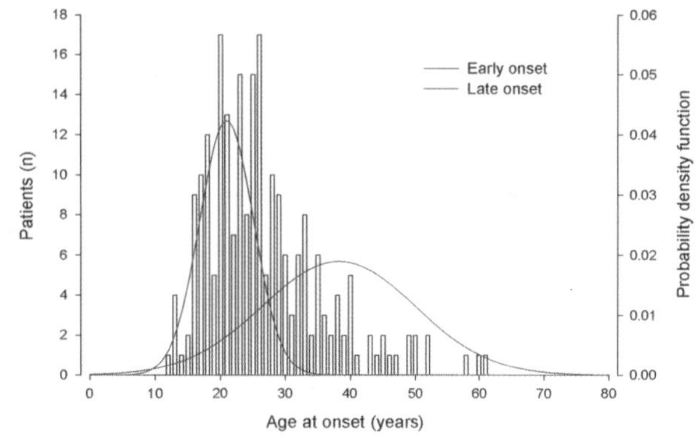

Fig. 2 Age at onset distribution in bipolar disorder type 2 patients ($N = 279$). Gaussian probability density function was derived by the estimated age at onset mixture function in bipolar disorder type 2 patients

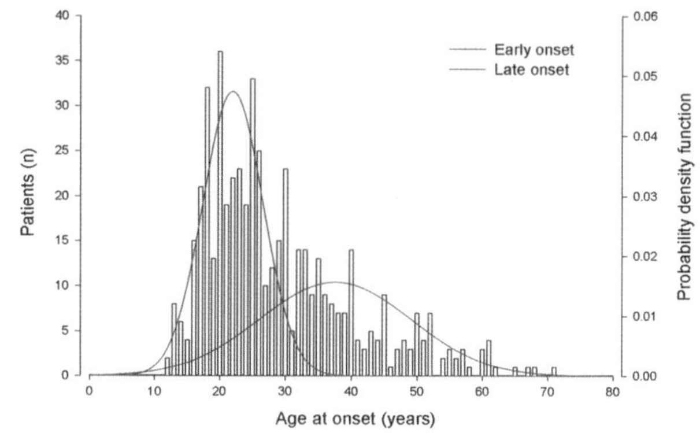

Fig. 4 Age at onset distribution in the whole sample of bipolar disorder patients ($N = 515$). Gaussian probability density function was derived by the estimated age at onset mixture function in the whole sample of bipolar disorder patients

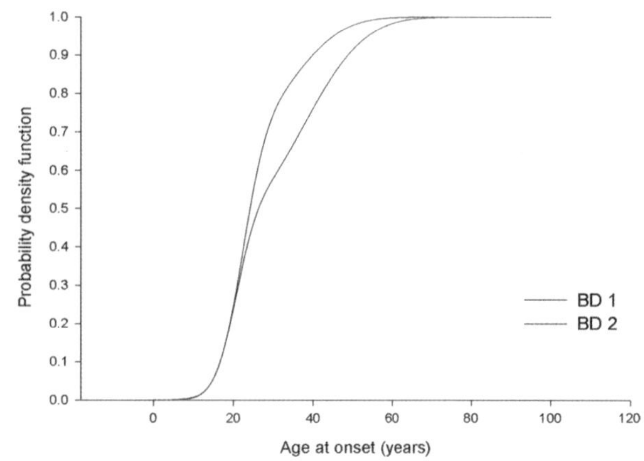

Fig. 3 Kolmogorov–Smirnov test between theoretical age at onset in bipolar disorder type 1 and type 2 patients. Probability density functions of the two estimated age at onset mixture function. *BD1* bipolar disorder type 1, *BD2* bipolar disorder type 2

of estimated AAO mixture of the two participating research centres ($D = 0.05$, $p = 0.57$). Finally, Gaussian mixture analysis confirmed a best fitting model of two normal components (detailed in Table 1) in the whole sample of 515 BD patients (216 males and 299 females), which included 12 subjects with BD NOS (Fig. 4). The cut-off point, derived by the Gaussian cumulative distribution function of this estimated AAO function, was at 30 years.

Clinical correlates of early onset: patterns of association in bipolar disorder type 1 and type 2 diagnostic subgroups

As shown in Table 2, a trend association ($p = 0.05$) was identified for the presence of family history of any DSM-IV-TR mood disorder, with LO BD1 having a higher rate than EO BD1. Early onset BD1 had a lower age at interview and a longer duration of illness than LO BD1.

Early onset BD2 had a higher rate of comorbidity with alcohol dependence, as well as a higher rate of family history of BD in EO BD2 compared to LO BD2 (Table 2). Further, they also had a lower age at interview and longer illness duration than LO BD2.

We then performed a multivariate logistic regression in BD2 confirming that family history of BD [odds ratio (OR) = 1.97, 95% confidence interval (CI) 1.04–3.73, $p = 0.04$], comorbidity with alcohol dependence (OR = 3.2, 95% CI 1.21–8.54, $p = 0.02$), and illness duration (OR = 1.03, 95% CI 1.008–1.048, $p = 0.006$) were associated with EO. As age at interview was used to calculate illness duration, and consequently significantly correlated with it ($r = -0.97$), it was not included in the logistic regression model. Multivariate analysis was not performed in BD1 since no clinical variable was significantly associated with AAO subgroup in univariate test.

Clinical correlates of early onset: comparison between bipolar disorder type 1 and type 2 diagnostic subgroups

The mean AAO was significantly lower in BD1 compared to BD2 (26.7 ± 9.2 vs. 30.6 ± 12.7; $t = -3.8$; $p < 0.0001$). The results of the univariate analysis are shown in Table 3. Early onset BD1 patients were older than EO BD2. Conversely, EO BD2 had a higher rate of comorbidity with alcohol dependence. In addition, a higher number of EO BD2 presented with a DMI course, while a higher rate of MDI course was found in EO BD1. The multivariate binary logistic regression confirmed the association of comorbidity with alcohol dependence with EO BD2 (OR = 0.4, 95% CI 0.18–0.90, $p = 0.02$).

Table 2 Comparison of clinical correlates between early and late onset bipolar disorder type 1 and type 2 patients

Clinical variable	Bipolar disorder type 1 ($N = 224$)		χ^2 or t	P
	Early onset ($N = 169$)	Late onset ($N = 55$)		
Female (%)	73 (43.2)	26 (47.3)	0.3	0.6
Age at interview, mean (SD)	45.3 (13.5)	53.1 (8.8)	4.0	*<0.0001*
Presence of family history of any psychiatric disorder (%)[a]	99 (58.9)	37 (67.3)	1.2	0.3
Presence of family history of mood disorder (%)[b]	85 (52.5)	34 (68.0)	3.7	0.05
Presence of family history of bipolar disorder (%)[c]	31 (18.5)	13 (23.6)	0.7	0.4
Number of manic/hypomanic episodes, mean (SD)[d]	4.4 (5.1)	3.6 (3.2)	−1.1	0.3
Number of depressive episodes, mean (SD)[e]	5.5 (4.7)	4.8 (4.4)	−0.9	0.3
Number of mixed episodes, mean (SD)[f]	0.6 (1.6)	0.8 (1.3)	0.8	0.4
Illness duration, mean (SD)	22.5 (12.8)	13.5 (8.6)	−4.9	*<0.0001*
Lifetime comorbidity with substance dependence (%)	15 (8.9)	4 (7.3)	0.1	0.7
Lifetime comorbidity with alcohol dependence (%)	10 (5.9)	1 (1.8)	1.5	0.2
Presence of suicidal behaviour (%)	47 (28)	11 (20)	1.4	0.2
Type of clinical course cycle				
MDI (%)	75 (44.4)	22 (40.0)	3.7	0.45
DMI (%)	20 (11.8)	11 (20.0)		
Irregular cycling (%)	65 (38.5)	21 (38.2)		
Continuous cycling (%)	5 (3.0)	1 (1.8)		
Rapid cycling (%)	4 (2.4)	0 (0.0)		
Clinical variable	**Bipolar disorder type 2 ($N = 279$)**		**χ^2 or t**	**p**
	Early onset ($N = 142$)	**Late onset ($N = 137$)**		
Female (%)	85 (59.9)	80 (58.4)	0.06	0.8
Age at interview, mean (SD)	42.8 (14.4)	58.7 (10.1)	10.6	*<0.0001*
Presence of family history of any psychiatric disorder (%)	93 (65.5)	87 (63.5)	0.1	0.7
Presence of family history of mood disorder (%)[b]	84 (60.0)	79 (58.5)	0.06	0.8
Presence of family history of bipolar disorder (%)	36 (25.4)	19 (13.9)	5.8	*0.02*
Number of manic/hypomanic episodes, mean (SD)[d]	4.3 (4.2)	3.7 (4.3)	−1.1	0.3
Number of depressive episodes, mean (SD)[e]	6.0 (5.6)	5.4 (5.3)	−1.0	0.3
Illness duration, mean (SD)[g]	22.0 (13.7)	17.8 (11.2)	−2.8	*0.005*
Lifetime comorbidity with substance dependence (%)	8 (5.6)	6 (4.4)	0.2	0.6
Lifetime comorbidity with alcohol dependence (%)	19 (13.4)	6 (4.4)	6.9	*0.01*
Presence of suicidal behaviour (%)	45 (31.7)	29 (21.2)	3.9	0.06
Type of clinical course cycle				
MDI (%)	51 (35.9)	45 (32.8)	3.9	0.4
DMI (%)	31 (21.8)	35 (25.5)		
Irregular cycling (%)	58 (40.8)	52 (38.0)		
Continuous cycling (%)	2 (1.4)	2 (1.5)		
Rapid cycling (%)	0 (0.0)	3 (2.2)		

Significant values are typed in italics

MDI (hypo)mania-depression-free interval, *DMI* depression-(hypo)mania-free interval, *SD* Standard Deviation, *p* p value

[a] BD1: missing data for 1 patient

[b] BD1: missing data for 12 patients, BD2: missing data for 4 patients

[c] BD1: missing data for 1 patient

[d] BD1: missing data for 1 patient, BD2: missing data for 4 patients

[e] BD1: missing data for 1 patient, BD2: missing data for 4 patients

[f] BD1: missing data for 1 patient, BD2: missing data for 3 patients

[g] BD2: missing data for 2 patients

Table 3 Comparison of clinical correlates between early onset bipolar disorder type 1 and type 2 patients

Clinical variable	Early onset diagnostic subgroup		χ^2 or *t*	*P*
	Bipolar disorder type 1 (*N* = 169)	Bipolar disorder type 2 (*N* = 142)		
Female (%)	96 (56.8)	85 (59.9)	0.3	0.6
Age at interview, mean (SD)	45.3 (13.5)	42.8 (14.4)	1.5	*0.01*
Presence of family history of any psychiatric disorder (%)	99 (58.9)	93 (65.5)	1.4	0.2
Presence of family history of mood disorder (%)	85 (52.5)	84 (60.0)	1.7	0.2
Presence of family history of bipolar disorder (%)	31 (18.5)	36 (25.4)	2.2	0.1
Number of manic/hypomanic episodes, mean (SD)	4.4 (5.1)	4.3 (4.2)	0.2	0.8
Number of depressive episodes, mean (SD)	5.5 (4.7)	6.0 (5.6)	−0.8	0.4
Illness duration, mean (SD)	22.5 (12.8)	21.9 (13.7)	0.4	0.7
Lifetime comorbidity with substance dependence (%)	15 (8.9)	8 (5.6)	1.2	0.3
Lifetime comorbidity with alcohol dependence (%)	10 (5.9)	19 (13.4)	5.1	*0.02*
Presence of suicidal behaviour (%)	47 (28.0)	45 (31.7)	0.5	0.5
Type of clinical course cycle				
MDI (%)	75 (44.4)	51 (35.9)	10.4	*0.035*
DMI (%)	20 (11.8)	31 (21.8)		
Irregular cycling (%)	65 (38.5)	58 (40.8)		
Continuous cycling (%)	5 (3.0)	2 (1.4)		
Rapid cycling (%)	4 (2.4)	0 (0.0)		

Significant values are typed in italics

MDI (hypo)mania-depression-free interval, *DMI* depression-(hypo)mania-free interval, *SD* Standard Deviation, *p* p value

Discussion

The present study highlighted that a two normal component model in BD1 as well as in BD2 diagnostic subgroup best described the distribution of AAO. This finding was not reflected, however, in similar distributional properties of AAO, as well as in comparable pattern of association with clinical variables between the two diagnostic subgroups. In fact, our study found that EO BD2 patients had a higher rate of alcohol dependence compared to both LO BD2 and EO BD1. Further, EO BD2 patients had more frequently a DMI type of clinical course, while the MDI type was more frequently associated with EO BD1. Finally, EO BD2 showed a higher familial load for BD compared to LO BD.

The bimodal AAO distribution found in both BD diagnostic subgroups and in the whole sample of 515 patients is consistent with some studies (Ortiz et al. 2011; Kennedy et al. 2005; Javaid et al. 2011). Conversely, the majority of studies on mixture analysis of AAO showed a trimodal distribution in samples comprising mainly BD1 patients (Bellivier et al. 2001, 2003; Lin et al. 2006; Severino et al. 2009; Hamshere et al. 2009; Tozzi et al. 2011; Bellivier et al. 2014; Golmard et al. 2015). Of note, a recent study showed that bimodal and trimodal distribution fit equally well the AAO of BD (Grigoroiu-Serbanescu et al. 2014). Further research is needed to determine which distribution (bi- or tri-modal) better describes AAO in BD and which is (or which are) the best cut-off(s) before investigating clinical correlates and genetic differences between subgroups based on AAO. In fact, thresholds between subgroups found in different studies differed [e.g. thresholds between the intermediate and late AAO subgroups differed from 25 in one study (Tozzi et al. 2011) to 40 years in another (Hamshere et al. 2009)] as well as percentages of patients in each AAO subgroups [e.g. percentages of patients attributed to the early onset subgroup varied between 21.4% (Bellivier et al. 2001) and 79.7% (Lin et al. 2006)]. Discrepancies in the identified AAO distributions, cut-off points, and proportions of patients in each AAO subgroups may depend on diverse assessment methods, recall bias, study design (Montlahuc et al. 2016), and differences in characteristics of samples studied, including geographic location (Post et al. 2008; Bellivier et al. 2014) and birth cohort (Bauer et al. 2015; Golmard et al. 2015). Concerning study design, Montlahuc et al. (2016) tested whether cross-sectional designs (which cause right truncation), unreliable diagnosis for individuals younger than 10 years old (which causes left truncation), and the selection criterion used for admixture analysis impacted the number of identified AAO subgroups. Importantly, a combination of left and right truncation, which is common in previously published studies of AAO admixture analysis, appeared to significantly influence the number of AAO subgroups detected (Montlahuc et al. 2016). Geographical location appears also to impact on AAO admixture analysis findings. Bellivier et al. (2014) found significant differences in the theoretical AAO functions between USA and European BD samples, mainly led by the higher proportion of patients in the EO subgroup and the lower mean AAO in the USA sample. Finally, birth cohort effect might also influence the estimation of AAO subgroups parameters. In this regard, Golmard et al. (2015) found that the proportion of EO cases increased substantially among BD cases born after 1960 compared to those born before the same year.

Several other findings deserve a comment. In our sample, BD type 1 patients had an earlier mean AAO (26.7 years) than BD2 patients (30.6 years), in agreement with existing data showing that BD1 first manifest their symptoms at an earlier age (Merikangas et al. 2011). In keeping, admixture analyses indicated a larger proportion of EO cases among BD1 patients (67%) compared to BD2 patients (44%). As a consequence, the EO BD1 group had a later mean AAO (22.6 years), compared to EO BD2 patients (20.9 years), reflecting in a higher AAO cut-off point (32 years for BD1 and 28 years for BD2).

These distributional properties of AAO distinguishing EO BD1 from EO BD2 resulted also in diverse patterns of clinical correlates of EO. Indeed, EO BD2 patients had a higher rate of alcohol dependence compared to both LO BD2 and EO BD1. Similarly, previous studies investigating clinical correlates of AAO subgroups found that EO BD patients have higher rates of alcohol abuse (Javaid et al. 2011; Lin et al. 2006). However, these studies either analysed only BD1 individuals (Lin et al. 2006) or did not specify the diagnostic stratification (Javaid et al. 2011). Interestingly, a recent study from Propper et al. (2015) did not find differences in rates of alcohol abuse among AAO subgroups in a sample with a BD1:BD2 ratio of 2:1.

Early onset BD2 patients had more frequently a DMI type of clinical course, while the MDI type was more frequently associated with EO BD1. Although not directly comparable with our study, the findings reported by Perlis et al. (2004) and Propper et al. (2015) in their samples relatively balanced in terms of BD1:BD2 ratio, indicated that very EO and EO BD patients have more frequently onset episodes of depressive polarity compared to later onset subgroups. In addition, our findings were consistent with the work of Koukopoulos et al. (2013), which found that patients with a DMI illness course are more likely to be BD2, while MDI illness course is overrepresented in BD1 patients.

Differently from what reported in the literature, our study failed to confirm in the BD1 subgroup the well-established association of EO BD with a higher familial load for BD and for mood disorders in general, as well as with higher rates of suicidal behaviour (Geoffroy et al. 2013). On the contrary, EO BD2 showed a higher familial load for BD ($p = 0.02$) compared to LO BD. Finally, although not statistically significant, EO BD2 showed higher rates of family history for BD as well as for mood disorders, compared to EO BD1. Similarly, Baek et al. (2011) found higher rates of major depression, but not of BD, in BD2 patients compared to BD1, although their sample was not stratified according to AAO. Further, another recent study showed that both BD1 and BD2 presented a similar familial load for mood disorders (Dell'Osso et al. 2016)

There is compelling evidence that EO BD patients appear also to be more frequently associated with rapid cycling, drug abuse, higher rates of obsessive–compulsive disorder, and possibly for psychotic features, and panic disorder (Geoffroy et al. 2013). Although our study did not test for association most of these clinical correlates, there were no statistically significant associations with EO for drug dependence. Of note, most of this evidence is derived from BD1 samples as there is a lack of data on the analysis of AAO in BD2, while only a few studies investigated mixed samples with both BD1 and BD2 patients (Perlis et al. 2004; Severino et al. 2009; Tozzi et al. 2011; Ortiz et al. 2011; Propper et al. 2015).

Our results should be interpreted in the context of some limitations. The retrospective assessment of AAO might have been subject to recall bias. However, data were gathered through direct interview of the patients as well as with systematic review of medical charts decreasing the probability of a systematic bias in the assessment of AAO. An additional limitation is the lack of a systematic approach in collecting family history data, which might have influenced the assessment of familial load in our sample. Moreover, external corroboration for AAO was obtained, whenever possible, by directly interviewing a first-degree family member or other significant individuals. Further, our samples of BD1 and BD2 patients might not have had an adequate statistical power to detect association signals of small to moderate magnitude. Finally, our study did not consider birth cohort effect in our analysis.

Conclusions

To our knowledge, this is the first study specifically aimed at comparing clinical correlates of EO between BD1 and BD2 patients' populations using admixture analysis. Our work found that, beside diverse distributional properties of AAO, BD1 and BD2 EO subgroups differed also in their clinical characteristics. Of note, our study identified a subgroup of EO BD2 with an AAO even earlier than in the EO BD1 subgroup, characterised by a higher genetic load (i.e. higher familial load for BD) and at greater risk of developing alcohol dependence. Should our findings be replicated in other studies directly comparing AAO BD1 subgroups with AAO BD2 subgroups, future work will be able to focus also on the differences in the genetic and biological makeup, possibly facilitating the search for reliable disease biomarkers.

Abbreviations
BD: bipolar disorder; BD1: BD type 1; BD2: BD type 2; AAO: age at onset; EO: early onset; LO: late onset; NOS: not otherwise specified; BIC: Schwarz's Bayesian information criteria; DMI: depression-(hypo)mania-free interval; MDI: (hypo)mania-depression-free interval; SCID-I/P: structured clinical interview for DSM-IV-TR Axis I disorders; KS: Kolmogorov–Smirnov.

Authors' contributions
MM performed the statistical analysis and wrote the initial draft of the manuscript. GM designed the study, oversaw data analysis, and critically revised the manuscript. BC contributed to the study design, and critically revised the manuscript. FP contributed to the study design, and critically revised the manuscript. LS, VDA, and VS collected clinical data, and critically revised the manuscript. MA oversaw data analysis, and critically revised the manuscript. AT designed the study, oversaw data analysis, and performed some of the writing. UA designed the study, oversaw data analysis, and performed some of the writing. All authors read and approved the final manuscript.

Author details
[1] Section of Psychiatry, Department of Medical Science and Public Health, University of Cagliari, Via Liguria, 13, 09127 Cagliari, Italy. [2] Department of Pharmacology, Dalhousie University, Halifax, NS, Canada. [3] Department of Mental Health, "San Luigi-Gonzaga" Hospital, University of Turin, Orbassano, Italy. [4] Department of Psychiatry, University of Naples SUN, Naples, Italy. [5] Department of Psychiatry, Dalhousie University, Halifax, NS, Canada. [6] Rita Levi Montalcini Department of Neuroscience, Anxiety and Mood Disorders Unit, University of Turin, Turin, Italy.

Acknowledgements
None.

Competing interests
The authors have no other relevant affiliations or financial involvement with any organisation or entity with a financial interest in or financial conflict with the subject matter or materials discussed in the manuscript.

Funding
This research did not receive any specific grant from funding agencies in the public, commercial, or not-for-profit sectors.

References
Alda M. The phenotypic spectra of bipolar disorder. Eur Neuropsychopharmacol. 2004;14(Suppl 2):S94–9.

Alda M, Grof P, Rouleau GA, Turecki G, Young LT. Investigating responders to lithium prophylaxis as a strategy for mapping susceptibility genes for bipolar disorder. Prog Neuropsychopharmacol Biol Psychiatry. 2005;29(6):1038–45.

American Psychiatric Association. Diagnostic and statistical manual of mental disorders (4th ed. text rev.). 1st ed. Washington, DC: American Psychiatric Association; 2000.

Baek JH, Park DY, Choi J, Kim JS, Choi JS, Ha K, et al. Differences between bipolar I and bipolar II disorders in clinical features, comorbidity, and family history. J Affect Disord. 2011;131(1–3):59–67.

Bauer M, Glenn T, Alda M, Andreassen OA, Angelopoulos E, Ardau R, et al. Influence of birth cohort on age of onset cluster analysis in bipolar I disorder. Eur Psychiatry. 2015;30(1):99–105.

Bellivier F, Etain B, Malafosse A, Henry C, Kahn JP, Elgrabli-Wajsbrot O, et al. Age at onset in bipolar I affective disorder in the USA and Europe. World J Biol Psychiatry. 2014;15(5):369–76.

Bellivier F, Golmard JL, Henry C, Leboyer M, Schurhoff F. Admixture analysis of age at onset in bipolar I affective disorder. Arch Gen Psychiatry. 2001;58(5):510–2.

Bellivier F, Golmard JL, Rietschel M, Schulze TG, Malafosse A, Preisig M, et al. Age at onset in bipolar I affective disorder: further evidence for three subgroups. Am J Psychiatry. 2003;160(5):999–1001.

Belmonte MP, Pirooznia M, Goes FS, Seifuddin F, Steele J, Lee PH, et al. Genome-wide association analysis of age at onset and psychotic symptoms in bipolar disorder. Am J Med Genet B Neuropsychiatr Genet. 2011;156B(3):370–8.

Benaglia T, Chauveau D, Hunter DR, Young D. mixtools: an R package for analyzing finite mixture models. J Stat Softw. 2009;32(6):1–29.

Dell'Osso B, Dobrea C, Cremaschi L, Buoli M, Miller S, Ketter TA et al. Italian bipolar II vs I patients have better individual functioning, in spite of overall similar illness severity. CNS Spectr 2016;1–8.

Etain B, Dumaine A, Mathieu F, Chevalier F, Henry C, Kahn JP, et al. A SNAP25 promoter variant is associated with early-onset bipolar disorder and a high expression level in brain. Mol Psychiatry. 2010;15(7):748–55.

Etain B, Mathieu F, Rietschel M, Maier W, Albus M, McKeon P, et al. Genome-wide scan for genes involved in bipolar affective disorder in 70 European families ascertained through a bipolar type I early-onset proband: supportive evidence for linkage at 3p14. Mol Psychiatry. 2006;11(7):685–94.

First MB, Spitzer RL, Gibbon M, Williams JBW. Structured clinical interview for DSM-IV-TR Axis I disorders, Research Version, Patient Edition. (SCID-I/P). New York: Biometrics Research, New York State Psychiatric Institute;2002.

Fraley C, Raftery A. MCLUST: software for model-based cluster analysis. J Classif. 1999;16(2):297–306.

Fraley C, Raftery A, Scrucca L. Normal mixture modeling for model-based clustering, classification, and density estimation. R 2014;(4.3).

Fraley C, Raftery AE. Model-based methods of classification: using the mclust software in chemometrics. J Stat Softw. 2007;18(6):1–13.

Geoffroy PA, Etain B, Scott J, Henry C, Jamain S, Leboyer M, et al. Reconsideration of bipolar disorder as a developmental disorder: importance of the time of onset. J Physiol Paris. 2013;107(4):278–85.

Goes FS, Zandi PP, Miao K, McMahon FJ, Steele J, Willour VL, et al. Mood-incongruent psychotic features in bipolar disorder: familial aggregation and suggestive linkage to 2p11-q14 and 13q21-33. Am J Psychiatry. 2007;164(2):236–47.

Golmard JL, Scott J, Etain B, Preisig M, Aubry JM, Henry C, et al. Using admixture analysis to examine birth-cohort effects on age at onset of bipolar disorder. Acta Psychiatr Scand. 2015;133(3):205–13.

Goodwin FK, Jamison KR. Course and outcome. In: Goodwin FK, Jamison KR, editors. Manic-depressive illness. New York: Oxford University Press; 2007. p. 119–54.

Grigoroiu-Serbanescu M, Rietschel M, Hauser J, Czerski PM, Herms S, Sun X, et al. Commingling analysis of age-of-onset in bipolar I disorder and the morbid risk for major psychoses in first degree relatives of bipolar I probands. J Affect Disord. 2014;168:197–204.

Hamshere ML, Gordon-Smith K, Forty L, Jones L, Caesar S, Fraser C, et al. Age-at-onset in bipolar-I disorder: mixture analysis of 1369 cases identifies three distinct clinical sub-groups. J Affect Disord. 2009;116(1–2):23–9.

Jamain S, Cichon S, Etain B, Muhleisen TW, Georgi A, Zidane N, et al. Common and rare variant analysis in early-onset bipolar disorder vulnerability. PLoS ONE. 2014;9(8):e104326.

Javaid N, Kennedy JL, De Luca V. Ethnicity and age at onset in bipolar spectrum disorders. CNS Spectr. 2011;16(6):127–34.

Kennedy N, Everitt B, Boydell J, VAN Os J, Jones PB, Murray RM. Incidence and distribution of first-episode mania by age: results from a 35-year study. Psychol Med. 2005;35(6):855–63.

Koukopoulos A, Reginaldi D, Tondo L, Visioli C, Baldessarini RJ. Course sequences in bipolar disorder: depressions preceding or following manias or hypomanias. J Affect Disord. 2013;151(1):105–10.
Lin PI, McInnis MG, Potash JB, Willour V, MacKinnon DF, Depaulo JR, et al. Clinical correlates and familial aggregation of age at onset in bipolar disorder. Am J Psychiatry. 2006;163(2):240–6.
Lin PI, McInnis MG, Potash JB, Willour VL, MacKinnon DF, Miao K, et al. Assessment of the effect of age at onset on linkage to bipolar disorder: evidence on chromosomes 18p and 21q. Am J Hum Genet. 2005;77(4):545–55.
Manchia M, Lampus S, Chillotti C, Sardu C, Ardau R, Severino G, et al. Age at onset in Sardinian bipolar I patients: evidence for three subgroups. Bipolar Disord. 2008;10(3):443–6.
Merikangas KR, Jin R, He JP, Kessler RC, Lee S, Sampson NA, et al. Prevalence and correlates of bipolar spectrum disorder in the world mental health survey initiative. Arch Gen Psychiatry. 2011;68(3):241–51.
Montlahuc C, Curis E, Jonas SF, Bellivier F, Chevret S. Age-at-onset subsets of bipolar I disorders: a critical insight into admixture analyses. Int J Methods Psychiatr Res. 2016;1–8.
Ortiz A, Bradler K, Slaney C, Garnham J, Ruzickova M, O'Donovan C, et al. An admixture analysis of the age at index episodes in bipolar disorder. Psychiatry Res. 2011;188(1):34–9.
Perlis RH, Miyahara S, Marangell LB, Wisniewski SR, Ostacher M, DelBello MP, et al. Long-term implications of early onset in bipolar disorder: data from the first 1000 participants in the systematic treatment enhancement program for bipolar disorder (STEP-BD). Biol Psychiatry. 2004;55(9):875–81.
Post RM, Luckenbaugh DA, Leverich GS, Altshuler LL, Frye MA, Suppes T, et al. Incidence of childhood-onset bipolar illness in the USA and Europe. Br J Psychiatry. 2008;192(2):150–1.
Propper L, Ortiz A, Slaney C, Garnham J, Ruzickova M, Calkin CV, et al. Early-onset and very-early-onset bipolar disorder: distinct or similar clinical conditions? Bipolar Disord. 2015;17(8):814–20.
R Development Core Team. R: a language and environment for statistical computing. R 2008.
Severino G, Manchia M, Contu P, Squassina A, Lampus S, Ardau R, et al. Association study in a Sardinian sample between bipolar disorder and the nuclear receptor REV-ERBalpha gene, a critical component of the circadian clock system. Bipolar Disord. 2009;11(2):215–20.
Tozzi F, Manchia M, Galwey NW, Severino G, Del Zompo M, Day R, et al. Admixture analysis of age at onset in bipolar disorder. Psychiatry Res. 2011;185(1–2):27–32.

12

Monitoring of patients treated with lithium for bipolar disorder: an international survey

M. Nederlof[1,2], E. R. Heerdink[1,3,4*], A. C. G. Egberts[1,4], I. Wilting[4], L. J. Stoker[1], R. Hoekstra[5] and R. W. Kupka[6]

Abstract

Background: Adequate monitoring of patients using lithium is needed for optimal dosing and for early identification of patients with (potential) ADEs. The objective was to internationally assess how health care professionals monitor patients treated with lithium for bipolar disorder.

Methods: Using networks of various professional organizations, an anonymous online survey was conducted among health care professionals prescribing lithium. Target lithium serum levels and frequency of monitoring was assessed together with monitoring of physical and laboratory parameters. Reasons to and not to monitor and use of guidelines and institutional protocols, and local monitoring systems were investigated.

Results: The survey was completed by 117 health care professionals incorporating responses from twenty-four countries. All prescribers reported to monitor lithium serum levels on a regular basis, with varying target ranges. Almost all (> 97%) monitored thyroid and renal function before start and during maintenance treatment. Reported monitoring of other laboratory and physical parameters was variable. The majority of respondents (74%) used guidelines or institutional protocols for monitoring. In general, the prescriber was responsible for monitoring, had to request every monitoring parameter separately and only a minority of patients was automatically invited.

Conclusions: Lithium serum levels, renal and thyroid function were monitored by (almost) all physicians. However, there was considerable variation in other monitoring parameters. Our results help to understand why prescribers of lithium monitor patients and what their main reasons are not to monitor patients using lithium.

Keywords: Lithium, Bipolar disorder, Survey, Monitoring, Therapeutic drug monitoring

Background

Mood stabilizers play a pivotal role in the long-term treatment of patients with bipolar disorder. While it is known that mood stabilizers effectively treat symptoms of bipolar disorder, the potential for adverse drug events (ADEs) is of concern (Rothschild et al. 2007; Ayani et al. 2016; Mann et al. 2008). Some ADEs are preventable, and steps to minimize errors are needed to improve patient safety (Leendertse et al. 2008).

Lithium is the gold standard for maintenance treatment of patients with bipolar disorder (Sani et al. 2017). It is a drug with a narrow therapeutic index; therefore, careful therapeutic drug monitoring is needed to maximize effectiveness and to minimize ADEs and toxicity. Patients using lithium are known to have a high intra- and inter-patient variability in dose—concentration relationship, and external factors including drug–drug interactions, environmental temperature, and fluid and electrolyte intake may influence lithium serum levels (Amdisen 1980; Huang et al. 2008; Wilting et al. 2005; Wilting et al. 2007; Rej et al. 2014). Recommendations regarding optimal lithium serum levels differ among clinical practice guidelines, with the most common range being between 0.6 and 0.8 mmol/L for maintenance treatment (Malhi

*Correspondence: e.r.heerdink@uu.nl
[1] Division of Pharmacoepidemiology and Clinical Pharmacology, Utrecht Institute for Pharmaceutical Sciences, Utrecht University, 3508 TB Utrecht, The Netherlands
Full list of author information is available at the end of the article

et al. 2017). The illness stage may further require a different approach for lithium serum levels (Malhi et al. 2016).

Besides monitoring of lithium serum levels, clinical and biomarker monitoring of physical and laboratory parameters is required (Nederlof et al. 2015). Lithium use has been associated with a gradual decline in renal function: estimated glomerular filtration rate (eGFR) decreases by about 30% more than associated with aging alone (Tondo et al. 2017). This decline in renal function can become irreversible and may lead to renal failure (Gitlin 2016). Moreover, a decline in eGFR can lead to an increased risk of lithium toxicity due to accumulation (Lepkifker et al. 2004). Furthermore, lithium is known to affect thyroid function (van Melick et al. 2010); with up to 40% of patients experiencing goiter and about 20% hypothyroidism (Lazarus 2009), although the reported prevalence shows a wide range. A 10% higher value of parathyroid hormone (PTH) and calcium was found in a meta-analysis comparing patients using lithium to healthy controls or psychiatric patients not treated with lithium (McKnight et al. 2012). These elevations could stimulate pathological changes leading to the occurrence of hyperplasia or parathyroid adenomas (Giusti et al. 2012). In addition, physical parameters such as weight and blood pressure may be influenced during lithium use (Gitlin 2016; Bisogni et al. 2016).

Adequate monitoring of patients during lithium use is needed for early identification of patients with (potential) ADEs and for optimal dosing (Kirkham et al. 2013; Severus et al. 2008; Aral and Vecchio-Sadus 2008; Baird-Gunning et al. 2017). So far, it is not known how different health care professionals internationally aim to achieve safe and effective lithium treatment through monitoring. Local monitoring systems may differ and health care professionals may be influenced by different guidelines, institutional or laboratory protocols, scientific literature, and their own personal knowledge and experience. The objective of this study was therefore to internationally assess how health care professionals report to monitor patients treated with lithium.

Methods

Study design, participants and recruitment

An international survey was conducted between October 2016 and April 2017 among health care professionals prescribing lithium for patients with bipolar disorder. Health care professionals were recruited through networks of various professional organizations (Additional file 1: Appendix S1), and invited by email to participate. The email introduced the nature and purpose of the survey and proposed to further forward the survey to lithium prescribing colleagues. To maximize the response rate, attention was generated during presentations for the Dutch Foundation for Bipolar Disorders and the Belgian College of Neurological and Biological Psychiatry and through flyers at a meeting of the International Group for The Study of Lithium Treated Patients (IGSLi). The survey was conducted in English. Participation was voluntary and answers were kept with anonymized identity of participants. A reminder email was sent a few weeks following the initial request. Study data were analyzed at the Division of Pharmacoepidemiology and Clinical Pharmacology of Utrecht University. The study protocol was approved by the Institutional Review Board of the Division of Pharmacoepidemiology and Clinical Pharmacology of Utrecht University.

Questionnaire

Based on monitoring recommendations in various guidelines, a questionnaire was designed to assess how health care professionals prescribing lithium to patients with bipolar disorder report to monitor these patients. The primary researcher (MN) assessed all monitoring instructions in four guidelines (Kupka et al. 2015; National Institute for Health and Care Excellence 2014; Ng et al. 2009; Grunze et al. 2013), to explore relevant monitoring parameters and advised frequencies of monitoring: the Dutch Multidisciplinary guideline (Kupka et al. 2015), the International Society for Bipolar Disorders guidelines (Ng et al. 2009) and the World Federation of Societies of Biological Psychiatry guidelines (Grunze et al. 2013), and the guideline of the National Institute for Health and Care Excellence (2014). Actual utilization of guidelines was assessed, including explicatory reasons. In addition, we included questions on local monitoring systems. Most questions were multiple choice with an option offered for comments at the end, if relevant. The study group then composed a questionnaire in LimeSurvey version 2.5, an online accessible survey application. The survey was tested by eleven Dutch experts in the field of lithium treatment (Additional file 2: Appendix S2) to optimize content on appropriateness, relevance, and time to complete the survey, and it was adjusted accordingly.

The final questionnaire consisted of 41 questions divided into four parts. First, target lithium serum levels and frequency of monitoring were assessed. Second, monitoring frequency of physical and laboratory parameters was assessed. Third, to identify factors contributing to monitoring, reasons to monitor or not to monitor, and use of guidelines or institutional protocols were investigated. Fourth, personal characteristics of the respondent including age, gender, experience with prescribing lithium, and country of residence were collected. A condensed version of the questionnaire can be found in

Table 1 Aspects covered in the questionnaire on monitoring of patients using lithium

Aspect	Item number	Items of question
Lithium serum level monitoring	1–8	Target values for: acute manic episode in adults (18–60 years old), maintenance treatment in adults, acute manic episode in elderly patients (> 60 years old), maintenance treatment in elderly Frequency of monitoring lithium serum levels during the first month, months 2–6 and per year
Monitoring of physical and laboratory parameters	9–25	Assessment of the following monitoring parameters before, during the first 6 months and during maintenance treatment Physical parameters: bodyweight, body mass index (BMI), blood pressure, pulse, waist circumference, electrocardiogram (ECG), pregnancy test, 24 h urine examination Laboratory parameters: creatinine, urea, albumin, glomerular filtration rate (GFR), thyroid stimulating hormone (TSH), parathyroid hormone (PTH), thyroxine (T4), alanine aminotransferase (ALAT), aspartate aminotransferase (ASAT), bilirubin, sodium, potassium, calcium, full blood count, leukocytes, leukocyte differentiation, total cholesterol, high density lipoprotein (HDL), low density lipoprotein (LDL), very low density lipoprotein (vLDL), triglycerides, fasting glucose
Local system for ensuring monitoring	26–35	Reasons to and not to monitor, assessment usage of guidelines or institutional protocols, responsible health care professional for monitoring, usage of laboratory protocols, method of inviting patients for monitoring
Background information	36–41	Gender, age, profession, institution of employment, years of lithium prescribing, country

Table 1. The full questionnaire can be found in Additional file 3: Appendix 3.

Analysis

Responses were analyzed using the Statistical Package for Social Sciences Version 24.0 for Windows (SPSS 24.0; SPSS Inc, Chicago, IL). Data were analyzed using descriptive statistics. Target lithium serum levels were presented with the use of boxplot statistics using Tukey's Hinges (Tukey 1977).

Results

Study sample

A total of 117 respondents completed the survey. The majority of respondents were employed as psychiatrists (91%), followed by nurse practitioners (3%), psychiatric residents (5%), or as general practitioner (1%). Twenty percent of the respondents were self-employed. The duration of experience with prescribing lithium had a median of 22 years [interquartile range (IQR) 10–33]. Two-third (66%) of the respondents were male; the median age was 53 years (IQR 41–60).

Responses were collected from health care professionals residing in twenty-four different countries. Countries where prescribers were employed were diverse, with 63% of the respondents employed in Europe, 22% in North America, 9% in South America, 3% in Australia, 2% in Asia and 1% in Africa (Fig. 1).

Lithium serum level and frequency of monitoring

In Fig. 2, target values for minimum and maximum lithium plasma levels the respondents reported to pursue are presented for acute and maintenance treatment in adults and elderly patients.

For adults, the median lower target level for acute treatment was 0.8 mmol/L (IQR 0.1; range 0.5–1.0). The median for the upper level was 1.1 mmol/L (IQR 0.2; range 0.7–1.6). For maintenance treatment the median target serum level for adults was 0.6 mmol/L (IQR 0.1; range 0.4–0.8); with a median upper level of 0.8 mmol/L (IQR 0.1; range 0.5–1.2).

For elderly, the median target range for serum levels was 0.6 mmol/L (IQR 0.2; range 0.3–1.0), with 0.9 mmol/L (IQR 0.2; range 0.5–1.2) as upper level for acute treatment. During maintenance treatment the median lower level was 0.4 mmol/L (IQR 0.1; range 0.3–0.8); with 0.8 mmol/L (IQR 0.2; range 0.6–1.2) as upper level. Spread in target ranges for both adults and elderly patients during acute treatment was relatively larger compared to maintenance treatment.

All respondents monitored lithium serum levels during treatment, although there was variability in frequency. In the initial phase of lithium treatment, most respondents monitored lithium serum levels one to three times in the first month and between one and three times during months 2–6. During maintenance treatment half of the respondents monitored one to three times a year; others four or more times a year (44%) (Table 2). Many had difficulties explaining how often they monitored the lithium serum level during the first month, as they monitored lithium serum levels until they reached the target level. Thirteen respondents commented to monitor 5–7 days after every dose change.

Fig. 1 Demographic presentation of responses

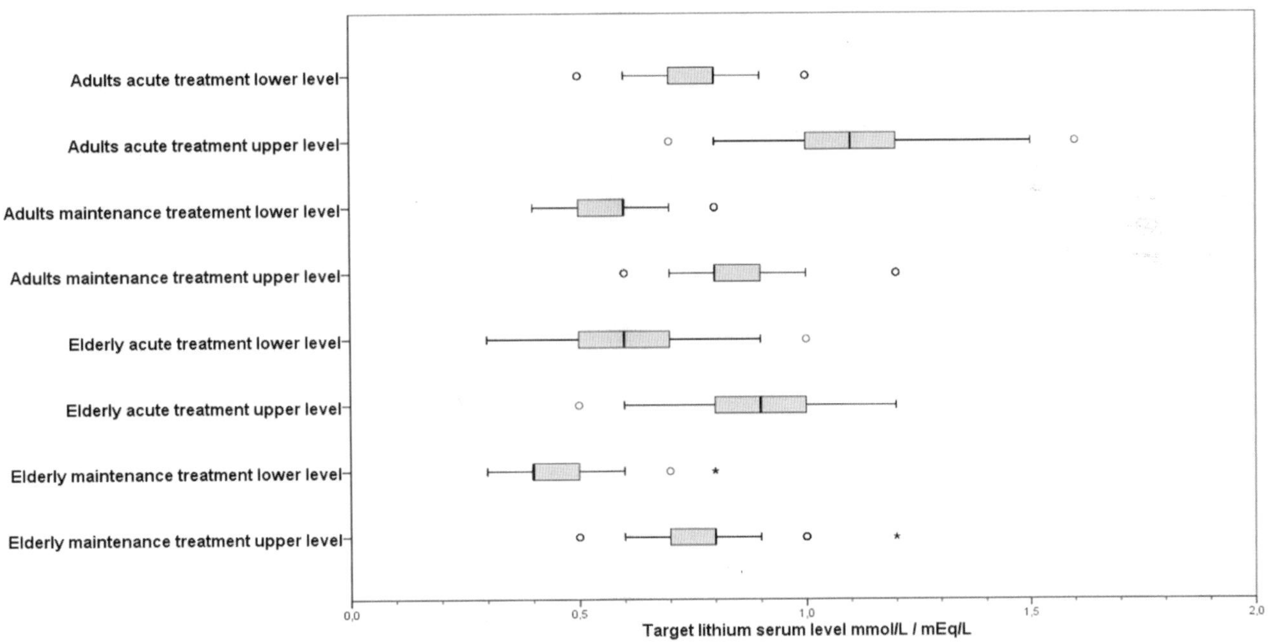

Fig. 2 Target lithium serum levels for both adults and elderly patients (> 60 years) during acute and maintenance treatment

Table 2 Frequency of monitoring lithium serum levels

Frequency of monitoring	Never	1–3 x	≥ 4 x
First month	0	75 (64%)	42 (36%)
Months 2–6	0	84 (72%)	33 (28%)
Per year (during maintenance treatment)	0	65 (56%)	52 (44%)

Monitoring of physical and laboratory parameters

All responders monitored at least one physical or laboratory parameter. Responses of monitoring of physical and laboratory monitoring are shown in Table 3.

Most respondents monitored bodyweight, blood pressure, pulse, and body mass index. Fewer respondents

Table 3 Monitoring of physical and laboratory parameters

Parameter	Monitoring before start of treatment	Frequency of monitoring during the first 6 months of treatment			Frequency of monitoring per year during maintenance treatment			
		Never	1–3 x	≥ 4 x	Never	Once	2–3 x	≥ 4 x
Physical parameters								
Physical parameters (at least one parameter)	104 (88%)	17 (14%)	*76 (64%)*	24 (21%)	12 (10%)	*58 (49%)*	28 (24%)	19 (16%)
Body weight	92 (79%)	32 (27%)	*70 (60%)*	15 (13%)	20 (17%)	*58 (50%)*	25 (21%)	14 (12%)
Blood pressure	88 (75%)	35 (30%)	*63 (54%)*	19 (16%)	28 (24%)	*51 (44%)*	24 (21%)	14 (12%)
Pulse	79 (68%)	43 (37%)	*56 (48%)*	18 (15%)	38 (32%)	*48 (41%)*	19 (16%)	12 (10%)
Body mass index (BMI)	63 (54%)	*54 (46%)*	*54 (46%)*	9 (8%)	45 (38%)	*47 (40%)*	16 (14%)	9 (8%)
Electrocardiogram (ECG)	51 (44%)	*66 (56%)*	46 (39%)	5 (4%)	*71 (61%)*	31 (27%)	12 (10%)	3 (3%)
Waist circumference	45 (38%)	*72 (62%)*	42 (36%)	3 (3%)	*65 (56%)*	38 (32%)	9 (8%)	5 (4%)
Pregnancy test	40 (34%)	*90 (77%)*	24 (21%)	3 (3%)	*102 (87%)*	7 (6%)	6 (5%)	2 (2%)
24 h urine examination	23 (20%)	*93 (79%)*	21 (18%)	3 (3%)	*88 (75%)*	23 (20%)	2 (2%)	4 (3%)
Renal function								
Renal function (at least one parameter)	116 (99%)	3 (3%)	*88 (75%)*	26 (22%)	0	25 (21%)	*60 (51%)*	32 (27%)
Creatinine	116 (99%)	3 (3%)	*88 (75%)*	26 (22%)	0	26 (22%)	*59 (50%)*	32 (27%)
Urea	101 (86%)	21 (18%)	*78 (67%)*	18 (15%)	18 (15%)	22 (19%)	*48 (41%)*	29 (25%)
Glomerular filtration rate (GFR)	100 (85%)	19 (16%)	*76 (65%)*	22 (19%)	13 (11%)	22 (19%)	*52 (44%)*	30 (26%)
Albumin	66 (56%)	46 (39%)	*60 (51%)*	11 (9%)	*42 (36%)*	21 (18%)	34 (29%)	20 (17%)
Thyroid function								
Thyroid function (at least one parameter)	115 (98%)	2 (2%)	*104 (89%)*	11 (9%)	0	43 (36%)	*54 (46%)*	20 (17%)
Thyroid stimulating hormone (TSH)	115 (98%)	2 (2%)	*104 (89%)*	11 (9%)	1 (1%)	42 (36%)	*54 (46%)*	20 (17%)
Thyroxine (T4)	82 (70%)	30 (26%)	*80 (68%)*	7 (6%)	28 (24%)	33 (28%)	*41 (35%)*	15 (13%)
Parathyroid function								
Parathyroid hormone (PTH)	32 (27%)	*79 (68%)*	35 (30%)	3 (3%)	*72 (62%)*	22 (19%)	17 (15%)	6 (5%)
Electrolytes								
Electrolytes (at least one parameter)	107 (91%)	10 (9%)	*86 (73%)*	21 (18%)	8 (7%)	34 (29%)	*49 (42%)*	26 (22%)
Sodium	103 (88%)	17 (15%)	*80 (68%)*	20 (17%)	14 (12%)	32 (27%)	*46 (39%)*	25 (21%)
Potassium	101 (86%)	18 (15%)	*79 (68%)*	20 (17%)	15 (13%)	32 (27%)	*45 (38%)*	25 (21%)
Calcium	94 (80%)	21 (18%)	*81 (69%)*	15 (13%)	19 (16%)	35 (30%)	*44 (38%)*	19 (16%)
Hematological parameters								
Hematological parameters (at least one parameter)	106 (90%)	26 (22%)	*79 (67%)*	12 (10%)	24 (21%)	*51 (44%)*	29 (25%)	13 (11%)
Full blood count	102 (87%)	32 (27%)	*73 (62%)*	12 (10%)	30 (26%)	*47 (40%)*	29 (25%)	11 (9%)
Leukocytes	101 (86%)	30 (26%)	*75 (64%)*	12 (10%)	27 (23%)	*50 (43%)*	27 (23%)	13 (11%)
Leukocyte differentiation	87 (74%)	40 (34%)	*67 (57%)*	10 (9%)	38 (32%)	*45 (38%)*	25 (21%)	9 (8%)
Lipid profile								
Lipid profile (at least one parameter)	73 (62%)	*57 (49%)*	55 (47%)	5 (4%)	42 (36%)	*53 (45%)*	18 (15%)	4 (3%)
Triglycerides	71 (61%)	*58 (50%)*	54 (46%)	5 (4%)	43 (37%)	*52 (44%)*	18 (15%)	4 (3%)
Total cholesterol	71 (61%)	*59 (50%)*	53 (45%)	5 (4%)	44 (38%)	*52 (44%)*	17 (15%)	4 (3%)
High density lipoprotein (HDL)	69 (59%)	*60 (51%)*	53 (45%)	4 (3%)	45 (38%)	*51 (44%)*	18 (15%)	3 (3%)
Low density lipoprotein (LDL)	67 (57%)	*63 (54%)*	50 (43%)	4 (3%)	48 (41%)	*49 (42%)*	17 (15%)	3 (3%)
Very low density lipoprotein (vLDL)	35 (30%)	*84 (72%)*	32 (27%)	1 (1%)	*71 (61%)*	35 (30%)	11 (9%)	0
Hepatic function								
Hepatic function (at least one parameter)	68 (58%)	*61 (52%)*	48 (41%)	8 (7%)	*54 (46%)*	37 (32%)	20 (17%)	6 (5%)
Alanine aminotransferase (ALAT)	68 (58%)	*62 (53%)*	47 (40%)	8 (7%)	*55 (47%)*	37 (32%)	19 (16%)	6 (5%)
Aspartate aminotransferase (ASAT)	66 (56%)	*64 (55%)*	46 (39%)	7 (6%)	*55 (47%)*	37 (32%)	19 (16%)	6 (5%)
Bilirubin	34 (29%)	*79 (68%)*	33 (28%)	5 (4%)	*71 (61%)*	27 (23%)	15 (13%)	3 (3%)
Other laboratory parameters								
Fasting glucose	79 (67%)	48 (41%)	*63 (54%)*	6 (5%)	35 (30%)	*56 (48%)*	20 (17%)	6 (5%)

Italicized cells represent most reported answers after initiation of lithium treatment made electrocardiograms, monitored waist circumference, performed pregnancy tests, or 24 h urine examinations. Renal function and thyroid function were monitored by almost all respondents before start and during maintenance treatment. Primarily creatinine, thyroid stimulating hormone (TSH), urea, and glomerular filtration rate were measured. PTH was considerably less often monitored, sometimes solely in case of a deviating calcium level. A few mentioned to measure anti-thyroid autoantibodies (n = 6), mostly in case of abnormal TSH. Electrolytes and hematological parameters were generally determined before start and often repeated during maintenance treatment. Slightly more than half of the respondents monitored a lipid profile and hepatic function before start. Most of them never monitored hepatic function after start, while lipids were monitoring more often once a year during maintenance treatment. Fasting glucose was monitored by about two-thirds of the respondents before start, and about half of the respondents monitored fasting glucose one to three times during the first 6 months and thereafter once a year during maintenance treatment.

Some respondents mentioned to monitor the following additional parameters: alkaline phosphatase (ALP) (n = 1), CRP (n = 1), cysteine (n = 1), EEG (n = 1), erythrocyte sedimentation rate (n = 1), folate (n = 2), gamma-glutamyltransferase (GGT) (n = 1), glycated hemoglobin (HbA1c) (n = 1), serum level of antipsychotic agents (n = 1), urine osmolality (n = 1) vitamin D (n = 4), physical examination (n = 1), vitamin B1 or vitamin B12 (n = 2).

Reasons for monitoring

The main reason to monitor patients using lithium was because of safety or adverse effects (99%). Respondents monitored additionally to aid in dose adjustment or optimization (94%), in case of possible lithium toxicity (85%), during start, stop, or dose-adjustment of interacting medication (67%), to verify therapeutic level, especially in case of insufficient efficacy (64%), due to co-morbidities of the patient (63%), and because it is recommended in guidelines (59%). Other mentioned reasons that were to assess compliance (3%), to monitor patients during pregnancy (1%) or in case of a new episode (1%), or if a medication brand changed (1%).

Reasons not to monitor patients during lithium treatment were a lack of resources to monitor (4%), non-cooperative patients (4%), if a guideline did not obligate monitoring (3%), if monitoring was unnecessary in the opinion of the respondent (3%), if an institutional protocol did not require monitoring (2%), or unawareness of the necessity of monitoring (2%). Still, 90% of the respondents reported they always monitored their patients. One psychiatrist commented that there are no good reasons *not* to monitor a patient on lithium.

Use of guidelines or institutional protocols for monitoring

The monitoring policy of 74% of the respondents was based upon a guideline or institutional protocol. A minority of respondents said not to use guidelines because personal experience and practice were more valuable to them (9%). A number of respondents thought guidelines were not explicit enough (7%) or the institutional protocol or Summary of Product Characteristics (SmPC) they used was overlapping (4%). Another reason not to use guidelines was a difficulty to apply them in daily clinical practice (4%), including a lack of resources in order to monitor (2%). Four psychiatrists (3%) reported the institutional protocol/SmPC they used was sufficient. Alternative reasons not to use guidelines were difficulties to apply guidelines to their patient population (3%) or an unawareness of the existence of such guidelines (2%). Additionally, respondents mentioned to perform monitoring based on individual patient characteristics (2%) or to experience a difficulty to choose between guidelines (1%). Sometimes guidelines were found to be excessive (1%) or they used their own reading of literature (1%).

Local systems for ensuring monitoring patients treated with lithium

The majority of respondents reported to be personally responsible for monitoring (91%). The health care professional responsible for monitoring was a psychiatrist (83%), psychiatric resident (3%), nurse practitioner (3%), or the head/clinic nurse (3%). A shared responsibility was mentioned by some respondents (3%). In a few responses, a general practitioner (2%), family physician (1%) or the doctor who continued treatment after discharge (1%) was responsible for monitoring.

Among the respondents, 74% had to request each parameter separately. For monitoring a combination of parameters during lithium treatment, 25% could make use of an existing laboratory protocol. For some health care professionals, the system for ensuring monitoring was organized in a way that patients were automatically invited by a laboratory or physician for determination of monitoring parameters (26%).

Discussion

We surveyed prescribers of lithium on monitoring of patients using lithium for bipolar disorder. All prescribers reported to monitor lithium serum levels on a regular basis, with varying intervals and target levels. Target levels for maintenance treatment were mostly consistent with target ranges in guidelines for bipolar disorders (Malhi et al. 2017). Target levels for acute treatment were more variable, which is in accordance with the variability among guidelines (Malhi et al. 2017).

Almost all health care professionals monitored thyroid and renal function before start, and all during maintenance treatment, indicating a higher priority was given to these parameters compared to other parameters. This does not mean that all respondents gave less priority to other monitoring physical or laboratory parameters. Some may consider other parameters equally important, but our results show that they reported to monitor at least renal and thyroid function. Respondents may not monitor these parameters in *all* patients using lithium in clinical practice. From studies in The Netherlands and the UK it is known that monitoring rates may be much lower than the health care professionals reported in our survey; showing that 8–22% of patients did not have any recorded test for renal or thyroid function (van de Beek et al. 2010; Paton et al. 2013). A difference between reported and actual monitoring in clinical practice can be a consequence of inadequate adherence to monitoring by patients (Collins et al. 2010). It is possible that respondents despite anonymity may have given socially desirable answers to our survey. If patients using lithium are not adequately monitored, ADEs may not be identified in time. On the other hand, excessive monitoring may have a negative impact on health care costs and provide an extra burden to patients and may even lead to a reduced treatment adherence (Tran et al. 2015).

Reported monitoring was more variable for other physical and laboratory parameters than thyroid and renal function. It would be of interest to assess reasons of health care professionals to monitor or not to monitor these parameters. Variability in monitoring between respondents can be a consequence of a lack of resources, difference in education, type of patient population, a different opinion on the need for monitoring or differences in recommendations in guidelines (Zivanovic 2017). The number of responses was not sufficient to compare responses between subgroups such as countries, type of health care professional or to determine guideline adherence.

Overall, respondents reported to use guidelines or institutional protocols for monitoring. Guidelines differ with respect to their recommendations, and studies have shown that there are discrepancies between guideline recommendations and actual monitoring in clinical practice (Malhi et al. 2017; van de Beek et al. 2010; Paton et al. 2013; Minay et al. 2013). Reasons to use or not to use guidelines were assessed in our survey. In line with previous research, several respondents reported not to follow guidelines because in their opinion they did not apply to their patient population (Perlis 2007). Guidelines are mainly based on literature such as randomized controlled trials that may not include specific patient populations, for instance children or older patients (Zarin et al. 2005). In our survey, health care professionals mentioned personal experience and practice to be the main reasons for not following a guideline. A lack of resources and non-cooperative patients could further complicate monitoring. Not all laboratories are equipped to perform all laboratory tests (Guo et al. 2013) and for prescribers of lithium not all monitoring facilities may be easily accessible, for example for making an electrocardiogram.

In the majority of cases the prescriber of lithium, generally a psychiatrist, was responsible for monitoring. The health care system should be organized in a way that continuity of monitoring is warranted. For instance, in the Dutch guideline, the prescriber is appointed to be responsible for monitoring (Kupka et al. 2015), but another health care professional can have a coordinating function. Among respondents, a small group reported that patients were automatically invited by a laboratory or physician for monitoring. Most responders had to request each monitoring parameter separately, which may increase the workload and demands awareness of health care professionals. A method to order all monitoring parameters after a prescription has been described, known as a corollary order (Wright and Sittig 2006). In this way, an order set of monitoring parameters could be developed to be used when a health care professional prescribes lithium. Clinical decision systems could be programmed in a way that all relevant monitoring parameters are automatically ordered after a lithium prescription.

Strengths and limitations

An advantage of using a survey is that we could assess anonymized reported monitoring and use of guidelines. Our results help to understand why prescribers of lithium monitor patients and what their main reasons are not to monitor patients according to guideline recommendations or even not at all. By using an international online survey we were able to include respondents from 24 countries worldwide.

A limitation is that the response was not sufficient to compare individual countries. The limited response could have been a result of a limited amount of time or a lack of interest in the subject. Since the survey was distributed via various networks, we do not know how many professionals actually have been reached. Prescribers who did participate in the survey, may have been a selection of prescribers who are more interested in the subject. The survey was sent to health care professionals who were members of professional health care organizations, including those with a specific focus on bipolar disorder. It is expected that they are better informed on lithium monitoring as some of them may have a special interest in lithium treatment. Respondents were relatively experienced, with a median of 22 years of prescribing lithium. Therefore, responses may not reflect monitoring in general clinical practice internationally.

Conclusions

Adequate monitoring of patients using lithium is needed for optimal dosing and early identification of patients with (potential) ADEs. In our survey, health care professionals prescribing lithium report to monitor lithium serum levels, renal and thyroid function on a regular basis. However, there was considerable variation in other monitoring parameters. Our results help to understand why prescribers of lithium monitor patients and what their main reasons are not to monitor patients. In future, it will be of interest to assess how prescribers respond to deviating parameters.

Abbreviations

ADE: adverse drug event; ALP: alkaline phosphatase; eGFR: estimated glomerular filtration rate; GGT: gamma-glUtamyltransferase; HbA1c: glycated hemoglobin; IGSLi: International Group for The Study of Lithium Treated Patients; IQR: interquartile range; PTH: parathyroid hormone; SmPC: Summary of Product Characteristics; TSH: thyroid stimulating hormone.

Authors' contributions

MN is the primary author and performed the survey, analyzing, writing and editing of the data. RK, EH, TE, IW, LS and RH helped spreading the survey and provided critical appraisal of the manuscript. All authors read and approved the final manuscript.

Author details

[1] Division of Pharmacoepidemiology and Clinical Pharmacology, Utrecht Institute for Pharmaceutical Sciences, Utrecht University, 3508 TB Utrecht, The Netherlands. [2] Brocacef Ziekenhuisfarmacie, 3600 AB Maarssen, The Netherlands. [3] Research Group Innovation of Pharmaceutical Care, University of Applied Sciences Utrecht, 3508 AD Utrecht, The Netherlands. [4] Department of Clinical Pharmacy, University Medical Center Utrecht, 3508 GA Utrecht, The Netherlands. [5] Antes, Delta Psychiatric Center, 3709 DZ Rotterdam, The Netherlands. [6] Department of Psychiatry, Amsterdam Public Health Research Institute, VU University Medical Center, A.J. Ernststraat 1187, 1081 HL Amsterdam, The Netherlands.

Acknowledgements

We would like to acknowledge all participants for their response to the survey. We additionally would like to thank Anouk Braam for her help in composing the survey.

Competing interests

The authors declare that they have no competing interests.

Funding

The authors received no financial support for the research, authorship, and/or publication of this article.

References

Amdisen A. Serum concentration and clinical supervision in monitoring of lithium treatment. Ther Drug Monit. 1980;2(1):73–83.

Aral H, Vecchio-Sadus A. Toxicity of lithium to humans and the environment–a literature review. Ecotoxicol Environ Saf. 2008;70(3):349–56.

Ayani N, Sakuma M, Morimoto T, Kikuchi T, Watanabe K, Narumoto J, et al. The epidemiology of adverse drug events and medication errors among psychiatric inpatients in Japan: the JADE study. BMC Psychiatry. 2016;30(16):303.

Baird-Gunning J, Lea-Henry T, Hoegberg LCG, Gosselin S, Roberts DM. Lithium poisoning. J Intensive Care Med. 2017;32(4):249–63.

Bisogni V, Rossitto G, Reghin F, Padrini R, Rossi GP. Antihypertensive therapy in patients on chronic lithium treatment for bipolar disorders. J Hypertens. 2016;34(1):20–8.

Collins N, Barnes TR, Shingleton-Smith A, Gerrett D, Paton C. Standards of lithium monitoring in mental health trusts in the UK. BMC Psychiatry. 2010;12(10):80.

Gitlin M. Lithium side effects and toxicity: prevalence and management strategies. Int J Bipolar Disord. 2016;4(1):27.

Giusti CF, Amorim SR, Guerra RA, Portes ES. Endocrine disturbances related to the use of lithium. Arq Bras Endocrinol Metabol. 2012;56(3):153–8.

Grunze H, Vieta E, Goodwin GM, Bowden C, Licht RW, Möller H-J, et al. The World Federation of Societies of Biological Psychiatry (WFSBP) guidelines for the biological treatment of bipolar disorders: update 2012 on the long-term treatment of bipolar disorder. World J Biol Psychiatry Off J World Fed Soc Biol Psychiatry. 2013;14(3):154–219.

Guo W, Guo G-X, Sun C, Zhang J, Rong Z, He J, et al. Therapeutic drug monitoring of psychotropic drugs in China: a nationwide survey. Ther Drug Monit. 2013;35(6):816–22.

Huang HC, Chang YL, Lan TH, Chiu HJ, Liu WM, Lee TJF. Prediction of optimal lithium doses for Taiwanese psychiatric patients. J Clin Pharm Ther. 2008;33(2):115–21.

Kirkham E, Bazire S, Anderson T, Wood J, Grassby P, Desborough JA. Impact of active monitoring on lithium management in Norfolk. Ther Adv Psychopharmacol. 2013;3(5):260–5.

Kupka RW, Goossens P, van Bendegem M, Daemen P, Daggenvoorde T, Daniels M, Dols A, van Duin D, Hillegers M, Hoogelander A, ter Kulve E, Peetom T, Schulte R, Stevens A. Dutch multidisciplinary guideline bipolar disorder. Nederlandse Vereniging voor Psychiatrie (NVvP); 2015. http://www.nvvp.net/stream/richtlijn-bipolaire-stoornissen-2015. Accessed 15 Sept 2016.

Lazarus JH. Lithium and thyroid. Best Pract Res Clin Endocrinol Metab. 2009;23(6):723–33.

Leendertse AJ, Egberts ACG, Stoker LJ, van den Bemt PMLA, HARM Study Group. Frequency of and risk factors for preventable medication-related hospital admissions in the Netherlands. Arch Intern Med. 2008;168(17):1890–6.

Lepkifker E, Sverdlik A, Iancu I, Ziv R, Segev S, Kotler M. Renal insufficiency in long-term lithium treatment. J Clin Psychiatry. 2004;65(6):850–6.

Malhi GS, Gershon S, Outhred T. Lithiumeter: version 2.0. Bipolar Disord. 2016;18(8):631–41.

Malhi GS, Gessler D, Outhred T. The use of lithium for the treatment of bipolar disorder: recommendations from clinical practice guidelines. J Affect Disord. 2017;27(217):266–80.

Mann K, Rothschild JM, Keohane CA, Chu JA, Bates DW. Adverse drug events and medication errors in psychiatry: methodological issues regarding identification and classification. World J Biol Psychiatry Off J World Fed Soc Biol Psychiatry. 2008;9(1):24–33.

McKnight RF, Adida M, Budge K, Stockton S, Goodwin GM, Geddes JR. Lithium toxicity profile: a systematic review and meta-analysis. Lancet Lond Engl. 2012;379(9817):721–8.

Minay J, Paul R, McGarvey D, Savage G, Stevenson M, Fogarty D, et al. Lithium usage and renal function testing in a large UK community population; a case-control study. Gen Hosp Psychiatry. 2013;35(6):631–5.

National Institute for Health and Care Excellence. NICE guideline bipolar disorder; 2014. http://www.nice.org.uk/guidance/cg185/. Accessed 15 Sept 2016.

Nederlof M, Stoker LJ, Egberts TCG, Heerdink ER. Instructions for clinical and biomarker monitoring in the summary of product characteristics (SmPC) for psychotropic drugs: overview and applicability in clinical practice. J Psychopharmacol Oxf Engl. 2015;29(12):1248–54.

Ng F, Mammen OK, Wilting I, Sachs GS, Ferrier IN, Cassidy F, et al. The International Society for Bipolar Disorders (ISBD) consensus guidelines for the safety monitoring of bipolar disorder treatments. Bipolar Disord. 2009;11(6):559–95.

Paton C, Adroer R, Barnes TRE. Monitoring lithium therapy: the impact of a quality improvement programme in the UK. Bipolar Disord. 2013;15(8):865–75.

Perlis RH. Use of treatment guidelines in clinical decision making in bipolar disorder: a pilot survey of clinicians. Curr Med Res Opin. 2007;23(3):467–75.

Rej S, AlAqeel B, Segal M, Low NCP, Mucsi I, Holcroft C, et al. Is environmental temperature related to renal symptoms, serum lithium levels, and other laboratory test results in current lithium users? Hum Psychopharmacol. 2014;29(4):392–6.

Rothschild JM, Mann K, Keohane CA, Williams DH, Foskett C, Rosen SL, et al. Medication safety in a psychiatric hospital. Gen Hosp Psychiatry. 2007;29(2):156–62.

Sani G, Perugi G, Tondo L. Treatment of bipolar disorder in a lifetime perspective: is lithium still the best choice? Clin Drug Investig. 2017;37(8):13–27.

Severus WE, Kleindienst N, Seemüller F, Frangou S, Möller HJ, Greil W. What is the optimal serum lithium level in the long-term treatment of bipolar disorder–a review? Bipolar Disord. 2008;10(2):231–7.

Tondo L, Abramowicz M, Alda M, Bauer M, Bocchetta A, Bolzani L, et al. Long-term lithium treatment in bipolar disorder: effects on glomerular filtration rate and other metabolic parameters. Int J Bipolar Disord. 2017;5(1):27.

Tran V-T, Barnes C, Montori VM, Falissard B, Ravaud P. Taxonomy of the burden of treatment: a multi-country web-based qualitative study of patients with chronic conditions. BMC Med. 2015;14(13):115.

Tukey JW. Exploratory data analysis. Boston: Addison-Wesley; 1977.

van de Beek LM, Ouwens MA, de Vries PL, Hummelen JW. Lithium levels need to be monitored: discrepancies between guidelines and practice. Tijdschr Voor Psychiatr. 2010;52(6):367–73.

van Melick EJM, Wilting I, Meinders AE, Egberts TCG. Prevalence and determinants of thyroid disorders in elderly patients with affective disorders: lithium and nonlithium patients. Am J Geriatr Psychiatry Off J Am Assoc Geriatr Psychiatry. 2010;18(5):395–403.

Wilting I, Movig KL, Moolenaar M, Hekster YA, Brouwers JR, Heerdink ER, et al. Drug-drug interactions as a determinant of elevated lithium serum levels in daily clinical practice. Bipolar Disord. 2005;7(3):274–80.

Wilting I, Fase S, Martens EP, Heerdink ER, Nolen WA, Egberts ACG. The impact of environmental temperature on lithium serum levels. Bipolar Disord. 2007;9(6):603–8.

Wright A, Sittig DF. Automated development of order sets and corollary orders by data mining in an ambulatory computerized physician order entry system. AMIA Annu Symp Proc AMIA Symp. 2006;2006:819–23.

Zarin DA, Young JL, West JC. Challenges to evidence-based medicine: a comparison of patients and treatments in randomized controlled trials with patients and treatments in a practice research network. Soc Psychiatry Psychiatr Epidemiol. 2005;40(1):27–35.

Zivanovic O. Lithium: a classic drug-Frequently discussed, but, sadly, seldom prescribed! Aust N Z J Psychiatry. 2017;1:4867417695889.

13

Mentalization deficit in bipolar patients during an acute depressive and manic episode: association with cognitive functions

Anna Bodnar and Janusz K. Rybakowski*

Abstract

Background: A number of studies in bipolar patients have shown a deficit in mentalization (theory of mind), one of the main aspects of social cognition. The aim of current study was to assess both cognitive and affective mentalization in well-defined groups of depressed and manic bipolar patients, compared to healthy control subjects, using a battery of tests measuring mentalization processes. The second aim was to investigate a possible relationship between cognitive and affective mentalization and cognitive functions in bipolar patients during a depressive and manic episode.

Methods: The study involved 25 bipolar disorder type I patients (10 male, 15 female) during a depressive episode (mean 24 ± 2 points in the 17-item Hamilton Depression Rating Scale) and 25 patients (10 male, 15 female) during a manic episode (mean 27 ± 4 points in the Young Mania Rating Scale). The control group consisted of 25 healthy subjects (10 male, 15 female) without psychiatric disorders. To measure mentalization, a revised version of the Reading the Mind in the Eyes (R-MET), the Strange Stories (SS), the Faux Pas Recognition (FPR), and the Moving Shapes Paradigm (MSP) tests were used. Assessment of cognitive functioning was made using the Digit Span, Trail Making, and Wisconsin Card Sorting Tests.

Results: In bipolar patients significant deficits in both cognitive and affective mentalization were demonstrated during both acute depressive and manic episodes. The impairment in FPR in manic patients was more severe than that in the depressive ones. On the other hand, in MSP, manic patients showed significantly increased intentionality for non-mentalization animations, compared with depressive patients and for "cause and effect" animations compared with control subjects. A significant relationship was found between the decrease in cognitive and affective mentalization and deficits of cognitive functions during both the depressive and manic episodes.

Conclusions: The results obtained confirm the deficits of mentalization in bipolar I patients, during both acute depressive and manic episodes. We found that in such patients mentalization deficits significantly correlated with cognitive dysfunctions more so during depressive episodes.

Keywords: Bipolar disorder, Mentalization, Theory of mind, Cognitive mentalization, Affective mentalization, Bipolar depression, Mania, Cognitive functions

Background

The ability to mentalize (mentalization, theory of mind—ToM) about other people's mental and emotional states forms one of the main aspects of social cognition. This term was introduced by Premack and Woodruff (1978), on the basis of their study of chimpanzees, as an ability to explain the activities and behaviors observed in other individuals by referring to their mental status. The past two decades of mentalization studies in humans have lead to a proposal that mentalization contains both cognitive and affective elements (Shamay-Tsoory et al. 2007). Cognitive mentalization is an inference about the

*Correspondence: janusz.rybakowski@gmail.com
Department of Adult Psychiatry, Poznan University of Medical Sciences, ul.Szpitalna 27/33, 60-572 Poznan, Poland

cognitive mental state, mainly beliefs, of other persons. Affective mentalization is an inference about the emotional state of other persons. Distinguishing cognitive and affective mentalization has also been proposed on the basis of studies which demonstrated different neural correlates of these two domains. Hynes et al. (2006), in a functional magnetic resonance study, showed that the medial orbitofrontal lobe, defined as Brodmann's areas 11 and 25, was preferentially involved in affective mentalization. This corresponded with Shamay-Tsoory et al. (2006) study showing an impairment of affective mentalizations in subjects having lesions in the ventromedial prefrontal cortex. On the other hand, Kalbe et al. (2010) using a repetitive transcranial magnetic stimulation (rTMS) approach, indicated the right dorsolateral prefrontal cortex (DLPFC) as the brain structure mostly connected with cognitive mentalization.

Previous research has suggested that impaired mentalization (ToM) forms the core handicap in autism subjects (Happé 1994). Also, two decades ago, a deficit in mentalization was demonstrated in schizophrenia (Frith and Corcoran 1996) and, in subsequent studies, it has been confirmed as an essential feature of this illness (Green et al. 2015). The first study on mentalization in bipolar disorder (BD) was performed by Kerr et al. (2003). This involved 20 patients during a manic episode, 15 in a depressive episode, 13 in remission, and 15 control subjects and used a method of six short stories. They found deficits in mentalization during manic and depressive episodes where the mean intensity of mania was 13 points, according to the Bech Mania Rating Scale, and 16 points for depression, according to the Beck Depression Inventory. In subsequent research, using tests of higher levels of complexity, the authors demonstrated that such deficits in BD also occur during remission periods (Inoue et al. 2004; Bora et al. 2005). Montag et al. (2010) demonstrated that bipolar patients scored significantly lower than control subjects for the cognitive aspect of ToM but not for the affective one. In recent meta-analyses of this topic, a deficit in ToM in bipolar patients in both acute episodes and during the euthymic state has been evidenced (Samamé et al. 2015; Bora et al. 2016). However, lately, Haag et al. (2016) did not show differences in visual theory of mind abilities between euthymic bipolar patients and healthy controls.

In some mentalization research studies, a concomitant assessment of cognitive functions has been performed. In a few, a possible relationship between mentalization and cognitive functions has been suggested. In the study of Bora et al. (2005), BD patients displayed an impairment in many cognitive tasks, including those related to sustained attention. Lahera et al. (2008) showed impaired sustained attention and executive functions in such patients. In the study of Ioannidi et al. (2015) BD patients had poorer performances in verbal memory and visuospatial working memory during both the acute and euthymic phases of the illness. Impaired immediate memory and executive functions were only noted during episodes of illness. Olley et al. (2005) showed an impaired performance on the Stroop task in remitted BD patients and a correlation between ToM and the CANTAB Stocking of Cambridge task. However, Wiener et al. (2011) while finding significant impairments on the subtests of CANTAB battery in BD patients, did not find a relationship between these tests and mentalization results. Recently, Van Rheenen et al. (2014) showed a significant correlation between tests measuring social cognition and neurocognition but not between neurocognition and emotional regulation.

It is thus conceivable that mentalization abnormalities could be connected with manic and/or depressive symptoms of BD. Therefore, in this study, an attempt was made to assess both cognitive and affective mentalization in well-defined groups of manic and depressed bipolar patients, compared to healthy control subjects, using a battery of tests measuring mentalization processes. We also hypothesized that, during an acute manic and depressive episode such abnormalities can be connected with cognitive functions. Therefore, the second aim of the study was to investigate a possible relationship between cognitive and affective mentalization and cognitive functions in these groups of bipolar patients and healthy subjects.

Methods

Participants

The study was performed on 50 patients with bipolar mood disorder type I (20 male, 30 female) aged 19–65 years, with a duration of illness of 11 $\pm$ 10 years. They were hospitalized in the inpatient clinic of the Department of Adult Psychiatry, Poznan University of Medical Sciences, on account of an acute manic or depressive episode of BD. A consensus diagnosis of BD was made for each patient by at least two psychiatrists according to DSM-IV criteria (SCID) (First et al. 1996). Exclusion criteria covered any other psychiatric co-morbidity or serious medical condition.

Twenty-five patients (10 male, 15 female), aged 41 $\pm$ 14 years, were studied during a depressive episode, and 25 patients (10 male, 15 female) aged 35 $\pm$ 14 years during an acute manic episode. The criterion for inclusion in the study for depressive patients was an intensity of depression, as assessed by the 17-item Hamilton Depression Rating Scale (HDRS) (Hamilton 1980)—of $\geq$ 18 points and for manic patients an intensity of mania, as assessed by the Young Mania Rating Scale (YMRS) (Young et al. 1978)—of $\geq$ 20 points.

On the day of study, the patients received pharmacological treatment: antidepressant and/or mood-stabilizing drugs in depression and antipsychotic and/or mood-stabilizing drugs in mania. The number of patients (in parentheses), taking individual drugs was as follows: lithium (23), olanzapine (20), valproate (20), quetiapine (16), venlafaxine (10), haloperidol (8), paroxetine (8), lamotrigine (5), aripiprazole (4), risperidone (4), carbamazepine (4), topiramate (2), bupropion (1), escitalopram (1), mirtazapine (1).

A comparison group consisted of ten healthy men and 15 healthy women, aged 36 ± 11 years who had volunteered to be studied in response to an internet advertisement. They did not report any psychiatric disturbance in themselves or in any 1st degree members of their family.

The number of years of education was 13 ± 3 years in depressed patients, in manic patients 15 ± 3 years, and in control subjects 16 ± 2 years.

Assessment of mentalization

A revised version of the Reading the Mind in the Eyes Test, the Strange Stories Test, the Faux Pas Recognition Test, and the Moving Shapes Paradigm were used for the measurement of mentalization. Previously, these scales had been translated into Polish by three independent translators, then, the best version was selected and back-translation performed. The reliability of the tests was assessed by the Cronbach's alpha factor.

The Reading Mind in Eyes Test (R-MET)

The revised version of the R-MET consists of 36 photos presenting the eyes and their adjacent areas. All the pictures show exactly the same region of the face—from the middle of the nose to the area above the brows. The subject being studied is asked to choose one of the four terms which best describes what the person on the picture is thinking or feeling. This test assesses the ability to identify both cognitive and affective mental states because, for inferring what the person on the picture is thinking or feeling it includes, among others, such terms as suspicious (cognitive component) and fearful (affective component) (Baron-Cohen et al. (2001)).

Strange Stories (SS)

This tool was introduced by Happé (1994) and it assesses the ability to understand a lie, a white lie, a figurative expression, irony, or persuasion. After presentation of each story, the subject is asked to answer a question connected with its content. A correct answer requires an inference about the mental state of the character in the story. In this study, five stories for assessing cognitive mentalization, as well as five control stories requiring inferences about physical causality are used.

The Faux Pas Recognition Test (FPR)

This test was introduced by Stone et al. (1998). By definition, a faux pas occurs when someone says something without thinking that the person who hears it may not wish to hear it or be offended or hurt by it. The test used in this study consists of ten stories arranged in random order—five stories with social condition mistakes and five control stories. The subject being studied is asked to read the story and answer a few questions connected with it. In the understanding and recognition of the Faux Pas, both cognitive and affective mentalizations are involved.

Moving Shapes Paradigm (MSP)

This is a collection of 12 computer animations designed by Abell et al. (2000). Each lasts 34–35 s and presents two moving triangles: one large red and one small blue. In this study three groups of four animations each, were used: (1) random animations: triangles moving about aimlessly without interactions; (2) cause-and-effect animations: the triangles are interacting: following, fighting, dancing, etc.; (3) mentalization animations: the triangles are mutually reacting to each other's mental states (e.g., 1 triangle is trying to seduce, to ridicule, or to scare the other). The subject studied is asked to view the animations which are presented in a pseudo-random sequence and answer a question: What happened during the animation? Two criteria are assessed: appropriateness of the attribution and the correctness of the intentionality of the story (random, cause-and-effect, mentalization).

Assessment of cognitive functioning

Assessment of cognitive functioning was made using The Digit Span, Trail Making and Wisconsin Card Sorting Tests.

Digit Span Test (DST)

This test is one of the subtests of the Wechsler Adult Intelligence Scale-Revised. The first part consists of remembering and presenting a series of digits in the correct order, and measures short-term auditory memory. The second part consists of remembering and presenting a series of digits in the reverse of the order presented, and measures verbal working memory.

Trail Making Test (TMT)

The Polish version of the Trail Making Test (TMT) is an element of the Halstead–Reitan Test battery (Reitan 1958). Part A of the test consists of connecting, by a continuous line, the points between 1 and 25 as quickly as possible and measures psychomotor speed and visual–motor coordination. Part B consists of connecting, by a continuous line as quickly as possible, the digits alternatively with consecutive letters i.e., $1 - A - 2 - B - 3 - C$, etc., and reflects the ability to shift strategy and assess executive function and visuospatial working memory. The results, separately for *A* and *B*, are presented as the duration of performance (in seconds), and the number of errors.

Wisconsin Card Sorting Test (WCST)

The Wisconsin Card Sorting Test (WCST) assesses the executive functions, controlling cognitive processes and the strategy of solving problems. It is also a tool for the assessment of working memory, abstract thinking, and "set shifting," i.e., the ability to display flexibility in the face of changing schedules of reinforcement. The subject is asked to match the 64 cards, according to color, shape, and number of elements. He/she is not told how to match. However, the subject is informed whether a particular match is right or wrong. After ten correct matches, the criterion is changed without informing the participant. The test is terminated when six categories are correctly arranged or all the cards are used. Percentages of errors, of perseverative responses, of conceptual responses, and the number of completed categories are calculated. A computer version of the WCST (Heaton 1981) was used in this study.

Experimental procedure

The experimental procedure consisted of two parts, over 2 days, each lasting about 1 h, performed by one of the authors (AB). On the first day, mentalization tests were performed. On the second day, empathy and cognitive functions were assessed. At the time of study, clinical assessment by the HDRS or YMRS scale in the patient was performed by a psychiatrist who was taking care of the patient in the ward.

Statistics

The one-way analysis of variance (ANOVA) with Tukey's post hoc test was performed. The belongingness to the three groups: depressed, manic, and control subjects made the independent variable. The dependent variables included selected components of mentalization and cognitive functions as well as clinical factors. The r-Pearson Test was used to determine any correlation between the variables. The calculations were done using the IBM SPSS 21.0. The level of statistical significance was determined at $p < 0.05$.

Results

As calculated by the analysis of variance, the three groups studied did not show differences due to age: $F(2,72) = 1.37$; $p = 0.26$. They did, however, differ as to years of education: $F(2,72) = 7.96$; $p = 0.001$. The control group had higher levels of education compared to the depressed group ($p < 0.01$) but not compared to the manic group: ($p = 0.32$). The patients with depression had marginally lower levels of education compared to the manic ones ($p = 0.06$).

On the day of study, the mean intensity of depression in the depressive patients, as measured with HDRS, was 24 ± 2 points and the mean intensity of mania in the manic patients, as measured by YMRS, was 27 ± 4 points.

For mentalization measures, assessed in the whole sample, the internal consistency coefficients were good, with a Cronbach's alpha for the Reading the Mind in the Eyes: total 0.72, affective 0.52, cognitive 0.63; for the Strange Stories: total 0.83, control stories 0.70, mentalization stories 0.77, for the Faux Pas Recognition: total 0.91, affective 0.68, cognitive 0.86; and for the Moving Shapes Paradigm Tests: appropriateness 0.70, intentionality 0.52.

The results of the Reading the Mind in the Eyes, Strange Stories, and Faux Pas Recognition Test are presented in Table 1.

There were significant differences between groups in the Reading the Mind in the Eyes Test. Post hoc comparisons revealed a deficit in mentalization, both cognitive and affective, measured by this test, in both the depressive and manic patients, compared to healthy subjects. This was also the case for the Strange Stories Test, where both depressive and manic patients obtained significantly worse results than the control subjects, for both mentalization and control stories.

Likewise, there were significant differences between groups in the Faux Pas Recognition Test. Post hoc comparisons revealed a significant reduction in ability for such recognition in both depressive and manic patients, compared to healthy subjects. Furthermore, manic patients scored worse in this test, compared to the depressive ones. Such an impairment applied to both cognitive and affective mentalization in both groups of bipolar patients, and the manic patients had greater deficits in affective mentalization, compared to depressed ones.

All the differences above remained valid after corrections for multiple testing.

The results of the Moving Shapes Paradigm are shown in Table 2.

Significant differences between groups were also observed for mentalization abilities as measured by the Moving Shapes Paradigm Test. Post hoc comparisons revealed a deficit in both cognitive and affective mentalization, measured by this test, in both depressive and manic patients, compared to healthy subjects. These differences remained valid after corrections for multiple testing.

For the mentalization and random animations both depressed and manic patients scored lower than the control subjects, while, in "cause and effect" animations, this

Table 1 The results of mentalization assessed by the Reading the Mind in the Eyes (R-MET), Strange Stories (SS), and Faux Pas Recognition (FPR) tests during depression (*A*), mania (*B*) and in healthy control subjects (*C*)

Mentalization	Group						Analysis of variance			Post hoc test		
	Depression		Mania		Controls							
	Mean	SD	Mean	SD	Mean	SD	$F(2,72)$	p	Eta^2	$A-B$	$A-C$	$B-C$
R-MET-total	21.36	5.12	23.32	3.94	28.12	3.41	16.99	< 0.001	0.32	0.235	< 0.001	< 0.001
R-MET-cognitive	11.16	3.08	12.04	2.68	15.00	1.83	15.17	< 0.001	0.30	0.454	< 0.001	< 0.001
R-MET-affective	10.20	2.87	11.28	2.34	13.12	2.55	8.08	≤ 0.001	0.18	0.311	< 0.001	0.038
SS-total	11.64	3.57	9.96	3.74	17.24	2.05	35.28	< 0.001	0.50	0.161	< 0.001	< 0.001
SS-mentalization stories	6.56	2.02	5.48	2.20	8.96	1.17	23.09	< 0.001	0.39	0.106	< 0.001	< 0.001
SS-control stories	5.08	2.23	4.48	2.33	8.24	1.45	24.43	< 0.001	0.40	0.555	< 0.001	< 0.001
FPR-total	64.52	7.63	59.00	9.82	75.08	4.01	29.3	< 0.001	0.45	0.031	< 0.001	< 0.001
FPR-cognitive	20.16	3.91	17.52	4.89	26.32	2.61	33.22	< 0.001	0.48	0.051	< 0.001	< 0.001
FPR-affective	7.64	1.63	6.36	1.80	9.20	1.04	21.74	< 0.001	0.38	0.011	0.002	< 0.001

Table 2 The results of mentalization assessed by the Moving Shapes Paradigm during depression (*A*), mania (*B*) and in healthy control subjects (*C*)

Moving Shapes Paradigm	Group						Analysis of variance			Post hoc test		
	Depression		Mania		Controls							
	Mean	SD	Mean	SD	Mean	SD	$F(2.72)$	p	Eta^2	$A-B$	$A-C$	$B-C$
Mentalization animations	2.00	1.12	2.24	1.16	3.16	0.75	8.89	< 0.001	0.20	0.688	< 0.001	0.006
Cause-and-effect animations	3.00	1.12	2.48	1.05	3.48	0.71	6.58	0.002	0.15	0.150	0.197	0.002
Random animations	2.08	1.29	1.12	1.01	3.16	0.99	21.34	< 0.001	0.37	0.008	0.003	< 0.001
Affective mentalization	2.96	1.57	2.88	1.45	4.24	1.59	6.16	0.003	0.15	0.982	0.012	0.007
Appropriateness total	11.24	4.08	9.64	2.84	17.00	3.77	28.75	< 0.001	0.44	0.266	< 0.001	< 0.001
Appropriateness mentalization	3.04	1.81	3.28	1.43	5.68	1.49	21.14	< 0.001	0.37	0.855	< 0.001	< 0.001
Appropriateness cause-and-effect	4.76	2.20	4.20	1.38	5.48	1.50	3.42	0.038	0.09	0.492	0.313	0.029
Appropriateness random	3.52	2.10	2.16	1.75	6.20	2.06	27.01	< 0.001	0.43	0.046	< 0.001	< 0.001
Intentionality total	26.80	6.27	32.84	5.24	28.28	3.62	9.30	< 0.001	0.21	< 0.001	0.571	0.007
Intentionality mentalization	12.72	3.16	13.96	2.61	16.28	2.05	11.69	< 0.001	0.25	0.228	< 0.001	0.008
Intentionality cause-and-effect	9.76	2.40	11.72	2.32	9.64	1.87	6.99	0.002	0.16	0.007	0.980	0.004
Intentionality random	4.72	3.59	7.56	3.68	2.36	2.66	15.20	< 0.001	0.30	0.010	0.039	< 0.001

was only the case for manic patients. Both groups were impaired in affective mentalization and on appropriateness for the total, mentalization and random animations. These differences remained valid after corrections for multiple testing.

However, for appropriateness of "cause and effect" animations, this was only observed in manic patients (not valid after multiple testing). For intentionality, both groups showed an impaired score in mentalization animation (valid after multiple testing) and increased scores in random animations (valid after multiple testing only for mania). For intentionality, total and "cause and effect," manic patients scored higher than those depressed (valid after multiple testing only for "cause and effect") and, in "cause and effect" animations higher than the control subjects (not valid after multiple testing).

For each of the four mentalization tests the differences between groups did not change when the results were controlled for the years of education.

The results of all the cognitive tests (Digit Span Test, TMT *A*, TMT *B*, WCST: percentage of errors, percentage of perseverative responses, completed categories, percentage of conceptual responses) were lower in both manic and depressive patients compared to healthy subjects while no difference between depressive and manic patients was found. To assess any possible relationship between mentalization measures and cognitive function tests, a correlation analysis of the results obtained in

Table 3 Relationship between mentalization assessed by the Reading the Mind in the Eyes (R-MET), Strange Stories (SS), Faux Pas Recognition (FPR), and Moving Shapes Paradigm (MSP) tests and the results of cognitive function tests: a correlation analysis in a depressive episode

	Digit Span Test	TMT A	TMT B	WCST percentage of errors	WCST percentage of perseverative responses	WCST completed categories	WCST percentage of conceptual responses
Mentalization R-MET-total	0.330	– 0.452*	– 0.341	– 0.622**	– 0.469*	0.575**	0.533**
Mentalization FPR-total	0.214	– 0.438*	– 0.507**	– 0.685**	– 0.430*	0.445*	0.704**
Cognitive mentalization R-MET	0.378	– 0.446*	– 0.277	– 0.556**	– 0.555**	0.473*	0.413*
Cognitive mentalization SS	0.302	– 0.257	– 0.065	– 0.532**	– 0.616**	0.504*	0.505*
Cognitive mentalization FPR	0.025	– 0.328	– 0.328	– 0.553**	– 0.272	0.330	0.618**
Cognitive mentalization MSP	0.164	– 0.420*	– 0.579**	– 0.561**	– 0.352	0.522**	0.631**
Affective mentalization R-MET	0.183	– 0.329	– 0.310	– 0.513**	– 0.241	0.519**	0.508**
Affective mentalization FPR	– 0.046	– 0.104	– 0.291	– 0.436*	– 0.220	0.228	0.552**
Affective mentalization MSP	0.216	– 0.165	– 0.305	– 0.342	– 0.301	0.372	0.282

* $p < 0.05$; ** $p < 0.01$

Table 4 Relationship between mentalization assessed by the Reading the Mind in the Eyes (R-MET), Strange Stories (SS), Faux Pas Recognition (FPR), and Moving Shapes Paradigm (MSP) tests and the results of cognitive function tests: a correlation analysis in a manic episode

	Digit Span Test	TMT *A*	TMT *B*	WCST percentage of errors	WCST percentage of perseverative responses	WCST completed categories	WCST percentage of conceptual responses
Mentalization R-MET-total	0.240	– 0.218	– 0.322	– 0.392	– 0.297	0.257	0.424*
Mentalization FPR-total	– 0.291	0.297	0.246	– 0.435*	– 0.257	0.420*	0.424*
Cognitive mentalization R-MET	0.292	– 0.184	– 0.458*	– 0.240	– 0.069	0.164	0.272
Cognitive mentalization SS	– 0.131	0.001	– 0.335	– 0.277	– 0.107	0.264	0.160
Cognitive mentalization FPR	0.112	– 0.157	– 0.095	– 0.430*	– 0.194	0.423*	0.442*
Cognitive mentalization MSP	0.225	– 0.518**	0.015	0.102	– 0.174	– 0.080	– 0.094
Affective mentalization R-MET	0.070	– 0.156	– 0.017	– 0.387	– 0.422*	0.246	0.403*
Affective mentalization FPR	– 0.132	0.019	– 0.048	– 0.546**	– 0.240	0.567**	0.583**
Affective mentalization MSP	– 0.037	– 0.488*	– 0.026	– 0.212	– 0.133	0.158	0.143

* $p < 0.05$; ** $p < 0.01$

depressive and manic episodes was performed and is presented in Tables 3 and 4.

An analysis of a relationship between mentalization and cognitive function tests during depression did not find any correlations between mentalization and the

Digit Span Test. On the other hand, 32 correlations were obtained between the four mentalization tests and the results of the TMT and WCST. A higher level of general mentalization was associated with better cognitive planning and efficiency of thinking, as well as with a fewer number of errors and perseverative responses in WCST. A better performance on the Faux Pas Recognition Test was connected with psychomotor speed, visual perception, visual–spatial coordination, and working memory. A higher level of cognitive mentalization was associated with better cognitive planning and efficiency of thinking (except for FPR), with a fewer number of errors and perseverative responses in WCST (R-MET and SS) and with psychomotor speed, visual perception, and visual–spatial coordination, and working memory (MSP). A higher level of affective mentalization was associated with a fewer number of errors and a higher percentage of conceptual responses in WCST (R-MET, FPR).

As in depression, the analysis of a relationship between mentalization and cognitive function tests during mania did not find any correlations between mentalization and the Digit Span Test. Fifteen correlations were obtained between the four mentalization tests and the results of the TMT and WCST. A higher level of general mentalization was associated with better cognitive planning. Better performance on the Faux Pas Recognition Test was connected with efficiency of thinking and fewer errors on WCST. A higher level of cognitive mentalization assessed by MSP was associated with better psychomotor speed and visual–spatial coordination and, when assessed by the R-MET test, with better attention and visual–spatial working memory. A higher level of affective mentalization was associated with better cognitive planning, a fewer number of perseverative responses (R-MET), better efficacy of thinking (FPR), and better psychomotor speed and visual–motor coordination.

In both tables no correlation coefficient was 0.64 or higher which would be necessary to withstand correction for multiple testing.

Discussion

The first finding of our study is the demonstration of deficits in mentalization (theory of mind) in bipolar patients, during both acute manic and depressive episodes. In our study, this was evidenced by the use of a number of tests for measuring mentalization These included the Reading the Mind in the Eyes, the Strange Stories, the Faux Pas Recognition Tests, and the Moving Shapes Paradigm Tests. The results obtained indicate an impairment of both cognitive and affective mentalization in the groups of bipolar patients studied. This corresponds to the results of recent meta-analyses (Samamé et al. 2015; Bora et al. 2016).

Further analysis of our mentalization results showed that there were some differences in this respect between depressive and manic patients. In the Faux Pas Recognition Test the impairments in manic patients were more severe than in the depressive ones in both the total as well as cognitive and affective scores. On the other hand, in the Moving Shapes Paradigm Test, manic patients showed significantly increased intentionality for non-mentalization animations, compared to depressive patients and, for "cause and effect" animations, compared to the control subjects. This may be connected with the fact that manic patients perceive social stimuli from strangers as more positive and directed at them and not as random behavior (Piff et al. 2012). Increased perception of intentionality in manic patients could also correspond with the increased affective empathy (over-empathising) we reported in bipolar patients during a manic episode (Bodnar and Rybakowski 2017).

The second finding of our study is that, in bipolar patients during an acute episode, mentalization deficits significantly correlated with cognitive dysfunctions. Impaired neurocognitive functioning in BD, more marked during an acute episode, is a well-demonstrated phenomenon (Tsitsipa and Fountoulakis 2015). In the current study we found many correlations between all the four mentalization tests applied and the results of such neuropsychological tests as TMT and WCST which measure psychomotor speed, visual–motor coordination, visuospatial working memory, and executive functions. Such correlations were more numerous in depressive than in manic patients. This may correspond to other studies pointing to cognitive dysfunctions in BD, concomitant to mentalization disturbances (Bora et al. 2005; Lahera et al. 2008; Wiener et al. 2011; Ioannidi et al. 2015), as well as to a relationship between mentalization and cognitive functions reported in such patients (Olley et al. 2005; Van Rheenen et al. 2014).

Disturbances of mentalization, as well as their relationship with cognitive dysfunctions during acute episodes of BD, should be regarded in the context of brain abnormalities in this illness. The neural circuits underlying the pathophysiology of mood disorders mostly include the prefrontal cortex and anatomically related limbic structures (Price and Drevets 2012). According to Strakowski et al. (2006) the main role is played by the anterior limbic network comprising the ventral and orbital parts of the prefrontal cortex, connected reciprocally with the amygdala, parahippocampal gyrus, insula, and the anterior part of the cingulated gyrus. As mentioned previously, the ventral and orbital parts of the prefrontal cortex have been suggested for affective mentalization (Hynes et al. 2006; Shamay-Tsoory et al. 2006) while Kalbe et al. (2010) suggests that the brain structure mostly associated with cognitive mentalization is the right dorsolateral prefrontal cortex (DLPFC). However, a recent study of Yeh et al. (2015) did not find differences between groups of patients having DLPFC vs ventromedial prefrontal cortex damage to both cognitive and affective aspects of mentalization.

In our study we obtained significant correlations between the results of the four tests measuring mentalization studies, and such cognitive function tests as the TMT and WCST. A meta-analysis of structural neuroimaging studies showed that the performance on these tests is related to the volume of the prefrontal cortex, mainly the lateral and medial parts of it (Yuan and Raz 2014). Recent studies have also shown an association between the dorsomedial prefrontal cortex and TMT B performance (Miskin et al. 2016) and between DLPFC and WCST (Boschin et al. 2016). This may indicate that a DLPFC abnormality in bipolar patients plays a role for both mentalization deficits and cognitive disorders. Such an abnormality and the resulting disturbances are less intense in BD patients than in schizophrenia (Bora and Pantelis 2016) as was confirmed in our study on WCST performance (Rybakowski et al. 2006).

Although the discussion above mainly concerned the prefrontal cortex it should be indicated that other areas of the brain may be also important for mentalization processes. According to a meta-analysis of Molenberghs et al. (2016), besides the prefrontal cortex, the second most important brain structure for mentalization is the temporoparietal junction. However, there is no data on the involvement of the temporoparietal junction in such cognitive tests as TMT and WCST.

Based on the differences obtained between manic and depressive patients, and especially for an increased intentionality for random and "cause and effect" animations in manic patients, it can be speculated that these are connected with differences in functional brain activities in these episodes. An example of this can be the right amygdala–hippocampal connectivity, increased in mania and decreased in depression (Li et al. 2015).

Conclusions

The limitation of our study is that the bipolar patients were actively treated during the study, receiving antidepressant and/or mood-normalizing drugs in depression and antipsychotic and/or mood-normalizing drugs in mania. Another limitation may be a difference in the mean education level between the bipolar depressive patients and the control group. On the other hand, the strength of our study is the use of four test for measuring mentalization and the well-designed groups of depressive and manic patients. Therefore, bearing these limitations in mind, we believe that our results strongly suggest that mentalization is significantly impaired during acute episodes of BD disorder although there may be some differences between depressive and manic episodes. Such impairments significantly correlate with the results of neuropsychological tests such as TMT and WCST.

Abbreviations

BD: bipolar disorder; DLPFC: dorsolateral prefrontal cortex; DST: Digit Span Test; FPR: Faux Pas Recognition Test; HDRS: Hamilton Depression Rating Scale; MSP: Moving Shapes Paradigm; R-MET: Reading the Mind in the Eyes Test; rTMS: repetitive transcranial magnetic stimulation; SS: Strange Stories; ToM: theory of mind; WCST: Wisconsin Card Sorting Test; YMRS: Young Mania Rating Scale.

Authors' contributions

AB designed the study, conducted the literature search, performed mentalization assessment, made statistical analysis, and wrote the first draft of the paper. JKR designed the study, recruited the patients, took part in the elaboration of results, and wrote the final version of the manuscript. Both authors read and approved the final manuscript.

Competing interests

The authors declare that they have no competing interests.

Funding

Not applicable.

References

Abell F, Happe F, Frith U. Do triangles play tricks? Attribution of mental states to animated shapes in normal and abnormal development. J Cogn Dev. 2000;15:1–20.

Baron-Cohen S, Wheelwright S, Hill J, Raste Y, Plumb I. The, "Reading the Mind in the Eyes" Test revised version: a study with normal adults, and adults with Asperger syndrome or high-functioning autism. J Child Psychol Psychiatry. 2001;42:241–51.

Bodnar A, Rybakowski JK. Increased affective empathy in bipolar patients during a manic episode. Rev Bras Psiquiatr. 2017. doi:10.1590/1516-4446-2016-2101.

Bora E, Pantelis C. Social cognition in schizophrenia in comparison to bipolar disorder: a meta-analysis. Schizophr Res. 2016;175:72–8.

Bora E, Vahip S, Gonul AS, Akdeniz F, Alkan M, Ogut M, et al. Evidence for theory of mind deficits in euthymic patients with bipolar disorder. Acta Psychiatr Scand. 2005;112:110–6.

Bora E, Bartholomeusz C, Pantelis C. Meta-analysis of theory of mind (ToM) impairment in bipolar disorder. Psychol Med. 2016;46:253–64.

Boschin EA, Mars RB, Buckley MJ. Transcranial magnetic stimulation to dorsolateral prefrontal cortex affects conflict-induced behavioural adaptation in a Wisconsin Card Sorting Test analogue. Neuropsychologia. 2016;94:36–43.

First MB, Spitzer RL, Gibbon M, Williams J. Structured clinical interview for DSM-IV axis I disorders. Clinician version (SCID-CV). Washington, DC: American Psychiatric Press Inc; 1996.

Frith CD, Corcoran R. Exploring 'theory of mind' in people with schizophrenia. Psychol Med. 1996;26:521–30.

Green MF, Horan WP, Lee J. Social cognition in schizophrenia. Nat Rev Neurosci. 2015;16:620–31.

Haag S, Haffner P, Quinlivan E, Brüne M, Stamm T. No differences in visual theory of mind abilities between euthymic bipolar patients and healthy controls. Int J Bipolar Disord. 2016;4:20.

Hamilton M. Rating depressive patients. J Clin Psychiatry. 1980;42:21–4.

Happé FG. An advanced test of theory of mind: understanding of story characters' thoughts and feelings by able autistic, mentally handicapped, and normal children and adults. J Autism Dev Disord. 1994;24:129–54.

Heaton RK. A manual for the Wisconsin Card Sorting Test. Odessa: Psychological Assessment Resources; 1981.
Hynes CA, Baird AA, Grafton ST. Differential role of the orbital frontal lobe in emotional versus cognitive perspective-taking. Neuropsychologia. 2006;44:374–83.
Ioannidi N, Konstantakopoulos G, Sakkas D, Oulis P. The relationship of Theory ofMind with symptoms and cognitive impairment in bipolar disorder: a prospective study.Psychiatriki 2015;26:17–27
Inoue Y, Tonooka Y, Yamada K, Kanba S. Deficiency of theory of mind in patients with remitted mood disorder. J Affect Disord. 2004;82:403–9.
Kalbe E, Schlegel M, Sack AT, Nowak DA, Dafotakis M, Bangard C, et al. Dissociating cognitive from affective theory of mind: a TMS study. Cortex. 2010;46:769–80.
Kerr N, Dunbar RI, Bentall RP. Theory of mind deficits in bipolar affective disorder. J Affect Disord. 2003;73:253–9.
Lahera G, Montes JM, Benito A, Valdivia M, Medina E, Mirapeix I, et al. Theory of mind deficit in bipolar disorder: is it related to a previous history of psychotic symptoms? Psychiatry Res. 2008;161:309–17.
Li M, Huang C, Deng W, Ma X, Han Y, Wang Q, et al. Contrasting and convergent patterns of amygdala connectivity in mania and depression: a resting-state study. J Affect Disord. 2015;173:53–8.
Miskin N, Thesen T, Barr WB, Butler T, Wang X, Dugan P, et al. Prefrontal lobe structural integrity and Trail Making Test, part B: converging findings from surface-based cortical thickness and voxel-based lesion symptom analyses. Brain Imaging Behav. 2016;10:675–85.
Molenberghs P, Johnson H, Henry JD, Mattingley JB. Understanding the minds of others: a neuroimaging meta-analysis. Neurosci Biobehav Rev. 2016;65:276–91.
Montag C, Ehrlich A, Neuhaus K, Dziobek I, Heekeren HR, Heinz A, et al. Theory of mind impairments in euthymic bipolar patients. J Affect Disord. 2010;123:264–9.
Olley AL, Malhi GS, Bachelor J, Cahill CM, Mitchell PB, Berk M. Executive functioning and theory of mind in euthymic bipolar disorder. Bipolar Disord. 2005;7(Suppl 5):43–52.
Piff PK, Purcell A, Gruber J, Hertenstein MJ, Keltner D. Contact high: mania proneness and positive perception of emotional touches. Cogn Emot. 2012;26:1116–23.
Premack D, Woodruff G. Chimpanzee problem-solving: a test for comprehension. Science. 1978;202:532–5.
Price JL, Drevets WC. Neural circuits underlying the pathophysiology of mood disorders. Trends Cogn Sci. 2012;16:61–71.
Reitan RM. The relation of the Trail Making Test to organic brain damage. J Cons Psychol. 1958;19:393–4.
Rybakowski JK, Borkowska A, Skibinska M, Hauser J. Illness-specific association of val66met BDNF polymorphism with performance on Wisconsin Card Sorting Test in bipolar mood disorder. Mol Psychiatry. 2006;11:122–4.
Samamé C, Martino DJ, Strejilevich SA. An individual task meta-analysis of social cognition in euthymic bipolar disorders. J Affect Disord. 2015;173:146–53.
Shamay-Tsoory SG, Tibi-Elhanany Y, Aharon-Peretz J. The ventromedial prefrontal cortex is involved in understanding affective but not cognitive theory of mind stories. Soc Neurosci. 2006;1:149–66.
Shamay-Tsoory SG, Shur S, Barcai-Goodman L, Medlovich S, Harari H, Levkovitz Y. Dissociation of cognitive from affective components of theory of mind in schizophrenia. Psychiatry Res. 2007;149:11–23.
Stone VE, Baron-Cohen S, Knight RT. Frontal lobe contributions to theory of mind. J Cogn Neurosci. 1998;10:640–56.
Strakowski SM, Adler CM, De Bello MP. Metabolic dysfunction within the anterior limbic network in bipolar disorder: a model for studying new treatments. Neuropsychiatry Neuropsychol. 2006;1:5–14.
Tsitsipa E, Fountoulakis KN. The neurocognitive functioning in bipolar disorder: a systematic review of data. Ann Gen Psychiatry. 2015;14:42.
Van Rheenen TE, Meyer D, Rossell SL. Pathways between neurocognition, social cognition and emotion regulation in bipolar disorder. Acta Psychiatr Scand. 2014;130:397–405.
Wiener D, Andrzejewska M, Bodnar A, Rybakowski J. Disturbances of theory of mind and empathy in schizophrenia and bipolar affective illness (in Polish). Neuropsychiatry Neuropsychol. 2011;6:85–92.
Yeh ZT, Lo CY, Tsai MD, Tsai MC. Mentalizing ability in patients with prefrontal cortex damage. J Clin Exp Neuropsychol. 2015;37:128–39.
Young RC, Biggs JT, Ziegler VE, Meyer DA. A rating scale for mania: reliability, validity and sensitivity. Br J Psychiatry. 1978;133:429–35.
Yuan P, Raz N. Prefrontal cortex and executive functions in healthy adults: a meta-analysis of structural neuroimaging studies. Neurosci Biobehav Rev. 2014;42:180–92.

14

Does perfectionism in bipolar disorder pedigrees mediate associations between anxiety/stress and mood symptoms?

Justine Corry[1,2], Melissa Green[1,2,4], Gloria Roberts[1,2], Janice M. Fullerton[4,5], Peter R. Schofield[4,5] and Philip B. Mitchell[1,2,3*]

Abstract

Background: Bipolar disorder (BD) and the anxiety disorders are highly comorbid. The present study sought to examine perfectionism and goal attainment values as potential mechanisms of known associations between anxiety, stress and BD symptomatology. Measures of perfectionism and goal attainment values were administered to 269 members of BD pedigrees, alongside measures of anxiety and stress, and BD mood symptoms. Regression analyses were used to determine whether perfectionism and goal attainment values were related to depressive and (hypo) manic symptoms; planned mediation models were then used to test the potential for perfectionism to mediate associations between anxiety/stress and BD symptoms.

Results: Self-oriented perfectionism was associated with chronic depressive symptoms; socially-prescribed perfectionism was associated with chronic (hypo)manic symptoms. Self-oriented perfectionism mediated relationships between anxiety/stress and chronic depressive symptoms even after controlling for chronic hypomanic symptoms. Similarly, socially-prescribed perfectionism mediated associations between anxiety/stress and chronic hypomanic symptoms after controlling for chronic depressive symptoms. Goal attainment beliefs were not uniquely associated with chronic depressive or (hypo)manic symptoms.

Conclusions: Cognitive styles of perfectionism may explain the co-occurrence of anxiety and stress symptoms and BD symptoms. Psychological interventions for anxiety and stress symptoms in BD might therefore address perfectionism in attempt to reduce depression and (hypo)manic symptoms in addition to appropriate pharmacotherapy.

Keywords: Bipolar disorder, Anxiety, Stress, Psychology

Background

The high rate of comorbidity between anxiety disorders and bipolar disorder is well established (Pavlova et al. 2015). Anxiety disorders have been shown to precede the onset of bipolar disorder (BD) (de Graaf et al. 2003; Perugi et al. 2001) and there are high rates of anxiety disorders in families affected by BD (Nurnberger et al. 2011; Perich et al. 2015; Merikangas et al. 2014). However, the mechanisms that underlie the comorbidity between anxiety disorders and BD are not fully understood (Mitchell 2015; Provencher et al. 2012). To move beyond purely descriptive studies, we propose that these disorders co-occur because they share common maintaining processes (Harvey et al. 2004). Cognitive styles are important maintaining factors in cognitive models of psychopathology (Harvey et al. 2004), and we propose that the cognitive style of perfectionism may be an explanatory factor in the high co-occurrence of BD and AD's. Here, we specifically examined perfectionism as a potential mediator of known associations between anxiety and stress symptoms and mood symptomatology (Alloy et al. 2006; Boylan et al. 2004; Corry et al. 2013), in a large family study.

*Correspondence: phil.mitchell@unsw.edu.au
[1] School of Psychiatry, University of New South Wales, Randwick, NSW 2031, Australia
Full list of author information is available at the end of the article

The development of BD is influenced strongly by genetics, accounting for as much as 85% of the variance in who develops mania (McGuffin et al. 2003). In families, a summary of 5 studies estimated that the risk of an affective disorder in first degree relatives of those with BD ranges from 24 to 31% and the risk of BD ranges from 7 to 22% (Merikangas et al. 2002). Given this high genetic contribution to the development of BD, there remains the task of identifying how and when this biological vulnerability is expressed with more proximal biological, psychological and environmental triggers being important factors (Johnson 2005; Jones and Bentall 2008) BD pedigrees have higher rates of Schizoaffective Disorder (BD type), BD-I, BD-II and Major Depressive Disorder that control families (Gershon et al. 1982). There is also emerging evidence that the family environment plays an important role in influencing the development of beliefs and attitudes related to achievement and attainment of goals (Johnson 2005; Chen and Johnson 2012). Hence, studies of extended families with some members diagnosed with BD may be useful to determine the contribution of perfectionistic cognitions and beliefs relating to goal attainment to anxiety, stress, and other core mood symptoms such as depression and hypomania.

Cognitive models of the development of psychopathology propose that cognitive, mood and behavioural symptoms arise when maladaptive beliefs and cognitions are triggered by congruent life events (Beck et al. 1979). Recently, cognitive models of BD symptoms and mood dysregulation have been proposed that attempt to explain both the depressive and (hypo)manic symptoms characteristic of BD (Holmes et al. 2008; Mansell et al. 2007). Mansell et al. (2007) have proposed a transdiagnostic model of mood dysregulation and bipolar disorder, within which it is proposed that self-critical or shaming beliefs may be important in driving anxious thoughts and cognitive appraisals of affect, as well as bodily sensations that ultimately influence the ascent into (hypo)mania or descent into depression (Mansell et al. 2007). In parallel, a separate cognitive model of BD emphasizes the role that anxiety plays in the development of BD symptoms (Holmes et al. 2008). The model of Mansell et al. (2007) in particular draws on findings that perfectionism is a core cognitive style of BD, along with high self-criticism and an emphasis on goal attainment and avoidance of failure (Alloy et al. 2009a; Lam et al. 2004; Mansell and Pedley 2008; Scott et al. 2000). For example, in a prospective study, self-criticism, performance focus and high self-standards interacted with congruent life events to predict both depressive and (hypo)manic symptoms in those with BD-II and cyclothymia (Francis-Raniere et al. 2006). Lam et al. (2004) found that beliefs related to goal attainment distinguished those with BD from normal controls and were correlated with number of hospitalizations for mania and BD episodes in general (Lam et al. 2004). Hewitt et al. (1998) examined perfectionism as a multidimensional construct in a mixed sample of unipolar and BD patients. Hewitt found that *self-oriented* perfectionism (whereby the individual has high standards for themselves) was uniquely associated with chronic depression symptoms, while *socially-prescribed* perfectionism (whereby individuals perceive that others have high standards for them) was been uniquely associated with chronic (hypo)manic symptoms (Hewitt et al. 1998). A perfectionistic cognitive style has also been associated with anxiety and stress symptoms (Hewitt and Flett 2002; Frost and DiBartolo 2002; Wheeler et al. 2011). Previous associations with perfectionism extend to variations in state and trait anxiety (Flett et al. 1995), social anxiety disorder (Juster et al. 1996), obsessive–compulsive disorder (Antony et al. 1998), panic disorder (Antony et al. 1998) and a tendency to worry (Chang 2000). Consistent with this, greater levels of perfectionism have also been associated with greater cortisol responses to stress in situations designed to induce a fear of negative evaluation (Wirtz et al. 2007) a core cognitive style in social anxiety disorder. These findings, which confirm perfectionism as a key cognitive style in both BD and the anxiety disorders, provided the impetus to examine perfectionism as a potential mediator of known associations between anxiety and stress symptoms and mood symptomatology.

Consistent with the psychological models of BD symptoms (Holmes et al. 2008; Mansell et al. 2007), we have previously reported that anxiety and stress symptoms mediated the effects of self-critical perfectionism and goal attainment beliefs on current bipolar depressive symptoms after controlling for current hypomanic symptoms (Corry et al. 2013). For hypomanic symptoms, stress symptoms were a significant mediator of the relationship between self-critical perfectionism and current hypomanic symptoms; however, these mediation models were no longer significant after controlling current depressive symptoms. Similar findings were reported by O'Garro-Moore et al. (2015) using prospective data from those with bipolar spectrum disorders. Of the six cognitive styles examined as mediators, only perfectionism was a significant mediator of the relationship between the presence of an anxiety disorder and depressive symptoms. No cognitive styles significantly mediated the relationship between anxiety disorder and hypomanic symptoms.

This study thus examined the hypotheses that perfectionism and goal attainment values would mediate the associations between (subclinical) anxiety/stress symptoms and hypomanic and depressive symptomatology, in BD patients and their unaffected relatives. We chose to extend the work of Hewitt et al. by examining perfectionism as a multidimensional construct in a family sample. We hypothesized that: (1) self-oriented perfectionism would mediate the relationship between anxiety and stress symptoms and chronic depressive symptoms; and (2) socially-prescribed perfectionism and goal attainment values would mediate the relationship between stress and anxiety symptoms and chronic (hypo)manic symptoms. In line with Hewitt et al. (1998) findings, these predictions reflected our expectation that: (1) self-oriented perfectionism would be uniquely related to chronic depression depressive symptoms; and (2) socially-prescribed perfectionism and goal attainment values would be uniquely related to chronic (hypo)manic symptoms.

Methods

Participants

The participants in the current study had previously been recruited through a BD molecular genetics pedigree research study (McAuley et al. 2009; Fullerton et al. 2010). All families were ascertained after initial consultation with a proband with BD (using the Family Interview for Genetic Studies; FIGS). Each pedigree member provided informed consent prior to inclusion in the study. All individuals were assessed using the Diagnostic Interview for Genetic Studies (DIGS) (Nurnberger et al. 1994), with interviews being undertaken by experienced medical practitioners, psychologists and psychiatric nurses trained in this instrument. Information obtained from the FIGS, DIGS and medical records was used to generate best-estimate Research Diagnostic Criteria (RDC) diagnoses for Bipolar I disorder (BD-I), Bipolar II Disorder (BD-II), Schizoaffective Disorder Manic Type (SZMA) or Recurrent Unipolar Major Depression (RUD). As we were interested in examining both sub-syndromal and syndromal mood disorder symptoms, we also included those participants who did not meet formal RDC criteria for a mood disorder but who may still be at greater risk of developing symptomatology due to increased familial risk.

The questionnaire for the current study was posted to all contactable first and second degree relatives of the proband in the 67 pedigrees ($n = 735$) with a return deadline of 24 days. After 37 days, 267 responses were received. At 45 days, a secondary mail-out was conducted to those individuals who had failed to respond, which yielded an additional 76 responses giving a 46.6% response rate. Of the 343 individuals who completed the questionnaires, 325 individuals responded to over 95% of the 164 items, and 297 individuals responded to over 99% of items. Of the 67 families included in the mail-out, 47 had 2 or more members complete over 95% of the survey. Missing data was imputed using the mean response of other items within the same questionnaire or sub-scale as applicable (Tabachnick and Fidell 2013). Respondents completing less than 95% of the survey were not included in the analysis in order to reduce the impact of non-randomly missing datapoints in the dataset (Tabachnick and Fidell 2013).

Measures

Internal State Scale (ISS)

The Internal State Scale is a 15-item self-report measure designed to provide a simple mood state ascertainment for those with BD (Bauer et al. 1991). There are four sub-scales—Activation, Well Being, Depression Index and Perceived Conflict—which are rated using a visual analogue line scale. An algorithm using scores from the Activation and Wellbeing sub-scales identifies individuals in euthymic, depressed, manic and mixed states. The ISS has been found to discriminate well, with moderate kappas found between clinician-determined diagnostic status and that determined by the ISS (Bauer et al. 1991; Bauer et al. 2000; Glick et al. 2003).

General Behaviour Inventory (GBI)

The GBI is a measure of chronic-intermittent forms of affective disorders and identifies the full range of severity of unipolar and BD—from sub-syndromal to syndromal (Depue et al. 1981, 1989). It consists of three clusters of items: depressive, hypomanic and biphasic (defined as the tendency to vacillate between depression and hypomania in the same item). The GBI has 73 items that are scored on a 0–4 Likert scale related to the chronicity of the symptom described. It is possible to use the scoring system of the GBI as a Likert scale yielding continuous scores of affective disturbance or dysregulation in the domains of depressive, hypomanic and biphasic symptoms. We used a selection of ten items from the depression domain of which the majority selected being consistent with a recent factor analysis informing the development of a shorter version of the GBI (Youngstrom et al. 2013). The items were: (1) Have you had periods of sadness and depression when almost everything gets on your nerves and makes you irritable or angry (other than related to the menstrual cycle)?; (2) Have there been times of several days or more when you were so sad that it was quite painful or you felt that you couldn't stand it?; (3) Have there been times when you looked back over your life and could see only failures or hardships?; (4) Have there been times when you were feeling low and depressed, and you also had to struggle very hard to control inner feelings of rage or an urge to smash or destroy things?; (5) Have there been times when you exploded at others and afterwards felt bad about yourself?; (6) Have there been times when you hated yourself or felt that you were stupid, ugly, unlovable, or useless? (7) Have there been times of several days or more when you really got down on yourself and felt worthless?; (8) Have you had periods when it seemed that the future was hopeless and things could not improve?; (9) Have there been periods lasting several days or more when you were so down in the dumps that you thought you might never snap out of it?; and (10) Have there been times when you have felt that you would be better off dead? All 27 items for the hypomanic and biphasic domains were administered. The GBI has been extensively validated and possesses good psychometric properties (Depue et al. 1981, 1989).

Depression, Anxiety and Stress Scale (DASS)

The DASS is a 42-item scale measuring the negative emotional states of depression, anxiety and stress with each sub-scale having 14 items (Lovibond and Lovibond 1995a). In the current study, we focused on the Anxiety and Stress sub-scales. The anxiety sub-scale is a measure of the acute autonomic fear response. The stress sub-scale measures the state of persistent arousal and tension with a low threshold for becoming upset or frustrated. For clinical utility, DASS scores can be categorized into normal, mild, moderate, severe and extreme severe categories for each emotional state (Lovibond and Lovibond 1995a). The DASS has been shown to have good psychometric properties (Lovibond and Lovibond 1995a; Lovibond and Lovibond 1995b).

Multidimensional Perfectionism Scale (MPS)

The MPS is a 45-item scale assessing three dimensions of perfectionism: (1) self-oriented perfectionism (i.e. the tendency to establish perfectionistic standards for oneself); (2) socially-prescribed perfectionism (i.e. The tendency to believe that others have unrealistic standards for oneself); and (3) other-oriented perfectionism (i.e. the tendency to have perfectionistic expectations of others) (Hewitt and Flett 1991). The MPS has been shown to have good reliability, internal consistency and validity (Hewitt and Flett 1991; Hewitt et al. 1991). The present study focused on self-oriented perfectionism (SO) and socially-prescribed perfectionism (SP) and therefore only these sub-scales of the MPS were administered.

Dysfunctional Attitudes Scale (DAS)

The original DAS consists of two 40-item parallel questionnaires items that tap various cognitive schemas proposed to place individuals at risk of depression (Weissman and Beck 1978). Factor analytic investigation of this scale has yielded various factors that relate to these cognitive schemas. We used the goal attainment factor from Lam et al. (2004) which is proposed to measure the intensity of beliefs related to positive affect, extraversion and achievement-striving (Lam et al. 2004). The goal attainment factor was found to be highly reliable (6 items; $\alpha = 0.79$).

Statistical analyses

Analyses were conducted using SPSS Statistics package and MPlus using procedures to account for the nested nature of the dataset. Pearson correlations were calculated for bivariate associations between the measures of cognitive style (perfectionism and goal attainment), chronic BD symptomatology (i.e., depression and hypomania), anxiety and stress symptoms, demographics and current episode. In order to test whether perfectionism and goal attainment values were uniquely related to BD symptomatology, we used generalized estimating equations (GEE procedure) to generate two regression models: one for chronic depressive symptoms and one for chronic (hypo)manic symptoms. We controlled for the effects of gender, age, presence vs absence of current BD episode and chronic depressive or (hypo)manic symptoms (depending on the independent variable). All variables were entered in one block so that the beta for any one independent variable represents the degree of association between that dependent variable and the independent variable after controlling for all other dependant variables in the model (Tabachnick and Fidell 2013).

Mediation analyses were conducted using nonparametric bootstrapping methods to test the significance of the proposed mediators in our models using Mplus (Muthén et al. 1998). Two separate mediation models were used for both chronic depressive symptoms and chronic (hypo) manic symptoms with the analysis comprising of four mediation models in total. In the first two models, the tendency to experience chronic depressive symptoms was the dependent variable, self-oriented and socially-prescribed perfectionism were entered simultaneously as the potential mediators, and anxiety and stress symptoms were the independent variables. These analyses were repeated for (hypo)manic symptoms as the dependent variable.

For demonstration of mediation, the independent variable (anxiety and stress symptoms) must be related to the dependent variable (chronic depressive and hypo/manic symptoms), the independent variable must be related to the proposed mediating variables (self-oriented perfectionism and socially-prescribed perfectionism and goal attainment values), and the relationship between the mediating variables and the dependent variable (the indirect effect) should be stronger than the relationship between the independent variable and the dependent variable (the direct effect). Using a nonparametric bootstrapping approach to mediation, the indirect effect is generated as a point estimate with 95% confidence intervals. If zero is not included in the 95% confidence intervals, it can be concluded that the indirect effects are significantly different from zero at $p < 0.05$ (two-tailed) and that partial or full mediation is present. We also included age, gender, the presence of a depressive, (hypo) manic or mixed episode as covariates in our analyses, and the opposing mood state (chronic depressive symptoms or chronic hypomanic/biphasic symptoms).

We also conducted additional analyses examining these four models separately for the affected group and unaffected group. These are reported in the Additional file 1.

Results

The sample comprised 269 subjects from 56 pedigrees of whom 17.5% ($n = 47$) had BD-I; 6.3% ($n = 17$) BD-II; 8.9% ($n = 24$) recurrent unipolar depression; 5.2% ($n = 14$) schizoaffective disorder (bipolar type); and 62.1% ($n = 167$) unaffected relatives who did not meet formal diagnostic criteria for any mood disorder. Descriptive statistics for the total sample are detailed in Table 1. *T* tests between affected and unaffected subjects showed significant differences between the two groups on the DASS stress sub-scale ($p < 0.001$). The same pattern of results was observed for anxiety scores: those with a mood disorder diagnosis had higher anxiety scores ($p < 0.001$). The mean scores for the stress and anxiety sub-scales of the DASS were low—in the normal range according the DASS severity categories (Lovibond and Lovibond 1995b). There were no significant differences between those affected and unaffected on current rates of depressive, (hypo)manic or mixed episodes (as measured by the ISS). Those in the affected groups, however, had higher levels of self-orientated perfectionism (mean = 14.36, SD = 6.12 v. mean = 16.89, SD = 6.86; $t(267) = -3.15$, $p < 0.001$). There were no significant differences between the two groups on measures socially-prescribed perfectionism or goal attainment values.

Correlation analyses

Table 2 shows Pearson's *r* correlations between the measures included in the analysis. All variables were correlated in the expected directions. Both measures of perfectionism (self-oriented and socially-prescribed) and goal attainment values were significantly correlated with chronic depression and (hypo)manic symptoms. Anxiety and stress symptoms were also significantly correlated with chronic depression and (hypo)manic symptoms.

Generalized estimating equation regression models

The first model demonstrates that self-oriented perfectionism was the only significant predictor of chronic depressive symptoms (as measured by the GBI), after controlling for other independent variables (Table 3).

Table 1 Participant characteristics

	Mean (SD)		
	Unaffected ($n = 167$)	Affected ($n = 102$)	Total sample ($n = 269$)
Demographics			
Age, years	51.86 (14.34)	52.51 (14.73)	52.11 (14.46)
Female, % (*n*)	60.5 (101)	60.8 (62)	60.6 (163)
Current episode			
ISS depressive episode, % (*n*)	13.8 (23)	22.5 (46)	17.1 (69)
ISS hypomanic episode, % (*n*)	17.4 (29)	23.5 (24)	19.7 (53)
ISS mixed episodes, % (*n*)	3.0 (5)	6.9 (7)	4.5 (12)
Chronic symptomatology			
GBI depression	13.05 (4.75)	18.71 (6.54)***	15.19 (6.13)
GBI hypomanic/biphasic	33.41 (10.21)	44.71 (14.12)***	37.70 (13.03)
DASS anxiety	3.68 (3.53)	7.17 (4.27)***	5.00 (4.18)
DASS stress	4.13 (3.42)	7.04 (4.37)***	5.23 (4.05)
Cognitive styles			
MPS: self-orientated perfectionism	14.36 (6.12)	16.89 (6.86)***	15.31 (6.51)
MPS: socially-prescribed perfectionism	21.70 (6.43)	21.96 (7.06)	21.80 (6.67)
DAS: goal attainment values	24.23 (7.35)	23.36 (8.18)	23.94 (7.67)

ISS Internal State Scale, *GBI Depression* General Behaviour Inventory Depression sub-scale, *GBI Hypomanic/Biphasic* General Behaviour Inventory Biphasic/Hypomanic sub-scale, *DASS Anxiety* Depression Anxiety Stress Scale-Anxiety sub-scale, *DASS Stress* Depression Anxiety Stress Scale-Stress scale, *MPS* Multidimensional Perfectionism Scale, *DAS* Dysfunctional Attitudes Scale

*** $p < 0.001$

Table 2 Zero-order correlations for all variables

	1	2	3	4	5	6	7	8	9	10	11
Age	–										
Gender	−0.06	–									
ISS depressive episode	0.08	0.00	–								
ISS hypomanic episode	−0.09	−0.08	−0.23	–							
ISS mixed episode	−0.01	−0.05	−0.10	−0.11	–						
GBI depression	−0.14*	0.05	0.15*	0.23**	0.15*	–					
GBI hypomanic/biphasic	−0.13*	−0.13*	0.06	0.34**	0.17**	0.73**	–				
DASS anxiety	−0.15*	−0.08	0.14*	0.32**	0.20**	0.74**	0.71**	–			
DASS stress	−0.21**	0.08	0.15*	0.33**	0.17**	0.74**	0.72**	0.85**	–		
MPS self-oriented	−0.09	−0.13*	0.10	0.24**	0.10	0.48**	0.45**	0.45**	0.47**	–	
MPS socially-prescribed	−0.18**	−0.10	−0.10	0.18**	0.12*	0.31**	0.40**	0.31**	0.32**	0.54**	–
DAS goal attainment	−0.16**	−0.14*	−0.06	0.25**	0.07	0.29**	0.38**	0.31**	0.34**	0.49**	0.55**

ISS Internal State Scale, *GBI depression* General Behaviour Inventory Depression sub-scale, *GBI hypomanic/biphasic* General Behaviour Inventory Biphasic/Hypomanic sub-scale, *DASS anxiety* Depression Anxiety Stress Scale-Anxiety sub-scale, *DASS stress* Depression Anxiety Stress Scale-Stress scale, *MPS self-oriented* Multidimensional Perfectionism scale Self-Oriented sub-scale, *MPS socially-prescribed* Multidimensional Perfectionism scale Socially-Prescribed sub-scale, *DAS goal attainment* Dysfunctional Attitudes Goal Attainment Factor

* $p < 0.05$; ** $p < 0.01$ (these analyses are exploratory and therefore no adjustments for multiple comparisons have been made)

No other cognitive style predicted depressive symptomatology, but other significant predictors were a current depressive episode (as determined by the ISS) and chronic (hypo)manic symptomatology (as measured by the GBI). Being female was also associated with higher levels of chronic depressive symptoms.

The second model showed that only socially-prescribed perfectionism significantly predicted chronic (hypo) manic symptomatology, after controlling for the other independent variables (Table 3). Self-oriented perfectionism was not a significant predictor. Other significant predictors of chronic (hypo)manic symptomatology were chronic depressive symptoms and a current hypomanic episode (as determined by the ISS). Goal attainment values only approached significance in this model ($p < 0.10$). Being male was also associated with higher levels of chronic (hypo)manic symptoms.

Mediation analyses

As goal attainment values was not a significant predictor in the generalized estimating equation regression models this cognitive style is not considered further in the mediation models. In the two mediation models where chronic depressive symptoms was the dependent variable, only self-oriented perfectionism mediated the relationship between both anxiety and stress symptoms and chronic depressive symptoms (Table 4). Socially-prescribed perfectionism was not a significant mediator. For anxiety symptoms, the true indirect effects was estimated to lie between 0.05 and 0.17. For stress symptoms, the true indirect effects were estimate to lie between 0.04 and 0.17.

Table 3 Generalized Estimating Equations Using Multidimensional Perfectionism Scale Dimensions and Goal Attainment Values to Predict Chronic Depressive and Chronic Hypomanic/Biphasic symptoms

Variable	Beta	SE
Predicting chronic unipolar symptoms		
Age	−0.02	0.02
Gender	−0.19	0.47***
ISS: depressed	−1.42	0.63*
ISS: hypomanic	0.10	0.82
ISS: mixed	−1.04	1.57
GBI: hypomanic/biphasic	0.31	0.02***
DAS: goal attainment factor	−0.02	0.04
MPS: self-oriented perfectionism	0.21	0.06***
MPS: socially-prescribed perfectionism	−0.04	0.05
Predicting chronic hypomanic/biphasic symptoms		
Age	−0.002	0.03
Gender	3.25	1.05**
ISS: depressed	−1.04	0.50
ISS: hypomanic	−5.41	1.45***
ISS: mixed	−4.46	2.49#
GBI: depression	1.34	0.13***
DAS: goal attainment factor	0.14	0.07#
MPS: self-oriented perfectionism	−0.04	0.13
MPS: socially-prescribed perfectionism	0.23	0.09**

ISS Internal State Scale, *GBI* General Behaviour Inventory, *DAS* Dysfunctional Attitudes Scale, *MPS* MultiDimensional Perfectionism Scale

\# $p < 0.10$, * $p < 0.05$, ** $p < 0.01$, *** $p < 0.001$

Table 4 Summary of mediation results for chronic depressive and hypomanic symptoms with self-oriented perfectionism and socially-prescribed perfectionism as mediators controlling for age, gender and opposing mood state

IV	Effect of IV on DV	Mediators	Effect of IV on M	Effect of M on DV	Indirect effect
Chronic depressive symptoms					
Anxiety	0.60***	SOP	0.70***	0.15**	0.11[a]
		SPP	0.50***	−0.05	−0.02
Stress	0.62***	SOP	0.75***	0.11**	0.12[a]
		SPP	0.53***	−0.02	0.01
Chronic (Hypo)manic symptoms					
Anxiety	0.91***	SOP	0.70***	−0.03	−0.02
		SPP	0.50***	0.30**	0.15[a]
Stress	1.03***	SOP	0.75***	−0.05	−0.04
		SPP	0.53***	0.30**	0.16[a]

IV independent variable, *M* mediating variable, *DV* dependent variable, *SOP* self-oriented perfectionism, *SPP* socially-prescribed perfectionism

* $p < 0.05$; ** $p < 0.01$; *** $p < 0.001$

[a] Significant point estimate $p < 0.05$

In the two mediation models where chronic hypomanic symptoms were the dependent variables, socially-prescribed perfectionism mediated the relationship between both anxiety and stress symptoms and chronic hypomanic symptoms. For anxiety symptoms, the true indirect effects were estimated to lie between 0.07 and 0.26. For stress symptoms, the true indirect effects were estimated to lie between 0.08 and 0.27. Self-oriented perfectionism was not a significant mediator.

Separate analyses for probands and non-affected family members are available in the supplementary analysis (see Additional file 1: Tables S1, S2). As the results replicate the combined sample, they were not included in the main results of this paper. The results in both groups are consistent with the combined sample with only self-oriented perfectionism significantly mediating the relationship between anxiety and stress symptoms and chronic depressive symptoms. For hypomanic symptoms, only socially-prescribed perfectionism significantly mediated the relationship between anxiety and stress symptoms and chronic hypomanic symptoms.

Discussion

The results highlight the potential role of perfectionism as a mechanism explaining the co-occurrence between BD and anxiety. The results further suggest that different dimensions of perfectionism are uniquely associated with chronic depressive and (hypo)manic symptoms. Univariate associations between self- and socially-prescribed perfectionism and BD symptomatology were consistent with previous reports (Lam et al. 2004; Hewitt et al. 1998). Similarly, we confirmed significant relationships between both self- and socially-prescribed perfectionism and anxiety and stress symptoms (Wheeler et al. 2011). Like Hewitt (Hewitt et al. 1998), we found that self-oriented perfectionism was uniquely associated with chronic depressive symptoms after controlling for chronic (hypo)manic symptoms; this suggests a preoccupation with high standards for oneself and a punitive response when mistakes are made, or when perfectionistic standards are not met. Previous studies have found self-oriented perfectionism to be associated with unipolar depressive symptoms (Hewitt and Flett 1993; Hewitt et al. 1996) and there are similarities between the cognitive styles of unipolar and bipolar depression (Scott and Pope 2003). The particular relevance of self-oriented perfectionism for depression (versus socially-prescribed perfectionism) is consistent with research highlighting the role of ruminative, self-focused attention in the onset and maintenance of depression (Nolen-Hoeksema 1991, 2000; Kuehner and Weber 1999). Self-analytical self-focus has been found to influence global negative self-judgments (e.g. "I am a failure") which increases depressive symptoms (Rimes and Watkins 2005).

For hypomanic symptoms, our findings suggest that an interpersonal focus is more important given that socially-prescribed perfectionism is defined as perceiving that others hold excessively high standards for oneself. We found that socially-prescribed perfectionism was uniquely associated with chronic (hypo)manic symptoms after controlling for chronic depressive symptoms. This is consistent with Shepero et al's (Shapero et al. 2015) finding that higher public self-consciousness (reflecting a person's awareness of other's view of themselves) distinguished BD patients from those with MDD (along with higher rumination on positive affect) (Shapero et al. 2015). Socially-prescribed perfectionism is also considered to be more maladaptive than self-oriented perfectionism, with self-criticism being the most problematic component (Blankstein and Dunkley 2002). In a sample of individuals with BD-II and cyclothymia, Alloy et al. found that higher autonomy (a construct related to perfectionism) and self-criticism predicted a greater likelihood of (hypo)manic episodes over 3.2 year follow-up (Alloy et al. 2009b). Our findings strengthen the hypothesis that a cognitive style characterized by a concern about the negative perceptions of others is associated with hypomanic symptoms.

The second aim of our study was to examine whether perfectionism mediates the relationship between stress and anxiety symptoms and BD symptoms in an attempt to understand mechanisms underlying the high comorbidity between anxiety symptoms and BD. For chronic bipolar depressive symptoms, the mediation models were significant with self-orientated perfectionism found to significantly mediate the relationship between anxiety and stress symptoms and bipolar depressive symptoms. These findings remained after controlling for the presence of chronic (hypo)manic symptoms. These findings are consistent with our previous finding in a clinical sample (Corry et al. 2013). Our hypothesis that socially-prescribed perfectionism and goal attainment values would mediate the relationship between anxiety and stress symptoms and chronic hypomanic symptoms was partially supported. Only socially-prescribed perfectionism (not goal attainment values) was uniquely associated with chronic hypomanic symptoms in the linear regression models in the current study; therefore, we considered only socially-prescribed perfectionism in the mediation models. In mediation models, socially-prescribed perfectionism significantly mediated associations between both anxiety and stress, and chronic hypomanic symptoms after controlling for the presence of chronic depressive symptoms. This finding is inconsistent with our previous study and likely represents methodological differences in the measurement of (hypo)mania (chronic in the present study versus current in our previous study) (Corry et al. 2013). It is important to note that the present findings do not imply that perfectionism is the only mediator between anxiety and stress symptoms and bipolar disorder symptoms. Perfectionism is only a partial mediator in the mediation models, leaving room for other constructs to play a role. For example, the perfectionism literature also highlights the importance of coping styles, emotional regulation strategies and congruent life events to explain the relationship between perfectionism and psychopathology [e.g. (Dunkley and Blankstein 2000; Dunkley et al. 2003)].

Our findings are consistent with current cognitive, transdiagnostic models of BD. Specifically, that self-critical, perfectionistic beliefs are related to both depressive and (hypo)manic symptoms (see Mansell et al. 2007; Mansell 2007) and that anxiety is likely a precursor to depressive symptoms in BD (Holmes et al. 2008). Consistent with Mansell et al.'s and Holmes' model it is proposed that depressive and/or (hypo)manic symptoms arise from the use of unhelpful emotional regulation strategies (ascent and descent behaviours) in response to anxiety and stress symptoms driven by perfectionistic and/or goal attainment beliefs [see (Mansell 2007) for an illustrative case formulation], (Holmes et al. 2008; Mansell et al. 2007). A key component of Mansell's model, the conflicted appraisals of an individual's internal state, was not examined here, but would be crucial in further understanding the transition from stress and anxiety symptoms to depressive and (hypo)manic symptoms. The role that perfectionism may play in these appraisals also warrants further investigation. It may be that anxiety/stress and depression are not merely co-occurring emotional states (or comorbid disorders) but that there is a dynamic, iterative process that occurs within an individual that sometimes produces a predominantly anxious presentation (i.e. meeting criteria for an anxiety disorder) and at other times produces symptoms consistent with a formal mood episode. Indeed, (Mansell 2007) proposes that the manner in which mood fluctuations express themselves over time should determine the diagnosis and that the nature of current symptoms will be a complex result of: (1) experiencing previous vicious cycles; (2) the nature of the underlying beliefs; and (3) the current environment.

The presence of these significant relationships in the current sample, comprising both affected and unaffected relatives within affected families, suggests that these processes are operating outside of formal episodes and may represent intermediate phenotypes in those at genetic risk of developing either depressive or (hypo)manic episodes. Perfectionism has been proposed to have developmental origins (Flett et al. 2002), with maternal criticism when standards are not met (Bleys et al. 2016; Greblo and Bratko 2014) and parental psychological control found to be particularly important (Soenens et al. 2005). Our findings are also consistent with perfectionism being a transdiagnostic psychological risk factor for psychopathology generally (Bieling et al. 2004; Egan et al. 2011). In BD, previous research suggests that family socialization plays a role in shaping beliefs towards goal attainment and achievement that conveys a vulnerability to developing the cognitions that are characteristic of (hypo)mania (Chen and Johnson 2012). Given that the presence of perfectionistic cognitions and anxiety/stress symptoms may be necessary but not the whole picture of risk for experiencing BD symptoms, future research is necessary to better understand what additional risk factors are present that give rise to BD symptomatology against a background of familial risk.

A number of limitations in this study are important to acknowledge. Firstly, the cross-sectional nature of the study means that caution must be exercised when inferring causality. Ultimately longitudinal data will be required to more definitively investigate relationships between perfectionism, anxiety/stress, and mood symptom development over time. The cross-sectional nature of the study also makes it impossible to be certain about the directionality of the relationship between the variables of interest. However, our hypotheses are proposed on the basis of other studies that have used longitudinal designs and have attained similar results (O'Garro-Moore et al. 2015; Alloy et al. 2009b). Secondly, the present study examined anxiety (and stress) symptoms dimensionally rather than using formal categorical diagnostic criteria; to better understand issues of comorbidity with BD, it will be useful to examine these relationships among people with specific categorical anxiety diagnoses, such as those defined by DSM-5. Thirdly, anxiety has been found to influence the course of bipolar disorder in other ways. Higher likelihood of relapse (Otto et al. 2006) increased suicidal behaviour (Dilsaver et al. 2006; Young et al. 1993) and greater number of episodes (Bauer et al. 2005) have all been found to be increased in those with comorbid BD and anxiety disorders compared to those with BD only. While beyond the scope of the current study it would be useful to examine the role of perfectionism mediating the relationship between anxiety and other markers of BD severity. For example, people with BD who exhibit a cognitive style characterized by rigidity and pessimism are less likely to recover from their BD depressive episode or, if able to recover, take longer to do so (Stange et al. 2013). Additionally, we did not measure the occurrence of life events in the current study. The cognitive-diathesis stress model of psychopathology proposes that negative cognitive styles or schemas interact with life events to trigger symptoms of psychopathology (Beck 1967, 1976); specific life events associated with achievement may be particularly relevant to the development of mood episodes in BD (Alloy et al. 2005; Koenders et al. 2014). Lastly, the variables of interest were assessed using retrospective, self-report measures and it therefore it could be argued that responses are unduly influenced by the current mood state of the participants. Future research using experience-sampling methodology would enable the relationships between anxiety and stress symptoms, perfectionism and BD symptoms to be more clearly elucidated.

Conclusions

In sum, this study provides support for the role of perfectionism in the co-occurrence of anxiety, stress, depression and (hypo)manic symptoms in BD. There are promising treatments for clinical perfectionism (Egan et al. 2014) and also transdiagnostic approaches to targeting both anxiety and BD symptoms (Ellard et al. 2012) that may be useful in psychological treatment approaches. These findings further suggest that BD patients and/or those considered at risk of BD should be routinely screened for the presence of maladaptive perfectionism and considered for the need for psychological intervention to address anxiety, depressive and (hypo)manic symptoms, in addition to appropriate pharmacotherapy.

Authors' contributions

JC: Conception and design of the study; data analysis and interpretation, drafting of the article, critical revision of the article, final approval of the version to be published. MG: Data analysis and interpretation, drafting of the article, final approval of the version to be published. GR: Data analysis and interpretation, critical revision of the article, final approval of the version to be published. JF: Conception and design of the study, data collection, critical revision of the article, final approval of the version to be published. PS: Data analysis and interpretation, critical revision of the article, final approval of the version to be published. PM: Conception and design of the study, data analysis and interpretation, drafting of the article, critical revision of the article, final approval of the version to be published. All authors read and approved the final manuscript.

Author details

[1] School of Psychiatry, University of New South Wales, Randwick, NSW 2031, Australia. [2] Black Dog Institute, Prince of Wales Hospital, Randwick, NSW 2031, Australia. [3] Prince of Wales Hospital, Randwick, NSW 2031, Australia. [4] Neuroscience Research Australia, Randwick, NSW, Australia. [5] School of Medical Sciences, University of New South Wales, Randwick, NSW, Australia.

Acknowledgements

We thank Dusan Hadzi-Pavlovic for his contribution to data analysis.

Competing interests

The authors declare that they have no competing interests.

Funding

This study was funded by an Australian National Health and Medical Research Council (NHMRC) Program Grant Number 1037196. MJG was funded by the NHMRC's R.D. Wright Biomedical Career Development Fellowship (APP108187). JMF was funded by a NHMRC Howard Florey Centenary Fellowship (325643), a NHMRC project grant (1063960) and the Janette Mary O'Neill Research Fellowship. The funding bodies acknowledged above had not role in the design of the study, collection and analysis of data, or the decision to publish.

References

Alloy LB, Abramson LY, Urosevic S, Walshaw PD, Nusslock R, Neeren AM. The psychosocial context of bipolar disorder: environmental, cognitive, and developmental risk factors. Clin Psychol Rev. 2005;25:1043–75.

Alloy LB, Abramson LY, Walshaw PD, Keyser J, Gerstein RK. A cognitive vulnerability-stress perspective on bipolar spectrum disorders in a normative adolescent brain, cognitive, and emotional development context. Dev Psychopathol. 2006;18(4):1055–103.

Alloy LB, Abramson LY, Flynn M, Liu RT, Grant DA, Jager-Hyman S, et al. Self-focused Cognitive Styles and Bipolar Spectrum Disorders: concurrent and Prospective Associations. Int J cognit Ther. 2009a;2(4):354.

Alloy LB, Abramson LY, Walshaw PD, Gerstein RK, Keyser JD, Whitehouse WG, et al. Behavioral approach system (BAS)-relevant cognitive styles and bipolar spectrum disorders: concurrent and prospective associations. J Abnorm Psychol. 2009b;118(3):459–71.

Antony MM, Purdon CL, Huta V, Swinson RP. Dimensions of perfectionism across the anxiety disorders. Behav Res Ther. 1998;36(12):1143–54.

Bauer S, Crits-Christoph P, Ball WA, Dewees E, McAllister T, Alahi P, et al. Independent assessment of manic and depressive symptoms by self-rating: scale characteristics and implications for the study of mania. Arch Gen Psychiatry. 1991;48:807–12.

Bauer MS, Vojta C, Kinosian B, Altshuler L, Glick H. The Internal State Scale: replication of its discriminating abilities in a multisite, public sector sample. Bipolar Disord. 2000;2:340–6.

Bauer MS, Altshuler L, Evans DR, Beresford T, Williford WO, Hauger R. Prevalence and distinct correlates of anxiety, substance, and combined comorbidity in a multi-site public sector sample with bipolar disorder. J Affect Disord. 2005;85(3):301–15.

Beck AT. Depression: clinical, experimental and clinical aspects. New York: Harper and Row; 1967.

Beck AT. Cognitive Therapy and the Emotional Disorders. New York: International Universities Press; 1976.

Beck AT, Rush AJ, Shaw BF, Emery G. Cognitive Therapy of Depression. New York: Guilford Press; 1979.

Bieling PJ, Summerfeldt LJ, Israeli AL, Antony MM. Perfectionism as an explanatory construct in comorbidity of axis I disorders. J Psychopathol Behav Assess. 2004;26:193–201.

Blankstein KR, Dunkley DM. Evaluative concerns, self-critical, and personal standards perfectionism: A structural equation modeling strategy. In: Flett DL, Hewitt PL, editors. Perfectionism: Theory, research and treatment. Washington, DC: American Psychological Association; 2002. p. 285–315.

Bleys D, Soenens B, Boone L, Claes S, Vliegen N, Luyten P. The role of intergenerational similarity and parenting in adolescent self-criticism: an actor-partner interdependence model. J Adolesc. 2016;49:68–76.

Boylan KR, Begin H, Young LT, Bieling PJ, Marriott M, MacQueen GM. Impact of comorbid anxiety disorders on outcome in a cohort of patients with bipolar disorder. J Clin Psychiatry. 2004;65(8):1106–13.

Chang EC. Perfectionism as a predictor of positive and negative psychological outcomes: examining a mediation model in younger and older adults. J Couns Psychol. 2000;47:18–26.

Chen SH, Johnson SL. Family influences on mania-relevant cognitions and beliefs: a cognitive model of mania and reward. J Clin Psychol. 2012;68(7):829–42.

Corry J, Green M, Roberts G, Frankland A, Wright A, Lau P, et al. Anxiety, stress and perfectionism in bipolar disorder. J Affect Disord. 2013;151(3):1016–24.

de Graaf R, Bijl RV, Spijker J, Beekman AT, Vollebergh WA. Temporal sequencing of lifetime mood disorders in relation to comorbid anxiety and substance use disorders–findings from the Netherlands Mental Health Survey and Incidence Study. Soc Psychiatry Psychiatr Epidemiol. 2003;38(1):1–11.

Depue RA, Slater JF, Wolfstetter-Kausch H, Klein D, Goplerud E, Farr D. A behavioral paradigm for identifying persons at risk for bipolar depressive disorder: a conceptual framework and five validation studies. J Abnorm Psychol. 1981;90(5):381–437.

Depue RA, Krauss S, Spoont MR, Arbisi P. General Behaviour Inventory identification of unipolar and bipolar affective conditions in a nonclinical university population. J Abnorm Psychol. 1989;98:117–26.

Dilsaver SC, Akiskal HS, Akiskal KK, Benazzi F. Dose-response relationship between number of comorbid anxiety disorders in adolescent bipolar/unipolar disorders, and psychosis, suicidality, substance abuse and familiality. J Affect Disord. 2006;96(3):249–58.

Dunkley DM, Blankstein KR. Self-critical perfectionism, coping, hassles and current distress: a structural equation modeling approach. Cognit Ther Res. 2000;24:713–30.

Dunkley DM, Zuroff DC, Blankstein KR. Self-critical perfectionism and daily affect: dispositional and situational influences on stress and coping. J Pers Soc Psychol. 2003;84:234–52.

Egan SJ, Wade TD, Shafran R. Perfectionism as a transdiagnostic process: a clinic review. Clin Psychol Rev. 2011;31:203–12.

Egan SJ, van Noort E, Chee A, Kane RT, Hoiles KJ, Shafran R, et al. A randomised controlled trial of face to face versus pure online self-help cognitive behavioural treatment for perfectionism. Behav Res Ther. 2014;63:107–13.

Ellard KK, Deckersbach T, Sylvia LG, Nierenberg AA, Barlow DH. Transdiagnostic treatment of bipolar disorder with comorbid anxiety with the unified protocol: a clinical replication series. Behav Modif. 2012;36(4):482–508.

Flett GL, Hewitt PL, Endler NS, Tassone C. Perfectionism and components of state and trait anxiety. Curr Psychol Dev Learn Personal Soc. 1995;13(4):326–50.

Flett GL, Hewitt PL, Oliver JM, Macdonald S. Perfectionism in children and their parents: a developmental analysis. Perfectionism: theory, research and treatment. Washington, D.C.: American Psychological Association; 2002. p. 89–132.

Francis-Raniere EL, Alloy LB, Abramson LY. Depressive personality styles and bipolar spectrum disorders: prospective tests of the event congruency hypothesis. Bipolar Disord. 2006;8:382–99.

Frost RO, DiBartolo PM. Perfectionism, anxiety, and obsessive-compulsive disorder. In: Flett DL, Hewitt PL, editors. Perfectionism: theory research and treatment. Washington, DC: American Psychological Association; 2002. p. 341–71.

Fullerton JM, Donald JA, Mitchell PB, Schofield PR. Two-dimensional genome scan identifies multiple genetic interactions in bipolar affective disorder. Biol Psychiatry. 2010;67(5):478–86.

Gershon ES, Hamovit J, Guroff JJ, Dibble E, Leckman JF, Sceery W, et al. A family study of schizoaffective, bipolar I, bipolar II, unipolar, and normal control probands. Arch Gen Psychiatry. 1982;39(10):1157–67.

Glick H, McBride L, Bauer MS. A manic-depressive symptom self-report in optical scanable format. Bipolar Disord. 2003;5:366–9.

Greblo Z, Bratko D. Parents' perfectionism and its relation to child rearing behaviors. Scand J Psychol. 2014;55:180–5.

Harvey AG, Watkins E, Mansell W, Shafran R. Cognitive behavioural processes accross the psychological disorders. A transdiagnostic approach to research and treatment. Oxford: Oxford University Press; 2004.

Hewitt PL, Flett DL. Perfectionism in the self and social contexts: conceptualisation, assessment and association with psychopathology. J Pers Soc Psychol. 1991;60(3):456–70.

Hewitt PL, Flett GL. Dimensions of perfectionism, daily stress, and depression: a test of the specific vulnerability hypothesis. J Abnorm Psychol. 1993;102(1):58–65.

Hewitt PL, Flett GL. Perfectionism and stress processes in psychopathology. In: Flett GL, Hewitt PL, editors. Perfectionism: theory, research and treatment. Washington: American Psychological Association; 2002. p. 255–84.

Hewitt PL, Flett GL, Turnbull-Donovan W, Mikail SF. The Multidimensional Perfectionism Scale: reliability, validity, and psychometric properties in psychiatric samples. Psychol Assess. 1991;3(3):464–8.

Hewitt PL, Flett GL, Ediger E. Perfectionism and depression: longitudinal assessment of a specific vulnerability hypothesis. J Abnorm Psychol. 1996;105:276–80.

Hewitt PL, Flett GL, Ediger E, Norton GR, Flynn CA. Perfectionism in chronic and state symptoms of depression. Can J Behav Sci. 1998;30(4):234–42.

Holmes EA, Geddes JR, Colom F, Goodwin GM. Mental imagery as an emotional amplifier: application to bipolar disorder. Behav Res Ther. 2008;46:1251–8.

Johnson SL. Mania and dysregulation in goal pursuit: a review. Clin Psychol Rev. 2005;25:241–62.

Jones SH, Bentall R. A review of potential cognitive and environmental risk markers in children of bipolar parents. Clin Psychol Rev. 2008;28:1083–95.

Juster HR, Heimberg RG, Frost RO, Holt CS, Mattia JI, Faccenda K. Social phobia and perfectionism. Personal Individ Differ. 1996;21:403–10.

Koenders MA, Giltay EJ, Spijker AT, Hoencamp E, Spinhoven P, Elzinga BM. Stressful life events in bipolar I and II disorder: cause or consequence of mood symptoms? J Affect Disord. 2014;161:55–64.

Kuehner C, Weber I. Responses to depression in unipolar depressed patients: an investigation of Nolen-Hoeksema's response styles theory. Psychol Med. 1999;29(6):1323–33.

Lam D, Wright K, Smith N. Dysfunctional assumptions in bipolar disorder. J Affec Disord. 2004;79(1–3):193–9.

Lovibond SH, Lovibond PF. Manual for the Depression Anxiety Stress Scales. Sydney: Psychological Foundation Monograph; 1995a.

Lovibond PF, Lovibond SH. The structure of negative emotional states: comparison of the Depression Anxiety Stress Scales (DASS) with the Beck Depression and Anxiety Inventories. Behav Res Ther. 1995b;33(3):335–43.

Mansell W. An integrative formulation-based cognitive treatment of bipolar disorders: application and illustration. J Clin Psychol. 2007;63(5):447–61.

Mansell W, Pedley R. The ascent into mania: a review of psychological processes associated with the development of manic symptoms. Clin Psychol Rev. 2008;28(3):494–520.

Mansell W, Morrison AP, Reid G, Lowens I, Tai S. The interpretation of, and responses to, changes in internal states: an integrative cognitive model of mood swings and bipolar disorders. Behav cognit Psychother. 2007;35:515–39.

McAuley EZ, Blair IP, Liu Z, Fullerton JM, Scimone A, Van Herten M, et al. A genome screen of 35 bipolar affective disorder pedigrees provides significant evidence for a susceptibility locus on chromosome 15q25-26. Mol psychiatry. 2009;14(5):492–500.

McGuffin P, Rijsdijk F, Andrew M, Sham P, Katz R, Cardno A. The heritability of bipolar affective disorder and the genetic relationship to unipolar depression. Arch Gen Psychiatry. 2003;60(5):497–502.

Merikangas KR, Chakravarti A, Moldin SO, Araj H, Blangero JC, Burmeister M, et al. Future of genetics of mood disorders research. Biol Psychiatry. 2002;52(6):457–77.

Merikangas KR, Cui L, Heaton L, Nakamura E, Roca C, Ding J, et al. Independence of familial transmission of mania and depression: results of the NIMH family study of affective spectrum disorders. Mol Psychiatry. 2014;19(2):214–9.

Mitchell PB. Bipolar disorder and anxiety: a comorbidity needing better treatments. Lancet Psychiatry. 2015;2(8):671–2.

Muthén LK, Muthén BO. Mplus User's Guide, 8th Edition. Los Angeles: Muthén & Muthén; 1998–2017.

Nolen-Hoeksema S. Responses to depression and their effects on the duration of depressed mood. J Abnorm Psychol. 1991;100:569–82.

Nolen-Hoeksema S. The role of rumination in depressive disorders and mixed anxiety/depressive symptoms. J Abnorm Psychol. 2000;109(3):504–11.

Nurnberger JI Jr, Blehar MC, Kaufmann CA, York-Cooler C, Simpson SG, Harkavy-Friedman J, et al. Diagnostic interview for genetic studies. Rationale, unique features, and training. NIMH Genetics Initiative. Arch Gen Psychiatry. 1994;51(11):849–59.

Nurnberger JI Jr, McInnis M, Reich W, Kastelic E, Wilcox HC, Glowinski A, et al. A high-risk study of bipolar disorder. Childhood clinical phenotypes as precursors of major mood disorders. Arch Gen Psychiatry. 2011;68(10):1012–20.

O'Garro-Moore JK, Adams AM, Abramson LY, Alloy LB. Anxiety comorbidity in bipolar spectrum disorders: the mediational role of perfectionism in prospective depressive symptoms. J Affect Disord. 2015;174:180–7.

Otto MW, Simon NM, Wisniewski SR, Miklowitz DJ, Kogan JN, Reilly-Harrington NA, et al. Prospective 12-month course of bipolar disorder in out-patients with and without comorbid anxiety disorders. Br J Psychiatry. 2006;189:20–5.

Pavlova B, Perlis RH, Alda M, Uher R. Lifetime prevalence of anxiety disorders in people with bipolar disorder: a systematic review and meta-analysis. Lancet Psychiatry. 2015;2(8):710–7.

Perich T, Lau P, Hadzi-Pavlovic D, Roberts G, Frankland A, Wright A, et al. What clinical features precede the onset of bipolar disorder? J Psychiatr Res. 2015;62:71–7.

Perugi G, Akiskal HS, Toni C, Simonini E, Gemignani A. The temporal relationship between anxiety disorders and (hypo)mania: a retrospective examination of 63 panic, social phobic and obsessive-compulsive patients with comorbid bipolar disorder. J Affect Disord. 2001;1–3:199–206.

Provencher MD, Guimond AJ, Hawke LD. Comorbid anxiety in bipolar spectrum disorders: a neglected research and treatment issue? J Affect Disord. 2012;137(1–3):161–4.

Rimes KA, Watkins E. The effects of self-focused rumination on global negative self-judgements in depression. Behav Res Ther. 2005;43(12):1673–81.

Scott J, Pope M. Cognitive styles in individuals with bipolar disorders. Psychol Med. 2003;6:1081–8.

Scott J, Stanton B, Garland A, Ferrier IN. Cognitive vulnerability in patients with bipolar disorder. Psychol Med. 2000;30(2):467–72.

Shapero BG, Stange JP, Goldstein KE, Black CL, Molz AR, Hamlat EJ, et al. Cognitive Styles in Mood Disorders: discriminative Ability of Unipolar and Bipolar Cognitive Profiles. Int J Cognit Ther. 2015;8(1):35–60.

Soenens B, Elliot AJ, Goossens L, Vansteenkiste M, Luyten P, Duriez B. The intergenerational transmission of perfectionism: parents' psychological control as an intervening variable. J Fam Psychol. 2005;19(3):358–66.

Stange JP, Sylvia LG, da Silva Magalhaes PV, Miklowitz DJ, Otto MW, Frank E, et al. Extreme attributions predict the course of bipolar depression: results from the STEP-BD randomized controlled trial of psychosocial treatment. J Clin Psychiatry. 2013;74(3):249–55.

Tabachnick BG, Fidell LS. Using Multivariate Statistics. 6th ed. MA: Allyn & Bacon; 2013.

Weissman AN, Beck AT. Development and validation of the Dysfunctional Attitude Scale: a preliminary investigation. In: Paper presented at the 62nd annual meeting of the American educational research association, Toronto, Canada. Washington, DC: ERIC Clearinghouse; 1978. http://www.eric.ed.gov/contentdelivery/serviet/ERICServiet?accno=ED167619.

Wheeler HA, Blankstein KR, Antony MM, McCabe RE, Bieling PJ. Perfectionism in anxiety and depression: comparisons across disorders, relations with symptoms severity, and role of comorbidity. Int J Cognit Psychother. 2011;4:66–91.

Wirtz PH, Elsenbruch S, Emini L, Rudisuli K, Groessbauer S, Ehlert U. Perfectionism and the cortisol response to psychosocial stress in men. Psychosom Med. 2007;69(3):249–55.

Young LT, Cooke RG, Robb JC, Levitt AJ, Joffe RT. Anxious and non-anxious bipolar disorder. J Affect Disord. 1993;29(1):49–52.

Youngstrom EA, Murray G, Johnson SL, Findling RL. The 7 up 7 down inventory: a 14-item measure of manic and depressive tendencies carved from the General Behavior Inventory. Psychol Assess. 2013;25(4):1377–83.

15

Circulating antithyroid antibodies contribute to the decrease of glomerular filtration rate in lithium-treated patients: a longitudinal study

Alberto Bocchetta[1,2*], Luca Ambrosiani[1], Gioia Baggiani[1], Claudia Pisanu[1], Caterina Chillotti[2], Raffaella Ardau[2], Fernanda Velluzzi[3], Doloretta Piras[4], Andrea Loviselli[3] and Antonello Pani[4]

Abstract

Background: Concerns about the adverse effects of long-term treatment with lithium include reduced renal function. In the present study, we examined comorbidities which may be associated with chronic kidney disease in a cohort of patients treated with lithium for up to 41 years.

Methods: We studied 394 patients who were treated with lithium for ≥ 5 years. The potential role of comorbidities (diabetes, concurrent antihypertensive medication, treatment with L-thyroxine, and presence of antithyroid peroxidase/microsomes, anti-thyroglobulin, and/or anti-thyrotropin-receptor antibodies) was analysed. We focused on the categories of patients with an estimated glomerular filtration rate (eGFR) lower than 60 or 45 mL/min/1.73 m^2 as calculated from serum creatinine according to the Modification of Diet in Renal Disease Study Group. We applied multivariate regression analysis and Cox survival analysis to study the effects exerted by sex, age, duration of lithium treatment, and comorbidities using eGFR categories as the dependent variable. Kaplan–Meier curves were generated to measure the time to decline to an eGFR lower than 45 mL/min/1.73 m^2 in patients with positive or negative thyroid antibodies.

Results: Age was associated with a decline to an eGFR lower than 60 mL/min/1.73 m^2 after controlling for sex, duration of lithium treatment, and comorbidities. Circulating thyroid antibodies were associated with a decline to an eGFR lower than 45 mL/min/1.73 m^2.

Conclusions: The present study is the first to suggest a potential role of circulating thyroid antibodies in the severe decline of eGFR in lithium-treated patients.

Keywords: Lithium, Renal insufficiency, Chronic, Glomerular filtration rate, Thyroid microsomal antibodies, Anti-thyroglobulin

Background

Adverse renal effects of lithium have long been known, varying from very frequent reversible polyuria (Schou 1958) to irreversible kidney damage (Hestbech et al. 1977; Aurell et al. 1981). New studies have raised concern especially for patients treated for many years (Bendz et al. 2010) and the debate has been revived in 2012 by a review and meta-analysis of the lithium toxicity profile (McKnight et al. 2012). Thereafter, several studies based on various kinds of data sources have addressed the potential risk factors for chronic kidney disease (CKD) in lithium-treated patients. Principal factors under study include sex, age, duration of lithium treatment,

*Correspondence: bocchett@unica.it
[1] Section of Neuroscience and Clinical Pharmacology, Department of Biomedical Sciences, University of Cagliari, Via Ospedale 54, 09124 Cagliari, Italy
Full list of author information is available at the end of the article

concurrent medications, and comorbidities that are already known to predispose to CKD.

In an initial study of 139 patients from our lithium clinic, we found a positive correlation between the duration of lithium treatment and reduced estimated glomerular filtration rate (eGFR) (Bocchetta et al. 2013). Subsequently, we extended the study to 953 patients treated for at least one year and found that eGFR was lower in women, in older patients, and in patients with longer duration of lithium treatment (Bocchetta et al. 2015).

In the meantime, several studies began to be published exploring population-based health records, mostly European, to identify factors which are potentially associated with CKD in lithium-treated cohorts. According to three large studies based on thousands of subjects from UK and Denmark, it can be concluded that long-term exposure to lithium is associated with increased rates of CKD (Close et al. 2014; Kessing et al. 2015; Hayes et al. 2016). Diabetes and the use of antihypertensive diuretic drugs were found among potential risk factors for CKD (Close et al. 2014). On the contrary, a Scottish population-based cohort study including 305 patients exposed to lithium has come up with the different conclusion that there is no effect of stable lithium maintenance therapy on the rate of change in eGFR over time (Clos et al. 2015). However, it must be noted that the mean duration of exposure to lithium was only for 55 months. In the Scottish study, significant predictors for eGFR decline included age, baseline eGFR, comorbidities, co-prescriptions of nephrotoxic drugs, and episodes of lithium toxicity (Clos et al. 2015).

More recently, we took part in a survey from 12 collaborating international sites including 312 patients treated in the lithium clinics for at least 8 years (Tondo et al. 2017). Medical comorbidities were found among risk factors for low eGFR, but were not examined in the details.

Aims of the study

As we are in possession of the detailed clinical data regarding patients on maintenance lithium treatment over the last four decades, the aims of this study were to determine whether comorbidities (hypertension, diabetes, thyroid function, and presence of circulating thyroid antibodies) or their treatments were associated with incident CKD.

Methods

Clinical records of the patients in the database of the Unit of Clinical Pharmacology, Azienda Ospedaliero-Universitaria, Cagliari, were examined. Our unit has been one of the reference centres for lithium monitoring in the Cagliari area since its introduction in the 1970s.

Lithium monitoring was in line with the international guidelines. Our current therapeutic range for lithium maintenance is 0.50–0.80 mmol/L, after it had been lowered from the range 0.60–1.0 mmol/L which was used up to the 1990s (Baldessarini 1996).

The subjects included in this study were all the consecutive patients from the database who had been followed at the lithium clinic between 1976 and 2016 for at least 5 years and whose thyroid-antibody status was known.

For the purpose of this study, we extracted the following variables from the charts of the patients: demographic characteristics, age of onset of lithium treatment, duration of lithium treatment, concurrent antihypertensive medications, diagnosis of diabetes, data on renal and thyroid function.

Renal function

Serum creatinine concentrations were taken from the panel of laboratory tests requested on an annual basis. We used the traditional standardisation method for serum creatinine. The estimated glomerular filtration rate (eGFR) was calculated from serum creatinine values using the equation proposed by the Modification of Diet in Renal Disease (MDRD) Study Group (Levey et al. 2009; Earley et al. 2012), with the '186' correction factor, which takes age, sex and ethnicity into account. The following categories of eGFR were considered: higher than 90 mL/min/1.73 m^2 (G1); 60–89 mL/min/1.73 m^2 (G2); 45–59 mL/min/1.73 m^2 (G3a); 30–44 mL/min/1.73 m^2 (G3b); 15–29 mL/min/1.73 m^2 (G4); lower than 15 mL/min/1.73 m^2 (G5). The abbreviations and ranges recall those used by Kidney Disease Improving Global Outcomes (KDIGO) 2012 Clinical Practice Guidelines for the Evaluation and Management of Chronic Kidney Disease (CKD) (2012), but it must be noted that KDIGO CKD stages are also based on albuminuria categories, which were not included in the present study.

Concomitant medical conditions and related treatments

We studied the following conditions potentially predisposing to CKD:

a. Long-term treatment with any antihypertensive agent before declining to an eGFR lower than 60 mL/min/1.73 m^2.
b. Long-term treatment with oral hypoglycemic agents or insulin, or dietary treatment after receiving an established diagnosis of diabetes.
c. Long-term treatment with L-thyroxine or antithyroid agents.
d. Presence of one or more of the following circulating antibodies: anti-thyroid peroxidase (AbTPO), anti-thyroid microsomes (AbM), anti-thyroglobulin

(AbTG), anti-thyrotropin receptors (TRAb). The laboratory tests varied over the decades. The antibodies were considered positive when they exceeded the upper end of the laboratory range in use at that time. For example, the cut-off was an AbM or AbTG titre $\geq$ 1:100 in the 1990s or an AbTPO $\geq$ 20 or $\geq$ 35 IU/mL (depending on the laboratory) in the more recent tests.

Statistical analysis

We used Student's t test to compare mean and Fisher's exact test to analyse contingency tables. We applied multivariate regression analysis to study the effect exerted by demographic and clinical variables on renal function, using the eGFR category as the dependent variable. The independent variables which were analysed include: sex, age, duration of lithium treatment, diabetes, treatment with antihypertensive medication, treatment with L-thyroxine, and presence of thyroid antibodies. We used Cox survival analysis to study the effects exerted by sex, age, duration of lithium treatment, and comorbidities on renal function. Kaplan–Meier curves were generated to measure the time taken to enter stage G3b in the subgroups of the patients with positive or negative circulating thyroid antibodies. The Log-rank (Mantel–Cox) test was used to compare the survival distributions of the subgroups with positive or negative circulating thyroid antibodies.

Statistical analysis was performed using the SPSS statistical software package v20 (SPSS, Inc., USA).

Results

Psychiatric diagnoses according to ICD-10 were the following: bipolar affective disorder (F31), $N = 280$ (bipolar I, 198; bipolar II, 82); schizoaffective disorder (F25), $N = 33$ (manic type, 20; depressive type, 13); recurrent depressive disorder (F33) $N = 81$.

Table 1 shows demographic and clinical characteristics of the 394 patients studied. Men had started lithium treatment earlier than women and were younger when studied. Duration of lithium treatment did not differ significantly between the sexes.

Similar proportions of women and men were taking long-term antihypertensive drugs before declining to an eGFR lower than 60 mL/min/1.73 m^2.

Diabetes was diagnosed in 89 (23%) patients: when last observed, 14 patients (9 women, 5 men) were being treated with insulin, 34 (21 women, 13 men) with oral hypoglycemic agents, and 41 (33 women, 8 men) with dietary treatment.

Only four patients (1%) had been treated with methimazole for hyperthyroidism, whereas treatment with L-thyroxine regarded as many as 125 (32%) patients. More women than men were taking treatment with L-thyroxine.

Prevalence of circulating thyroid antibodies was significantly higher in women. Antibodies were principally represented by AbTPO (or AbM in older tests prior to the identification of TPO as the specific thyroid microsomal antigen) alone or associated with AbTG (79% of cases). AbTG without AbTPO/AbM were found in 18 women and 1 man. We found only two cases of TRAb with no other circulating antibodies. However, it must be noted that TRAb is not in the panel of first instance thyroid function tests.

Antibody-positive women were taking L-thyroxine more frequently ($54/90 = 60\%$) compared to the antibody-negative ($60/199 = 30\%$) ($P = 0.0001$).

Table 2 shows demographic and clinical characteristics of patients by their final eGFR category. Overall, 84 patients had declined to an eGFR lower than 45 mL/min/1.73 m^2 (CKD3b). A greater proportion of patients in the G3b subgroup had been treated with antihypertensive agents before the diagnosis of CKD compared to the G1–G2 subgroup.

In the regression analysis using three different eGFR categories (G1/G2; G3a; G3b) as the dependent variable, age was the only independent variable with significant effects (Table 3). When the regression analysis was limited to the severest stage (G3b), the effect of circulating

Table 1 Demographic and clinical characteristics by sex

	Total sample ($N = 394$)	Women ($N = 289$)	Men ($N = 105$)	P value
Age of onset of lithium treatment, mean ± SD	39.2 ± 13.0	40.7 ± 13.1	35.0 ± 11.8	0.0001
Years with lithium treatment, mean ± SD	15.1 ± 7.5	15.2 ± 7.7	14.7 ± 6.9	0.56
Current age, mean ± SD	55.0 ± 13.6	56.5 ± 13.6	50.8 ± 12.9	0.0002
Treatment with antihypertensive agents	132 (34%)	99 (34%)	33 (31%)	0.63
Diabetes	89 (23%)	63 (22%)	26 (25%)	0.59
Treatment with L-thyroxine	125 (32%)	114 (39%)	11 (10%)	0.0001
Circulating thyroid antibodies	102 (26%)	90 (31%)	12 (11%)	0.0001

Table 2 Demographic and clinical characteristics by the patient's final eGFR category

	G3b ($N = 84$)	G3a ($N = 55$)	G1–G2 ($N = 255$)	Between-group differences (P value)
Number of males	13 (15%)[a]	18 (33%)	74 (29%)[b]	$a < b$ (0.01)
Current age, mean ± SD	59 ± 11[c]	56 ± 13[d]	48 ± 21[e]	$c > e$ (0.0001); $d > e$ (0.007)
Treatment with antihypertensive agents before declining to eGFR < 60 mL/min/1.73 m^2	38 (45%)[f]	22 (40%)	72 (28%)[g]	$f > g$ (0.005)
Diabetes	21 (25%)	18 (33%)	50 (20%)	–
Treatment with L-thyroxine				
Males	4 (31%)[h]	2 (11%)	5 (7%)[i]	$h > i$ (0.03)
Females	32 (45%)	14 (38%)	68 (38%)	
Total	36 (43%)[j]	16 (29%)	73 (29%)[k]	$l > m$ (0.02)
Circulating thyroid antibodies				
Males	4 (31%)[l]	2 (11%)	6 (8%)[m]	$n > o$ (0.04)
Females	29 (41%)	8 (22%)	53 (29%)	–
Total	33 (39%)[n]	10 (18%)	59 (23%)[o]	$p > q$ (0.005)

Superscripts a–o are used to indicate significant between-group differences

G1–G2, eGFR ≥ 60 mL/min/1.73 m^2

G3a, eGFR = 45–59 mL/min/1.73 m^2

G3b, eGFR < 45 mL/min/1.73 m^2

Table 3 Regression analysis using three different eGFR categories (G1/G2; G3a; G3b) as the dependent variable

Independent variables	P value	Coefficient beta (95% CI)
Sex	0.99	0.001 (− 0.21 to 0.21)
Age	0.009	0.007 (0.002 to 0.012)
Duration of lithium treatment	0.08	0.01 (− 0.001 to 0.022)
Treatment with antihypertensive drugs	0.15	0.13 (− 0.05 to 0.31)
Diabetes	0.89	0.01 (− 0.18 to 0.21)
Treatment with L-thyroxine	0.48	0.07 (− 0.12 to 0.25)
Circulating thyroid antibodies	0.10	0.16 (− 0.03 to 0.35)

thyroid antibodies was the only significant variable (Table 4).

The presence of circulating antibodies was the only significant variable in the Log-rank test or Cox survival analysis (Table 5).

Table 4 Regression analysis using two different eGFR categories (G1/G2/G3a; G3b) as the dependent variable

Independent variables	P value	Coefficient beta (95% CI)
Sex	0.55	− 0.03 (− 0.14 to 0.07)
Age	0.054	0.003 (− 5.3 to 0.005)
Duration of lithium treatment	0.38	0.003 (− 0.003 to 0.009)
Treatment with antihypertensive drugs	0.13	0.07 (− 0.02 to 0.16)
Diabetes	0.69	− 0.02 (− 0.12 to 0.08)
Treatment with L-thyroxine	0.39	0.04 (− 0.05 to 0.13)
Circulating thyroid antibodies	0.03	0.11 (0.01 to 0.20)

Figure 1 shows the Kaplan–Meier curves measuring the time taken to enter stage CKD3b in the subgroups of patients positive ($N = 102$; 33 events; 32%) or negative ($N = 292$; 51 events; 17%) for circulating thyroid antibodies. In this case, the Log-rank (Mantel–Cox) test used to compare the survival distributions provided significant results ($P = 0.044$).

Discussion

The problem of lithium-associated renal dysfunction has recently been addressed by several research studies and reviews. As already mentioned in the introduction, recent large studies agree that long-term exposure to lithium is associated with increased rates of CKD (Close et al. 2014; Bocchetta et al. 2015; Kessing et al. 2015; Hayes et al. 2016). Current interest has been devoted principally to risk factors that are already known to predispose to CKD. Results vary according to study setting, sample size, duration of lithium exposure, quality of data on confounders, and availability of a control group.

The purpose of the present study was to help clarify the role of concomitant conditions which may have been associated with CKD in our cohort of patients. From the beginning of lithium treatment, we have recorded any concurrent medication taken regularly in our clinical charts, as well as laboratory tests which are requested on an annual basis, and reports from consulting cardiologists, endocrinologists, and nephrologists. The main focus of the study was on antihypertensive treatment, diabetes and thyroid function with particular regard to thyroid antibodies. Although international guidelines do not generally include circulating thyroid antibodies

Table 5 Log-rank test and Cox regression analysis of the time taken to enter CKD3b

	Univariate (Log-rank test)	Multivariate (Cox regression analysis)		
	P value	Hazard ratio	95% CI	*P* value
Age[a]	0.21	0.98	0.96–1.0	0.19
Sex	0.21	0.66	0.35–1.25	0.20
Treatment with antihypertensive drugs	0.74	1.02	0.64–1.60	0.93
Circulating thyroid antibodies	0.05	1.57	1.00–2.49	0.05
Treatment with L-thyroxine	0.91	0.83	0.52–1.34	0.45
Diabetes	0.49	0.93	0.56–1.57	0.80

[a] In the univariate analysis, three categories of age (< 45 years; 45–65 years; > 65 years) were used

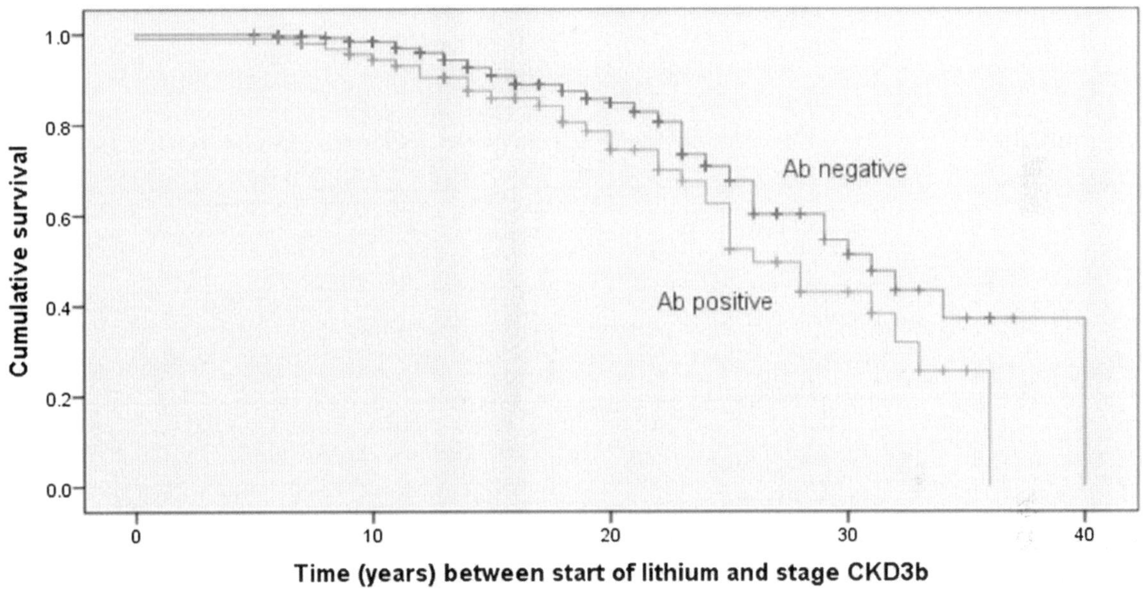

Fig. 1 Kaplan–Meier curve showing the time taken between start of lithium treatment and the decline to stage CKD3b

among the routine laboratory tests for lithium patients, we have started recommending the search for antibodies since the late 1980s, when we first found evidence of high prevalence of AbM and/or AbTG in our cohort of patients (Bocchetta et al. 1991). Thereafter, as AbTPO had been identified as the specific thyroid microsomal antigen (Mariotti et al. 1987), we switched from AbM to AbTPO in our series of follow-up studies (for a review, see Bocchetta and Loviselli 2006).

Diabetes and hypertension

In the present study, we were not able to reveal the role of diabetes and hypertension, that are already known to predispose to CKD in the general population (Stenvinkel 2010) and have also been associated with renal failure in patients treated with lithium (Close et al. 2014; Clos et al. 2015). It must be noted that we found only 14 cases of type-I diabetes, whereas cases of type-II diabetes were typically found in older patients and their effect was perhaps included in the age-related decline of eGFR that we already found in the entire cohort of patients treated with lithium (Bocchetta et al. 2015). A similar conclusion can also be made regarding the treatment with antihypertensive agents, whose apparent role (as shown in Table 2) vanished after controlling for age in the regression analysis. Similar results were observed in the UK study of the patients treated with lithium, (Close et al. 2014) that reported that hypertension itself was not associated with renal disease in fully adjusted models. Moreover, hypertension may not only predispose to CKD, but may also be a consequence of CKD (Sternlicht and Bakris 2017). It must also be noted that certain agents (namely ACE inhibitors and sartans) are prescribed to CKD patients even in the absence of hypertension to prevent further decline in eGFR (Ruggenenti et al. 2012), and this might influence results obtained by studies using the database of antihypertensive prescriptions as a proxy of a diagnosis of hypertension.

Thyroid function

In the present study, we did not observe cases of clinical hypothyroidism or hyperthyroidism because patients were referred to the endocrinologist in case of abnormal TSH concentrations. Therefore, we focused on treatment with L-thyroxine or antithyroid agents as a measure of thyroid dysfunction. It must be noted that the large proportion of patients taking L-thyroxine in the present sample (one-third) may be due to the over-surveillance bias in patients treated with lithium as well as to the multiple indications for treatment: hypothyroidism (lithium- and/or autoimmunity-related), hormone replacement after thyroidectomy (for goitre or cancer), and TSH-suppressing therapy of nodular goitre. The apparent association between treatment with L-thyroxine and stage G3b (Table 2) vanished in the adjusted analyses (Tables 3 and 4).

At variance with the present study which was based on specific treatments, population-based surveys of renal and thyroid function have focused on clinical or subclinical hypothyroidism (increased TSH concentrations with normal thyroid hormone concentrations). Hypothyroidism or increased TSH have been found associated with lower eGFR or impaired kidney function in several cross-sectional surveys, mostly European (Lo et al. 2005; Chonchol et al. 2008; Targher et al. 2009; Asvold et al. 2011; Ye et al. 2013; Meuwese et al. 2014; Rhee et al. 2015). On the other hand, results from prospective studies have not been consistent. In fact, for example, an American and a Chinese survey reported that elevated TSH were not associated with the development of incident CKD during follow-up (Schultheiss et al. 2016; Huang et al. 2016), a large South Korean study reported that high levels of TSH were associated with an increased risk of incident CKD (Zhang et al. 2014), whereas the Rotterdam Study reported that higher TSH levels were associated with lower CKD incidence (Chaker et al. 2016).

Thyroid antibodies

With regard to the role of thyroid antibodies, the absence of control groups of either lithium naïve patients or healthy individuals does not allow us to determine whether the long-term exposure to lithium is a necessary condition or thyroid antibodies may be nephrotoxic in themselves.

Thyroid function has been studied in the general population or in clinical samples with various degrees of CKD (for review, see Iglesias et al. 2017), but the inclusion of antibodies in the panel of thyroid markers has been very rare. To our knowledge, there are only two relevant but contrasting studies (Targher et al. 2009; Schultheiss et al. 2016).

Targher et al. (2009) surveyed cross-sectionally the database of a clinical chemistry laboratory in the north of Italy and found an excess of AbTPO and/or AbTG among individuals with an eGFR lower than 60 mL/min/1.73 m^2 (18/53 = 34%) compared to the remaining individuals (195/862 = 23%). Age- and sex-adjusted P value in logistic regression analysis was significant (0.01). Data included 16 participants with an eGFR lower than 45 mL/min/1.73 m^2. On the contrary, the Atherosclerosis Risk in Communities study, a large prospective study of middle-aged American adults (Schultheiss et al. 2016) found no association between AbTPO and reduced kidney function. In their prospective evaluation over a median follow-up time of 19.6 years, incidence of CKD (eGFR lower than 60 mL/min/1.73 m^2) did not differ between AbTPO-positive and AbTPO-negative participants (odds ratio 0.79; 95% CI = 0.5–1.25; $P = 0.32$; total N of events = 1488) (Schultheiss et al. 2016).

We first suspected that thyroid antibodies may play a role in CKD of patients treated with lithium when we collected the data for our recent collaboration study (Tondo et al. 2017). In fact, we contributed with 30 patients to the study and we were impressed by the high prevalence of circulating thyroid antibodies among the patients who had eventually manifested severe CKD (7/14 = 50%). The present study confirms that circulating thyroid antibodies can contribute to the severe decline of eGFR in patients treated with lithium.

Mechanisms

We can only speculate about the potential mechanisms involved in the excess of thyroid-antibody-related CKD in our cohort of patients treated with lithium, because no renal biopsy data were available.

Case reports have repeatedly associated nephropathy with thyroid antibodies over the last four decades. In some cases, deposition of immune complexes was documented. For example, Jordan et al. (1978) reported a case with immune complex glomerulonephritis and hypothyroidism. Granular glomerular basement membrane and mesangial staining were detected by indirect immunofluorescence, with antibody specific for thyroglobulin and thyroid microsomal antigen.

From the clinical point of view, the majority of the cases reported to date were nephrotic syndrome rather than reduced eGFR (for review, see Santoro et al. 2017). With regard to the relationship between pathological and clinical findings, the most informative contribution has been provided by Koçak et al. (2012) who reviewed retrospectively 28 patients with Hashimoto's thyroiditis referred to their department because of unexplained haematuria, proteinuria or renal impairment. They concluded that glomerular pathologies associated with Hashimoto's thyroiditis are similar to those in the general population. The most common lesions were membranous glomerulonephritis, focal segmental glomerulosclerosis and immunoglobulin A nephritis. Proteinuria and glomerular filtration rate were found independent of thyroid hormone concentrations and thyroid antibodies titres. Of the 28 cases, 12 (43%) had an eGFR lower than 60 mL/min/1.73 m^2, whereas proteinuria was found in 24 (86%), nephrotic range proteinuria in 11 (39%), and haematuria in 11 (39%).

Data on prevalence of proteinuria and haematuria were not available for the present study.

Besides the potential deposition of immune complexes, other mechanisms have been involved in the various diseases that have been found associated with circulating thyroid antibodies. This does not necessarily mean that thyroid antibodies play a direct role in all the observed cases. As circulating thyroid antibodies are very prevalent in the population, their concomitant occurrence with other prevalent diseases may be a coincidence. For example, a Sardinian survey found an overall prevalence of AbTPO of 174/789 (22%) in women and 30/444 (7%) in men (Loviselli et al. 1999). With regard to the psychiatric presentation of the so-called Hashimoto's encephalopathy, we have suggested that it may be dependent on a diffuse vasculitis (Bocchetta et al. 2007, 2016). In turn, vasculitis may be due to concurrent antibodies: for example, Yoneda et al. (2007) have suggested that antibodies against the amino terminal region of alpha-enolase play a role in Hashimoto's encephalopathy. Because alpha-enolase is expressed in vascular endothelial cells, autoantibodies against this enzyme may be associated with vasculitis. Moreover, alpha-enolase has been identified among intrinsic renal antigens that are targets of nephritogenic antibodies. Indeed, in situ formation of immune complexes is a well-recognised mechanism of renal injury, as observed in systemic autoimmune disorders (Migliorini et al. 2002).

On the other hand, vasculitis or cross-reactivity between antigens are among the mechanisms suggested to explain the cases of glomerulopathies associated with autoimmune thyroiditis (Santoro et al. 2017).

Conclusions

Whatever the mechanism, the potential role of thyroid antibodies in the decline of glomerular filtration in patients with mood disorders is relevant, given their frequent co-occurrence.

Given the current uncertainty regarding the potential role of thyroid antibodies in CKD due to the paucity of studies on the general population and the lack of a control group of patients with mood disorders never treated with lithium in the present study, it is yet to be established whether the long-term exposure to lithium is a necessary condition to allow the manifestation of the effects of thyroid antibodies or thyroid antibodies are nephrotoxic in themselves.

If our finding will be confirmed, it might have some clinical implications when discussing the role of lithium with consultant nephrologists in cases of patients with declining eGFR. We suggest the inclusion of thyroid antibodies in the list of risk factors potentially associated with CKD.

Abbreviations

CI: confidence interval; CKD: chronic kidney disease; eGFR: estimated glomerular filtration rate; AbTPO: anti-thyroid peroxidase antibodies; AbM: anti-thyroid microsomes antibodies; AbTG: anti-thyroglobulin antibodies; TRAb: anti-thyrotropin receptors; TSH: thyroid stimulating hormone; FT4: free thyroxine; T3: triiodothyronine; FT3: free triiodothyronine.

Authors' contributions

AB devised the study, participated in its design and coordination, and drafted the manuscript. RA and CC participated in the study design, literature search, and data collection and interpretation. LA and GB participated in data collection and interpretation. CP and DP participated in the study design, performed statistical analysis, and participated in data interpretation. FV and AL performed the assessment of thyroid function and participated in data interpretation and drafting of the manuscript. DP and AP performed the assessment of renal function and participated in data interpretation and drafting of the manuscript. All authors read and approved the final manuscript.

Author details

[1] Section of Neuroscience and Clinical Pharmacology, Department of Biomedical Sciences, University of Cagliari, Via Ospedale 54, 09124 Cagliari, Italy. [2] Unit of Clinical Pharmacology, Cagliari University Hospital, Cagliari, Italy. [3] Department of Medical Sciences and Public Health, University of Cagliari, Cagliari, Italy. [4] Nephrology, Dialysis and Transplantation Unit, 'Giuseppe Brotzu' Hospital, Cagliari, Italy.

Acknowledgements

None.

Competing interests

The authors declare that they have no competing interests.

Funding

This work was supported by a supplementary fund for research from the University of Cagliari.

References

Asvold BO, Bjøro T, Vatten LJ. Association of thyroid function with estimated glomerular filtration rate in a population-based study: the HUNT study. Eur J Endocrinol. 2011;164:101–5.

Aurell M, Svalander C, Wallin L, Alling C. Renal function and biopsy findings in patients on long-term lithium treatment. Kidney Int. 1981;20:663–70.

Baldessarini RJ. Drugs and the treatment of psychiatric disorders: depression and mania. In: Hardman JG, Limbird LE, editors. Goodman and Gilman's the pharmacological basis of therapeutics. 9th ed. New York: McGraw-Hill; 1996. p. 431–59.

Bendz H, Schön S, Attman PO, Aurell M. Renal failure occurs in chronic lithium treatment but is uncommon. Kidney Int. 2010;77:219–24.

Bocchetta A, Loviselli A. Lithium treatment and thyroid abnormalities. Clin Pract Epidemiol Ment Health. 2006;2:23.

Bocchetta A, Bernardi F, Pedditzi M, et al. Thyroid abnormalities during lithium treatment. Acta Psychiatr Scand. 1991;83:193–8.

Bocchetta A, Tamburini G, Cavolina P, Serra A, Loviselli A, Piga M. Affective psychosis, Hashimoto's thyroiditis, and brain perfusion abnormalities: case report. Clin Pract Epidemiol Ment Health. 2007;3:31.

Bocchetta A, Ardau R, Carta P, et al. Duration of lithium treatment is a risk factor for reduced glomerular function: a cross sectional study. BMC Med. 2013;11:33.

Bocchetta A, Ardau R, Fanni T, et al. Renal function during long-term lithium treatment: a cross-sectional and longitudinal study. BMC Med. 2015;13:12.

Bocchetta A, Traccis F, Mosca E, Serra A, Tamburini G, Loviselli A. Bipolar disorder and antithyroid antibodies: review and case series. Int J Bipolar Disord. 2016;4:5.

Chaker L, Sedaghat S, Hoorn EJ, et al. The association of thyroid function and the risk of kidney function decline: a population-based cohort study. Eur J Endocrinol. 2016;175:653–60.

Chonchol M, Lippi G, Salvagno G, Zoppini G, Muggeo M, Targher G. Prevalence of subclinical hypothyroidism in patients with chronic kidney disease. Clin J Am Soc Nephrol. 2008;3:1296–300.

Clos S, Rauchhaus P, Severn A, Cochrane L, Donnan PT. Long-term effect of lithium maintenance therapy on estimated glomerular filtration rate in patients with affective disorders: a population-based cohort study. Lancet Psychiatry. 2015;2:1075–83.

Close H, Reilly J, Mason JM, et al. Renal failure in lithium-treated bipolar disorder: a retrospective cohort study. PLoS ONE. 2014;9:e90169.

Earley A, Miskulin D, Lamb EJ, Levey AS, Uhlig K. Estimating equations for glomerular filtration rate in the era of creatinine standardization: a systematic review. Ann Intern Med. 2012;156:785–95.

Hayes JF, Marston L, Walters K, Geddes JR, King M, Osborn DP. Adverse renal, endocrine, hepatic, and metabolic events during maintenance mood stabilizer treatment for bipolar disorder: a population-based cohort study. PLoS Med. 2016;3:e1002058.

Hestbech J, Hansen HE, Amdisen A, Olsen S. Chronic renal lesions following long-term treatment with lithium. Kidney Int. 1977;12:205–13.

Huang X, Ding L, Peng K, et al. Thyroid hormones associate with risk of incident chronic kidney disease and rapid decline in renal function: a prospective investigation. J Transl Med. 2016;14:336.

Iglesias P, Bajo MA, Selgas R, Díez JJ. Thyroid dysfunction and kidney disease: an update. Rev Endocr Metab Disord. 2017;18:131–44.

Jordan SC, Johnston WH, Bergstein JM. Immune complex glomerulonephritis mediated by thyroid antigens. Arch Pathol Lab Med. 1978;102:530–3.

Kessing LV, Gerds TA, Feldt-Rasmussen B, Andersen PK, Licht RW. Use of lithium and anticonvulsants and the rate of chronic kidney disease: a nationwide population-based study. JAMA Psychiatry. 2015;72:1182–91.

Koçak G, Huddam B, Azak A, Ortabozkoyun L, Duranay M. Coexistent findings of renal glomerular disease with Hashimoto's thyroiditis. Clin Endocrinol (Oxf). 2012;76:759–62.

Levey AS, Stevens LA, Schmid CH, et al. A new equation to estimate glomerular filtration rate. Ann Intern Med. 2009;150:604–12.

Lo JC, Chertow GM, Go AS, Hsu CY. Increased prevalence of subclinical and clinical hypothyroidism in persons with chronic kidney disease. Kidney Int. 2005;67:1047–52.

Loviselli A, Oppo A, Velluzzi F, et al. Independent expression of serological markers of thyroid autoimmunity and hepatitis virus C infection in the general population: results of a community-based study in north-western Sardinia. J Endocrinol Invest. 1999;22:660–5.

Mariotti S, Anelli S, Ruf J, et al. Comparison of serum thyroid microsomal and thyroid peroxidase autoantibodies in thyroid diseases. J Clin Endocrinol Metab. 1987;65:987–93.

McKnight RF, Adida M, Budge K, Stockton S, Goodwin GM, Geddes JR. Lithium toxicity profile: a systematic review and meta-analysis. Lancet. 2012;379:721–8.

Meuwese CL, Gussekloo J, de Craen AJ, Dekker FW, den Elzen WP. Thyroid status and renal function in older persons in the general population. J Clin Endocrinol Metab. 2014;99:2689–96.

Migliorini P, Pratesi F, Bongiorni F, Moscato S, Scavuzzo M, Bombardieri S. The targets of nephritogenic antibodies in systemic autoimmune disorders. Autoimmun Rev. 2002;1:168–73.

Rhee CM, Kalantar-Zadeh K, Streja E, et al. The relationship between thyroid function and estimated glomerular filtration rate in patients with chronic kidney disease. Nephrol Dial Transplant. 2015;30:282–7.

Ruggenenti P, Cravedi P, Remuzzi G. Mechanisms and treatment of CKD. J Am Soc Nephrol. 2012;23:1917–28.

Santoro D, Vadalà C, Siligato R, Buemi M, Benvenga S. Autoimmune thyroiditis and glomerulopathies. Front Endocrinol (Lausanne). 2017;8:119.

Schou M. Lithium studies. 1. Toxicity. Acta Pharmacol Toxicol (Copenh). 1958;15:70–84.

Schultheiss UT, Daya N, Grams ME, et al. Thyroid function, reduced kidney function and incident chronic kidney disease in a community-based population: the atherosclerosis risk in communities study. Nephrol Dial Transplant. 2016. https://doi.org/10.1093/ndt/gfw301.

Stenvinkel P. Chronic kidney disease: a public health priority and harbinger of premature cardiovascular disease. J Intern Med. 2010;268:456–67.

Sternlicht H, Bakris GL. The kidney in hypertension. Med Clin North Am. 2017;101:207–17.

Targher G, Chonchol M, Zoppini G, et al. Prevalence of thyroid autoimmunity and subclinical hypothyroidism in persons with chronic kidney disease not requiring chronic dialysis. Clin Chem Lab Med. 2009;47:1367–71.

Tondo L, Abramowicz M, Alda M, et al. Long-term lithium treatment in bipolar disorder: effects on glomerular filtration rate and other metabolic parameters. Int J Bipolar Disord. 2017;5:27.

Ye Y, Gai X, Xie H, Jiao L, Zhang S. Impact of thyroid function on serum cystatin C and estimated glomerular filtration rate: a cross-sectional study. Endocr Pract. 2013;19:397–403.

Yoneda M, Fujii A, Ito A, Yokoyama H, Nakagawa H, Kuriyama M. High prevalence of serum autoantibodies against the amino terminal of alpha-enolase in Hashimoto's encephalopathy. J Neuroimmunol. 2007;185(1–2):195–200.

Zhang Y, Chang Y, Ryu S, et al. Thyroid hormone levels and incident chronic kidney disease in euthyroid individuals: the Kangbuk Samsung Health Study. Int J Epidemiol. 2014;43:1624–32.

Anxiety, irritability, and agitation as indicators of bipolar mania with depressive symptoms: a post hoc analysis of two clinical trials

Trisha Suppes[1*], Jonas Eberhard[2,3,4], Ole Lemming[2], Allan H. Young[4] and Roger S. McIntyre[5]

Abstract

Background: Symptoms of anxiety, irritability, and agitation (AIA) are prevalent among patients with bipolar I disorder (BD-I) mania with depressive symptoms, and could potentially be used to aid physicians in the identification of this more severe form of BD-I. Using data from two clinical trials, the aims of this post hoc analysis were to describe the phenomenology of bipolar mania in terms of AIA and depressive symptoms, and to evaluate the influence of these symptoms on the likelihood of remission during treatment.

Methods: Patients with a BD-I manic or mixed episode (Diagnostic and Statistical Manual of Mental Disorders IV criteria) were randomised to 3 weeks of double-blind treatment with asenapine, placebo, or olanzapine (active comparator). Anxiety was defined as a score of ≥3 on the Positive and Negative Syndrome Scale 'anxiety' item, irritability as a score of ≥4 on the Young Mania Rating Scale (YMRS) 'irritability' item, and agitation as a score of ≥3 on the YMRS 'increased motor activity–energy' item. Depressive symptoms were defined as a score of ≥1 on three or more individual Montgomery–Åsberg Depression Rating Scale (MADRS) items, or a MADRS Total score of ≥20.

Results: A total of 960 patients with BD-I were analysed, 665 with a manic episode and 295 with a mixed episode. At baseline, 61.4% had anxiety, 62.4% had irritability, 76.4% had agitation, and 34.0% had all three AIA symptoms ('severe AIA'); 47.3% had three or more depressive symptoms, and 13.5% had a MADRS total score of ≥20. Anxiety, irritability, and severe AIA (but not agitation) were statistically significantly more common in patients with depressive symptoms. Patients with anxiety or severe AIA at baseline were statistically significantly less likely to achieve remission (YMRS total <12). In general, remission rates were higher with asenapine and olanzapine than with placebo, irrespective of baseline AIA or depressive symptoms.

Conclusions: Assessment of AIA symptoms in bipolar mania could enable physicians to identify patients with more severe depressive symptoms, allowing for appropriate intervention. Assessment and monitoring of AIA may help physicians to predict which patients may be harder to treat and at risk for self-harm.

Keywords: Bipolar disorder, Mixed features, Depression, Anxiety, Irritability, Agitation, Remission

*Correspondence: tsuppes@stanford.edu
[1] VA Palo Alto Health Care System and Department of Psychiatry and Behavioral Sciences, Stanford University School of Medicine, Stanford, CA, USA
Full list of author information is available at the end of the article

Background

Bipolar I disorder (BD-I) is an illness that comprises more than just two discrete poles; between the extremes of 'pure' mania and 'pure' depression, patients can experience 'mixed' states in which various manic and depressive symptoms are present at the same time. Mixed states were described by Kraepelin in the early 20th century, and have been well characterised and operationally defined in the 100 years since (Kraepelin 1921; Swann et al. 2013). The fourth edition of the Diagnostic and Statistical Manual of Mental Disorders (DSM-IV) defined a 'mixed episode' as the coexistence of the full symptomatology of a manic and a depressive episode—a restrictive, categorical approach that neglects those patients with subsyndromal depressive symptoms (Vieta and Valentí 2013; American Psychiatric Association 1994). Since the DSM-IV, studies have shown that this definition does not reflect clinical reality and that patients with bipolar disorder [as well as patients with major depressive disorder (MDD)] have a complex symptom presentation (Suppes et al. 2005; Vieta and Valentí 2013; Targum and Nierenberg 2011). Consequently, the fifth edition of the DSM (DSM-5) changed to a dimensional approach for the diagnosis of BD-I (Vieta and Valentí 2013). The DSM-5 includes a 'with mixed features' specifier that applies to a manic or hypomanic episode with three or more depressive symptoms (or, alternatively, to a depressive episode with three or more manic symptoms) (American Psychiatric Association 2013). In a retrospective chart review, three times as many patients with bipolar disorder were diagnosed with mixed features using the DSM-5 criteria compared with the DSM-IV text revision (DSM-IV-TR) criteria for a mixed episode (Shim et al. 2015). In an observational study, around half of patients with DSM-IV bipolar mania did not meet the criteria for DSM-5 bipolar mania, due to the additional requirement of increased activity or energy levels (Machado-Vieira et al. 2017). However, 45% of these patients now met the DSM-5 criteria for a major depressive episode with mixed features, showing the value of the mixed features specifier for making diagnoses across the continuum of mood disorders (Machado-Vieira et al. 2017).

Patients with BD-I mixed states have a worse clinical course than those with 'pure' manic states, since they tend to experience more episodes, and since episodes are of longer duration (Swann et al. 2013). Mania with depressive symptoms is also associated with a high rate of comorbid conditions, such as anxiety disorders and substance abuse (Swann et al. 2013). These patients are harder to treat and physicians of patients meeting the DSM-5 criteria for mania 'with mixed features' report greater treatment dissatisfaction than do physicians of patients without mixed features (Swann et al. 2013; Young and Eberhard 2015). Furthermore, there is a higher risk of suicidality among patients with mixed features; these patients are more likely to have made at least one suicide attempt during their lifetime, and during their current manic episode, compared with patients without mixed features (Swann et al. 2013; Young and Eberhard 2015). Thus, the presence of depressive symptoms during a manic episode is indicative of a more severe form of BD-I.

The symptoms observed in manic episodes and depressive episodes are not mutually exclusive, with anxiety, irritability, and agitation (AIA), for example, occurring in both mania and depression. Since they are not specific to either pole, AIA symptoms are not included in the DSM-5 'with mixed features' specifier (Cassidy 2010; Koukopoulos et al. 2013). [Anxiety is, however, covered by the DSM-5 'with anxious distress' specifier (American Psychiatric Association 2013)]. According to physicians, AIA symptoms show an increased prevalence, and greater severity, in patients with mixed features in BD-I mania compared with those without mixed features (Young and Eberhard 2015). Similarly, in an online survey, patients with mania with depressive symptoms self-reported the combination of 'anxiety or worry' and 'irritability or agitation' more frequently than those without depressive symptoms (Vieta et al. 2014). A recent prospective study from the Stanley Bipolar Network found increased irritability in bipolar patients with mixed depression compared with pure depression (Miller et al. 2016). Due to their high frequency among such patients, AIA symptoms could potentially be used as indicators (albeit non-specific indicators) to aid physicians in the identification of patients whose mania is complicated by depressive symptoms.

Using data from two pivotal, randomised, placebo-controlled asenapine trials, the aims of the present post hoc analysis were (1) to describe the phenomenology of bipolar mania in terms of AIA and depressive symptoms, (2) to evaluate if the presence of AIA and depressive symptoms can be used to predict non-remission, and (3) to evaluate the effect of asenapine, placebo, and olanzapine on remission in patients with AIA, and in patients with depressive symptoms.

Methods

This was a post hoc analysis of patient-level data from two 3-week, randomised, placebo-controlled trials (ARES 7501004 and ARES 7501005; ClinicalTrials.gov identifiers NCT00159744 and NCT00159796, respectively) of asenapine in patients with BD-I experiencing an acute DSM-IV manic or mixed episode (McIntyre et al. 2009, 2010). Olanzapine was included as active comparator.

Study design and patients

The two primary studies had identical designs, which have been described previously (McIntyre et al. 2009, 2010). In brief, eligible patients were aged ≥18 years with a current DSM-IV diagnosis of BD-I. Patients were required to have a manic or mixed episode that began in the 3 months prior to screening, a Young Mania Rating Scale (YMRS; Young et al. 1978). Total score of ≥20 at screening and baseline, and a documented history of at least one previous moderate-to-severe mood episode, with or without psychotic features. Patients were excluded if they had a primary diagnosis other than BD-I, a psychotic disorder, rapid-cycling bipolar disorder, or substance abuse or dependence.

Eligible patients entered a single-blind placebo run-in (washout) period of up to 7 days in an inpatient treatment centre. Following the run-in period, patients were randomised in a 2:1:2 ratio to 3 weeks of double-blind treatment with oral asenapine (20 mg on Day 1, flexible-dose 10 or 20 mg/day thereafter; dose divided across morning and evening), placebo, or olanzapine (15 mg on Day 1, flexible-dose 5–20 mg thereafter; once daily). Patients remained in the inpatient centre for at least the first 7 days of treatment, after which they could complete the trial as outpatients if they were deemed stable and suitable for discharge by the investigator. Benzodiazepines (lorazepam ≤4 mg/day for agitation; temazepam ≤30 mg/day for insomnia; or others with comparable half-lives) were permitted for the first 7 days of treatment only.

Assessments

In the two primary studies, efficacy was assessed using psychiatric rating scales including the YMRS, the Clinical Global Impressions-Bipolar version (CGI-BP; Spearing et al. 1997; Guy 1976), the Montgomery–Åsberg Depression Rating Scale (MADRS; Montgomery and Åsberg 1979), and the Positive and Negative Syndrome Scale (PANSS; Kay et al. 1987). YMRS and CGI-BP assessments were made at screening, baseline, and Days 2, 4, 7, 14, and 21 (or end of treatment). MADRS assessments were made at baseline, Day 7, and at Day 21 or study endpoint.

In this post hoc analysis, the presence or absence of AIA symptoms at baseline was assessed using the following definitions. Anxiety was defined as a score of ≥3 ("mild") on the PANSS anxiety item (item G2; possible score range from 1 "absent" to 7 "extreme"; Kay et al. 1987). Irritability was defined as a score of ≥4 ("irritable at times during interview, recent episodes of anger or annoyance on ward") on the YMRS irritability item (item 5; possible score range from 0 "absent" to 8 "hostile, uncooperative; interview impossible"; Young et al. 1978). Agitation was defined as a score of ≥3 ("excessive energy, hyperactive at times, restless [can be calmed]") on the YMRS increased motor activity–energy item (item 2; possible score range from 0 "absent" to 4 "motor excitement; continuous hyperactivity [cannot be calmed]"; Young et al. 1978). 'Severe AIA' was defined as meeting the above criteria for all three AIA symptoms.

Two definitions were used, in separate analyses, for the presence of depressive symptoms at baseline: (1) a score of ≥1 on three or more individual MADRS items; (2) a MADRS Total score of ≥20.

Two definitions were used, in separate analyses, for YMRS remission: (1) a YMRS Total score of <12 at endpoint (Day 21); (2) a YMRS Total score of <8 at endpoint (Day 21).

Safety and tolerability were assessed in the primary studies; please refer to the primary sources for these analyses (McIntyre et al. 2009, 2010).

Statistical analyses

This post hoc analysis was performed on the full analysis set (FAS), which comprised all randomised patients who took at least one dose of study medication, and had at least one valid post-baseline YMRS assessment.

For baseline analyses of the incidence of AIA symptoms stratified by the number and severity of depressive symptoms, between-group comparisons were made using a Chi squared test. Incidence of remission, stratified by the presence or absence of baseline AIA and depressive symptoms, was analysed using two criteria—YMRS Total score of <12, and YMRS Total score of <8, at Day 21—also using a Chi squared test for between-group comparisons. Due to repeated testing, a significance level of 0.01 was applied in the remission analyses (Bonferroni adjustment for multiplicity); a significance level of 0.05 was applied elsewhere. A footnote on relevant comparisons indicates where the significance level is 0.01.

The AIA parameters that were found to be statistically significant predictors of non-remission were then examined using an analysis of covariance (ANCOVA), in order to determine the effects of treatment (asenapine, placebo, or olanzapine) on change in YMRS Total score over time. Between-group comparisons were made using a *t* test.

Results

Disposition

Across the two primary studies, a total of 977 patients were randomised and 976 were treated. The FAS comprised 960 patients (480 from each study), split into asenapine ($n = 372$), placebo ($n = 197$), and olanzapine ($n = 391$) treatment groups.

Baseline characteristics: phenomenology of bipolar mania in terms of AIA and depressive symptoms

Patient baseline demographic and clinical characteristics are presented in Table 1. Slightly over half of patients were male, and the majority were unemployed. The ratio of manic to mixed episodes of BD-I was approximately 7:3. On average, patients had pronounced mania at baseline (mean [SD] YMRS Total score of 28.9 [6.2] and CGI-BP Mania severity of 4.6 [0.8]—markedly ill), and mild depression (mean [SD] MADRS Total score of 11.3 [7.3] and CGI-BP Depression severity of 2.1 [1.3]—minimally ill). Patients were well matched between treatment groups for all measurements.

Overall, 589 patients (61.4%) had anxiety at baseline, 599 patients (62.4%) had irritability at baseline, and 733 patients (76.4%) had agitation at baseline. Severe AIA (i.e., all three AIA symptoms) was present in 326 patients (34.0%). The proportion of patients with each AIA

Table 1 Baseline demographic and clinical characteristics

	Asenapine ($n = 372$)	Placebo ($n = 197$)	Olanzapine ($n = 391$)	Total ($N = 960$)
Male, *n* (%)	203 (54.6)	98 (49.7)	230 (58.8)	531 (55.3)
Age (years), median (range)	40 (18–76)	39 (18–69)	39 (18–67)	39 (18–76)
Unemployed, *n* (%)	270 (72.6)	139 (70.6)	285 (72.9)	694 (72.3)
DSM-IV BD-I diagnosis, *n* (%)				
Manic episode	265 (71.2)	131 (66.5)	269 (68.8)	665 (69.3)
Mixed episode	107 (28.8)	66 (33.5)	122 (31.2)	295 (30.7)
YMRS total score[a], mean (SD)	28.8 (6.2)	28.7 (6.2)	29.2 (6.3)	28.9 (6.2)
MADRS total score[a], mean (SD)	10.8 (7.0)	12.4 (7.8)	11.3 (7.3)	11.3 (7.3)
CGI-BP mania severity score[a], mean (SD)	4.7 (0.8)	4.6 (0.8)	4.6 (0.8)	4.6 (0.8)
CGI-BP depression severity score[a], mean (SD)	2.0 (1.2)	2.2 (1.3)	2.1 (1.3)	2.1 (1.3)
Number of depressive symptoms[b], *n* (%)				
0–2	201 (54.0)	100 (50.8)	205 (52.4)	506 (52.7)
3 or more	171 (46.0)	97 (49.2)	186 (47.6)	454 (47.3)
Severity of depressive symptoms, n (%)				
MADRS Total score <20	328 (88.2)	164 (83.2)	338 (86.4)	830 (86.5)
MADRS Total score ≥20	44 (11.8)	33 (16.8)	53 (13.6)	130 (13.5)
Anxiety[c], *n* (%)				
Absent or minimal	144 (38.7)	73 (37.1)	150 (38.4)	367 (38.2)
Present	227 (61.0)	124 (62.9)	238 (60.9)	589 (61.4)
Not rated	1 (0.3)	0 (0.0)	3 (0.8)	4 (0.4)
Irritability[d], *n* (%)				
Absent or low	150 (40.3)	65 (33.0)	134 (34.3)	349 (36.4)
Present	218 (58.6)	128 (65.0)	253 (64.7)	599 (62.4)
Not rated	4 (1.1)	4 (2.0)	4 (1.0)	12 (1.3)
Agitation[e], *n* (%)				
Absent or low	83 (22.3)	48 (24.4)	84 (21.5)	215 (22.4)
Present	285 (76.6)	145 (73.6)	303 (77.5)	733 (76.4)
Not rated	4 (1.1)	4 (2.0)	4 (1.0)	12 (1.3)
Severe AIA[f], *n* (%)				
Not present	247 (66.4)	123 (62.4)	248 (63.4)	618 (64.4)
Present	120 (32.3)	70 (35.5)	136 (34.8)	326 (34.0)
One or more symptom not rated	5 (1.3)	4 (2.0)	7 (1.8)	16 (1.7)

AIA, anxiety, irritability, and agitation; BD-I, bipolar I disorder; CGI-BP, Clinical Global Impressions-Bipolar version; DSM-IV, Diagnostic and Statistical Manual of Mental Disorders, Fourth Edition; MADRS, Montgomery–Åsberg Depression Rating Scale; PANSS, Positive and Negative Syndrome Scale; SD, standard deviation; YMRS, Young Mania Rating Scale

[a] For patients missing a value at baseline, the value was used from the screening visit

[b] Based on the number of individual MADRS items with a score of ≥1

[c] Based on the PANSS anxiety item: 'absent or minimal' indicates a score of ≤2; 'present' indicates a score of ≥3

[d] Based on the YMRS irritability item: 'absent or low' indicates a score of ≤3; 'present' indicates a score of ≥4

[e] Based on the YMRS increased motor activity–energy item: 'absent or low' indicates a score of ≤2; 'present' indicates a score of ≥3

[f] Meeting the above criteria for all three AIA symptoms

symptom, and the overlap between symptoms, is shown in Fig. 1.

Considering depressive symptoms, 454 patients (47.3%) had three or more depressive symptoms at baseline based on individual MADRS items, and 130 patients (13.5%) had a MADRS Total score of ≥20.

Figure 2 shows the relationships between depressive symptoms and AIA symptoms at baseline. Anxiety and irritability were statistically significantly more common in patients with depressive symptoms at baseline, both for patients with three or more individual depressive symptoms, and for patients with a MADRS Total score of ≥20. Agitation, in contrast, was not more common in patients with depressive symptoms at baseline. Finally, severe AIA (all three symptoms) was statistically significantly more common in patients with depressive symptoms at baseline.

Can the presence of AIA and depressive symptoms be used to predict non-remission?

As shown in Fig. 3a, patients with anxiety at baseline were statistically significantly less likely to achieve remission than those without anxiety at baseline, according to both definitions of remission (YMRS Total score of <12 and <8 at Day 21). The presence of severe AIA at baseline also had a statistically significant negative effect on remission,

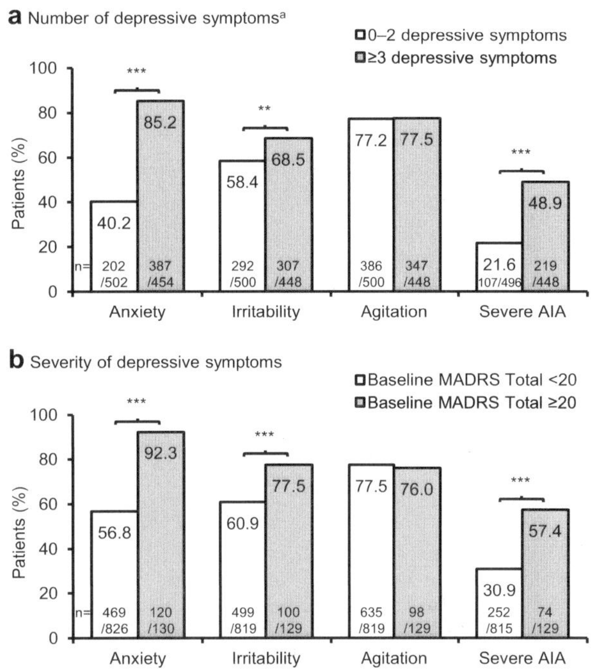

Fig. 2 Incidence of baseline AIA symptoms in BD-I mania, stratified by the number/severity of depressive symptoms. $^{**}p < 0.01$, $^{***}p < 0.001$, Chi squared test. Anxiety was defined as a PANSS anxiety item score of ≥3 at baseline. Irritability was defined as a YMRS irritability item score of ≥4 at baseline. Agitation was defined as a YMRS increased motor activity–energy item score of ≥3 at baseline. Severe AIA was defined as meeting the above criteria for all three AIA symptoms. Patients missing a value for the corresponding symptom at baseline were not included in the analysis. [a] Based on the number of individual MADRS items with a score of ≥1. AIA, anxiety, irritability, and agitation; BD-I, bipolar I disorder; MADRS, Montgomery–Åsberg Depression Rating Scale; PANSS, Positive and Negative Syndrome Scale; YMRS, Young Mania Rating Scale. **a** Number of depressive symptoms of 0-2 symptoms versus 3 or more symptoms, and **b** severity of depressive symptoms baseline MADRS <20 versus ≥ to 20

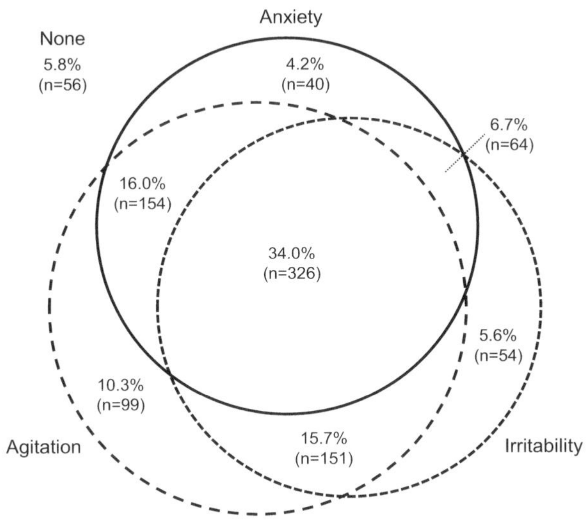

Fig. 1 Venn diagram displaying the overlap of comorbid AIA symptoms in BD-I mania. Sixteen patients (1.7%) were missing a value for one or more AIA symptom at baseline and are not shown on the figure. Anxiety was defined as a PANSS anxiety item score of ≥3 at baseline. Irritability was defined as a YMRS irritability item score of ≥4 at baseline. Agitation was defined as a YMRS increased motor activity–energy item score of ≥3 at baseline. Percentages are calculated from the full analysis set, which comprised 960 patients. AIA, anxiety, irritability, and agitation; BD-I, bipolar I disorder; PANSS, Positive and Negative Syndrome Scale; YMRS, Young Mania Rating Scale

when defined as a YMRS Total score of <12. The presence of agitation at baseline reduced the incidence of remission by 8–10% points, but this did not meet the criteria for statistical significance. The only AIA symptom without a notable effect on remission was irritability.

As shown in Fig. 3b, the presence of three or more depressive symptoms at baseline reduced the incidence of remission by 6–9% points, but this did not meet the criteria for statistical significance. In contrast, the presence of depressive symptoms defined by a MADRS Total score of ≥20 had no notable effect on remission rate.

Effect of treatment on remission in patients with AIA and depressive symptoms

With remission defined as a YMRS Total score of <12 at Day 21, remission rates were higher with asenapine

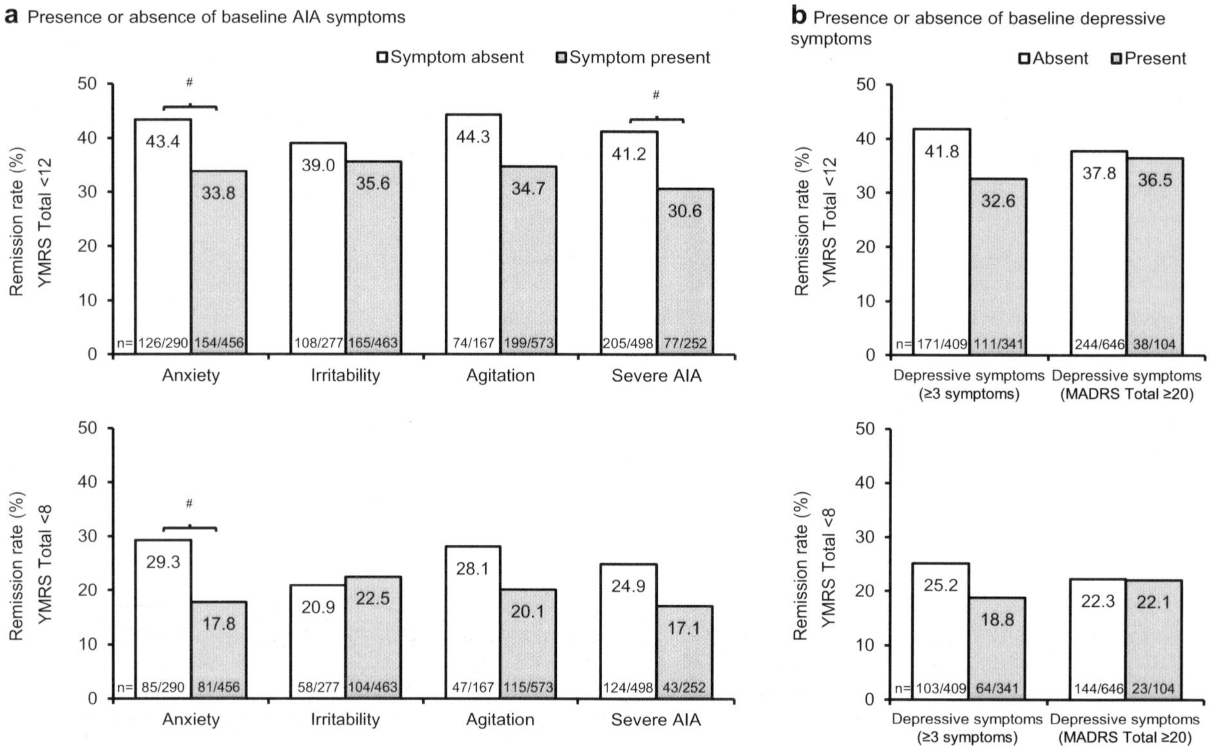

Fig. 3 Incidence of remission in BD-I mania, stratified by baseline AIA/depressive symptoms. #*p*-value significant (when adjusted for multiplicity), Chi squared test. Anxiety was defined as a PANSS anxiety item score of ≥3 at baseline. Irritability was defined as a YMRS irritability item score of ≥4 at baseline. Agitation was defined as a YMRS increased motor activity–energy item score of ≥3 at baseline. Severe AIA was defined as meeting the above criteria for all three AIA symptoms. Patients missing a value for the corresponding symptom at baseline were not included in the analysis. Two definitions were used for remission: a YMRS Total score of <12 at Day 21 (upper figures); and a YMRS Total score of <8 at Day 21 (lower figures) (observed cases). Depressive symptoms were defined in two ways: ≥3 individual MADRS items with a score of ≥1, or a MADRS Total score of ≥20 at baseline. AIA, anxiety, irritability, and agitation; BD-I, bipolar I disorder; MADRS, Montgomery–Åsberg Depression Rating Scale; PANSS, Positive and Negative Syndrome Scale; YMRS, Young Mania Rating Scale. **a** Presence or absence of baseline AIA symptoms and **b** presence or absence of baseline depressive symptoms

and olanzapine than with placebo among patients with anxiety, irritability, agitation, or severe AIA at baseline, as shown in Fig. 4a. With remission defined as a YMRS Total score of <8 at Day 21, remission rates were only higher than placebo with asenapine and olanzapine among patients with irritability or agitation at baseline. For patients with depressive symptoms at baseline, remission rates were generally higher with asenapine and olanzapine than with placebo, as shown in Fig. 4b. These differences were not tested for statistical significance.

Since baseline anxiety and severe AIA were identified as statistically significant predictors of non-remission (see Fig. 3a), stratified analyses according to feature present or not present were carried out, to determine the effect of treatment on change in YMRS Total score over time. As shown in Fig. 5, asenapine and olanzapine produced a statistically significant benefit on YMRS Total score at the majority of time points among patients with anxiety at baseline (Day 21 effect sizes: 0.33 for asenapine, and 0.34 for olanzapine). The benefits were even greater among patients without anxiety at baseline (Day 21 effect sizes: 0.76 for asenapine, and 0.95 for olanzapine). A statistically significant benefit on YMRS Total score was also observed at the majority of time points among patients with severe AIA at baseline (Day 21 effect sizes: 0.42 for asenapine, and 0.45 for olanzapine).

Discussion

This post hoc analysis of two randomised, controlled trials revealed that symptoms of anxiety, irritability, and agitation were present in around two-thirds-to-three-quarters of patients with BD-I mania. In addition, around a third of patients had all three AIA symptoms. While different studies have defined the presence of AIA symptoms in different ways, there is agreement in the literature that AIA symptoms are common among patients with BD-I mania (Hantouche et al. 2006; Vieta et al. 2014; Young and Eberhard 2015).

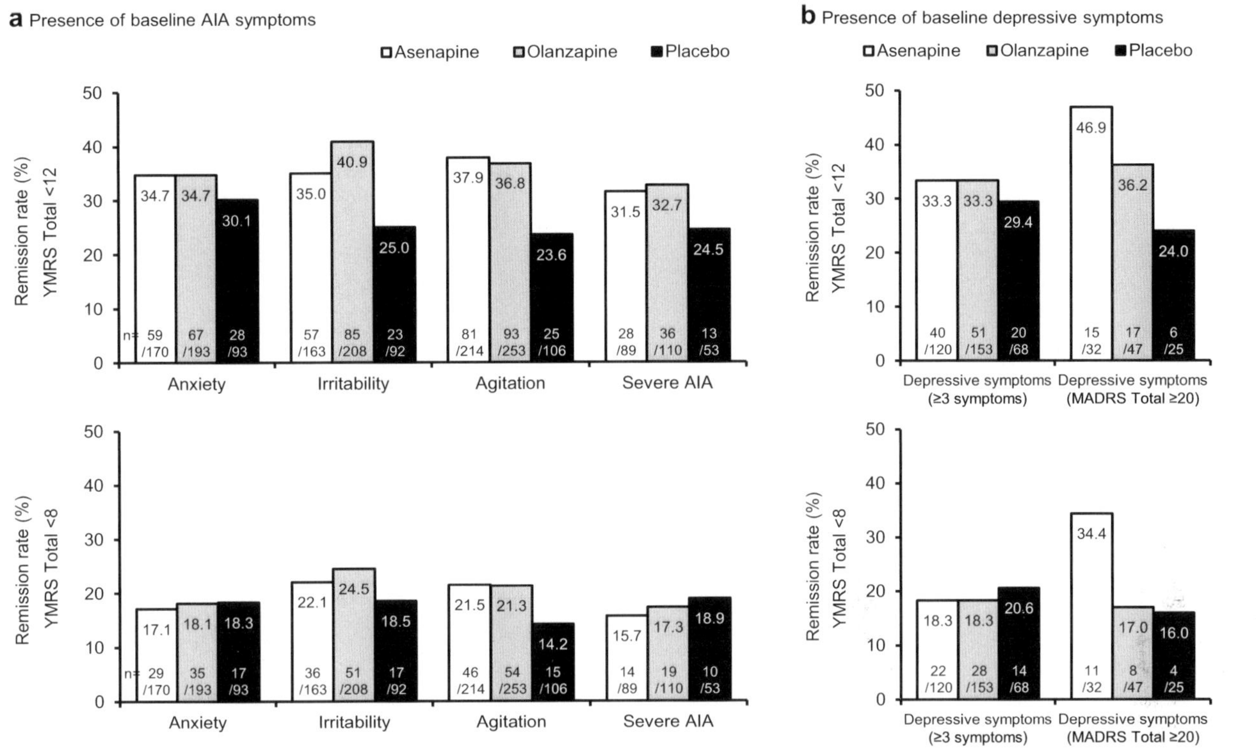

Fig. 4 Incidence of remission by treatment group in BD-I mania, stratified by baseline AIA/depressive symptoms. Anxiety was defined as a PANSS anxiety item score of ≥3 at baseline. Irritability was defined as a YMRS irritability item score of ≥4 at baseline. Agitation was defined as a YMRS increased motor activity–energy item score of ≥3 at baseline. Severe AIA was defined as meeting the above criteria for all three AIA symptoms. Patients missing a value for the corresponding symptom at baseline were not included in the analysis. Two definitions were used for remission: a YMRS Total score of <12 at Day 21 (upper figures); and a YMRS Total score of <8 at Day 21 (lower figures) (observed cases). Depressive symptoms were defined in two ways: ≥3 individual MADRS items with a score of ≥1, or a MADRS Total score of ≥20 at baseline. AIA, anxiety, irritability, and agitation; BD-I, bipolar I disorder; MADRS, Montgomery–Åsberg Depression Rating Scale; PANSS, Positive and Negative Syndrome Scale; YMRS, Young Mania Rating Scale. **a** Presence of baseline AIA symptoms and **b** presence of baseline depressive symptoms

The present analysis also showed that half of patients with BD-I mania had at least three depressive symptoms, whereas less than one in seven patients had a MADRS Total score of ≥20. A previous post hoc analysis in the same dataset found that 4–34% of patients met proxy criteria for the DSM-5 'with mixed features' specifier, depending on the severity cut-offs used (McIntyre et al. 2013a). In general, the incidence of depressive symptoms among bipolar disorder patients with mania is around 30–40%, though the incidence varies widely according to how the presence of depressive symptoms is defined (McElroy et al. 1992; Akiskal et al. 1998; Hantouche et al. 2006; Azorin et al. 2009; Vieta et al. 2014; Young and Eberhard 2015; McIntyre et al. 2015). In a prospective study of patients with bipolar hypomania, the likelihood of having depressive symptoms was significantly greater for women (72%) than for men (42%) (Suppes et al. 2005).

With regard to the relationship between AIA and depressive symptoms, the analysis showed that anxiety, irritability, and the AIA combination—but not agitation alone—were more common in patients with depressive symptoms at baseline. This replicates the findings of a naturalistic study, in which anxiety and irritability were more common in BD-I patients with three or more depressive symptoms, whereas agitation was not (Young and Eberhard 2015). Thus, anxiety and irritability, and the combination of all three AIA symptoms, could potentially be used as non-specific indicators, or 'gateway symptoms', to help psychiatrists identify bipolar mania with depressive symptoms (Eberhard and Weiller 2016). At present, the DSM-5 does not highlight or discuss AIA symptoms in the 'with mixed features' specifier section. Future iterations of the DSM may want to consider how to discuss the findings of this study and related studies in terms of the mixed specifier. While our findings are not definitive, given the retrospective nature of these analyses and limits of the studies themselves, they do highlight the need for further assessment of the best components to make up the mixed specifier for future DSM-5 editions.

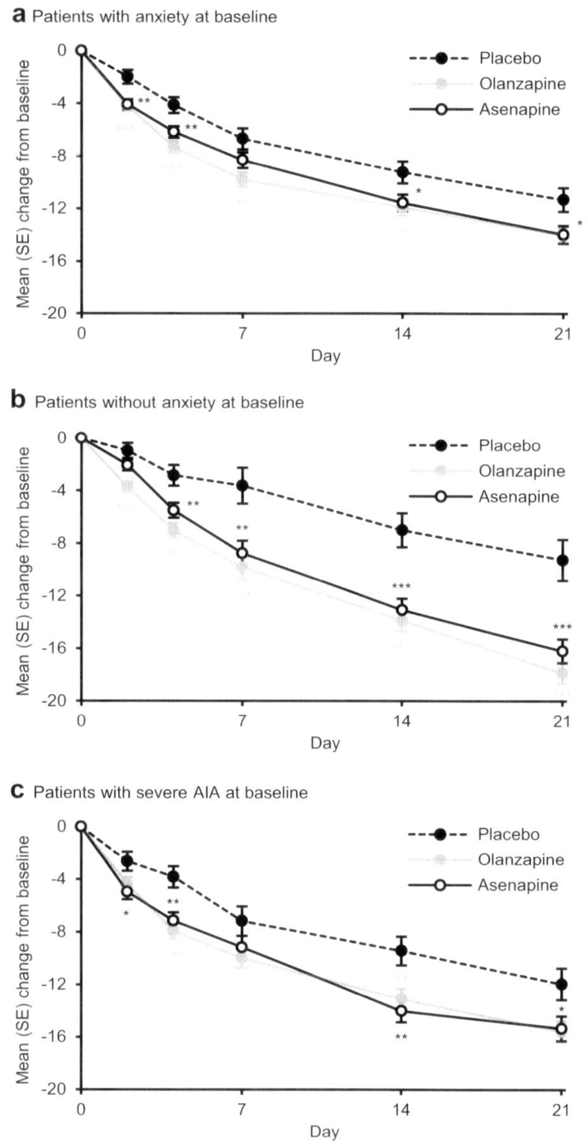

Fig. 5 Change from baseline in YMRS Total score by treatment group in BD-I mania. **p* < 0.05, ***p* < 0.01, ****p* < 0.001 versus placebo, *t* test. Anxiety was defined as a PANSS anxiety item score of ≥3 at baseline. Irritability was defined as a YMRS irritability item score of ≥4 at baseline. Agitation was defined as a YMRS increased motor activity–energy item score of ≥3 at baseline. Severe AIA was defined as meeting the above criteria for all three AIA symptoms. Patients missing a value for the corresponding symptom at baseline were not included in the analysis. AIA, anxiety, irritability, and agitation; BD-I, bipolar I disorder; PANSS, Positive and Negative Syndrome Scale; SE, standard error; YMRS, Young Mania Rating Scale. **a** Patients with anxiety at baseline, **b** patients without anxiety at baseline, and **c** patients with severe AIA at baseline

These results support the importance of assessing carefully any patient presenting with significant anxiety, irritability, and agitation for underlying symptoms of depression, especially during mania or hypomanic episodes. While it is routine practice to administer depression scales in some settings, this is not universal. The presence of these symptoms supports that it is a time to review carefully whether they herald less visible symptomology that could inform both clinical care and address patient concerns such as self-harm. As noted in a recent article by Solé and colleagues (2017) and consistent with the findings reported here, indicators of mixity may be key to appropriate treatment choices and addressing suicide prevention effectively (Solé et al. 2017).

Of interest, a recent pilot study examined the use of actigraphy to assess prediction for different bipolar clinical states including mania, depression, and mixed (Scott et al. 2017). In this small sample with 24 h of observation, the researchers were able to predict with 79% accuracy which state a subject was experiencing (Scott et al. 2017). It is to be hoped these types of objective measures may assist us to understand, prevent, and treat mixed symptoms more efficiently.

The presence of anxiety in patients with bipolar disorder has previously been associated with a longer time to remission (Feske et al. 2000). The present analysis extended this observation—showing that patients with anxiety or a combination of all three AIA symptoms are less likely to achieve remission than those without the corresponding symptom(s). Thus, these data support the notion that AIA symptoms identify a more severe or complicated phenotype of mania that is less likely to respond to treatment.

Similarly, patients with three or more depressive symptoms were less likely to achieve remission, although this outcome did not meet the criteria for statistical significance. However, patients with a MADRS Total score of ≥20 showed similar remission rates to those below this depression threshold. The previous post hoc analysis in this same dataset also found that the remission rate (defined as a YMRS Total score of ≤12) was not influenced by the number or severity of depressive symptoms (with the exception of the most severely depressed patients, who showed a *higher* remission rate) (McIntyre et al. 2013a). It may be that those patients who are the most ill may also be the most responsive to the medications under study; and thus most likely to show a larger degree of improvement.

In BD-I (unlike in MDD) there has been relatively little prior investigation into whether patient characteristics (including AIA) within an episode can affect treatment response and other health outcomes (Feske et al. 2000). A recent analysis showed that the presence of AIA symptoms raises the already high suicide risk among patients with BD-I mania with depressive symptoms (Eberhard and Weiller 2016). Additionally, a subtype of bipolar depression, characterised by anxiety and irritability among other symptoms, is associated with a greater likelihood of receiving government financial support, suggesting that this pattern of symptoms is particularly malignant (Perich et al. 2016). From a clinical point of view, given the hazards associated with AIA, clinicians should routinely probe for AIA, and should systematically target these symptoms with treatment. In MDD, for example, many physicians reserve adjunctive antipsychotics for use in patients presenting with agitation or irritability, among other symptoms (McIntyre and Weiller 2015). Furthermore, the 2015 update to the Florida Best Practice Psychotherapeutic Medication Guidelines provides different algorithms for the treatment of MDD according to the presence or absence of mixed features (University of South Florida 2015); this is an unmet need for BD-I.

In the present analysis, both asenapine and olanzapine demonstrated higher remission rates (defined as a YMRS score of <12) than placebo among patients with AIA symptoms. A more stringent definition of remission was also considered (a YMRS score of <8); remission rates were low (<25%) with this definition regardless of treatment, demonstrating the difficulty in reducing symptoms to this level over such a short time period. Asenapine and olanzapine also showed consistent benefits over placebo in terms of mean change from baseline in YMRS Total score among patients with anxiety and all three AIA symptoms. In general, second-generation antipsychotics are efficacious in the treatment of mixed episodes with predominant manic symptoms, and have been described as the treatment of choice in the management of bipolar disorder mixed states (Muralidharan et al. 2013; Fagiolini et al. 2015). In mania with DSM-5 mixed features, asenapine, aripiprazole, and olanzapine have been evaluated and have shown efficacy as potential treatment options (McIntyre et al. 2013a, b; Tohen et al. 2014).

In line with considerations of best treatment choices, a range of guideline efforts for the treatment of bipolar disorder have recently been developed (Stahl et al. 2017; Fountoulakis et al. 2016; Goodwin et al. 2016) or are in revision, such as the CANMAT guidelines (Yatham et al. 2013). The importance of the results reported in this present post hoc analysis is highlighted as the best definition for mixed symptoms is sought and the understanding of the implications for treatment and course of illness is developed. It is clear from both past and more recent efforts that mixed symptoms herald a more severe course of illness, but the optimal definition is still under enquiry (Swann et al. 2013; Barbuti et al. 2017).

This present study is limited in that it is a post hoc analysis of studies that were not designed for this purpose. In particular, as these were regulatory studies, patients with current suicidality or complex comorbidities were excluded from study entry, thus limiting generalizability. In terms of study design, participants were inpatients for at least the first week of treatment, which may have selected for agitation. The results may also have been influenced by the use of benzodiazepines for agitation. Benzodiazepines were not permitted beyond Day 7 of treatment; however, 131 patients (13.6%) in the FAS received one or more doses of benzodiazepines beyond Day 7. The use of proxies for AIA and depressive symptoms was another limitation of the analysis—especially for agitation, which was based on the YMRS increased motor activity–energy item because no agitation item was available. Since irritability and agitation were based upon YMRS items, they were not independent with regard to YMRS remission. It is important to keep in mind that this proxy for depression symptoms (MADRS ≥3), and thus potential mixed symptoms, does not itself assess for the DSM-5 Mixed Specifier criteria and must be viewed as a limit of the study design. Finally, the analysis does not rule out the possibility of pseudospecificity: that AIA and depressive symptoms are discrete, overlapping phenomena.

Conclusions

Assessment of AIA symptoms in bipolar mania could enable physicians to identify patients with more severe depressive symptoms and who may be at increased risk of suicide, allowing for appropriate intervention. Furthermore, assessment and monitoring of AIA may help physicians to predict which patients may be harder to treat.

Abbreviations

AIA: anxiety, irritability, and agitation; ANCOVA: analysis of covariance; BD-I: bipolar I disorder; CGI-BP: Clinical Global Impressions-Bipolar version; DSM: Diagnostic and Statistical Manual of Mental Disorders; FAS: full analysis set; MADRS: Montgomery–Åsberg Depression Rating Scale; MDD: major depressive disorder; PANSS: Positive and Negative Syndrome Scale; SD: standard deviation; SE: standard error; YMRS: Young Mania Rating Scale.

Authors' contributions

OL performed the statistical analyses. TS, JE, OL, AY, and RM contributed to the data interpretation and to the drafting and revisions of the manuscript. All authors read and approved the final manuscript.

Author details

[1] VA Palo Alto Health Care System and Department of Psychiatry and Behavioral Sciences, Stanford University School of Medicine, Stanford, CA, USA. [2] H. Lundbeck A/S, Valby, Copenhagen, Denmark. [3] Department of Clinical Sciences, Lund University, Lund, Sweden. [4] Department of Psychological Medicine, Institute of Psychiatry, Psychology & Neuroscience (IoPPN), King's College London, London, UK. [5] Mood Disorders Psychopharmacology Unit, University Health Network, University of Toronto, Toronto, ON, Canada.

Acknowledgements

Writing services were provided by Cambridge Medical Communication Ltd (Cambridge, UK).

Competing interests

TS in the past 5 years has received grants from the National Institute of Mental Health, VA Cooperative Studies Program, Pathway Genomics, Stanley Medical Research Institute, Elan Pharma International Ltd, and Sunovion Pharmaceuticals; consulting fees from H. Lundbeck A/S, Sunovion, Merck & Co, and AstraZeneca; honoraria from Medscape Education, Global Medical Education, CMEology, Omnia-Prova Education Collaborative Inc, and ISBD Columbia; royalties from Jones & Bartlett and UpToDate; and travel reimbursement from Sunovion, Omnia-Prova Education Collaborative Inc, American Psychiatric Association, International Society of Bipolar Disorders (ISBD) Columbia, Global Medical Education, CMEology, H. Lundbeck A/S, Merck & Co and AstraZeneca.

JE and OL are employees of H. Lundbeck A/S.

AY has received grants/research support for investigator-initiated studies from AstraZeneca, Eli Lilly, and Lundbeck; and has received honoraria or consultation fees for paid lectures and advisory boards from all major pharmaceutical companies with drugs used in affective and related disorders.

RM has received research grants from the Stanley Medical Research Institute (non-profit organisation), and from Allergan, AstraZeneca, Janssen Ortho, Lundbeck, Otsuka, Pfizer, Purdue, and Shire. He has been part of advisory boards for, and received speaker's fees from, AstraZeneca, Bristol-Myers Squibb, Eli Lilly, Forest, Janssen Ortho, Johnson & Johnson, Lundbeck, Mitsubishi, Moksha8, Otsuka, Pfizer, Purdue, Shire, Sunovion, and Takeda.

Funding

Study NCT00159796 was funded by Schering-Plough and Pfizer Inc. Study NCT00159744 was funded by Merck and Pfizer Inc. Funding for the writing of this manuscript was provided by H. Lundbeck A/S (Valby, Denmark).

References

Akiskal HS, Hantouche EG, Bourgeois ML, Azorin JM, Sechter D, Allilaire JF, et al. Gender, temperament, and the clinical picture in dysphoric mixed mania: findings from a French national study (EPIMAN). J Affect Disord. 1998;50(2–3):175–86.

American Psychiatric Association. Diagnostic and statistical manual of mental disorders. 4th ed. Washington, DC: American Psychiatric Association; 1994.

American Psychiatric Association. Diagnostic and statistical manual of mental disorders. 5th ed. Arlington: American Psychiatric Association; 2013.

Azorin JM, Aubrun E, Bertsch J, Reed C, Gerard S, Lukasiewicz M. Mixed states vs. pure mania in the French sample of the EMBLEM study: results at baseline and 24 months—European mania in bipolar longitudinal evaluation of medication. BMC Psychiatry. 2009;9:33.

Barbuti M, Pacchiarotti I, Vieta E, Azorin JM, Angst J, Bowden CL, et al. Antidepressant-induced hypomania/mania in patients with major depression: evidence from the BRIDGE-II-MIX study. J Affect Disord. 2017;219:187–92.

Cassidy F. Anxiety as a symptom of mixed mania: implications for DSM-5. Bipolar Disord. 2010;12(4):437–9.

Eberhard J, Weiller E. Suicidality and symptoms of anxiety, irritability, and agitation in patients experiencing manic episodes with depressive symptoms: a naturalistic study. Neuropsychiatr Dis Treat. 2016;12:2265–71.

Fagiolini A, Coluccia A, Maina G, Forgione RN, Goracci A, Cuomo A, Young AH. Diagnosis, epidemiology and management of mixed states in bipolar disorder. CNS Drugs. 2015;29(9):725–40.

Feske U, Frank E, Mallinger AG, Houck PR, Fagiolini A, Shear MK, et al. Anxiety as a correlate of response to the acute treatment of bipolar I disorder. Am J Psychiatry. 2000;157(6):956–62.

Fountoulakis KN, Grunze H, Vieta E, Young A, Yatham L, Blier P, et al. The International College of Neuro-Psychopharmacology (CINP) treatment guidelines for Bipolar disorder in adults (CINP-BD-2017), part 3: the clinical guidelines. Int J Neuropsychopharmacol. 2016. [Epub ahead of print].

Goodwin GM, Haddad PM, Ferrier IN, Aronson JK, Barnes T, Cipriani A, et al. Evidence-based guidelines for treating bipolar disorder: Revised third edition recommendations from the British Association for Psychopharmacology. J Psychopharmacol. 2016;30(6):495–553.

Guy W. ECDEU assessment manual for psychopharmacology, revised. Rockville: National Institute of Mental Health; 1976.

Hantouche EG, Akiskal HS, Azorin JM, Châtenet-Duchêne L, Lancrenon S. Clinical and psychometric characterization of depression in mixed mania: a report from the French National Cohort of 1090 manic patients. J Affect Disord. 2006;96(3):225–32.

Kay SR, Fiszbein A, Opler LA. The positive and negative syndrome scale (PANSS) for schizophrenia. Schizophr Bull. 1987;13(2):261–76.

Koukopoulos A, Sani G, Ghaemi SN. Mixed features of depression: why DSM-5 is wrong (and so was DSM-IV). Br J Psychiatry. 2013;203(1):3–5.

Kraepelin E. Manic–depressive insanity and paranoia. Edinburgh: E&S Livingstone; 1921.

Machado-Vieira R, Luckenbaugh DA, Ballard ED, Henter ID, Tohen M, Suppes T, Zarate CA Jr. Increased activity or energy as a primary criterion for the diagnosis of bipolar mania in DSM-5: findings from the STEP-BD study. Am J Psychiatry. 2017;174(1):70–6.

McElroy SL, Keck PE Jr, Pope HG Jr, Hudson JI, Faedda GL, Swann AC. Clinical and research implications of the diagnosis of dysphoric or mixed mania or hypomania. Am J Psychiatry. 1992;149(12):1633–44.

McIntyre RS, Weiller E. Real-world determinants of adjunctive antipsychotic prescribing for patients with major depressive disorder and inadequate response to antidepressants: a case review study. Adv Ther. 2015;32(5):429–44.

McIntyre RS, Cohen M, Zhao J, Alphs L, Macek TA, Panagides J. A 3-week, randomized, placebo-controlled trial of asenapine in the treatment of acute mania in bipolar mania and mixed states. Bipolar Disord. 2009;11(7):673–86.

McIntyre RS, Cohen M, Zhao J, Alphs L, Macek TA, Panagides J. Asenapine in the treatment of acute mania in bipolar I disorder: a randomized, double-blind, placebo-controlled trial. J Affect Disord. 2010;122(1–2):27–38.

McIntyre RS, Tohen M, Berk M, Zhao J, Weiller E. DSM-5 mixed specifier for manic episodes: evaluating the effect of depressive features on severity and treatment outcome using asenapine clinical trial data. J Affect Disord. 2013a;150(2):378–83.

McIntyre RS, Miguelez M, Vogel Marler S, Baker RA, Rahman Z. Analysis of aripiprazole clinical data using the proposed DSM-5 diagnostic criteria for mixed features in bipolar disorder. Poster abstract NR8-08 at American Psychiatric Association 2013 Annual Meeting. 2013b. http://www.psychiatry.org/psychiatrists/search-directories-databases/library-and-archive. Accessed 18 May 2017.

McIntyre RS, Soczynska JK, Cha DS, Woldeyohannes HO, Dale RS, Alsuwaidan MT, et al. The prevalence and illness characteristics of DSM-5-defined "mixed feature specifier" in adults with major depressive disorder and bipolar disorder: results from the International Mood Disorders Collaborative Project. J Affect Disord. 2015;172:259–64.

Miller S, Suppes T, Mintz J, Hellemann G, Frye MA, McElroy SL, et al. Mixed depression in bipolar disorder: prevalence rate and clinical correlates during naturalistic follow-up in the Stanley Bipolar Network. Am J Psychiatry. 2016;173(10):1015–23.

Montgomery SA, Åsberg M. A new depression scale designed to be sensitive to change. Br J Psychiatry. 1979;134:382–9.

Muralidharan K, Ali M, Silveira LE, Bond DJ, Fountoulakis KN, Lam RW, Yatham LN. Efficacy of second generation antipsychotics in treating acute mixed episodes in bipolar disorder: a meta-analysis of placebo-controlled trials. J Affect Disord. 2013;150(2):408–14.

Perich T, Hadzi-Pavlovic D, Frankland A, Breakspear M, Loo C, Roberts G, et al. Are there subtypes of bipolar depression? Acta Psychiatr Scand. 2016;134(3):260–7.

Scott J, Vaaler AE, Fasmer OB, Morken G, Krane-Gartiser K. A pilot study to determine whether combinations of objectively measured activity parameters can be used to differentiate between mixed states, mania, and bipolar depression. Int J Bipolar Disord. 2017;5(1):5.

Shim IH, Woo YS, Bahk WM. Prevalence rates and clinical implications of bipolar disorder "with mixed features" as defined by DSM-5. J Affect Disord. 2015;173:120–5.

Solé E, Garriga M, Valentí M, Vieta E. Mixed features in bipolar disorder. CNS Spectr. 2017;22(2):134–40.

Spearing MK, Post RM, Leverich GS, Brandt D, Nolen W. Modification of the Clinical Global Impressions (CGI) scale for use in bipolar illness (BP): the CGI-BP. Psychiatry Res. 1997;73(3):159–71.
Stahl SM, Morrissette DA, Faedda G, Fava M, Goldberg JF, Keck PE, et al. Guidelines for the recognition and management of mixed depression. CNS Spectr. 2017;22(2):203–19.
Suppes T, Mintz J, McElroy SL, Altshuler LL, Kupka RW, Frye MA, et al. Mixed hypomania in 908 patients with bipolar disorder evaluated prospectively in the Stanley Foundation Bipolar Treatment Network: a sex-specific phenomenon. Arch Gen Psychiatry. 2005;62(10):1089–96.
Swann AC, Lafer B, Perugi G, Frye MA, Bauer M, Bahk WM, et al. Bipolar mixed states: an International Society for Bipolar Disorders task force report of symptom structure, course of illness, and diagnosis. Am J Psychiatry. 2013;170(1):31–42.
Targum SD, Nierenberg A. The complexity of "mixed" depression: a common clinical presentation. Innov Clin Neurosci. 2011;8(6):38–42.
Tohen M, McIntyre RS, Kanba S, Fujikoshi S, Katagiri H. Efficacy of olanzapine in the treatment of bipolar mania with mixed features defined by DSM-5. J Affect Disord. 2014;168:136–41.
University of South Florida. Florida Medicaid Drug Therapy Management Program sponsored by the Florida Agency for Health Care Administration. 2015 Florida Best Practice Psychotherapeutic Medication Guidelines for Adults. 2015. http://www.medicaidmentalhealth.org/_assets/file/Guidelines/Web_2015-Psychotherapeutic%20Medication%20Guidelines%20for%20Adults_Final_Approved1.pdf. Accessed 18 May 2017.
Vieta E, Valentí M. Mixed states in DSM-5: implications for clinical care, education, and research. J Affect Disord. 2013;148(1):28–36.
Vieta E, Grunze H, Azorin JM, Fagiolini A. Phenomenology of manic episodes according to the presence or absence of depressive features as defined in DSM-5: results from the IMPACT self-reported online survey. J Affect Disord. 2014;156:206–13.
Yatham LN, Kennedy SH, Parikh SV, Schaffer A, Beaulieu S, Alda M, et al. Canadian Network for Mood and Anxiety Treatments (CANMAT) and International Society for Bipolar Disorders (ISBD) collaborative update of CANMAT guidelines for the management of patients with bipolar disorder: update 2013. Bipolar Disord. 2013;15(1):1–44.
Young AH, Eberhard J. Evaluating depressive symptoms in mania: a naturalistic study of patients with bipolar disorder. Neuropsychiatr Dis Treat. 2015;11:1137–43.
Young RC, Biggs JT, Ziegler VE, Meyer DA. A rating scale for mania: reliability, validity and sensitivity. Br J Psychiatry. 1978;133:429–35.

Aripiprazole once-monthly as maintenance treatment for bipolar I disorder: a 52-week, multicenter, open-label study

Joseph R. Calabrese[1*], Na Jin[2], Brian Johnson[2], Pedro Such[3], Ross A. Baker[2], Jessica Madera[2], Peter Hertel[3], Jocelyn Ottinger[2], Joan Amatniek[2] and Hiroaki Kawasaki[4]

Abstract

Background: The long-acting injectable antipsychotic aripiprazole once-monthly 400 mg (AOM 400) was recently approved for maintenance treatment of bipolar I disorder (BP-I). The purpose of this study was to evaluate the safety, tolerability, and efficacy of AOM 400 as long-term maintenance treatment for BP-I.

Methods: This open-label multicenter study evaluated the effectiveness of AOM 400 as maintenance treatment for BP-I by assessing safety and tolerability (primary objective) and efficacy (secondary objective). The study enrolled AOM 400-naive ("de novo") patients as well as AOM 400-experienced ("rollover") patients with BP-I from a lead-in randomized, placebo-controlled clinical trial that demonstrated the efficacy of AOM 400 in the maintenance treatment of BP-I (Calabrese et al. in J Clin Psychiatry 78:324–331, 2017). Safety variables included frequency and severity of treatment-emergent adverse events (TEAEs) and TEAEs resulting in study discontinuation. Efficacy was assessed by the proportion of patients maintaining stability throughout the maintenance phase, as well as mean changes from baseline in Young Mania Rating Scale (YMRS), Montgomery–Asberg Depression Rating Scale, and Clinical Global Impressions for Bipolar Disorder–Severity of Illness Scale (CGI-BP-S) total scores. Patient acceptability and tolerability of treatment was assessed using the Patient Satisfaction with Medication Questionnaire-Modified.

Results: Of 464 patients entering the maintenance phase, 379 (82%) were de novo and 85 (18%) were rollover. TEAEs were more common in de novo than rollover patients. The overall discontinuation rate due to TEAEs was 10.3% (48/464). Improvements in YMRS and CGI-BP-S total scores were maintained during the study, and the vast majority of both de novo (87.0%) and rollover (97.6%) patients maintained stability through their last visit. Overall, the need for rescue medication during the maintenance phase was minimal (< 10% of patients). Patient satisfaction levels were high, with both de novo and rollover patients rating the side effect burden of AOM 400 as greatly improved relative to previous medications.

Conclusion: AOM 400 was safe, effective, and well tolerated by both de novo and AOM 400-experienced patients with BP-I for long-term maintenance treatment.

Keywords: Aripiprazole once-monthly, Bipolar I disorder, Maintenance treatment, Safety, Patient satisfaction

*Correspondence: joseph.calabrese@uhhospitals.org
[1] University Hospitals Cleveland Medical Center, 10524 Euclid Avenue, Cleveland, OH 44106, USA
Full list of author information is available at the end of the article

Background

Bipolar I disorder (BP-I) is a lifelong neuropsychiatric disorder characterized by manic episodes, and frequently includes depressive states intermixed with periods of remission. BP-I is specifically defined by periods of debilitating mania that impair social and occupational functioning and can include psychotic symptoms and the need for hospitalization (Grande et al. 2016). It has been shown that even during periods of remission, patients with BP-I exhibit high levels of functional and cognitive impairment, leading to a reduced quality of life (Martinez-Aran et al. 2004; Martino et al. 2009). Combined, these data suggest that treatment during both mood episodes and periods of remission is warranted.

Long-term pharmacologic therapy may be required to maintain periods of remission, prevent relapse of symptoms, and preserve function (Work Group on Bipolar Disorder 2002). The most commonly used medications for BP-I include mood stabilizers, anticonvulsants, and second-generation (atypical) antipsychotics (SGAs) (Grande et al. 2016). For patients with BP-I who experience severe episodes of mania, SGAs have frequently been used in conjunction with drugs such as lithium or valproate for stabilization during crises. Oftentimes these SGAs are then continued as adjunctive maintenance treatments (Lindström et al. 2017). More recently, certain SGAs have been approved for use as maintenance monotherapy, including risperidone and aripiprazole oral or bi-weekly and monthly formulations (Kishi et al. 2016; McIntyre et al. 2011). Oral therapy has traditionally been used for treatment of BP-I, but newer long-acting injectable (LAI) antipsychotic formulations may allow for better adherence rates, more consistent dosing, more regular contact between patients and their healthcare team, and improved patient outcomes (Brissos et al. 2014).

Though there are numerous oral options for maintenance treatment of BP-I, until recently, bimonthly risperidone LAI was the only LAI atypical antipsychotic approved by the US Food and Drug Administration (FDA) for maintenance treatment of BP-I (Risperdal Consta 2016). Randomized controlled trials have demonstrated the efficacy of bi-weekly risperidone LAI as monotherapy and adjunctive therapy in delaying time to recurrence of mood episodes in patients with BP-I (Macfadden et al. 2009; Quiroz et al. 2010). In an open-label trial involving a small study population ($N = 11$), patients on risperidone LAI maintenance treatment maintained symptom stability over a 12-month period (Han et al. 2007). Clinically relevant weight gain and glucose metabolism-related adverse events (AEs) have been more frequently reported in patients receiving risperidone LAI versus placebo (Quiroz et al. 2010). The recently approved once-monthly formulation of aripiprazole, aripiprazole once-monthly 400 mg (AOM 400), with its prolactin-sparing profile and low rate of sexual dysfunction side effects (Calabrese et al. 2017; Abilify Maintena 2016; De Hert et al. 2014), adds an additional treatment option for long-term maintenance treatment of BP-I.

Aripiprazole has also demonstrated a favorable metabolic side effect profile relative to other antipsychotic medications, which is important given that patients with BP-I exhibit increased risk for cardiometabolic disorders (Correll et al. 2015; Vancampfort et al. 2015). This bears even greater clinical significance considering that patients are typically required to take the medication long term for maintenance therapy. It has been shown that antipsychotic medications further exacerbate the risk for several cardiovascular and metabolic conditions beyond those experienced inherently by patients with bipolar disorder (Correll et al. 2015). Therefore, implementing the use of LAI antipsychotic medication formulations, which can make lower doses clinically effective (Kishi et al. 2016; Spanarello and Ferla 2014), should be a priority.

The primary and secondary objectives of the open-label trial reported here were to evaluate the safety/tolerability and efficacy, respectively, of AOM 400 for long-term maintenance treatment of BP-I in a mixed cohort of adult patients, some with no exposure to AOM 400 (de novo patients) and others stabilized and/or maintained on AOM 400 in the lead-in study (rollover patients). This is the first trial to study AOM 400 maintenance treatment in patients with BP-I not previously exposed to AOM 400 monotherapy and in those requiring rescue medication during maintenance treatment with AOM 400.

Methods

Study overview

This open-label, multicenter study (ClinicalTrials.gov, NCT01710709) was performed as a follow-on to a previous double-blind, placebo-controlled, randomized withdrawal study of AOM 400 monotherapy in the maintenance treatment of BP-I, as previously published (Calabrese et al. 2017). The study reported here enrolled both rollover patients from the aforementioned study and AOM 400-naive (de novo) patients to assess the long-term safety and efficacy of AOM 400 during ≥ 1 year of maintenance treatment in patients with BP-I. Unlike the patients rolling over from the lead-in study, de novo patients were not stabilized on AOM 400 before the maintenance phase (although they were required to be stable on oral aripiprazole to enter the study), and use of adjunct rescue medications was permitted.

This trial was conducted from November 2012 to November 2016 at 149 sites in 10 countries (Canada, France, Hungary, Japan, Malaysia, Poland, Romania,

South Korea, Taiwan, and the United States) in compliance with the International Conference of Harmonisation and Good Clinical Practice consolidated guideline (2016). The protocol was approved by an institutional review board or independent ethics committee, as appropriate. Informed consent was obtained from all patients or their legal representatives as necessary.

Safety was assessed by the frequency, severity, seriousness, and discontinuation of AOM 400 due to treatment-emergent adverse events (TEAEs). Efficacy was assessed by (a) the proportion of patients meeting stabilization criteria at the beginning of the maintenance phase who remained stable at the last visit; (b) mean changes from baseline in Young Mania Rating Scale (YMRS) (Young et al. 1978) and Montgomery–Asberg Depression Rating Scale (MADRS) (Montgomery and Asberg 1979) total scores, as well as in Clinical Global Impressions for Bipolar Disorder-Severity of Illness Scale (CGI-BP-S) (Spearing et al. 1997) scores (overall, mania, and depression); and (c) proportion of patients requiring use of a rescue medication, as well as the frequency and duration of use of the rescue medication. Patient acceptability and tolerability of treatment was assessed by (a) patient satisfaction with AOM 400 and (b) side effects of AOM 400 versus previous medication, both measured using the Patient Satisfaction with Medication Questionnaire–Modified (PSMQ-M) (Kalali 1999).

Patients

This study enrolled 2 cohorts of patients, defined as de novo or rollover. De novo patients consisted of male and female outpatients aged 18–65 years with a diagnosis of BP-I according to *Diagnostic and Statistical Manual of Mental Disorders, Fourth Edition, Text Revision* (American Psychiatric Association 2000) criteria, and confirmed by the Mini-International Neuropsychiatric Interview (Sheehan et al. 1998). Eligible patients had experienced ≥ 1 previous manic or mixed episode of sufficient severity to require hospitalization, treatment with a mood stabilizer, or treatment with an antipsychotic agent. Patients with a current depressive episode or a history of ≥ 9 episodes in the past year were excluded. Eligibility criteria for this study were generally similar to those of the lead-in study (Calabrese et al. 2017) except that the lead-in study excluded patients with either a mixed or depressive episode, whereas the present study excluded only patients experiencing a depressive episode. Additionally, there was no YMRS score criterion for entry into this open-label study.

Rollover patients were derived from the lead-in double-blind, placebo-controlled randomized withdrawal trial as previously published (Calabrese et al. 2017). Patients were required to have completed the maintenance phase without recurrence to be eligible for this extension study. Because the final phase of the lead-in trial was randomized, patients entering the current study were from both the placebo and AOM 400 maintenance arms, resulting in patients with different levels of AOM 400 exposure before inclusion in the current study. However, all rollover patients had some level of AOM 400 exposure owing to the 12- to 28-week AOM 400 stabilization phase included as part of the lead-in trial protocol (Calabrese et al. 2017).

Study design

This trial had distinct protocols for de novo versus rollover patients. For de novo patients, the study consisted of 2 or 3 of the following phases: a 4- to 6-week oral aripiprazole cross-titration phase, if the patient was receiving an oral antipsychotic other than aripiprazole at enrollment, a 4- to 12-week oral aripiprazole stabilization phase, and an open-label 52-week maintenance phase where AOM 400 was administered by single-site gluteal intramuscular injection every 4 weeks. Of note, no stabilization on AOM 400 was performed before the AOM 400 maintenance phase. De novo patients entered the study at screening and then proceeded to oral conversion or oral stabilization, depending on their current antipsychotic treatment regimen.

Because cross-titration and stabilization were completed as part of the lead-in trial, rollover patients entered this study directly at the AOM 400 maintenance phase (Calabrese et al. 2017). Importantly, only those patients completing the lead-in study through the full 52-week maintenance phase without recurrence of a mood episode were eligible for participation in the current study. In both de novo and rollover patients, dose decrease to 300 mg was permitted for tolerability, as was return to the 400-mg dose at any point.

Use of rescue medications was permitted if a patient became unstable. Patients requiring rescue therapy were permitted use of one adjunct medication at a time, as follows: lithium or valproate (immediate release or controlled release), benzodiazepines (lorazepam equivalents) at ≤ 4 mg/day (≤ 12 mg/week) during the oral aripiprazole stabilization phase, and ≤ 2 mg/day (≤ 8 mg/week) during the AOM 400 maintenance phase.

Stability assessments

Before entering the AOM 400 maintenance phase, de novo patients were required to meet the following stability criteria: outpatient status, YMRS total score ≤ 12, MADRS total score ≤ 12, and no active suicidality, with active suicidality defined as MADRS item 10 score ≥ 4, or "yes" on question 4 or 5 of the Columbia Suicide Severity Rating Scale (C-SSRS) (Posner et al. 2009).

Safety and tolerability

All patients who received ≥ 1 dose of AOM 400 in the open-label maintenance phase were analyzed for safety. Safety data were summarized using descriptive statistics for the open-label AOM 400 maintenance phase. AEs were coded according to Medical Dictionary for Regulatory Activities definitions. A TEAE was defined as an AE that emerged after the start of treatment or an AE that continued from baseline of one phase and became serious; was drug related; or resulted in death, discontinuation, interruption, or reduction of dosing during the subsequent phase. Suicidality was measured using the C-SSRS. Injection site reaction was assessed using the patient-reported Visual Analog Scale (VAS) and investigator evaluations. Extrapyramidal symptoms were reported as the change from baseline (beginning of AOM 400 maintenance phase) in Simpson–Angus Scale (used in countries other than Japan) (Simpson and Angus 1970), Drug-Induced Extrapyramidal Symptoms Scale (used in Japan) (Kim et al. 2002), Abnormal Involuntary Movement Scale (Guy 1976), and Barnes Akathisia Rating Scale (Barnes 1989) scores. Standard safety measurements, including clinical laboratory tests (including serum prolactin concentrations), vital signs, electrocardiogram (ECG), body weight, and general physical examination, were recorded. Central laboratories designated by the sponsor were used for all laboratory testing and ECG review.

Efficacy

All patients with ≥ 1 postbaseline effectiveness evaluation in the open-label AOM 400 maintenance phase were analyzed for efficacy. The proportion of patients stable at baseline who were also stable at the last visit of the maintenance phase was calculated using descriptive statistics. The mean changes from baseline to end of study (up to week 52) in YMRS and MADRS total scores and in CGI-BP-S overall score were calculated using descriptive statistics with the last-observation-carried-forward method.

Briefly, the YMRS is based on a clinical interview with patients in which they report on 11 items that assess the core symptoms of mania. Total score can range from 0 to 60, with higher scores indicating more severe mania (Young et al. 1978). The MADRS is a structured interview that assesses the patient's depressive symptoms. Using a scale consisting of 10 items scored on 7 defined grades of severity (0–6), the total score can range from 0 to 60, with higher scores indicating greater severity of depressive symptoms (Montgomery and Asberg 1979). Finally, the CGI-BP-S is a 7-point scale that rates a patient's severity of bipolar illness in 3 categories: mania, depression, and overall; higher scores indicate more severe disease (Spearing et al. 1997). All raters of efficacy assessments received structured training.

Patient satisfaction and patient-assessed tolerability

The PSMQ-M (Kalali 1999) was used to evaluate patient satisfaction with AOM 400 and to determine the side effect burden of AOM 400 relative to the patient's previous medications. These data were interpreted as patient-assessed tolerability of AOM 400 as maintenance therapy for BP-I. The PSMQ-M is a simple 4-part questionnaire that patients complete independently, requiring little to no clinician aid.

Results

Patients

A total of 464 patients entered the AOM 400 maintenance phase of this study. Figure 1a details the proportion of patients who were de novo (n = 379; 82%), rollover from the placebo arm of the lead-in study (n = 30; 6%), and rollover from the AOM 400 arm of the lead-in study (n = 55; 12%). This distinction is important because it indicates different pre-maintenance stabilization protocols for de novo versus rollover patients and different total AOM 400 exposure times for placebo arm versus AOM 400 arm rollover patients. De novo patients were stabilized on oral aripiprazole only (before entering the trial, or after if previously on a different oral antipsychotic), with no stabilization on AOM 400 before the AOM 400 maintenance phase of this study, while all rollover patients were stabilized for 12–28 weeks on AOM 400 according to lead-in study protocol. Rollover patients randomized to the placebo arm had no further exposure to AOM 400 before this study, while rollover patients randomized to the AOM 400 arm of the lead-in study received 52 weeks of AOM 400 during the randomized phase, resulting in a total of 64–80 weeks of exposure to AOM 400 before the 52-week maintenance phase of the current study.

Of 958 de novo patients screened, 663 met eligibility criteria. Figure 1b details patient disposition during each treatment phase of the study, and denotes the entry point of rollover patients from the lead-in trial. Of the 464 patients who entered the open-label AOM 400 maintenance phase, 379 were de novo and 85 were rollover patients. Of these, 291 (63%) completed 52 weeks of treatment. The most frequent reasons for discontinuation were withdrawal of consent (53/464; 11.4%) and AEs (48/464; 10.3%). Lack of efficacy led to study discontinuation in a small number of patients (3/464; 0.6%).

Demographic (Additional file 1: Table S1) and clinical characteristics at baseline of the open-label AOM 400 maintenance phase were similar between de novo and rollover patients. Briefly, 57.8% of patients were female, the mean age was 41.1 years, the mean BMI was 30.2 kg/m^2, and age at first BP-I diagnosis was 29.1 years. Mean (SD) YMRS total score was 2.3 (2.9), MADRS score was 3.2 (3.2), CGI-BP-S mania score was 1.5 (0.8), CGI-BP-S

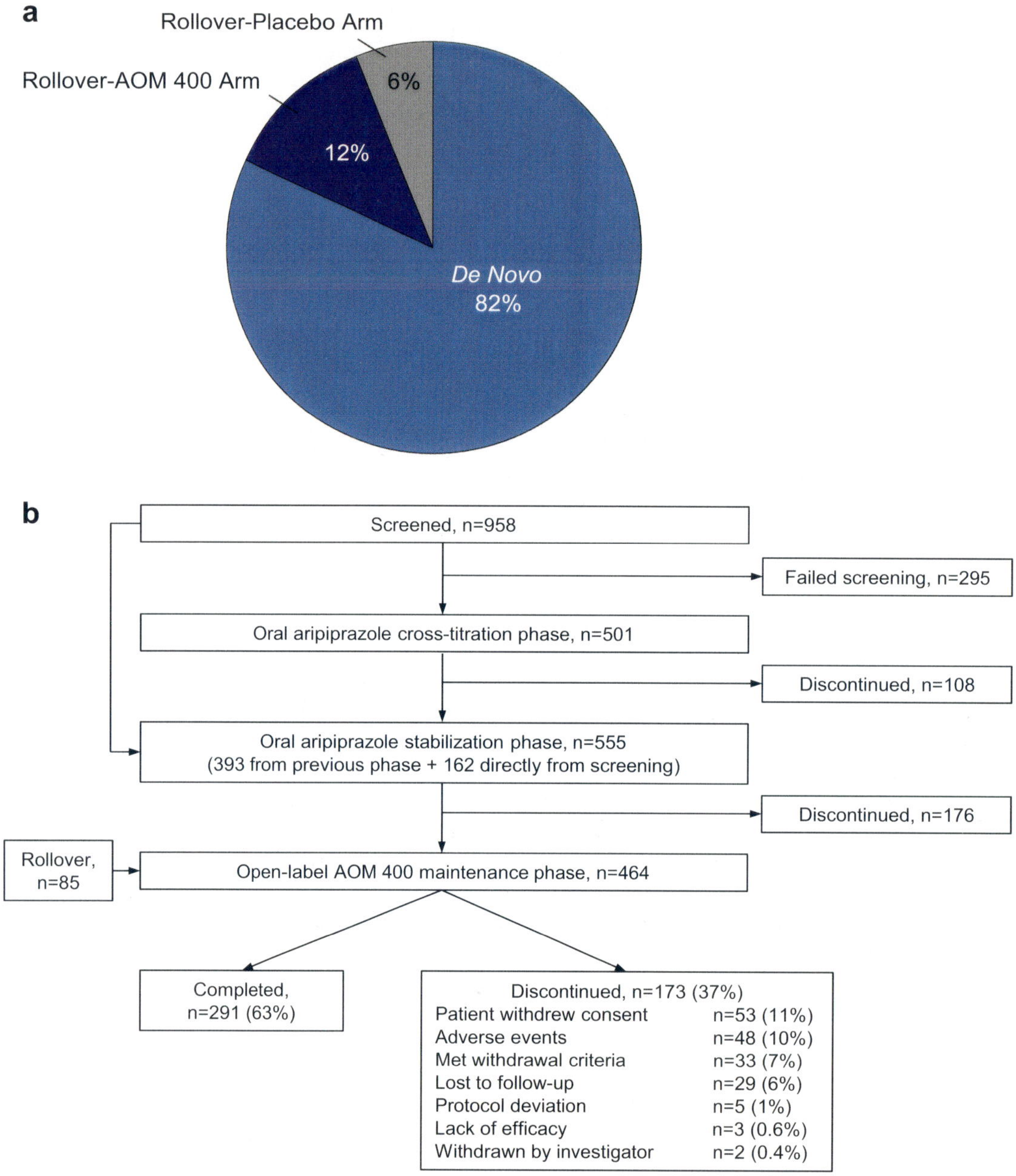

Fig. 1 **a** Source of patients participating in this clinical trial. de novo = patients who did not participate in the lead-in study and had no prior AOM 400 exposure; Rollover-AOM 400 Arm = rollover patients from the lead-in study who had been randomized to the AOM 400 arm; Rollover-Placebo Arm = rollover patients from the lead-in study who had been randomized to the placebo arm. **b** Patient disposition across the study. Patients entered the oral aripiprazole cross-titration phase if they were not already receiving oral aripiprazole in their treatment regimen at screening. Those already on aripiprazole therapy at screening entered directly into the oral aripiprazole stabilization phase. *AOM 400* aripiprazole once-monthly 400 mg

depression score was 1.6 (0.8), and CGI-BP-S overall score was 1.7 (0.8).

Safety and tolerability

The primary objective of this study was to evaluate the safety of AOM 400 administered every 4 weeks over up to 52 weeks of maintenance therapy for BP-I. During the AOM 400 maintenance phase, patients received up to 13 injections in the gluteal muscle. Injection site AEs occurred in 42 out of 464 patients (9.1%) across de novo and rollover patients, and included pain (n = 34; 7.3%), swelling (n = 4; 0.9%), bruising (n = 2; 0.4%), mass (n = 2;

0.4%), erythema (n = 1; 0.2%), and induration (n = 1; 0.2%). VAS assessment of the injections remained low, with mean patient ratings remaining at 5 or below on a scale of 0–100 throughout the maintenance phase (injections 1–13). Overall, injection site pain and reactions were minimal, decreased with subsequent injections, and were consistent with those reported in the lead-in study (Calabrese et al. 2017).

Throughout the maintenance phase, 374 of 464 patients (80.6%) experienced ≥ 1 TEAE, with 85.2% of de novo and 60.0% of rollover patients experiencing any TEAE, and 11.6% of de novo and 3.5% of rollover patients discontinuing the study owing to TEAEs (Table 1). Among AEs leading to discontinuation, bipolar I disorder, bipolar disorder, major depression, and mania were reported in 4 (0.9%), 2 (0.4%), 1 (0.2%), and 3 (0.4%) patients, respectively.

The most commonly occurring TEAEs, occurring in ≥ 5% of patients overall, are shown in Fig. 2, with the most common for de novo and rollover being akathisia (15.8% vs 9.4%), weight increase (14.8% vs 7.1%), nasopharyngitis (12.7% vs 9.4%), and insomnia (12.9% vs 2.4%). Mean (SD) change in weight from baseline to the last visit of the AOM 400 maintenance phase was 0.5 (7.0) kg for de novo patients and 0.6 (4.8) kg for rollover patients. Potentially clinically relevant weight gain (≥ 7%) at the last visit of the maintenance phase was observed in 61/370 de novo patients (16.5%) and 10/84 rollover patients (11.9%), while potentially clinically relevant weight loss was observed in 42 de novo patients (11.4%) and 6 rollover patients (7.1%). Overall, the incidence of TEAEs was low, and TEAEs occurred early and did not appear to increase with time on treatment. Mean changes from baseline in extrapyramidal symptoms, as assessed by specific rating scales, were minimal and not clinically meaningful (Additional file 2: Table S2). No clinically meaningful changes in clinical laboratory parameters were observed.

Treatment-emergent adverse events related to suicidal ideation/suicide were reported in 11/464 patients (2.4%) during the maintenance phase, with the events considered serious in 4 patients. Treatment-emergent possible suicidal events assessed using the C-SSRS were reported in 46/464 patients (9.9%), including suicidal ideation (9.9%), non-suicidal self-injurious behavior (0.9%), suicide attempt (0.6%), and preparatory action toward imminent suicidal behavior (0.9%).

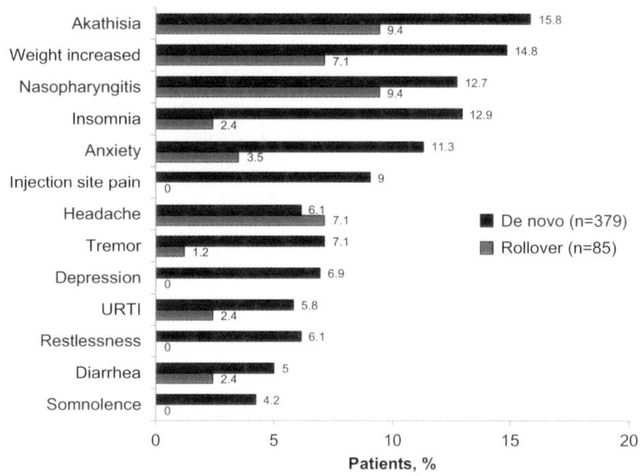

Fig. 2 TEAEs occurring in ≥ 5% of patients during the AOM 400 maintenance phase, by enrollment source. TEAEs displayed from most common overall at top to least common overall at bottom, displayed as percent incidence in de novo and rollover patients. AOM 400 = aripiprazole once-monthly 400 mg; *TEAE* treatment-emergent adverse event, *URTI* upper respiratory tract infection

Although serious AEs (SAEs) were rare, 27 de novo (7.1%) and 3 rollover (3.5%) patients reported SAEs during maintenance treatment with AOM 400, including 1 death in the de novo cohort (acute myocardial infarction) that was not considered related to study drug. SAEs considered related to study drug included BP-I (2 patients) and diabetes mellitus, obesity, somnolence, tardive dyskinesia, bipolar disorder, major depression, mania, and dyspnea (1 patient each).

Efficacy

The secondary objective of this study was to evaluate the long-term therapeutic effect of AOM 400 as maintenance

Table 1 Incidence of AEs during the AOM 400 maintenance phase

AE, n (%)	De novo, n = 379	Rollover, n = 85	Total, N = 464
TEAEs	323 (85.2)	51 (60.0)	374 (80.6)
Serious TEAEs	27 (7.1)	3 (3.5)	30 (6.5)
Nonserious TEAEs	318 (83.9)	49 (57.6)	367 (79.1)
Severe TEAEs	39 (10.3)	2 (2.4)	41 (8.8)
Discontinued AOM 400 due to TEAEs	44 (11.6)	3 (3.5)	47 (10.1)
Discontinued AOM 400 due to AE/death	45 (11.9)	3 (3.5)	48 (10.3)
Deaths	1 (0.3)	0	1 (0.2)

AE adverse event, *AOM 400* aripiprazole once-monthly 400 mg, *TEAE* treatment-emergent AE

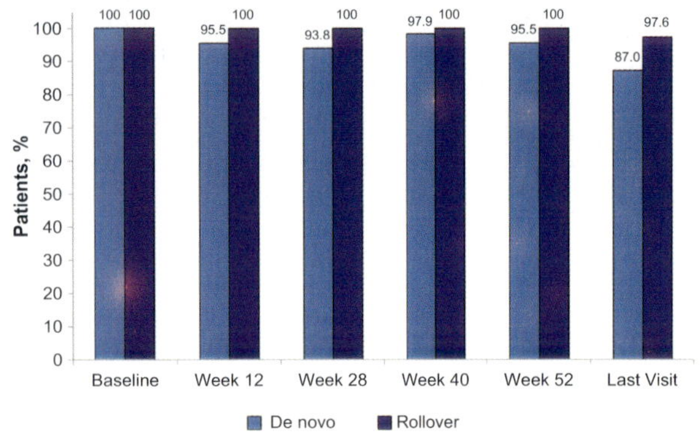

Fig. 3 Percentage of patients remaining stable throughout the AOM 400 maintenance phase, by enrollment source. Stability defined as (1) outpatient status, (2) Young Mania Rating Scale total score ≤ 12, (3) MADRS total score ≤ 12, and (4) no active suicidality, with active suicidality defined as MADRS item 10 score ≥ 4, or "yes" on question 4 or 5 of the Columbia Suicide Severity Rating Scale. *MADRS* Montgomery–Asberg Depression Rating Scale, *n* number evaluable

treatment for BP-I in de novo and rollover patients. Efficacy was measured first as the proportion of patients stable at baseline (beginning of the AOM 400 maintenance phase) who remained stable at the end of AOM 400 maintenance treatment (Fig. 3). Overall, 89% of patients who were stable at baseline were stable at their last visit of the maintenance treatment phase.

Efficacy was also measured by assessing the change in key clinical stability indicators, including YMRS total score, MADRS total score, CGI-BP-S overall score, CGI-BP-S mania score, and CGI-BP-S depression score, as outlined in Table 2. The mean YMRS and CGI-BP-S (overall, mania, and depression) scores were largely unchanged, with slight improvement from baseline.

Use of rescue medication during the AOM 400 maintenance phase is shown in Table 3. Less than 8% of patients used lithium (6.0%) or valproate (7.8%), all but one of whom were de novo patients.

Patient satisfaction and patient-assessed tolerability

An additional secondary objective was to assess the acceptability and long-term tolerability of AOM 400 from a patient perspective, using qualitative patient satisfaction and side effect profiles as evaluation measures. Using the PSMQ-M, patients could directly share their

Table 2 Change in clinical stability indicators during the AOM 400 maintenance phase

Mean (SD) change from baseline to last visit (up to week 52; LOCF)						
Assessment	De novo		Rollover		Total	
	N	Result	N	Result	N	Result
YMRS total score	377	−0.33 (3.87)	85	−0.16 (4.42)	462	−0.30 (3.97)
MADRS total score	377	1.36 (6.93)	85	0.67 (3.16)	462	1.24 (6.41)
CGI-BP-S overall score	353	0.13 (1.20)	84	−0.01 (0.69)	437	0.10 (1.12)
CGI-BP-S mania score	353	−0.07 (0.83)	84	−0.08 (0.71)	437	−0.07 (0.81)
CGI-BP-S depression score	353	0.18 (1.14)	84	0.12 (0.52)	437	0.17 (1.05)

AOM 400 aripiprazole once-monthly 400 mg, *CGI-BP-S* Clinical Global Impressions for Bipolar Disorder-Severity of Illness Scale, *LOCF* last observation carried forward, *MADRS* Montgomery–Asberg Depression Rating Scale, *SD* standard deviation, *YMRS* Young Mania Rating Scale

Table 3 Rescue medication use during the AOM 400 maintenance phase

Medication	Enrollment source	Number of patients	Number (%) taking rescue medication	Duration (days)[a]		
				Mean	SD	Median
Lithium	De novo	379	28 (7.4)	147.9	101.8	131.5
	Rollover	85	0	–	–	–
	Total	464	28 (6.0)	147.9	101.8	131.5
Valproate	De novo	379	35 (9.2)	114.5	96.6	100
	Rollover	85	1 (1.2)	84.0	–	84.0
	Total	464	36 (7.8)	113.7	95.4	92.0

Rescue medication (lithium [immediate or controlled release] or valproate [immediate or extended release]) was recommended for patients not meeting stability criteria. Only one type of rescue medication was permitted at a time. Patients meeting stability criteria were not eligible for rescue medication

AOM 400 aripiprazole once-monthly 400 mg, *SD* standard deviation

[a] Calculated for patients receiving AOM 400 during maintenance phase who took rescue medication during maintenance phase

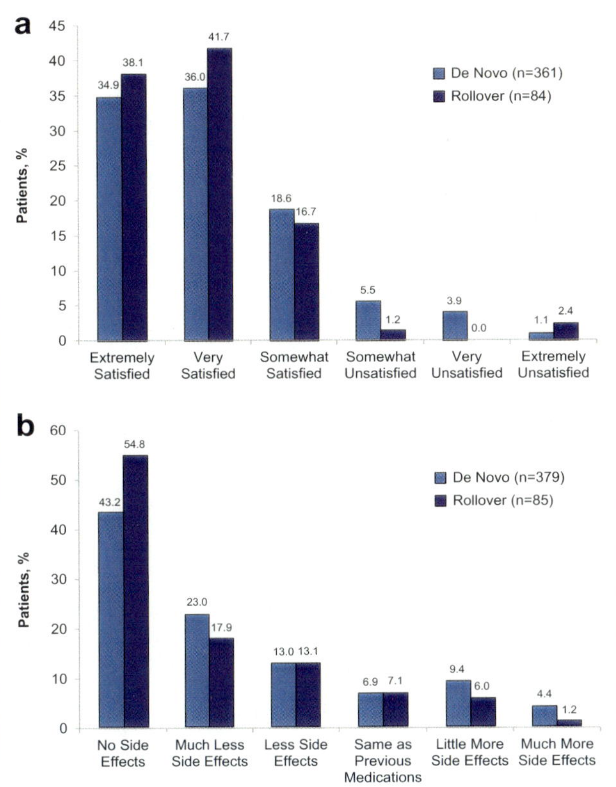

Fig. 4 Patient evaluation of own satisfaction with AOM 400 (**a**) and patient assessment of side effects on AOM 400 relative to previous medication (**b**) using the Patient Satisfaction with Medication Questionnaire-Modified; data collected at last visit of the AOM 400 maintenance phase. *AOM 400* aripiprazole once-monthly 400 mg

experience of taking AOM 400 with clinicians. Figure 4a, b show that > 70% of patients in either group were extremely or very satisfied with AOM 400 treatment, and > 65% had either no side effects or many fewer side effects than with previous medications.

Discussion

Overall, these data demonstrate the safety and efficacy of AOM 400 for the maintenance treatment of BP-I. The finding that, after switching from a previous antipsychotic, patients stable on oral aripiprazole can be safely switched to AOM 400 is important because it opens the use of AOM 400 for maintenance treatment by patients in the clinic without the need for lengthy pre-stabilization protocols. Making the switch to AOM 400 for long-term maintenance may prove to be a simple and effective clinical next step. With maintained efficacy and a good tolerability profile, patient satisfaction was high, suggesting AOM 400 may be well accepted with broader clinical use.

This study, combined with the previously published lead-in study (Calabrese et al. 2017), provides robust data on the only once-monthly LAI atypical antipsychotic approved by the FDA for maintenance monotherapy of BP-I (Citrome 2017). The 2 cohorts of patients included in this study (de novo and rollover) exhibited similar maintenance phase outcomes, including low discontinuation rates, low need for rescue medications, high rates of stability, and high levels of patient-assessed satisfaction relative to previous medications. Rollover patients provide the longest maintenance treatment period data for analysis, and de novo patients represent a real-world practice setting, in which patients on other treatments could be effectively switched to AOM 400. Because LAI formulations of antipsychotics have been shown to reduce relapse rates and hospitalizations, and improve brain health and long-term societal functioning (Kishimoto et al. 2013; Subotnik et al. 2015), a more general shift from oral to LAI aripiprazole may be justified for eligible patients.

The majority of randomized controlled trials that have been performed to assess the efficacy of SGAs in patients with bipolar disorder are enriched for responders (Lindström et al. 2017); in contrast, this trial cohort was not. The majority of participants in this study (82%) were classified as de novo patients, meaning they were not stabilized on AOM 400 before being maintained on AOM 400. Instead, these patients were stabilized on oral aripiprazole and then switched to AOM 400 for maintenance. As a result, the high percentage of de novo patients with stable disease seen in our study is not due to selection bias; instead, it reflects the efficacy of AOM 400 for maintenance treatment of BP-I in a population of patients and a clinical scenario more closely representing those routinely encountered in clinical practice. Furthermore, the rate of study discontinuation due to lack of treatment efficacy was very low, and overall study completion rate was high. Notably, de novo patients demonstrated a low rate of discontinuation due to TEAEs and expressed high levels of satisfaction with the medication, suggesting a safety and tolerability profile similar to that seen in the earlier randomized withdrawal study (Calabrese et al. 2017).

The remaining 18% of the study population consisted of patients previously stabilized on AOM 400, and thus represent a subset of respondent-enriched participants (Calabrese et al. 2017). All TEAEs were less common in rollover versus de novo patients, which might be due to the enriched population. It could also reflect a tendency for some TEAEs to emerge earlier in the treatment course. As with de novo patients, a large proportion of rollover patients reported high satisfaction with their treatment and less bothersome side effects versus their previous medication. To be eligible to rollover into this study, these participants had to have completed the full trial mentioned above, which for some individuals resulted in exposure to AOM 400 exceeding 2 years (up to 2.5 years) across the 2 studies.

The 2 notable aspects of this trial, the relative lack of enrichment design (because the patients did not require prior stabilization on AOM 400) and the permitted use of rescue medications, allow the results to more closely reflect what may be seen if AOM 400 were to be used for maintenance treatment of BP-I in the clinic. In most cases, healthcare providers may choose to use oral antipsychotics for management of acute mood crises, while LAI forms may be preferred for long-term maintenance in an outpatient setting (Citrome 2017).

The efficacy of AOM 400 as maintenance treatment in reducing the occurrence of mood episodes in BP-I has been reported previously (Calabrese et al. 2017); however, data on relapse rates was not collected in this study, limiting the ability to directly compare the effectiveness of long-term AOM 400 maintenance treatment for BP-I with other similar studies in long-term treatment settings.

Conclusion

To our knowledge, this is the longest recorded evidence of safety and efficacy of any formulation of an atypical LAI antipsychotic and the only one approved for monthly injection for the maintenance treatment of BP-I. We have shown long-term safety and efficacy in a large data set in which a majority of patients maintained stability through 52 weeks of AOM 400 treatment with minimal need for rescue medication. These data support the broader use of AOM 400 for maintenance treatment of BP-I.

Abbreviations

AE: adverse event; AOM 400: aripiprazole once-monthly 400 mg; BP-I: bipolar I disorder; CGI-BP-S: Clinical Global Impressions for Bipolar Disorder-Severity of Illness Scale; C-SSRS: Columbia Suicide Severity Rating Scale; ECG: electrocardiogram; LAI: long-acting injectable; MADRS: Montgomery–Asberg Depression Rating Scale; PSMQ-M: Patient Satisfaction with Medication Questionnaire-Modified; SAE: serious adverse event; SGA: second-generation antipsychotic; TEAE: treatment-emergent adverse event; VAS: Visual Analog Scale; YMRS: Young Mania Rating Scale.

Authors' contributions

All authors had full access to the data included in the paper, interpreted the data, and critically reviewed drafts of the paper. All authors read and approved the final manuscript.

Author details

[1] University Hospitals Cleveland Medical Center, 10524 Euclid Avenue, Cleveland, OH 44106, USA. [2] Otsuka Pharmaceutical Development & Commercialization, Inc., Princeton, NJ, USA. [3] H. Lundbeck A/S, Valby, Denmark. [4] Department of Psychiatry, Faculty of Medicine, Fukuoka University, Fukuoka, Japan.

Acknowledgements

Editorial support for manuscript development was provided by C4 MedSolutions, LLC (Yardley, PA, USA), a CHC Group company. Funding was provided by Otsuka Pharmaceutical Development & Commercialization, Inc. (Princeton, NJ, USA), and H. Lundbeck A/S (Valby, Denmark).

Competing interests

JC has received federal funding from the Department of Defense, Health Resources Services Administration, and National Institute of Mental Health; and grant support from Abbott Laboratories, AstraZeneca, Bristol-Myers Squibb Company, Cephalon, Inc. (now Teva Pharmaceutical Industries Ltd.), Dainippon Sumitomo Pharma Co., Ltd., GlaxoSmithKline, Janssen Pharmaceuticals, Inc., Eli Lilly and Company, Intra-Cellular Therapies, Inc., Pfizer Inc, H. Lundbeck A/S, Sunovion Pharmaceuticals Inc., and Takeda Pharmaceutical Company Limited. He has also served as a consultant/advisory board member/speaker for Abbott Laboratories, Allergan, AstraZeneca, Bristol-Myers Squibb Company, Cephalon, Inc. (now Teva Pharmaceutical Industries Ltd.), Dainippon Sumitomo Pharma Co., Ltd., GlaxoSmithKline, Janssen Pharmaceuticals, Inc., H. Lundbeck A/S, Merck & Co., Inc., Otsuka Pharmaceutical Co., Ltd., Pfizer Inc, Repligen Corporation, Servier, Sunovion Pharmaceuticals Inc., Solvay Pharmaceuticals, Inc., and Takeda Pharmaceutical Company Limited. PS and PH are employees of H. Lundbeck A/S. NJ, BJ, RB, JM, JO, and JA are employees of Otsuka Pharmaceutical Development & Commercialization, Inc. HK has received honoraria for lectures and/or consulting from Dainippon Sumitomo Pharma Co., Ltd., Lundbeck Japan K.K., Mochida Pharmaceutical Co., Ltd., Otsuka Pharmaceutical Co., Ltd., and Pfizer Japan Inc.

Funding

Study funded by Otsuka Pharmaceutical Development & Commercialization, Inc., and H. Lundbeck A/S.

References

Abilify Maintena® US (aripiprazole). Full prescribing information. Tokyo: Otsuka Pharmaceutical Co., Ltd.; 2016.

American Psychiatric Association. Diagnostic and statistical manual of mental disorders, fourth edition, text revision. Washington, DC: American Psychiatric Association; 2000.

Barnes TR. A rating scale for drug-induced akathisia. Br J Psychiatry Suppl. 1989;154:672–6.

Brissos S, Veguilla MR, Taylor D, Balanza-Martinez V. The role of long-acting injectable antipsychotics in schizophrenia: a critical appraisal. Ther Adv Psychopharmacol. 2014;4(5):198–219.

Calabrese JR, Sanchez R, Jin N, Amatniek J, Cox K, Johnson B, et al. Efficacy and safety of aripiprazole once-monthly in the maintenance treatment of bipolar I disorder: a double-blind, placebo-controlled, 52-week randomized withdrawal study. J Clin Psychiatry. 2017;78:324–31.

Citrome L. Long-acting injectable antipsychotics update: lengthening the dosing interval and expanding the diagnostic indications. Expert Rev Neurother. 2017;17(10):1029–43.

Correll CU, Detraux J, De Lepeleire J, De Hert M. Effects of antipsychotics, antidepressants and mood stabilizers on risk for physical diseases in people with schizophrenia, depression and bipolar disorder. World Psychiatry. 2015;14(2):119–36.

De Hert M, Detraux J, Peuskens J. Second-generation and newly approved antipsychotics, serum prolactin levels and sexual dysfunctions: a critical literature review. Expert Opin Drug Saf. 2014;13(5):605–24.

Grande I, Berk M, Birmaher B, Vieta E. Bipolar disorder. Lancet. 2016;387(10027):1561–72.

Guy W. Abnormal Involuntary Movement Scale (AIMS). ECDEU Assessment Manual for Psychopharmacology. Rockville: US Department of Health, Education, and Welfare, Public Health Service, Alcohol, Drug Abuse, and Mental Health Administration, National Institute of Mental Health, Psychopharmacology Research Branch, Division of Extramural Research Programs; 1976. p. 534–7.

Han C, Lee MS, Pae CU, Ko YH, Patkar AA, Jung IK. Usefulness of long-acting injectable risperidone during 12-month maintenance therapy of bipolar disorder. Prog Neuropsychopharmacol Biol Psychiatry. 2007;31(6):1219–23.

International Conference on Harmonisation. E6: Good clinical practice: consolidated guideline. http://www.ich.org. Accessed July 26 2016.
Kalali A. Patient satisfaction with, and acceptability of, atypical antipsychotics. Curr Med Res Opin. 1999;15(2):135–7.
Kim JH, Jung HY, Kang UG, Jeong SH, Ahn YM, Byun HJ, et al. Metric characteristics of the Drug-Induced Extrapyramidal Symptoms Scale (DIEPSS): a practical combined rating scale for drug-induced movement disorders. Mov Disord. 2002;17(6):1354–9.
Kishi T, Oya K, Iwata N. Long-acting injectable antipsychotics for prevention of relapse in bipolar disorder: a systematic review and meta-analyses of randomized controlled trials. Int J Neuropsychopharmacol. 2016;19(9):1–10.
Kishimoto T, Nitta M, Borenstein M, Kane JM, Correll CU. Long-acting injectable versus oral antipsychotics in schizophrenia: a systematic review and meta-analysis of mirror-image studies. J Clin Psychiatry. 2013;74(10):957–65.
Lindström L, Lindström E, Nilsson M, Höistad M. Maintenance therapy with second generation antipsychotics for bipolar disorder—a systematic review and meta-analysis. J Affect Disord. 2017;213:138–50.
Macfadden W, Alphs L, Haskins JT, Turner N, Turkoz I, Bossie C, et al. A randomized, double-blind, placebo-controlled study of maintenance treatment with adjunctive risperidone long-acting therapy in patients with bipolar I disorder who relapse frequently. Bipolar Disord. 2009;11(8):827–39.
Martinez-Aran A, Vieta E, Reinares M, Colom F, Torrent C, Sanchez-Moreno J, et al. Cognitive function across manic or hypomanic, depressed, and euthymic states in bipolar disorder. Am J Psychiatry. 2004;161(2):262–70.
Martino DJ, Marengo E, Igoa A, Scapola M, Ais ED, Perinot L, et al. Neurocognitive and symptomatic predictors of functional outcome in bipolar disorders: a prospective 1 year follow-up study. J Affect Disord. 2009;116(1–2):37–42.
McIntyre RS, Yoon J, Jerrell JM, Liauw SS. Aripiprazole for the maintenance treatment of bipolar disorder: a review of available evidence. Neuropsychiatr Dis Treat. 2011;7:319–23.
Montgomery SA, Asberg M. A new depression scale designed to be sensitive to change. Br J Psychiatry Suppl. 1979;134:382–9.
Posner K, Brent D, Lucas C, Gould M, Stanley B, Brown G, et al. Columbia Suicide Severity Rating Scale. 2009. http://cssrs.columbia.edu/docs/C-SSRS_1_14_09_Baseline.pdf. Accessed 19 Apr 2016.
Quiroz JA, Yatham LN, Palumbo JM, Karcher K, Kushner S, Kusumakar V. Risperidone long-acting injectable monotherapy in the maintenance treatment of bipolar I disorder. Biol Psychiatry. 2010;68(2):156–62.
Risperdal Consta® (risperidone long-acting injection). Full prescribing information. Titusville: Janssen Pharmaceuticals, Inc.; 2016.
Sheehan DV, Lecrubier Y, Sheehan KH, Amorim P, Janavs J, Weiller E, et al. The Mini-International Neuropsychiatric Interview (M.I.N.I.): the development and validation of a structured diagnostic psychiatric interview for DSM-IV and ICD-10. J Clin Psychiatry. 1998;59(suppl 20):22–33.
Simpson GM, Angus JW. A rating scale for extrapyramidal side effects. Acta Psychiatr Scand Suppl. 1970;212:11–9.
Spanarello S, Ferla TL. The pharmacokinetics of long-acting antipsychotic medications. Current Clinical Pharmacology. 2014;9(3):310–7.
Spearing MK, Post RM, Leverich GS, Brandt D, Nolen W. Modification of the Clinical Global Impressions (CGI) scale for use in bipolar illness (BP): the CGI-BP. Psychiatry Res. 1997;73(3):159–71.
Subotnik KL, Casaus LR, Ventura J, Luo JS, Hellemann GS, Gretchen-Doorly D, et al. Long-acting injectable risperidone for relapse prevention and control of breakthrough symptoms after a recent first episode of schizophrenia. A randomized clinical trial. JAMA Psychiatry. 2015;72(8):822–9.
Vancampfort D, Stubbs B, Mitchell AJ, De Hert M, Wampers M, Ward PB, et al. Risk of metabolic syndrome and its components in people with schizophrenia and related psychotic disorders, bipolar disorder and major depressive disorder: a systematic review and meta-analysis. World Psychiatry. 2015;14(3):339–47.
Work Group on Bipolar Disorder. Practice guideline for the treatment of patients with bipolar disorder. 2nd ed. Washington, DC: American Psychiatric Association; 2002.
Young RC, Biggs JT, Ziegler VE, Meyer DA. A rating scale for mania: reliability, validity and sensitivity. Br J Psychiatry Suppl. 1978;133:429–35.

18

A nationwide study on concordance with multimodal treatment guidelines in bipolar disorder

Joannes W. Renes[1*], Eline J. Regeer[1], Adriaan W. Hoogendoorn[2], Willem A. Nolen[3] and Ralph W. Kupka[1,2]

Abstract

Background: Most previous studies on concordance with treatment guidelines for bipolar disorder focused on pharmacotherapy. Few studies have included other treatment modalities.

Aims: To study concordance with the Dutch guideline of various treatment modalities in outpatient treatment settings for patients with bipolar disorder and to identity factors associated with concordance.

Methods: A nationwide non-interventional study using psychiatrists' and patients' surveys.

Results: 839 patients with bipolar or schizoaffective disorder bipolar type were included. Concordance with the guideline was highest for participation of a psychiatrist in the treatment (98%) and for maintenance pharmacotherapy (96%), but lower for supportive treatment (73.5%), use of an emergency plan (70.6%), psychotherapy (52.2%), group psychoeducation (47.2%), and mood monitoring (47%). Presence of a written treatment plan, a more specialized treatment setting, more years of education, and diagnosis of bipolar I disorder versus bipolar II, bipolar NOS, or schizoaffective disorder were significantly associated with better concordance.

Conclusion: In contrast to pharmacotherapy, psychosocial treatments are only implemented to a limited extend in everyday clinical practice in bipolar disorder. More effort is needed to implement non-pharmacological guideline recommendations for bipolar disorder.

Keywords: Bipolar, Guidelines, Concordance

Background

To improve the quality of care, several guidelines for the treatment of bipolar disorder (BD) have been published in the past two decades, including in the Netherlands (Kupka et al. 2015; Nolen et al. 2008). Studies on the naturalistic treatment of BD show that concordance with these guidelines varies considerably from less than 50% (Altinbas et al. 2011; Baek et al. 2014; Busch et al. 2007; Lim et al. 2001), 50–70% (Arvilommi et al. 2007; Bauer et al. 2009; Farrelly et al. 2006; Freeland et al. 2015; Huang et al. 2014; Marcus et al. 1999; Simon et al. 2004; Smith et al. 2008; Wang et al. 2014a, 2015), or up to 90% (Altinbas et al. 2011; Farrelly et al. 2006; Kilbourne et al. 2005; Paterniti and Bisserbe 2013; Unutzer et al. 2000; Walpoth-Niederwanger et al. 2012; Wang et al. 2014b) on the primary outcome measure of concordance. These concordance rates are difficult to compare due to differences in study design, treatment settings, and in what phase of the illness concordance was studied. Most studies focused on pharmacotherapy only (including monitoring of plasma levels), and were retrospective in design. Few studies have included other treatment modalities, such as psychoeducation or psychotherapy, or visits with health care providers (Busch et al. 2007; Farrelly et al. 2006; Kilbourne et al. 2005; Unutzer et al. 2000).

In these naturalistic studies on concordance with treatment guidelines, factors that have been found to be of influence are type of mood episode (Baek et al. 2014; Farrelly et al. 2006; Huang et al. 2014; Paterniti and Bisserbe

*Correspondence: j.renes@altrecht.nl
[1] Altrecht Institute for Mental Health Care, Utrecht, Nieuwe Houtenseweg 12, 3524 SH Utrecht, The Netherlands
Full list of author information is available at the end of the article

2013), psychotic features (Altinbas et al. 2011; Lim et al. 2001), bipolar disorder subtype (Simon et al. 2004), age at onset (Dennehy et al. 2007), rapid cycling (Arvilommi et al. 2007), treatment setting (Arvilommi et al. 2007; Busch et al. 2007), race (Kilbourne et al. 2005), and higher medical complexity in elderly patients (Huang et al. 2014).

In 2008 a revised guideline on the treatment of bipolar disorder in the Netherlands was published (Nolen et al. 2008). In this paper we present the outcomes of a nationwide naturalistic prospective study on treatment practice and concordance with this Dutch guideline in various treatment settings for patients with BD or schizoaffective disorder, bipolar type (SZA). We hypothesized that the guideline would be better implemented in centers specialized in the treatment of mood disorders, and in patients with bipolar I disorder (BD I) versus those with bipolar II disorder (BD II), bipolar disorder NOS (BD NOS), or SZA. Since BD I is more clearly defined by the lifetime occurrence of full manic episodes, this diagnosis will represent a more homogeneous group of patients, for which providers probably better recognize treatment recommendations in the guideline. Moreover, guidelines often take BD I as their main focus. We further examined the relationship of demographic, illness, and treatment variables with concordance with the guideline.

Methods

The Treatment of Bipolar Disorder in the Netherlands study (TBDN) is a nationwide, multicenter, non-intervention study on concordance with guideline recommendations for the long-term treatment of BD and SZA in mental health outpatient treatment settings (Renes et al. 2014). The study was performed between December 2009 and June 2014.

Selection of psychiatrists and patients

Between December 2009 and February 2010 all psychiatrists registered as member of the Dutch Psychiatric Association received a short survey about their treatment setting and whether they would be willing to participate in this study. All psychiatrists who indicated that they were treating adult patients with BD or SZA in an outpatient setting and were interested in participating in the study, received a questionnaire about their treatment setting, organization of care, and the number of patients currently in treatment for BD or SZA. Furthermore, they were asked to send a letter to all these patients inviting them to participate in the study.

All patients who returned an informed consent form were sent two questionnaires: one for themselves and one for a spouse, relative or significant other. The patients' questionnaire concerned care they had received in the previous 12 months or earlier for some treatment modalities, lifetime illness characteristics, clinical outcome, quality of life and functioning, satisfaction with care, and adherence to treatment. For each patient a clinical diagnosis, according to DSM-IV-TR (American Psychiatric Association 2000), was supplied by the treating psychiatrist, including comorbid diagnoses. The study was approved by the Medical Ethical Committee of the University Medical Center Utrecht, the Netherlands, and independently reviewed by the scientific committees of the two main participating research centers, Altrecht Institute for Mental Health Care, Utrecht, the Netherlands, and GGZ inGeest/VU University Medical Center, Amsterdam, the Netherlands. All participating patients gave written informed consent.

Outcome measures

Treatment modalities

Patients were asked to tick the medication they were currently using from a list of maintenance medications (lithium, carbamazepine, valproate, lamotrigine, olanzapine, quetiapine, risperidone, or aripiprazole), and to add any other medication they were currently using for BD, and were asked if, and with what frequency, laboratory tests were part of the treatment with lithium, valproate or carbamazepine. For psychosocial treatments, patients were asked if they ever had participated in a group psychoeducation program, if they had ever received psychotherapy, and if so, whether they had received it in the previous year, if they had received supportive treatment in the previous year, if they had an emergency plan on how to deal with early symptoms of an impending mood episode, and if they regularly monitored their mood by completing prospective LifeCharts according to the NIMH Life-Chart Method (Leverich and Post 1998), which is well-known in the Netherlands.

Measurement of concordance with the Dutch guideline

In the Dutch guideline recommendations may differ for patients with specific clinical profiles. For our study we distinguished four clinical profiles. Table 1 indicates which treatment modalities are, and which are not, recommended to be part of the treatment for patients with these profiles.

Maintenance pharmacotherapy is recommended for patients after three or more mood episodes, and for patients after two episodes if at least one of the episodes was severe, or when the patient has a first degree relative with BD. Furthermore, maintenance pharmacotherapy may be considered: (1) after a single severe manic episode, (2) after a single manic episode of any severity and having a first degree relative with BD, or (3) after two non-severe episodes without a family history of BD.

Table 1 Treatment modalities that are recommended by the Dutch guideline for the treatment of BD in patients with differential clinical profiles

	Clinical profiles			
	Currently asymptomatic and no indication for maintenance pharmacotherapy	Currently asymptomatic, with an indication for maintenance pharmacotherapy, and *no* episode in the previous year	Currently asymptomatic, with an indication for maintenance pharmacotherapy, and an episode in the previous year	Currently symptomatic
Treatment modality[a]				
Participation of a psychiatrist[b]	+	+	+	+
Group psychoeducation	+	+	+	+
Emergency plan	+/−[c]	+/−[c]	+	+
Maintenance pharmacotherapy	–	+	+	+
Life charting	−	−	+	+
Supportive treatment[d]	−	−	+	+
Psychotherapy[e]	−	−	−	+

[a] "+" indicates the modality is recommended to be part of the treatment in case of that particular clinical profile, and "−" indicates the modality is not recommended to be part of the treatment

[b] Patients with BD should have at least one visit/year with a psychiatrist or physician, when health care providers other than a psychiatrist/physician are part of the treatment team

[c] For these patients an emergency plan is recommended as optional

[d] At least three visits with a psychiatrist or mental health nurse in the previous year

[e] Any form of psychotherapy in the previous year

Finally, maintenance pharmacotherapy is not recommended for patients with a single non-severe manic episode in the absence of a first degree relative with BD.

To assess concordance with the Dutch guideline, a composite score ranging from 0 to 100 for the degree of concordance was developed based on the sum of scores for each treatment modality, taking into account an assumed impact factor of each treatment modality on treatment outcome as determined by consensus among the authors (JR, ER, WN, RK), when taking into account the level of scientific evidence of recommendations as described in the guideline. Of notice, WN and RK had been involved in the development of the guideline. The impact factors were rated as follows: pharmacotherapy 40 points, group psychoeducation 20, psychotherapy 20, participation of a psychiatrist 5, having an emergency plan on how to deal with emerging symptoms 5, mood monitoring 5, and supportive treatment 5 points.

If, according to the guideline, a treatment modality was recommended and accordingly applied, points were added to the total score; and similarly if a treatment modality was not recommended and accordingly not applied. If a treatment modality was recommended but not applied, or applied despite not being recommended, no points were added. The latter was based on the assumption that a more intensive treatment is not necessarily beneficial and might even pose a psychological or biological burden on the patient. No points were subtracted in case of non-concordance.

Assessment of symptoms and illness characteristics

The Quick Inventory of Depressive Symptomatology (QIDS) (Rush et al. 1996), and the Altman Self-Rating Mania Scale (ASRM) (Altman et al. 1997), were part of the patient questionnaire to measure current severity of mood symptoms. The questionnaire also addressed various lifetime illness characteristics. Because these data were obtained through self-reporting, some data could be missing or conflicting. When data were conflicting, consensus was first reached between the first two authors (JR, ER). The other authors (WN, RK) were consulted when necessarily. Data that remained inconclusive were excluded from analysis.

Statistical analyses

SPSS 22 was used for statistical analysis. Descriptive statistics were used for demographics and illness characteristics of the sample. Relationships with the total score of concordance were tested using simple and multiple regression analyses.

* based on anonymous logs with number of patients invited by psychiatrists, or number of letters for patients provided to the psychiatrists

Fig. 1 Inclusion of psychiatrists and patients

Results

Inclusion

The inclusion of psychiatrists and patients is presented in Fig. 1.

Socio-demographic and illness characteristics

Five hundred and fifty-five respondents (66.2%) were women. The average age was 49.5 years (s.d. 11.2). Five hundred and one out of 833 (60.1%) respondents were married or living together. The mean years of education (n=837) was 16.1 years (s.d. 4.3). Diagnoses were BD I (n=551; 65.7%), BD II (n=211; 25.1%), BD NOS (n=32; 3.8%), and SZA (n=45; 5.4%). At least one comorbid psychiatric diagnosis was present in 238 respondents (28.4%). The mean duration of illness (n=712) was 23.8 years (s.d. 12.3). The average age at onset for (hypo)manic symptoms was 30.1 years (s.d. 11.8), and for depressive symptoms 26.1 years (s.d. 11.7). Only nine respondents (1.1%) experienced one single manic episode, 28 (3.3%) had two mood episodes, all other 718 respondents (85.6%) had three or more mood episodes. Data on total lifetime number of mood episodes were inconclusive or missing in 84 respondents (10%). Hospital admission because of a mood episode was reported by 532 (63.4%) respondents. Data on admission were missing in 65 respondents (7.7%). Of the respondents, 283 (33.7%) had a first degree relative with bipolar disorder.

Treatments

The number of respondents receiving maintenance pharmacotherapy and various forms of psychosocial treatments is reported in Table 2.

Maintenance pharmacotherapy

Lithium, carbamazepine, valproate, lamotrigine or an antipsychotic as maintenance medication was used by 804 (96.1%) respondents. Of the remaining 32 (3.9%) who currently did not use any pharmacotherapy, 15 had BD I, 13 BD II, three BD NOS, and one SZA; all reported at least two previous mood episodes (data missing in one),

Table 2 Elements of current treatment as reported by the patients

Treatment modalities[a]	*n*	%
Current use of maintenance medication (n=836)		
Lithium	590	70.6
Anticonvulsants[b]	281	33.6
Atypical antipsychotics[c]	318	38.0
Conventional antipsychotics	30	3.6
Ever participated in group psychoeducation (n=836)	394	47.1
Emergency plan (n=836)	484	57.9
Participation of a psychiatrist (n=819)	803	98.0
Mood monitoring (n=835)	229	27.4
Psychotherapy in the previous year (n=681)	133	15.9
Supportive treatment (n=809)	749	92.6
Patient reports that a treatment plan has been made (n=825)		
Yes	502	60.8
No	323	39.2
Patient is involved in decision-making (n=827)		
Never	52	6.3
Sometimes	166	20.1
Mostly	279	33.7
Always	330	39.9
Significant others have been asked to participate in the treatment (n=828)		
Yes	677	81.8
No	151	18.2
Patient uses the internet for information on bipolar disorders and treatments (n=836)		
Yes	357	42.7
No	479	57.3

[a] Sample size may differ among variables, depending on missing data points

[b] Valproate, lamotrigine, carbamazepine

[c] Olanzapine, quetiapine, risperidone, aripiprazole, clozapine

and eight had been admitted at least once (data missing in two).

Polypharmacy was common. When all medications, excluding benzodiazepines and somatic medications, were taken together, 328 (39.1%) respondents used two drugs, and 117 (13.9%) three or more drugs with a maximum of five. In addition to the medication already listed in the questionnaire, 169 (20.1%) respondents reported the use of an antidepressant (14.2% BD I; 35.5% BD II; 25.0% BD NOS; 17.8% SZA). In 15 of these 169 respondents (BD I n=4; BD II=10; BD NOS=1) the antidepressant was not combined with lithium, an anticonvulsant or an antipsychotic. Of the respondents using either lithium, valproate or carbamazepine (n=711), almost all (n=702) reported an adequate frequency of laboratory testing.

Psychotherapy

Of the 133 respondents that received psychotherapy in the previous year, 77 (57.8%) reported that the therapy was specifically aimed at treating their BD, and 50 (37.6%) reported that the therapy had another focus.

Concordance with treatment guideline

Concordance with the guideline for each treatment modality was as follows: participation of a psychiatrist in 757 of 773 respondents (97.9%), maintenance pharmacotherapy in 754 of 786 (95.9%), supportive treatment in 560 of 762 (73.5%), use of an emergency plan in 556 of 787 (70.6%), psychotherapy in 399 of 765 (52.2%), group psychoeducation in 371 of 786 (47.2%), and mood monitoring in 369 of 785 respondents (47%). A guideline recommendation for maintenance pharmacotherapy applied to almost all respondents. In only two respondents, both BD I, maintenance pharmacotherapy was not recommended according to the guideline, however one was symptomatic and therefore concordance was scored according to clinical profile "currently symptomatic" as described in Table 1. For 30 respondents, data necessary to determine the need for maintenance pharmacotherapy were either missing or inconclusive.

Factors associated with concordance

Factors associated with concordance are presented in Table 3. Specialization for mood disorder of treatment setting, whether the respondents reported that a treatment plan had been made, total years of education, bipolar diagnosis, whether one or more significant others had been asked to participate in the treatment, duration of illness, absence of psychiatric comorbidity, and age were all significantly associated with being better concordant with the guideline. Age and duration of illness were negatively correlated with concordance (see Table 3).

In a multiple regression analysis age, absence of psychiatric comorbidity, duration of illness, and whether or not it was asked to involve significant others in the treatment, did not contribute significantly to the model, although the latter almost reached significance. All other factors were significant. The model explained almost 10% of variance in concordance scores (see Table 3).

Discussion

In this nationwide study of guideline concordance in routine clinical practice, we found that the use of maintenance pharmacotherapy was highly concordant with the recommendations in the Dutch guideline for BD. This resembles outcomes in some of the previous studies in euthymic or unspecified BD. The high frequency of lithium use (70.6%) in our study is remarkable. In a recent study in Denmark, lithium was prescribed less frequently, 41.7% during a 12-year study period, and its use had declined over the years (Kessing et al. 2016). In contrast to pharmacotherapy, applying psychosocial treatments was much less concordant with the Dutch guideline, even in specialized centers for mood disorders. Especially the low rate of concordance with the participation in (group) psychoeducation is relevant since its efficacy in the maintenance treatment of bipolar disorder has been well established (Colom et al. 2003) and it is thus recommended in the guideline for all BD patients. Moreover, group psychoeducation is widely available in the Netherlands. Concordance-rates for mood monitoring and psychotherapy were also relatively low. For psychotherapy, this may be due to the fact that in the 2008 guideline the indications are still described in general terms. As a consequence, measuring its concordance is less straightforward. Moreover, psychotherapy may have a wider focus than only BD, as was indicated by a considerable number of participants. Specialization of treatment center, years of education, type of diagnosis, and the fact that the patient was informed that a written treatment plan had been made, were all significantly associated with guideline concordance. This is an important finding since some of these factors (making a treatment plan and informing patients about this, and taking into account the level of education of patient) can be easily optimized in everyday clinical practice. Especially the level of understanding of verbal communication can easily be overestimated. Together with inviting a significant other to be involved in the treatment, these findings point in the direction that shared decision-making may result in more guideline-concordant treatments. However, little is currently known if and how shared decision-making may influence clinical outcome in mental health care (Duncan et al. 2010). Although significant in univariate analysis, the presence or absence of psychiatric comorbidity, duration

Table 3 Demographic, illness related and treatment related factors for concordance with the Dutch guideline for BD: univariate and multivariate analyses

	Univariate model[a]			Multivariate model[b]		
	B	*SE*	*P*	*B*	*SE*	*P*
Demographic factors						
Gender: female (male)[c]	−0.65	1.38	.640			
Age	−0.15	0.06	.010	0.03	0.07	.670
Marital status: living together or married (living alone, divorced, widowed)[c]	1.34	1.32	.309			
Education: total years of education	0.52	0.15	<.001	0.49	0.16	.002
Illness related factors						
Diagnosis: BD I (BD II, BD NOS or SZA)[c]	3.74	1.34	.005	2.98	1.43	.037
Psychiatric comorbidity: absent (present)[c]	2.97	1.40	.035	2.63	1.50	.080
Duration of illness	−0.15	0.06	.007	−0.09	0.07	.193
Treatment related factors						
Treatment setting: specialized centers (non-specialized center)[c]	7.36	1.50	<.001	5.67	1.64	.001
Patient reports that a treatment plan has been made: yes (no)[c]	5.65	1.32	<.001	5.37	1.44	<.001
Significant others have been asked to participate in the treatment: yes (no)[c]	4.86	1.69	.004	3.43	1.81	.059
Patient is involved in decision-making: (never)[c]						
Sometimes	−0.08	3.09	.979			
Mostly	0.04	2.96	.989			
Always	0.67	2.92	.818			
Other factor						
Patient uses the internet for information on bipolar disorder and treatments: yes (no)[c]	1.56	1.30	.229			

[a] Univariate analysis from simple regression. *Note*: constants in the simple regression models with categorical factors: gender: 72.8, marital status: 72.6, diagnosis: 72.1, psychiatric comorbidity: 72.1, treatment setting: 70.7, whether or not a treatment plan has been made: 72.0, whether or not significant others have been asked to participate: 71.1, patients' involvement in decision-making: 72.6, and patients' use of internet: 72.8

[b] The multivariate analysis includes all factors that are univariately associated with concordance (at the level of statistical significance of $a = 0.05$). The coefficient of determination of the multivariate model $R^2 = 0.09$ ($p < 0.001$)

[c] Reference category

of illness, and age did not contribute significantly in the regression model. In contrast to our hypothesis, gender, marital status, and use of internet by the patient, were not associated with better concordance with the guideline. The involvement of the patient in decision-making in the treatment was also not associated with better concordance, although this was probably due to the fact that the majority of patients stated that they were involved.

Strengths and limitations

Our study has several strong points. To the best of our knowledge this is a first nation-wide study that it includes a large number of patients in long-term psychiatric outpatient treatment. Moreover, concordance with the treatment guideline was assessed for a wide variety of guideline recommended treatment modalities, and quantified in a composite score taking into account different clinical profiles of patients in maintenance treatment. Dennehey et al. (2005) used a composite score for adherence to the medication guidelines from the Texas Medication Algorithm Project (TMAP). This score measured visit schedules, medication/dosing, and response to patient symptoms. In that study a multifaceted treatment program including the medication guidelines was studied in several intervention clinics, and compared with treatment as usual in non-intervention clinics. Adherence to the guideline was only studied in the intervention clinics. Kilbourne et al. (2010) implemented composite quality metrics to measure the quality of processes of care from various treatment guidelines in a study using medical records, including assessments of symptoms, comorbidity, cardiometabolic outcomes, and documentation of patient treatment experience.

Our study has several limitations. First, although a great effort was made to include a representative cohort in a wide variety of mental health care treatment settings, it is likely that a bias towards psychiatrists and patients with particular interest in our study will have occurred, since many participating patients were treated in specialized mood disorder centers. This will limit the generalizability of our results to non-specialized centers and private practice. Therefore, outcomes may reflect more guideline-concordant care than in settings where psychiatrists (and therefore their patients) did not participate in this study. On the other hand, this could suggest that measures to improve guideline concordance may be even more vital in those settings. A second limitation is that maintenance pharmacotherapy was not assessed in detail but was defined as the use of at least one maintenance drug recommended in the guideline. Whether the choice or dosage of medication was optimized according to guideline recommendations, was not taken into account. Use of antidepressants may have been underreported since information was provided at the initiative of the respondent. As will be the case in studies using patient surveys, not all nuances of individual treatments could be included in the assessment of concordance with the guideline, and answers may have been incomplete or inconsistent. Although an updated guideline was published in 2015, after the study was completed, we assume that the findings of our study are still relevant today, since there were no major changes in the recommendations for long-term treatment strategies in the 2015 guideline. The differences between these guidelines concern recommendations in pharmacotherapy and psychological treatment of a more detailed level than addressed in our study.

Conclusions

Overall, we conclude that in everyday clinical practice, more than pharmacotherapy, the implementation of psychosocial treatments still needs considerable effort. Actively involving the patient in the treatment may improve concordance rates, although further research in this field is needed. Future studies on psychosocial treatments for bipolar disorder may result in more specific indications for which treatment is needed for which patient in which phase of the illness. Eventually, one can expect that a more personalized approach in treatment guidelines will greatly enhance their utility and implementation.

Abbreviations

BD: bipolar disorder; SZA: schizoaffective disorder, bipolar type; BD I: bipolar I disorder; BD II: bipolar II disorder; BD NOS: bipolar disorder NOS.

Authors' contributions

JWR drafted this paper and it was modified by all authors. WAN and RWK conceived the study, JWR and EJR contributed to the design and study protocol. All authors read and approved the final manuscript.

Author details

[1] Altrecht Institute for Mental Health Care, Utrecht, Nieuwe Houtenseweg 12, 3524 SH Utrecht, The Netherlands. [2] Amsterdam UMC, Vrije Universiteit Amsterdam, Psychiatry, Amsterdam Public Health, De Boelelaan 1117, 1081 HV Amsterdam, The Netherlands. [3] Department of Psychiatry, University Medical Center Groningen, University of Groningen, Hanzeplein 1, 9713 GZ Groningen, The Netherlands.

Acknowledgements

The authors thank the participating psychiatrists and patients for their contribution to the study.

Competing interests

J.W. Renes and E.J. Regeer received speaker's fees from AstraZeneca, Bristol-Myers Squibb, and Ely Lilly. A. W. Hoogendoorn reports no potential competing interests. W.A. Nolen has received grants from the Netherlands Organization for Health Research and Development, the European Union; has received honoraria/speaker's fees from Lundbeck and Aristo Pharma, and has served as consultant for Daleco Pharma. R.W. Kupka received speaker's fees for lectures on symposia sponsored by AstraZeneca, Bristol-Myers Squibb, Lundbeck, Sanofi, and Janssen. W.A. Nolen and R.W. Kupka were member of subsequent Dutch bipolar disorder guideline committees.

Funding

R.W. Kupka received an unrestricted research grant for this study from AstraZeneca.

References

Altinbas K, Smith D, Oral ET. Adherence to Turkish psychiatric association guideline for bipolar depression treatment in a specialized mood disorders outpatient unit. Psychiatr Danub. 2011;23(2):189–93.

Altman EG, Hedeker D, Peterson JL, Davis JM. The Altman self-rating mania scale. Biol Psychiatry. 1997;42(10):948–55.

American Psychiatric Association. Diagnostic and statistical manual of mental disorders, Text Revision. 4th ed. Washington, D.C: American Psychiatric Association; 2000.

Arvilommi P, Suominen KS, Mantere OK, Leppamaki S, Valtonen H, Isometsa ET. Adequacy of treatment received by diagnosed and undiagnosed patients with bipolar I and II disorders. J Clin Psychiatry. 2007;68(1):102–10.

Baek JH, Ha K, Yatham LN, Chang JS, Ha TH, Jeon HJ, et al. Pattern of pharmacotherapy by episode types for patients with bipolar disorders and its concordance with treatment guidelines. J Clin Psychopharmacol. 2014;34(5):577–87.

Bauer MS, Biswas K, Kilbourne AM. Enhancing multiyear guideline concordance for bipolar disorder through collaborative care. Am J Psychiatry. 2009;166(11):1244–50.

Busch AB, Huskamp HA, Landrum MB. Quality of care in a Medicaid population with bipolar I disorder. Psychiatr Serv. 2007;58(6):848–54.

Colom F, Vieta E, Martinez-Aran A, Reinares M, Goikolea JM, Benabarre A, et al. A randomized trial on the efficacy of group psychoeducation in the prophylaxis of recurrences in bipolar patients whose disease is in remission. Arch Gen Psychiatry. 2003;60(4):402–7.

Dennehy EB, Bauer MS, Perlis RH, Kogan JN, Sachs GS. Concordance with treatment guidelines for bipolar disorder: data from the systematic treatment enhancement program for bipolar disorder. Psychopharmacol Bull. 2007;40(3):72–84.

Dennehy EB, Suppes T, Rush AJ, Miller AL, Trivedi MH, Crismon ML, et al. Does provider adherence to a treatment guideline change clinical outcomes for patients with bipolar disorder? Results from the Texas Medication Algorithm Project. Psychol Med. 2005;35(12):1695–706.

Duncan E, Best C, Hagen S. Shared decision making interventions for people with mental health conditions. Cochrane Database Syst Rev. 2010. https://doi.org/10.1002/14651858.CD007297.pub2.

Farrelly N, Dibben C, Hunt N. Current management of bipolar affective disorder: is it reflective of the BAP guidelines? J Psychopharmacol. 2006;20(1):128–31.

Freeland K, Cogdili B, Ross C, Sullivan C, Drayton S. Adherence to evidence-based treatment guidelines for bipolar depression in an inpatient setting. Am J Health Pharm. 2015;72(suppl 3):S156–61.

Huang H, Goren JL, Chan YF, Katon W, Russo J, Hogan D, et al. Pharmacologic management of bipolar disorder in a medicare advantage population. Psychosomatics. 2014;55(6):572–7.

Kessing LV, Vradi E, Andersen PK. Nationwide and population-based prescription patterns in bipolar disorder. Bipolar Disord. 2016;18(2):174–82.

Kilbourne AM, Bauer MS, Han X, Haas GL, Elder P, Good CB, et al. Racial differences in the treatment of veterans with bipolar disorder. Psychiatr Serv. 2005;56(12):1549–55.

Kilbourne AM, Farmer Teh C, Welsh D, Pincus HA, Lasky E, Perron B, et al. Implementing composite quality metrics for bipolar disorder: towards a more comprehensive approach to quality measurement. Gen Hosp Psychiatry. 2010;32(6):636–43.

Kupka RW, Goossens PJJ, van Bendegem M, Daemen P, Daggenvoorde T, Daniels M, et al. Multidisciplinaire richtlijn bipolaire stoornissen. Utrecht: Nederlandse Vereniging voor Psychiatrie, De Tijdstroom; 2015.

Leverich GS, Post RM. Life charting of affective disorders. CNS Spectr. 1998;3(5):21–37.

Lim PZ, Tunis SL, Edell WS, Jensik SE, Tohen M. Medication prescribing patterns for patients with bipolar I disorder in hospital settings: adherence to published practice guidelines. Bipolar Disord. 2001;3(4):165–73.

Marcus SC, Olfson M, Pincus HA, Zarin DA, Kupfer DJ. Therapeutic drug monitoring of mood stabilizers in Medicaid patients with bipolar disorder. Am J Psychiatry. 1999;156(7):1014–8.

Nolen WA, Kupka RW, Schulte PFJ, Knoppert-van der Klein EAM, Honig A, Reichart CG, et al. Richtlijn Bipolaire stoornissen. Nederlandse Vereniging voor Psychiatrie. Utrecht: De Tijdstroom; 2008.

Paterniti S, Bisserbe JC. Pharmacotherapy for bipolar disorder and concordance with treatment guidelines: survey of a general population sample referred to a tertiary care service. BMC Psychiatry. 2013;13:211.

Renes JW, Regeer EJ, van der Voort TY, Nolen WA, Kupka RW. Treatment of bipolar disorder in the Netherlands and concordance with treatment guidelines: study protocol of an observational, longitudinal study on naturalistic treatment of bipolar disorder in everyday clinical practice. BMC Psychiatry. 2014;14:58.

Rush AJ, Gullion CM, Basco MR, Jarrett RB, Trivedi MH. The inventory of depressive symptomatology (IDS): psychometric properties. Psychol Med. 1996;26(3):477–86.

Simon NM, Otto MW, Weiss RD, Bauer MS, Miyahara S, Wisniewski SR, et al. Pharmacotherapy for bipolar disorder and comorbid conditions: baseline data from STEP-BD. J Clin Psychopharmacol. 2004;24(5):512–20.

Smith TE, Levine SB, Hampel J. A successful effort to improve adherence to treatment guidelines for bipolar disorder. Harv Rev Psychiatry. 2008;16(3):210–3.

Unutzer J, Simon G, Pabiniak C, Bond K, Katon W. The use of administrative data to assess quality of care for bipolar disorder in a large staff model HMO. Gen Hosp Psychiatry. 2000;22(1):1–10.

Walpoth-Niederwanger M, Kemmler G, Grunze H, Weiss U, Hortnagl C, Strauss R, et al. Treatment patterns in inpatients with bipolar disorder at a psychiatric university hospital over a 9-year period: focus on mood stabilizers. Int Clin Psychopharmacol. 2012;27(5):256–66.

Wang Z, Chen J, Zhang C, Gao K, Hong W, Xing M, et al. Guidelines concordance of maintenance treatment in euthymic patients with bipolar disorder: data from the national bipolar mania pathway survey (BIPAS) in mainland China. J Affect Disord. 2015;182:101–5.

Wang Z, Gao K, Hong W, Xing M, Wu Z, Chen J, et al. Guidelines disconcordance in acute bipolar depression: data from the national bipolar mania pathway survey (BIPAS) in mainland China. PLoS ONE. 2014a;9(4):1–6.

Wang Z, Gao K, Hong W, Xing M, Wu Z, Chen J, et al. Pharmacotherapy for acute mania and disconcordance with treatment guidelines: bipolar mania pathway survey (BIPAS) in mainland China. BMC Psychiatry. 2014b;14:167.

Regional cortical thinning in young adults with schizophrenia but not psychotic or non-psychotic bipolar I disorder

Douglass Godwin[1], Kathryn I. Alpert[2], Lei Wang[2] and Daniel Mamah[1*]

Abstract

Background: Schizophrenia shares some genetic risk and clinical symptoms with bipolar disorder. Clinical heterogeneity across subjects is thought to contribute to variable structural imaging findings across studies. The current study investigates cortical thickness in young adults diagnosed with schizophrenia or bipolar I disorder with a history of hyperthymic mania. We hypothesize that cortical thickness will be most similar between SCZ and the psychotic bipolar 1 disorder subtype.

Methods: Patients with schizophrenia ($n=52$), psychotic bipolar I disorder (PBD; $n=49$) and non-psychotic bipolar I disorder (NPBD; $n=24$) and healthy controls ($n=40$) were scanned in a 3T Trio MRI. The thickness of 34 cortical regions was estimated with FreeSurfer, and analyzed using univariate analyses of variance. Relationships to psychotic (SAPS) and negative (SANS) symptoms were investigated using linear regression.

Results: Cortical thickness showed significant group effects, after covarying for sex, age, and intracranial volume ($p=0.001$). SCZ subjects had thinner paracentral, inferior parietal, supramarginal and fusiform cortices compared to CON. Caudal anterior cingulate cortical thickness was increased in SCZ, PBD and NPBD. Cortical thickness in PBD and NPBD were not significantly different from controls. Significant partial correlations were observed for SAPS severity with middle temporal ($r=-0.26$; $p=0.001$) and fusiform (-0.26; $p=0.001$) cortical thickness.

Conclusions: Individuals with SCZ displayed significantly reduced cortical thickness in several cortical regions compared to both CON and bipolar. We found that SCZ participants had significant cortical thinning relative to CON and bipolar disorder most significantly in the frontal (i.e. paracentral), parietal (i.e. inferior parietal, supramarginal), and temporal (i.e. middle temporal, fusiform) cortices.

Keywords: Bipolar disorder, Schizophrenia, Cortical thickness, MRI

Background

Bipolar disorder has substantial genetic and familiar overlap with schizophrenia and often share clinical features, including the presence of psychotic symptoms (Cardno and Owen 2014; Moskvina et al. 2009; Mamah and Barch 2011; Fischer and Carpenter 2009). Over 60% of bipolar disorder patients have had a lifetime history of at least one psychotic symptom (Keck et al. 2003; Coryell et al. 2001; Goodwin and Jamison 2007). Some studies have also found that schizophrenia susceptibility genes are more commonly shared with psychotic bipolar patients, compared to bipolar patients without a psychotic disorder history (Moskvina et al. 2009; Ivleva et al. 2008, 2010; Green et al. 2005; Potash 2006; Tamminga et al. 2013).

There has been continued interest in the use of neuroimaging to investigate intermediate phenotypes common across schizophrenia and bipolar disorder. The cortical structure of the brain is commonly quantitatively measured via gray matter volume, a measurement that is dependent on both cortical thickness and surface area of a region. These structural measures are thought to be

*Correspondence: mamahd@wustl.edu
[1] Department of Psychiatry, Washington University Medical School, St. Louis, USA
Full list of author information is available at the end of the article

heritable (Panizzon et al. 2009) and can therefore provide insight into the genetic differences between patient populations. However, the surface area and cortical thickness appear to be genetically uncorrelated (Panizzon et al. 2009). Thus, volume measurements, which combine aspects of both traits, are likely influenced by some combination of these genetic factors. Cortical thickness is thought to be dependent on the size, number, and arrangement of neurons and neuroglia in the cortex (Hatton et al. 2013; Goldman-Rakic 1988; Kuperberg et al. 2003; Rakic and Caviness 1995; Winkler et al. 2010). As such, cortical thinning relative to normal populations has implications about the preservation of, or lack thereof, network architecture in the cortex. To the extent abnormal function in cortical and subcortical networks, which are thought to be perturbed in both diseases (Uhlhaas 2013; Hulshoff Pol et al. 2012; Menon 2011), can be explained by abnormality of structure, the region-specific nature of cortical thinning could provide insight into differential developmental trajectories of brain disorders (Fischl et al. 1999; Fischl and Dale 2000).

Several brain studies investigating cortical structure have been conducted in schizophrenia and bipolar disorder patients. A meta-analysis of voxel-based morphometric studies in schizophrenia and bipolar disorder identified overlap of gray matter deficits in paralimbic cortical regions (including the anterior cingulate and insula) across the two diagnoses, with schizophrenia patients showing more extensive cortical deficits, also including neocortical and limbic regions (Ellison-Wright and Bullmore 2010). A recent large meta-analysis by the ENIGMA schizophrenia working group found widespread cortical thinning in schizophrenia, as well as reduced surface area (van Erp et al. 2017). Similarly, Rimol et al. (2012) found widespread cortical thinning and circumscribed cortical area reductions in schizophrenia patients, but not in bipolar disorder patients. However, the largest study of cortical thickness and surface area in bipolar disorder was conducted within the ENIGMA Consortium, and involved 2447 adult bipolar disorder patients (Hibar et al. 2018). These authors found cortical thinning in frontal, temporal and parietal regions, as well as an association of reduced cortical surface area with psychosis history (Hibar et al. 2018).

Heterogeneity in patient populations studied can influence the structural imaging findings observed (Zhang et al. 2015). Thus, studying more homogenous populations may provide greater understanding of cortical thickness in disease. For example, investigating a wide age range of subjects can introduce confounds unrelated to the illness and associated with older age. Studying cortical thickness in younger and older bipolar disorder populations separately, have provided additional insights into the disease, showing substantial cortical thinning only in the older bipolar patients (Hibar et al. 2018). Studying the clinical subtypes separately, can also be valuable. Patients with bipolar I disorder and bipolar II disorder are sometimes pooled as one group, despite the former representing a subtype with longer duration clinical episodes ("mania") than the latter ("hypomania") (American_Psychiatric_Association 2013). Significant reductions in cortical volume and thickness however has been reported by some authors to be limited to bipolar I disorder patients (Maller et al. 2014; Abe et al. 2016; Rimol et al. 2010). Finally, separating bipolar patients based on psychotic disorder histories often show differential effects, usually with the psychotic bipolar patients showing structural changes more closely related to that of schizophrenia patients (Strasser et al. 2005; Mamah et al. 2016; Womer et al. 2014).

The current study compares cortical thickness between young adult (aged 18–30 years) control subjects and patients with schizophrenia, psychotic bipolar I disorder and non-psychotic bipolar I disorder. Bipolar disorder subjects all had a history of hyperthymic manic episodes, while patients with a history of exclusively irritable manic episodes were excluded. In addition, none of our participants met criteria for a substance use disorder in the past 6 months of assessment, to minimize substance related effects on cortical thickness. We hypothesized that patterns of cortical thinning in schizophrenia patients will share some similarity with psychotic but not non-psychotic bipolar disorder patients.

Methods

Participants

All participants provided written informed consent and experimental procedures were approved by the Washington University School of Medicine institutional review board. Four diagnostic groups were included in the current study: healthy controls (CON; n = 40), schizophrenia (SCZ, n = 52), psychotic bipolar I disorder (PBD, n = 49) and non-psychotic bipolar I disorder (NPBD, n = 24). Participant groups were diagnosed on the basis of a consensus between a research psychiatrist and a trained research assistant who used the Structured Clinical Interview for DSM-IV Axis I Disorder (First et al. 2002; Lobbestael et al. 2011). CON subjects were required to have no lifetime history of psychotic or mood disorders. Bipolar (BD) participant patients were required to meet DSM-IV criteria for Bipolar I Disorder and were classified as psychotic BD if the participant had a psychotic event over the course of their lifetime, as assessed via the Structured Clinical Interview for the DSM (SCID). All psychotic events were reported to have occurred during manic episodes in bipolar participants. Participants were excluded if they: (a) met DSM-IV criteria for substance dependence or severe/moderate abuse during the prior 6 months; (b) had a clinically unstable or severe general medical disorder; or (c) had a history of head injury with documented neurological sequelae or loss of consciousness. Additionally, to minimize clinical heterogeneity within the BD group, only participants with a history of euphoric mania (versus mania characterized by primarily irritable mood) were included in the study.

Table 1 shows demographic data across the four participant groups. All patients were on stable medication for at least 4 weeks prior to assessment. Based on the results of the Young Mania Rating Scale (YMRS), the majority of bipolar participants were euthymic at the time of admission into the study. Four participants (3 PBD, 1 NPBD) scored between 13 and 20 suggesting a potential case of hyper- or hypomania. Three participants (2 PBD, 1 NPBD) scored above 20 indicating a probable case of hyper- or hypomania (Young et al. 1978; Marchand et al. 2005). The YMRS was only collected for bipolar patients. The average duration of illness for the psychotic bipolar group was 7.87 years while the average duration of illness for the non-psychotic group was 8.58 years.

Clinical assessment

Symptoms were assessed using the Scale for the Assessment of Negative Symptoms (SANS) and the Scale for the Assessment of Positive Symptoms (SAPS). Specific subscale scores were summed to derive measures of positive symptoms (i.e. hallucination, delusion) and negative symptoms (i.e. flat affect, alogia, anhedonia, attention and amotivation subscales). Disorganized symptoms were not included in SAPS scores so as to only reflect the presence of positive symptoms.

Image and cortical thickness acquisition

Magnetic resonance (MR) scans were obtained using a Siemens (Erlangen, Germany) 3T Tim TRIO Scanner at Washington University Medical School. T1-weighted images were acquired using a sagittal MPRAGE 3D sequence (TR = 2400 ms, TE = 3.16 ms, flip = 8°; voxel size = 1 × 1 × 1 mm).

Cortical thickness of 34 brain cortical regions for each hemisphere were obtained using FreeSurfer version 5.1.0 software (Fischl et al. 1999; Dale et al. 1999). Gray-matter (GM) and white-matter (WM) boundaries were reconstructed in order to estimate the distance between those surfaces across the cortex in order to calculate the cortical thickness (Dale et al. 1999; Han et al. 2006; Rosas et al. 2002). Our preprocessing included automated skull stripping, removal of subcortical surfaces, transformation into Talairach space, and a spatial smoothing algorithm (Dale et al. 1999). Measurements of intracranial volume (ICV) were determined via the automated Freesurfer pipeline. These surfaces were then inflated into spheres in order to be registered to a common space via an automated procedure based on identification of cortical features identified in a predefined atlas (Fischl et al. 1999). Thickness for each region of interest (ROI) was calculated on a per-vertex basis based on the distance between closest points between gray and white-matter surfaces and then averaged across vertices within each region of interest (Fischl et al. 1999; Dale et al. 1999).

Statistical analysis

Statistical analyses were performed using IBM's SPSS software (IBM SPSS Statistics for Macintosh, Version 24.0, Armonk, NY). We examined group differences in SAPS and SANS measures using a multivariate analysis of covariance, covarying for age and sex. Differences in cortical thickness between subjects of different diagnostic groups were initially tested using a repeated measures analysis of covariance, covaried for age, sex, and ICV, treating hemisphere and region as repeated-measures. ICV was used here as a covariate given past evidence of cranial size differences in individuals with schizophrenia (Ward et al. 1996). This repeated-measures test revealed no main effect of hemisphere. Thus, subsequent testing was performed on cortical thickness values averaged across hemisphere in order to reduce the number tests for multiple comparisons considerations. We then tested for univariate effects of diagnostic group on cortical thickness within each region, with post hoc analyses of pairwise differences in groups in regions showing a univariate effect. To assess the relationship between clinical variables and cortical thickness, we performed a set of linear regressions to predict SAPS and SANS scores for each ROI. Included in these models were predictors for age, sex, ICV as well as dummy predictors for SCZ, PBD, and NPBD group membership in addition to a cortical thickness regressor. Given the number of regions tested, multiple comparisons corrections are noted when performed.

Results

Clinical measures

Based on multivariate testing, there was a significant main effect of diagnosis ($F_{(6,310)} = 20.530$, Wilk's $\Lambda = 0.512$, $p < 0.001$, $\eta^2 = 0.284$) after controlling for age and sex, indicating a difference in SAPS and SANS scores between groups. Differences in scores were driven by higher ratings in the SCZ and PBD groups relative to controls (CON) in the SAPS data, and SCZ relative to all other groups in the SANS scores (Table 1; Fig. 1).

Table 1 Demographics and Clinical Information

Characteristics	CON (n=40)	SCZ (n=52)	PBD (n=49)	NPBD (n=24)
Mean age (SD)	24.9 (5.0)	26.1 (4.1)	25.3 (3.7)	26.2 (3.7)
Sex (%)				
Male	20 (50.0)	38 (73.1)	20 (40.8)	8 (33.3)
Female	20 (50.0)	14 (26.9)	29 (59.2)	16 (66.7)
Race (%)				
Asian	2 (5.0)	0	1 (2.0)	2 (8.3)
Black	20 (50.0)	27 (51.9)	13 (26.5)	2 (8.3)
Hispanic	0	0	3 (6.1)	0
White	18 (45.0)	25 (48.1)	30 (61.2)	18 (75.0)
Multiracial	0	0	2 (4.1)	2 (8.3)
Handedness (%)				
Left	4 (10.0)	2 (3.8)	4 (8.2)	3 (12.5)
Right	36 (90.0)	50 (96.2)	45 (91.8)	21 (87.5)
History of use disorder (%)[a]				
Alcohol	4 (10.0)	17 (32.7)	23 (46.9)	12 (50.0)
Cannabis	0	21 (40.4)	17 (34.7)	6 (25.0)
Stimulant	1 (2.5)	1 (1.9)	1 (2.0)	0
Opioid	0	1 (1.9)	2 (4.1)	0
Cocaine	0	0	6 (12.2)	1 (4.2)
Hallucinogen	0	0	2 (4.1)	1 (4.2)
Psychotropic medication (%)				
Typical antipsychotic	0	8 (13.6)	3 (6.1)	0
Atypical antipsychotic	0	37 (72.5)	30 (62.2)	6 (25.0)
SSRI	0	15 (29.4)	24 (49.0)	10 (41.7)
Other antidepressants[b]	0	3 (5.8)	12 (24.5)	7 (29.2)
Stimulant	0	0	4 (8.2)	3 (12.5)
Mood stabilizer	0	11 (21.6)	33 (67.3)	18 (75.0)
Benzodiazepines	0	1 (2.0)	20 (40.8)	6 (25.0)
Anticholinergic	0	0	8 (16.3)	2 (8.3)
None	40 (100.0)	13 (25.5)	6 (12.2)	1 (4.2)
Symptom domains (SD)				
SAPS[c]	0.25 (.2)	3.56 (3.0)	1.35 (1.9)	0.42 (0.8)
Hallucination subscale	0	1.40 (1.8)	0.39 (0.9)	0
Delusion subscale	0.05 (.221)	2.12 (1.4)	0.96 (1.3)	0.42 (0.8)
SANS[d]	2.30 (2.3)	10.25 (3.9)	3.18 (3.8)	3.42 (2.4)
Flat Affect subscale	0.08 (0.4)	1.85 (1.3)	0.59 (0.9)	0.71 (1.2)
Alogia subscale	0.05 (0.3)	1.23 (1.8)	0.16 (0.5)	0.13 (0.4)
Anhedonia subscale	0.38 (0.8)	2.48 (1.1)	1.31 (1.4)	1.04 (1.1)
Amotivation subscale	0.73 (1.1)	3.02 (1.0)	1.24 (1.4)	0.92 (1.2)
Attention subscale	1.08 (1.3)	1.67 (1.3)	0.88 (1.1)	0.63 (1.0)

[a] Other than for nicotine use disorder, participants did not meet criteria for a use disorder in the last 6 months

[b] Refers to antidepressants other than selective serotonin reuptake inhibitors (SSRI)

[c] Maximum possible score on the Structured Assessment of Positive Symptoms (SAPS) is 16

[d] Maximum possible score on the Structured Assessment of Negative Symptoms (SANS) is 20

Group analysis of cortical thickness

Covarying for sex, age, and ICV, a repeated-measures test of cortical thickness showed a significant main effect of diagnosis ($F_{(3,158)}=5.664$, $p=0.001$, $\eta^2=0.058$; Fig. 2) and region ($F_{(33,514)}=23.074$, $p<0.001$, $\eta^2=0.127$), but no effect of hemisphere ($F_{(1,158)}=3.650$, $p=0.057$, $\eta^2=0.021$). We observed a group by hemisphere interaction ($F_{(3,158)}=8.879$, $p<0.001$, $\eta^2=0.144$), driven by

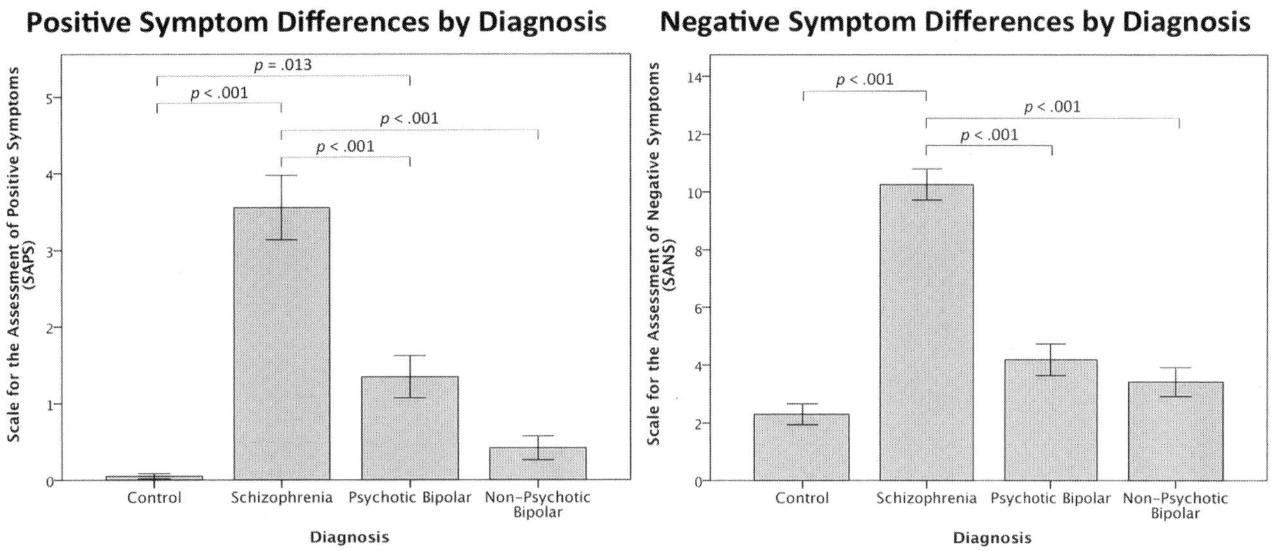

Fig. 1 Clinical measures of positive and negative symptoms by diagnosis. (left) Relationship between positive symptoms by diagnosis as assessed by SAPS. (right) Negative symptom scores as assessed by SANS by diagnosis. Significant pairwise comparisons shown in both figures, Bonferroni corrected for multiple comparisons. Error bars represent within-group standard error

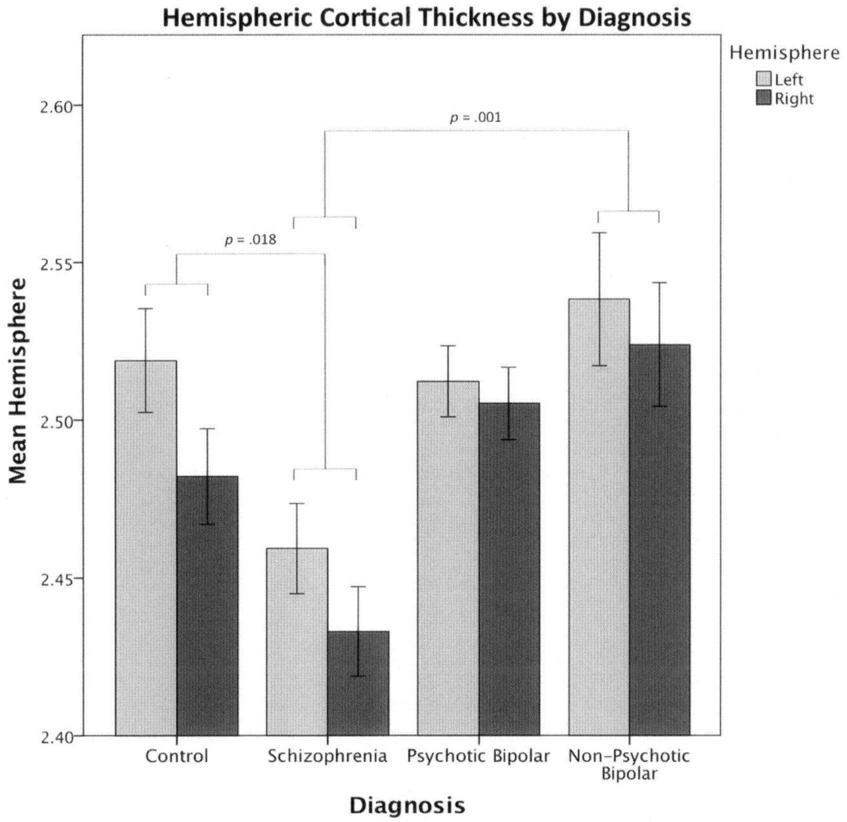

Fig. 2 Average cortical thickness per hemisphere by diagnosis. In repeated-measures testing, a significant main effect of diagnosis was observed, with no significant main effect of hemisphere. Significance comparisons represent pairwise contrasts between diagnostic groups. Significance values greater than 0.05 not shown. Pairwise comparisons were Bonferroni corrected for multiple comparisons. Error bars represent within-group standard error

decreased right hemisphere thickness in the CON and SCZ groups relative to BD groups.

Further tests of cortical thickness averaged values across hemisphere to produce 34 cortical regions of interest to reduce the number of tests performed, given the lack of a main effect of hemisphere. Table 2 shows the results of 34 univariate tests, one for each region. After Bonferroni correction, significant effect of diagnosis was observed for the superior frontal cortex, paracentral cortex, the fusiform gyrus, as well as the caudal anterior and posterior portions of the cingulate. For visualization purposes, mean, z-scored cortical thickness values of the 34 cortical regions are depicted in Fig. 3.

Results of post hoc analyses, comparing cortical thickness between individual groups in regions that showed an omnibus group effect (prior to Bonferroni correction), are shown in Table 3. After Bonferroni correction, pairwise comparisons showed cortical thinning in SCZ participants relative to other groups, most notably in specific

Table 2 Estimated marginal means

	ROI	CON	SCZ	PBD	NPBD	$F_{(3,156)}$ (p value)
Frontal	1. Frontal pole	2.736	2.675	2.650	2.696	1.279 (0.284)
	2. Superior fontal	*2.697*	*2.645*	*2.723*	*2.753*	*6.281 (< 0.001)*
	3. Rostral middle frontal	2.284	2.302	2.320	2.355	2.239 (0.062)
	4. Caudal middle frontal	2.569	2.516	2.564	2.577	3.091 (0.029)
	5. Pars opercularis	2.612	2.590	2.599	2.645	1.660 (0.178)
	6. Pars triangularis	2.483	2.456	2.454	2.447	0.353 (0.787)
	7. Pars orbitalis	2.654	2.607	2.601	2.618	1.254 (0.292)
	8. Precentral	2.447	2.529	2.591	2.558	4.490 (0.005)
	9. Paracentral	*2.431*	*2.369*	*2.464*	*2.458*	*7.764 (< 0.001)*
	10. Lateral orbitofrontal	2.537	2.519	2.503	2.584	2.274 (0.082)
	11. Medial orbitofrontal	2.327	2.308	2.330	2.395	2.019 (0.114)
Parietal	12. Superior parietal	2.276	2.209	2.225	2.259	2.153 (0.096)
	13. Inferior parietal	2.516	2.437	2.488	2.526	5.136 (0.002)
	14. Supramarginal	2.585	2.522	2.569	2.575	4.586 (0.004)
	15. Postcentral	2.110	2.107	2.089	2.074	0.512 (0.675)
	16. Precuneus	2.447	2.388	2.395	2.455	2.569 (0.062)
Temporal	17. Temporal pole	3.670	3.618	3.751	3.810	3.095 (0.029)
	18. Superior temporal	2.868	2.817	2.827	2.854	2.676 (0.049)
	19. Middle temporal	2.937	2.839	2.867	2.909	3.841 (0.011)
	20. Inferior temporal	2.819	2.710	2.756	2.767	4.029 (0.009)
	21. Bank Sup. Temp. Sulcus	2.627	2.566	2.542	2.568	1.438 (0.234)
	22. Fusiform	*2.744*	*2.663*	*2.726*	*2.778*	*7.476 (< 0.001)*
	23. Transverse temporal	2.520	2.488	2.462	2.494	2.351 (0.074)
	24. Parahippocampal	2.808	2.718	2.770	2.795	2.740 (0.045)
	25. Entorhinal	3.428	3.359	3.534	3.521	3.486 (0.017)
Occipital	26. Lateral occipital	2.242	2.171	2.184	2.193	2.274 (0.082)
	27. Lingual	2.097	2.053	2.019	2.030	0.852 (0.467)
	28. Cuneus	1.928	1.889	1.878	1.917	1.799 (0.150)
	29. Pericalcarine	1.725	1.703	1.734	1.618	0.446 (0.721)
Cingulate	30. Rostral Ant. cingulate	2.776	2.777	2.851	2.856	2.501 (0.062)
	31. Caudal Ant. cingulate	*2.525*	*2.554*	*2.560*	*2.568*	*6.441 (< 0.001)*
	32. Posterior cingulate	*2.508*	*2.468*	*2.499*	*2.615*	*7.062 (< 0.001)*
	33. Isthmus of cingulate	2.439	2.409	2.419	2.482	1.321 (0.270)
Insula	34. Insula	3.050	3.001	3.054	3.049	3.858 (0.011)

Values indicate estimated means of subject groups, controlled for age, sex, race and total intracranial volume. Significance values are uncorrected for multiple comparisons. Italicized regions were significant after Bonferroni correcting for 34 comparisons

ROI region of interest, *CON* control, *SCZ* schizophrenia, *PBD* psychotic bipolar disorder, *NPBD* non-psychotic, bipolar disorder, *Temp.* temporal, *Sup.* superior, *Ant.* anterior

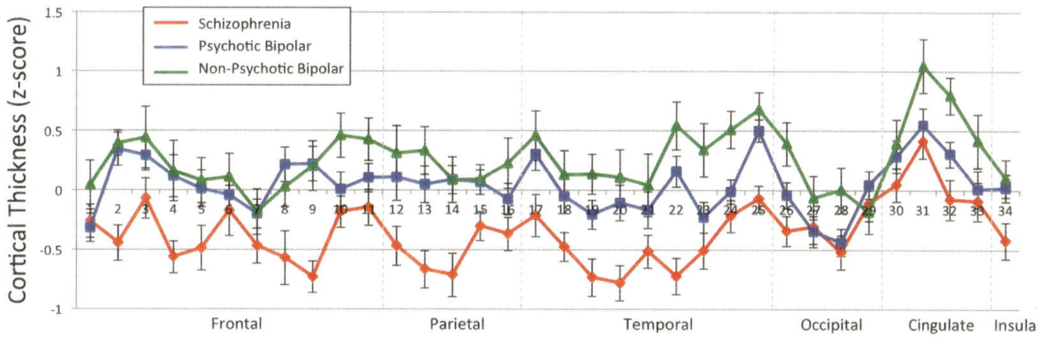

Fig. 3 Z-scored, average cortical thickness values per region of interest. Region of interest labels correspond to those identified in Table 2. Z-scores were computed by using the mean and standard deviation of the control group as reference, and as such the healthy controls lie on the horizontal axis. Error bars represent within-group standard error

Table 3 Pair-wise cortical thickness comparisons by diagnostic group

	ROI	CON vs. SCZ	CON vs. PBD	CON vs. NPBD	SCZ vs. PBD	SCZ vs. NPBD
Frontal	2. Superior fontal				PBD > SCZ $p=0.001$	NPBD > SCZ $p=0.004$
	4. Caud. Mid. frontal				PBD > SCZ $p=0.033$	
	8. Precentral				PBD > SCZ $p=0.003$	
	9. Paracentral	CON > SCZ $p=0.004$			PBD > SCZ $p<0.001$	NPBD > SCZ $p=0.004$
Parietal	13. Inferior parietal	CON > SCZ $p=0.033$			PBD > SCZ $p=0.035$	NPBD > SCZ $p=0.003$
	14. Supramarginal	CON > SCZ $p=0.015$			PBD > SCZ $p=0.009$	
Temporal	17. Temporal pole					
	18. Sup. temporal					
	19. Mid. temporal	CON > SCZ $p=0.027$				NPBD > SCZ $p=0.032$
	22. Fusiform	CON > SCZ $p=0.032$			PBD > SCZ $p=0.004$	NPBD > SCZ $p<0.001$
	24. Parahippocampal					NPBD > SCZ $p=0.042$
	25. Entorhinal					
Cingulate	31. Caud. Ant. cingulate	*SCZ > CON* $p=0.028$	*PBD > CON* $p=0.005$	*NPBD > CON* $p<0.001$		
	32. Post. cingulate			*NPBD > CON* $p<0.001$		NPBD > SCZ $p<0.001$
Insula	34. Insula					NPBD > SCZ $p=0.016$

Values shown reflect *p* values Bonferroni corrected for multiple comparisons for five comparisons within each region. Italicized values indicate regions that are smaller in control participants

Blank cells indicate a *p* value greater than 0.05 after correcting for multiple comparisons. No differences in PBD and NPBD groups was observed

ROI region of interest, *CON* control, *SCZ* schizophrenia, *PBD* psychotic bipolar disorder, *NPBD* non-psychotic bipolar disorder, *Ant.* anterior, *Sup.* superior, *Post.* posterior, *Caud.* caudal, *Mid.* middle

frontal, parietal and temporal regions. However, the thickness of the anterior cingulate cortex was increased in SCZ, PBD, and NPBD participants compared to CON participants. Cortical thickness in the posterior cingulate was larger in NPBD compared to CON participants. There were no other significant cortical thickness abnormalities in either PBD or NPBD compared to CON.

Clinical relationships of cortical thickness

We performed linear regressions to predict SAPS and SANS scores based on cortical thickness, diagnostic group membership, and covariates (age, sex, and ICV). All regression models significantly predicted SAPS scores ($F's_{(7,157)} > 11.601$, $p's < 0.001$) and a diagnosis of SCZ (p's < 0.001) or bipolar disorder with psychotic symptoms (p's < 0.005) predicted higher SAPS. The partial correlations associated with the cortical thickness of each region, as well as the significance of those parameter estimates is shown in Table 4. After Bonferroni correction for multiple (34) tests, two regions showed significant correlations with SAPS: the middle temporal gyrus (r = − 0.257) and the fusiform area (r = − 0.255). Several additional regions were significant prior to correction for multiple comparisons including frontal (pars triangularis, lateral orbitofrontal), parietal (inferior parietal, supramarginal, precuneus) and temporal (inferior temporal, bank of the superior temporal sulcus, entorhinal) areas.

All regression models also significantly predicted SANS scores ($F's_{(7,157)} > 23.780$, $p's < 0.001$), with SCZ (p's < 0.001) or psychotic BD (p's < 0.005) predicting higher SANS scores. After correcting for multiple comparisons, no region's cortical thickness predicted negative symptom scores. Partial correlations prior to multiple comparisons correction are shown in Table 5. Regions that were significant prior to multiple comparisons correction included frontal (middle frontal gyrus), parietal (inferior parietal), and temporal (inferior temporal, fusiform) regions.

Table 4 Partial correlations predicting SAPS scores

	ROI	Partial correlation	p value
Frontal	1. Frontal pole	0.045	0.569
	2. Superior fontal	− 0.074	0.352
	3. Rostral middle frontal	− 0.026	0.748
	4. Caudal middle frontal	− 0.120	0.133
	5. Pars opercularis	− 0.141	0.075
	6. Pars triangularis	*− 0.175*	*0.027*
	7. Pars orbitalis	− 0.167	0.036
	8. Precentral	− 0.117	0.142
	9. Paracentral	− 0.114	0.154
	10. Lateral orbitofrontal	*− 0.163*	*0.040*
	11. Medial orbitofrontal	− 0.088	0.269
Parietal	12. Superior parietal	− 0.090	0.260
	13. Inferior Parietal	*− 0.207*	*0.009*
	14. Supramarginal	*− 0.172*	*0.030*
	15. Postcentral	− 0.056	0.483
	16. Precuneus	*− 0.188*	*0.018*
Temporal	17. Temporal pole	− 0.099	0.217
	18. Superior temporal	− 0.107	0.179
	19. Middle temporal	***− 0.257***	***0.001***
	20. Inferior temporal	*− 0.246*	*0.002*
	21. Bank Sup. Temp. sulcus	*− 0.217*	*0.006*
	22. Fusiform	***− 0.255***	***0.001***
	23. Transverse temporal	0.040	0.614
	24. Parahippocampal	− 0.043	0.591
	25. Entorhinal	*− 0.157*	*0.048*
Occipital	26. Lateral occipital	− 0.154	0.053
	27. Lingual	− 0.111	0.162
	28. Cuneus	− 0.037	0.643
	29. Pericalcarine	− 0.016	0.845
Cingulate	30. Rostral Ant. cingulate	0.028	0.730
	31. Caudal Ant. cingulate	0.074	0.356
	32. Posterior cingulate	− 0.115	0.151
	33. Isthmus of cingulate	0.012	0.882
Insula	34. Insula	− 0.065	0.417

Values derived from linear regression predicting SAPS scores. Significance values are uncorrected for multiple comparisons. Italicized regions indicate significance prior to multiple comparisons correction. Bolditalic regions were significant after Bonferroni correcting for 34 comparisons

ROI region of interest, *CON* control, *SCZ* schizophrenia, *PBD* psychotic bipolar disorder, *NPBD* non-psychotic, bipolar disorder, *Temp.* temporal, *Sup.* superior, *Ant.* anterior

Discussion

Our study investigated cortical thickness in young adult patients with schizophrenia and relatively homogenous clinical subgroups of bipolar I disorder patients, comprising of psychotic—(PBD) and non-psychotic (NPBD) patients with hyperthymic mania histories. We found that SCZ participants had significant cortical thinning relative to CON and BD most significantly in the frontal (i.e. paracentral), parietal (i.e. inferior parietal, supramarginal), and temporal (i.e. middle temporal, fusiform) cortices. Our results are consistent with that of most other studies which found cortical thinning in SCZ relative to control populations across a wide range of cortical regions, usually including parts of the frontal and temporal cortex (van Erp et al. 2017; Rimol et al. 2012; Sugihara et al. 2017; Knochel et al. 2016; Besteher et al. 2016; Nenadic et al. 2015; Goldman et al. 2009). A recent meta-analysis of 4474 SCZ subjects found that the largest effect sizes for lower cortical thickness compared to controls were present in the fusiform, inferior frontal (pars opercularis), lateral orbitofrontal, temporal (inferior/medial/superior), parahippocampal, insula, isthmus cingulate, and the posterior cingulate cortices (van Erp et al. 2017). Despite some inconsistencies in the specific affected regions across schizophrenia studies, which likely reflects the biological heterogeneity of patients and methodological differences, cortical thinning is considered a key pathology underlying schizophrenia. Interestingly, we also found increased cortical thickness in an isolated region—the anterior cingulate cortex (ACC)—in the

Table 5 Partial correlations predicting SANS scores

	ROI	Partial correlation	*p*-value
Frontal	1. Frontal pole	0.131	0.099
	2. Superior fontal	0.081	0.308
	3. Rostral middle frontal	*0.191*	*0.016*
	4. Caudal middle frontal	−0.014	0.863
	5. Pars opercularis	−0.009	0.915
	6. Pars triangularis	0.067	0.399
	7. Pars orbitalis	−0.061	0.442
	8. Precentral	−0.012	0.880
	9. Paracentral	0.084	0.295
	10. Lateral orbitofrontal	−0.085	0.286
	11. Medial orbitofrontal	0.096	0.229
Parietal	12. Superior parietal	−0.047	0.557
	13. Inferior parietal	*−0.161*	*0.043*
	14. Supramarginal	−0.059	0.457
	15. Postcentral	0.014	0.863
	16. Precuneus	0.001	0.994
Temporal	17. Temporal pole	−0.085	0.286
	18. Superior temporal	−0.019	0.816
	19. Middle temporal	−0.108	0.174
	20. Inferior temporal	*−0.142*	*0.073*
	21. Bank Sup. Temp. sulcus	−0.083	0.296
	22. Fusiform	*−0.217*	*0.006*
	23. Transverse temporal		
	24. Parahippocampal	−0.021	0.789
	25. Entorhinal	−0.067	0.398
Occipital	26. Lateral occipital	−0.114	0.154
	27. Lingual	−0.005	0.946
	28. Cuneus	−0.042	0.599
	29. Pericalcarine	0.038	0.631
Cingulate	30. Rostral Ant. cingulate	0.05	0.533
	31. Caudal Ant. cingulate	−0.012	0.882
	32. Posterior cingulate	0.055	0.491
	33. Isthmus of cingulate	−0.02	0.802
Insula	34. Insula	0.05	0.532

Values derived from linear regression predicting SANS scores. Significance values are uncorrected for multiple comparisons. Italicized regions indicate significance prior to multiple comparisons correction. No regions were significant after Bonferroni correcting for 34 comparisons

ROI region of interest, *CON* control, *SCZ* schizophrenia, *PBD* psychotic bipolar disorder, *NPBD* non-psychotic, bipolar disorder, *Temp.* temporal, *Sup.* superior, *Ant.* anterior

schizophrenia group, as well as in both groups of bipolar disorder subjects. The ACC is a brain region critical for integrating cognitive and emotional functions in support of adaptive, goal-directed behavior (Devinsky et al. 1995). Increased ACC thickness in our subjects do not appear to be driven primarily by their relatively young age, as ACC thinning has also been seen in youth at clinically high risk for developing schizophrenia (Jung et al. 2011; Yucel et al. 2003). These findings in our patient groups differ from other studies that found gray matter reduction in the ACC in schizophrenia (Fornito et al. 2009a; Bouras et al. 2001; Hanford et al. 2016). However, increased ACC thickness has been reported in male first episode psychosis in bipolar disorder (Fornito et al. 2009b). These authors suggested that hypertrophy of regions critical for regulating the HPA axis, including the ACC, amygdala and pituitary gland, in early psychosis may be associated with an elevated stress response, which ultimately results in volumetric contraction with chronic illness. A few other authors also found increased ACC thickness in either first-episode (Adler et al. 2007) or chronic (Adler et al. 2005; Bearden et al. 2007) bipolar disorder, which was also been attributable to lithium effects in one study (Bearden et al. 2007) but not others (Fornito et al. 2009; Adler et al. 2007). Taken together, these findings suggest that while widespread cortical thinning is pathognomonic of schizophrenia, increased ACC thickness in some schizophrenia cohorts may reflect a hyperfunctional abnormality that produces an excessive stress response.

Contrary to our hypothesis, we did not find similar cortical thinning in PBD as we found in schizophrenia. Cortical thickness in both PBD and NPBD were comparable into controls, other than the increased ACC discussed above. It is notable that several other regions were larger in bipolar patients than in controls, albeit nonsignificantly. While these findings differ from those from a recent systematic review of bipolar disorder which reported cortical thinning in bipolar disorder (Hanford et al. 2016), normal cortical thickness have also been reported (Rimol et al. 2010, 2012). The ENIGMA Consortium conducted the largest cortical analysis of bipolar disorder patients, involving 6503 subjects and found bilateral frontal, temporal and parietal cortical thinning, especially in the left pars opercularis, fusiform gyrus and rostral middle frontal cortex (Hibar et al. 2018). When cortical thinning is observed in bipolar disorder, it is however not as pronounced as it is in schizophrenia and sometimes involves different brain regions (Knochel et al. 2016). Cortical thinning found in some bipolar disorder studies but not others appears to be due to differences in the populations studied. For example, older age and illness chronicity would be expected to lead to greater cortical thinning in bipolar disorder patients. Our study involved bipolar disorder subjects who on average, were in their mid-twenties, while most other bipolar studies include older populations. The ENIGMA bipolar study included older patients (grand mean age across sites was 37.5 years) found notably greater cortical thinning when comparing older BD patients to controls, than when younger bipolar patients were compared to controls

(Hibar et al. 2018). Thus, cortical thinning may be a later presentation of bipolar disorder, which would not be evident in younger adults. Our bipolar disorder population also consisted of a more homogenous clinical cohort than those in most other studies, including only bipolar 1 disorder patients with hyperthymic manic histories. Although not directly investigated, it is plausible that bipolar disorder with hyperthymic mania may be associated with less cortical thinning than with irritable mania. Future studies comparing bipolar disorder patients based on their manic presentation, may clarify their relationship to brain structure. Finally, differences in cortical findings across studies may be related to differences in the medication and recreational drug use of the patient cohorts. Psychotropic medications used in bipolar disorder have been associated with both increased cortical thickness (e.g. lithium) (Giakoumatos et al. 2015) and cortical thinning (e.g. typical antipsychotics) (van Haren et al. 2011). Similarly, recreational substances can also exacerbate cortical thinning in patients (Hartberg et al. 2018). Our study design excluded those with a significant substance use comorbidity (i.e. substance use disorder in last 6 months), and therefore may have represented a healthier cohort with less cortical abnormality.

We did not find any notable differences between our clinical subgroups of bipolar disorder subjects. Cortical and subcortical volumetric deficits have been reported in psychotic compared to nonpsychotic bipolar disorder (Strasser et al. 2005; Altamura et al. 2017). However, consistent with our study, the ENIGMA group did not find a relationship of psychosis history and cortical thickness in bipolar subjects, although they reported an association of psychosis with surface area in isolated brain regions (Hibar et al. 2018). Thus, cortical surface or volume, which were not investigated in our study, may be more sensitive in discriminating these clinical subtypes of bipolar disorder. PBD has been reported to represent a clinical construct more closely related to schizophrenia than NPBD, based on clinical presentation, familial and genetic overlap (Moskvina et al. 2009; Ivleva et al. 2008, 2010; Green et al. 2005; Potash 2006; Tamminga et al. 2013). PBD patients also show greater cognitive dysfunction compared to NPBD, approximating that seen in schizophrenia (Martinez-Aran et al. 2008; Simonsen et al. 2011; Bourne et al. 2013).

Our results showed that the cortical thickness of several brain regions correlated with measures of positive and negative symptoms, although only relationships between temporal regions and positive symptoms survived multiple comparisons correction. The observed correlations however may have been minimized by confounders, which were not adequately corrected. For example, the recorded SAPS and SANS scores reflect symptom severity within the previous 2 weeks, and often fluctuate over time. Additionally, dimensional ratings for depression were not collected for the current study. Considering that the period between symptom assessment and brain scanning varied across patients and were in some cases lengthy (median: 14 days; mean: 19 days), clinical symptoms during scanning may not be properly captured by our instruments. In the future, studying associations with clinical measures of chronic symptoms severity, such as the Washington Early Recognition Affectivity and Psychosis (WERCAP) Screen (Hsieh et al. 2016; Mamah et al. 2014), may be more accurate in uncovering brain-behavior relationships.

Numerous factors may contribute to cortical thinning, including changes in the number, density and arrangement of cells in the cortical sheet (Hatton et al. 2013; Goldman-Rakic 1988; Kuperberg et al. 2003; Rakic and Caviness 1995). Post-mortem examination of SCZ have shown reduced neuronal size and neuropil (Rimol et al. 2012; Tandon et al. 2008; Harrison 1999). Others have reported decreases in glial density and proliferation, indicating a relative lack of gliosis (Tandon et al. 2008; Harrison 1999; Phillips et al. 2008) as well as an increase in synaptic apoptosis leading to reduced synaptic integrity in pyramidal neurons (Glantz and Lewis 2000). Decreased glial density, reduced neuronal size, and synaptic degeneration have also been observed in BD to a lesser extent than in SCZ (Tandon et al. 2008; Harrison 2002). Most of these changes are believed to be neurodevelopmental in origin (Harrison 1999, 2002; Phillips et al. 2008; Rapoport et al. 2005; Lewis and Levitt 2002) supported by reports of cortical thinning in medication naïve subjects (Narr et al. 2005a, b; Lyoo et al. 2006), as well as prior to disease onset (Ellison-Wright and Bullmore 2010; Tandon et al. 2008; Harrison 1999) and in unaffected relatives (Goghari et al. 2007).

There are some limitations to our study. Firstly, medications can influence cortical thickness, which could disproportionately affect SCZ and BD participants. Considering our sample size and the complexity of medications and doses, our current study was not adequately designed to decipher medication related effects. Typical antipsychotics, such as haloperidol, have been found to cause regional cortical thinning across wide ranges of cortical regions including frontal, temporal, and parietal areas (Dazzan et al. 2005; Lieberman et al. 2005; Navari and Dazzan 2009), in addition to increased basal ganglia volumes (Dazzan et al. 2005; Smieskova et al. 2009). Atypical antipsychotics have been associated with more muted cortical thinning compared to typical antipsychotics (Navari and Dazzan 2009; Mamah et al. 2012), and antidepressants (Duman and Monteggia 2006; Lim et al. 2012) and lithium (Bearden et al. 2007; Hafeman et al.

2012) have neurotrophic effects, which are believed to underlie symptomatic improvement. Secondly, our study results may also have been influenced by gender disparity across groups. Our subjects consisted of more males than females in the SCZ group, and more females in the BD groups. Thicker cortices have been found in regionally in women compared to men in some (Sowell et al. 2007; Koolschijn and Crone 2013; Savic and Arver 2014) but not all (Raznahan et al. 2011) studies. Sex related differences have also been reported in cortical surface area, as well as neuronal and synaptic density (Rabinowicz et al. 1999; Luders et al. 2004; Alonso-Nanclares et al. 2008). While our statistical design, treating gender as a covariate, may reduce some of this potential confound, matching studies by gender would lead to more accurate results. Finally, our study was not well powered to investigate group differences in each individual brain region. In order to reduce the number of tests performed when examining relationships between cortical thickness and symptom measures, we collapsed across hemisphere. While cortical thickness in most regions correlated across hemispheres, a group by hemisphere interaction was observed. Thus, group differences in regional cortical thickness in our patients may be specific to individual hemispheres.

Conclusions

In conclusion, our studies investigated cortical thickness in a relatively homogenous groups of young adult schizophrenia patients and bipolar I disorder patients with hyperthymic manic histories. Regions of decreased cortical thickness were observed in schizophrenia patients, but not in either psychotic or non-psychotic bipolar patients. Thickness of the anterior cingulate cortex was increased in all patient groups. Clinical and demographic heterogeneity in patient populations may explain inconsistent findings across studies.

Abbreviations

B-SNIP: Bipolar–Schizophrenia Network on Intermediate Phenotypes; BD: bipolar disorder; CON: healthy controls; ICV: intracranial volume; GM: gray matter; MRI: magnetic resonance imaging; NPBD: bipolar disorder with no psychotic features; PBD: bipolar disorder with psychotic features; ROI: region of interest; SANS: Scale for the Assessment of Negative Symptoms; SAPS: Scale for the Assessment of Positive Symptoms; SCID-I: Structured Clinical Interview for DSM-IV Axis I Disorders; SCID-II: Structured Clinical Interview for DSM-IV Axis II Disorders; SCZ: schizophrenia; WM: white matter; YMRS: Young Mania Rating Scale.

Authors' contributions

DM and LW were involved in the design and data acquisition of the study. DG and DM wrote the manuscript. DG and KA provided data and statistical analysis. LW and DM oversaw the research and provided additional interpretation of data. All authors read and approved the final manuscript.

Author details

[1] Department of Psychiatry, Washington University Medical School, St. Louis, USA. [2] Department of Psychiatry and Behavioral Sciences, Northwestern University Feinberg School of Medicine, Chicago, USA.

Acknowledgements

None.

Competing interests

The authors declare that they have no competing interests.

Funding

This study was funded by NIMH grants K08 MH085958 and R01 MH104414 to Dr. Daniel Mamah. Additionally, this work was funded by the Taylor Family Institute and the Center for Brain Research on Mood Disorders in the department of Psychiatry, Washington University School of Medicine.

References

Abe C, Ekman CJ, Sellgren C, Petrovic P, Ingvar M, Landen M. Cortical thickness, volume and surface area in patients with bipolar disorder types I and II. J Psychiatry Neurosci. 2016;41(4):240–50.

Adler CM, Levine AD, DelBello MP, Strakowski SM. Changes in gray matter volume in patients with bipolar disorder. Biol Psychiatry. 2005;58(2):151–7.

Adler CM, DelBello MP, Jarvis K, Levine A, Adams J, Strakowski SM. Voxel-based study of structural changes in first-episode patients with bipolar disorder. Biol Psychiatry. 2007;61(6):776–81.

Alonso-Nanclares L, Gonzalez-Soriano J, Rodriguez JR, DeFelipe J. Gender differences in human cortical synaptic density. Proc Natl Acad Sci USA. 2008;105(38):14615–9.

Altamura AC, Maggioni E, Dhanoa T, et al. The impact of psychosis on brain anatomy in bipolar disorder: a structural MRI study. J Affect Disord. 2017. https://doi.org/10.1016/j.jad.2017.11.092.

American_Psychiatric_Association. Diagnostic and statistical manual of mental disorders. 5th ed. Arlington: American Psychiatric Publishing; 2013.

Bearden CE, Thompson PM, Dalwani M, et al. Greater cortical gray matter density in lithium-treated patients with bipolar disorder. Biol Psychiatry. 2007;62(1):7–16.

Besteher B, Wagner G, Koch K, et al. Pronounced prefronto-temporal cortical thinning in schizophrenia: neuroanatomical correlate of suicidal behavior? Schizophr Res. 2016;176(2–3):151–7.

Bouras C, Kovari E, Hof PR, Riederer BM, Giannakopoulos P. Anterior cingulate cortex pathology in schizophrenia and bipolar disorder. Acta Neuropathol. 2001;102(4):373–9.

Bourne C, Aydemir O, Balanza-Martinez V, et al. Neuropsychological testing of cognitive impairment in euthymic bipolar disorder: an individual patient data meta-analysis. Acta Psychiatr Scand. 2013;128(3):149–62.

Cardno AG, Owen MJ. Genetic relationships between schizophrenia, bipolar disorder, and schizoaffective disorder. Schizophr Bull. 2014;40(3):504–15.

Coryell W, Leon AC, Turvey C, Akiskal HS, Mueller T, Endicott J. The significance of psychotic features in manic episodes: a report from the NIMH collaborative study. J Affect Disord. 2001;67(1–3):79–88.

Dale AM, Fischl B, Sereno MI. Cortical surface-based analysis. I. Segmentation and surface reconstruction. Neuroimage. 1999;9(2):179–94.

Dazzan P, Morgan KD, Orr K, et al. Different effects of typical and atypical antipsychotics on grey matter in first episode psychosis: the AESOP study. Neuropsychopharmacology. 2005;30(4):765–74.

Devinsky O, Morrell MJ, Vogt BA. Contributions of anterior cingulate cortex to behaviour. Brain. 1995;118(Pt 1):279–306.

Duman RS, Monteggia LM. A neurotrophic model for stress-related mood disorders. Biol Psychiatry. 2006;59(12):1116–27.

Ellison-Wright I, Bullmore E. Anatomy of bipolar disorder and schizophrenia: a meta-analysis. Schizophr Res. 2010;117(1):1–12.

First M, Spitzer R, Gibbon M, Williams J. Structured clinical interview for DSM-IV-TR Axis I disorders, research version, patient edition (SCID-I/P). New York: New York State Psychiatric Institute, Biometrics Research; 2002.
Fischer BA, Carpenter WT Jr. Will the Kraepelinian dichotomy survive DSM-V? Neuropsychopharmacology. 2009;34(9):2081–7.
Fischl B, Dale AM. Measuring the thickness of the human cerebral cortex from magnetic resonance images. Proc Natl Acad Sci USA. 2000;97(20):11050–5.
Fischl B, Sereno MI, Dale AM. Cortical surface-based analysis. II: inflation, flattening, and a surface-based coordinate system. Neuroimage. 1999;9(2):195–207.
Fornito A, Yucel M, Dean B, Wood SJ, Pantelis C. Anatomical abnormalities of the anterior cingulate cortex in schizophrenia: bridging the gap between neuroimaging and neuropathology. Schizophr Bull. 2009a;35(5):973–93.
Fornito A, Yucel M, Wood SJ, et al. Anterior cingulate cortex abnormalities associated with a first psychotic episode in bipolar disorder. Br J Psychiatry. 2009b;194(5):426–33.
Giakoumatos CI, Nanda P, Mathew IT, et al. Effects of lithium on cortical thickness and hippocampal subfield volumes in psychotic bipolar disorder. J Psychiatr Res. 2015;61:180–7.
Glantz LA, Lewis DA. Decreased dendritic spine density on prefrontal cortical pyramidal neurons in schizophrenia. Arch Gen Psychiatry. 2000;57(1):65–73.
Goghari VM, Rehm K, Carter CS, MacDonald AW 3rd. Regionally specific cortical thinning and gray matter abnormalities in the healthy relatives of schizophrenia patients. Cereb Cortex. 2007;17(2):415–24.
Goldman AL, Pezawas L, Mattay VS, et al. Widespread reductions of cortical thickness in schizophrenia and spectrum disorders and evidence of heritability. Arch Gen Psychiatry. 2009;66(5):467–77.
Goldman-Rakic PS. Topography of cognition: parallel distributed networks in primate association cortex. Annu Rev Neurosci. 1988;11:137–56.
Goodwin FK, Jamison KR. Manic-depressive illness. Oxford: Oxford University Press; 2007.
Green EK, Raybould R, Macgregor S, et al. Operation of the schizophrenia susceptibility gene, neuregulin 1, across traditional diagnostic boundaries to increase risk for bipolar disorder. Arch Gen Psychiatry. 2005;62(6):642–8.
Hafeman DM, Chang KD, Garrett AS, Sanders EM, Phillips ML. Effects of medication on neuroimaging findings in bipolar disorder: an updated review. Bipolar Disord. 2012;14(4):375–410.
Han X, Jovicich J, Salat D, et al. Reliability of MRI-derived measurements of human cerebral cortical thickness: the effects of field strength, scanner upgrade and manufacturer. Neuroimage. 2006;32(1):180–94.
Hanford LC, Nazarov A, Hall GB, Sassi RB. Cortical thickness in bipolar disorder: a systematic review. Bipolar Disord. 2016;18(1):4–18.
Harrison PJ. The neuropathology of schizophrenia. A critical review of the data and their interpretation. Brain. 1999;122(Pt 4):593–624.
Harrison PJ. The neuropathology of primary mood disorder. Brain. 2002;125(Pt 7):1428–49.
Hartberg CB, Lange EH, Lagerberg TV, et al. Cortical thickness, cortical surface area and subcortical volumes in schizophrenia and bipolar disorder patients with cannabis use. Eur Neuropsychopharmacol. 2018;28(1):37–47.
Hatton SN, Lagopoulos J, Hermens DF, Scott E, Hickie IB, Bennett MR. Cortical thinning in young psychosis and bipolar patients correlate with common neurocognitive deficits. Int J Bipolar Disord. 2013;1:3.
Hibar DP, Westlye LT, Doan NT, et al. Cortical abnormalities in bipolar disorder: an MRI analysis of 6503 individuals from the ENIGMA Bipolar Disorder Working Group. Mol Psychiatry. 2018;23(4):932–42.
Hsieh CJ, Godwin D, Mamah D. Utility of washington early recognition center self-report screening questionnaires in the assessment of patients with schizophrenia and bipolar disorder. Front Psychiatry. 2016;7:149.
Hulshoff Pol HE, van Baal GC, Schnack HG, et al. Overlapping and segregating structural brain abnormalities in twins with schizophrenia or bipolar disorder. Arch Gen Psychiatry. 2012;69(4):349–59.
Ivleva E, Thaker G, Tamminga CA. Comparing genes and phenomenology in the major psychoses: schizophrenia and bipolar 1 disorder. Schizophr Bull. 2008;34(4):734–42.
Ivleva EI, Morris DW, Moates AF, Suppes T, Thaker GK, Tamminga CA. Genetics and intermediate phenotypes of the schizophrenia–bipolar disorder boundary. Neurosci Biobehav Rev. 2010;34(6):897–921.
Jung WH, Kim JS, Jang JH, et al. Cortical thickness reduction in individuals at ultra-high-risk for psychosis. Schizophr Bull. 2011;37(4):839–49.
Keck PE Jr, McElroy SL, Havens JR, et al. Psychosis in bipolar disorder: phenomenology and impact on morbidity and course of illness. Compr Psychiatry. 2003;44(4):263–9.
Knochel C, Reuter J, Reinke B, et al. Cortical thinning in bipolar disorder and schizophrenia. Schizophr Res. 2016;172(1–3):78–85.
Koolschijn PC, Crone EA. Sex differences and structural brain maturation from childhood to early adulthood. Dev Cogn Neurosci. 2013;5:106–18.
Kuperberg GR, Broome MR, McGuire PK, et al. Regionally localized thinning of the cerebral cortex in schizophrenia. Arch Gen Psychiatry. 2003;60(9):878–88.
Lewis DA, Levitt P. Schizophrenia as a disorder of neurodevelopment. Annu Rev Neurosci. 2002;25:409–32.
Lieberman JA, Tollefson GD, Charles C, et al. Antipsychotic drug effects on brain morphology in first-episode psychosis. Arch Gen Psychiatry. 2005;62(4):361–70.
Lim HK, Jung WS, Ahn KJ, et al. Regional cortical thickness and subcortical volume changes are associated with cognitive impairments in the drug-naive patients with late-onset depression. Neuropsychopharmacology. 2012;37(3):838–49.
Lobbestael J, Leurgans M, Arntz A. Inter-rater reliability of the structured clinical interview for DSM-IV Axis I disorders (SCID I) and Axis II disorders (SCID II). Clin Psychol Psychother. 2011;18(1):75–9.
Luders E, Narr KL, Thompson PM, et al. Gender differences in cortical complexity. Nat Neurosci. 2004;7(8):799–800.
Lyoo IK, Sung YH, Dager SR, et al. Regional cerebral cortical thinning in bipolar disorder. Bipolar Disord. 2006;8(1):65–74.
Maller JJ, Thaveenthiran P, Thomson RH, McQueen S, Fitzgerald PB. Volumetric, cortical thickness and white matter integrity alterations in bipolar disorder type I and II. J Affect Disord. 2014;169:118–27.
Mamah D, Barch DM. Diagnosis and classification of the schizophrenia spectrum disorders. In: Ritsner MS, editor. Handbook of schizophrenia spectrum disorders, vol. 1. Dordrecht: Springer; 2011. p. 45–83.
Mamah D, Harms MP, Barch D, Styner M, Lieberman JA, Wang L. Hippocampal shape and volume changes with antipsychotics in early stage psychotic illness. Front Psychiatry. 2012;3:96.
Mamah D, Owoso A, Sheffield JM, Bayer C. The WERCAP screen and the WERC stress screen: psychometrics of self-rated instruments for assessing bipolar and psychotic disorder risk and perceived stress burden. Compr Psychiatry. 2014;55(7):1757–71.
Mamah D, Alpert KI, Barch DM, Csernansky JG, Wang L. Subcortical neuromorphometry in schizophrenia spectrum and bipolar disorders. Neuroimage Clin. 2016;11:276–86.
Marchand WR, Clark SC, Wirth L, Simon C. Validity of the parent young mania rating scale in a community mental health setting. Psychiatry (Edgmont). 2005;2(3):31–5.
Martinez-Aran A, Torrent C, Tabares-Seisdedos R, et al. Neurocognitive impairment in bipolar patients with and without history of psychosis. J Clin Psychiatry. 2008;69(2):233–9.
Menon V. Large-scale brain networks and psychopathology: a unifying triple network model. Trends Cogn Sci. 2011;15(10):483–506.
Moskvina V, Craddock N, Holmans P, et al. Gene-wide analyses of genome-wide association data sets: evidence for multiple common risk alleles for schizophrenia and bipolar disorder and for overlap in genetic risk. Mol Psychiatry. 2009;14(3):252–60.
Narr KL, Bilder RM, Toga AW, et al. Mapping cortical thickness and gray matter concentration in first episode schizophrenia. Cereb Cortex. 2005a;15(6):708–19.
Narr KL, Toga AW, Szeszko P, et al. Cortical thinning in cingulate and occipital cortices in first episode schizophrenia. Biol Psychiatry. 2005b;58(1):32–40.
Navari S, Dazzan P. Do antipsychotic drugs affect brain structure? A systematic and critical review of MRI findings. Psychol Med. 2009;39(11):1763–77.
Nenadic I, Yotter RA, Sauer H, Gaser C. Patterns of cortical thinning in different subgroups of schizophrenia. Br J Psychiatry. 2015;206(6):479–83.
Panizzon MS, Fennema-Notestine C, Eyler LT, et al. Distinct genetic influences on cortical surface area and cortical thickness. Cereb Cortex. 2009;19(11):2728–35.
Phillips ML, Ladouceur CD, Drevets WC. A neural model of voluntary and automatic emotion regulation: implications for understanding the pathophysiology and neurodevelopment of bipolar disorder. Mol Psychiatry. 2008;13(9):829, 833–57.

Potash JB. Carving chaos: genetics and the classification of mood and psychotic syndromes. Harv Rev Psychiatry. 2006;14(2):47–63.
Rabinowicz T, Dean DE, Petetot JM, de Courten-Myers GM. Gender differences in the human cerebral cortex: more neurons in males; more processes in females. J Child Neurol. 1999;14(2):98–107.
Rakic P, Caviness VS Jr. Cortical development: view from neurological mutants two decades later. Neuron. 1995;14(6):1101–4.
Rapoport JL, Addington AM, Frangou S, Psych MR. The neurodevelopmental model of schizophrenia: update 2005. Mol Psychiatry. 2005;10(5):434–49.
Raznahan A, Shaw P, Lalonde F, et al. How does your cortex grow? J Neurosci. 2011;31(19):7174–7.
Rimol LM, Hartberg CB, Nesvag R, et al. Cortical thickness and subcortical volumes in schizophrenia and bipolar disorder. Biol Psychiatry. 2010;68(1):41–50.
Rimol LM, Nesvag R, Hagler DJ Jr, et al. Cortical volume, surface area, and thickness in schizophrenia and bipolar disorder. Biol Psychiatry. 2012;71(6):552–60.
Rosas HD, Liu AK, Hersch S, et al. Regional and progressive thinning of the cortical ribbon in Huntington's disease. Neurology. 2002;58(5):695–701.
Savic I, Arver S. Sex differences in cortical thickness and their possible genetic and sex hormonal underpinnings. Cereb Cortex. 2014;24(12):3246–57.
Simonsen C, Sundet K, Vaskinn A, et al. Neurocognitive dysfunction in bipolar and schizophrenia spectrum disorders depends on history of psychosis rather than diagnostic group. Schizophr Bull. 2011;37(1):73–83.
Smieskova R, Fusar-Poli P, Allen P, et al. The effects of antipsychotics on the brain: what have we learnt from structural imaging of schizophrenia?—a systematic review. Curr Pharm Des. 2009;15(22):2535–49.
Sowell ER, Peterson BS, Kan E, et al. Sex differences in cortical thickness mapped in 176 healthy individuals between 7 and 87 years of age. Cereb Cortex. 2007;17(7):1550–60.
Strasser HC, Lilyestrom J, Ashby ER, et al. Hippocampal and ventricular volumes in psychotic and nonpsychotic bipolar patients compared with schizophrenia patients and community control subjects: a pilot study. Biol Psychiatry. 2005;57(6):633–9.
Sugihara G, Oishi N, Son S, Kubota M, Takahashi H, Murai T. Distinct patterns of cerebral cortical thinning in schizophrenia: a neuroimaging data-driven approach. Schizophr Bull. 2017;43(4):900–6.
Tamminga CA, Ivleva EI, Keshavan MS, et al. Clinical phenotypes of psychosis in the bipolar–schizophrenia network on intermediate phenotypes (B-SNIP). Am J Psychiatry. 2013;170(11):1263–74.
Tandon R, Keshavan MS, Nasrallah HA. Schizophrenia, "Just the Facts": what we know in 2008 part 1: overview. Schizophr Res. 2008;100(1–3):4–19.
Uhlhaas PJ. Dysconnectivity, large-scale networks and neuronal dynamics in schizophrenia. Curr Opin Neurobiol. 2013;23(2):283–90.
van Erp T, Hibar D, Walton E, et al. Cortical abnormalities in schizophrenia: an ENIGMA schizophrenia working group meta-analysis. Organization of Human Brain Mapping, Annual Meeting; June 26, 2017; Vancouver, Canada.
van Haren NE, Schnack HG, Cahn W, et al. Changes in cortical thickness during the course of illness in schizophrenia. Arch Gen Psychiatry. 2011;68(9):871–80.
Ward KE, Friedman L, Wise A, Schulz SC. Meta-analysis of brain and cranial size in schizophrenia. Schizophr Res. 1996;22(3):197–213.
Winkler AM, Kochunov P, Blangero J, et al. Cortical thickness or grey matter volume? The importance of selecting the phenotype for imaging genetics studies. Neuroimage. 2010;53(3):1135–46.
Womer FY, Wang L, Alpert KI, et al. Basal ganglia and thalamic morphology in schizophrenia and bipolar disorder. Psychiatry Res. 2014;223(2):75–83.
Young RC, Biggs JT, Ziegler VE, Meyer DA. A rating scale for mania: reliability, validity and sensitivity. Br J Psychiatry. 1978;133:429–35.
Yucel M, Wood SJ, Phillips LJ, et al. Morphology of the anterior cingulate cortex in young men at ultra-high risk of developing a psychotic illness. Br J Psychiatry. 2003;182:518–24.
Zhang T, Koutsouleris N, Meisenzahl E, Davatzikos C. Heterogeneity of structural brain changes in subtypes of schizophrenia revealed using magnetic resonance imaging pattern analysis. Schizophr Bull. 2015;41(1):74–84.

20

Thyroid and renal tumors in patients treated with long-term lithium: case series from a lithium clinic, review of the literature and international pharmacovigilance reports

Luca Ambrosiani[1], Claudia Pisanu[1], Arianna Deidda[2], Caterina Chillotti[3], Maria Erminia Stochino[2] and Alberto Bocchetta[1,3*]

Abstract

Background: Cancer had never been considered as a relevant problem in patients treated with lithium until 2015, when a document published by the European Medicine Agency concluded that long-term use of lithium might induce renal tumors. A few months later, we observed the case of a woman treated with lithium for 18 years who was diagnosed with both thyroid and renal tumors.

Methods: This study aimed to investigate the correlation between lithium treatment and thyroid or renal tumors. We analyzed clinical records in our lithium clinic database, causes of death of patients who had been visited at least once at the lithium clinic, reports of lithium adverse reactions in the European and WHO pharmacovigilance databases, and published cases of thyroid and renal tumors in long-term lithium-treated patients.

Results: Of the 1871 lithium patients who had been visited at least once between 1980 and 2013, eight had been diagnosed with thyroid papillary carcinoma and two with clear-cell renal-cell carcinoma. No cases of thyroid cancer and only one case of renal tumor were the cause of death according to the 375 available death certificates. VigiAccess database contained a total of 29 and 14 cases of renal and thyroid tumors, respectively. EudraVigilance database contained 21 cases of renal and 8 of thyroid neoplasms. Literature search yielded 6 published cases of thyroid papillary carcinoma and 25 cases of various renal tumors. However, two population-based studies did not find any increased risks of cancer in patients exposed to lithium, whereas two nationwide studies did not find any excess of renal tumors.

Conclusion: So far it has not been possible epidemiologically to confirm an increased risk of thyroid or renal cancers associated with lithium. Such a conclusion is supported by the findings of low rates and mortalities of thyroid or renal cancers from the present lithium clinic data.

Keywords: Lithium, Thyroid cancer, Renal cancer, VigiAccess, EudraVigilance

*Correspondence: bocchett@unica.it
[1] Section of Neuroscience and Clinical Pharmacology, Department of Biomedical Sciences, University of Cagliari, S.S. 554, km 4,500, Monserrato, Italy
Full list of author information is available at the end of the article

Background

Lithium has been essential in the maintenance therapy of patients with recurrent mood disorders since the discovery of its effects in mania in 1949 and in the prophylaxis of manic depression thereafter (for review see Bauer and Gitlin 2016). Lithium has also been shown to prevent suicide mortality, which is particularly high in patients with mood disorders (Lewitzka et al. 2015). Lithium is increasingly recommended as one of first line treatment or as the single preferred first-line drug in the long-term treatment of bipolar disorder (Nolen 2015).

Compared to common adverse events (for review see McKnight et al. 2012), cancer has long been considered a secondary problem in patients treated with lithium. However, the interest in the potential association between lithium therapy and tumors has recently been revived by a document issued by the European Medicine Agency (EMA) (2015), which adopted the following recommendation: "in light of the data available, the PRAC (Pharmacovigilance Risk Assessment Committee) has agreed that the evidence is sufficient to conclude that long-term use of lithium may induce microcysts, oncocytomas and collecting duct renal carcinomas. Therefore, the Marketing Authorisation Holders of lithium containing medicinal products should submit a variation within 2 months, to amend the product information. The document also recommends that routine pharmacovigilance should be performed in order to better characterize the risk (http://www.ema.europa.eu/docs/en_GB/document_library/PRAC_recommendation_on_signal/2015/01/WC500181043.pdf). The present study was prompted by a series of circumstances: (a) our group serves as the Sardinian Pharmacovigilance Center; (b) our group has been running a lithium clinic since the 1970s and is in possession of detailed clinical data regarding patients on maintenance treatment with lithium; (c) in 2015, a few months after the publication of the aforementioned EMA document, we observed the case of a woman treated with lithium for 18 years who was diagnosed with both thyroid and renal tumors.

We started this study aiming to investigate the possible correlation between lithium treatment and thyroid or renal tumors from different perspectives: (a) a retrospective analysis of the clinical records in the lithium clinic database; (b) an analysis of the causes of death of the patients who had been visited at least once at the lithium clinic between 1980 and 2013; (c) an analysis of the reports of lithium adverse reactions to the European and the WHO pharmacovigilance databases; and (d) a review of the literature on thyroid and renal tumors in patients treated with lithium.

Methods

Lithium clinic database

Clinical records of the patients in the database of the Unit of Clinical Pharmacology, Azienda Ospedaliero-Universitaria, Cagliari, were examined. Our Unit has been one of the reference centers for lithium monitoring in the Cagliari area since its introduction in the 1970s.

Lithium monitoring was in line with international guidelines. For the purpose of this study, we extracted the clinical data of patients who had been diagnosed with thyroid or renal tumors.

Causes of death

In 2002, we started to analyze systematically mortality and causes of death of patients in our lithium clinic database (Bocchetta 2005; Bocchetta et al. 2007b). Life status was assessed through Population Registers from the last known town of residence. Population registers also constituted the source of death certificates up to 1984, whereas the Register of the Causes of Death of the Local Health Unit has been the source from 1985 onwards. We retrieved the information about life status for 1391 of 1411 (99%) patients in the database from 1980 to 2000. Death certificates were obtained for 191 of the 201 (95%) who had deceased up to 2002. Causes of death were reviewed and coded using the International Classification of Diseases-9th revision.

Mortality and causes of death were analyzed again in 2013. We retrieved the information about life status for 1826 of 1840 (99%) patients treated with lithium who had been visited at least once since 1980. Certificates of death were available for 375 cases.

Pharmacovigilance databases

In January 2018 we searched VigiAccess, EudraVigilance. VigiAccess is a global database supervised by the Uppsala Monitoring Centre Vigibase, the World Health Organization (WHO) adverse drug reaction database (ADR) database. It provides free access to all individual case safety reports (ICSRs) spontaneously collected by over 110 national drug authorities (including Europe and US) since 1968, even though it does not allow analysis of the individual ADRs collected.

EudraVigilance is a European database managed by EMA, which is freely accessible and collects and processes suspected ADRs since December 2001. The databases were searched for the active ingredient "lithium", and data were extracted according to the medical dictionary for regulatory activity (MedDRA). MedDRA terms are classified in system organ classes (SOC). Standardized MedDRA queries (SMQs) are tools developed to facilitate retrieval of MedDRA-coded data in pharmacovigilance.

Unfortunately, an official list of SMQs used for classifying thyroid and renal cancers is not available (https://www.meddra.org/standardised-meddra-queries). Therefore, any MedDRA term that could be related was searched under the SOC "neoplasms benign, malignant and unspecified". General terms which did not relate to thyroid or kidney, such as "neoplasm", "metastasis" or "adenocarcinoma" were excluded from the analysis. Cases of tumors of the renal pelvis were also excluded. Due to the overlap of the WHO and the European databases, a duplication of cases may have occurred.

Review of the literature

A systematic review of the literature was conducted using PubMed and Scopus without date restrictions, to identify studies reporting cases of thyroid and renal tumors occurred in patients chronically treated with lithium. The search was conducted using the following search strategies with "English language" as a filter:

a. "kidney tumor AND lithium", "renal cancer AND lithium", "renal carcinoma AND lithium", "oncocytoma AND lithium";
b. combinations of the MeSH terms "kidney neoplasms", "lithium/toxicity", "cell proliferation/drug effects", "lithium compounds/adverse effects";
c. "thyroid carcinoma AND lithium", "thyroid tumor AND lithium", "thyroid cancer AND lithium";
d. combinations of the MeSH terms "lithium compounds" AND "thyroid neoplasms".

Bibliographic references of relevant articles were reviewed for additional studies.

Preclinical studies, as well as studies in which lithium was used as an adjuvant to ^{131}I therapy of thyroid cancer were excluded, as were studies of non-malignant thyroid tumors (adenoma or goiter).

From each selected study we collected the following information: number of reported cases, pathological diagnosis, duration of exposure to lithium treatment. For renal tumors we also indicated, when available, presence of cysts and estimated glomerular filtration rate (eGFR).

Results

Case report

The following case was observed in 2015, a few months after the publication of the EMA document.

A 52-year-old woman had been treated with lithium carbonate, haloperidol and risperidone for schizoaffective disorder since 1997. The patient also received benzodiazepines. From 1998 to 2004, carbamazepine was added as a second mood stabilizer. Lithium doses varied throughout the years from 600 to 1050 mg/day, in order to keep serum concentration within the therapeutic range (0.6–0.8 mmol/L). No episodes of lithium intoxication occurred. Comorbidities included increased body mass index, repeated findings of abnormally high fasting plasma glucose, hypertension (treated with amlodipine, 5 mg/day). Over the last 10 years, her estimated glomerular filtration rate (eGFR) had gradually declined to 40 ml/min/1.73 m^2, which falls into the category G3b [moderately to severely decreased chronic kidney disease (CKD)] according to KDIGO (kidney disease improving global outcomes) (KDIGO 2017). She developed a multinodular goiter that eventually caused dysphagia and dyspepsia. After an ultrasound scan, she underwent a medical workup in September 2015. Computer tomography scans showed abnormal thyroid images, multiple pulmonary metastasis, increased adrenal gland, a renal mass in the left kidney (maximum diameter, 38 mm), and multiple hyperdense nodules in the contralateral kidney (maximum diameter, 13 mm). She underwent thyroidectomy and the histological examination was consistent with the presence of two different tumors. A papillary thyroid carcinoma within adenomatous goiter tissue was identified within the left lobe, whereas an epithelial, sarcomatoid-like tumor was found in the right lobe. The latter was consistent with renal origin according to immunohistochemistry. A subsequent renal biopsy led to the diagnosis of oncocytoma, stage IV (M1). The patient died in May 2016 for respiratory failure due to pulmonary metastases.

We reported the case to the national pharmacovigilance agency in April 2016. The adverse reaction was codified as severe (life threatening). The causality assessment, evaluated by the Regional Centre of Pharmacovigilance according to the Naranjo algorithm (Naranjo et al. 1981), was considered "possible" based on the chronological criteria (18 years of lithium treatment), and the presence of objective evidence and previous conclusive reports. In fact, the ADR renal tumor has been included in the package leaflet since the 2015 EMA document.

Lithium-clinic database

Of the 1871 patients treated with lithium who had been visited at least once between 1980 and 2013, 562 had been followed up with regular monitoring for at least 5 years (total = 7639 patient/years). The number of patients followed up for at least 10 years was 345 (total = 6212 patient/years).

Out of 19 (18 women, one man) who underwent thyroidectomy, 9 cases were diagnosed with thyroid cancer. The remaining were 9 cases of multinodular goiter and one case of adenoma. Characteristics of the patients with thyroid cancer are shown in Table 1. At the time of thyroidectomy, the median age of the patients was 53 years

Table 1 Characteristics of the 9 patients with thyroid cancer from our lithium clinic

Sex	Age at thyroidectomy	Years on lithium at thyroidectomy	Pathological diagnosis	Radio-iodine therapy
F	60	25	Papillary carcinoma, follicular variant, with focal invasion of the capsule	Yes
F	53	25	Papillary carcinoma	Yes
M	44	15	Papillary carcinoma, follicular variant	Yes
F	53	12	Papillary carcinoma	No
F	52	19	Papillary carcinoma[a]	No
F	54	26	Multifocal papillary carcinoma[b]	Yes
F	66	23	Papillary carcinoma	Yes
F	61	22	Papillary carcinoma	Yes
F	53	23	Papillary carcinoma	No

[a] Case report with concurrent renal oncocytoma described in this paper

[b] Case already reported in a follow-up study of a cohort of 150 patients (Bocchetta et al. 2007a)

and their median duration of lithium therapy was 23 years.

With regard to renal tumors, only the following two cases were retrieved from our retrospective analysis of the lithium clinic database, besides the aforementioned case report.

A 58-year-old man had been diagnosed with clear-cell renal cancer and bilateral adrenal gland hyperplasia in 2003. He had been prescribed lithium since the age of 50 for Bipolar I Disorder. He also suffered from hypertension, dyslipidemia, hepatitis C virus infection with related chronic liver disease, and insulin-treated diabetes. He underwent nephrectomy and his eGFR decreased from 86 to 50 ml/min/1.73 m^2. In 2005 he was also diagnosed with non-small-cell lung cancer and died in 2010 for cerebral metastases originated from the pulmonary neoplasm.

The second case regarded a man who had been treated with lithium since 1991 for Bipolar II Disorder. In November 2005, at age 55, during a medical work up including abdominal ultrasound examination, an abnormal image was found in the right kidney. After further investigation (including a CT scan) he underwent nephrectomy in September 2006. The histological diagnosis was clear-cell renal cancer. Thereafter, his eGFR decreased from 105 to 75 ml/min/1.73 m^2 and lithium was replaced with valproate. The patient died in 2013 due to complications of his alcoholic cirrhosis which had been first diagnosed in 2006.

Causes of death

Out of 375 death certificates regarding patients who had been visited at least once from 1980 to 2013, no cases of thyroid cancer and only one case of renal tumor were registered as the principal cause of death. The latter regarded a 68-year-old man who had been prescribed lithium 5 years earlier but had taken the therapy only for a few months.

The total number of patient/years calculated for the 1840 patients visited at least once from 1980 to 2013 amounted to 33,801, including 8263 patient/years on regular monitoring of lithium therapy. Causes of death were represented by other malignancies in 35 cases and by suicide in 64 cases (only one during regular maintenance with lithium).

Pharmacovigilance databases

VigiAccess

A search on VigiAccess database performed in January 2018 retrieved a total of 22,280 lithium-related ADRs. Only 220 (1%) were classified under the System Organ Class (SOC) "neoplasms benign, malignant and unspecified". We found a total of 29 and 14 individual cases of renal and thyroid tumors, respectively, codified with the MedDRA terms shown in Table 2.

EudraVigilance

A search on EudraVigilance database performed in January 2018 retrieved a total of 9833 individual cases of ADRs related to lithium. Only 150 (1.53%) of them were classified as "neoplasms benign, malignant and unspecified". Table 2 shows the MedDRA terms for those codified as renal (N = 21) or thyroid (N = 8) neoplasms. Demographic characteristics and outcome are shown in Table 3. All renal cases were reported by healthcare professionals, while non-healthcare professionals reported two of the 8 thyroid cases.

Table 2 Number of reports of renal and thyroid neoplasms (classified by MedDRA terms) from the pharmacovigilance databases EudraVigilance and VigiAccess

	EudraVigilance	VigiAccess
Renal neoplasms, total cases	21	29
Renal-cell carcinoma	10	9
Oncocytoma	0	5
Renal oncocytoma	5	2
Renal cancer	4	5
Clear-cell renal-cell carcinoma	1	5
Renal neoplasm	1	2
Renal adenoma	0	1
Thyroid neoplasms, total cases	8	14
Thyroid cancer	2	9
Thyroid adenoma	5	0
Thyroid neoplasm	0	3
Medullary thyroid cancer	1	1
Benign neoplasm of thyroid gland	0	1

Table 3 Demographic characteristics and outcome in renal and thyroid neoplasm from the EudraVigilance database

	Renal neoplasms (N=21)	Thyroid neoplasms (N=8)
Sex		
Male	5	2
Female	12	6
Not specified	4	–
Age groups (years)		
18–64	7	7
65–85	10	1
Not specified	4	–
Outcome		
Not recovered	1	2
Recovered with sequelae	1	–
Recovered	6	2
Unknown	8	4
Not specified	5	–

Review of the literature: thyroid tumors

Our search retrieved six articles identified as potentially relevant. Among the retrieved articles, one was excluded because it reported the case of a benign adenoma, one because it was not pertinent, while four articles were identified as meeting the inclusion criteria.

We only found six published cases of thyroid cancer in patients treated with lithium (Table 4). The first was observed in a 55-year-old woman who had been treated with lithium for 3.5 years. She presented with unilateral thyroid enlargement causing tracheal deviation. She underwent thyroidectomy and was diagnosed with a papillary-cell carcinoma. In particular, histological examination revealed a multinodular goiter with multiple areas of sclerosis with juxtaposed groups of malignant cells, some showing papillary structures. She was administered ^{131}Iodine in an attempt to ablate the remnant thyroid tissue (Brownlie et al. 1980).

In a series of seven parathyroid or thyroid surgical cases in Canada, McHenry et al. (1990) reported three cases of thyroid carcinoma after long-term lithium therapy. All three cases were associated with multinodular goiter, hypothyroidism, and hyperparathyroidism (McHenry et al. 1990).

The fifth case was seen in a 45-year-old man who had been treated with lithium for 4 years who underwent thyroid workup for hypothyroidism. Fine needle aspiration revealed papillary carcinoma and the patient underwent thyroidectomy. Histopathological examination showed multifocal papillary carcinoma and Hashimoto thyroiditis (Aksoy et al. 2006).

The sixth published case was found in the context of a follow-up study of a cohort of 150 patients treated with lithium at our facility. It regarded a 54-year-old woman taking lithium since the age of 28. Histology revealed a multicentric papillary carcinoma. She was treated with ^{131}Iodine after surgery (Bocchetta et al. 2007a).

Review of the literature: renal tumors

Seventeen articles identified as potentially relevant were retrieved for evaluation of the full text. Among the

Table 4 Characteristics of thyroid tumors from the literature and from the present case series

Authors	N.	Pathological diagnosis	Years on lithium	Sex	Age	Notes
Brownlie et al. (1980)	1	Papillary-cell carcinoma	3.5	F	55	Multinodular goiter
McHenry et al. (1990)	3	Papillary carcinoma	3	F	48	Myxedema, multinodular goiter, radio-iodine therapy
		Papillary carcinoma	4	F	52	Myxedema, multinodular goiter
		Papillary carcinoma	6	F	78	Hypothyroidism, multinodular goiter, hyperparathyroidism
Aksoy et al. (2006)	1	Multifocal papillary carcinoma	4	M	45	Hypothyroidism, hashimoto thyroiditis
Bocchetta et al. (2007a), and present study	9	9 papillary carcinoma	12–26	8F 1M	44–66	Radio-iodine therapy in 6 cases

retrieved articles, two were excluded because they considered renal tumors together with cancers of the renal pelvis or ureter, nine because they were not pertinent, while six articles were identified as meeting the inclusion criteria. Cases reported in these studies were excluded in case a histological diagnosis was missing. The six studies included in the review reported 25 cases of renal tumors occurred in patients chronically treated with lithium and meeting our inclusion criteria (Table 5). Among included cases, there was a high percentage of oncocytomas and collecting-ducts carcinomas, which are usually reported as uncommon or rare. In addition, the presence of cysts is very frequent, involving 72% of cases. The vast majority of cases (84%) presented an eGFR <60 ml/min/1.73 m^2 (CKD, G3 to G5). When the eGFR was not available, it was calculated from the plasma creatinine reported in the paper, using the Modification of Diet in Renal Disease (MDRD) Study Group equation (Levey et al. 1999).

Besides the case reports meeting the above-mentioned criteria, we retrieved two nationwide population-based studies that were prompted in order to estimate rates of renal tumors among individuals exposed to lithium.

Kessing et al. (2015) analyzed time-specific data from all individuals exposed to lithium (n=24,272)

Table 5 Case reports of histologically confirmed renal tumor associated with lithium treatment from the literature and from the present case series

Authors	Pathological diagnosis	Cysts	Years on lithium	Sex	Age	eGFR ml/min/1.73 m^2 (CKD category)[a]
Markowitz et al. (2000) (2 cases)	Oncocytoma	+	20	M	50	13 (G5)
	Papillary renal-cell carcinoma	+	25	M	56	27 (G4)
Rookmaaker et al. (2012) (6 cases)	Collecting-ducts carcinoma	+	17	M	69	11 (G5)
	Collecting-ducts carcinoma	+	12	M	59	50 (G3a)
	Collecting-ducts carcinoma	+	15	M	61	48 (G3a)
	Oncocytoma	+	30	M	70	6 (G5)
	Oncocytoma	+	41	F	65	35 (G3b)
	Oncocytoma + collecting-ducts carcinoma	+	30	F	71	37 (3b)
Kjaersgaard et al. (2012)	Renal-cell carcinoma	+	28	M	71	Not available
Zardawi et al. (2013)	Renal-cell carcinoma	+	12	F	72	21 (G4)
Zaidan et al. (2014b) (14 cases)	Clear-cell renal-cell carcinoma	–	17	M	69	48 (G3a)
	Clear-cell renal-cell carcinoma	+	31	F	75	27 (G4)
	Clear-cell renal-cell carcinoma	–	18	F	70	24 (G4)
	Clear-cell renal-cell carcinoma + leiomyomatous stroma	–	41	F	71	55 (G3a)
	Oncocytomas + papillary adenomas	+	23	M	60	10 (G5)
	Oncocytoma	+	32	M	66	33 (G3b)
	Oncocytoma	+	16	M	68	52 (G3a)
	Oncocytoma	+	26	F	59	34 (G3b)
	Angiomyolipoma	–	21	F	65	24 (G4)
	Angiomyolipoma	–	>10	F	77	68 (G2)
	Papillary renal-cell carcinoma	+	15	M	56	52 (G3a)
	Papillary renal-cell carcinoma	–	35	M	54	61 (G2)
	Oncocytoma + chromophobe renal-cell carcinoma	+	10	F	66	5 (G5)
	Mixed epithelial and stromal tumor	+	3	F	46	71 (G2)
Jung (2016)	Renal-cell carcinoma	–	15	F	54	29 (G4)
This study (3 cases)	Clear-cell renal-cell carcinoma	–	8	M	56	86 (G2)
	Clear-cell renal-cell carcinoma	–	14	M	55	105 (G1)
	Oncocytoma[b]	–	18	F	52	40 (G3b)

[a] eGFR was calculated from reported serum creatinine concentrations using the Modification of Diet in Renal Disease Study Group equation (Levey et al. 1999). The following are the categories of chronic kidney disease (CKD) according to KDIGO (2017) based on eGFR: G1, "Normal or high" (≥ 90 ml/min/1.73 m^2); G2, "Mildly decreased" (60–89 ml/min/1.73 m^2); G3a, "Mildly to moderately decreased" (45–59 ml/min/1.73 m^2); G3b, "Moderately to severely decreased" (30–44 ml/min/1.73 m^2); G4, "Severely decreased" (15–29 ml/min/1.73 m^2); G5, "Kidney failure" (< 15 ml/min/1.73 m^2). It must be noted that KDIGO CKD stages are also based on albuminuria categories, which were not included in the present table

[b] Case with concurrent thyroid carcinoma described in this paper

or anticonvulsants (n = 386,255), all individuals with a diagnosis of bipolar disorder (n = 9651), and a randomly selected sample of 1500,000 from the Danish population. The study period was from 1995 to 2012. Analyses were adjusted for the number of prescriptions for lithium/anticonvulsants, antipsychotic agents, antidepressants, use of all other types of medication, sociodemographic variables, and a diagnosis of bipolar disorder. Continued treatment with lithium, but also with anticonvulsants, was not associated with increased rates of renal and upper urinary tract tumors.

Pottegård et al. (2016) identified all histologically verified upper urinary tract cancer cases in Denmark between 2000 and 2012 from the Danish Cancer Registry. A total of 6477 cases were matched by age and sex to 259,080 cancer-free controls. Data on lithium use from 1995 to 2012 were obtained from the Danish Prescription Registry. The study estimated the association between long-term use of lithium (≥ 5 years) and risk of upper urinary tract cancer using conditional logistic regression with adjustment for potential confounders. The number of renal cancers amounted to 11 cases among 5648 subjects exposed to lithium (1.9 per 1000 subjects) compared to 377 cases among 225,920 subjects not exposed to lithium (1.7 per 1000 subjects) resulting in non-significant odd ratios after adjustment for sociodemographic variables and comorbidities.

Discussion

With this study, we sought to shed light on the issue of renal and thyroid cancer during long-term lithium therapy.

Of the 1871 lithium patients who had been visited at least once between 1980 and 2013, eight had been diagnosed with thyroid papillary carcinoma and two with clear-cell renal-cell carcinoma. No cases of thyroid cancer and only one case of renal tumor were the cause of death according to the 375 available death certificates.

Compared to other adverse events of lithium (McKnight et al. 2012), cancer has long been neglected until the publication of the 2015 EMA document. Indeed, very few clinical studies had investigated the association between cancer risk and lithium. There have been occasional reports of leukemia in patients treated with lithium (Lyskowski and Nasrallah 1981; Moreb and Hershko 1985; Volf and Crismon 1991), but a causal relationship has not yet been established. Cohen et al. (1998) studied 609 patients treated with lithium carbonate and 2396 controls. They found a non-significant lower risk to develop non-epithelial tumors among psychiatric patients treated with lithium as compared to controls. They also observed a significantly inverse trend of cancer occurrence with lithium dose. The risk of developing cancer among psychiatric patients was found to be significantly lower than in the general population and the study concluded that mental patients had a lower cancer prevalence and that lithium may exert a protective effect.

More recently, Huang et al. (2016) studied retrospectively a cohort of patients treated with lithium (N = 370) or anticonvulsants (N = 3250) for bipolar disorder in Taiwan. Lithium exposure was associated with significantly lower cancer risk compared with anticonvulsants exposure. They also observed a dose–response relationship for cancer risk reduction with lithium. For site-specific cancer, lithium users showed trends of decreased cancer risks, except for bone, skin, connective and other soft tissue as well as genitourinary cancer risk. However, the authors suggested to interpret these results with caution in light of the possibly limited statistical power due to the low number of specific cancer cases.

Renal tumors

Apart from individual case reports (Table 5), the EMA document was principally based on two studies which were conducted in nephrology departments, one Dutch (Rookmaaker et al. 2012) and one French (Zaidan et al. 2014b).

Over a time period of 15 years, Rookmaaker et al. (2012) identified six patients with one or more solid renal tumors in their population of approximately 50 patients with chronic lithium-associated nephropathy. All patients were on lithium therapy for over 10 years and suffered from varying degrees of lithium nephropathy and renal diabetes insipidus. The renal tumors were incidental findings during workup for renal dysfunction or upon analysis of nonspecific abdominal complaints. The abdominal scans showed multiple uncomplicated renal cysts in all patients and a complicated cyst in the contralateral kidney in one patient. The tumors were all of collecting-duct origin and comprised both oncocytomas and collecting-duct carcinomas. The authors underscored that the latter differed from the "classical" collecting-duct-cell carcinomas, which are very rare with an incidence of less than 2 per 1000,000 person years (Storkel et al. 1997). They concluded that the 4 cases of collecting-duct-cell carcinomas in their population of approximately 50 patients with lithium nephropathy represent a much higher incidence. Other differences from the "classical" collecting-duct-cell carcinomas included histological appearance, multifocal presentation and non-aggressive clinical behavior. In fact, "classical" collecting-duct-cell carcinomas are aggressive tumors with 80% lymph node metastases at presentation and a median survival of only 22 months (Peyromaure et al. 2003).

Over a 16-year period, Zaidan et al. (2014b) found that 14 of 170 lithium-treated patients, followed at two nephrology departments in Paris and with available renal imaging, had various types of renal tumors (Table 5). The mean duration of lithium exposure at tumor diagnosis was above 20 years. Mean age at diagnosis was 64.4 ± 8.6 years. The percentage of renal tumors, particularly cancers and oncocytomas, was significantly higher in lithium treated patients compared with 340 gender-, age-, and eGFR-matched lithium free patients. Additionally, the Standardized Incidence Ratio of renal cancer was significantly higher in lithium treated patients compared with the French general population.

The EMA document has raised an intense debate, particularly in the context of the scientific community involved in the study of lithium therapy, because the epidemiological evidence leading to the recommendation was considered somewhat limited (Baldessarini and Tondo 2014; Licht et al. 2014; Zaidan et al. 2014a; Conell et al. 2015). For example, Licht et al. (2014) commented that, as all patients initiated on lithium (and controls) were not identified and followed over time, time at risk and cumulative events over time were not determined. Therefore, risks or incidence rate ratios as reported in the French study cannot be estimated. The observed difference in prevalence of tumors between the two patient samples may be explained by other factors than the effects of lithium, such as differential use of medications and differential referral patterns. Licht et al. concluded that no causal relationship between lithium and solid renal tumors can be inferred from the French study.

Zaidan et al. (2014a) replied that they had not estimated relative risks and incidence rate ratios between the two groups. Instead, they had calculated the number of expected cases of renal cancer in lithium-treated patients by gender and for each 5-year stratum using the French national estimates of renal cancer and showed increased standardized incidence ratios of renal cancers in lithium-treated patients compared to the general population. Moreover, they had reported an association and not a causal effect.

Baldessarini and Tondo (2014) commented that the French study did not report risks among lithium-treated patients without renal impairment. As the rates of severe impairment of renal function among lithium-treated patients may be as low as 0.5% (McKnight et al. 2012) and given an estimated risk of solid renal tumors of 8.24% of lithium-treated patients with significant renal impairment according to the French study, a tentative estimate of risk of kidney tumors among all patients exposed to lithium long-term would be approximately 0.041% (0.0824×0.005). This estimate suggests a risk of one case of solid renal tumor in approximately 2400 lithium-treated patients. However, as shown in Table 5, the patients referred to the French nephrology departments included cases with mildly decreased eGFR, so that Baldessarini and Tondo's estimates are questionable. Moreover, McKnight et al.'s estimates are also questionable because they were based on prospective studies with a mean observation time of 1 year, whereas, in our survey, including patients followed for several decades, as many as half of the patients treated for longer than 20 years had an eGFR lower than 60 ml/min/1.73 m^2 (Bocchetta et al. 2015).

In any case, Baldessarini and Tondo (2014) also mentioned that "based on consulting international colleagues who lead large mood disorder clinical programs, no reports of renal cancers have emerged in a collective experience involving thousands of psychiatric patients treated long-term with lithium (IGSLI centers, http://www.igsli.org; personal written communication, 28 March 2014; and clinical records of the Lucio Bini Mood Disorders Centers, Rome and Cagliari, March 2014)." The latter comment was one of the reasons that encouraged us to analyze retrospectively our lithium clinic database in order to overcome a potential recall bias. We thus identified the two cases of renal-cell cancer out of 1871 patients up to 2013. Curiously, the third case was observed in 2015, right after the publication of the EMA document.

Conell et al. (2015) warned about uncritical reactions including withdrawal of lithium in successfully treated patients after the adjustment within the lithium package leaflet was required by the European authorities concerning the increased risk for kidney tumors. We agree that any decision must weigh pros and cons.

The above-mentioned statements (Baldessarini and Tondo 2014; Licht et al. 2014; Zaidan et al. 2014a; Conell et al. 2015) were made prior to the two epidemiological studies clearly showing with overwhelming statistical power that long-term use of lithium is not associated with increased risk of renal tumors or cancer (Kessing et al. 2015; Pottegård et al. 2016).

Thyroid cancer

As goiter was beyond the scope of this review, we found less literature on thyroid tumors in patients treated with lithium as compared to renal tumors. We retrieved only five case reports of thyroid cancer in addition to the one we had already reported in 2007 (Bocchetta et al. 2007a). The latter was found in the context of a follow-up study of a cohort of 150 patients at various stages of lithium treatment at our facility. We had detected nodules with ultrasonic scan in a large proportion of patients from that cohort (Licht et al. 2014). However, we observed only one case of malignancy during the 15-year follow-up (Bocchetta et al. 1996), concluding that it may be consistent with chance. In any case, we also acknowledged that, as further diagnostic evaluation of nodules (such as fine-needle aspiration biopsy) was not performed systematically, incidence might have been underestimated. Moreover, only three patients from that cohort had undergone thyroidectomy. Now, the present updated analysis of our entire cohort of lithium patients has revealed 16 additional cases of thyroidectomy, including the new 8 cases of thyroid cancer. All the nine cases observed (Table 1) were represented by papillary carcinoma and had occurred in middle-aged patients (mean 55 years) after an average of above 20 years of lithium exposure.

With our case series, the total number of reported cases amounts now to 14 (Table 4).

Pharmacovigilance databases and epidemiological studies

We are aware that the number of ADR reports serves principally to generate or confirm an alarm, but its epidemiological value is limited. Reporting is subject to different influences, including the presence of previous literature reports. On the other hand, there may be overlapping across the different pharmacovigilance databases and with cases reported in the literature. We expect that the rate of reports of renal tumors is going to increase after the EMA document encouraged routine pharmacovigilance in order to better characterize the risk.

The analysis of data from the Pharmacovigilance systems has many limitations, including the underreporting and underestimation of the events and the impossibility to estimate the incidence of ADRs. Unfortunately, some ADRs were codified as "renal neoplasm" or "renal cancer", with no histological characterization. The different terms used to classify the ADRs (e.g. oncocytoma, renal oncocytoma) further limit the analysis.

In any case, after the alarming finding of an increased risk of renal tumors among long-term lithium users, besides the routine pharmacovigilance reports, the two nationwide Danish population-based studies clearly showed with overwhelming statistical power that long-term use of lithium is not associated with increased risk of renal tumors or cancer (Kessing et al. 2015; Pottegård et al. 2016).

It appears that no epidemiological studies have addressed the issue of lithium-related thyroid cancer. We can just estimate an incidence of 9 cases over approximately 6200 patient/years in our cohort of 345 patients followed up for more than 10 years of lithium therapy.

It must be underscored that patients treated with lithium may receive a particular attention as regard to assessment of thyroid and renal functions, so that a surveillance bias cannot be ruled out in epidemiological studies. This issue was for example addressed by Licht et al. (2014): "lithium-treated patients are generally under careful observation for renal symptoms, even if not causally related to lithium, and non-lithium-treated patients may suffer from even serious renal problems that never lead to tertiary referral or renal imaging".

Potential mechanisms

Whatever the epidemiological relevance, some mechanisms potentially involved in lithium-related tumors are worth being discussed.

The cases of thyroid cancer reported so far in patients treated with lithium (Table 4) were invariably papillary carcinoma, which is the most common type also in the general population. Therefore, it cannot be concluded that lithium is a direct cause. However, given the known goitrogenic effect of lithium and the frequent finding of increased thyrotropin concentrations (for review see Bocchetta and Loviselli 2006), it is possible that lithium contributes to the propagation of incidental differentiated thyroid cancers. Moreover, it has been shown that lithium has a direct stimulatory effect on the growth of thyroid cells in culture (Tsuchiya et al. 1990).

The question of the potential role of lithium in renal tumors is somewhat different. In fact, beyond clear-cell renal-cell and papillary renal-cell cancer, other rare subtypes of renal cancers have been reported in patients treated with lithium (Table 5). Rookmaaker et al. (2012), who observed several cases of collecting-duct carcinoma, commented that the latter are derived from principal cells in the collecting duct, where lithium can reach very high concentrations. They hypothesized that a prolonged stimulation of principal cell proliferation by lithium, via its inhibition of the enzyme glycogen synthase kinase 3 beta and the increased availability of β-catenin in tubular cells (Kjaersgaard et al. 2012; Nielsen et al. 2008; Saadi-Kheddouci et al. 2001) can eventually induce adenomas and carcinomas.

On the other hand, the relatively high proportion of cases of the otherwise rare renal oncocytoma that have been reported in lithium patient is intriguing. Renal oncocytomas are derived from intercalated cells (Kuroda et al. 2003). Animal experiments have shown that lithium treatment not only induces the proliferation of principal cells, but also causes an increase in the number of intercalated cells, possibly resulting from proliferation and differentiation of progenitor cells or the conversion of principal cells into intercalated cells (Christensen et al. 2006). Zaidan et al. (2014b) suggested that similar mechanisms may be involved in the development of oncocytomas in patients on lithium therapy.

Outcome

The possibility that tumors may be favored by long-term therapy with lithium must be weighted also in view of their outcome. It appears that the cases of thyroid cancer reported in patients treated with lithium do not differ from that found in the general population. They were invariably represented by papillary carcinoma, whose prognosis is generally considered good provided that diagnostic and therapeutic guidelines are followed (Mitchell et al. 2016). Common procedures include imaging (ultrasound and nuclear scan), fine needle aspiration biopsy, thyroidectomy, and radioiodine therapy. In our survey of the causes of death of the 375 deceased patients of the 1840 who had been visited at least once from 1980 to 2013, no cases of thyroid cancer were found. The total number of patient/years was 33,801, including 8263 patient/years on regular monitoring of lithium therapy.

With regard to renal tumors, the most common subtype in the general population is the conventional clear-cell carcinoma followed by papillary renal-cell carcinoma (Eble et al. 2004). The latter can be differentiated into two subgroups: an organ-confined/localized subgroup with a significantly better prognosis and an advanced/metastatic subgroup with a worse prognosis compared to the clear-cell carcinoma (Steffens et al. 2012).

In our survey of the causes of death, of the 375 deceased patients updated to 2013, we found only one case of renal tumor, not otherwise specified. The relationship with lithium therapy is doubtful, as this regarded a man who had taken the therapy only for a few months.

On the contrary, the case of the woman who died for metastatic oncocytoma in 2016 warrants a particular discussion. Renal oncocytomas represent 3–7% of all renal tumors. Although in the past decades malignant oncocytomas have seldom been described (Perez-Ordonez et al. 1997; Oxley et al. 2007), they are classified as benign tumors, since neoplastic cells are usually well differentiated and they are generally encapsulated and not invasive or associated with metastases (Eble et al. 2004).

Our case report is extremely unusual given the presence of lung and thyroid metastases at diagnosis. However, cases with concomitant oncocytomas and renal-cell cancers have been reported (Licht et al. 1993; Dechet et al. 1999), especially if there are diffuse nodules involving parenchyma in the same or contralateral kidney, as in the case described. We acknowledge that the histological analysis of thyroid metastasis only described the compatibility with renal origin without confirming the oncocytic nature, and no histological confirmation of the nodules in the contralateral kidney was available. Furthermore, histological diagnosis of oncocytoma may be difficult, and cases of chromophobe renal-cell cancer described as metastatic oncocytomas have been reported. Both oncocytomas and chromophobe renal-cell cancer derive from the intercalating cells of distal renal tubules, and their similar histologic features make it difficult to distinguish them, thus leading to possible misdiagnosis (Chao et al. 2002; Van der Kwast and Perez-Ordonez 2007).

Clinical recommendations

We agree with the suggestions by Baldessarini and Tondo (2014) that tumors and other medical risks "are to be balanced against the extraordinary body of evidence that lithium, more than any other mood stabilizer, not only has short-term antimanic effects but can also reduce risks of recurrences of various components of bipolar disorder and may reduce the risks of suicide as well as of mortality associated with cardiovascular and respiratory illnesses, which are more frequent in bipolar patients compared to the general population (Bauer et al. 2006; Ahrens et al. 1995; Baldessarini et al. 2006; Grof and Müller-Oerlinghausen 2009)". In this regard, we would like to remark our data on 375 death certificates of patients previously treated with lithium collected between 1980 and 2013 that included no cases of thyroid cancer and only one case of renal cancer (before the case identified in 2016). Even the total number of malignancies ($N=35$) is outnumbered by the 64 cases of suicide, 63 of which had occurred in patients who had abandoned regular maintenance with lithium.

Nevertheless, the findings of several cases of thyroid and renal tumors as reviewed in this paper, makes us agree with the other comment on Zaidan et al results by Baldessarini and Tondo (2014): "Clinically the findings underscore the importance of close medical monitoring of patients treated with lithium, especially for more than several years" and, in particular, "consideration of renal scanning examinations for cysts and tumors among those with clinically identified, progressive impairment of renal function".

In this regard, Rookmaaker et al. (2012) raised the question of "whether patients with chronic lithium nephropathy should be screened for renal cysts and which strategy should be applied in case a complex cyst or solid tumor is found. A subset of these tumors are oncocytomas, which are often slow-growing benign neoplasms that require only surgical intervention in the case of rapid growth or a large tumor volume (Chao et al. 2002). The benign clinical behavior challenges the indication for surgery, which results in loss of renal mass in patients with already compromised renal function. Until more information is obtained "on the incidence and natural history of lithium-related proliferative renal disease, we do not suggest radiological screening in patients with lithium nephropathy" (Rookmaaker et al. 2012).

It must be underscored that Rookmaaker et al comment dates back to 2012 before the report of excessive rates in the French nephrology department (Zaidan et al.

2014b) from one hand and the findings of rates similar to general Danish population (Kessing et al. 2015; Pottegård et al. 2016) on the other hand.

Rookmaaker et al. (2012) also suggested a biopsy "in the case of a renal mass found incidentally in a patient on chronic lithium therapy"; and "if an oncocytoma is found, careful radiological follow-up would be sufficient. If a collecting-duct-cell carcinoma is found, the same strategy could be considered in view of the benign clinical behavior of the tumours in our cases. However, treatment should be individualized and surgical removal may be preferred if a biopsy is technically not feasible, the tumour grows rapidly or removal of the tumour would imply only minimal loss of renal mass" (Rookmaaker et al. 2012).

Zaidan et al. (2014a, b) commented that "similarly to lithium-induced nephropathy, which develops slowly over decades, usually after 10–20 years, renal tumor development in lithium-treated patients may also be considered as a late complication, as assessed by a mean duration of 20 years of lithium exposure at diagnosis in our study and other reports. Thus, lithium-treated patients who have received lithium for more than 10 years and have developed CKD would be the most likely to benefit of a screening for renal tumors. Zaidan et al. (2014a, b) recommended the prescription of a renal ultrasound every 3 years. However, it is premature and unbalanced to suggest such screenings as there is simply no evidence for an increased risk of renal tumors/cancers so far.

Conclusions

With regard to the cases of thyroid cancer, it cannot be concluded that lithium is a direct cause, because thyroid papillary carcinoma is the most common type also in the general population. No large-scale epidemiological studies have been performed. However, the prognosis is generally considered good, provided that diagnostic and therapeutic guidelines are followed.

On the other hand, the possible association between long-term lithium treatment and the occurrence of renal neoplasms is still to be assessed. So far, two population-based studies clearly showed that long-term use of lithium is not associated with increased risk of renal tumors or cancer. However, the seriousness of the alert should lead to further investigations through international cohort studies as well as implementation of the ADRs reporting.

Abbreviations

EMA: European Medicine Agency; PRAC: Pharmacovigilance Risk Assessment Committee; ADR: adverse drug reaction; ICSRs: individual case safety reports; MedDRA: medical dictionary for regulatory activity; SOC: system organ classes; SMQs: standardized MedDRA queries; MeSH: medical subject headings; eGFR: estimated glomerular filtration rate; KDIGO: kidney disease improving global outcomes; CKD: chronic kidney disease.

Authors' contributions

AB devised the study, participated in its design and coordination, and drafted the manuscript. LA participated in the study design, literature search, data collection and interpretation, and drafting of the manuscript. CP participated in the literature search and interpretation. AD and MES participated in the interpretation of pharmacovigilance data. CC participated in the collection of clinical data. All authors read and approved the final manuscript.

Author details

[1] Section of Neuroscience and Clinical Pharmacology, Department of Biomedical Sciences, University of Cagliari, S.S. 554, km 4,500, Monserrato, Italy. [2] Sardinian Regional Centre of Pharmacovigilance, Azienda Ospedaliero-Universitaria, Cagliari, Italy. [3] Unit of Clinical Pharmacology, "San Giovanni di Dio Hospital", Azienda Ospedaliero-Universitaria, Cagliari, Italy.

Acknowledgements

The authors thank Ms. Enrica Mosca for reviewing and editing the manuscript.

Competing interests

The authors declare they have no competing interests.

Funding

The authors and institutions involved did not receive any grant for the collection and analysis of data and the writing of the manuscript.

References

Ahrens B, Grof P, Möller HJ, Müller-Oerlinghausen B, Wolf T. Extended survival of patients on long-term lithium treatment. Can J Psychiatry. 1995;40:241–6.

Aksoy S, Kilickap S, Erman M. Lithium-associated hypothyroidism and thyroid papillary carcinoma: a case report. South Med J. 2006;99:279–81.

Baldessarini RJ, Tondo L. Are renal tumors associated with lithium treatment? Int J Bipolar Disord. 2014;2:6.

Baldessarini RJ, Tondo L, Davis P, Pompili M, Goodwin FK, Hennen J. Decreased risk of suicides and attempts during long-term lithium treatment: meta-analytic review. Bipolar Disord. 2006;8:625–39.

Bauer M, Gitlin M. The essential guide to lithium treatment. Berlin: Springer; 2016.

Bauer M, Grof P, Müller-Oerlinghausen B. Lithium in neuropsychiatry: the comprehensive guide. London: Taylor & Francis; 2006.

Bocchetta A. Mortality follow-up of patients since commencing lithium therapy. J Clin Psychopharmacol. 2005;25:197–9.

Bocchetta A, Loviselli A. Lithium treatment and thyroid abnormalities. Clin Pract Epidemiol Ment Health. 2006;2:23.

Bocchetta A, Cherchi A, Loviselli A, Mossa P, Velluzzi F, Derai R, Del Zompo M. Six-year follow-up of thyroid function during lithium treatment. Acta Psychiatr Scand. 1996;94:45–8.

Bocchetta A, Cocco F, Velluzzi F, Del Zompo M, Mariotti S, Loviselli A. A fifteen-year follow-up of thyroid function in lithium patients. J Endocrinol Invest. 2007a;30:363–6.

Bocchetta A, Fadda D, Satta G, Del Zompo M, Gessa GL, Cocco P. Long-term lithium treatment and survival from external causes including suicide. J Clin Psychopharmacol. 2007b;27:544–6.

Bocchetta A, Ardau R, Fanni T, Sardu C, Piras D, Pani A, Del Zompo M. Renal function during long-term lithium treatment: a cross-sectional and longitudinal study. BMC Med. 2015;13:12.

Brownlie BE, Turner JG, Millner GM, Perry EG, Ding L. Lithium associated thyroid cancer. Aust NZ J Med. 1980;10:62–3.

Chao DH, Zisman A, Pantuck AJ, Freedland SJ, Said JW, Belldegrun AS. Changing concepts in the management of renal oncocytom. Urology. 2002;59:635–42.

Christensen BM, Kim YH, Kwon TH, Nielsen S. Lithium treatment induces a marked proliferation of primarily principal cells in rat kidney inner medullary collecting duct. Am J Physiol Renal Physiol. 2006;291:F39–48.

Cohen Y, Chetrit A, Cohen Y, Sirota P, Modan B. Cancer morbidity in psychiatric patients: influence of lithium carbonate treatment. Med Oncol. 1998;15:32–6.

Conell J, Lewitzka U, Ritter P, Severus E, Pilhatsch M, Pfennig A, et al. Is there an increased risk for renal tumors during long-term treatment with lithium? Nervenarzt. 2015;86:1157–61.

Dechet CB, Bostwick DG, Blute ML, Bryant SC, Zincke H. Renal oncocytoma: multifocality, bilateralism, metachronous tumor development and coexistent renal cell carcinoma. J Urol. 1999;162:40–2.

Eble JN, Sauter G, Epstein JI, Sesterhenn IA. World Health Organization classification of tumours. Pathology and genetics of tumours of the urinary system and male genital organs. Lyon: IARC Press; 2004.

European Medicines Agency, Pharmacovigilance Risk Assessment Committee (PRAC). PRAC recommendations on signals, adopted at the PRAC meeting of 6–9 January 2015. 2015. http://www.ema.europa.eu/docs/en_GB/document_library/PRAC_recommendation_on_signal/2015/01/WC500181043.pdf. Accessed 3 May 2018.

Grof P, Müller-Oerlinghausen B. A critical appraisal of lithium's efficacy and effectiveness: the last 60 years. Bipolar Disord. 2009;11(Suppl 2):10–9.

Huang RY, Hsieh KP, Huang WW, Yang YH. Use of lithium and cancer risk in patients with bipolar disorder: population-based cohort study. Br J Psychiatry. 2016;209:393–9.

Jung JH. Renal cell carcinoma recognized incidentally during long-term lithium treatment. Chonnam Med J. 2016;52:143–4.

KDIGO 2017 Clinical Practice Guideline Update for the Diagnosis, Evaluation, Prevention, and Treatment of Chronic Kidney. Disease-mineral and bone disorder (CKD-MBD). Kidney Int. 2017;7:1–59.

Kessing LV, Gerds TA, Feldt-Rasmussen B, Andersen PK, Licht RW. Lithium and renal and upper urinary tract tumours—results from a nationwide population-based study. Bipolar Disord. 2015;17:805–13.

Kjaersgaard G, Madsen K, Marcussen N, Christensen S, Walter S, Jensen BL. Tissue injury after lithium treatment in human and rat postnatal kidney involves glycogen synthase kinase-3β-positive epithelium. Am J Physiol Renal Physiol. 2012;302:F455–65.

Kuroda N, Toi M, Hiroi M, Shuin T, Enzan H. Review of renal oncocytoma with focus on clinical and pathobiological aspects. Histol Histopathol. 2003;18:935–42.

Levey AS, Bosch JP, Lewis JB, Greene T, Rogers N, Roth D. A more accurate method to estimate glomerular filtration rate from serum creatinine: a new prediction equation. Modification of Diet in Renal Disease Study Group. Ann Intern Med. 1999;130:461–70.

Lewitzka U, Severus E, Bauer R, Ritter P, Müller-Oerlinghausen B, Bauer M. The suicide prevention effect of lithium: more than 20 years of evidence—a narrative review. Int J Bipolar Disord. 2015;3:32.

Licht MR, Novick AC, Tubbs RR, Klein EA, Levin HS, Streem SB. Renal oncocytoma: clinical and biological correlates. J Urol. 1993;150:1380–3.

Licht RW, Grabenhenrich LB, Nielsen RE, Berghöfer A, International Group for the Study of Lithium (IGSLi). Lithium and renal tumours: a critical comment to the report by Zaidan et al. Kidney Int. 2014;86:857.

Lyskowski J, Nasrallah HA. Lithium therapy and the risk for leukemia. Br J Psychiatry. 1981;139:256.

Markowitz GS, Radhakrishnan J, Kambham N, Valeri AM, Hines WH, D'Agati VD. Lithium nephrotoxicity: a progressive combined glomerular and tubulointerstitial nephropathy. J Am Soc Nephrol. 2000;11:1439–48.

McHenry CR, Rosen IB, Rotstein LE, Forbath N, Walfish PG. Lithiumogenic disorders of the thyroid and parathyroid glands as surgical disease. Surgery. 1990;108:1001–5.

McKnight RF, Adida M, Budge K, Stockton S, Goodwin GM, Geddes JR. Lithium toxicity profile: a systematic review and meta-analysis. Lancet. 2012;379:721–8.

Medical Dictionary for Regulatory Activities (MedDRA), Standardised MedDRA Queries. 2007. https://www.meddra.org/standardised-meddra-queries. Accessed 3 May 2018.

Mitchell AL, Gandhi A, Scott-Coombes D, Perros P. Management of thyroid cancer: united Kingdom National Multidisciplinary Guidelines. J Laryngol Otol. 2016;130:S150–60.

Moreb J, Hershko C. Increased leucocyte alkaline phosphatase and transcobalamin III in chronic myeloid leukaemia associated with lithium therapy. Scand J Haematol. 1985;34:238–41.

Naranjo CA, Busto U, Sellers EM, Sandor P, Ruiz I, Roberts EA, et al. A method for estimating the probability of adverse drug reactions. Clin Pharmacol Ther. 1981;30:239–45.

Nielsen J, Hoffert JD, Knepper MA, Agre P, Nielsen S, Fenton RA. Proteomic analysis of lithium-induced nephrogenic diabetes insipidus: mechanisms for aquaporin 2 down-regulation and cellular proliferation. Proc Natl Acad Sci USA. 2008;105:3634–9.

Nolen WA. More robust evidence for the efficacy of lithium in the long-term treatment of bipolar disorder: should lithium (again) be recommended as the single preferred first-line treatment? Int J Bipolar Disord. 2015;3:1.

Oxley JD, Sullivan J, Mitchelmore A, Gillatt DA. Metastatic renal oncocytoma. J Clin Pathol. 2007;60:720–2.

Perez-Ordonez B, Hamed G, Campbell S, Erlandson RA, Russo P, Gaudin PB, Reuter VE. Renal oncocytoma: a clinicopathologic study of 70 cases. Am J Surg Pathol. 1997;21:871–83.

Peyromaure M, Thiounn N, Scotté F, Vieillefond A, Debré B, Oudard S. Collecting duct carcinoma of the kidney: a clinicopathological study of 9 cases. J Urol. 2003;170:1138–40.

Pottegård A, Hallas J, Jensen BL, Madsen K, Friis S. Long-term lithium use and risk of renal and upper urinary tract cancers. J Am Soc Nephrol. 2016;27:249–55.

Rookmaaker MB, van Gerven HA, Goldschmeding R, Boer WH. Solid renal tumours of collecting duct origin in patients on chronic lithium therapy. Clin Kidney J. 2012;5:412–5.

Saadi-Kheddouci S, Berrebi D, Romagnolo B, Cluzeaud F, Peuchmaur M, Kahn A. Early development of polycystic kidney disease in transgenic mice expressing an activated mutant of the beta-catenin gene. Oncogene. 2001;20:5972–81.

Steffens S, Janssen M, Roos FC, Becker F, Schumacher S, Seidel C. Incidence and long-term prognosis of papillary compared to clear cell renal cell carcinoma—a multicentre study. Eur J Cancer. 2012;48:2347–52.

Storkel S, Eble JN, Adlakha K, Amin M, Blute ML, Bostwick DG, et al. Classification of renal cell carcinoma: workgroup No. 1. Union Internationale Contre le Cancer (UICC) and the American Joint Committee on Cancer (AJCC). Cancer. 1997;80:987–9.

Tsuchiya Y, Saji M, Isozaki O, Arai M, Tsushima T, Shizume K. Effect of lithium on deoxyribonucleic acid synthesis and iodide uptake in porcine thyroid cells in culture. Endocrinology. 1990;126:460–5.

Van der Kwast T, Perez-Ordoñez B. Renal oncocytoma, yet another tumour that does not fit in the dualistic benign/malignant paradigm? J Clin Pathol. 2007;60:585–6.

Volf N, Crismon ML. Leukemia in bipolar mood disorder: is lithium contraindicated? DICP. 1991;25:948–51.

Zaidan M, Landais P, Grünfeld JP, Servais A. The authors repl. Kidney Int. 2014a;86:857–8.

Zaidan M, Stucker F, Stengel B, Vasiliu V, Hummel A, Landais P, et al. Increased risk of solid renal tumours in lithium-treated patients. Kidney Int. 2014b;86:184–90.

Zardawi I, Nagonkar S, Patel P. Renal cell carcinoma in a setting of chronic lithium toxicity. Am J Case Rep. 2013;14:300–3.

21

Shared decision making in pharmacotherapy decisions, perceived by patients with bipolar disorder

Doris Verwijmeren[1*] and Koen P. Grootens[1,2]

Abstract

Background: Shared decision making has been promoted as standard care, but there has been debate on the possible types. On the one hand, there is a more 'instrumental'/objective approach focused on the exchange of information, but an 'interpersonal'/subjective patient involvement has been suggested as well. In this study we aim to investigate this further by assessing both actual and perceived patient involvement in medical decisions.

Methods: Eighty-one consultations between patients with bipolar disorder and their clinicians were observed and scored using the OPTION scale. Afterwards, the patients' experienced involvement was explored with the SDM-Q-9. Furthermore, several patient characteristics were gathered. Correlations between the scores were examined.

Results: The clinicians scored on average 34.6 points on the OPTION scale. In contrast, patients scored on average 77.5 points on the SDM-Q-9, suggesting that patients felt more involved in the consultation than was observable.

Conclusion: Our patients with bipolar disorder feel involved in pharmacotherapy decisions, but this is not scored in objective observations. Our data suggest that there are implicit, interpersonal aspects of patient involvement in shared decision making, a concept that deserves further attention and conceptualisation.

Keywords: Communication, Bipolar disorders, Pharmacotherapy

Background

Shared decision making

In recent decades, patient participation in medical decisions has increased enormously and has become the new standard (de Cuevas et al. 2011; Hamann et al. 2011; Zijlstra and Goossensen 2007). This patient-centred care has been promoted by an increased emphasis on clinical interaction with respect to patients' values, preferences and experiences (Elwyn et al. 2014). To explore these values and preferences, the model of shared decision making (SDM) has gradually evolved. In SDM, patient and physician discuss the pros and cons of all treatment options using the best available evidence for the individual situation. In addition, the clinician is encouraged to examine the patient's preferences and fears and his or her preferred level of participation in the decision making (Elwyn et al. 2014; Goossensen et al. 2007; Morant et al. 2016). The most important aspect is that at the end of the process a decision is made that matches the patient's values, is informed based on evidence, and has the full agreement of both doctor and patient (Simmons et al. 2010).

Importance of SDM

The importance of SDM is widely recognised. The benefits, such as improved self-management (Goossensen et al. 2007), patient satisfaction (Ilgen et al. 2009) and treatment adherence (Simmons et al. 2010; Hamann et al. 2003; McCabe et al. 2013; Stacey et al. 2008; Sylvia et al. 2013) have already been described in several studies throughout the medical field. Some studies even report an improvement in clinical outcomes due to a higher level of SDM (Hamann et al. 2003; Os et al. 2005; Rathert et al. 2013). In psychiatry, a similar shift towards interest

*Correspondence: d.verwijmeren@reiniervanarkel.nl
[1] Reinier van Arkel Mental Health Institute, Postbus 70058, 5201 DZ 's-Hertogenbosch, The Netherlands
Full list of author information is available at the end of the article

in SDM has taken place as in general medicine. Os et al. (2005) showed an improvement in patient outcomes in depression where the antidepressant treatment was provided by a doctor with good communicative skills (Os et al. 2005). Nevertheless, compared to the large number of studies assessing patient participation in decision making in somatic medicine, SDM in the mental health field is a relatively understudied topic (Morant et al. 2016; Hamann et al. 2003).

SDM in patients with bipolar disorder

Bipolar patients are an outstanding group to involve in SDM. Patients with bipolar disorder have a great responsibility in self-managing their disease to prevent a relapse or recurrence (Fisher et al. 2016). The intermittent nature of the disorder makes it convenient to apply SDM in the symptom-free intervals. There are a variety of options for maintenance treatment that need further explanation and consideration, each with more or less similar efficacy but different side effects and monitoring aspects (Kupka et al. 2015).

Finally, treatment adherence remains a major challenge due to the significant side effects of the drugs described, such as lithium-induced renal failure. This makes a balanced consideration of the choice of treatment especially relevant (Fisher et al. 2016; Sajatovic et al. 2005). Nevertheless, a recent systematic review showed only 13 studies on SDM in bipolar patients, with only two bipolar-only samples and eleven mixed psychiatric patient samples with a minority of bipolar patients (Fisher et al. 2016).

In the studies in that review, bipolar patients preferred making decisions together with their clinician or making the decision alone. Less than a third of patients reported preferring a passive decision style. Most patients wanted to rely on the professional advice of their clinician and preferred the clinician to make the final treatment decisions (Fisher et al. 2016).

Differences between 'being' and 'feeling' involved?

Research and policy on SDM so far seem to focus predominantly on the objective part of SDM, such as the exchange of information or treatment options. However, a more subjective approach has been suggested as well, concerning a more patient-oriented style and subjective phenomena that play a part in the consult. For instance, Fisher et al. (2016) separates the patient involvement in 'instrumental' and 'interpersonal'. Also Goossensen et al. (2007) conducted a study for comparing doctor skills (measured by the OPTION scale) versus patient satisfaction and concluded that although the skills of SDM from the doctor did not always score that high, the patient satisfaction did. Entwistle and Watt (2006) suggests several aspects of involvement in decision-making., such as the patient's views and feelings about their role and contributions in relation to decision-making. In addition, the patient's views and feelings about their relationship with their clinician can be taken into account. Patients themselves also talk in terms of feeling involved, not just being. The authors notice that less attention has been paid to these aspects (Entwistle and Watt 2006).

Most ideally, this topic should be addressed in a qualitative study. Because there are no validated quantitative tests aligning this topic, we aim to look for directions pointing out a possible difference between this 'being' and 'feeling' involved by assessing the patient's perspective about SDM with the SDM-Q-9.

Study aims and hypotheses

In this study, we aimed to research the preferences of patients with bipolar disorder in the decision-making process regarding pharmacotherapeutic options. The study was designed to explore possible differences between the subjective and observable aspects of SDM. By focusing on this particular patient group and only on pharmacotherapeutic decisions, we attempt to obtain a clear and complete image of SDM. We hypothesised that patients with bipolar disorder wanted to be involved in the decision-making process, as has already been described in other studies with different patient samples in both psychiatric and somatic medicine (Blumenthal-Barby et al. 2015; Cuevas et al. 2014; Zheng et al. 2006).

In addition, we expected to find indications for a distinction between implicit, experienced and explicit, observed patient involvement. We explicit use the term indications, because we realise that the SDM-Q-9 is a scale to measure the patient's perspective more than pure implicit communication.

Methods

Participants

Consultations between psychiatrists, residents, nurse practitioners and their patients were observed by the first author during real-time observation, after informed consent. No audio-or video-recordings were made. Most clinicians were partly instructed about the topic, by telling them the communication would be observed, but not revealing our hypotheses. The consultations took place in two specialised outpatient clinics for bipolar disorder in 's-Hertogenbosch and Nijmegen in the Netherlands. The following inclusion criteria were used: age over 18 years, a known DSM-IV diagnosis of bipolar disorder I, II or 'not otherwise specified' (NOS) diagnosed by a psychiatrist, and a consultation which was expected to involve a pharmacotherapy decision. We specifically did not place any limitations related to current mood symptoms to create a representative image of a consultation with a patient with bipolar disorder. Patients were asked to answer a questionnaire afterwards. Participants provided both written and verbal informed consent prior to the consultation. Patients were included in the study during 8 weeks. The study was approved by the local ethics committee.

Of the 91 patients who were asked to join the research, only eight refused informed consent. Two patients did not have a bipolar disorder and were subsequently excluded from the study. Three patients did not return the questionnaire and were treated as lost to follow-up. Forty-two patients did not complete the full questionnaire. As shown in Table 1, most of the 81 patients had a DSM-IV bipolar I disorder and more than half had been admitted to hospital at least once in their lifetime.

Table 1 Patient characteristics

Characteristics	Sample, N=81		
	N	%	*SD*
Gender			
Female	52	64.2	
Male	29	35.9	
Age (mean in years)	52.0		13.6
Ethnic origin			
Dutch	78	96.3	
American	1	1.2	
Asian	1	1.2	
African	1	1.2	
Diagnosis			
Bipolar I	50	61.7	
Bipolar II	23	28.4	
Bipolar NOS	8	9.9	
Clinician			
Psychiatrist	61	75.3	
Trainee	5	6.2	
Nurse practitioner	15	18.5	
Time of consultation (mean in minutes)	40.1		15.2
Total duration of treatment (years)			
<1	34	42.0	
1–5	33	40.7	
5–10	12	14.8	
>10	2	2.5	
Number of clinical admissions			
0	13	18.8	
1–3	49	71.1	
4–5	5	6.2	
>5	2	2.4	

Instruments

Explicit aspects of SDM were observed and scored using OPTION (Observing Patient Involvement in Treatment Choices), an instrument that measures (on a scale from 0 to 100) the degree to which clinicians involve patients in decision making (Elwyn et al. 2005a, b). The instrument consists of 12 items to observe verbal behaviour displayed by the clinician. The instrument can be applied using audio- or video-recording, or live rating (Elwyn et al. 2005a).

After the consultation, we asked the participant to fill in a questionnaire exploring the preceding process of SDM from the patient's perspective (the implicit SDM), using the nine-item Shared Decision-Making Questionnaire (SDM-Q-9). The SDM-Q-9 is developed to measure the process of SDM by self-assessment of the patient. It consists of 9 items, each addressing a step of the SDM process (Kriston et al. 2010). In addition, the Decision Self-Efficacy Scale was used to measure the patient's self-confidence or belief in their abilities in decision making, including SDM. Third, the WHO Disability Assessment Schedule 2.0 (WHODAS 2.0) (WHO 2017) was scored to obtain a clear image of the severity of the disease in the last 3 months. The WHODAS 2.0 is developed by the WHO organization to measure disability levels on six domains of functioning: cognition, mobility, self-care, getting along, life activities, participation (WHO 2017). The scale is available in a 36-item scale and a 12-item scale. In this research, the 12-item scale is used.

Finally, the patients were asked to answer eight self-designed multiple choice questions about the communication with their physician and their preferences regarding the communication (see Table 3). This questionnaire was designed to evaluate possible bias in our design and to further underpin our results.

Data analysis

We used descriptives and a Pearson correlation to test the correlation between OPTION and SDM-Q-9. For statistical testing of the answers to the multiple choice questions, crosstabs with Chi square were used. Furthermore, we used a Pearson correlation and two-way ANOVA with Least Significant Difference for statistical testing of the influence of the different variables on the OPTION and SDM-Q-9 scales. A significance level of 0.05 was used. Data were analysed with SPSS, Version 22.

Results

Quality of SDM scored by observer

The mean OPTION score of all clinicians over the remaining 78 consultations was 34.6 ($SD = 16.4$). The mean scores per clinician ranged from 0.0 to 64.6. We explored the associations between the OPTION scale and the following variables: different clinicians, patient sex, patient age, diagnosis, self-confidence for making a decision, severity of bipolar symptoms (WHODAS 2.0 and number of clinical admissions), duration of total treatment by the same clinician and duration of the consultation.

Only duration of consultation was found to have a statistically significant relationship with the observed OPTION scale. The correlation was: the longer the consultation, the higher the OPTION score (see Table 2).

Quality of SDM scored by the patient

The mean SDM-Q-9 score for the patients was 77.5 (*SD* 23.5, range 6.7–100). We also explored the relationships between the patient characteristics and the SDM-Q-9. We found a positive relationship between the number of clinical admissions and the SDM-Q-9 ($p=0.046$), suggesting that the severity of the disease influences the patient's feeling of being involved in the decision-making process.

We also found a significant relationship between the Decision Self-Efficacy Scale and the SDM-Q-9 (Table 2). In contrast to our hypothesis, we found no correlation between the SDM-Q-9 and the total duration of treatment.

In line with our hypothesis, there was no correlation between the OPTION score and SDM-Q-9 ($r=0.08$ and statistically not significant). Despite the fact that the two scales cannot be compared, we found a higher mean on the SDM-Q-9 of 42.9, indicating that, in the patients' opinion or feeling, the use of SDM is higher than the researcher observed.

Table 2 Correlation between different patient- and consultation-specific variables and the OPTION scale (explicit shared decision making) and the SDM-Q-9 (implicit shared decision making)

Variable	OPTION		SDM-Q-9	
	*R***	*p*	*R*	*p*
Duration of consultation	0.39	*0.00**	0.14	0.25
Number of clinical admissions	−0.20	0.11	−0.25	*0.046**
Decision Self-Efficacy Scale	−0.07	0.59	0.52	*0.00**
Duration of total treatment	−0.15	0.19	−0.09	0.45
OPTION	–	–	0.08	0.51

Statistically significant results are in italics

* Correlation is significant at the 0.05 level

** R = Pearson correlation

Needs of patients with bipolar disorder

The results of the multiple choice questions are presented in Table 3. As shown in the table, the majority of patients find it very important that both doctor and patient agree on the final decision. Furthermore, it is clear that most patients prefer that both patient and doctor are involved in the decision. If the patient were (theoretically) forced to choose between the two, half of the patients said they would make the decision themselves and the other half would let the clinician decide. Only 'age of the patient' was found to be significantly related to this aspect. It appeared that the older the patient is, the more he or she prefers a final decision by the doctor ($p=0.021$).

Multiple analysis

In the two-way ANOVA of all the independent factors mentioned in "Quality of SDM scored by the patient" section we found only duration of consultation to be of influence on the OPTION scale ($F=5.51$ and $p=0.01$) (Table 4). After adjustment for multiple comparisons by Least Significant Difference we found comparison of the shortest duration of consultation (0–25 min) with the longest duration of consultation (51–75 min) to be still significant ($p=0.003$). Comparison of the 26–50 min group with the longest time was also significant, with a p-value of 0.017.

In the two-way ANOVA of the SDM-Q-9 the only independent factor of influence on the SDM-Q-9 was the Decision Self-Efficacy Scale ($F=3.82$ and $p=0.35$) (Table 5). After adjustment for multiple comparisons by Least Significant Difference we found a significant difference between the lowest score on this scale (0–50) and the highest score (76–100) with a p-value of 0.02.

Discussion

The study presented here was designed to research the opinion of patients with bipolar disorder about their desired and experienced (implicit) involvement, combined with the observed (explicit) involvement in the shared decision-making process.

The clinicians in our sample scored relatively high on the OPTION scale in comparison with other psychiatrists (Goossensen et al. 2007; McCabe et al. 2013) and with paediatricians (Brinkman et al. 2011), general practitioners (Hamann et al. 2003) and oncologists (Arend 2006). Although direct comparisons between the OPTION scale and SDM-Q-9 are not possible, we state that the implicit SDM (experienced involvement) is higher than the observed/explicit SDM. There is no correlation found between the SDM-Q-9 and the OPTION scores.

Although the SDM-Q-9 is not developed for the interpersonal aspect of SDM, the fact that the patient

Table 3 Patients' answers to multiple choice questions in the qualitative interview

Question	Answer *N*	%
1. How did you experience the communication concerning the decision making by your doctor in comparison with previous consultations?		
A. In this conversation I was more involved in the decision-making process than usually	12	16.2
B. In this conversation I was less involved in the decision-making process than usually	1	1.4
C. The doctor behaved in the same way as usually	61	82.4
2. Did you ever use decision aids to make a decision about your treatment? If yes: which decision aids did you use?[a]		
A. Yes	18	25.0
B. No	54	75.0
3. Do you think you would benefit from different tools when making a decision about your treatment? E.g. on the internet, a flyer or an app. If yes, go to question 4. If no, go to question 6		
A. Yes	26	38.2
B. No	42	61.8
4. In the previous question you indicated your need for decision aids. Which tools would you prefer? Multiple answers possible		
A. The pros and cons of each treatment	24	77.4
B. The effects and side effects of each treatment	23	74.2
C. Questions about your preferences which guide you to make a decision about your treatment	7	22.6
D. A proposal of critical questions to ask your doctor for more information about the different treatment options	11	35.5
5. What kind of format would you prefer to present the above chosen aids?		
A. Folder	18	54.5
B. Website	12	36.4
C. An app for your smartphone	3	9.1
6. How important do you think it is that you and your doctor agree on the decision made? (on a scale from 0 to 5)		
0: Not important at all	0	0.0
1: Mostly not important	1	1.9
2: Partly not important	0	0.0
3: Partly important	5	9.6
4: Mostly important	13	25.0
5: Very important	33	63.5
7. If you and your doctor have to make a decision, who makes the decision in the end?		
A. Your doctor	7	13.5
B. You	11	21.2
C. Both of you	34	65.4
8. If you and your doctor disagree about a decision, whose opinion do you eventually follow?		
A. The doctor's opinion	25	52.1
B. Your own opinion	23	47.9

[a] Patients who did use decision aids before used mostly internet, books and advice from their social environment/support group

rated the consultation much higher than the observer, supports our hypothesis that SDM involves both an explicit, observable aspect (information, patient values, consideration of all options) and an implicit, interpersonal aspect that needs further attention, as suggested in the literature mentioned in "Differences between 'being' and 'feeling' involved?" section.

The difference between the implicit and explicit SDM might be explained by the importance of the clinicians' non-verbal behaviour in contrast to the verbal exchange and explanations. The inner feeling of the patient, and possibly the confidence and the relationship with the clinician may be much more important.

In addition, it is possible that patients have a blind spot for possible improvement in their treatment. Patients are content with this communication because they don't realize that improvement is possible. In addition, from a methodically point of view, in general patients tend to be positive about their clinicians in questionnaire research (Edwards et al. 2004).

In exploring the different variables influencing both the OPTION score and SDM-Q-9, only time of consultation and self-efficacy and number of clinical

Table 4 ANOVA summary table for OPTION scale

Source	*df*	MS	F	*p*	Effect size
Gender	1	2.293	0.009	0.924	0.000
Diagnosis	2	91.247	0.365	0.697	0.026
Age	3	262.605	1.052	0.386	0.105
Clinician	2	206.761	0.828	0.448	0.058
Duration of total treatment	3	263.793	1.056	0.384	0.105
SDM-Q-9	1	5.781	0.023	0.880	0.001
WHODAS 2.0	1	350.003	1.402	0.247	0.049
Duration of consultation	2	1374.875	5.506	*0.010**	0.290
Decision Self-Efficacy scale	2	489.703	1.961	0.160	0.127
Error	27	249.719			
Total	47				

Statistically significant results are in italics, $R^2 = 0.508$ (adjusted $R^2 = 0.161$)

MS mean squares, effect size = partial η^2

* Statistically significant at the 0.05 level

Table 5 ANOVA summary table for SDM-Q-9

Source	*df*	MS	F	*p*	Effect size
Gender	1	521.908	1.051	0.314	0.037
Diagnosis	2	674.905	1.360	0.274	0.091
Age	3	931.708	1.877	0.157	0.173
Clinician	2	167.655	0.338	0.716	0.024
Duration of total treatment	3	333.630	0.672	0.577	0.069
OPTION	1	16.581	0.033	0.856	0.001
WHODAS 2.0	1	830.694	1.673	0.207	0.058
Duration of consultation	2	734.410	1.479	0.246	0.099
Decision Self-Efficacy scale	2	1897.546	3.822	*0.035**	0.221
Error	27	496.420			
Total	47				

Statistically significant results are in italics, $R^2 = 0.549$ (adjusted $R^2 = 0.232$)

MS mean squares, effect size = partial η^2

* Statistically significant at the 0.05 level

admissions were correlated with OPTION respectively SDM-Q-9. Interestingly, experienced involvement was not correlated with the duration of the consultation, another clue that involvement is not only about the transmission of information. In contrast to our hypothesis, the duration of the total treatment history had no influence on the implicit and the explicit SDM. This may be partly because there is no normal distribution in our sample, as around 80% of the patients had a treatment duration of < 5 years. Unfortunately, there are no studies focusing on the duration of treatment as a possible influence on SDM.

Cuevas et al. (2014) found that having low efficacy predicted for the patient's experience that the doctor used a passive decision-making style, and little use of SDM. This is in accordance with our findings that a lower score on the Decision Self-Efficacy Scale led to a lower score on the SDM-Q-9. This is not surprising, as it described in literature that there is increased use of a more passive decision-making style by the doctor in a conversation when a patient feels less self-assured about his/her decision making skills (Hamann et al. 2011).

The patients in our sample wanted to be involved in the decision process about their treatment options, in line with previous studies (Cuevas et al. 2014; Klingaman et al. 2015). When in the end the final decision has to be made, we see a pattern emerging regarding differentiation by age. It appears that being older predicted stronger preferences for deciding together or 'letting the doctor decide'. These results were also found by Cuevas et al. (2014). This could be explained by the fact that a few decades ago, a more passive decision making style was commonly used, so older patients are used to this. However, our study was not designed to study this hypothesis. It might be interested to investigate this further in future research.

If patients were (theoretically) forced to choose who made the final decision, half of them would prefer to make it on their own and the other half would prefer the doctor to decide. This was also found by, Park et al. (2014) who showed that more than half of patients preferred the doctor to decide. Therefore, it seems that patients in our sample do want to be involved *in the process*, but not so much in the *actual decision* made at the end. Note that none of the clinicians in our sample discussed explicitly, on a meta-level, the patient's preferences with regard to making health decisions in general.

Strengths and limitations

The strength of this study is its focus on one specific psychiatric disorder and only on pharmacotherapy decisions. Furthermore, this is the first study to explore the occurrence, needs and expectations of SDM in this number of only bipolar patients. The few studies which also included bipolar-only samples were aimed at researching the quality of patient-clinician interactions and the influence of SDM on clinical outcomes (Ilgen et al. 2009; Sylvia et al. 2013; Sajatovic et al. 2005).

The results of this study should be read with some limitations in mind. We used methods in order to find a quick overview of patient experiences and opinions of SDM. Further qualitative analyses of patient-clinician interactions are necessary to deepen our understanding of how patients and clinicians take a position in decisions.

It is important to note that the OPTION scale only scores the clinician's behaviour and does not directly score the interaction between patient and clinician.

Imagining the most extreme situation, in which an 'empowered' patient enters the consultation room and spontaneously states his or her opinion and concerns about the treatment options, the clinician would score zero on several scoring points, resulting in the overall SDM score being lower. Future research methods should focus primarily on the interaction between patients and clinicians.

Finally, it should be mentioned that no data was available about the socio-cultural-economic background of the patients. Thereby the influences of these variables are not researched in this study.

Conclusion and recommendations

The patients with bipolar disorder in our sample want to be involved in pharmacotherapy decisions, especially younger patients. We advise clinicians to tailor SDM and actively explore the patient's preferences with regard to information, the style of the decision process, and the final call in the decision.

In accordance to Fisher et al. (2016), Goossensen et al. (2007) and Etwistle et al. (2006), our data suggest that there are implicit and explicit aspects of patient involvement in SDM, and the two aspects are uncorrelated. Research and policy on SDM so far seem to focus predominantly on the objective part. The interpersonal part may not have been addressed sufficiently in the literature. Clinicians and patients might deduce each other's treatment options and wishes in a more intuitive manner, based for example on their previous treatment history or non-verbal signals. Future (qualitative) research could deepen our understanding of the interactions that take place between clinicians and patients in decision making and should develop new measuring scales to make this implicit part observable.

Our quantitative data suggest that age, self-efficacy and duration of the consultation may be variables to consider in further research.

Finally, modern health care is shifting from doctor-centred to patient-centred care. SDM, our dominant paradigm in decision making, is more than the exchange of information and values. There are indications that there is an interpersonal aspect to SDM in the consultation room which deserves the attention of researchers, clinical training providers and policy makers.

Abbreviation

SDM: shared decision making.

Authors' contributions

Each author have contributed substantial to conception and design, and analysis and interpretation of data. Each author have contributed substantial to drafting the article or revising it critically for important intellectual content and the final approval of the version to be published. In addition, the corresponding author ensures that there is no one else who fulfils the criteria but has not been included as an author. DV also affirms that there was no editorial direction or censorship from any sponsors. Both authors indeed read and approved the final manuscript.

Author details

[1] Reinier van Arkel Mental Health Institute, Postbus 70058, 5201 DZ 's-Hertogenbosch, The Netherlands. [2] Department of Psychiatry, Radboud University Medical Centre, Nijmegen, The Netherlands.

Acknowledgements

None.

Competing interests

The authors declare that they have no competing interests.

Disclosure

Doris Verwijmeren reports no financial relationships with commercial interests. Dr. Grootens reports no financial relationships with commercial interests.

Funding

This research did not receive any specific grant from funding agencies in the public, commercial, or not-for-profit sectors.

References

Arend L. Clinical decisionmaking in oncology care. Rotterdam: Erasmus University; 2006.

Blumenthal-Barby JS, Kostick KM, Delgado ED, Volk RJ, Kaplan HM, Wilhelms LA, et al. Assessment of patients' and caregivers' informational and decisional needs for left ventricular assist device placement: implications for informed consent and shared decision-making. J Heart Lung Transpl. 2015;34(9):1182–9.

Brinkman WB, Hartl J, Rawe LM, Epstein JN. Physicians' shared decision-making behaviors in attention-deficit/hyperactivity disorder care. Arch Pediatr Adolesc Med. 2011;165(11):1013–9.

de Cuevas C, Rivero A, Perestelo-Perez L, Gonzalez M, Perez J, Peñate W. Psychiatric patients' attitudes towards concordance and shared decision making. Patient Educ Couns. 2011;85(3):245–50.

de Cuevas C, Peñate W, de Rivera L. To what extent is treatment adherence of psychiatric patients influenced by their participation in shared decision making? Patient Pref Adher. 2014;8:1547–53.

Edwards C, Staniszweska S, Crichton N. Investigation of the ways in which patients' reports of their satisfaction with healthcare are constructed. Sociol Health Illn. 2004;26(2):159–83.

Elwyn G, Edwards A, Wensing M, Grol R. Shared decision making. Measurement using the OPTION instrument. Leeds: Cardiff University; 2005a.

Elwyn G, Hutchings H, Edwards A, Rapport F, Wensing M, Cheung WY, Grol R. The OPTION scale: measuring the extent that clinicians involve patients in decision-making tasks. Health Expect. 2005b;8(1):34–42.

Elwyn G, Dehlendorf C, Epstein RM, Marrin K, White J, Frosch DL. Shared decision making and motivational interviewing: achieving patient-centered care across the spectrum of health care problems. Ann Fam Med. 2014;12(4):270–5.

Entwistle VA, Watt IS. Patient involvement in treatment decision-making: the case for a broader conceptual framework. Patient Educ Couns. 2006;63:268–78.

Fisher A, Manicavasagar V, Kiln F, Juraskova I. Communication and decision-making in mental health: a systematic review focusing on Bipolar disorder. Patient Educ Couns. 2016;99(7):1106–20.

Goossensen A, Zijlstra P, Koopmanschap M. Measuring shared decision making processes in psychiatry: skills versus patient satisfaction. Patient Educ Couns. 2007;67(1–2):50–6.

Hamann J, Leucht S, Kissling W. Shared decision making in psychiatry. Acta Psychiatr Scand. 2003;107(6):403–9.

Hamann J, Mendel R, Meier A, Asani F, Pausch E, Leucht S, Kissling W. "How to speak to your psychiatrist": shared decision-making training for inpatients with schizophrenia. Psychiatr Serv. 2011a;62(10):1218–21.

Hamann J, Mendel R, Reiter S, Cohen R, Bühner M, Schebit M, et al. Why do some patients with schizophrenia want to be engaged in medical decision making and others do not? J Clin Psychiatry. 2011b;72(12):1636–43.

Ilgen MA, Czyz EK, Welsh DE, Zeber JE, Bauer MS, Kilbourne AM. A collaborative therapeutic relationship and the risk of suicidal ideation in patients with bipolar disorder. J Affect Disord. 2009;115(1–2):246–51.

Klingaman EA, Medof DR, Park SG, Brown CH, Fang L, Dixon LB, et al. Consumer satisfaction with psychiatric services: the role of shared decision making and the therapeutic relationship. Psychiatr Rehabil J. 2015;38(3):242–8.

Kriston L, Scholl I, Hölzel L, Simon D, Loh A, Härter M. The 9-item Shared Decision Making Questionnaire (SDM-Q-9). Development and psychometric properties in a primary care sample. Patient Educ Couns. 2010;80(1):94–9.

Kupka R, Goossens P, Bendegem M, Daemen P, Daggenvoorde T, Daniels M, et al. Multidisciplinaire richtlijn bipolaire stoornissen. De Tijdstroom: Leed; 2015.

McCabe R, Khanom H, Bailey P, Priebe S. Shared decision-making in ongoing outpatient psychiatric treatment. Patient Educ Couns. 2013;91(3):326–8.

Morant N, Kaminskiy E, Ramon S. Shared decision making for psychiatric medication management: beyond the micro-social. Health Expect. 2016;19(5):1002–14.

Park SG, Derman M, Dixon LB, Brown CH, Klingaman EA, Fang L, Medoff DR, Kreyenbuhl J. Factors associated with shared decision-making preferences among veterans with serious mental illness. Psychiatric Serv. 2014;64(12):1409–13.

Rathert C, Wyrwich MD, Boren SA. Patient-centered care and outcomes: a systematic review of the literature. Med Care Res Rev. 2013;70(4):351–79.

Sajatovic M, Davies M, Bauer MS, McBride L, Hays RW, Safavi R, et al. Attitudes regarding the collaborative practice model and treatment adherence among individuals with bipolar disorder. Compr Psychiatry. 2005;46(4):272–7.

Simmons M, Hetrick S, Jorm A. Shared decision-making: benefits, barriers and current opportunities for application. Australas Psychiatry. 2010;18(5):394–7.

Stacey D, Menard P, Gaboury I, Jacobsen M, Sharif F, Ritchie L, et al. Decision-making needs of patients with depression: a descriptive study. J Psychiatr Ment Health Nurs. 2008;15(4):287–95.

Sylvia LG, Hay A, Ostacher MJ, Miklowitz DJ, Nierenberg AA, Thase ME, et al. Association between therapeutic alliance, care satisfaction and pharmacological adherence in bipolar disorder. J Clin Psychopharmac. 2013;33(3):343–50.

van Os TW, van den Brink RH, Tiemens BG, Jenner JA, van der Meer K, Ormel J. Communicative skills of general practitioners augment the effectiveness of guideline-based depression treatment. J Affect Disord. 2005;84(1):43–51.

WHO. DAS 2.0. 2017. http://www.who.int/classifications/icf/more_whodas/en/. Accessed 15 Jan 2018

Zheng Y, Huang W, Xiao B, Qu B, Peng W, Liu B, et al. Preferences for participation in shared decision-making among cataract patients in urban southern China: a cross-sectional study. Lancet. 2006;388(1):56.

Zijlstra P, Goossensen A. Shared decision making in de psychiatrie. Tijdschrift voor Gezondheidswetenschappen. 2007;85(2):92–7.

Lack of emotional gaze preferences using eye-tracking in remitted bipolar I disorder

John R. Purcell[1], Monika Lohani[2], Christie Musket[3], Aleena C. Hay[4], Derek M. Isaacowitz[5] and June Gruber[6*]

Abstract

Background: Bipolar disorder is associated with heightened and persistent positive emotion (Gruber in Curr Dir Psychol Sci 20:217–221, 2011; Johnson in Clin Psychol Rev 25:241–262, 2005). Yet little is known about information processing biases that may influence these patterns of emotion responding.

Methods: The current study adopted eye-tracking methodology as a continuous measure of sustained overt attention to monitor gaze preferences during passive viewing of positive, negative, and neutral standardized photo stimuli among remitted bipolar adults and healthy controls. Percentage fixation durations were recorded for predetermined areas of interest across the entire image presentation, and exploratory analyses were conducted to examine early versus late temporal phases of image processing.

Results: Results suggest that the bipolar and healthy control groups did not differ in patterns of attention bias.

Conclusions: Findings provide insight into apparently intact attention processing despite disrupted emotional responding in bipolar disorder.

Keywords: Emotion, Attention, Eye-tracking, Bipolar disorder

Background

Bipolar disorder (BD) is a severe and chronic psychiatric condition associated with functional impairment and disability (Fagiolini et al. 2005; Michalak et al. 2007). Recent models of BD stress the importance of difficulties in positive emotion processing (Gruber 2011; Phillips and Vieta 2007). An important next step is to characterize processes that may underlie and contribute to these patterns of emotion disturbance. One promising route is to explore attentional biases, which have been shown to play an important role in depression (e.g., Gotlib et al. 2004; Joormann et al. 2007). However, comparably less is known about how attentional biases contribute to disturbances in positive emotion characteristic of BD.

*Correspondence: june.gruber@colorado.edu
[6] Department of Psychology and Neuroscience, University of Colorado Boulder, 345 UCB, Muenzinger D321C, Boulder, CO 80309, USA
Full list of author information is available at the end of the article

Emotion disturbance in BD

Recent models suggest that individuals with BD experience heightened and persistent elevations in positive emotionality (e.g., Gruber 2011). This pattern is consistent with psychosocial models of BD that implicate heightened reward seeking and goal-striving (e.g., Alloy et al. 2009; Johnson 2005). For example, individuals at risk for BD and remitted BD adults self-report greater positive affect than healthy controls in response to emotional films (Gruber et al. 2011a, b), photos (M'Bailara et al. 2009), and at the prospect of earning rewards (Meyer et al. 2001). BD individuals and individuals at risk for BD also exhibit increased parasympathetic reactivity in response to emotional stimuli such as films, photos, and memories (Gruber et al. 2008, 2009; Sutton and Johnson 2002). Neuroimaging studies reveal that people with BD exhibit increased activity in brain regions typically associated with reward (e.g., ventral striatum) to positive stimuli (e.g., Dutra et al. 2015; Wessa et al. 2007). Heightened positive emotionality differentiates BD from major depressive disorder (Gruber et al. 2011a), and has important implications for psychosocial treatments aimed at reducing positive emotionality and subsequent manic episodes (e.g., Johnson 2005).

Abnormalities in negative emotionality might also be expected in BD, given the characteristic frequent and recurrent episodes of depression (Judd et al. 2003). However, the current literature suggests that people diagnosed with and at risk for BD may not differ from healthy controls in their emotional responses to negative stimuli including negative social feedback (e.g., Ruggero and Johnson 2006) and interpersonal criticism (Cuellar et al. 2009). At the same time, individuals with BD do report increased tendencies toward behavioral inhibition and neuroticism which is associated with increased negative affect (e.g., Alloy et al. 2008; Meyer et al. 2001; Murray et al. 2007).

Coinciding cognitive and emotional processes

Though many studies have evaluated abnormal emotional reactivity in a variety of populations, a critical next step includes isolating the correspondingly impaired cognitive processes in BD (Gruber 2011). Cognitive processes such as attention have long been recognized as contributing to, and being affected by, emotion (e.g. Schwarz 2000; Shimojo et al. 2003), and visual attention in particular has been shown to impact emotional responding (e.g., Cacioppo et al. 2000). One methodology well-suited to examine visual attention for emotional events is eye-tracking technology, which has allowed researchers to elucidate different patterns of visual attention to negative stimuli in mood disorders such as depression and BD (Gotlib and Joormann 2010; Gotlib et al. 2004; Mathews and MacLeod 2005).

Research suggests that adults diagnosed with depression take longer to disengage attention away from sad faces, which has been predictive of sustained negative mood (Kellough et al. 2008; Sanchez et al. 2013). A meta-analytic review of eye-tracking studies has also found that failing to attend to positive events was associated with reductions in pleasure in depressed individuals (Armstrong and Olatunji 2012). Research on BD has found impaired recognition of negative facial expressions, failure to demonstrate attentional biases towards negative stimuli (Elliott et al. 2000; Lembke and Ketter 2002), and difficulties maintaining negative emotional information (Gruber et al. 2013). These findings suggest that BD may be associated with attention *away* from negative stimuli, while depression is associated with attention *toward* it.

There has been comparatively less work examining attentional biases underlying *positive* emotion. Wadlinger and Isaacowitz (2008) found that after experimentally training healthy adult participants to selectively attend to positive information, they spent significantly less time looking at negative stimuli following the attentional training. Similarly, trait happiness is associated with increased attentional bias toward a variety of positive stimuli (Raila et al. 2015), and optimism is associated with gaze preferences away from negative health-related images (e.g., cancer tumor images; Isaacowitz 2005). Furthermore, older adults, who report higher and more stable levels of positive emotional states relative to younger adults (for review, see Lohani et al. 2013), display attentional preferences toward positive and away from negative faces (Isaacowitz et al. 2006b, 2008) and negative images (Noh et al. 2011).

However, studies on visual attention to emotional stimuli in BD have suggested that biases may be mood-congruent. For example, research has found that mildly depressed BD participants demonstrate bias towards negative and away from positive words using a modified dot-probe task compared with controls (Jongen et al. 2007). Other studies have utilized "free-looking" tasks to simultaneously display several images to subjects have demonstrated that currently manic BD adults attend more to positive images, and currently depressed BD adults attend less to positive images, as compared to controls (García-Blanco et al. 2013, 2014, 2015, 2017; Leyman et al. 2009).

These recent studies have suggested that selective attention may coincide with positive and negative mood states in BD, and that these attentional biases are not present during periods of remission. This theory has been bolstered by studies that report no group differences between those with remitted BD and healthy controls in attention bias for positive or negative faces using emotional dot-probe, and free-view, tasks (e.g., Peckham et al. 2015, 2016). Thus far, a substantial body of literature suggests that attentional processes may not harmoniously fit into the model of BD as a disorder of positive emotionality throughout all mood phases of the disorder. However, findings thus far have only investigated attentional biases to differently-valenced, simultaneously presented affective stimuli.

The present investigation

The present investigation aimed to explore attentional biases toward emotionally relevant stimuli in BD by employing continuous eye-tracking during individually presented images. By presenting images one at a time, the current study constrained participants' potential attentional biases to affectively salient vs. non-salient areas, mimicking visual field processing in a more ecologically valid way. Using this methodology, individual and age-group differences in attentional biases have been found within non-clinical populations (Isaacowitz and Choi 2011; Wadlinger and Isaacowitz 2008). For instance, compared to younger adults, older adults have been found to focus their visual attention away from more negative regions and towards non-affective regions of an image (Noh et al. 2011). Using this method, we investigated whether individuals with remitted BD would deploy attention toward more salient negative or positive regions, as opposed to the non-emotional regions, of images, and whether or not these patterns of gaze fixation would differ from healthy controls. Considering the positive emotion persistence observed in remitted BD, two hypotheses were formed (Gruber 2011). The first predicted that individuals with BD would demonstrate specific attention biases towards positive emotional stimuli (i.e. *positive amplification).* The other non-mutually exclusive hypothesis predicted that individuals with BD would demonstrate specific attentional biases away from negative emotional stimuli (i.e. *negative attenuation*).

We also conducted post hoc exploratory analyses to investigate early, relative to late, phases of image viewing as well as sustained attention across the entire duration of image viewing. This approach has shown promise in other domains of emotion and attention processing such that individuals who report higher trait levels of happiness have shown increased dwell time and fixation counts to positive compared to neutral stimuli in later, rather than early, stages of visual attention (e.g., Nakayama and Mackeben 1989; Raila et al. 2015).

Methods

Participants

Participants were recruited as part of a larger study using posted flyers, online advertisements (e.g., http://www.craigslist.org), and outpatient mental health referrals. Participant sample size was based on common standards in research with severe psychiatric samples at the time of recruitment (i.e., between 2012 and 2013) and included 35 individuals diagnosed with BD type I, currently remitted, and a healthy control (CTL) group comprising 32 individuals who did not meet current or lifetime criteria for any DSM-IV-TR Axis I disorder (First et al. 2007). BD participants were currently remitted (i.e., not in a current manic depressed, or mixed mood phase in the past month) to examine patterns of attention-related biases independent of current mood phase. Participants in the BD group were not excluded on the basis of comorbid Axis I disorders (aside from substance or alcohol abuse/dependence in the past 6 months) to ensure a more ecologically valid sample (e.g. Kessler et al. 2005). Exclusion criteria for all participants included head trauma, cognitive impairment, stroke, neurological disease, severe medical illness, or current alcohol or substance abuse/dependence in the past 6 months. All participants had normal or corrected vision by glasses or soft contact lenses. Additional tasks not relevant to the present study were also conducted the same day.[1]

Measures of clinical functioning, cognitive functioning, and visual acuity

Diagnostic evaluation and assessment of global functioning

Diagnoses were determined using the Structured Clinical Interview for DSM-IV (SCID-IV; First et al. 2007). As published in Hay et al. (2015), diagnostic ratings between the SCID interviewer matched an independent rater for a subset of participants from the larger study protocol.[2] The Global Assessment of Functioning (GAF; Luborsky 1962) Scale was used to assess current general functioning on a scale from 1 (lowest level of functioning) to 100 (highest level of functioning). Additional information about illness duration, age of onset, and lifetime number of mood episodes was also collected.

Mood symptoms

Clinician-rated symptoms of mania were assessed using the Young Mania Rating Scale (YMRS; Young et al. 1978)

[1] One other publication to date has arisen from the same broader protocol (e.g., Hay et al. 2015). The other tasks administered on the same day not yet published included experimental tasks measuring baseline emotion responding, attentional rubbernecking, and emotion and memory. We also administered a larger battery of questionnaires at the end of the study that included medication history, health information, suicidal history information, Care Satisfaction Questionnaire (e.g., Morris et al. 2005), Altman Self-Rating Mania Scale (Altman et al. 1997), BDI-SF (Beck and Beck 1972), STAI-state (Spielberger et al. 1970), SWLS (Diener et al. 1985), modified Differential Emotions Scale (Cohn et al. 2009), ERQ (Gross and John 2003), Response Style Questionnaire-Distraction subscale (Nolen-Hoeksema and Morrow 1991), Emotion Beliefs Survey (Tamir et al. 2007), Berkeley Expressivity Questionnaire (Gross and John 1997), Difficulty with Emotion Regulation Scale (Gratz and Roemer 2004), and a questionnaire assessing positive and negative affect for the Hay et al. (2015) study cited above.

[2] We provide additional details for interested readers beyond the typically brief description of inter-rater procedures common in mood-disordered studies (Gruber and Weinstock 2018). Specifically, we note for this study no consensus meetings took place for clinical diagnosis and severity ratings, as the rater performed the ratings independently (i.e., did not look at the interviewer's scores beforehand) and did not correct or modify her scores at any point. As is common practice, both the interviewers and rater consulted if diagnostic questions arose as needed. As such, the ratings reported above from Hay et al. (2015) reflect original (i.e., pre-meeting) values. Of note, this is distinct from other previously published studies from the same laboratory that do typically hold consensus meetings where major discrepancies (i.e., errors) are resolved and final ratings reflected post-meeting ratings (for a non-exaustive list of examples from our research team using this approach see: Dutra et al. 2015; Kang and Gruber 2013; Gruber et al. 2016; Ong et al. 2017). Both approaches with or without consensus meetings from this laboratory team frequently yield "almost perfect" (i.e., above 0.90) levels of agreement (e.g., McHugh 2012).

and current depression symptoms using the Inventory of Depressive Symptomatology (IDS-C; Rush et al. 1996). See Hay et al. (2015) for inter-rater reliability for the YMRS and IDS-C. Current remitted mood status was verified according to SCID-IV criteria and cutoff scores on the YMRS (≤ 7), and IDS-C (≤ 11), which reflected symptomatology within the last 7 days.

Working memory and mental status

Participants were administered the letter-number sequencing subtest of the Wechsler Adult Intelligence Scale-IV (WAIS-IV; Pearson 2008). Raw scores (ranging from 0 to 21) were calculated as the total number of trials correct, from which WAIS-IV age-normed scaled scores were computed. The Mini-Mental State Examination (MMSE) was used as a brief, objective measure of cognitive capability (Folstein et al. 1975). Raw scores (ranging from 0 to 30) were calculated as the total number of trials correct. Threshold eligibility was set at ≥ 24, and all participants met or exceeded this score.

Visual acuity

Visual acuity was measured using the Snellen Eye Chart Test (Snellen 1862) that tested participants' ability to distinguish small details by identifying different optotype letters. Participants were positioned 20 feet away from the Snellen chart in a well-lit room. Each score was given based upon a participant's ability to accurately read an entire line of the smallest distinguishable letters using the left eye (i.e. after covering the right eye).

Emotional stimuli

Emotional stimuli included 84 images from the International Affective Picture System classified according to valence intensity, and matched on normative arousal ratings across the 28 positive ($M=5.66$, $SD=0.83$) and 28 negative ($M=5.00$, $SD=0.98$) images (Lang et al. 1999). Less ideally, the 28 neutral images were less arousing on average ($M=3.15$, $SD=0.53$), but this is typical for research utilizing neutral IAPS stimuli (Schneider et al. 2016). For the present investigation, the affectively salient areas of each image were determined by tracing areas of interest (AOIs; e.g. Fig. 1) using a coding procedure similar to that of previous studies (e.g., Wadlinger and Isaacowitz 2008; Noh et al. 2011).

Emotion-related gaze task

An Applied Science Laboratories eye tracker, Model 504 (Bedford, MA) recorded the movements and position of participants' left eye sixty times per second with a camera and a non-invasive beam of infrared light. The visual fixations were defined as those series of gazes in which an individual stayed within 1° visual angle for 100 ms or longer (Manor and Gordon 2003). Visual fixations were recorded throughout the presentation of each image on a $15 \times 12''$ Dell desktop computer and calculated using GazeTracker software (Eye Response Technologies, Inc., Charlottesville, VA). To eliminate possible order effects, participants viewed all 84 images in one of three randomly generated orders, and were given the following instructions: "*Watch each image naturally, as you would if at home while watching TV. You can look anywhere on the screen, but try not to turn your head away from the screen.*" Each trial consisted of a single image, displayed at a size of 12×10.25 in. (5.0 s), followed by a buffer slide with a fixation cross (0.5 s) to realign gaze to the center of the screen.

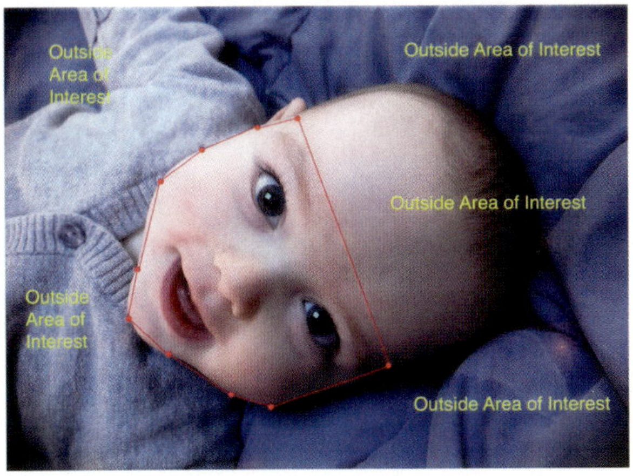

Fig. 1 Example area of interest (AOI). The area within the red lines would be coded as a positively valenced AOI and all surrounding content would be coded as outside of the AOI. No boundaries (i.e. red lines) identified the AOIs for participants during experimentation

Procedure

After obtaining informed consent, trained interviewers administered the diagnostic, symptom and cognitive measures. Next, participants' left eye visual acuity was tested. In an individual testing room, participants sat approximately 28″ away from a computer monitor. The height of the seat was also adjusted so that the participants' gaze would naturally fall in the middle of the screen while keeping their heads in a neutral position. Participants were oriented to the task both verbally by the experimenter and through a short slide presentation. The eye-tracker was then calibrated to each participant's left eye, using 17 points displayed in two concentric squares on the screen, ensuring that the tracker accurately recorded within 1° visual angle of each point (Isaacowitz et al. 2006a, b). Participants then viewed a series of images during the emotion-related gaze task. The entire task (instruction, calibration, and experimental

Table 1 Demographic, clinical and visual acuity participant characteristics

	BD ($n=24$)	Control ($n=25$)	Statistic
Demographic			
Age (years)	33.88 (12.82)	32.16 (9.59)	$F=0.29$
Female (%)	58.33%	52%	$\chi^2=0.20$
Caucasian (%)	87.50%	92%	$\chi^2=2.71$
Education (years)	14.88 (1.94)	15.86 (2.38)	$F=2.41$
Employed (%)	58.33%	64%	$\chi^2=1.66$
Partnered (%)	41.66%	60%	$\chi^2=1.64$
Number children	0.54 (0.98)	0.32 (0.80)	$F=0.76$
Annual income			$\chi^2=11.78$
< $10K	8 (33%)	3 (12%)	
$10K–$25K	10 (42%)	5 (20%)	
$26K–$50K	2 (8%)	5 (20%)	
$51K–$75K	1 (4%)	6 (24%)	
$76K–$100K	0	3 (12%)	
> $100K	3 (13%)	3 (12%)	
Cognitive			
Working memory	11.46 (2.73)	12.16 (3.39)	$F=0.63$
MMSE	28.13 (1.92)	28.88 (1.33)	$F=2.57$
Clinical			
YMRS	1.79 (2.06)	0.48 (0.71)	$F=8.99$*
IDS-C	4.25 (2.75)	2.12 (2.49)	$F=8.08$*
GAF	70.94 (8.33)	88.56 (4.78)	$F=83.121$
Age at onset (years)	16.42 (4.55)	–	–
Illness duration (years)	17.46 (13.57)	–	–
# Depressive episodes	22.48 (30.27)	–	–
# Manic episodes	15.65 (24.33)	–	–
Visual acuity			$\chi^2=2.78$
20/13	2 (8.3%)	2 (8%)	
20/15	1 (4.2%)	2 (8%)	
20/20	6 (25%)	9 (36%)	
20/25	6 (25%)	5 (20%)	
20/30	5 (20.8%)	4 (16%)	
20/40	4 (16.7%)	2 (8%)	
20/50	0 (0%)	1 (4%)	

BD bipolar I disorder group, *Employed* employed full-time or part-time; *Partnered* married or live-in-partner, *YMRS* Young Mania Rating Scale, *IDS-C* inventory to diagnose depression, *GAF* global assessment of functioning; *Age at Onset* age of first depressive or manic episode; *# Comorbid disorders* the number of current DSM-IV-TR axis I comorbidities. *# Medications* the number of psychotropic medications currently taken (including anticonvulsants, lithium, neuroleptics, anxiolytics, stimulants, antidepressants, and sedative-hypnotics). Mean values are displayed with standard deviations in parentheses where applicable

* $p<0.05$ for BD and CTL

trials) took approximately 30 min. Additional tasks unrelated to the eye-tracking task were also completed during this experimental session that same day. At the end, participants were debriefed and compensated.

Data analyses plan

The goal of this project was to compare differences in visual attention within and outside of emotional AOIs in the CTL versus BD group. First, we examined group differences in the average percent time participants fixated on emotional AOIs across the *entire* image presentation (5.0 s) to understand overall attentional biases for different image valences. Second, we examined group differences in early (0.0–2.5 s) and late (2.51–5.0 s) phases of image presentation separately (by examining the average percent time fixated on *emotional* AOI in late – early phases) to understand group differences in attentional focus towards images in the later phase of image viewing after accounting for fixation duration in the early phase. This analysis was exploratory in nature, and implemented post hoc after discovering that visual attention in later stages (i.e. 10–15 s compared to 1–10 s) of visual attention to positive stimuli has been positively associated with trait levels of happiness within non-clinical subjects (Raila et al. 2015). Whenever assumptions of sphericity were not met, adjusted degrees of freedom are reported in the results using Huynh–Feldt estimates of sphericity.

Results

Participant characteristics

Following convention in previous eye-tracking studies (e.g., Isaacowitz and Choi 2011), participants were excluded from the final analysis for incomplete data due to track ability issues including problematic pupils, glare from eyeglasses (10 BD, 5 CTL participants) and/or other technical problems experienced during their sessions (1 BD, 2 CTL participants). This left a remaining sample of 24 BD and 25 CTL participants available for final data analysis. These participants were successfully tracked for at least 65% of each eye-tracking session (e.g., Isaacowitz and Choi 2011), for an average of 91.20% successful tracking overall. Trackable and nontrackable participants within each group did not differ on demographic, cognitive, or visual measures ($ps>0.05$), and groups did not differ in percentage of trackable data (92.16 and 90.15% overall; $F(1,47)=0.92$, $p=0.34$, $\eta^2=0.001$).

As seen in Table 1, BD and CTL participants did not significantly differ with respect to age, gender, ethnicity, or education ($ps>0.05$). Not surprisingly, the BD group scored lower on global functioning than the CTL group. Although all groups scored below YMRS (≤ 7) and IDS-C (≤ 11) cutoffs, BD participants scored higher than CTL participants on the IDS-C and YMRS, and thus symptoms were controlled for in the main analyses. The groups did not differ on the baseline cognitive measures ($p>0.05$). There were no main effects for order ($ps>0.13$) or gender ($ps>0.12$) for all main variables. Finally, BD participants were currently remitted for an average of 27.57 months ($SD = 31.99$).

Validation of emotional stimuli

To ensure the validity of our emotional stimuli 100 independent judges (54.0% Female, 49.0% Caucasian, mean age = 33.69 years ($SD = 9.75$), recruited via Amazon Mechanical Turk (Buhrmester et al. 2011; Gosling et al. 2004), rated both the valence and arousal of each individual AOI, and surrounding non-AOI content, on 9-point, bipolar scales (e.g. *extremely unpleasant to extremely pleasant*). AOIs within positive images were rated as significantly more pleasant ($M = 6.34$, $SD = 0.67$) and arousing ($M = 5.02$, $SD = 0.91$) than the rest of image area (valence: $M = 5.96$, $SD = 0.71$; arousal: $M = 4.63$, $SD = 0.86$), $t(99) = 8.85$, $p < 0.001$ for valence and $t(99) = 6.14$, $p < 0.001$ for arousal. Similarly, AOIs within negative images ($M = 2.59$, $SD = 0.40$) were rated as significantly less pleasant ($M = 3.02$, $SD = 0.92$) and more arousing ($M = 5.90$, $SD = 1.07$) than the rest of the image areas (valence: $M = 3.90$, $SD = 0.98$ arousal: $M = 5.27$, $SD = 1.02$), $t(99) = -11.47$, $p < 0.001$ for valence and $t(99) = 8.234$, $p < 0.001$ for arousal.

Main analyses

In order to examine the differences in sustained attention between the BD and CTL groups we conducted a 2 (Group: BD, CTL) × 3 (Valence: Positive, Negative, Neutral) repeated-measures ANCOVA for the average percent time participants fixated on emotional AOI across the entire image presentation (5.0 s), while controlling for depression and manic symptom levels (YMRS and IDS-C scores).[3] Mauchly's test indicated that the assumption of sphericity had been violated ($p < 0.05$); therefore, degrees of freedom were corrected using Huynh–Feldt estimates of sphericity. Results revealed a main effect of Valence, $F(1.73, 77.84) = 54.35$, $p < 0.001$, $\eta^2 = 0.55$, with more percent time fixated on Neutral images ($M = 70.52$, $SE = 1.14$), followed by Positive images ($M = 67.85$, $SE = 1.20$), and Negative images ($M = 55.76$, $SE = 1.62$), thus not supporting the positive amplification nor negative attenuation hypotheses. The Group main effect ($p = 0.50$) and Group x Valence interaction were not significant ($p = 0.36$). Pairwise comparisons for each Valence type were conducted to compare the BD versus the CTL group but were not significant, ($ps > 0.21$). No significant differences were found in fixation duration patterns for the entire image presentation time.

[3] The same analyses were performed without controlling for symptomatology and results were still null.

Table 2 Mean percent fixation in non-emotional AOI regions in the early and late phases of image presentation for each picture type

Phase	Image-type	Control	BD
Early	Positive images	0.49 (0.03)	0.44 (0.04)
Late	Positive images	0.54 (0.03)	0.50 (0.004)
Early	Negative images	0.63 (0.04)	0.58 (0.05)
Late	Negative images	0.67 (0.04)	0.69 (0.06)
Early	Neutral images	0.45 (0.02)	0.41 (0.03)
Late	Neutral images	0.46 (0.03)	0.44 (0.05)

Mean values are displayed with standard error values in parentheses where applicable

BD bipolar I disorder group

Exploratory analyses

Next, we conducted exploratory analyses to explore whether attentional profiles were sensitive to the temporal dynamics of visual attention by examining the average percent time participants fixated at *emotional* AOI separately for the early and late phases of image presentation by computing a difference score by subtracting fixation % from the late − early phase scores (Table 2). There was a marginally significant effect of valence, $F(2, 90) = 2.95$, $p = 0.06$, $\eta^2 = 0.06$. No main effect of group ($p = 0.79$) or group × valence interaction effect was found, ($p = 0.43$). None of the between-subjects comparisons were found significant, $ps > 0.34$.[4]

Discussion

Bipolar disorder (BD) is a chronic psychiatric disorder that is associated with heightened and persistent positive emotion and reward sensitivity, even during periods of remission from mood episodes (M'Bailara et al. 2009; Gruber 2011; Johnson 2005). Attentional biases toward positive emotion stimuli have been shown to be related to trait positive emotionality in multiple populations, and BD individuals currently experiencing manic symptoms have been shown to show attentional biases to positive visual stimuli; however, recent literature suggests that

[4] Although not part of the main results reported in this study, for full transparency we note that we also examined the average percent time participants fixated at *non-emotional* AOI. We then computed a difference score by subtracting fixation % from the late − early phase scores. No significant effects of valence ($p = 0.11$), group ($p = 0.21$), or valence × group were significant ($p = 0.21$). A post hoc comparison of CTL versus BD group for negative images was significant: $t(47) = 2.58$, $p = 0.01$, Cohen's $d = 0.75$ (large effect). Examination of the mean values for the Early and Late phases of image presentation appear to suggest that the BD group fixated significantly more at non-emotional regions in the Late phase (versus the early phase) of viewing negative images compared to the CTL group. Given the small sample size and large effect size (especially in the absence of other significant group differences; $ps > 0.64$), we believe this finding should be interpreted with extreme caution.

these biases may not present in *remitted* BD (García-Blanco et al. 2013, 2014, 2015, 2017). The current study sought to clarify the potential attentional biases to emotionally-valenced stimuli in remitted BD patients, as compared to healthy controls, using a continuous eye-tracking methodology (which is novel in this population). Overall, we found no significant group differences in fixation time towards emotionally-valenced stimuli, suggesting an area of relative strength in remitted BD patients.

No support for positive amplification or negative attenuation perspectives

We examined whether remitted BD was associated with attentional bias towards positive stimuli or away from negative stimuli, both of which may facilitate sustained positive mood perhaps even independent of current mood state. Somewhat surprisingly, we did not find support for either perspective. The absence of support for the *positive amplification* hypothesis is consistent with previous findings suggesting that visual biases are mood-dependent in BD (Lembke and Ketter 2002), and do not differ from non-clinical controls during remission (García-Blanco et al. 2013, 2014, 2015, 2017; Peckham et al. 2015, 2016). However, these findings are somewhat inconsistent with previous research in which high trait hypomania (Putman et al. 2007) were associated with gaze preferences for positive stimuli.

The absence of support for the *negative attenuation* perspective is also surprising as those with BD have exhibited impaired recognition of negative facial expressions and failed to demonstrate attentional biases towards negative stimuli (Elliott et al. 2000; Lembke and Ketter 2002) and demonstrate difficulties maintaining negative emotional information (Gruber et al. 2013). However, this absence of group effects is consistent with other recent null group findings in remitted adults with BD across experimental dot-probe and free-viewing eye-tracking tasks (Peckham et al. 2015, 2016).

Implications of findings for positive emotion disturbance in BD

These findings are not necessarily inconsistent with positive emotion persistence in BD, which is quantified by emotion responsivity and reactivity. Rather, they suggest that persistent emotional reactivity and responsiveness may be unrelated to bottom-up involuntary attention biases to positive emotion stimuli. However, more research is required to elucidate the relationship between emotion, attention, and symptomatology in BD (for review, see Lima et al. 2017).

Conclusion

The current study expanded further upon the body of emotional visual biases in remitted BD by assessing fixation time within affective areas (i.e., AOIs) of an image. These findings broaden our understanding of emotion processing in BD by assessing whether visual attention is differentially allocated within a single emotional image, rather than between several emotionally valenced images. This distinction is important, as visual attentional tasks typically present simultaneous, distinct options for gaze, which may not mirror ecologically-valid visual scenes that include both emotionally salient regions as well as less emotionally salient regions. Overall, the results suggest that remitted BD is not characterized by differential visual attention biases to affective regions of stimuli compared to non-clinical controls.

Limitations

Findings from the present study should be interpreted within the confines of several limitations. First, although the images used in the present study are standardized and reliable elicitors of emotions, it could be argued that the results may not be generalizable to everyday emotional experiences or visual scenes in the lives of BD patients. Thus, it will be important for future studies to assess attention biases using stimuli that are more ecologically valid (e.g., personalized emotional images), and perhaps more dynamic in nature (e.g., remembering the temporal sequence of an emotional event) and personally salient (e.g., autobiographical memories). Second, the use of complex static images may have introduced variance in emotional gaze responses, which may have driven observed attentional patterns towards or away from the image (e.g., Raila et al. 2015). Third, we acknowledge that our sample sizes were relatively modest despite mirroring sample sizes typically reported in experimental psychopathology research among BD patients (e.g., Robinson et al. 2006). Future studies would benefit from larger sample sizes. Fourth, the sample consisted largely of Caucasian participants and results may not generalize to a more diverse sample. Fifth, individuals in the BD group were not excluded on the basis of comorbidities to ensure a more ecologically valid sample so future research should examine how the presence of specific comorbid disorders influences emotional attention biases. Finally, given the possible confound of psychotropic medication, future paradigms with random assignment to different medication classes are warranted. Specifically, future research might include a control group that is matched on the same comorbid conditions, as well as assignment of BD individuals on different medication classes (e.g., antidepressants, mood stabilizers, anxiolytics).

Future directions

While the current study was not designed to investigate emotion regulation, it sheds light on an important cognitive component of emotion regulation; namely attention allocation to affective stimuli or situations (Gross 2015). Difficulty with selecting and independently implementing appropriate positive emotion regulation strategies is characteristic of BD (Gruber et al. 2012; Hay et al. 2015). Despite these issues, visual attention to affective stimuli has not been associated with self-reported emotion regulation (Peckham et al. 2016). Our results indicate that BD is not inherently characterized by a universal attentional bias toward or away from affective stimuli; however, a more targeted evaluation of whether or not visual attention biases contribute to, or are impacted by, the implementation of emotion regulation strategies is necessary. If visual attention to affective stimuli is unaltered in individuals with BD during emotion regulation efforts, other components or stages of emotion regulation such as appraisal, reactivity, and strategy implementation could be targets of treatment and intervention to improve emotion regulation in individuals with BD.

Authors' contributions

JG, ML, and DI designed and piloted the task. JP, CM, AH, and JG oversaw data collection. ML, JG, JP, and CM complied and analyzed the data. AH oversaw and conducted the inter-rater reliability analyses. JG oversaw manuscript writing with substantial contributions and feedback from all authors. All authors read and approved the final manuscript.

Author details

[1] Department of Psychological and Brain Sciences, Indiana University, 1101 E. 10th St., Bloomington, IN 47405, USA. [2] Department of Psychology, University of Utah, 201 Presidents Circle, Salt Lake City, UT 84112, USA. [3] Department of Psychology, University of Pittsburgh, 210 South Bouquet St, #4209, Pittsburgh, PA 15260, USA. [4] Department of Psychological and Brain Sciences, Boston University, 648 Beacon St., 6th Floor, Boston, MA 02215, USA. [5] Department of Psychology, Northeastern University, 360 Huntington Ave., Boston, MA 02115, USA. [6] Department of Psychology and Neuroscience, University of Colorado Boulder, 345 UCB, Muenzinger D321C, Boulder, CO 80309, USA.

Acknowledgements

We thank Sohini Bandy, Colin Bosma, Anjali Ambani, Hillary Devlin, Anny Dow, Melissa DuBois, Sunny Dutra, Kirsten Gilbert, Franziska Goer, Amanda Purcell, Elizabeth Reeves, Razia Sukaina Sahi, and Corinne Sejourne for assistance.

Competing interests

The authors declare that they have no competing interests.

Funding

This work was supported by a CTSA Grant UL1 RR024139 from the National Center for Research Resources (NCRR) and the National Center for Advancing Translational Science (NCATS), NIH roadmap for Medical Research (JG), NIMH T32MH103213 (JP), and Indiana CTSI Predoctoral Award Grant UL1 TR001108 (JP). Its contents are solely the responsibility of the authors and do not necessarily represent the official view of NIH.

References

Alloy LB, Abramson LY, Walshaw PD, Cogswell A, Grandin LD, Hughes ME, Iacoviello BM, Whitehouse WG, Urosevic S, Nusslock R, Hogan ME. Behavioral approach system and behavioral inhibition system sensitivities and bipolar spectrum disorders: prospective prediction of bipolar mood episodes. Bipolar Disord. 2008;10(2):310–22. https://doi.org/10.1111/j.1399-5618.2007.00547.x.

Alloy LB, Abramson LY, Urosevic S, Bender RE, Wagner CA. Longitudinal predictors of bipolar spectrum disorders: a behavioral approach system perspective. Clin Psychol Sci Pract. 2009;16(2):206–26. https://doi.org/10.1111/j.1468-2850.2009.01160.x.

Altman EG, Hedeker D, Peterson JL, Davis JM. The altman self-rating mania scale. Biol Psychiat. 1997;42:948–55. https://doi.org/10.1016/S0006-3223(96)00548-3.

Armstrong T, Olatunji BO. Eye tracking of attention in the affective disorders: a meta-analytic review and synthesis. Clin Psychol Rev. 2012;32(8):704–23. https://doi.org/10.1016/j.cpr.2012.09.004.

Beck AT, Beck RW. Screening depressed patients in a family practice: a rapid technique. Postgrad Med. 1972;52:81–5.

Buhrmester M, Kwang T, Gosling SD. Amazon's mechanical turk: a new source of inexpensive, yet high-quality, data? Perspect Psychol Sci. 2011;6(1):3–5. https://doi.org/10.1177/1745691610393980.

Cacioppo JT, Berntson GG, Larsen JT, Poehlmann KM, Ito TA. The psychophysiology of emotion. Handbook Emotions. 2000;2:173–91. https://doi.org/10.1017/cbo9780511546396.025.

Cohn MA, Fredrickson BL, Brown SL, Mikels JA, Conway AM. Happiness unpacked: positive emotions increase life satisfaction by building resilience. Emotion. 2009;9(3):361–8. https://doi.org/10.1037/a0015952.

Cuellar AK, Johnson SL, Ruggero CJ. Affective reactivity in response to criticism in remitted bipolar disorder: a laboratory analog of expressed emotion. J Clin Psychol. 2009;65(9):925–41. https://doi.org/10.1002/jclp.20596.

Diener E, Emmons RA, Larsen RJ, Griffin S. The satisfaction with life scale. J Pers Assess. 1985;49:71–5. https://doi.org/10.1207/s15327752jpa4901_13.

Dutra SJ, Cunningham WA, Kober H, Gruber J. Elevated striatal reactivity across monetary and social rewards in bipolar I disorder. J Abnorm Psychol. 2015;124(4):890. https://doi.org/10.1037/abn0000092.supp.

Elliott R, Rubinsztein JS, Sahakian BJ, Dolan RJ. Selective attention to emotional stimuli in a verbal go/no-go task: an fMRI study. NeuroReport. 2000;11(8):1739–44. https://doi.org/10.1097/00001756-200006050-00028.

Fagiolini A, Kupfer DJ, Masalehdan A, Scott JA, Houck PR, Frank E. Functional impairment in the remission phase of bipolar disorder. Bipolar Disord. 2005;7(3):281–5. https://doi.org/10.1111/j.1399-5618.2005.00207.x.

First MB, Spitzer RL, Gibbon M, Williams J. Structured clinical interview for DSM-IV-TR axis I disorders, research version, patient edition (SCID-VP). New York: Biometrics Research, New York State Psychiatric Institute; 2007.

Folstein MF, Folstein SE, McHugh PR. "Mini-mental state": a practical method for grading the cognitive state of patients for the clinician. J Psychiatr Res. 1975;12(3):189–98. https://doi.org/10.1016/0022-3956(75)90026-6.

García-Blanco AC, Perea M, Livianos L. Mood-congruent bias and attention shifts in the different episodes of bipolar disorder. Cogn Emot. 2013;27(6):1114–21. https://doi.org/10.1080/02699931.2013.764281.

García-Blanco A, Salmerón L, Perea M, Livianos L. Attentional biases toward emotional images in the different episodes of bipolar disorder: an eye-tracking study. Psychiatry Res. 2014;215(3):628–33. https://doi.org/10.1016/j.psychres.2013.12.039.

García-Blanco A, Salmerón L, Perea M. Attentional capture by emotional scenes across episodes in bipolar disorder: evidence from a free-viewing task. Biol Psychol. 2015;108:36–42. https://doi.org/10.1016/j.biopsycho.2015.03.010.

García-Blanco A, Salmerón L, Perea M. Inhibitory control for emotional and neutral scenes in competition: an eye-tracking study in bipolar disorder. Biol Psychol. 2017;127:82–8. https://doi.org/10.1016/j.biopsycho.2017.05.006.

Gosling SD, Vazire S, Srivastava S, John OP. Should we trust web-based studies? A comparative analysis of six preconceptions about internet questionnaires. Am Psychol. 2004;59(2):93–104. https://doi.org/10.1037/0003-066x.59.2.93.

Gotlib IH, Joormann J. Cognition and depression: current status and future directions. Ann Rev Clin Psychol. 2010;6:285–312. https://doi.org/10.1146/annurev.clinpsy.121208.131305.

Gotlib IH, Krasnoperova E, Yue DN, Joormann J. Attentional biases for negative interpersonal stimuli in clinical depression. J Abnorm Psychol. 2004;113(1):127–35. https://doi.org/10.1037/0021-843x.113.1.121.

Gratz KL, Roemer L. Multidimensional assessment of emotion regulation and dysregulation: development, factor structure, and initial validation of the difficulties in emotion regulation scale. J Psychopathol Behav Assess. 2004;26(1):41–54.

Gross JJ. Emotion regulation: current status and future prospects. Psychol Inq. 2015;26(1):1–26.

Gross JJ, John OP. Revealing feelings: facets of emotional expressivity in self-reports, peer ratings, and behavior. J Pers Soc Psychol. 1997;72:435–48.

Gross JJ, John OP. Individual differences in two emotion regulation processes: implications for affect, relationships, and well-being. J Pers Soc Psychol. 2003;85:348–62.

Gruber J. Can feeling too good be bad? Positive emotion persistence (PEP) in bipolar disorder. Curr Dir Psychol Sci. 2011;20(4):217–21. https://doi.org/10.1177/0963721411414632.

Gruber J, Weinstock LM. Interrater reliability in bipolar disorder research: a brief note on current practices and suggestions for enhancing best practices. Int J Bipolar Dis. 2018. https://doi.org/10.1186/s40345-017-0111-7.

Gruber J, Johnson SL, Oveis C, Keltner D. Risk for mania and positive emotional responding: too much of a good thing? Emotion. 2008;8(1):23–33. https://doi.org/10.1037/1528-3542.8.1.23.

Gruber J, Harvey AG, Johnson SL. Reflective and ruminative processing of positive emotional memories in bipolar disorder and healthy controls. Behav Res Ther. 2009;47(8):697–704. https://doi.org/10.1016/j.brat.2009.05.005.

Gruber J, Harvey AG, Purcell AL. What goes up can come down? A preliminary investigation of emotion reactivity and emotion recovery in bipolar disorder. J Affect Disord. 2011a;133(3):457–66. https://doi.org/10.1016/j.jad.2011.05.009.

Gruber J, Oveis C, Keltner D, Johnson SL. A discrete emotions approach to positive emotion disturbance in depression. Cogn Emot. 2011b;25(1):40–52. https://doi.org/10.1080/02699931003615984.

Gruber J, Harvey AG, Gross JJ. When trying is not enough: emotion regulation and the effort–success gap in bipolar disorder. Emotion. 2012;12(5):997–1003. https://doi.org/10.1037/a0026822.

Gruber J, Purcell AL, Perna M, Mikels JA. Letting go of the bad: deficits in maintaining negative, but not positive, emotion in bipolar disorder. Emotion. 2013;13(1):168–75. https://doi.org/10.1037/a0029381.

Gruber J, Siegel EH, Purcell AL, Earls HA, Cooper G, Feldman Barrett L. Unseen positive and negative affective information influences social perception in bipolar I disorder and healthy adults. J Affect Disord. 2016;192:191–8. https://doi.org/10.1016/j.jad.2015.12.037.

Hay AC, Sheppes G, Gross JJ, Gruber J. Choosing how to feel: emotion regulation choice in bipolar I disorder. Emotion. 2015;15(2):139–45. https://doi.org/10.1037/emo0000024.

Isaacowitz DM. The gaze of the optimist. Pers Soc Psychol Bull. 2005;31(3):407–25. https://doi.org/10.1177/0146167204271599.

Isaacowitz DM, Choi Y. The malleability of age-related positive gaze preferences: training to change gaze and mood. Emotion. 2011;11(1):90–100. https://doi.org/10.1037/a0021551.

Isaacowitz DM, Wadlinger HA, Goren D, Wilson HR. Is there an age-related positivity effect in visual attention? A comparison of two methodologies. Emotion. 2006a;6(3):511–6. https://doi.org/10.1037/1528-3542.6.3.511.

Isaacowitz DM, Wadlinger HA, Goren D, Wilson HR. Selective preference in visual fixation away from negative images in old age? An eye tracking study. Psychol Aging. 2006b;21(1):40–8. https://doi.org/10.1037/0882-7974.21.1.40.

Isaacowitz DM, Toner K, Goren D, Wilson HR. Looking while unhappy: mood congruent gaze in young adults, positive gaze in older adults. Psychol Sci. 2008;19(9):848–53. https://doi.org/10.1111/j.1467-9280.2008.02167.x.

Johnson SL. Mania and dysregulation in goal pursuit: a review. Clin Psychol Rev. 2005;25(2):241–62. https://doi.org/10.1016/j.cpr.2004.11.002.

Jongen EM, Smulders FT, Ranson SM, Arts BM, Krabbendam L. Attentional bias and general orienting processes in bipolar disorder. J Behav Ther Exp Psychiatry. 2007;38(2):168–83. https://doi.org/10.1016/j.jbtep.2006.10.007.

Joormann J, Talbot L, Gotlib IH. Biased processing of emotional information in girls at risk for depression. J Abnorm Psychol. 2007;116(1):135–43. https://doi.org/10.1037/0021-843X.116.1.135.

Judd LL, Akiskal HS, Schettler PJ, Coryell W, Endicott J, Maser JD, Solomon DA, Leon AC, Keller MB. A prospective investigation of the natural history of the long-term weekly symptomatic status of bipolar II disorder. Arch Gen Psychiatry. 2003;60(3):261–9. https://doi.org/10.1001/archpsyc.60.3.261.

Kang Y, Gruber J. Harnessing happiness? Uncontrollable positive emotion in bipolar disorder, major depression, bipolar and healthy adults. Emotion. 2013;13(2):290–301. https://doi.org/10.1037/a0030780.

Kellough JL, Beevers CG, Ellis AJ, Wells TT. Time course of selective attention in clinically depressed young adults: an eye tracking study. Behav Res Ther. 2008;46(11):1238–43. https://doi.org/10.1016/j.brat.2008.07.004.

Kessler RC, Chiu WT, Demler O, Walters EE. Prevalence, severity, and comorbidity of 12-month DSM-IV disorders in the National Comorbidity Survey Replication. Arch Gen Psychiatry. 2005;62(6):617–27. https://doi.org/10.1001/archgenpsychiatry.2011.12.

Lang PJ, Bradley MM, Cuthbert BN. International affective picture system (IAPS): affective ratings of pictures and instruction manual. Technical Report A-6. Gainesville: University of Florida; 1999.

Lembke A, Ketter TA. Impaired recognition of facial emotion in mania. Am J Psychiatry. 2002;159(2):302–4. https://doi.org/10.1176/appi.ajp.159.2.302.

Leyman L, De Raedt R, Koster EH. Attentional biases for emotional facial stimuli in currently depressed patients with bipolar disorder. Int J Clin Health Psychol. 2009;9(3):393–410.

Lima IM, Peckham AD, Johnson SL. Cognitive deficits in bipolar disorders: implications for emotion. Clin Psychol Rev. 2017;56:126–36. https://doi.org/10.1016/j.cpr.2017.11.006.

Lohani M, Larcom MJ, Isaacowitz DM. Happier & older? Age-related effects on positive emotion. In: Gruber J, Moskowitz J, editors. The light and dark sides of positive emotion. Oxford: Oxford University Press; 2013.

Luborsky L. Clinicians' judgments of mental health: a proposed scale. Arch Gen Psychiatry. 1962;7(6):407–17. https://doi.org/10.1001/archpsyc.1962.01720060019002.

M'Bailara K, Demotes-Mainard J, Swendsen J, Mathieu F, Leboyer M, Henry C. Emotional hyper-reactivity in normothymic bipolar patients. Bipolar Disord. 2009;11(1):63–9. https://doi.org/10.1111/j.1399-5618.2008.00656.x.

Manor BR, Gordon E. Defining the temporal threshold for ocular fixation in free-viewing visuocognitive tasks. J Neurosci Methods. 2003;128(1–2):85–93. https://doi.org/10.1016/s0165-0270(03)00151-1.

Mathews A, MacLeod C. Cognitive vulnerability to emotional disorders. Ann Rev Clin Psychol. 2005;1:167–95. https://doi.org/10.1146/annurev.clinpsy.1.102803.143916.

McHugh ML. Interrater reliability: the kappa statistic. Biochemica Medica. 2012;22(3):276–82.

Meyer B, Johnson SL, Winters R. Responsiveness to threat and incentive in bipolar disorder: relations of the BIS/BAS scales with symptoms. J Psychopathol Behav Assess. 2001;23(3):133–43. https://doi.org/10.1023/a:1010929402770.

Michalak EE, Yatham LN, Maxwell V, Hale S, Lam RW. The impact of bipolar disorder upon work functioning: a qualitative analysis. Bipolar Disord. 2007;9(1–2):126–43. https://doi.org/10.1111/j.1399-5618.2007.00436.x.

Morris CD, Miklowitz DJ, Wisniewski SR, Giese AA, Thomas MR, Allen MH. Care satisfaction, hope, and life functioning among adults with bipolar disorder: data from the first 1000 participants in the Systematic Treatment Enhancement Program. Compr Psychiatry. 2005;46(2):98–104.

Murray G, Goldstone E, Cunningham E. Personality and the predisposition(s) to bipolar disorder: heuristic benefits of a two-dimensional model. Bipolar Disord. 2007;9(5):453–61. https://doi.org/10.1111/j.1399-5618.2007.00456.x.

Nakayama K, Mackeben M. Sustained and transient components of focal visual attention. Vision Res. 1989;29:1631–47. https://doi.org/10.1016/0042-6989(89)90144-2.

Noh SR, Lohani M, Isaacowitz DM. Deliberate real-time mood regulation in adulthood: the importance of age, fixation and attentional functioning. Cogn Emot. 2011;25(6):998–1013. https://doi.org/10.1080/02699931.2010.541668.

Nolen-Hoeksema S, Morrow J. A prospective study of depression and post-traumatic stress symptoms after a natural disaster: the 1989 Loma Prieta earthquake. J Pers Soc Psychol. 1991;61:115–21. https://doi.org/10.1037/0022-3514.61.1.115.

Ong DC, Zaki J, Gruber J. Increased cooperative behavior across remitted bipolar I disorder and major depression: insights utilizing a behavioral economic trust game. J Abnorm Psychol. 2017;126(1):1–7. https://doi.org/10.1037/xge0000252.

Pearson. WAIS-IV technical and interpretive manual. San Antonio: Pearson; 2008.

Peckham AD, Johnson SL, Gotlib IH. Attentional bias in euthymic bipolar I disorder. Cogn Emot. 2015. https://doi.org/10.1080/02699931.2015.1014313.

Peckham AD, Johnson SL, Tharp JA. Eye tracking of attention to emotion in bipolar I disorder: links to emotion regulation and anxiety comorbidity. Int J Cogn Ther. 2016;9(4):295–312. https://doi.org/10.1521/ijct_2016_09_12.

Phillips ML, Vieta E. Identifying functional neuroimaging markers of bipolar disorder: towards DSM-V. Schizophr Bull. 2007;33(4):893–904. https://doi.org/10.1093/schbul/sbm060.

Putman P, Saevarsson S, Van Honk J. Hypomanic trait is associated with a hypovigilant automatic attentional response to social cues of danger. Bipolar Disord. 2007;9(7):779–83. https://doi.org/10.1111/j.1399-5618.2007.00425.x.

Raila H, Scholl BJ, Gruber J. Seeing the world through rose-colored glasses: people who are happy and satisfied with life preferentially attend to positive stimuli. Emotion. 2015;15(4):449. https://doi.org/10.1037/emo0000049.

Robinson LJ, Thompson JM, Gallagher P, Goswami U, Young AH, Ferrier IN, Moore PB. A meta-analysis of cognitive deficits in euthymic patients with bipolar disorder. J Affect Disord. 2006;93(1):105–15. https://doi.org/10.1016/j.jad.2006.02.016.

Ruggero C, Johnson SL. Reactivity to a laboratory stressor among individuals with bipolar I disorder in full or partial remission. J Abnorm Psychol. 2006;115(3):539–44. https://doi.org/10.1037/0021-843x.115.3.539.

Rush AJ, Gullion CM, Basco MR, Jarrett RB, Trivedi MH. The inventory of depressive symptomatology (IDS): psychometric properties. Psychol Med. 1996;26:477–86. https://doi.org/10.1017/s0033291700035558.

Sanchez A, Vazquez C, Marker C, LeMoult J, Joormann J. Attentional disengagement predicts stress recovery in depression: an eye-tracking study. J Abnorm Psychol. 2013;122(2):303–13. https://doi.org/10.1037/a0031529.

Schneider IK, Veenstra L, van Harreveld F, Schwarz N, Koole SL. Let's not be indifferent about neutrality: neutral ratings in the International Affective Picture System (IAPS) mask mixed affective responses. Emotion. 2016;16(4):426.

Schwarz N. Emotion, cognition, and decision making. Cogn Emot. 2000;14(4):433–40. https://doi.org/10.1080/026999300402745.

Shimojo S, Simion C, Shimojo E, Scheier C. Gaze bias both reflects and influences preference. Nat Neurosci. 2003;6(12):1317.

Snellen H. Letterproeven tot bepaling der gezichtsscherpte. Utrecht: Van de Weyer; 1862.

Spielberger CD, Gorsuch RL, Lushene RE. Manual for the state-trait anxiety inventory. Palo Alto: Consulting Psychologists Press; 1970.

Sutton SK, Johnson SL. Hypomanic tendencies predict lower startle magnitudes during pleasant pictures. Psychophysiology. 2002;S39:80.

Tamir M, John OP, Srivastava S, Gross JJ. Implicit theories of emotion: affective and social outcomes across a major life transition. J Pers Soc Psychol. 2007;92(4):731–44. https://doi.org/10.1037/0022-3514.92.4.731.

Wadlinger HA, Isaacowitz DM. Looking happy: the experimental manipulation of a positive visual attention bias. Emotion. 2008;8(1):121–6. https://doi.org/10.1037/1528-3542.8.1.121.

Wessa M, Houenou J, Paillère-Martinot ML, Berthoz S, Artiges E, Leboyer M, Martinot JL. Fronto-striatal overactivation in euthymic bipolar patients during an emotional go/nogo task. Am J Psychiatry. 2007;164(4):638–46. https://doi.org/10.1176/appi.ajp.164.4.638.

Young RC, Biggs JT, Ziegler VE, Meyer DA. A rating scale for mania: reliability, validity, and sensitivity. Br J Psychiatry. 1978;133:429–35. https://doi.org/10.1192/bjp.133.5.429.

23

The challenges of living with bipolar disorder: a qualitative study of the implications for health care and research

Eva F. Maassen[1,2*], Barbara J. Regeer[1], Eline J. Regeer[2], Joske F. G. Bunders[1] and Ralph W. Kupka[2,3]

Abstract

Background: In mental health care, clinical practice is often based on the best available research evidence. However, research findings are difficult to apply to clinical practice, resulting in an implementation gap. To bridge the gap between research and clinical practice, patients' perspectives should be used in health care and research. This study aimed to understand the challenges people with bipolar disorder (BD) experience and examine what these challenges imply for health care and research needs.

Methods: Two qualitative studies were used, one to formulate research needs and another to formulate healthcare needs. In both studies focus group discussions were conducted with patients to explore their challenges in living with BD and associated needs, focusing on the themes diagnosis, treatment and recovery.

Results: Patients' needs are clustered in 'disorder-specific' and 'generic' needs. Specific needs concern preventing late or incorrect diagnosis, support in search for individualized treatment and supporting clinical, functional, social and personal recovery. Generic needs concern health professionals, communication and the healthcare system.

Conclusion: Patients with BD address disorder-specific and generic healthcare and research needs. This indicates that disorder-specific treatment guidelines address only in part the needs of patients in everyday clinical practice.

Background

Bipolar disorder (BD) is a major mood disorder characterized by recurrent episodes of depression and (hypo) mania (Goodwin and Jamison 2007). According to the Diagnostic and Statistical Manual 5 (DSM-5), the two main subtypes are BD-I (manic episodes, often combined with depression) and BD-II (hypomanic episodes, combined with depression) (APA 2014). The estimated lifetime prevalence of BD is 1.3% in the Dutch adult population (de Graaf et al. 2012), and BD is associated with high direct (health expenditure) and indirect (e.g. unemployment) costs (Fajutrao et al. 2009; Michalak et al. 2012), making it an important public health issue. In addition to the economic impact on society, BD has a tremendous impact on patients and their caregivers (Granek et al. 2016; Rusner et al. 2009). Even between mood episodes, BD is often associated with functional impairment (Van Der Voort et al. 2015; Strejilevich et al. 2013), such as occupational or psychosocial impairment (Huxley and Baldessarini 2007; MacQueen et al. 2001; Yasuyama et al. 2017). Apart from symptomatic recovery, treatment can help to overcome these impairments and so improve the person's quality of life (IsHak et al. 2012).

Evidence Based Medicine (EBM), introduced in the early 1990s, is a prominent paradigm in modern (mental) health care. It strives to deliver health care based on the best available research evidence, integrated with individual clinical expertise (Sackett et al. 1996). EBM was introduced as a new paradigm to *'de-emphasize intuition'* and '*unsystematic clinical experience*' (Guyatt et al. 1992) (p. 2420). Despite its popularity *in principle* (Barratt 2008), EBM has also been criticized. One such criticism is the ignorance of patients' preferences and healthcare needs (Bensing 2000). A second criticism relates to the difficulty

*Correspondence: e.maassen@altrecht.nl
[2] Altrecht Institute for Mental Health Care, Nieuwe Houtenseweg 12, 3524 SH Utrecht, Netherlands
Full list of author information is available at the end of the article

of adopting evidence-based treatment options in clinical practice (Bensing 2000), due to the fact that research outcomes measured in 'the gold standard' randomized-controlled trials (RCTs) seldom correspond to the outcomes clinical practice seeks and are not responsive to patients' needs (Newnham and Page 2010). Moreover, EBM provides an overview on population level instead of individual level (Darlenski et al. 2010). Thus, adopting research evidence in clinical practice entails difficulties, resulting in an implementation gap.

To bridge the gap between research and clinical practice, it is argued that patients' perspectives should be used in both health care and research. Patients have experiential knowledge about their illness, living with it in their personal context and their care needs (Tait 2005). This is valuable for both clinical practice and research as their knowledge complements that of health professionals and researchers (Tait 2005; Broerse et al. 2010; Caron-Flinterman et al. 2005). This source of knowledge can be used in the process of translating evidence into clinical practice (Schrevel 2015). Moreover, patient participation can enhance the clinical relevance of and support for research and the outcomes in practice (Abma and Broerse 2010). Hence, it is argued that these perspectives should be explicated and integrated into clinical guidelines, clinical practice, and research (Misak 2010; Rycroft-Malone et al. 2004).

Given the advantages of including patients' perspectives, patients are increasingly involved in healthcare services (Bagchus et al. 2014; Larsson et al. 2007), healthcare quality (e.g. guideline development) (Pittens et al. 2013) and health-related research (e.g. agenda setting, research design) (Broerse et al. 2010; Boote et al. 2010; Elberse et al. 2012; Teunissen et al. 2011). However, patients' perspectives on health care and on research are often studied separately. We argue that to be able to provide care focused on the patients and their needs, care and research must closely interact.

We hypothesize that the challenges BD patients experience and the associated care and research needs are interwoven, and that combining them would provide a more comprehensive understanding. We hypothesize that this more comprehensive understanding would help to close the gap between clinical practice and research. For this reason, this study aims to understand the challenges people with BD experience and examine what these challenges imply for healthcare and research needs.

Methods

To understand the challenges and needs of people with BD, we undertook two qualitative studies. The first aimed to formulate a research agenda for BD from a patient's perspective, by gaining insights into their challenges and research needs. A second study yielded an understanding of the care needs from a patient's perspective. In this article, the results of these two studies are combined in order to investigate the relationship between research needs and care needs. Challenges are defined as 'difficulties patients face, due to having BD'. Care needs are defined as that what patients 'desire to receive from healthcare services to improve overall health' (Asadi-Lari et al. 2004) (p. 2). Research needs are defined as that what patients 'desire to receive from research to improve overall health'.

Study on research needs

In this study, mixed-methods were used to formulate research needs from a patient's perspective. First six focus group discussions (FGDs) with 35 patients were conducted to formulate challenges in living with BD and hopes for the future, and to formulate research needs arising from these difficulties and aspirations. These research needs were validated in a larger sample ($n=219$) by means of a questionnaire. We have reported this study in detail elsewhere (Maassen et al. 2018).

Study on care needs

This study was part of a nationwide Dutch project to generate a practical guideline for BD: a translation of the existing clinical guideline to clinical practice, resulting in a standard of care that patients with BD could expect. The practical guideline (Netwerk Kwaliteitsontwikkeling GGZ 2017) was written by a taskforce comprising health professionals, patients. In addition to the involvement of three BD patients in the taskforce, a systematic qualitative study was conducted to gain insight into the needs of a broader group of patients.

Participants and data collection

To formulate the care needs of people with BD, seven FGDs were conducted, with a total of 56 participants, including patients ($n=49$) and caregivers ($n=9$); some participants were both patient and caregiver. The inclusion criteria for patients were having been diagnosed with BD, aged 18 years or older and euthymic at time of the FGDs. Inclusion criteria for caregivers were caring for someone with BD and aged 18 years or older. To recruit participants, a maximum variation sampling strategy was used to collect a broad range of care needs (Kuper et al. 2008). First, all outpatient clinics specialized in BD affiliated with the Dutch Foundation for Bipolar Disorder (Dutch: Kenniscentrum Bipolaire Stoornissen) were contacted by means of an announcement at regular meetings and by email if they were interested to participate. From these outpatient clinics, patients were recruited by means of flyers and posters. Second, patients were recruited at a quarterly meeting of the Dutch patient and caregiver association for bipolar disorder. The FGDs were conducted between March and May 2016.

The FGDs were designed to address challenges experienced in BD health care and areas of improvement for health care for people with BD. The FGDs were structured by means of a guide and each session was facilitated by two moderators. The leading moderator was either BJR or EFM, having both extensive experience with FGD's from previous studies. The first FGD explored a broad range of needs. The subsequent six FGDs aimed to gain a deeper understanding of these care needs, and were structured according to the outline of the practical guideline (Netwerk Kwaliteitsontwikkeling GGZ 2017). Three chapters were of particular interest: diagnosis, treatment and recovery. These themes were discussed in the FGDs, two in each session, all themes three times in total. Moreover, questions on specific aspects of care formulated by the members of the workgroup were posed. The sessions took 90–120 min. The FGDs were audiotaped and transcribed verbatim. A summary of the FGDs was sent to the participants for a member check.

Data analysis

To analyze the data on challenges and needs, a framework for thematic analysis to identify, analyze and report patterns (themes) in qualitative data sets by Braun and Clarke (2006) was used. First, we familiarized ourselves with the data by carefully reading the transcripts. Second, open coding was used to derive initial codes from the data. These codes were provided to quotes that reflected a certain challenge or care need. Third, we searched for patterns within the codes reflecting challenges and within those reflecting needs. For both challenges and needs, similar or overlapping codes were clustered into themes. Subsequently, all needs were categorized as 'specific' or 'generic'. The former are specific to BD and the latter are relevant for a broad range of psychiatric illnesses. Finally, a causal analysis provided a clear understanding of how challenges related to each other and how they related to the described needs.

To analyze the data on needs regarding recovery, four domains were distinguished, namely clinical, functional, social and personal recovery (Lloyd et al. 2008; van der Stel 2015). Clinical recovery refers to symptomatic remission; functional recovery concerns recovery of functioning that is impaired due to the disorder, particularly in the domain of executive functions; social recovery concerns the improvement of the patient's position in society; personal recovery concerns the ability of the patient to give meaning to what had happened and to get a grip on their own life. The analyses were discussed between BR and EM. The qualitative software program MAX QDA 11.1.2 was used (MaxQDA).

Ethical considerations

According to the Medical Ethical Committee of VU University Medical Center, the Medical Research Involving Human Subjects Act does not apply to the current study. All participants gave written or verbal informed consent regarding the aim of the study and for audiotaping and its use for analysis and scientific publications. Participation was voluntary and participants could withdraw from the study at any time. Anonymity was ensured.

Results

This section is in three parts. The first presents the participants' characteristics. The second presents the challenges BD patients face, derived from both studies, and the disorder-specific care and research needs associated with these challenges. The third part describes the generic care needs that patients formulated.

Characteristics of the participants

In the study on care needs, 56 patients and caregivers participated. The mean age of the participants was 52 years (24–75), of whom 67.8% were women. The groups varied from four to sixteen participants, and all groups included men and women. Of all participants 87.5% was diagnosed with BD, of whom 48.9% was diagnosed with BD I. 3.5% was both caregivers and diagnosed with BD. Of 4 patients the age was missing, and from 6 patients the bipolar subtype.

Diagnosis

Despite the fact that participants acknowledge the inevitable diagnostic difficulties of a complex disorder like BD, in both studies they describe a range of challenges in different phases of the diagnostic process (Fig. 1). Patients explained that the general practitioner (GP) and society in general did not recognize early-warning signs and mood swings were not well interpreted, resulting in late or incorrect diagnosis. Patients formulated a need for more research on what early-warning signs could be and on how to improve GPs' knowledge about BD. Formulated care needs were associated with GPs using this knowledge to recognize early-warning signs in individual patients. One participant explained that certain symptoms must be noticed and placed in the right context:

> *I call it, 'testing overflow of ideas'. [....] When it happens for the first time you yourself do not recognize it. Someone else close to you or the health professional, who is often not involved yet, must signal it. (FG6)*

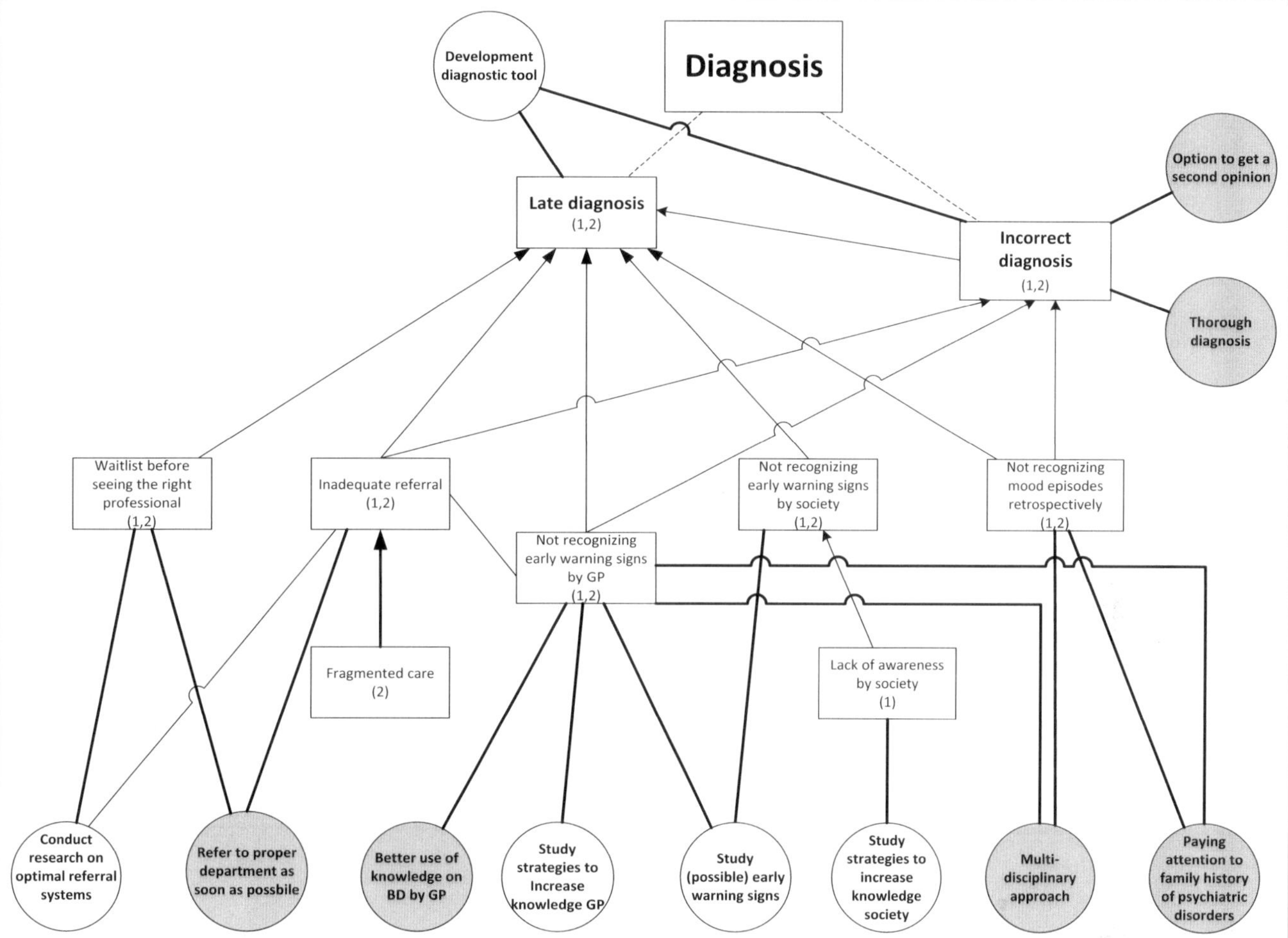

Fig. 1 Challenges with diagnosis (squares) including relating research needs (white circles) and care needs (grey circles). (1): mentioned in study on research needs; (2): mentioned in study on care needs. Dotted lines: division of challenges into sub challenges. Arrows: causal relation between challenges

Moreover, these challenges are associated with the need to pay attention to family history and to use a multidisciplinary approach to diagnosis to benefit from multiple perspectives. The untimely recognition of early symptoms also results in another challenge: inadequate referral to the right specialized health professional. After referral, people often face a waiting list, again causing delay in the diagnostic process. These challenges result in the need for research on optimal referral systems and the care need for timely referral. One participant described her process after the GP decided to refer her:

> *But, yes, at that moment the communication wasn't good at all. Because the general practitioner said: 'she urgently has to be seen by someone'. Subsequently, three weeks went by, until I finally arrived at depression [department]. And at that department they said: 'well, you are in the wrong place, you need to go to bipolar [department]'. (FG1)*

The challenge of being misdiagnosed is associated with the need to be able to ask for a second opinion and to have a timely and thorough diagnosis. On the one hand, it is important for patients that health professionals quickly understand what is going on, on the other hand that health professionals take the time to thoroughly investigate the symptoms by making several appointments.

Treatment

From both studies, two main challenges related to the treatment of BD were derived (Fig. 2). The first is finding appropriate and satisfactory treatment. Participants explained that it is difficult to find the right medication and dosage that is effective and has acceptable side-effects. One participant illustrates:

> *I think, at one point, we have to choose, either overweight or depressed. (FG1)*

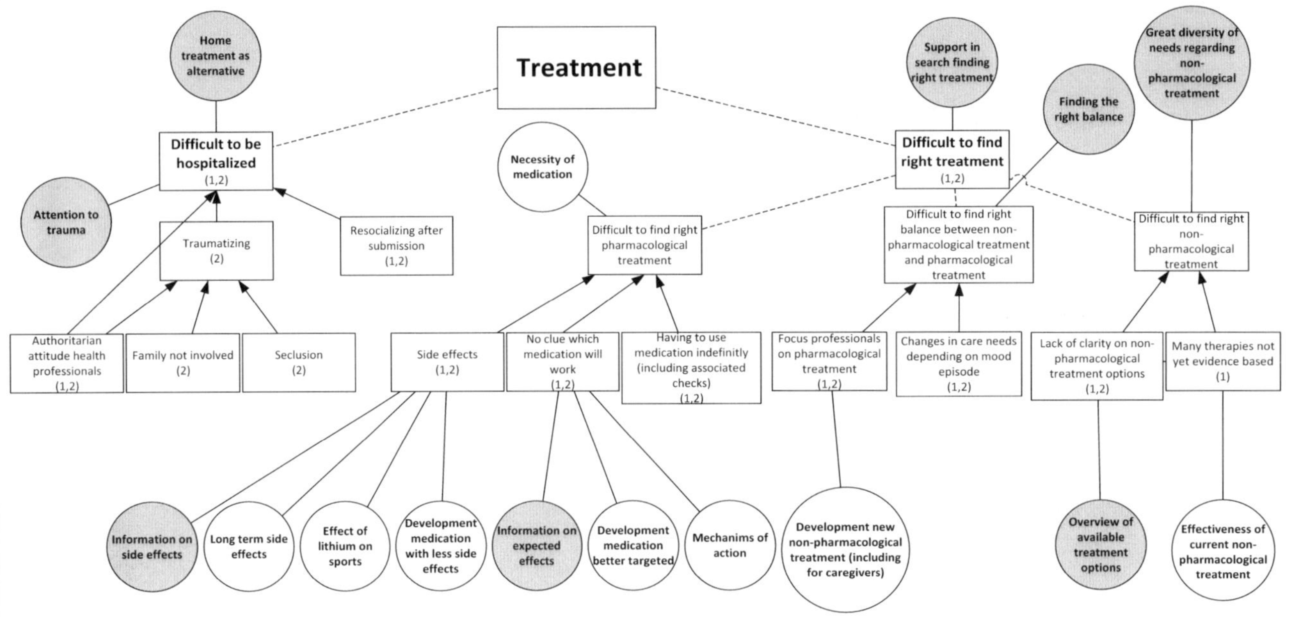

Fig. 2 Challenges with treatment (squares) including relating research needs (white circles) and care needs (grey circles). (1): mentioned in study on research needs; (2): mentioned in study on care needs. Dotted lines: division of challenges into sub challenges. Arrows: causal relation between challenges

Some participants said that they struggle with having to use medication indefinitely, including the associated medical checks. The difficult search for the right pharmacological treatment results in the need for research on long-term side-effects, on the mechanism of action of medicine and on the development of better targeted medication with fewer adverse side-effects. In care, patients would appreciate all the known information on the side-effects and intended effects. One participant explained the importance of being properly informed about medication:

> *I don't read anything [about medication], because then I wouldn't dare taking it. But I do think, when you explain it well, the advantages, the disadvantages, the treatment, the idea behind it, that would help a lot in compliance. (FG1)*

A second aspect is the challenge of finding non-pharmacological therapies that fit patients' needs. They said they and the health professionals often do not know which non-pharmacological therapies are available and effective:

> *But we found the carefarm ourselves[1] [....]. You have to search for yourself completely. Yes, I actually hoped that that would be presented to you, like: 'this would be something for you.' (FG3)*

Participants mentioned a variety of non-pharmacological therapies they found useful, namely cognitive behavior therapy (CBT), EMDR, running therapy, social-rhythm training, light therapy, mindfulness, psychotherapy, psychoeducation, and training in living with mood swings. They formulated the care need to receive an overview of all available treatment options in order to find a treatment best suited to their needs. They would appreciate research on the effectiveness of non-pharmacological treatments.

A third aspect within this challenge is finding the right balance between non-pharmacological and pharmacological treatment. Participants differed in their opinion about the need for medication. Whereas some participants stated that they need medication to function, others pointed out that they found non-pharmacological treatments effective, resulting in less or no medication use. They explained that the preferred balance can also change over time, depending on their mood. However, they experience a dominant focus on pharmacological treatment by the health professionals. To address this challenge, patients need support in searching for an appropriate balance.

[1] Care farm: farms that combine agriculture and services for people with disabilities (Iancu 2013). These farms are used as interventions in mental care throughout Europe and the USA to facilitate recovery (Iancu et al. 2014).

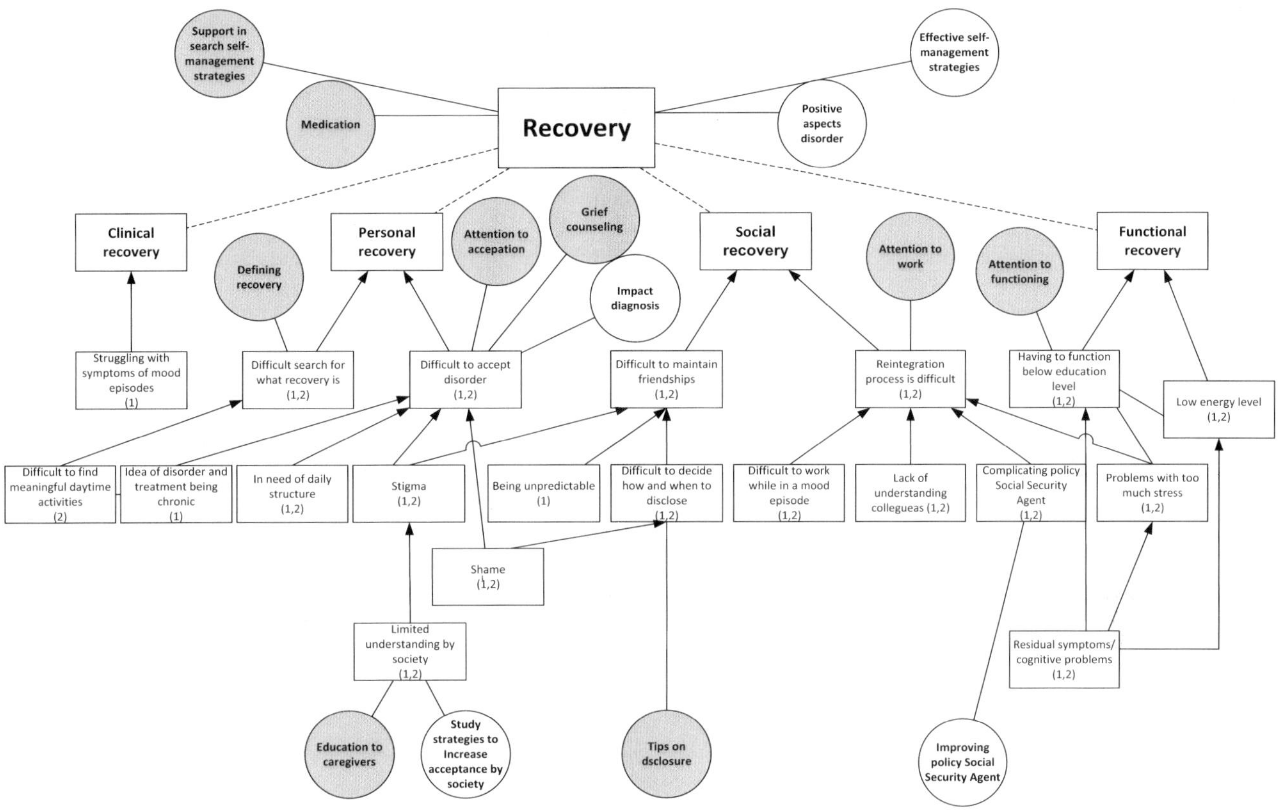

Fig. 3 Challenges with recovery (squares) including relating research needs (white circles) and care needs (grey circles). (1): mentioned in study on research needs; (2): mentioned in study on care needs. Dotted lines: division of challenges into sub challenges. Arrows: causal relation between challenges

Next to the challenge of finding appropriate and satisfactory treatment, a second treatment-related challenge is hospitalization. Participants often had a traumatic experience, due to seclusion, the authoritarian attitudes of clinical staff, and not involving their family. Patients therefore found it important to try preventing being hospitalized, for example by means of home treatment, which some participants experienced positively. Despite the challenges relating to hospitalization, participants did acknowledge that in some cases it cannot be avoided, in which case they urged for close family involvement, open communication and being treated by their own psychiatrist. Still, in the study on research needs, hospitalization did not emerge as an important research theme.

Recovery

In both studies, participants described challenges in all four domains of recovery: clinical, functional, social and personal (Fig. 3). In relation to clinical recovery, participants struggled with the symptoms of mood episodes, the psychosis and the fear of a future episode. In contrast, some participants mentioned that they sometimes miss the hypomanic state they had experienced previously due to effective medical treatment. In the domain of functional recovery, participants contended with having to function below their educational level due to residual symptoms, such as cognitive problems, due to the importance of preventing stress in order to reduce the risk of a new episode, and because of low energy levels. This leads to the care need that health professionals should pay attention to the level of functioning of their patients.

In the domain of social recovery, participants described challenges with maintaining friendships, due to stigma, being unpredictable and with deciding when to disclose the disorder. The latter resulted in the care need for tips on disclosure. Moreover, patients experienced challenges with reintegration to work, due to colleagues' lack of understanding, problems with functioning during an episode, the complicating policy of the (Dutch) Employee Insurance Agency[2] in relation to the fluctuating course of BD and the negative impact of stress. These challenges are associated with the care need that health

[2] A government agency involved in the implementation of employee insurance and providing labor market and data services.

professionals should pay attention to work and the need for research on how to improve the Social Security Agency's policy.

For their personal recovery, participants struggled with acceptance of the disorder, due to shame, stigma, having to live by structured rules and disciplines, and the chronic nature of BD. This results in care needs for grief counselling and attention to acceptance and the need for research on the impact of being diagnosed with BD. Limited understanding within society also causes problems with acceptance, corresponding with the care need for education for caregivers and for research on how to increase social acceptance. Another challenge in personal recovery was discovering what recovery means and what constitute meaningful daily activities. Patients appreciated the support of health professionals in this area. One participant described the difficult search for the meaning of recovery:

> *I have been looking to recover towards the situation [before diagnosis] for a long time; that I could do what I always did and what I liked. But then I was confronted with the fact that I shouldn't expect that to happen, or only with a lot of effort. (...) Then you start thinking, now what? A compromise. I don't want to call that recovery, but it is a recovered, partly accepted, situation. But it is not recovery as I expected it to be. (FG5)*

In general, participants considered frequent contact with a nurse or psychiatrist supportive, to help them monitor their mood and help them find (efficient) self-management strategies. Most participants appreciated the involvement of caregivers in the treatment and contact with peers.

Generic care needs

We have described BD-specific needs, but patients mentioned also mentioned several generic care needs. The latter are clustered into three categories. The first concerns *the health professionals*. Participants stressed the importance of a good health professional, who carefully listens, takes time, and makes them feel understood, resulting in a sense of connection. Furthermore, a good health professional treats beyond the guideline, and focuses on the needs of the individual patient. When there is no sense of connection, it should be possible to change to another health professional. The second category concerns *communication between the patient and the health professional*. Health professionals should communicate in an open, honest and clear way both in the early diagnostic phase and during treatment. Open communication facilitates individualized care, in which the patient is involved in decision making. In addition, participants wanted to be treated as a person, not as a patient, and according to a strength-based approach. The third category concerns needs at the level of *the healthcare system*. Participants struggled with the availability of the health professionals and preferred access to good care 24/7 and being able to contact their health professional quickly when necessary. Currently, according to the participants, the care system is not geared to the mood swings of BD, because patients often faced waiting lists before they could see a health professional.

> *Is adequate treatment also having a number from a mental health institution you can always call when you are in need, that you can go there? And not that you can go in three weeks, but on a really short notice. So at least a phone call. (FG3)*

Participants were often frustrated by the limited collaboration between health professionals, within their own team, between departments of the organization, and between different organizations, including complementary health professionals. They would appreciate being able to merge their conventional and complementary treatment, with greater collaboration among the different health professionals. Furthermore, they would like continuity of health professionals as this improves both the diagnostic phase and treatment, and because that health professional gets to know the patient.

Discussion

We hypothesized that research and care needs of patients are closely intertwined and that understanding these, by explicating patients' perspectives, could contribute to closing the gap between research and care. Therefore, this study aimed to understand the challenges patients with BD face and examine what these imply for both healthcare and research. In the study on needs for research and in the study on care needs, patients formulated challenges relating to receiving the correct diagnosis, finding the right treatment, including the proper balance between non-pharmacological and pharmacological treatment, and to their individual search for clinical, functional, social and personal recovery. The formulated needs in both studies clearly reflected these challenges, leading to closely corresponding needs. Another important finding of our study is that patients not only formulate disorder-specific needs, but also many generic needs.

The needs found in our study are in line with the current literature on the needs of patients with BD, namely for more non-pharmacological treatment (Malmström et al. 2016; Nestsiarovich et al. 2017), timely recognition of early-warning signs and self-management strategies to prevent a new episode (Goossens et al. 2014), better information on treatment and treatment alternatives

(Malmström et al. 2016; Neogi et al. 2016) and coping with grief (Goossens et al. 2014). Moreover, the need for frequent contact with health professionals, being listened to, receiving enough time, shared decision-making on pharmacological treatment, involving caregivers (Malmström et al. 2016; Fisher et al. 2017; Skelly et al. 2013), and the urge for better access to health care and continuity of health professionals (Nestsiarovich et al. 2017; Skelly et al. 2013) are confirmed by the literature. Our study added to this set of literature by providing insights in patients' needs in the diagnostic process and illustrating the interrelation between research needs and care needs from a patient's perspective.

The generic healthcare needs patients addressed in this study are clustered into three categories: *the health professional, communication between the patient and the health professional* and *the health system.* These categories all fit in a model of patient-centered care (PCC) by Maassen et al. (2016) In their review, patients' perspectives on good care are compared with academic perspectives of PCC and a model of PCC is created comprising four dimensions: *patient, health professional, pattent–professional interaction* and *healthcare organization.* All the generic needs formulated in this study fit into these four dimensions. The need to be treated as a person with strengths fits the dimension 'patient', and the need for a good health professional who carefully listens, takes time and makes them feel understood, resulting in a good connection with the professional, fits the dimension 'health professional' of this model. Furthermore, patients in this study stressed the importance of open communication in order to provide individualized care, which fits the dimension of 'patient–professional interaction'. The urge for better access to health care, geared to patients' mood swings and the need for better collaboration between health professionals and continuity of health professionals fits the dimension of 'health care organization' of the model. This study confirms the findings from the review and contributes to the literature stressing the importance of a patient-centered care approach (Mills et al. 2014; Scholl et al. 2014).

In the prevailing healthcare paradigm, EBM, the best available evidence should guide treatment of patients (Sackett et al. 1996; Darlenski et al. 2010). This evidence is translated into clinical and practical guidelines, which thus facilitate EBM and could be used as a decision-making tool in clinical practice (Skelly et al. 2013). For many psychiatric disorders, treatment is based on such *disorder-specific* clinical and practical guidelines. However, this disease-focused healthcare system has contributed to its fragmented nature Stange (2009) argues that this fragmented care system has expanded without the corresponding ability to integrate and personalize accordingly. We argue that acknowledging that *disorder-specific* clinical and practical guidelines address only parts of the care needs is of major importance, since otherwise important aspects of the patients' needs will be ignored. Because there is an increasing acknowledgement that health care should be responsive to the needs of patients and should change from being disease-focused towards being patient-focused (Mead and Bower 2000; Sidani and Fox 2014), currently in the Netherlands generic practical guidelines are written on specific care themes (e.g. comorbidity, side-effects, daily activity and participation). These generic practical guidelines address some of the generic needs formulated by the patients in our study. We argue that in addition to disorder-specific guidelines, these generic practical guidelines should increasingly be integrated into clinical practice, while health professionals should continuously be sensitive to other emerging needs. We believe that an integration of a disorder-centered and a patient-centered focus is essential to address all needs a patient.

Strengths, limitations and future research

This study has several strengths. First, it contributes to the literature on the challenges and needs of patients with BD. Second, the study is conducted from a patient's perspective. Moreover, addressing this aim by conducting two separate studies enabled us to triangulate the data.

This study also has several limitations. First, this study reflects the challenges, care needs and research needs of Dutch patient with BD and caregivers. Despite the fact that a maximum variation sampling strategy was used to derive a broad range of challenges and needs throughout the Netherlands, the Dutch setting of the study may limit the transferability to other countries. To understand the overlap and differences between countries, similar research should be conducted in other contexts. Second, given the design of the study, we could not differentiate between patients and caregivers since they participated together in the FGDs. More patients than caregivers participated in the study. For a more in-depth understanding of the challenges and needs faced by caregivers, in future research separate FGDs should be conducted. Third, due to the fixed outline of the practical guideline used to conduct the FGDs, only the healthcare needs for diagnosis, treatment and recovery of BD are studied. Despite the fact that these themes might cover a broad range of health care, it could have resulted in overlooking certain needs in related areas of well-being. Therefore, future research should focus on needs outside of these themes in order to provide a complete set of healthcare needs.

Conclusion

Patients and their caregivers face many challenges in living with BD. Our study contributes to the literature on care and research needs from a patient perspective. Needs specific for BD are preventing late or incorrect diagnosis, support in search for individualized treatment, and supporting clinical, functional, social and personal recovery. Generic healthcare needs concern health professionals, communication and the healthcare system. This explication of both disorder-specific and generic needs indicates that clinical practice guidelines should address and integrate both in order to be responsive to the needs of patients and their caregivers.

Authors' contributions

EFM designed the study, contributed to the data collection, managed the analysis and wrote the first draft of the manuscript. BJR designed the study and contributed to the data collection, data analysis, and writing of the manuscript. JFGB contributed to the study design and critical revision of the manuscript. EJR contributed to the study conception and critical revision of the manuscript. RWK contributed to the study design, acquisition of data, and critical revision of the manuscript. All authors contributed to the final manuscript. All authors read and approved the final manuscript.

Author details

[1] Athena Institute, Faculty of Earth and Life Sciences, VU University Amsterdam, Boelelaan 1085, 1081HV Amsterdam, Netherlands. [2] Altrecht Institute for Mental Health Care, Nieuwe Houtenseweg 12, 3524 SH Utrecht, Netherlands. [3] Amsterdam Public Health Research Institute, Amsterdam UMC, Vrije Universiteit Amsterdam, Psychiatry, De Boelelaan 1117, Amsterdam, Netherlands.

Competing interests

The authors declare that they have no competing interests.

Funding

The authors received no financial support for the research.

References

Abma T, Broerse J. Patient participation as dialogue: setting research agendas. Health Expect. 2010;13(2):160–73.

APA. Beknopt overzicht van de criteria (DSM-5). Nederlands vertaling van de Desk Reference to the Diagnostic Criteria from DSM-5. Amsterdam: Boom; 2014.

Asadi-Lari M, Tamburini M, Gray D. Patients' needs, satisfaction, and health related quality of life: towards a comprehensive model. Health Qual Life Outcomes. 2004;2:1–15.

Bagchus C, Dedding C, Bunders JFG. "I"m happy that I can still walk'—participation of the elderly in home care as a specific group with specific needs and wishes. Health Expect. 2014;18(6):1–9.

Barratt A. Evidence based medicine and shared decision making: the challenge of getting both evidence and preferences into health care. Patient Educ Couns. 2008;73(3):407–12.

Bensing J. Bridging the gap. The separate worlds of evidence-based medicine and patient-centered medicine. Patient Educ Couns. 2000;39:17–25.

Boote J, Baird W, Beecroft C. Public involvement at the design stage of primary health research: a narrative review of case examples. Health Policy. 2010;95(1):10–23.

Braun V, Clarke V. Using thematic analysis in psychology. Qual Res Psychol. 2006;3(2):77–101.

Broerse J, Zweekhorst M, van Rensen A, de Haan M. Involving burn survivors in agenda setting on burn research: an added value? Burns. 2010;36(2):217–31.

Caron-Flinterman JF, Broerse JEW, Bunders JFG. The experiential knowledge of patients: a new resource for biomedical research? Soc Sci Med. 2005;60(11):2575–84.

Darlenski RB, Neykov NV, Vlahov VD, Tsankov NK. Evidence-based medicine: facts and controversies. Clin Dermatol. 2010;28(5):553–7.

de Graaf R, ten Have M, van Gool C, van Dorsselaer S. Prevalence of mental disorders and trends from 1996 to 2009. Results from the Netherlands Mental Health Survey and Incidence Study-2. Soc Psychiatry Psychiatr Epidemiol. 2012;47(2):203–13.

Elberse J, Pittens C, de Cock Buning T, Broerse J. Patient involvement in a scientific advisory process: setting the research agenda for medical products. Health Policy. 2012;107(2–3):231–42.

Fajutrao L, Locklear J, Priaulx J, Heyes A. A systematic review of the evidence of the burden of bipolar disorder in Europe. Clin Pract Epidemiol Ment Health. 2009;5(1):3.

Fisher A, Manicavasagar V, Sharpe L, Laidsaar-Powell R, Juraskova I. A qualitative exploration of patient and family views and experiences of treatment decision-making in bipolar II disorder. J Ment Health. 2017;27(1):66–79.

Goodwin FK, Jamison KR. Manic-depressive illness: bipolar disorder and recurrent depression. 2nd ed. New York: Oxford University Press; 2007.

Goossens P, Knoopert-van der Klein E, Kroon H, Achterberg T. Self reported care needs of outpatients with a bipolar disorder in the Netherlands: a quantitative study. J Psychiatr Ment Health Nurs. 2014;14:549–57.

Granek L, Danan D, Bersudsky Y, Osher Y. Living with bipolar disorder: the impact on patients, spouses, and their marital relationship. Bipolar Disord. 2016;18(2):192–9.

Guyatt G, Cairns J, Churchill D, Cook D, Haynes B, Hirsh J, Irvine J, Levine M, Levine M, Nishikawa J, Sackett D, Brill-Edwards P, Gerstein H, Gibson J, Jaeschke R, Kerigan A, Neville A, Panju A, Detsky A, Enkin M, Frid P, Gerrity M, Laupacis A, Lawrence V, Menard J, Moyer V, Mulrow C, Links P, Oxman A, Sinclair J, Tugwell P. Evidence-based medicine: a new approach to teaching the practice of medicine. JAMA. 1992;268(17):2420–5.

Huxley N, Baldessarini R. Disability and its treatment in bipolar disorder patients. Bipolar Disord. 2007;9(1–2):183–96.

Iancu SC. New dynamics in mental health recovery and rehabilitation. Amsterdam: Vu University; 2013.

Iancu SC, Zweekhorst MBM, Veltman DJ, Van Balkom AJLM, Bunders JFG. Mental health recovery on care farms and day centres: a qualitative comparative study of users' perspectives. Disabil Rehabil. 2014;36(7):573–83.

IsHak WW, Brown K, Aye SS, Kahloon M, Mobaraki S, Hanna R. Health-related quality of life in bipolar disorder. Bipolar Disord. 2012;14(1):6–18.

Kuper A, Lingard L, Levinson W. Critically appraising qualitative research. BMJ. 2008;337(7671):687–9.

Larsson IE, Sahlsten MJM, Sjöström B, Lindencrona CSC, Plos KAE. Patient participation in nursing care from a patient perspective: a grounded theory study. Scand J Caring Sci. 2007;21(3):313–20.

Lloyd C, Waghorn G, Williams PL. Conceptualising recovery in mental health. Br J Occup Ther. 2008;71:321–8.

Maassen EF, Schrevel SJC, Dedding CWM, Broerse JEW, Regeer BJ. Comparing patients' perspectives of "good care" in Dutch outpatient psychiatric services with academic perspectives of patient-centred care. J Ment Health. 2016;26(1):1–11.

Maassen EF, Regeer BJ, Bunders JGF, Regeer EJ, Kupka RW. A research agenda for bipolar disorder developed from a patient's perspective. J Affect Disord. 2018;239:11–17. https://doi.org/10.1016/j.jad.2018.05.061.

MacQueen GM, Young LT, Joffe RT. A review of psychosocial outcome in patients with bipolar disorder. Acta Psychiatr Scand. 2001;103(3):163–70.

Malmström E, Hörberg N, Kouros I, Haglund K, Ramklint M. Young patients' views about provided psychiatric care. Nord J Psychiatry. 2016;70(7):521–7.

MaxQDA [Internet]. Available from: https://www.maxqda.com/. Accessed 2 Aug 2018.

Mead N, Bower P. Patient-centredness: a conceptual framework and review of the empirical literature. Soc Sci Med. 2000;51(7):1087–110.

Michalak EE, Hole R, Livingston JD, Murray G, Parikh SV, Lapsley S, et al. Improving care and wellness in bipolar disorder: origins, evolution and future

directions of a collaborative knowledge exchange network. Int J Ment Health Syst. 2012;6:16.
Mills I, Frost J, Cooper C, Moles DR, Kay E. Patient-centred care in general dental practice—a systematic review of the literature. BMC Oral Health. 2014;14(1):64.
Misak CJ. Narrative evidence and evidence-based medicine. J Eval Clin Pract. 2010;16(2):392–7.
Neogi R, Chakrabarti S, Grover S. Health-care needs of remitted patients with bipolar disorder: a comparison with schizophrenia. World J Psychiatry. 2016;6(4):431–41.
Nestsiarovich A, Hurwitz NG, Nelson SJ, Crisanti AS, Kerner B, Kuntz MJ, et al. Systemic challenges in bipolar disorder management: a patient-centered approach. Bipolar Disord. 2017;19(8):676–88.
Netwerk Kwaliteitsontwikkeling GGZ. Zorgstandaard Bipolaire stoornissen. 2017;1–54.
Newnham EA, Page AC. Bridging the gap between best evidence and best practice in mental health. Clin Psychol Rev. 2010;30(1):127–42.
Pittens C, Noordegraaf A, van Veen S, Broerse J. The involvement of gynaecological patients in the development of a clinical guideline for resumption of (work) activities in the Netherlands. Health Expect. 2013;18:1397–412.
Rusner M, Carlsson G, Brunt D, Nyström M. Extra dimensions in all aspects of life—the meaning of life with bipolar disorder. Int J Qual Stud Health Well-being. 2009;4(3):159–69.
Rycroft-Malone J, Seers K, Titchen A, Harvey G, Kitson A, McCormack B. What counts as evidence in evidence-based practice? J Adv Nurs. 2004;47(1):81–90.
Sackett D, Rosenberg W, Gray J, Haynes R, Richardson W. Evidence based medicine: what it is and what it isn't. Br Med J. 1996;312(7023):71–2.
Scholl I, Zill JM, Härter M, Dirmaier J. An integrative model of patient-centeredness—a systematic review and concept analysis. PLoS ONE. 2014;9(9):e107828.
Schrevel SJC. Surrounded by controversy: perspectives of adults with ADHD and health professionals on mental healthcare. Amsterdam: VU University; 2015.
Sidani S, Fox M. Patient-centered care: clarification of its specific elements to facilitate interprofessional care. J Interprof Care. 2014;28(2):134–41.
Skelly N, Schnittger RI, Butterly L, Frorath C, Morgan C, McLoughlin DM, et al. Quality of care in psychosis and bipolar disorder from the service user perspective. Qual Health Res. 2013;23(12):1672–85.
Stange KC. The problem of fragmentation and the need for integrative solutions. Ann Fam Med. 2009;7(2):100–3.
Strejilevich SA, Martino DJ, Murru A, Teitelbaum J, Fassi G, Marengo E, et al. Mood instability and functional recovery in bipolar disorders. Acta Psychiatr Scand. 2013;128(3):194–202.
Tait L. Encouraging user involvement in mental health services. Adv Psychiatr Treat. 2005;11(3):168–75.
Teunissen T, Visse M, De Boer P, Abma TA. Patient issues in health research and quality of care: an inventory and data synthesis. Health Expect. 2011;16:308–22.
van der Stel. Het begrip herstel in de psychische gezondheidzorg, Leiden; 2015. p. 1–3.
Van Der Voort TYG, Van Meijel B, Hoogendoorn AW, Goossens PJJ, Beekman ATF, Kupka RW. Collaborative care for patients with bipolar disorder: effects on functioning and quality of life. J Affect Disord. 2015;179:14–22.
Yasuyama T, Ohi K, Shimada T, Uehara T, Kawasaki Y. Differences in social functioning among patients with major psychiatric disorders: interpersonal communication is impaired in patients with schizophrenia and correlates with an increase in schizotypal traits. Psychiatry Res. 2017;249:30–4.

24

Clinical characteristics of patients with bipolar disorder and premorbid traumatic brain injury

Ole Kristian Drange[1,2*], Arne Einar Vaaler[1,2], Gunnar Morken[1,2], Ole Andreas Andreassen[3,4], Ulrik Fredrik Malt[3,5] and Per Ivar Finseth[6]

Abstract

Background: About one in ten diagnosed with bipolar disorder (BD) has experienced a premorbid traumatic brain injury (TBI), while not fulfilling the criteria of bipolar and related disorder due to another medical condition (BD due to TBI). We investigated whether these patients have similar clinical characteristics as previously described in BD due to TBI (i.e. more aggression and irritability and an increased hypomania/mania:depression ratio) and other distinct clinical characteristics.

Methods: Five hundred five patients diagnosed with BD type I, type II, or not otherwise specified, or cyclothymia were interviewed about family, medical, and psychiatric history, and assessed with the Young Mania Rating Scale (YMRS) and the Inventory of Depressive Symptoms Clinician Rated 30 (IDS-C_{30}). Principal component analyses of YMRS and IDS-C_{30} were conducted. Bivariate analyses and logistic regression analyses were used to compare clinical characteristics between patients with (n = 37) and without (n = 468) premorbid TBI.

Results: Premorbid TBI was associated with a higher YMRS disruptive component score (OR 1.7, 95% CI 1.1–2.4, p = 0.0077) and more comorbid migraine (OR 4.6, 95% CI 1.9–11, p = 0.00090) independently of several possible confounders. Items on disruptive/aggressive behaviour and irritability had the highest loadings on the YMRS disruptive component. Premorbid TBI was not associated with an increased hypomania/mania:depression ratio.

Conclusions: Disruptive symptoms and comorbid migraine characterize BD with premorbid TBI. Further studies should examine whether the partial phenomenological overlap with BD due to TBI could be explained by a continuum of pathophysiological effects of TBI across the diagnostic dichotomy.

Keywords: Bipolar disorder, Brain injuries, Diagnosis, Principal component analysis, Irritable mood, Migraine disorders

Background

About one in ten diagnosed with bipolar disorder (BD) has experienced a premorbid traumatic brain injury (TBI) (Sagduyu 2002; Orlovska et al. 2014; Chi et al. 2016). An association between TBI and risk of BD is established by nation-wide cohort studies from Denmark (Orlovska et al. 2014) and Taiwan (Chi et al. 2016) and a meta-analysis of prior smaller studies (Perry et al. 2016). The nature of this association could theoretically include inverse causation, confounding, and causation (Malaspina et al. 2001). A review on the topic using Bradford Hill's criteria finds evidence for a causal relationship in some cases (van Reekum and Cohen 2000). The American Psychiatric Association also acknowledges that TBI can cause BD (American Psychiatric Association 2013).

The Diagnostic and Statistical Manual of Mental Disorders 5th edition (DSM 5) distinguishes between a diagnosis of BD and a diagnosis of bipolar and related disorder due to another medical condition (in the context of this

*Correspondence: ole.kristian.drange@gmail.com
[2] Department of Østmarka, Division of Mental Health Care, St. Olavs Hospital, Trondheim University Hospital, Trondheim, Norway
Full list of author information is available at the end of the article

paper abbreviated to BD due to TBI) (American Psychiatric Association 2013). To fulfil the criteria of the latter, there must be evidence from the history (e.g. an acute or subacute onset of the mood disturbance after the onset of the general medical condition), physical examination, or laboratory findings that the mood disturbance is the direct physiological consequence of the general medical condition. Similar criteria exist for the corresponding diagnosis in the DSM fourth edition (DSM IV) (American Psychiatric Organization 1994). Thus, among patients with symptoms of BD, a premorbid TBI does not per se qualify for a diagnosis of BD due to TBI.

The validity of this dichotomy between BD *with* premorbid TBI and BD *due to* TBI is questionable (Kendell and Jablensky 2003). First, BD has a non-absolute monozygotic concordance (Craddock and Sklar 2013). Environmental factors must thus be of some etiological importance in both diagnoses. Second, a latency in the onset of BD after TBI does not exclude a pathophysiological impact of the latter. In a nation-wide sibling-controlled cohort study from Sweden (Sariaslan et al. 2016), TBI predicted risks of later psychiatric visits and hospitalizations. The risks were also increased among those with TBI in childhood and of mild severity. Even though these findings were not stratified by diagnoses, they highlight the possibility of a causative effect of TBI in childhood on psychiatric disorders in adulthood. Third, TBI can induce a range of pathophysiological processes which are not necessarily detected by standard radiological or electrophysiological assessment (Mayer et al. 2010; Nuwer et al. 2005; Blennow et al. 2012).

It is thus possible that TBI could have had an impact in the pathophysiological trajectory of BD in some patients who do not fulfil the criteria of BD due to TBI. If so, these patients would be expected to have some of the same clinical characteristics as previously described in BD due to TBI. Such clinical characteristics are more aggression and irritability, and a high hypomania/mania:depression ratio (Shukla et al. 1987; Jorge et al. 1993). Clinical characteristics of BD with premorbid TBI could obviously be influenced by other factors than the TBI. Family history of mental illness is particularly of relevance, since it is associated with both risk of TBI (Malaspina et al. 2001) and more severe clinical characteristics of BD (Antypa and Serretti 2014). Also, some clinical characteristics (e.g. levels of aggression and irritability) could be sensitive to potential differences between those with and without premorbid TBI in regard to BD subtypes (Baek et al. 2011; Serretti and Olgiati 2005), and mood states (Young et al. 1978) and pharmacological treatment (Müller-Oerlinghausen and Lewitzka 2010) at assessment.

The aim of the present study was to identify clinical characteristics in patients with BD and premorbid TBI, using a large sample of patients from psychiatric care. We hypothesized to find more aggression and irritability, a higher hypomania/mania:depression ratio, and other clinical characteristics distinguishing patients with premorbid TBI from those without. Further, we hypothesized that eventual findings would be independent of possible confounders.

Methods

Study design

The study has a cross-sectional design.

Setting

Psychiatric health care services in Norway are publicly funded and the hospitals have catchment area responsibilities. From 2003 to 2012 data were collected from 17 psychiatric hospitals and outpatient clinics collaborating in the Bipolar Research And Innovation Network Norway (BRAIN) study (Morken et al. 2009).

Participants

Patients diagnosed with BD type I, type II, or not otherwise specified (NOS), or cyclothymia were invited to participate. Diagnoses were confirmed by trained clinicians with the Structured Clinical Interview for DSM IV Axis I Disorders (SCID I) (First et al. 1997) or the Mini-International Neuropsychiatric Interview (M.I.N.I.) (Sheehan et al. 1998). The only exclusion criterion was inability to give informed consent. There is no information available on the number of patients who refused to participate. A total of 549 patients were included. The present study consists of the 505 patients who answered the questions about TBI and age at onset of BD.

Data sources

All patients were assessed with a Norwegian adaptation of the Network Entry Questionnaire (NEQ). NEQ is a semi-structured interview developed by the Bipolar Collaboration Network (Leverich et al. 2001). The Norwegian adaptation of NEQ was used to obtain data on TBI, demographic factors, family history, course of illness, pharmacological treatment, somatic comorbidity, and psychiatric comorbidity in childhood. The Young Mania Rating Scale (YMRS) (Young et al. 1978) and the Inventory of Depressive Symptomatology Clinician Rated 30 (IDS-C_{30}) (Rush et al. 1996) were used to obtain data on symptom composition and burden. The SCID I or the M.I.N.I. were used to obtain data on current mood state.

Variables

The grouping variable was premorbid TBI. Patients were asked if they had had a head injury with loss of consciousness (LOC) and if they had had a head injury without LOC. The questions could be answered *yes (diagnosed)*, *no*, or *don't know*. An answer of *yes (diagnosed)* thus implicated a prior diagnostic evaluation of a general practitioner or hospital doctor. In Norway, head injuries are in general practice defined according to the International Classification of Primary Care (ICPC) (Brage et al. 1996; Lamberts and Wood 1987), and in hospital settings according to the International Classification of Diseases (ICD) 10th revision (World Health Organization 1993). An ICPC diagnosis of head injury (N79–N80) requires loss of consciousness, neurological sequela, or cerebral injury, while an ICD-10 diagnosis of head injury implies that the criteria for hospital admission (i.e. loss of consciousness, amnesia, reduced responsiveness, focal neurological deficits, or Glasgow Coma Scale Score < 15) in Norway have been met (Lamberts and Wood 1987; Ingebrigtsen et al. 2000). If answering *yes (diagnosed)*, patients where further asked about their age at the time of diagnosis. We defined premorbid TBI as having received a diagnosis of head injury of any severity at an age lower than age at onset of BD. The definition of age at onset of BD was age at first depressive symptoms associated with dysfunction or first hypomanic or manic symptoms similar to those experienced in adulthood (Morken et al. 2009).

Years of education refers to the accumulated time spent at upper secondary schools, university colleges, and universities.

From variables of family history of mental illness, we computed answers of *yes (diagnosed)* as positive and *probable* or *no* as negative to questions of schizophrenia, BD, and depression in 1st degree relatives.

Duration of illness was calculated as the difference between age at inclusion and age at onset. Variables on affective episodes per year were calculated as fractions of number of episodes above duration of illness. Rapid cycling was dichotomized from a question of four or more episodes per year during lifetime, where answers of *yes* were defined as positive and *no* or *uncertain* were defined as negative. The variable on serious suicidal attempts was defined by lifetime history of suicidal attempts leading to medical assistance, emergency room visit, or hospitalization.

Variables on pharmacological treatment were defined by current use of lithium, anticonvulsants, antipsychotics, and antidepressants.

History of epileptic seizures and comorbid migraine were defined by answers of *yes (diagnosed)* to questions of lifetime history of the two, while answers of *no* or *don't know* were regarded as negative. Obesity was defined as body mass index ≥ 30 kg/m^2 as calculated from self-reported height and weight. Psychiatric comorbidity was defined by one variable on abuse or dependence of alcohol and a similar variable on other substances, both defined by SCID-I or M.I.N.I., as well as one variable on self-reported diagnosis of childhood attention deficit (hyperactivity) disorder (AD(H)D) obtained from the NEQ.

Variables on symptom composition and burden were obtained from principal components and total scores, respectively, of YMRS and IDS-C_{30} at inclusion (see statistical methods).

Bias

As an indirect test of bias in self-reported variables, we compared the groups on a four-point ordinal item in the NEQ on the clinicians' judgement of the reliability of the patients' answers. The item scores ranged from 1 to 4, corresponding to very reliable and unreliable answers, respectively.

Statistical methods

R (version 3.4.0) (2018) and RStudio (version 1.0.143) (2018) were used for statistical analyses.

The R package psych was used for principal component analyses (PCA) of items in the YMRS and IDS-C_{30}. The purpose of conducting a PCA was to limit the number of comparisons in analyses of symptomatology. Items on appetite and weight in the IDS-C_{30} are pair-wise optional and were excluded to avoid large amounts of missing data. Cronbach's alpha was used to test the internal reliability of the rating scales. A Kaiser-Meyer-Olkin (KMO) test was used to measure sample size adequacy. A determinant cut-off at > 0.00001 was used to avoid multicollinearity. The Velicer's map criterion was used to determine the number of components to retain. Direct oblimin oblique rotation was used since components were assumed to be correlated. Pattern matrices of component loadings > 0.4 were used to interpret the results. Standardized component scores were saved for each participant.

Bivariate analyses of differences between the groups were undertaken for all variables. Pearson's Chi squared tests, Fisher's exact tests, Mann–Whitney U-tests, and independent samples t-tests were used as appropriate. The alpha level was set to < 0.05. A Bonferroni correction of 40 comparisons, two of which were not included in the paper due to large amounts of missing data, yielded a p-value threshold of < 0.0013. The beta level for each comparison was not calculated.

A backward likelihood ratio logistic regression analysis was conducted in order to find clinical characteristics associated with premorbid TBI independent of each other and possible confounders. We included variables with p-values < 0.1 from bivariate analyses, and possible confounding variables based on the literature and clinical experience. These were age, sex, years of education, 1st degree family members with schizophrenia, BD, or depression, rapid cycling, migraine, AD(H)D in childhood, comorbid alcohol abuse or dependence, comorbid substance abuse or dependence, YMRS total score, IDS-C_{30} total score, YMRS disruptive component score, and IDS-C_{30} activated component score. Depressive episodes per year and hypomanic episodes per year were not included due to large amounts of missing data. YMRS total score had a skewed distribution with large amounts of null scores. Logarithmic transformation of total score plus one was therefore used in the regression model.

Further, we built additional logistic regression models to test whether our findings from the backward likelihood ratio logistic regression analysis were dependent on BD subtypes, mood states, and pharmacological treatments. First, we built a base model (Model 1) including sociodemographic factors (age, gender, and years of education), family history of mental illness (schizophrenia, BD, and depression), and clinical characteristics significantly associated with premorbid TBI in the backward likelihood ratio logistic regression analysis (YMRS disruptive component score and comorbid migraine) as independent variables. Then, we added and removed dummy variables of BD subtypes (Model 2a: type 1 vs. others; Model 2b: type 2 vs. others), mood states (Model 3a: depressed vs. others; Model 3b: euthymic vs. others etc.), and pharmacological treatments (Model 4a: lithium vs. others; Model 4b: anticonvulsants vs. others etc.) in successive models.

Variance inflation factors (VIF) between all independent variables were calculated to assess for multicollinearity.

Results

Sample characteristics

Five hundred five patients were included. Mean age was 42 years (SD 14), 286 (57%) were women, and 256 (53%) had BD type I. Thirty-seven patients (7.3%) reported a premorbid TBI, of whom 23 (4.6%) had LOC. Age at TBI and years from age at TBI to age at onset of BD had mean values of 10 years (SD 9.0) and 8.9 years (SD 7.3), respectively.

Clinicians judged the reliability of the patients' answers as high in both groups (median 1 vs. 1 (interquartile range 1 vs. 1), $p=0.45$).

Principal component analyses

Cronbach's alpha was 0.90 for both YMRS and IDS-C_{30}, which implicates a very good internal reliability of the rating scales.

Two components were extracted from items in both YMRS (Table 1) and IDS-C_{30} (Table 2). The KMO measure of sampling adequacy was 0.89 and 0.93, respectively. Barlett's test of spherity was significant for both. The determinant was 0.0017 and 0.000029, respectively. The components accounted for 62% of the variance in the YMRS and 39% of the variance in the IDS-C_{30}.

Table 1 Items loadings on principal components of the Young Mania Rating Scale

Item	Components (variance explained)	
	Elated (37%)	Disruptive (24%)
Elevated mood	0.95	
Increased motor activity/energy	0.93	
Speech	0.84	
Language/thought disorder	0.75	
Sexual interest	0.70	
Content	0.56	
Disruptive/aggressive behavior		0.89
Irritability		0.76
Appearance		0.69
Insight		0.65

Bivariate analyses

By applying bivariate analyses with correction for multiple testing, we found more comorbid migraine (36 vs. 13%, $p=0.00030$) among patients with premorbid TBI (Table 3).

Logistic regression analyses

Data for 395 of 505 participants (78%) were complete and thereby included in the backward likelihood ratio logistic regression analysis. Among clinical characteristics, the YMRS disruptive component score (OR 1.7, 95% CI 1.1–2.4, $p=0.0077$) and comorbid migraine (OR 4.6, 95% CI 1.9–11, $p=0.00090$) were independently associated with premorbid TBI (Table 4). Family history of schizophrenia (OR 11, 95% CI 2.3–51, $p=0.0025$) was also independently associated with premorbid TBI.

The associations between premorbid TBI and YMRS disruptive component score and comorbid migraine remained significant after correction for BD subtypes, mood states, and pharmacological treatments (Additional file 1: Table S1).

Nagelkerke R^2 of 0.31 implied a low relationship between prediction and grouping in the backward likelihood ratio logistic regression analysis. VIF was <3.0

Table 2 Item loadings on principal components of the Inventory of Depressive Symptomatology Clinican Rated 30

Item	Components (variance explained)	
	Depressed (31%)	Activated (9%)
Energy/fatiguability	0.86	
Pleasure/enjoyment	0.86	
Involvement	0.85	
Mood (sad)	0.78	
Outlook (future)	0.78	
Reactivity of mood	0.74	
Psychomotor slowing	0.68	
Sexual interest	0.67	
Outlook (self)	0.64	
Suicidal ideation	0.64	
Mood (anxious)	0.64	
Leaden paralysis/physical energy	0.63	
Concentration/decision making	0.53	
Mood variation	0.41	
Psychomotor agitation		0.60
Mid-nocturnal insomnia		0.60
Early morning insomnia		0.60
Sleep onset insomnia		0.53
Mood (irritable)		0.41

between all independent variables in all logistic regression models.

Discussion

We found that premorbid TBI was associated with comorbid migraine in bivariate analyses with correction for multiple comparisons. In a logistic regression model, we found that premorbid TBI was associated with disruptive symptoms and comorbid migraine independently of a range of possible confounders. Family history of schizophrenia was also independently associated with premorbid TBI. We did not find associations between premorbid TBI and any other clinical characteristics and specifically not with hypomania/mania:depression ratio.

The finding of more disruptive symptoms corresponds with our hypothesis of finding similar clinical characteristics in BD with premorbid TBI as previously described in BD due to TBI (Shukla et al. 1987; Jorge et al. 1993). Aggression and irritability, which in our study had the highest loadings on the disruptive component, are common symptoms after TBI of all severities (Lique Sté Fan and Mathé 2015; Hammond et al. 2016). A cross-sectional study on 89 patients with and without aggression after TBI of all severities, found that aggression was associated with premorbid substance use disorders, affective disorders, and poor social functioning (Tateno et al. 2003). Similarly, a study on 97 children with severe TBI found that preinjury affective lability and psychosocial adversity predicted affective lability (including irritability and temper outbursts) at one year follow-up (Vasa et al. 2015). These studies suggest that TBI could result in more disruptive symptoms among patients with a disposition to affective symptoms and lower social function/support. Further, aggression after TBI was in the same studies associated with frontal lobe lesions (Tateno et al. 2003; Vasa et al. 2015), highlighting a possible structural substrate for disruptive symptoms after TBI. Frontal lobe regions are also implicated in mania secondary to focal brain lesions in general (Satzer and Bond 2016), and are on average thinner among patients with BD than among healthy controls (Hibar et al. 2018).

The mean YMRS score in the premorbid TBI group in our study was low. Further, the association between the YMRS disruptive component score and premorbid TBI remained significant after corrections for BD subtypes, mood states, and pharmacological treatments (Additional file 1: Table S1). It is thus a possibility that the disruptive symptoms in most patients represent a personality trait related to premorbid TBI rather than a mood state related to BD. However; disruptive symptoms after TBI could also be rapidly alternating (Arciniegas and Wortzel 2014) and thereby resemble, and possibly fulfil the criteria of, short lasting manic states (Coetzer 2008).

Our results are in line with previous findings that migraine is a common headache after TBI (Lucas et al. 2014; Stacey et al. 2017). Inflammation and impaired pain modulation after TBI are two of the suggested pathophysiological mechanisms (Ruff et al. 2016). Furthermore, migraine and BD are bi-directionally associated (Fornaro et al. 2015) and possibly influenced by shared environmental and genetic factors (Sucksdorff et al. 2016). It is thus difficult to conclude on the nature behind our finding of an association between migraine and premorbid TBI among patients with BD.

Although it was not a primary outcome of our study, our finding of more family history of schizophrenia among those with premorbid TBI harmonizes with findings in a study of Malaspina et al. (Malaspina et al. 2001). They assessed for TBI in members of families where at least two 1st degree-relatives had schizophrenia or BD. Members of the schizophrenia pedigrees had an increased risk of TBI which was independent of their own diagnoses. The effect of family history of schizophrenia on risk of premorbid TBI could be mediated by several factors. Examples are co-inherited motor coordination

Table 3 Demographics, family history, and clinical characteristics in patients with and without premorbid traumatic brain injury

	All (n = 505)	+pTBI (n = 37)	−pTBI (n = 468)	p-value
Demographics				
Age	505	41 (15)	42 (13)	0.74[a]
Female sex	505	21/37 (57)	265/468 (57)	1.0[c]
Years of education	495	4.8 (3.1)	4.4 (3.1)	0.55[b]
Family history				
Schizophrenia	496	4/37 (11)	9/459 (2.0)	0.012[d]
Bipolar disorder	497	5/37 (14)	105/460 (23)	0.27[c]
Depression	497	26/37 (70)	199/460 (43)	0.0027[c]
Any	497	27/37 (73)	247/460 (54)	0.036[c]
Mood state				
Depressed	504	28/37 (76)	305/467 (65)	0.27[c]
Euthymic	504	1/37 (2.7)	12/467 (2.6)	1.0[c]
Mixed	504	1/37 (2.7)	22/467 (4.7)	0.88[c]
Hypomanic	504	0/37 (0)	10/467 (2.1)	0.77[c]
Manic	504	7/37 (19)	118/467 (25)	0.51[c]
Course of illness				
Age at onset	505	20 (12)	19 (11)	0.81[b]
Duration of illness	505	21 (14)	23 (14)	0.45[b]
Bipolar disorder subtype	505			0.57[d]
Type I		18/37 (49)	247/468 (53)	
Type II		18/37 (49)	213/468 (46)	
Cyclothymia		0/37 (0)	1/468 (2)	
Not otherwise specified		1/37 (3)	7/468 (1)	
Depressive episodes per year	420	1.3 (1.8)	0.78 (1.1)	0.014[b]
Hypomanic episodes per year	424	1.4 (2.0)	0.92 (2.2)	0.025[b]
Manic episodes per year	461	0.073 (0.15)	0.091 (0.21)	0.23[b]
Hypomania/mania:depression ratio	405	1.3 (1.1)	2.1 (5.2)	0.59[b]
Admissions per decade	449	0.82 (1.1)	1.4 (2.6)	0.24[b]
Rapid cycling	491	14/35 (40)	103/456 (23)	0.034[c]
Serious suicidal attempt(s)	500	14/37 (38)	202/463 (44)	0.61[c]
Current pharmacological treatment				
Lithium	483	12/33 (36)	102/450 (23)	0.11[c]
Anticonvulsants	483	20/33 (61)	302/450 (67)	0.57[c]
Antipsychotics	483	19/33 (58)	270/450 (60)	0.93[c]
Antidepressants	483	12/33 (36)	165/450 (37)	1.0[c]
Comorbidity				
Epileptic seizures	505	1/37 (2.7)	9/468 (1.9)	0.54[d]
Migraine	501	13/36 (36)	59/465 (13)	0.00030[c]*
Obesity	498	4/36 (11)	79/462 (17)	0.49[c]
Alcohol, abuse or dependence	505	5/37 (14)	64/468 (14)	1.0[c]
Other substances, abuse or dependence	505	2/37 (5.4)	28/468 (6.0)	1.0[d]
Childhood AD(H)D	497	6/37 (16)	33/460 (7.2)	0.059[c]
Symptom composition				
YMRS elated component score	484	0.12 (1.2)	−0.020 (0.98)	0.77[b]
YMRS disruptive component score	484	0.54 (1.7)	−0.050 (0.90)	0.0044[b]
IDS-C_{30} depressed component score	446	0.19 (1.0)	0.011 (1.0)	0.30[b]
IDS-C_{30} activated component score	446	0.21 (0.86)	−0.046 (0.99)	0.041[b]

Table 3 (continued)

	All (n = 505)	+pTBI (n = 37)	−pTBI (n = 468)	p-value
Symptom burden				
YMRS total score	497	7.9 (11)	5.4 (7.8)	0.16[b]
IDS-C_{30} total score	490	28 (14)	24 (15)	0.087[b]

Results are presented by fraction (%) for categorical variables and mean (SD) for continuous variables. +pTBI premorbid traumatic brain injury. −pTBI no premorbid traumatic brain injury

* Multiple comparisons p-value threshold = 0.0013

[a] Independent samples t-test

[b] Mann–Whitney-U test

[c] Pearson's Chi squared test

[d] Fisher's exact test

Table 4 Final step of the backward likelihood ratio logistic regression analysis on variables independently associated with premorbid traumatic brain injury among patients with bipolar disorder

	Coefficient	S.E.	OR	95% CI	Wald Z	p-value
Intercept	− 1.2	0.36	0.29	0.14–0.60	− 3.4	0.00078
Family history schizophrenia	2.4	0.79	11	2.3–51	3.0	0.0025
Comorbid migraine	1.5	0.46	4.6	1.9–11	3.3	0.00090
YMRS disruptive component	0.51	0.19	1.7	1.1–2.4	2.7	0.0077

S.E. standard error, *OR* odds ratio, *CI* confidence interval

problems (Ismail et al. 1998; Burton et al. 2017), and co-inherited susceptibility to risk-taking behaviour (Strawbridge et al. 2018).

Regarding course of illness, the findings of more rapid cycling, depressive episodes per year and hypomanic episodes per year were not significant after correction for multiple testing. Due to missing data in the latter two variables, only rapid cycling was included in the regression model, and it was not independently associated with premorbid TBI. In the Systematic Treatment Enhancement Program for Bipolar Disorder (STEP-BD) study, mild TBI after age at onset of BD, but not before, was associated with rapid cycling (Sagduyu 2002). One of several possible explanations to our and the STEP-BD study's findings is that the co-occurrence of TBI and more rapid cycling are epiphenomena of increased genetic susceptibility to BD (Antypa and Serretti 2014). We found a hypomania/mania:depression ratio of 1:1 in the premorbid TBI group, which was not higher than among those without premorbid TBI. In comparison, Shukla et al. reported a ratio of 15:1 in a study on patients with BD due to TBI (Shukla et al. 1987). Several differences between the samples, e.g. regarding clinical setting, severity of TBI, and frequency of comorbid epilepsy, make it difficult to conclude on the cause(s) of this discrepancy.

There were no differences between the groups on current treatment with lithium, anticonvulsants, antipsychotics or antidepressants. Previous studies have found increased treatment response to valproate among patients with BD and a history of TBI (Pope et al. 1988; Stoll et al. 1994). However, treatment response is not directly comparable to our measures, which could be influenced by the prescribing clinicians' preferences and discontinuation due to side effects.

Epilepsy is previously suggested as the pathophysiological mechanism in BD due to TBI (van Reekum and Cohen 2000). In our study of BD with premorbid TBI, self-report did not unveil higher frequencies of epileptic seizures. Nevertheless, not all seizures are recognized by patients (Elger and Hoppe 2018).

The prevalence of premorbid TBI in our study from Norway (7.3%) was lower than in the STEP-BD study from the United States (10% with premorbid mild TBI) (Sagduyu 2002) and in register-based studies from Denmark (11%) (Orlovska et al. 2014) and Taiwan (25%) (Chi et al. 2016). However, both variation in prevalence of TBI across nations and different methodologies across studies (Corrigan et al. 2010) warrant caution when interpreting these differences.

Our study has several limitations that should be taken into account. The reliability and validity of the definition of TBI in the NEQ is unknown. While the definition implies an ICPC or ICD-10 diagnosis of head injury, the NEQ did not harvest data on specific symptoms of head injury or on diagnostic codes from the patients' health records. Self-reported data implies risk of recall bias. It is possible that patients with disruptive symptoms and comorbid migraine look for explanations in the past and thus report a higher prevalence of premorbid TBI. The inter-rater reliability of the diagnostic evaluations was not measured. There exists no data on the overall participation rate. The generalizability of our findings to all patients in psychiatric care is thus unknown. We included patients with all BD subtypes, mood states, and pharmacological treatments. It is possible that our results would have been different if the sample had been restricted to more selected groups, e.g. patients with medication naïve first manic episodes. The Bonferroni correction for multiple testing in the bivariate analyses implies a high risk of type II errors. However, interpretation of the results should be based not only on the Bonferroni corrected p-values alone, but also on the strength of effects, prior knowledge, and biological plausibility of the associations. The design of our study makes it impossible draw conclusions about whether the findings of more disruptive symptoms and comorbid migraine are causal. Inverse causation is an alternative explanation. In regard the association between premorbid TBI and disruptive symptoms, a review found that aggression and irritability are common parts of the distal prodrome of BD (Skjelstad et al. 2010). Aggression and irritability might even characterize a prodromal subgroup of BD type II with neurocognitive deficits (Skjelstad et al. 2011), which can be hypothesized to be more prone to injuries including TBI. Residual confounding could also explain the associations. In our study, disruptive symptoms, comorbid migraine, and family history of schizophrenia were independently associated with premorbid TBI. Taken together, these variables represent a pattern of symptomatology (Hanwella and de Silva 2011), comorbidity (Fornaro et al. 2015), and heritability (Cross-Disorder Group of the Psychiatric Genomics Consortium 2013) typical for BD. We emphasize the possibility that their apparently independent associations with premorbid TBI could be a consequence of residual confounding by genetic susceptibility to BD. Examples of other factors that could have contributed to residual confounding are AD(H)D, which was probably seldom evaluated when the majority of patients in our study grew up, and psychological trauma, on which we have no data despite its known association with more severe clinical characteristics (Leverich and Post 2006) and possibly also with physical trauma including TBI.

Conclusions

Premorbid TBI is associated with disruptive symptoms and comorbid migraine independently of the measured possible confounders including family history of mental disorders, while it is not associated with an increased hypomania/mania:depression ratio. The finding of more disruptive symptoms is in line with our hypothesis of finding similar clinical characteristics in BD with premorbid TBI as in BD due to TBI. Studies designed to draw conclusions of causal inference from observational data, e.g. by using family-based quasi-experimental designs (D'Onofrio et al. 2013), are warranted to clarify whether our findings could be explained by a continuum of pathophysiological effects of premorbid TBI across the diagnostic dichotomy of BD with premorbid TBI and BD due to TBI.

Abbreviations

BD: bipolar disorder; BRAIN: Bipolar Research And Innovation Network Norway; DSM: Diagnostic and Statistical Manual of Mental Disorders; ICD: International Classification of Diseases; ICPC: International Classification of Primary Care; IDS-C30: Inventory of Depressive Symptoms Clinician Rated 30; KMO: Kaiser-Meyer-Olkin; LOC: loss of consciousness; MINI: Mini-International Neuropsychiatric Interview; NEQ: Network Entry Questionnaire; NOS: not otherwise specified; PCA: principal component analysis; SCID I: Structured Clinical Interview for DSM IV Axis I Disorders; STEP-BD: Systematic Treatment Enhancement Program for Bipolar Disorder; TBI: traumatic brain injury; VIF: variance inflation factor; YMRS: Young Mania Rating Scale.

Authors' contributions

UFM, OAA, GM, and AEV designed the BRAIN study. OKD, AEV, and PIF wrote the protocol for the present study. All authors included patients to the BRAIN study. OKD and PIF conducted the analyses. All authors interpreted the results. OKD drafted the manuscript under supervision of AEV and PIF. All authors contributed with the further writing of the manuscript. All authors read and approved the final manuscript.

Author details

[1] Department of Mental Health, Norwegian University of Science and Technology, Trondheim, Norway. [2] Department of Østmarka, Division of Mental Health Care, St. Olavs Hospital, Trondheim University Hospital, Trondheim, Norway. [3] Institute of Clinical Medicine, University of Oslo, Oslo, Norway. [4] NORMENT, Division of Mental Health and Addiction, Oslo University Hospital, Oslo, Norway. [5] Department of Research and Education, Division of Clinical Neuroscience, Oslo University Hospital, Oslo, Norway. [6] Department of Brøset, Division of Mental Health Care, St. Olavs Hospital, Trondheim University Hospital, Trondheim, Norway.

Acknowledgements

We want to thank the patients for participating in the study, colleagues for recruitment and interviews, and Thomas D. Bjella for preparation of data.

Competing interests

UFM has received honoraria from Takeda and Lundbeck for lectures about mood disorders to primary care physicians and psychiatrists. He has also received honoraria from Takeda and Lundbeck Norway for giving scientific advice. OAA has received speaker's honoraria from GSK and Lundbeck. OKD, AEV, GM and PIF report no competing interests.

Funding

The study was supported by the South-East Norway Health Authority, the KG Jebsen Foundation, and the Research Council of Norway. The funding bodies have not been involved in the design of the present study, in the collection, analysis, or interpretation of data, or in the writing of the manuscript.

References

American Psychiatric Association. Diagnostic and statistical manual of mental disorders. 5th ed. Washington, DC: American Psychiatric Association; 2013.

American Psychiatric Organization. Diagnostic and statistical manual of mental disorders. 4th ed. Washington, DC: American Psychiatric Organization; 1994.

Antypa N, Serretti A. Family history of a mood disorder indicates a more severe bipolar disorder. J Affect Disord. 2014;156:178–86.

Arciniegas DB, Wortzel HS. Emotional and behavioral dyscontrol after traumatic brain injury. Psychiatr Clin North Am. 2014;37:31–53.

Baek JH, Park DY, Choi J, Kim JS, Choi JS, Ha K, et al. Differences between bipolar I and bipolar II disorders in clinical features, comorbidity, and family history. J Affect Disord. 2011;131:59–67.

Blennow K, Hardy J, Zetterberg H. The neuropathology and neurobiology of traumatic brain injury. Neuron. 2012;76:886–99.

Brage S, Bentsen BG, Bjerkedal T, Nygård JF, Tellnes G. ICPC as a standard classification in Norway. Fam Pract. 1996;13:391–6.

Burton BK, Thorup AAE, Jepsen JR, Poulsen G, Ellersgaard D, Spang KS, et al. Impairments of motor function among children with a familial risk of schizophrenia or bipolar disorder at 7 years old in Denmark: an observational cohort study. Lancet Psychiatry. 2017;4:400–8.

Chi Y-C, Wu H-L, Chu C-P, Huang M-C, Lee P-C, Chen Y-Y. Traumatic brain injury and affective disorder: a nationwide cohort study in Taiwan, 2000–2010. J Affect Disord. 2016;191:56–61.

Coetzer R. Diagnostic dilemmas associated with bipolar disorder after traumatic brain injury. CNS Spectr. 2008;13:1022–3.

Corrigan JD, Selassie AW, Orman JAL. The epidemiology of traumatic brain injury. J Head Trauma Rehabil. 2010;25:72–80.

Craddock N, Sklar P. Genetics of bipolar disorder. Lancet. 2013;381:1654–62.

Cross-Disorder Group of the Psychiatric Genomics Consortium. Genetic relationship between five psychiatric disorders estimated from genome-wide SNPs. Nat Genet. 2013;45:984–94.

D'Onofrio BM, Lahey BB, Turkheimer E, Lichtenstein P. Critical need for family-based, quasi-experimental designs in integrating genetic and social science research. Am J Public Health. 2013;103(Suppl 1):46–55.

Elger CE, Hoppe C. Diagnostic challenges in epilepsy: seizure under-reporting and seizure detection. Lancet Neurol. 2018;17:279–88.

First MB, Spitzer R, Gibbon M, Williams JB. Structured clinical interview for DSM-IV—patient version. Washington, DC: Am Psychiatr Press; 1997.

Fornaro M, De Berardis D, De Pasquale C, Indelicato L, Pollice R, Valchera A, et al. Prevalence and clinical features associated to bipolar disorder-migraine comorbidity: a systematic review. Compr Psychiatry. 2015;56:1–16.

Hammond FM, Davis C, Cook JR, Philbrick P, Hirsch MA. A conceptual model of irritability following traumatic brain injury. J Head Trauma Rehabil. 2016. https://doi.org/10.1097/HTR.0000000000000136.

Hanwella R, de Silva VA. Signs and symptoms of acute mania: a factor analysis. BMC Psychiatry. 2011;11:137.

Hibar DP, Westlye LT, Doan NT, Jahanshad N, Cheung JW, Ching CRK, et al. Cortical abnormalities in bipolar disorder: an MRI analysis of 6503 individuals from the ENIGMA Bipolar Disorder Working Group. Mol Psychiatry. 2018;23:932–42.

Ingebrigtsen T, Rise IR, Wester K, Romner B, Kock-Jensen C. Scandinavian guidelines for management of minimal, mild and moderate head injuries. Tidsskr den Nor Laegeforen. 2000;120:1985–90.

Ismail B, Cantor-Graae E, McNeil TF. Neurological abnormalities in schizophrenic patients and their siblings. Am J Psychiatry. 1998;155:84–9.

Jorge RE, Robinson RG, Starkstein SE, Arndt SV, Forrester AW, Geisler FH. Secondary mania following traumatic brain injury. Am J Psychiatry. 1993;150:916–21.

Kendell R, Jablensky A. Distinguishing between the validity and utility of psychiatric diagnoses. Am J Psychiatry. 2003;160:4–12.

Lamberts H, Wood M. International Classification of Primary Care (ICPC). Oxford: Oxford University Press; 1987.

Leverich GS, Post RM. Course of bipolar illness after history of childhood trauma. Lancet. 2006;367:1040–2.

Leverich GS, Nolen WA, Rush AJ, McElroy SL, Keck PE, Denicoff KD, et al. The Stanley Foundation Bipolar Treatment Outcome Network: I longitudinal methodology. J Affect Disord. 2001;67:33–44.

Lique Sté Fan A, Mathé J-F. What are the disruptive symptoms of behavioral disorders after traumatic brain injury? A systematic review leading to recommendations for good practices. Ann Phys Rehabil Med. 2015;59:5–17.

Lucas S, Hoffman JM, Bell KR, Dikmen S. A prospective study of prevalence and characterization of headache following mild traumatic brain injury. Cephalalgia. 2014;34:93–102.

Malaspina D, Goetz RR, Friedman JH, Kaufmann CA, Faraone SV, Tsuang M, et al. Traumatic brain injury and schizophrenia in members of schizophrenia and bipolar disorder pedigrees. Am J Psychiatry. 2001;158:440–6.

Mayer AR, Ling J, Mannell MV, Gasparovic C, Phillips JP, Doezema D, et al. A prospective diffusion tensor imaging study in mild traumatic brain injury. Neurology. 2010;74:643–50.

Morken G, Vaaler AE, Folden GE, Andreassen OA, Malt UF. Age at onset of first episode and time to treatment in in-patients with bipolar disorder. Br J Psychiatry. 2009;194:559–60.

Müller-Oerlinghausen B, Lewitzka U. Lithium reduces pathological aggression and suicidality: a mini-review. Neuropsychobiology. 2010;62:43–9.

Nuwer MR, Hovda DA, Schrader LM, Vespa PM. Routine and quantitative EEG in mild traumatic brain injury. Clin Neurophysiol. 2005;116:2001–25.

Orlovska S, Pedersen MS, Benros ME, Mortensen PB, Agerbo E, Nordentoft M. Head injury as risk factor for psychiatric disorders: a nationwide register-based follow-up study of 113,906 persons with head injury. Am J Psychiatry. 2014;171:463–9.

Perry DC, Sturm VE, Peterson MJ, Pieper CF, Bullock T, Boeve BF, et al. Association of traumatic brain injury with subsequent neurological and psychiatric disease: a meta-analysis. J Neurosurg. 2016;124:511–26.

Pope HG, Mcelroy SL, Satlin A, Hudson JI, Keck PE, Kalish R. Head injury, bipolar disorder, and response to valproate. Compr Psychiatry. 1988;29:34–8.

R Core Team. R: A language and environment for statistical computing. R Foundation for Statistical Computing, Vienna, Austria. https://www.r-project.org/. Accessed 8 July 2018.

RStudio Team. RStudio: Integrated Development for R. RStudio, Inc., Boston, MA. http://www.rstudio.com/. Assessed 8 July 2018.

Ruff RL, Blake K. Pathophysiological links between traumatic brain injury and post-traumatic headaches. F1000Res. 2016. https://doi.org/10.12688/f1000research.9017.1.

Rush AJ, Gullion CM, Basco MR, Jarrett RB, Trivedi MH. The inventory of depressive symptomatology (IDS): psychometric properties. Psychol Med. 1996;26:477–86.

Sagduyu K. Association of mild traumatic brain injury with bipolar disorder. J Clin Psychiatry. 2002;63:595–8.

Sariaslan A, Sharp DJ, D'Onofrio BM, Larsson H, Fazel S. Long-term outcomes associated with traumatic brain injury in childhood and adolescence: a Nationwide Swedish Cohort Study of a wide range of medical and social outcomes. PLOS Med. 2016. https://doi.org/10.1371/journal.pmed.1002103.

Satzer D, Bond DJ. Mania secondary to focal brain lesions: implications for understanding the functional neuroanatomy of bipolar disorder. Bipolar Disord. 2016;18:205–20.

Serretti A, Olgiati P. Profiles of "manic" symptoms in bipolar I, bipolar II and major depressive disorders. J Affect Disord. 2005;84:159–66.

Sheehan DV, Lecrubier Y, Sheehan KH, Amorim P, Janavs J, Weiller E, et al. The Mini-International Neuropsychiatric Interview (M.I.N.I.): the development and validation of a structured diagnostic psychiatric interview for DSM-IV and ICD-10. J Clin Psychiatry. 1998;59(Suppl 2):22–33.

Shukla S, Cook BL, Mukherjee S, Godwin C, Miller MG. Mania following head trauma. Am J Psychiatry. 1987;144:93–6.

Skjelstad DV, Malt UF, Holte A. Symptoms and signs of the initial prodrome of bipolar disorder: a systematic review. J Affect Disord. 2010;126:1–13.

Skjelstad DV, Malt UF, Holte A. Symptoms and behaviors prior to the first major affective episode of bipolar II disorder. An exploratory study. J Affect Disord. 2011;132:333–43.

Stacey A, Lucas S, Dikmen S, Braden CA, Brown AW, Brunner R, et al. Natural history of headache five years after traumatic brain injury. J Neurotrauma. 2017;34:1558–64.

Stoll AL, Banov M, Kolbrener M, Mayer PV, Tohen M, Strakowski SM, et al. Neurologic factors predict a favorable valproate response in bipolar and schizoaffective disorders. J Clin Psychopharmacol. 1994;14:311–3.

Strawbridge RJ, Ward J, Cullen B, Tunbridge EM, Hartz S, et al. Genome-wide analysis of self-reported risk-taking behaviour and cross-disorder genetic correlations in the UK Biobank cohort. Transl Psychiatry. 2018;8:39.

Sucksdorff D, Brown AS, Chudal R, Heinimaa M, Suominen A, Sourander A. Parental and comorbid migraine in individuals with bipolar disorder: a nationwide register study. J Affect Disord. 2016;206:109–14.

Tateno A, Jorge RE, Robinson RG. Clinical correlates of aggressive behavior after traumatic brain injury. J Neuropsychiatry Clin Neurosci. 2003;15:155–60.

van Reekum R, Cohen T. Can traumatic brain injury cause psychiatric disorders? J Neuropsychiatry Clin Neurosci. 2000;12:316–27.

Vasa RA, Suskauer SJ, Thorn JM, Kalb L, Grados MA, Slomine BS, et al. Prevalence and predictors of affective lability after paediatric traumatic brain injury. Brain Inj. 2015;29:921–8.

World Health Organization. The ICD-10 classification of mental and behavioural disorders: Diagnostic criteria for research. Geneva: World Health Organization; 1993.

Young RC, Biggs JT, Ziegler VE, Meyer DA. A rating scale for mania: reliability, validity and sensitivity. Br J Psychiatry. 1978;133:429–35.

25

Detecting significant genotype–phenotype association rules in bipolar disorder: market research meets complex genetics

René Breuer[1†], Manuel Mattheisen[2,3,4,40†], Josef Frank[1], Bertram Krumm[5], Jens Treutlein[1], Layla Kassem[6], Jana Strohmaier[1], Stefan Herms[2,3], Thomas W. Mühleisen[2,3], Franziska Degenhardt[2,3], Sven Cichon[2,3,7,8], Markus M. Nöthen[2,3], George Karypis[9], John Kelsoe[10], Tiffany Greenwood[10,11], Caroline Nievergelt[10], Paul Shilling[10], Tatyana Shekhtman[10], Howard Edenberg[12], David Craig[13], Szabolcs Szelinger[13], John Nurnberger[14], Elliot Gershon[15], Ney Alliey-Rodriguez[15], Peter Zandi[16], Fernando Goes[17], Nicholas Schork[13,18], Erin Smith[19,20], Daniel Koller[21], Peng Zhang[22], Judith Badner[15], Wade Berrettini[23], Cinnamon Bloss[24], William Byerley[25], William Coryell[26], Tatiana Foroud[21], Yirin Guo[27], Maria Hipolito[28], Brendan Keating[29,30], William Lawson[31], Chunyu Liu[32], Pamela Mahon[17], Melvin McInnis[33], Sarah Murray[19,34], Evaristus Nwulia[31], James Potash[35], John Rice[36], William Scheftner[37], Sebastian Zöllner[22], Francis J. McMahon[6], Marcella Rietschel[1] and Thomas G. Schulze[1,6,38,39*]

Abstract

Background: Disentangling the etiology of common, complex diseases is a major challenge in genetic research. For bipolar disorder (BD), several genome-wide association studies (GWAS) have been performed. Similar to other complex disorders, major breakthroughs in explaining the high heritability of BD through GWAS have remained elusive. To overcome this dilemma, genetic research into BD, has embraced a variety of strategies such as the formation of large consortia to increase sample size and sequencing approaches. Here we advocate a complementary approach making use of already existing GWAS data: a novel data mining procedure to identify yet undetected genotype–phenotype relationships. We adapted association rule mining, a data mining technique traditionally used in retail market research, to identify frequent and characteristic genotype patterns showing strong associations to phenotype clusters. We applied this strategy to three independent GWAS datasets from 2835 phenotypically characterized patients with BD. In a discovery step, 20,882 candidate association rules were extracted.

Results: Two of these rules—one associated with eating disorder and the other with anxiety—remained significant in an independent dataset after robust correction for multiple testing. Both showed considerable effect sizes (odds ratio ~ 3.4 and 3.0, respectively) and support previously reported molecular biological findings.

Conclusion: Our approach detected novel specific genotype–phenotype relationships in BD that were missed by standard analyses like GWAS. While we developed and applied our method within the context of BD gene discovery, it may facilitate identifying highly specific genotype–phenotype relationships in subsets of genome-wide data sets of other complex phenotype with similar epidemiological properties and challenges to gene discovery efforts.

Keywords: Bipolar disorder, Subphenotypes, Rule discovery, Data mining, Genotype–phenotype patterns

*Correspondence: tschulze@med.lmu.de
[†]René Breuer and Manuel Mattheisen contributed equally to this work
[39] Institute of Psychiatric Phenomics and Genomics (IPPG), Ludwig-Maximilians-University, Munich, Nußbaumstr. 7, 80336 Munich, Germany
Full list of author information is available at the end of the article

Background

It is widely accepted that the high heritability of around 80% for bipolar disorder (BD) is conferred by a polygenic component yet to be understood in its complexity (McGuffin et al. 2003; Craddock et al. 2005). Genome-wide association studies of BD have identified several genome-wide significant variants and also hinted at the existence of many more variants which fail to achieve the rigorous threshold of genome-wide significance ($p < 5.0e-08$) but contribute to the overall variance when considered within the context of polygenicity (Lee et al. 2012a, b; Sullivan et al. 2012; Schulze et al. 2014). However, the number of newly identified variants is far below original expectations, with limited sample sizes being one of the explanatory factors. The largest sample for a meta-analysis of GWAS of BD to date comprised nearly 64,000 participants (Sklar et al. 2011). Although this is an impressive sample size, GWAS of other phenotypes, such as adult height, have demonstrated that samples three-times this figure are required to achieve an adequate number of significant findings (Lango Allen et al. 2010). Recent successes of the Psychiatric Genomics Consortium (https://pgc.unc.edu/) in schizophrenia genetics where case–control samples have already exceeded 100,000 individuals suggest that continued enlargement of sample size will also increase the yield of genome-wide significant findings for BD. Clinical heterogeneity of the BD phenotype may also have hampered success in identifying vulnerability genes. DSM (American Psychiatric Association 2000) and ICD (World Health Organization 2011) present a list of possible symptoms, each of which must persist for a minimum period of time for the diagnosis to be assigned. Since a diagnosis of BD is based upon the presence of a minimum number of these symptoms, the diagnosis can be assigned for varying symptom constellations. Thus the nature and number of the underlying clinical symptoms, as well as the time periods over which they occur, show substantial variation between patients. Thus, the clinical presentation is diverse, and differing disease courses are observed within each diagnostic category.

We hypothesize that heterogeneity can be reduced and the number of identified variants increased by analyzing the joint effect of several genetic variants on specific subsets of clinical items identified in BD patients (Purcell et al. 2009; Lee et al. 2011). We hypothesize that systematic data mining approaches from other fields can be applied to analyses of GWAS data. Popular methods such as support vector machines, Bayesian networks, and association rule mining (ARM) have been successfully applied in industry. ARM is one of the most important and well researched techniques of data mining (Kotsiantis and Kanellopoulos 2006). It aims to extract casual structures among sets of items in data bases for discovering and predicting regularities and has been applied extensively to market research (Agrawal et al. 1993; Ngai et al. 2009) in order to analyze customer habits. For several years now, it has been applied to biological data, in particular microarray data for gene expression analysis (Martinez et al. 2008; Liu et al. 2011). We consider this approach highly appropriate for genome-wide data, since its main goal is to unravel unknown associations between source data, i.e. customer profiles in market research, and potential targets, i.e. their buying behavior, which can then be used for target prediction (Fig. 1). Within the context of genome-wide data, the source data are genetic variants and the potential targets are symptom clusters. The aim of the present study is to apply this data mining approach to GWAS datasets of BD in order to identify yet undetected genotype–phenotype associations, searching for associations between frequently occurring genotype combinations and symptom clusters.

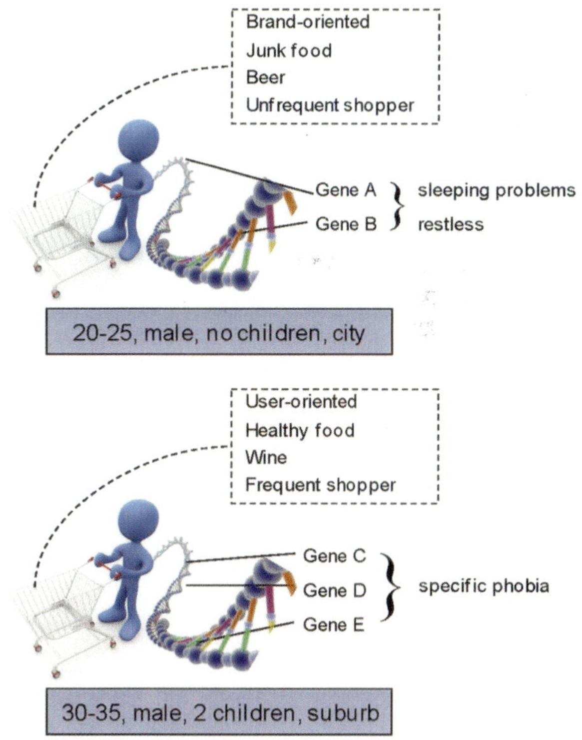

Fig. 1 Outline of the overall approach. A main goal of market research is to identify rules that predict customer habits based on market baskets. In the cartoon, a male customer between 20 and 25 without children living in the city favours junk food and beer and when he goes shopping he will most likely buy brands. Adapting this idea to genetic research we try to identify those genetic factors from the plethora of genetic factors in the "market basket" that are characterized by specific phenotypic features (like specific phobia or restlessness). The cartoon contains graphical depictions by Benjamin Albiach Galan and Konstantinos Kokkinis

Methods

Samples

Genotype and phenotype data were obtained from three independent BD case–control samples, the US-American GAIN (1000 cases, 1033 controls) (Smith et al. 2009) and TGEN (1190 cases, 401 controls) collections (Smith et al. 2011) and the German BoMa (645 cases, 1310 controls) sample (Cichon et al. 2011). Clinical symptoms, sociodemographic and environmental features were ascertained using structured interviews (DIGS (Nurnberger et al. 1994) for GAIIN and SCID-I for BoMa (Spitzer et al. 1992). All phenotypes were retrieved from professionally curated databases (Potash et al. 2007; Fangerau et al. 2004). Detailed information on the samples can be found elsewhere (Smith et al. 2009, 2011; Baum et al. 2008). Descriptive statistics for both samples are provided in Additional file 1: Table S1. The total sample for the present study comprised $n=5579$ subjects (2835 cases and 2744 controls). The GAIN sample was used for the discovery step, and the TGEN and BoMa samples were used for the replication step. Prior to study inclusion, written informed consent was obtained from all subjects.

Selection of clinical features

In addition to the two phenotypic specifiers age at onset (AAO) and sex, we included a variety of other phenotypic feature, for the selection of which we applied the following criteria: (i) evidence of familiality and/or heritability (Schulze 2006); (ii) a frequency of at least 5% across all three samples; (iii) a missing data rate of less than 10%; (iv) availability in at least two of the three data sets; and/or (v) clinical features with a high frequency among BD patients, including co-morbid features not being part of the diagnosis of BD. In total, we selected 23 clinical features (Additional file 2: Table S2), the frequency of which was similar across all three samples (Additional file 3: Figure S1), and ranged from < 10% (e.g. eating disorder) to 80% (e.g. reckless behavior).

Selection of single markers and genetic model

The GAIN and TGEN samples were genome-wide genotyped on the Affymetrix 6.0 SNP array. For the BoMa sample, the Illumina HumanHap550 BeadChip was used. All genotypes were imputed based on 2.1 million HapMap Phase 2 markers (McMahon et al. 2010). Due to computational runtime constraints, our analysis is based on a selected number of markers. We included only those SNPs that showed an association p-value of less than 0.001 in a recent meta-analysis of 4961 BD patients and 7294 controls (Additional file 4: Text S1, Methods-*SNP selection*). Our resulting SNP set comprised 5487 SNPs, on which LD pruning (Additional file 4: Text S1, Methods-*Linkage disequilibrium*) was performed in order to reduce redundancy within the genotype data before the discovery step and to decrease runtime. This left us with a total of 1599 SNPs. Of these, 1581 SNPs were available in all three samples studied. As the ARM approach requires binary variables we had to transform the genotype information into a binary format (Additional file 4: Text S1, Methods-*Genetic Models*).

Algorithm for association rule mining

The basic idea for identifying genotype–phenotype data using these binary genotype data is to (i) receive frequent genotype patterns, (ii) to look for significantly associated phenotypes as candidates, or in terms of the original algorithm *candidate association rules*, in a discovery dataset, and (iii) to validate these candidate association rules in an independent replication dataset. Figure 2 illustrates the basic idea of combining genotypic information in order to identify frequent genotype patterns (left) and evaluate the patterns regarding interesting phenotype traits in order to receive a candidate association rule like genotype-pattern A implies phenotype-pattern B ($A \Rightarrow B$) (right).

Identifying frequent genotype patterns

The frequent genotype patterns can be identified in a systematic manner. Several approaches have been developed for association rule mining (Han and Kamber 2006; Maimon and Rokach 2005). Here we use the most common Apriori algorithm, as it can be implemented in a straightforward manner and shows a good performance for short patterns, making it an ideal choice for the present study. For details, see Additional file 4: Text S1, Methods-*Runtime, Apriori algorithm*, and *Closed frequent itemsets.*

Discovery of candidate association rules

Once a frequent genotype pattern is identified it is tested for association with each phenotypic trait, i.e. each of the 23 selected clinical features. This step involves the generation of a contingency table for the frequent genotype pattern and each clinical feature. Based on this contingency table, the interestingness of an association rule is assessed. For details, see Additional file 4: Text S1, Methods-*Association rule discovery.*

Replication of candidate association rules

The third stage of our rule mining approach is the replication of the candidate rules. Significance testing is rarely investigated in rule mining (Webb 2006). However, we considered this to be important as an inherent aspect of rule mining is the occurrence of false positive

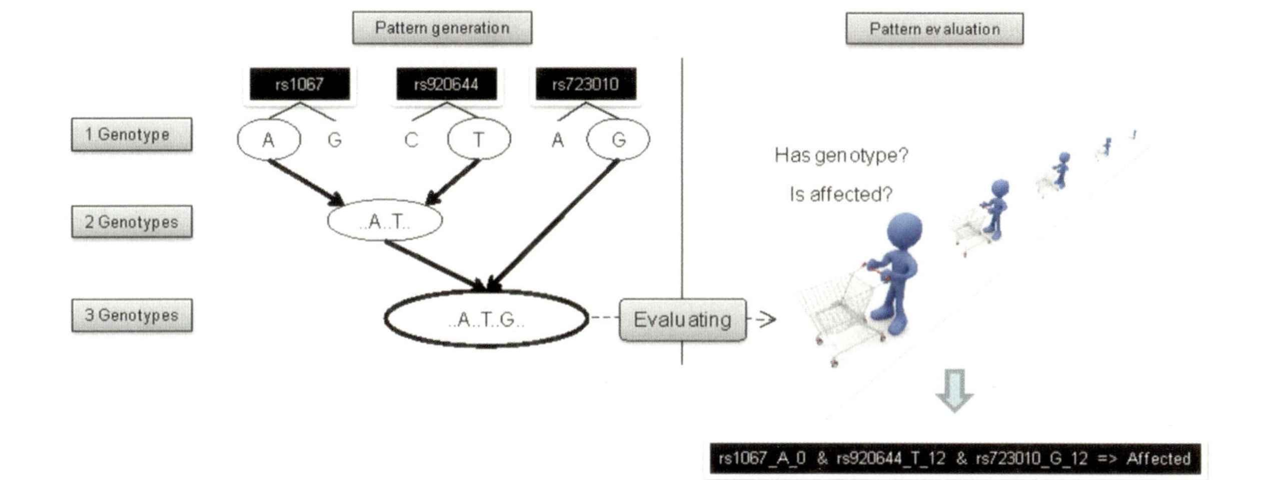

Fig. 2 Illustration of the implemented version of the association rule mining algorithm. The lattice shown left is traversed starting from root {} to all leaves. Each genotype pattern (node in the tree) represents a subgroup of patients shown in the genotype matrix G. Additionally, using the p phenotype information of the patients from matrix P, we can count genotype and phenotype occurrences in contingency tables. Here illustrated for the genotype pattern $g_1g_2g_n$ with 'a' counting all patients where genotype $g_1g_2g_n$ and phenotype p_i are present, 'd' were neither of both are present, and 'b' and 'c' counting patients with presentation of genotype $g_1g_2g_n$ but not phenotype p_i and visa versa. The lattice is traversed as long as there are unprocessed genotype patterns that cannot be pruned before

results. We anticipated 50,000 false positives per one million tests on the basis of the widely used type I error rate of 5%. One approach to correct for this is to assume that the association rules are independent and apply Bonferroni correction to the test statistics in the discovery data only. However, several simulations have shown that as well as reducing the rate of false discoveries, the Bonferroni approach also reduces the rate of true positive findings (Webb 2006). Alternatively, permutation tests can be performed to test whether or not the association between a genotype pattern and a phenotype cluster is random (Additional file 4: Text S1, Methods-*Permutation tests*). However, when constrained to a single dataset, both methods are susceptible to overfitting. Thus, we considered the performance of a replication of all candidate rules n_{CR} in an independent dataset a more appropriate alternative as this adjusts for potentially spurious sample effects and random associations. Using the latter approach and the Bonferroni method, we defined a primary test-wide significance level α_{adj} for the replication as:

$$\alpha_{adj} = 0.05/n_{CR}.$$

However, as shown by our findings and those of Webb (2006), when extracting a set of association rules using the ARM approach, the rules are unlikely to be independent. Thus, this significance testing remains conservative and is likely to reject true positive results. Therefore, we also report p-values adjusted using the false discovery rate (FDR). This is an alternative statistical method to adjust for multiple testing: FDR assumes sub-groups of tests to be dependent. FDR is less conservative, resulting in an increase in power at the cost of an increased likelihood of type I errors (Benjamini and Hochberg 1995; Benjamini 2010).

Analyses

In order to apply our approach to the GWAS data, we developed a software tool, termed RUDI (*RUle Discoverer*; http://www.rudi-genetics.net; see also Additional file 4: Text S1). A rule discovery analysis of 1581 SNPs (3162 variables) and 23 phenotypic traits in the 1000 cases from the GAIN sample was performed. Around 4.286e+09 genotype patterns were tested using the following settings: (a) z-score of 5.0; (b) maximum length of the genotype pattern of 3, and (c) absolute minimum support of individuals matching the particular genotype pattern of 50 (Additional file 4: Text S1, Methods-*Parameter selection*). The runtime on an Intel Xeon X3220 with 2.4 GHz was around 18 h on a single processor using the described settings. A second run was performed to replicate the candidate rules in our replication dataset of n = 1835 BD patients (TGEN + BoMa).

Results

N = 20,882 candidate rules satisfied the required thresholds in the discovery data set. The strongest association rule showed a p-value of 3.457e−15 (#962) and thus reached significance after correction for multiple testing using the Bonferroni method (adjusted p-value = 3.260e−04). When all candidate rules were compared, 15 disjunct phenotype clusters were observed. Of these, 11 consisted of a single clinical feature. The remaining four consisted of two clinical features (Additional file 5: Table S3).

Replication of the n = 20,882 candidate rules was then performed in our replication dataset of n = 1835 BD patients. The level of significance after adjustment using the Bonferroni method was 2.394e−06 for a default alpha of 5%. Although replication of the top finding from the discovery step (#962) failed, two rules met the significance threshold:

(i) rule #12978

rs6733011_A_0, rs4113925_T_0, rs3769745_T_0=> 'eating disorder' (ED)

with a p-value = 3.576e−08 and an odds ratio (OR) = 3.566 [0.95 confidence interval (CI) 2.169–5.681];

and (ii) rule #6221

rs858057_G_0, rs4757144_G_0, rs3130781_C_0=> 'simple phobia' (SP)

with a p-value = 1.780e−06 and an OR = 2.995 [0.95 CI 1.841–4.730]. Three further rules remained significant after FDR correction (Additional file 4: Text S1, *Further results*). A total of 1252 (6.0%) of the candidate rules reached nominal significance in the replication sample. The distribution of the p-values for all candidate rules in the replication dataset fits the expected Chi squared distribution (Additional file 6: Figure S2).

Association finding with eating disorder

Our top finding, rule #12978, showed a genotype pattern frequency of 5.2–7.4% in the case samples and of around 5.2–5.8% in the control populations (Additional file 7: Table S4). Further details of the genotype pattern are shown in Additional file 8: Table S7. In addition to the primary replication within the discovery-replication framework, two types of permutation tests (Additional file 4: Text S1, Methods-*Permutation tests*) were performed to estimate: (a) the probability of finding a more significant association with the genotype pattern by re-sampling the phenotype; and (b) the probability of randomly choosing a genotype pattern that shows at least the same level of significance. Both reject the hypothesis of a random association based on the empirical p-values observed (4.000e−06 and 7.000e−06, respectively), based on 1e + 06 trials in the discovery data. In a subsequent step, we combined the data of all n = 2835 patients and re-evaluated rule #12978, i.e. we compared patients with and without an eating disorder (BD_ED and BD_nonED, respectively) in terms of the genotype pattern of this rule. This combined analysis of cases showed a p-value = 5.300e−14 and an OR = 4.120 [0.95 CI 2.740–6.068]. Thus, within the group of patients carrying the genotype pattern, the frequency of a co-morbid eating disorder is increased on average by a factor of 4. An association analysis was then performed for each of the three SNPs of the genotype pattern to determine whether the observed association was due to the combination of the three SNPs or conferred by only one of them. Single trend tests for the phenotype 'eating disorder' was performed in each of the three datasets using PLINK (Purcell et al. 2007). No significant evidence was found to support the hypothesis that the association with the phenotype of the rule is driven by a single SNP (Additional file 9: Table S6).

We furthermore performed an association study of the genotype pattern of rule #12978 in cases versus controls. No differential distribution of the genotype pattern was observed between (a) the BD_nonED cases and controls and (b) between all BD cases and controls: However, the genotype pattern was significantly associated with BD_ED cases compared to controls (p-value = 4.937e−14, OR = 4.107 [0.95 CI 2.735–6.040]) (Additional file 10: Table S5).

Association finding with simple phobia

The second finding, rule #6221, showed an association with 'simple phobia'. The genotype frequencies were 5.4–6.9% in cases and 5.1–7.2% in controls. In the combined analysis of all cases, we observed a p-value = 3.476e−13 (adjusted p-value = 3.427e−02) and an OR = 3.551 [0.95 CI 2.453–5.063]. Thus, within the group of patients carrying the genotype pattern, the frequency of a co-morbid simple phobia increased on average by a factor of 3.5. As was the case for the rule including eating disorder, the association was not conferred by the single SNPs taken separately but only in combination (Additional file 9: Table S6). Likewise a case–control analysis showed: (a) no differential distribution of the genotype pattern between the BD_nonSP cases and controls nor (b) between all BD cases and controls. However, we observed (c) a significant differential distribution between BD_SP cases and controls (p-value = 1.686e−11, OR = 3.195 [0.95 CI 2.220–4.523]) (Additional file 10: Table S5).

Discussion

Application of the ARM data mining approach identified significant associations between sets of candidate SNPs and BD subgroups characterized by two specific comorbid conditions: eating disorder and simple phobia.

Our top finding (rule #12978) highlights an association between the genotype pattern of rule #12978 and the subgroup of BD patients with an eating disorder. The association was conferred by the combination of three SNPs but not by the individual SNPs. While the proportion of BD patients with an eating disorder was very small (n = 192 patients; i.e. 6.8% of our sample), this frequency is comparable to that reported in other studies (McElroy et al. 2006, 2011). Thirty-seven of these patients displayed the genotype pattern of rule #12978, which was present in 182 of all BD patients. Despite the small sample size, the association finding (p-value = 4.937e−14) is rather strong with an OR = 4.107 in the combined case–control analysis, an effect size typically not seen for diagnosis-based studies.

The likelihood that our findings may be due to chance is further decreased when considering the following two points: Firstly, the replication sample was comprised of two smaller samples, and in both of these samples, the effect was in the same direction (with test-wide significance being achieved in neither). Secondly, our findings fall in line with reports on the function of the genes involved. SNP rs3769745 of rule #12978 is located in the intron region of the cyclic nucleotide gated channel alpha 3 gene (*CNGA3*) on chromosome 2. In humans, *CNGA3* is implicated in total color blindness (achromatopsia) (Ding et al. 2010; Lam et al. 2011). Animal studies have shown that *CNGA3* is required for normal vision (Biel et al. 1999), olfactory signal transduction (Leinders-Zufall et al. 2007), and involved in nociceptive processing (Heine et al. 2011). Further, it is expressed in the mouse brain and is reported to influence synaptic plasticity and behaviour (Michalakis et al. 2011). Research has also shown that the specialized olfactory subsystem to which CNGA3 belongs is required for the acquisition of socially transmitted food preferences (STFPs) in mice. Mice that lack this gene fail to acquire STFPs from other mice, and exhibit an absence of neuronal activation of the ventral subiculum of the hippocampus, a brain region implicated in STFP retrieval (Munger et al. 2010). According to the KEGG Database, *CNGA3* is in a common pathway, i.e. olfactory transduction (KEGG ID hsa04740), with *CALM1*, a candidate gene for anorexia nervosa (Pinheiro et al. 2010). To the best of our knowledge, no association between this variant and eating disorder has been reported so far. For the other two variants, a plausible support from biological data is not available. SNP rs6733011 is located in an intron region of the KIAA1211-like (*KIAA1211L*) gene on chromosome 2 that encodes the uncharacterized protein *C2orf55* (chromosome 2 open reading frame 55). The location is within a 500 kb window to rs3769745, but not in the same LD block ($r^2 = 0.027$ and D' = 0.343 in the discovery dataset). Its function remains unknown. SNP rs4113925 is located on chromosome 12q24.21 in an intron of the T-box transcription factor (*TBX5*) gene. This T-box gene has been implicated in heart development and disease as well as specification of limb identity (Wang et al. 2011).

To investigate whether our finding identified genetic markers specific to BD with an eating disorder subphenotype or eating disorder per se, we tested a potential association of the genotype pattern of rule #12978 with an eating disorder phenotype comprising anorexia and bulimia in a population-based sample from Australia (n = 1672, 12.9% with a diagnosis of anorexia or bulimia). We did not see an association of the genotype pattern of rule #12978, suggesting that our approach has detected a genetic marker for BD with comorbid eating disorder rather than for eating disorder per se.

Our second finding, rule #6221, showed an association with simple phobia. Two of the three contributing SNPs are located within genes. SNP rs4757144 is located in an intron region of the aryl hydrocarbon receptor nuclear translocator-like (*ARNTL*) gene, and rs3130781 is located in an intron region of the diffuse panbronchiolitis critical region 1 (*DPCR1*) gene. The third SNP, rs858057, is located at an intergenic region of 20p11.21. An implication of ARNTL in the etiology disorders via its influence on the circadian system has been discussed repeatedly (Mansour et al. 2006; Le-Niculescu et al. 2009; Nakatani 2006; Nievergelt et al. 2006; Shi et al. 2008; Sipilä et al. 2010). There is further report that genes homologous to *ARNTL* may be implicated in the etiology of anxiety. Sipilä and colleagues (Sipilä et al. 2010) tested several anxiety phenotypes for association with 13 circadian genes and found association between social phobia and *ARNTL2*. Thus the *ARNTL* gene family may be involved in this co-morbid phenotype. The second gene, *DPCR1*, is located in the major histocompatibility complex (MHC), which hosts genes that are crucial for the functioning of the immune system.

While we observed several other genotype–phenotype rules that may warrant further in-depth investigation (Table 1 and Additional file 4: Text S1, *Further results*), we focused on the rules implicating BD subtypes with comorbid eating disorder and simple phobia, respectively, as only these two survived our stringent multi-tiered evaluation of potential type I error. These steps help minimize—if not eliminate- type I error rate in ARM due to the overfitting of rules in a particular dataset (Han and Kamber 2006).

We would like to point out that the two reported association rules were associated with very low frequency phenotypes. This is due to the characteristics of the z-score approach applied. Since small proportions of the data are more likely to deviate strongly from the random distribution, larger effects and thus larger z-scores are expected. As only those rules that show a z-score of greater or equal 5 are extracted as candidates, this particular rule measure is biased towards associations with low frequency phenotypes. This further explains the relatively small number, i.e. 4 out of 15 (Additional file 4: Text S1, Methods-*Phenotype cluster*), of phenotype clusters

Table 1 Top 10 association rules regarding their p-values in the replication dataset (TGEN + BoMa)

PID	Groups				Statistics		Adjusted p-value	
	GP	Gp	gP	gp	p_chisq	Odds ratio (0.95 CI)	Bonferroni	FDR
12978	25	105	107	1598	3.576e−08	3.566 [2.169–5.681]	0.00075	0.00075
6221	26	84	162	1563	1.780e−06	2.995 [1.841–4.730]	0.03717	0.01859
12681	33	103	187	1512	4.648e−06	2.596 [1.682–3.917]	0.09706	0.02771
12981	25	129	107	1574	5.720e−06	2.860 [1.751–4.520]	0.11944	0.02771
6225	25	84	163	1563	6.635e−06	2.862 [1.747–4.545]	0.13855	0.02771
6228	26	93	162	1554	1.585e−05	2.690 [1.661–4.225]	0.33102	0.05517
4428	31	88	212	1504	2.021e−05	2.505 [1.600–3.830]	0.42198	0.06028
6111	21	109	111	1594	4.096e−05	2.779 [1.636–4.529]	0.85530	0.10654
6183	20	66	168	1581	4.592e−05	2.864 [1.652–4.765]	0.95887	0.10654
6178	20	68	168	1579	7.577e−05	2.777 [1.604–4.611]	1	0.15823

Listed are the rule identifier (PID), the counts per group of the contingency tables, the p-values based on the Chi squared test along with the odds ratios including confidence intervals (CI), and results from two multiple correction methods (based on 20,882 tests). The coding of the groups is as follow: G, if genotype pattern is present, g if not; P, if phenotype pattern is present, p if not. *FDR* false discovery rate

that consisted of more than one phenotype. We may thus have discarded many potentially true findings. Given that our study can be considered a proof-of-concept for the application of ARM on GWAS-derived data for a complex phenotype, we opted for statistical stringency rather than a merely exploratory pattern mining. While this approach resulted in only two findings, they are characterized by effect sizes up to four times larger than typically seen in GWAS of BD or other complex traits.

Conclusions

In summary, using already available GWAS data sets on BD, we have established and implemented a novel data mining process for complex genetic data. We identified genotype–phenotype patterns highlighting subtypes of BD characterized by specific comorbid conditions. These two comorbid conditions, eating disorder and simple phobia, may delineate more homogenous subgroups of BD that warrant further study in genomic studies of BD.

An important limitation of our approach is that our approach was only based on 5487 SNPs that showed some evidence of association with BD. As association rule mining may detect hidden association of specific phenotypes with previously un-identified SNPs, our approach may have missed several novel associations. This restriction, however, was due to our motivation to perform genotype–phenotype dissection on SNPs that showed some evidence of association. We were further bound by some computational runtime constraints. Further extensions of the algorithm will be required to allow for a variety of assumed genetic models (here we used a dominant genetic model), to optimize computational feasibility for an increased number of SNPs (Additional file 4: Text S1, Methods-*Runtime*), and to determine the optimal correction methodology for highly correlated data.

Our approach highlights a strategy for genotype–phenotype dissection and for the identification of genetic susceptibility variants beyond initial GWAS of heterogeneous disorders. Finally, our results emphasize the importance of thorough phenotyping, particularly with regard to comorbidity.

Additional files

Additional file 1: Table S1. Descriptive data for patients with bipolar disorder and controls.

Additional file 2: Table S2. Details on the 23 phenotypic traits included into the study.

Additional file 3: Figure S1. Frequencies of the selected phenotype variables in the patients for each bipolar disorder sample. Non-binary variables are mapped to binary variables. Abbreviations: aao = age at onset; M = during mania; D = during depression.

Additional file 4: Text S1. Supplementary notes on methods.

Additional file 5: Table S3. Overview of all distinct phenotype clusters received from the candidate rules of the discovery step.

Additional file 6: Figure S2. QQ-Plot of all chi-squared values of the replications step (n=20,882). Expected quantiles are based on a 1 degree of freedom distribution. Confidence intervals are based on a 5% error rate. The inflation factor was estimated to be 1.140.

Additional file 7: Table S4. Association results for each data set of our top finding, pattern #12978.

Additional file 8: Table S7. Details regarding the genotype patterns of the top 5 association rules.

Additional file 9: Table S6. Single SNP association results for each SNP of our two test-wide significant findings (Bonferroni) regarding the phenotype cluster of the corresponding association rule.

Additional file 10: Table S5. Association results of the case-control analyses for the top 5 replication patterns.

Authors' contributions
RB: study design, analysis, writing the first draft, software programming; MM: study design, analysis, interpretation of data; JF, BK, JT: analysis, interpretation of data; ; LK: study design, phenotyping; JS: phenotyping; SH, TWM, FD: molecular genetic analyses; SC: molecular genetic analyses, interpretation of the data; MMN: study design, interpretation of data, securing funding; GK: method development, study design, interpretation of data; JK, TG, CN, PS, TS, HE, DC, SS, JN, EG, NAR, PZ, FG, NS, ES, DK, PZ, JB, WB, CB, WB, WC, TF, YG, MH, BK, WL, CL, PM, MM, SM, EN, JP, JR, WS, SZ: study design, interpretation of data, securing funding; FJM: study design, interpretation of data, securing funding; MR: study design, interpretation of data, securing funding; TGS: lead PI, overall study design, interpretation of data, securing funding, writing of the manuscript. All authors read and approved the final manuscript.

Author details
[1] Department of Genetic Epidemiology in Psychiatry, Central Institute of Mental Health, Medical Faculty Mannheim/Heidelberg University, Mannheim, Germany. [2] Department of Genomics, Life & Brain Center, University of Bonn, Bonn, Germany. [3] Institute of Human Genetics, University of Bonn, Bonn, Germany. [4] Center for Integrative Sequencing, iSEQ, Department of Biomedicine, Aarhus University, Aarhus, Denmark. [5] Department for Biostatistics, Central Institute of Mental Health, Medical Faculty Mannheim/Heidelberg University, Mannheim, Germany. [6] Human Genetics Branch, Intramural Research Program, National Institute of Mental Health, National Institutes of Health, US Department of Health and Human Services, Bethesda, MD, USA. [7] Institute of Neuroscience and Medicine (INM-1), Structural and Functional Organisation of the Brain, Genomic Imaging, Research Centre Juelich, Juelich, Germany. [8] Department of Biomedicine, University of Basel, Basel, Switzerland. [9] Department of Computer Science & Engineering, University of Minnesota, Minneapolis, MN, USA. [10] Department of Psychiatry, University of California San Diego, San Diego, USA. [11] BGI-Shenzhen, Beishan Industrial Zone, Yantian District, Shenzhen, China. [12] Department of Biochemistry and Molecular Biology, Indiana University School of Medicine, Indianapolis, USA. [13] The Translational Genomics Research Institute, Phoenix, USA. [14] Department of Psychiatry, Indiana University School of Medicine, Indianapolis, USA. [15] Department of Psychiatry and Behavioral Neuroscience, University of Chicago, Chicago, USA. [16] Department of Mental Health, John Hopkins Bloomberg School of Public Health, Baltimore, USA. [17] Department of Psychiatry and Behavioral Sciences, John Hopkins School of Medicine, Baltimore, USA. [18] J. Craig Venter Institute, La Jolla, USA. [19] Scripps Genomic Medicine & The Scripps Translational Sciences Institute (STSI), La Jolla, USA. [20] Department of Pediatrics and Rady's Children's Hospital, School of Medicine, University of California San Diego, La Jolla, USA. [21] Department of Medical and Molecular Genetics, Indiana University School of Medicine, Indianapolis, USA. [22] Department of Computational Medicine and Bioinformatics, University of Michigan, Ann Arbor, USA. [23] Department of Psychiatry, University of Pennsylvania, Philadelphia, USA. [24] University of California, San Diego, La Jolla, USA. [25] Department of Psychiatry, University of California at San Francisco, San Francisco, USA. [26] University of Iowa Hospitals and Clinics, Iowa City, USA. [27] Center for Applied Genomics, Children's Hospital of Philadelphia, Abramson Research Center, Philadelphia, USA. [28] Department of Psychiatry and Behavioral Sciences, Howard University Hospital, Washington, USA. [29] Cardiovascular Institute, University of Pennsylvania School of Medicine, Philadelphia, PA, USA. [30] Institute for Translational Medicine and Therapeutics, School of Medicine, University of Pennsylvania, Philadelphia, PA, USA. [31] Dell Medical School, University of Texas at Austin, Austin, USA. [32] Department of Psychiatry, University of Illinois at Chicago, Chicago, USA. [33] Department of Psychiatry, University of Michigan, Ann Arbor, USA. [34] Department of Pathology, University of California San Diego, La Jolla, USA. [35] Department of Psychiatry, Carver College of Medicine, University of Iowa School of Medicine, Iowa City, USA. [36] Department of Psychiatry, Washington University School of Medicine in St. Louis, St. Louis, USA. [37] Rush University Medical Center, Chicago, USA. [38] Department of Psychiatry and Psychotherapy, University of Göttingen, Göttingen, Germany. [39] Institute of Psychiatric Phenomics and Genomics (IPPG), Ludwig-Maximilians-University, Munich, Nußbaumstr. 7, 80336 Munich, Germany. [40] Department of Psychiatry, Psychosomatics, and Psychotherapy, University of Würzburg, Würzburg, Germany.

Acknowledgements
We gratefully acknowledge critical input from Nicholas Martin, Scott Gordon, and Cynthia Bulik.

Competing interests
The authors declare that they have no competing interests.

Funding
This study is part of the *Systematic Investigation of the Molecular Causes of Major Mood Disorders and Schizophrenia* (*MooDS*) network, which is funded by the Federal Ministry of Education and Research (BMBF) through the framework of National Genomic Research Network (NGFN) (Grant 01GS08144 to SC and MMN; Grant 01GS08147 to MR). MR was also supported by the Seventh Framework Program of the European Union (FP7/2007–2011) under grant agreement no. 242257 (ADAMS). MMN also received support from the Alfried Krupp von Bohlen und Halbach-Stiftung. LK, FJM, and TGS were also supported through Intramural Research Program of the National Institute of Mental Health (NIHM) at the National Institutes of Health (NIH) of the US Government. TGS is supported through grants from the *Deutsche Forschungsgemeinschaft* (DFG; SCHU 1603/4-1 & 5-1) and the *Dr. Lisa Oehler Foundation* (Kassel, Germany).

References

Agrawal R, Imielinski T, Swami A. Mining association rules between sets of items in large databases. In: Proceedings of the 1993 ACM SIGMOD international conference on management of data. 2. Washington DC: ACM Press; 1993. p. 207–16.

American Psychiatric Association. Diagnostic and statistical manual of mental disorders: DSM-IV-TR. Washington, DC: American Psychiatric Association; 2000.

Baum AE, Akula N, Cabanero M, Cardona I, Corona W, et al. A genome-wide association study implicates diacylglycerol kinase eta (DGKH) and several other genes in the etiology of bipolar disorder. Mol Psychiatry. 2008;13:197–207. https://doi.org/10.1038/sj.mp.4002012.

Benjamini Y. Simultaneous and selective inference: current successes and future challenges. Biom J. 2010;52:708–21. https://doi.org/10.1002/bimj.200900299.

Benjamini Y, Hochberg Y. Controlling the false discovery rate: a practical and powerful approach to multiple testing. J R Stat Soc Ser B (Methodological). 1995;57:289–300.

Biel M, Seeliger M, Pfeifer A, Kohler K, Gerstner A, Ludwig A, Jaissle G, Fauser S, Zrenner E, Hofmann F. Selective loss of cone function in mice lacking the cyclic nucleotide-gated channel CNG3. Proc Natl Acad Sci USA. 1999;96:7553–7.

Cichon S, Mühleisen TW, Degenhardt FA, Mattheisen M, Miró X, et al. Genome-wide association study identifies genetic variation in neurocan as a susceptibility factor for bipolar disorder. Am J Hum Genet. 2011;88:372–81. https://doi.org/10.1016/j.ajhg.2011.01.017.

Craddock N, O'Donovan MC, Owen MJ. The genetics of schizophrenia and bipolar disorder: dissecting psychosis. J Med Genet. 2005;42:193–204. https://doi.org/10.1136/jmg.2005.030718.

Ding X-Q, Fitzgerald JB, Quiambao AB, Harry CS, Malykhina AP. Molecular pathogenesis of achromatopsia associated with mutations in the cone cyclic nucleotide-gated channel CNGA3 subunit. Adv Exp Med Biol. 2010;664:245–53. https://doi.org/10.1007/978-1-4419-1399-9_28.

Fangerau H, Ohlraun S, Granath RO, Nöthen MM, Rietschel M, et al. Computer-assisted phenotype characterization for genetic research in psychiatry. Hum Hered. 2004;58:122–30. https://doi.org/10.1159/000083538.

Han J, Kamber M. Data mining concepts and techniques, second edition. 2nd ed. Amsterdam: Elsevier; Morgan Kaufmann Publishers; 2006.

Heine S, Michalakis S, Kallenborn-Gerhardt W, Lu R, Lim HY, Weiland J, Del Turco D, Deller T, Tegeder I, Biel M, Geisslinger G, Schmidtko A. CNGA3: a target of spinal nitric oxide/cGMP signaling and modulator of inflammatory pain hypersensitivity. J Neurosci. 2011;31:11184–92.

Kotsiantis S, Kanellopoulos D. Association rules mining: a recent overview. Int Trans Comput Sci Eng. 2006;32:71–82.

Lam K, Guo H, Wilson GA, Kohl S, Wong F. Identification of variants in CNGA3 as cause for achromatopsia by exome sequencing of a single patient. Arch Ophthalmol. 2011;129:1212–7. https://doi.org/10.1001/archophthalmol.2011.254.

Lango Allen H, Estrada K, Lettre G, Berndt SI, Weedon MN, et al. Hundreds of variants clustered in genomic loci and biological pathways affect human height. Nature. 2010;467:832–8. https://doi.org/10.1038/nature09410.

Lee SH, Wray NR, Goddard ME, Visscher PM. Estimating missing heritability for disease from genome-wide association studies. Am J Hum Genet. 2011;88:294–305. https://doi.org/10.1016/j.ajhg.2011.02.002.

Lee KW, Woon PS, Teo YY, Sim K. Genome wide association studies (GWAS) and copy number variation (CNV) studies of the major psychoses: what have we learnt? Neurosci Biobehav Rev. 2012a;36:556–71. https://doi.org/10.1016/j.neubiorev.2011.09.001.

Lee SH, DeCandia TR, Ripke S, Yang J, Schizophrenia Psychiatric Genome-Wide Association Study Consortium (PGC-SCZ), International Schizophrenia Consortium (ISC), Molecular Genetics of Schizophrenia Collaboration (MGS), Sullivan PF, Goddard ME, Keller MC, Visscher PM, Wray NR. Estimating the proportion of variation in susceptibility to schizophrenia captured by common SNPs. Nat Genet. 2012b;44:247–50.

Leinders-Zufall T, Cockerham RE, Michalakis S, Biel M, Garbers DL, Reed RR, Zufall F, Munger SD. Contribution of the receptor guanylyl cyclase GC-D to chemosensory function in the olfactory epithelium. Proc Natl Acad Sci USA. 2007;104(36):14507–12.

Le-Niculescu H, Patel SD, Bhat M, Kuczenski R, Faraone SV, et al. Convergent functional genomics of genome-wide association data for bipolar disorder: comprehensive identification of candidate genes, pathways and mechanisms. Am J Med Genet Part B Neuropsychiatr Genet. 2009;150B:155–81. https://doi.org/10.1002/ajmg.b.30887.

Liu Y-C, Cheng C-P, Tseng VS. Discovering relational-based association rules with multiple minimum supports on microarray datasets. Bioinformatics. 2011;27:3142–8. https://doi.org/10.1093/bioinformatics/btr526.

Maimon OZ, Rokach L. Data mining and knowledge discovery handbook. New York: Springer; 2005.

Mansour HA, Wood J, Logue T, Chowdari KV, Dayal M, et al. Association study of eight circadian genes with bipolar I disorder, schizoaffective disorder and schizophrenia. Genes Brain Behav. 2006;5:150–7. https://doi.org/10.1111/j.1601-183X.2005.00147.x.

Martinez R, Pasquier N, Pasquier C. GenMiner: mining non-redundant association rules from integrated gene expression data and annotations. Bioinformatics. 2008;24:2643–4. https://doi.org/10.1093/bioinformatics/btn490.

McElroy SL, Kotwal R, Keck PE Jr. Comorbidity of eating disorders with bipolar disorder and treatment implications. Bipolar Disord. 2006;8:686–95. https://doi.org/10.1111/j.1399-5618.2006.00401.x.

McElroy SL, Frye MA, Hellemann G, Altshuler L, Leverich GS, et al. Prevalence and correlates of eating disorders in 875 patients with bipolar disorder. J Affect Disord. 2011;128:191–8. https://doi.org/10.1016/j.jad.2010.06.037.

McGuffin P, Rijsdijk F, Andrew M, Sham P, Katz R, et al. The heritability of bipolar affective disorder and the genetic relationship to unipolar depression. Arch Gen Psychiatry. 2003;60:497–502. https://doi.org/10.1001/archpsyc.60.5.497.

McMahon FJ, Akula N, Schulze TG, Muglia P, Tozzi F, et al. Meta-analysis of genome-wide association data identifies a risk locus for major mood disorders on 3p21.1. Nat Genet. 2010;42:128–31. https://doi.org/10.1038/ng.523.

Michalakis S, Kleppisch T, Polta SA, Wotjak CT, Koch S, et al. Altered synaptic plasticity and behavioral abnormalities in CNGA3-deficient mice. Genes Brain Behav. 2011;10:137–48. https://doi.org/10.1111/j.1601-183X.2010.00646.x.

Munger SD, Leinders-Zufall T, McDougall LM, Cockerham RE, Schmid A, et al. An olfactory subsystem that detects carbon disulfide and mediates food-related social learning. Curr Biol. 2010;20:1438–44. https://doi.org/10.1016/j.cub.2010.06.021.

Nakatani N. Genome-wide expression analysis detects eight genes with robust alterations specific to bipolar I disorder: relevance to neuronal network perturbation. Hum Mol Genet. 2006;15:1949–62. https://doi.org/10.1093/hmg/ddl118.

Ngai EWT, Xiu L, Chau DCK. Application of data mining techniques in customer relationship management: a literature review and classification. Expert Syst Appl. 2009;36:2592–602. https://doi.org/10.1016/j.eswa.2008.02.021.

Nievergelt CM, Kripke DF, Barrett TB, Burg E, Remick RA, et al. Suggestive evidence for association of the circadian genes PERIOD3 and ARNTL with bipolar disorder. Am J Med Genet B Neuropsychiatr Genet. 2006;141B:234–41. https://doi.org/10.1002/ajmg.b.30252.

Nurnberger JI Jr, Blehar MC, Kaufmann CA, York-Cooler C, Simpson SG, et al. Diagnostic interview for genetic studies. Rationale, unique features, and training. NIMH Genetics Initiative. Arch Gen Psychiatry. 1994;51:849–59 **(discussion 863–864)**.

Pinheiro AP, Bulik CM, Thornton LM, Sullivan PF, Root TL, et al. Association study of 182 candidate genes in anorexia nervosa. Am J Med Genet B Neuropsychiatr Genet. 2010;153B:1070–80. https://doi.org/10.1002/ajmg.b.31082.

Potash JB, Toolan J, Steele J, Miller EB, Pearl J, et al. The bipolar disorder phenome database: a resource for genetic studies. Am J Psychiatry. 2007;164:1229–37. https://doi.org/10.1176/appi.ajp.2007.06122045.

Purcell S, Neale B, Todd-Brown K, Thomas L, Ferreira MAR, et al. PLINK: a tool set for whole-genome association and population-based linkage analyses. Am J Hum Genet. 2007;81:559–75. https://doi.org/10.1086/519795.

Purcell SM, Wray NR, Stone JL, Visscher PM, O'Donovan MC, et al. Common polygenic variation contributes to risk of schizophrenia and bipolar disorder. Nature. 2009;460:748–52. https://doi.org/10.1038/nature08185.

Schulze TG. What is familial about familial bipolar disorder? Resemblance among relatives across a broad spectrum of phenotypic characteristics. Arch Gen Psychiatry. 2006;63:1368. https://doi.org/10.1001/archpsyc.63.12.1368.

Schulze TG, Akula N, Breuer R, Steele J, Nalls MA, Singleton AB, Degenhardt FA, Nöthen MM, Cichon S, Rietschel M, Bipolar Genome Study, McMahon FJ. Molecular genetic overlap in bipolar disorder, schizophrenia, and major depressive disorder. World J Biol Psychiatry. 2014;15:200–8.

Shi J, Wittke-Thompson JK, Badner JA, Hattori E, Potash JB, et al. Clock genes may influence bipolar disorder susceptibility and dysfunctional circadian rhythm. Am J Med Genet Part B Neuropsychiatr Genet. 2008;147B:1047–55. https://doi.org/10.1002/ajmg.b.30714.

Sipilä T, Kananen L, Greco D, Donner J, Silander K, et al. An association analysis of circadian genes in anxiety disorders. Biol Psychiatry. 2010;67:1163–70. https://doi.org/10.1016/j.biopsych.2009.12.011.

Sklar P, Ripke S, Scott LJ, Andreassen OA, Cichon S, et al. Large-scale genome-wide association analysis of bipolar disorder identifies a new susceptibility locus near ODZ4. Nat Genet. 2011;43:977–83. https://doi.org/10.1038/ng.943.

Smith EN, Bloss CS, Badner JA, Barrett T, Belmonte PL, et al. Genome-wide association study of bipolar disorder in European American and African American individuals. Mol Psychiatry. 2009;14:755–63. https://doi.org/10.1038/mp.2009.43.

Smith EN, Koller DL, Panganiban C, Szelinger S, Zhang P, et al. Genome-wide association of bipolar disorder suggests an enrichment of replicable associations in regions near genes. PLoS Genet. 2011;7:e1002134. https://doi.org/10.1371/journal.pgen.1002134.

Spitzer RL, Williams JB, Gibbon M, First MB. The structured clinical interview for DSM-III-R (SCID). I: history, rationale, and description. Arch Gen Psychiatry. 1992;49:624–9.

Sullivan PF, Daly MJ, O'Donovan M. Genetic architectures of psychiatric disorders: the emerging picture and its implications. Nat Rev Genet. 2012;13:537–51. https://doi.org/10.1038/nrg3240.

Wang C, Cao D, Wang Q, Wang D-Z. Synergistic activation of cardiac genes by myocardin and Tbx5. PLoS ONE. 2011;6:e24242. https://doi.org/10.1371/journal.pone.0024242.

Webb GI. Discovering significant rules. In: Proceedings of the 12th ACM SIGKDD international conference on Knowledge discovery and data mining. New York: ACM Press; 2006. p. 434–43. https://doi.org/10.1145/1150402.1150451.

World Health Organization. International statistical classification of diseases and related health problems. Geneva: World Health Organization; 2011.

Permissions

All chapters in this book were first published in IJBD, by Springer; hereby published with permission under the Creative Commons Attribution License or equivalent. Every chapter published in this book has been scrutinized by our experts. Their significance has been extensively debated. The topics covered herein carry significant findings which will fuel the growth of the discipline. They may even be implemented as practical applications or may be referred to as a beginning point for another development.

The contributors of this book come from diverse backgrounds, making this book a truly international effort. This book will bring forth new frontiers with its revolutionizing research information and detailed analysis of the nascent developments around the world.

We would like to thank all the contributing authors for lending their expertise to make the book truly unique. They have played a crucial role in the development of this book. Without their invaluable contributions this book wouldn't have been possible. They have made vital efforts to compile up to date information on the varied aspects of this subject to make this book a valuable addition to the collection of many professionals and students.

This book was conceptualized with the vision of imparting up-to-date information and advanced data in this field. To ensure the same, a matchless editorial board was set up. Every individual on the board went through rigorous rounds of assessment to prove their worth. After which they invested a large part of their time researching and compiling the most relevant data for our readers.

The editorial board has been involved in producing this book since its inception. They have spent rigorous hours researching and exploring the diverse topics which have resulted in the successful publishing of this book. They have passed on their knowledge of decades through this book. To expedite this challenging task, the publisher supported the team at every step. A small team of assistant editors was also appointed to further simplify the editing procedure and attain best results for the readers.

Apart from the editorial board, the designing team has also invested a significant amount of their time in understanding the subject and creating the most relevant covers. They scrutinized every image to scout for the most suitable representation of the subject and create an appropriate cover for the book.

The publishing team has been an ardent support to the editorial, designing and production team. Their endless efforts to recruit the best for this project, has resulted in the accomplishment of this book. They are a veteran in the field of academics and their pool of knowledge is as vast as their experience in printing. Their expertise and guidance has proved useful at every step. Their uncompromising quality standards have made this book an exceptional effort. Their encouragement from time to time has been an inspiration for everyone.

The publisher and the editorial board hope that this book will prove to be a valuable piece of knowledge for researchers, students, practitioners and scholars across the globe.

List of Contributors

Connie Thuroee Nielsen
Institute of Regional Health Services Research, Faculty of Health Sciences, University of Southern Denmark, Odense, Denmark
Mental Health Service Vejle, Odense, The Region of Southern Denmark, Denmark

Pernille Kempel Ellegaard
Institute of Regional Health Services Research, Faculty of Health Sciences, University of Southern Denmark, Odense, Denmark
Research Unit, Mental Health Service Esbjerg, Gl. Vardevej 101, 6715 Esbjerg N, The Region of Southern Denmark, Denmark
OPEN, Odense Patient Data Explorative Network, Odense University Hospital, Institute of Clinical Research, University of Southern Denmark, Odense, Denmark

Rasmus Wentzer Licht and René Ernst Nielsen
Unit for Psychiatric Research, Psychiatry, Aalborg University Hospital, Aalborg, Denmark
Department of Clinical Medicine, Faculty of Medicine, Aalborg University, Aalborg, Denmark

Henrik Enghusen Poulsen
Clinical Pharmacology, Bispebjerg Frederiksberg Hospital, Copenhagen, Denmark
Institute of Clinical Medicine, Faculty of Health and Medical Sciences, University of Copenhagen, Copenhagen, Denmark

Michael Berk and Olivia May Dean
IMPACT Strategic Research Centre, School of Medicine, Barwon Health, Deakin University, Geelong, Australia
Florey Institute for Neuroscience and Mental Health, University of Melbourne, Parkville, Australia
Department of Psychiatry, University of Melbourne, Royal Melbourne Hospital, Parkville, Australia

Mohammadreza Mohebbi
Biostatistics Unit, Faculty of Health, Deakin University, Geelong, Australia

Karoline Krane-Gartiser, Gunnar Morken and Arne E. Vaaler
Department of Mental Health, NTNU, Norwegian University of Science and Technology, Sluppen, 7006 Trondheim, Norway
Department of Psychiatry, St. Olav's University Hospital, Trondheim, Norway

Jan Scott
Department of Mental Health, NTNU, Norwegian University of Science and Technology, Sluppen, 7006 Trondheim, Norway Academic Psychiatry, Institute of Neuroscience, Newcastle University, Newcastle upon Tyne, UK

Andreas Asheim
Department of Mathematical Sciences, NTNU, Norwegian University of Science and Technology, Trondheim, Norway
Center for Health Care Improvement in Mid-Norway, St. Olav's University Hospital, Trondheim, Norway

Ole Bernt Fasmer
Section for Psychiatry, Department of Clinical Medicine, Faculty of Medicine and Dentistry, University of Bergen, Bergen, Norway
Division of Psychiatry, Haukeland University Hospital, Bergen, Norway

Dominik K. E. Beyer and Nadja Freund
Experimental and Molecular Psychiatry, LWL University Hospital, Ruhr University Bochum, Universitätsstr. 150, 44801 Bochum, Germany

Lisa P. Henry
Orygen, The National Centre of Excellence in Youth Mental Health, 35 Poplar Road, Parkville, VIC 3052, Australia

Rothanthi Daglas, Kelly Allott and Sue M. Cotton
Orygen, The National Centre of Excellence in Youth Mental Health, 35 Poplar Road, Parkville, VIC 3052, Australia
Centre for Youth Mental Health, University of Melbourne, 35 Poplar Road, Parkville, VIC 3052, Australia

Michael Berk
Orygen, The National Centre of Excellence in Youth Mental Health, 35 Poplar Road, Parkville, VIC 3052, Australia
Centre for Youth Mental Health, University of Melbourne, 35 Poplar Road, Parkville, VIC 3052, Australia

IMPACT Strategic Research Centre, School of Medicine, Deakin University, Geelong 3220, Australia
Barwon Health and the Geelong Clinic, Swanston Centre, Geelong, VIC 3220, Australia Florey Institute for Neuroscience and Mental Health, Kenneth Myer Building, Royal Parade, Parkville, Australia

Murat Yücel
Brain and Mental Health Laboratory, School of Psychological Sciences and Monash Biomedical Imaging Facility, Monash University, Clayton, Australia

Craig A. Macneil and Melissa K. Hasty
Orygen Youth Health-Clinical Program, 35 Poplar Road, Parkville 3052, Australia

Robert Gonzalez and Angelica Forero
Department of Psychiatry, Texas Tech University Health Sciences Center El Paso, El Paso, TX, USA

Trisha Suppes and Jamie Zeitzer
VA Palo Alto Health Care System, Department of Psychiatry and Behavioral Sciences, Stanford University School of Medicine, Palo Alto, CA, USA

Colleen McClung
Department of Psychiatry, University of Pittsburgh Medical Center, Pittsburgh, PA, USA

Carol Tamminga
Department of Psychiatry, University of Texas, Southwestern Medical School, Dallas, TX, USA

Mauricio Tohen
Department of Psychiatry, University of New Mexico Medical School, Albuquerque, NM, USA

Alok Dwivedi and Andres Alvarado
Department of Biomedical Sciences, Texas Tech University Health Sciences Center El Paso, El Paso, TX, USA

Georgina M. Hosang
Psychology Department, Goldsmiths, University of London, Lewisham Way, London SE14 6NW, UK

Helen L. Fisher, Barbara Maughan, Peter McGuffin and Anne E. Farmer
MRC Social, Genetic and Developmental Psychiatry Centre, Institute of Psychiatry, Psychology and Neuroscience, King's College London, De Crespigny Park, London SE5 8AF, UK

Rudolf Uher
Department of Psychiatry, Dalhousie University, 5909 Veterans' Memorial Lane, Halifax, NS B3H 2E2, Canada

Sarah Cohen-Woods
School of Psychology, Flinders University, Adelaide, SA 5001, Australia

Maria D. L. A. Vazquez-Montes, Richard Stevens and Rafael Perera
Nuffield Department of Primary Care Health Sciences, University of Oxford, Radcliffe Observatory Quarter, Woodstock Road, Oxford OX2 6GG, UK

Kate Saunders and John R. Geddes
Department of Psychiatry, Warneford Hospital, University of Oxford, Warneford Lane, Oxford OX3 7JX, UK

David G. Angeler
Department of Aquatic Sciences and Assessment, Swedish University of Agricultural Sciences, 750 07 Uppsala, Sweden

Craig R. Allen
U.S. Geological Survey, Nebraska Cooperative Fish and Wildlife Research Unit, School of Natural Resources, University of Nebraska-Lincoln, Lincoln, NE, USA

Maj-Liz Persson
PRIMA Adult Psychiatric Ward, Katrinebergsvägen 6, 117 43 Stockholm, Sweden

Maximilian Pilhatsch, Emanuel Severus, Rita Bauer, Philipp Ritter and Michael Bauer
Department of Psychiatry and Psychotherapy, Medical Faculty, University Hospital Carl Gustav Carus, Technische Universität Dresden, Fetscherstr. 74, 01307 Dresden, Germany

Tasha Glenn
ChronoRecord Association Inc., Fullerton, CA, USA

Natalie Rasgon
Department of Psychiatry and Behavioral Sciences, Stanford School of Medicine, Palo Alto, CA, USA

Martin Alda
Department of Psychiatry, Dalhousie University, Halifax, NS, Canada

Kemal Sagduyu
Department of Psychiatry, University of Missouri Kansas City School of Medicine, Kansas City, MO, USA

Paul Grof
Mood Disorders Center of Ottawa, University of Toronto, Toronto, Canada

Rodrigo Munoz
Department of Psychiatry, University of California San Diego, San Diego, CA, USA

Wendy Marsh
Department of Psychiatry, University of Massachusetts, Worcester, MA, USA

Scott Monteith
Michigan State University College of Human Medicine, Traverse City Campus, Traverse City, MI, USA

Peter C. Whybrow
Department of Psychiatry and Biobehavioral Sciences, Semel Institute for Neuroscience and Human Behavior, University of California Los Angeles (UCLA), Los Angeles, CA, USA

A. Duffy
Student Wellness Centre, Department of Psychiatry, Queen's University, 146 Stuart Street, Kingston, ON K7L3N6, Canada

C. Vandeleur and M. Preisig
Department of Psychiatry Lausanne, University Hospital of Lausanne, Lausanne, Switzerland

N. Heffer
Medical Sciences Division, University of Oxford, Oxford, UK

Bernardo Carpiniello and Federica Pinna
Section of Psychiatry, Department of Medical Science and Public Health, University of Cagliari, Via Liguria, 13, 09127 Cagliari, Italy

Mirko Manchia
Section of Psychiatry, Department of Medical Science and Public Health, University of Cagliari, Via Liguria, 13, 09127 Cagliari, Italy
Department of Pharmacology, Dalhousie University, Halifax, NS, Canada

Giuseppe Maina, Virginia D'Ambrosio and Virginio Salvi
Department of Mental Health, "San Luigi-Gonzaga" Hospital, University of Turin, Orbassano, Italy

Luca Steardo and Alfonso Tortorella
Department of Psychiatry, University of Naples SUN, Naples, Italy

Martin Alda
Department of Psychiatry, Dalhousie University, Halifax, NS, Canada

Umberto Albert
Rita Levi Montalcini Department of Neuroscience, Anxiety and Mood Disorders Unit, University of Turin, Turin, Italy

L. J. Stoker
Division of Pharmacoepidemiology and Clinical Pharmacology, Utrecht Institute for Pharmaceutical Sciences, Utrecht University, 3508 TB Utrecht, The Netherlands

M. Nederlof
Division of Pharmacoepidemiology and Clinical Pharmacology, Utrecht Institute for Pharmaceutical Sciences, Utrecht University, 3508 TB Utrecht, The Netherlands
Brocacef Ziekenhuisfarmacie, 3600 AB Maarssen, The Netherlands

A. C. G. Egberts
Division of Pharmacoepidemiology and Clinical Pharmacology, Utrecht Institute for Pharmaceutical Sciences, Utrecht University, 3508 TB Utrecht, The Netherlands
Department of Clinical Pharmacy, University Medical Center Utrecht, 3508 GA Utrecht, The Netherlands

E. R. Heerdink
Division of Pharmacoepidemiology and Clinical Pharmacology, Utrecht Institute for Pharmaceutical Sciences, Utrecht University, 3508 TB Utrecht, The Netherlands
Research Group Innovation of Pharmaceutical Care, University of Applied Sciences Utrecht, 3508 AD Utrecht, The Netherlands
Department of Clinical Pharmacy, University Medical Center Utrecht, 3508 GA Utrecht, The Netherlands

I. Wilting
Department of Clinical Pharmacy, University Medical Center Utrecht, 3508 GA Utrecht, The Netherlands

R. Hoekstra
Antes, Delta Psychiatric Center, 3709 DZ Rotterdam, The Netherlands

R. W. Kupka
Department of Psychiatry, Amsterdam Public Health Research Institute, VU University Medical Center, A.J. Ernststraat 1187, 1081 HL Amsterdam, The Netherlands

Anna Bodnar and Janusz K. Rybakowski
Department of Adult Psychiatry, Poznan University of Medical Sciences, ul.Szpitalna 27/33, 60-572 Poznan, Poland

Justine Corry and Gloria Roberts
School of Psychiatry, University of New South Wales, Randwick, NSW 2031, Australia
Black Dog Institute, Prince of Wales Hospital, Randwick, NSW 2031, Australia

Philip B. Mitchell
School of Psychiatry, University of New South Wales, Randwick, NSW 2031, Australia
Black Dog Institute, Prince of Wales Hospital, Randwick, NSW 2031, Australia
Prince of Wales Hospital, Randwick, NSW 2031, Australia

Melissa Green
School of Psychiatry, University of New South Wales, Randwick, NSW 2031, Australia
Black Dog Institute, Prince of Wales Hospital, Randwick, NSW 2031, Australia
Neuroscience Research Australia, Randwick, NSW, Australia

Janice M. Fullerton and Peter R. Schofield
Neuroscience Research Australia, Randwick, NSW, Australia
School of Medical Sciences, University of New South Wales, Randwick, NSW, Australia

Luca Ambrosiani, Gioia Baggiani and Claudia Pisanu
Section of Neuroscience and Clinical Pharmacology, Department of Biomedical Sciences, University of Cagliari, Via Ospedale 54, 09124 Cagliari, Italy

Alberto Bocchetta
Section of Neuroscience and Clinical Pharmacology, Department of Biomedical Sciences, University of Cagliari, Via Ospedale 54, 09124 Cagliari, Italy
Unit of Clinical Pharmacology, Cagliari University Hospital, Cagliari, Italy

Caterina Chillotti and Raffaella Ardau
Unit of Clinical Pharmacology, Cagliari University Hospital, Cagliari, Italy

Fernanda Velluzzi and Andrea Loviselli
Department of Medical Sciences and Public Health, University of Cagliari, Cagliari, Italy

Doloretta Piras and Antonello Pani
Nephrology, Dialysis and Transplantation Unit, 'Giuseppe Brotzu' Hospital, Cagliari, Italy

Trisha Suppes
VA Palo Alto Health Care System and Department of Psychiatry and Behavioral Sciences, Stanford University School of Medicine, Stanford, CA, USA

Ole Lemming
H. Lundbeck A/S, Valby, Copenhagen, Denmark

Jonas Eberhard
H. Lundbeck A/S, Valby, Copenhagen, Denmark
Department of Clinical Sciences, Lund University, Lund, Sweden
Department of Psychological Medicine, Institute of Psychiatry, Psychology and Neuroscience (IoPPN), King's College London, London, UK

Allan H. Young
Department of Psychological Medicine, Institute of Psychiatry, Psychology and Neuroscience (IoPPN), King's College London, London, UK

Roger S. McIntyre
Mood Disorders Psychopharmacology Unit, University Health Network, University of Toronto, Toronto, ON, Canada

Joseph R. Calabrese
University Hospitals Cleveland Medical Center, 10524 Euclid Avenue, Cleveland, OH 44106, USA

Na Jin, Brian Johnson, Ross A. Baker, Jessica Madera, Jocelyn Ottinger and Joan Amatniek
Otsuka Pharmaceutical Development and Commercialization, Inc., Princeton, NJ, USA

Pedro Such and Peter Hertel
H. Lundbeck A/S, Valby, Denmark

Hiroaki Kawasaki
Department of Psychiatry, Faculty of Medicine, Fukuoka University, Fukuoka, Japan

Joannes W. Renes and Eline J. Regeer
Altrecht Institute for Mental Health Care, Utrecht, Nieuwe Houtenseweg 12, 3524 SH Utrecht, The Netherlands

Ralph W. Kupka
Altrecht Institute for Mental Health Care, Utrecht, Nieuwe Houtenseweg 12, 3524 SH Utrecht, The Netherlands
Amsterdam UMC, Vrije Universiteit Amsterdam, Psychiatry, Amsterdam Public Health, De Boelelaan 1117, 1081 HV Amsterdam, The Netherlands

Adriaan W. Hoogendoorn
Amsterdam UMC, Vrije Universiteit Amsterdam, Psychiatry, Amsterdam Public Health, De Boelelaan 1117, 1081 HV Amsterdam, The Netherlands

Willem A. Nolen
Department of Psychiatry, University Medical Center Groningen, University of Groningen, Hanzeplein 1, 9713 GZ Groningen, The Netherlands

Douglass Godwin and Daniel Mamah
Department of Psychiatry, Washington University Medical School, St. Louis, USA

Kathryn I. Alpert and Lei Wang
Department of Psychiatry and Behavioral Sciences, Northwestern University Feinberg School of Medicine, Chicago, USA

Luca Ambrosiani and Claudia Pisanu
Section of Neuroscience and Clinical Pharmacology, Department of Biomedical Sciences, University of Cagliari, S.S. 554, km 4, 500, Monserrato, Italy

Alberto Bocchetta
Section of Neuroscience and Clinical Pharmacology, Department of Biomedical Sciences, University of Cagliari, S.S. 554, km 4, 500, Monserrato, Italy
Unit of Clinical Pharmacology, "San Giovanni di Dio Hospital", Azienda Ospedaliero-Universitaria, Cagliari, Italy

Arianna Deidda and Maria Erminia Stochino
Sardinian Regional Centre of Pharmacovigilance, Azienda Ospedaliero-Universitaria, Cagliari, Italy

Caterina Chillotti
Unit of Clinical Pharmacology, "San Giovanni di Dio Hospital", Azienda Ospedaliero-Universitaria, Cagliari, Italy

Doris Verwijmeren
Reinier van Arkel Mental Health Institute, Postbus 70058, 5201 DZ 's-Hertogenbosch, The Netherlands

Koen P. Grootens
Reinier van Arkel Mental Health Institute, Postbus 70058, 5201 DZ 's-Hertogenbosch, The Netherlands
Department of Psychiatry, Radboud University Medical Centre, Nijmegen, The Netherlands

John R. Purcell
Department of Psychological and Brain Sciences, Indiana University, 1101 E. 10th St., Bloomington, IN 47405, USA

Monika Lohani
Department of Psychology, University of Utah, 201 Presidents Circle, Salt Lake City, UT 84112, USA

Christie Musket
Department of Psychology, University of Pittsburgh, 210 South Bouquet St, #4209, Pittsburgh, PA 15260, USA

Aleena C. Hay
Department of Psychological and Brain Sciences, Boston University, 648 Beacon St., 6th Floor, Boston, MA 02215, USA

Derek M. Isaacowitz
Department of Psychology, Northeastern University, 360 Huntington Ave., Boston, MA 02115, USA

June Gruber
Department of Psychology and Neuroscience, University of Colorado Boulder, 345 UCB, Muenzinger D321C, Boulder, CO 80309, USA

Barbara J. Regeer and Joske F. G. Bunders
Athena Institute, Faculty of Earth and Life Sciences, VU University Amsterdam, Boelelaan 1085, 1081HV Amsterdam, Netherlands

Eva F. Maassen
Athena Institute, Faculty of Earth and Life Sciences, VU University Amsterdam, Boelelaan 1085, 1081HV Amsterdam, Netherlands
Altrecht Institute for Mental Health Care, Nieuwe Houtenseweg 12, 3524 SH Utrecht, Netherlands

Eline J. Regeer
Altrecht Institute for Mental Health Care, Nieuwe Houtenseweg 12, 3524 SH Utrecht, Netherlands

Ralph W. Kupka
Altrecht Institute for Mental Health Care, Nieuwe Houtenseweg 12, 3524 SH Utrecht, Netherlands
Amsterdam Public Health Research Institute, Amsterdam UMC, Vrije Universiteit Amsterdam, Psychiatry, De Boelelaan 1117, Amsterdam, Netherlands

Ole Kristian Drange, Arne Einar Vaaler and Gunnar Morken
Department of Mental Health, Norwegian University of Science and Technology, Trondheim, Norway
Department of Østmarka, Division of Mental Health Care, St. Olavs Hospital, Trondheim University Hospital, Trondheim, Norway

Ole Andreas Andreassen
Institute of Clinical Medicine, University of Oslo, Oslo, Norway
NORMENT, Division of Mental Health and Addiction, Oslo University Hospital, Oslo, Norway

Ulrik Fredrik Malt
Institute of Clinical Medicine, University of Oslo, Oslo, Norway
Department of Research and Education, Division of Clinical Neuroscience, Oslo University Hospital, Oslo, Norway

Per Ivar Finseth
Department of Brøset, Division of Mental Health Care, St. Olavs Hospital, Trondheim University Hospital, Trondheim, Norway

René Breuer, Josef Frank, Jens Treutlein, Jana Strohmaier and Marcella Rietschel
Department of Genetic Epidemiology in Psychiatry, Central Institute of Mental Health, Medical Faculty Mannheim/Heidelberg University, Mannheim, Germany

Thomas G. Schulze
Department of Genetic Epidemiology in Psychiatry, Central Institute of Mental Health, Medical Faculty Mannheim/Heidelberg University, Mannheim, Germany
Human Genetics Branch, Intramural Research Program, National Institute of Mental Health, National Institutes of Health, US Department of Health and Human Services, Bethesda, MD, USA
Department of Psychiatry and Psychotherapy, University of Göttingen, Göttingen, Germany
Institute of Psychiatric Phenomics and Genomics (IPPG), Ludwig-Maximilians-University, Munich, Nußbaumstr. 7, 80336 Munich, Germany

Stefan Herms, Thomas W. Mühleisen, Franziska Degenhardt and Markus M. Nöthen
Department of Genomics, Life and Brain Center, University of Bonn, Bonn, Germany
Institute of Human Genetics, University of Bonn, Bonn, Germany

Sven Cichon
Department of Genomics, Life and Brain Center, University of Bonn, Bonn, Germany
Institute of Human Genetics, University of Bonn, Bonn, Germany
Institute of Neuroscience and Medicine (INM-1), Structural and Functional Organisation of the Brain, Genomic Imaging, Research Centre Juelich, Juelich, Germany
Department of Biomedicine, University of Basel, Basel, Switzerland

Manuel Mattheisen
Department of Genomics, Life and Brain Center, University of Bonn, Bonn, Germany
Institute of Human Genetics, University of Bonn, Bonn, Germany
Center for Integrative Sequencing, iSEQ, Department of Biomedicine, Aarhus University, Aarhus, Denmark
Department of Psychiatry, Psychosomatics, and Psychotherapy, University of Würzburg, Würzburg, Germany

Bertram Krumm
Department for Biostatistics, Central Institute of Mental Health, Medical Faculty Mannheim/Heidelberg University, Mannheim, Germany

Layla Kassem and Francis J. McMahon
Human Genetics Branch, Intramural Research Program, National Institute of Mental Health, National Institutes of Health, US Department of Health and Human Services, Bethesda, MD, USA

George Karypis
Department of Computer Science and Engineering, University of Minnesota, Minneapolis, MN, USA

John Kelsoe, Caroline Nievergelt, Paul Shilling and Tatyana Shekhtman
Department of Psychiatry, University of California San Diego, San Diego, USA

Tiffany Greenwood
Department of Psychiatry, University of California San Diego, San Diego, USA
BGI-Shenzhen, Beishan Industrial Zone, Yantian District, Shenzhen, China

Howard Edenberg
Department of Biochemistry and Molecular Biology, Indiana University School of Medicine, Indianapolis, USA

David Craig and Szabolcs Szelinger
The Translational Genomics Research Institute, Phoenix, USA

Nicholas Schork
The Translational Genomics Research Institute, Phoenix, USA
J. Craig Venter Institute, La Jolla, USA

John Nurnberger
Department of Psychiatry, Indiana University School of Medicine, Indianapolis, USA

Elliot Gershon, Ney Alliey-Rodriguez and Judith Badner
Department of Psychiatry and Behavioral Neuroscience, University of Chicago, Chicago, USA

Peter Zandi
Department of Mental Health, John Hopkins Bloomberg School of Public Health, Baltimore, USA

Fernando Goes and Pamela Mahon
Department of Psychiatry and Behavioral Sciences, John Hopkins School of Medicine, Baltimore, USA

Erin Smith
Scripps Genomic Medicine and The Scripps Translational Sciences Institute (STSI), La Jolla, USA
Department of Pediatrics and Rady's Children's Hospital, School of Medicine, University of California San Diego, La Jolla, USA

Sarah Murray
Scripps Genomic Medicine and The Scripps Translational Sciences Institute (STSI), La Jolla, USA
Department of Pathology, University of California San Diego, La Jolla, USA

Daniel Koller and Tatiana Foroud
Department of Medical and Molecular Genetics, Indiana University School of Medicine, Indianapolis, USA

Peng Zhang and Sebastian Zöllner
Department of Computational Medicine and Bioinformatics, University of Michigan, Ann Arbor, USA

Wade Berrettini
Department of Psychiatry, University of Pennsylvania, Philadelphia, USA

Cinnamon Bloss
University of California, San Diego, La Jolla, USA

William Byerley
Department of Psychiatry, University of California at San Francisco, San Francisco, USA

William Coryell
University of Iowa Hospitals and Clinics, Iowa City, USA

Yirin Guo
Center for Applied Genomics, Children's Hospital of Philadelphia, Abramson Research Center, Philadelphia, USA

Maria Hipolito
Department of Psychiatry and Behavioral Sciences, Howard University Hospital, Washington, USA

Brendan Keating
Cardiovascular Institute, University of Pennsylvania School of Medicine, Philadelphia, PA, USA
Institute for Translational Medicine and Therapeutics, School of Medicine, University of Pennsylvania, Philadelphia, PA, USA

William Lawson and Evaristus Nwulia
Dell Medical School, University of Texas at Austin, Austin, USA

Chunyu Liu
Department of Psychiatry, University of Illinois at Chicago, Chicago, USA

Melvin McInnis
Department of Psychiatry, University of Michigan, Ann Arbor, USA
Department of Pathology, University of California San Diego, La Jolla, USA

James Potash
Department of Psychiatry, Carver College of Medicine, University of Iowa School of Medicine, Iowa City, USA

John Rice
Department of Psychiatry, Washington University School of Medicine in St. Louis, St. Louis, USA

William Scheftner
Rush University Medical Center, Chicago, USA

Index